A·N·N·U·A·L E·D·I·T·I·O·N·S

PSYCHOLOGY

99/00

Twenty-Ninth Edition

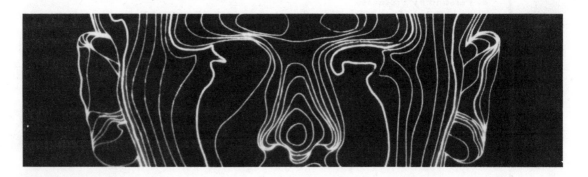

EDITOR

Karen G. Duffy
SUNY College, Geneseo

Karen G. Duffy holds a doctorate in psychology from Michigan State University and is currently a professor of psychology at SUNY at Geneseo. She sits on the executive board of the New York State Employees Assistance Program and is a certified community and family mediator. She is a member of the American Psychological Society and the Eastern Psychological Association.

Dushkin/McGraw-Hill
Sluice Dock, Guilford, Connecticut 06437

Visit us on the Internet
http://www.dushkin.com/annualeditions/

Credits

1. The Science of Psychology
Facing overview—Dushkin Publishing Group illustration by Mike Eagle.
2. Biological Bases of Behavior
Facing overview—Medical World News photo.
3. Perceptual Processes
Facing overview—UN Photo/Shelley Rotner.
4. Learning and Remembering
Facing overview—© 1998 by Cleo Photography.
5. Cognitive Processes
Facing overview—© 1998 by Cleo Photography.
6. Emotion and Motivation
Facing overview—UN photo/John Isaac
7. Development
Facing overview—© 1998 by Cleo Photography. 120—APA Monitor photo.
8. Personality Processes
Facing overview—Card 12F from the *Thematic Apperception Text.* © *1971 by Harvard University Press. All rights reserved.*
9. Social Processes
Facing overview—© 1998 by Cleo Photography.
10. Psychological Disorders
Facing overview—© 1998 by Cleo Photography.
11. Psychological Treatments
Facing overview—Photo © Gerd Ludwig/Woodfin Camp & Associates.

Cataloging in Publication Data
Main entry under title: Annual Editions: Psychology. 1999/2000.
1. Psychology—Periodicals. I. Duffy, Karen G., *comp.*II. Title: Psychology.
BF 149.A58   150'   79-180263   ISBN 0-07-041372-X   ISSN 0272-3794

Twenty-Ninth Edition

Cover image © 1999 PhotoDisc, Inc.

Printed in the United States of America   1234567890BAHBAH54321098   Printed on Recycled Paper

To the Reader

In publishing ANNUAL EDITIONS we recognize the enormous role played by the magazines, newspapers, and journals of the public press in providing current, first-rate educational information in a broad spectrum of interest areas. Many of these articles are appropriate for students, researchers, and professionals seeking accurate, current material to help bridge the gap between principles and theories and the real world. These articles, however, become more useful for study when those of lasting value are carefully collected, organized, indexed, and reproduced in a low-cost format, which provides easy and permanent access when the material is needed. That is the role played by ANNUAL EDITIONS.

New to ANNUAL EDITIONS is the inclusion of related World Wide Web sites. These sites have been selected by our editorial staff to represent some of the best resources found on the World Wide Web today. Through our carefully developed topic guide, we have linked these Web resources to the articles covered in this ANNUAL EDITIONS reader. We think that you will find this volume useful, and we hope that you will take a moment to visit us on the Web at *http://www.dushkin.com/* to tell us what you think.

Ronnie's parents couldn't understand why he didn't want to be picked up and cuddled as did his older sister when she was a baby. As an infant, Ronnie did not respond to his parents' smiles, words, or attempts to amuse him. By the age of two, Ronnie's parents knew that he was not like other children. He spoke no words, was very temperamental, and often rocked himself for hours. Ronnie is autistic. His parents feel that some of Ronnie's behavior may be their fault; they both work long hours as young professionals and leave both children with a woman caregiver on the weekdays. Ronnie's pediatrician assures his parents that their reasoning, while logical, probably holds no merit, because the causes of autism are little understood and are likely to be physiological rather than parental. What can we do about children like Ronnie? What is the source of autism? Can autism be treated or reversed? Can it be prevented?

Psychologists attempt to answer these and other questions in a specific way. Researchers use carefully planned methods to discover the causes of complex human behavior, normal or not. The scientific results of most psychological research are published in professional journals and therefore may be difficult for the lay person to understand.

Annual Editions: Psychology 99/00 is designed to meet the needs of lay people and introductory-level students who are curious about psychology. This book provides a vast selection of readable and informative articles, primarily from popular magazines and newspapers. These articles are typically written by journalists, but a few are written by psychologists and retain the excitement of the discovery of scientific knowledge.

The particular writings in this volume were chosen to be representative of the most current work in psychology. They were selected because they are accurate in their reporting and provide examples of the types of psychological research discussed in most introductory psychology classes. As in any science, some of the findings discussed in this collection are startling, while others confirm what we already know. Some entries invite speculation about social and personal issues; others demand careful thought about potential misuse of the applications of research findings. Readers are expected to make the investment of effort and critical reasoning needed to discuss questions and concerns.

I believe that you will find *Annual Editions: Psychology 99/00* readable and useful. I suggest that students just look at the organization of this book and compare it to the organization of their textbook and course syllabus. By examining the *topic guide* that follows the *table of contents*, you can identify those readings most appropriate for any particular unit of study in your course. The *World Wide Web* sites that follow the topic guide can be used to further explore the topics. These sites are cross-referenced by number to subjects in the topic guide.

Your instructor may provide some help in assigning certain articles to supplement the text. As you read the selections, try to connect their contents with the principles you are learning from your text and classroom lectures. Some of the articles will help you better understand specific areas of research, while others will help you connect and integrate information from various research areas. Both of these strategies are important in learning about psychology or any other science. It is only through intensive investigation and subsequent integration of the findings from many studies that we are able to discover and apply new knowledge.

Please take time to provide us with feedback to guide the annual revision of this anthology by completing and returning the *article rating form* in the back of the book. With your help, this collection will be even better next year. Thank you.

Karen Grover Duffy

Karen Grover Duffy
Editor

Contents

UNIT 1

The Science of Psychology

Three articles examine psychology as the science of behavior.

UNIT 2

Biological Bases of Behavior

Four selections discuss the biological bases of behavior. Topics include brain functions and the brain's control over the body.

The concepts in bold italics are developed in the article. For further expansion please refer to the Topic Guide, the Glossary, and the Index.

UNIT 3

Perceptual Processes

Four articles discuss the impact of the senses on human perceptual processes.

UNIT 4

Learning and Remembering

Four selections examine how operant conditioning, positive reinforcement, and memory interact during the learning process.

UNIT 5

Cognitive Processes

Four articles examine how
social skills, common sense,
and intelligence affect human
cognitive processes.

UNIT 6

Emotion and Motivation

Six articles discuss the influences of stress, mental states, and emotion on the mental and physical health of the individual.

UNIT 7

Development

Four articles consider the importance of experience, discipline, familial support, and physiological aging during the normal human development process.

The concepts in bold italics are developed in the article. For further expansion please refer to the Topic Guide, the Glossary, and the Index.

UNIT 8

Personality Processes

Four selections discuss a few of the processes by which personalities are developed. Topics include sex differences, state of mind, and hostility.

The concepts in bold italics are developed in the article. For further expansion please refer to the Topic Guide, the Glossary, and the Index.

UNIT 9

Social Processes

Four selections discuss how the individual's social development is affected by genes, stereotypes, prejudice, and self-help.

UNIT 10

Psychological Disorders

Five articles examine several psychological disorders. Topics include unexpected behavior, the impact of depression on a person's well-being, and physical abuse.

x

The concepts in bold italics are developed in the article. For further expansion please refer to the Topic Guide, the Glossary, and the Index.

UNIT 11

Psychological Treatments

Four selections discuss a few
psychological treatments, including
psychoanalysis, psychotherapy to
alleviate depression, self-care,
and the use of drugs.

This topic guide suggests how the selections and World Wide Web sites found in the next section of this book relate to topics of traditional concern to psychology students and professionals. It is useful for locating interrelated articles and Web sites for reading and research. The guide is arranged alphabetically according to topic.

The relevant Web sites, which are numbered and annotated on pages 4 and 5, are easily identified by the Web icon (☉) under the topic articles. By linking the articles and the Web sites by topic, this ANNUAL EDITIONS reader becomes a powerful learning and research tool.

TOPIC AREA	TREATED IN	TOPIC AREA	TREATED IN
Abuse	41. Patterns of Abuse ☉ **25, 26, 27, 29**	**Depression**	45. Quest for a Cure ☉ **25, 26, 27, 30, 32**
Adolescents	28. Rethinking Puberty: The Development of Sexual Attraction ☉ **8, 14, 19, 21, 22, 25**	**Development**	16. Your Child's Brain 26. Behaviors of a Newborn Can Be Traced to the Fetus 27. Do Parents Really Matter? 28. Rethinking Puberty: The Development of Sexual Attraction 29. Slowing Down Alzheimer's 39. Mother's Little Helper ☉ **8, 9, 15, 21, 22**
Adults	29. Slowing Down Alzheimer's ☉ **22**		
Aging	29. Slowing Down Alzheimer's ☉ **22**		
Alzheimer's	29. Slowing Down Alzheimer's ☉ **22**	**Diet/Dieting**	24. Weight Loss for Grown-Ups ☉ **20, 28**
Animals/Animal Research	2. Benefits and Ethics of Animal Research ☉ **5, 6, 7**	**Domestic Violence**	41. Patterns of Abuse ☉ **25, 26, 27, 29**
Anxiety/Anxiety Disorder	40. Why Worry? ☉ **25, 26, 27**	**Dreams**	11. Dream Catchers ☉ **31, 33**
Attention Deficit Disorder	39. Mother's Little Helper ☉ **25, 26, 27**	**Drugs/Drug Treatment**	39. Mother's Little Helper 44. Prescription for Happiness? 45. Quest for a Cure 46. New Treatments for Schizophrenia—Part I ☉ **31, 32, 33**
Audition	9. Gain in Years Can Mean Loss in Hearing ☉ **12**		
Brain	4. Nature, Nurture, Not Mutually Exclusive 6. Secrets of the Brain 7. Revealing the Brain's Secrets 16. Your Child's Brain 29. Slowing Down Alzheimer's ☉ **8, 9, 10, 11, 15, 17, 19, 22**	**Emotions**	21. EQ Factor 22. Doubtful Device 23. Biology of Joy 24. Weight Loss for Grown-Ups ☉ **20, 22, 23**
		Freud/Psychoanalysis	1. Why Freud Isn't Dead ☉ **5, 33**
Children	16. Your Child's Brain 26. Behaviors of a Newborn Can Be Traced to the Fetus 27. Do Parents Really Matter? 28. Rethinking Puberty: The Development of Sexual Attraction 39. Mother's Little Helper ☉ **15, 17, 20, 21, 22**	**Gender**	36. Laughter May Be No Laughing Matter 37. Brain Sex and the Language of Love ☉ **29**
		Genes/Genetics	4. Nature, Nurture, Not Mutually Exclusive 5. What We Learn from Twins 20. Is It Nature or Nurture? 30. Personality Genes ☉ **8, 9, 10, 11, 22, 23**
Cognition	16. Your Child's Brain 19. On the Trail of Language: Neuropsychologist Angelica Freiderici ☉ **15, 17, 21, 22**	**History of Psychology**	1. Why Freud Isn't Dead ☉ **5, 31, 33**
Crime	34. Disintegration of the Family Is the Real Root Cause of Violent Crime ☉ **24**	**Intelligence**	17. To Be Intelligent 18. Reflections on Multiple Intelligences ☉ **15, 16, 17, 18**

Annual Editions: Psychology

The following World Wide Web sites have been carefully researched and selected to support the articles found in this reader. If you are interested in learning more about specific topics found in this book, these Web sites are a good place to start. The sites are cross-referenced by number and appear in the topic guide on the previous two pages. Also, you can link to these Web sites through our DUSHKIN ONLINE support site at *http://www.dushkin.com/online/*.

The following sites were available at the time of publication. Visit our Web site—we update DUSHKIN ONLINE regularly to reflect any changes.

General Sources

1. Mental Health Net
http://www.cmhc.com/
Comprehensive guide to mental health online, featuring more than 6,300 individual resources. Covers information on mental disorders and professional resources in psychology, psychiatry, and social work.

2. Psychnet
http://www.apa.org/psychnet/
Use the site map or search engine to access *APA Monitor*, the American Psychological Association newspaper, APA books on a wide range of topics, PsychINFO, an electronic database of abstracts on over 1,350 scholarly journals, and the HelpCenter.

3. The Psych.com: Internet Psychology Resource
http://www.thepsych.com/
Over 3000 psychology resources are currently indexed at this site. Psychology Disciplines, Psychology Areas, Conditions & Disorders, Psychiatry, Assistance, and Self-Development are among the most useful.

4. Resources in the History of Psychology
http://198.49.179.4/pages/awalsh/psych-history.html
Maintained by Dr. Anthony Walsh at Salve Regina University, this site includes pages (and links) on the history of various areas and topics in psychology.

The Science of Psychology

5. Abraham A. Brill Library
http://plaza.interport.net/nypsan/service.html
The Abraham A. Brill Library contains data on over 40,000 books, periodicals, and reprints in psychoanalysis and related fields. Its holdings span the literature of psychoanalysis from its beginning to the present day.

6. American Psychological Society (APS)
http://www.psychologicalscience.org/links.htm
The APS is dedicated to advancing the best of scientific psychology in research, application, and the improvement of human conditions. Links to teaching, research, and graduate studies resources are available.

7. Psychology Research on the Net
http://psych.hanover.edu/APS/exponnet.html
Psychologically related experiments on the Net can be found at this site. Biological psychology/neuropsychology, clinical psychology, cognition, developmental psychology, emotions, health psychology, personality, sensation/perception, and social psychology are some of the areas covered.

Biological Bases of Behavior

8. Biological Changes in Adolescence
http://www.personal.psu.edu/faculty/n/x/nxd10/biologic2.htm

This site offers a discussion of puberty, sexuality, biological changes, cross-cultural differences, and nutrition for adolescents, including obesity and its effects on adolescent development.

9. Division of Hereditary Diseases and Family Studies, Indiana University School of Medicine
http://medgen.iupui.edu/divisions/hereditary/
This division of the Department of Medical and Molecular Genetics is primarily concerned with determining the genetic basis of disease. It consists of a multifaceted program with a variety of interdisciplinary projects. The areas of twin studies and linkage analysis are particularly explored.

10. Institute for Behavioral Genetics
http://ibgwww.colorado.edu/index.html
This organized research unit at the University of Colorado is dedicated to conducting and facilitating research on the genetic and environmental bases of individual differences in behavior. The site leads to Genetic Sites, Statistical Sites, and Biology Meta Index, as well as search engines.

11. Serendip
http://serendip.brynmawr.edu/serendip/
Organized into five subject areas (brain and behavior, complex systems, genes and behavior, science and culture, and science education), Serendip contains interactive exhibits, articles, links to other resources, and a forum area.

Perceptual Processes

12. Psychology Tutorials
http://psych.hanover.edu/Krantz/tutor.html
A collection of interactive tutorials and simulations, primarily in the area of sensation and perception, is available here.

13. Your Mind's Eye
http://illusionworks.com/html/jump_page.html
This multimedia museum exhibit on illusions will inform and delight about how we think and perceive.

Learning and Remembering

14. The Opportunity of Adolescence
http://www.winternet.com/~webpage/adolescencepaper.html
This paper calls adolescence the turning point, after which the future is redirected and confirmed. The opportunities and problems of this period are discussed, using quotations from Erik Erikson, Jean Piaget, and others.

15. Project Zero
http://pzweb.harvard.edu/
Harvard Project Zero has investigated the development of learning processes in children and adults for 30 years. Today, Project Zero's mission is to understand and enhance learning, thinking, and creativity in the arts and other disciplines for individuals and institutions. Research projects include one based on Howard Gardner's Theory of Multiple Intelligences.

Cognitive Processes

16. Chess: Kasparov v. Deep Blue: The Rematch
  http://www.chess.ibm.com/home/html/b.html
Find here clips from the rematch and commentaries on chess, computers, artificial intelligence, and what it all means.

17. Cognitive Science Article Archive
  http://www.helsinki.fi/hum/kognitiotiede/archive.html
This excellent Finnish source contains articles on various fields of cognitive science.

18. Introduction to Artificial Intelligence (AI)
  http://www-formal.stanford.edu/jmc/aiintro/aiintro.html
This site states what AI is. Click on John McCarthy's home page for a list of additional papers.

Emotion and Motivation

19. CYFERNET-Youth Development
  http://www.cyfernet.mes.umn.edu/youthdev.html
An excellent source of many articles on youth development, including a statement on the concept of normal adolescence and impediments to healthy development.

20. Nature vs. Nature: Gergen Dialogue with Winifred Gallagher
  http://www.pbs.org/newshour/gergen/gallagher_5-14.html
The author of *I.D.: How Heredity and Experience Make You Who You Are* explains a current theory about, for example, temperament: Nature and nurture are not oil and water but, rather, flour and water that make bread. Experience modifies temperament, according to this interesting television interview.

Development

21. American Association for Child and Adolescent Psychiatry
  http://www.aacap.org/factsfam/index.htm
This site is designed to aid in the understanding and treatment of the developmental, behavioral, and mental disorders that could affect children and adolescents. There is a specific link just for families about common childhood problems that may or may not require professional intervention.

22. Behavioral Genetics
  http://www.uams.edu/department_of_psychiatry/slides/html/genetics/index.htm
Dr. Jeff Clothier's site consists of a slide show on Behavioral Genetics, which includes objectives, methods of genetic investigation, family and twin studies, personality, intelligence, mental disorders, and Alzheimer's Disease.

Personality Processes

23. The Personality Project
  http://fas.psych.nwu.edu/personality.html
The Personality Project of William Revelle, director of the Graduate Program in Personality at Northwestern University, is meant to guide those interested in personality theory and research to the current personality research literature.

Social Processes

24. National Clearinghouse for Alcohol and Drug Information
  http://www.health.org/

This is an excellent general site for information on drug and alcohol facts that might relate to adolescence and the issues of peer pressure and youth culture. Resources, referrals, research and statistics, databases, and related Internet links are among the options available at this site.

Psychological Disorders

25. Anxiety Disorders in Children and Adolescents
  http://www.adaa.org/4_info/4i_child/4i_01.htm
The Anxiety Disorders Association of America (ADAA) discusses anxiety disorders in children and adolescents under seven headings on this page. Included is a glossary.

26. Ask NOAH About: Mental Health
  http://www.noah.cuny.edu/illness/mentalhealth/mental.html
This enormous resource contains information about child and adolescent family problems, mental conditions and disorders, suicide prevention, and much more.

27. Mental Health Infosource: Disorders
  http://www.mhsource.com/disorders/
This no-nonsense page lists hotlinks to psychological disorders pages, including anxiety, panic, phobic disorders, schizophrenia, and violent/self-destructive behaviors.

28. Mental Health Net: Eating Disorder Resources
  http://www.cmhc.com/guide/eating.htm
This is a very complete list of Web references on eating disorders, including anorexia, bulimia, and obesity.

29. National Women's Health Resource Center
  http://www.healthywomen.org/
This site contains links to resources related to women's substance abuse and mental illnesses.

30. Suicide Awareness: Voices of Education
  http://www.save.org/
This is the most popular suicide site on the Internet. It is very thorough, with information on dealing with suicide.

Psychological Treatments

31. JungWeb
  http://www.onlinepsych.com/jungweb/
Dedicated to the work of Carl Jung, this site is a comprehensive resource for Jungian psychology. Links to reference materials, graduate programs, dreams, and multilingual sites.

32. Knowledge Exchange Network (KEN)
  http://www.mentalhealth.org/about/index.htm
KEN provides information about mental health via toll-free telephone services, an electronic bulletin board, and publications. Source for information and resources on prevention, treatment, and rehabilitation services for mental illness.

33. Sigmund Freud and the Freud Archives
  http://plaza.interport.net/nypsan/freudarc.html
Internet resources related to Sigmund Freud can be accessed through this site. A collection of libraries, museums, and biographical materials can be found here.

We highly recommend that you review our Web site for expanded information and our other product lines. We are continually updating and adding links to our Web site in order to offer you the most usable and useful information that will support and expand the value of your Annual Editions. You can reach us at: *http://www.dushkin.com/annualeditions/*.

www.dushkin.com/online/

Unit Selections

1. **Why Freud Isn't Dead,** John Horgan
2. **The Benefits and Ethics of Animal Research,** Andrew N. Rowan
3. **On the Validity of Psychology Experiments,** John F. Kihlstrom

Key Points to Consider

❖ Which area of psychology do you think is the most valuable and why? Many people are most aware of clinical psychology, for example. Is this the most valuable area of the discipline? About which other areas of psychology do you think the public ought to be informed? What trends shaped psychology and psychiatry as we know them today? How might psychology be related to other scientific disciplines?

❖ Do you think psychologists will ever be able to piece together a single grand theory of human psychology? How close does psychoanalysis come to being that grand theory? Defend your answer. What are the various definitions of consciousness or the mind that have emerged over the years? How is psychology related to psychiatry? How do the two disciplines differ?

❖ How do you feel about animal research for psychology or another scientific discipline? Discuss how psychological research with animals might differ from medical research using animals. Why might some animals not be good models for studying human behavior? What characteristics would enable us to extrapolate knowledge from animals to humans?

❖ Why is research important to psychology? What kinds of information can be gleaned from psychological research? What types of problems are inherent in poorly designed research? How can psychological research be improved? What general conclusion about laboratory experiments must we always remember, according to John Kihlstrom (see "On the Validity of Psychology Experiments)?

 **Links** | **www.dushkin.com/online/**

These sites are annotated on pages 4 and 5.

Little did Wilhelm Wundt realize his monumental contribution to science when in 1879, in Germany, he opened the first psychological laboratory to examine consciousness. Wundt would barely recognize today's science of psychology, so much has it changed from his own practice.

Contemporary psychology is defined as the science or study of individual mental activity and behavior. This definition reflects the two parent disciplines from which psychology emerged: philosophy and biology. Compared to its parents, psychology is very much a new discipline. Some aspects of modern psychology are particularly biological, such as neuroscience, perception, psychophysics, and behavioral genetics. Other aspects are more philosophical, such as the study of personality. Still others approximate sociology, as does social psychology.

Today's psychologists work in a variety of settings. Many psychologists are academics, teaching and researching psychology on university campuses. Others work in applied settings such as hospitals, mental health clinics, industry, and schools. Most psychologists specialize after some graduate training. Industrial psychologists deal with human performance in organizational settings.

Clinical psychologists are concerned about the assessment, diagnosis, and treatment of individuals with a variety of mental disorders.

Some psychologists think that psychology is still in its adolescence and that the field is experiencing some growing pains. Since its establishment, the field has expanded to many different areas. As mentioned, some areas are very applied; others emphasize theory and research. The growing pains have resulted in some conflict over what the agenda of the first national psychological association, the American Psychological Association, should be. Because academics perceived this association as mainly serving practitioners, academics and researchers established their own competing association, the American Psychological Society. But, despite its varied nature and growing pains, psychology remains a viable and exciting field. The first unit of this book is designed to introduce you to the nature and history of psychology.

In the first article, "Why Freud Isn't Dead," John Horgan guides the reader through some of the controversial history and concepts of psychoanalysis, an early psychological theory, which was developed by Sigmund Freud. Horgan goes further; he explores some of the history of psychology and psychiatry with special attention to the controversy over the use of drugs versus psychotherapy.

In the next article, "The Benefits and Ethics of Animal Research," Andrew Rowan weighs the pros and cons of using animals in scientific research. Because psychology is a science, psychological researchers sometimes utilize the ubiquitous white rat as a model for human behavior. Other animals frequently seen in psychologists' laboratories are the dog, the cat, and the pigeon. Whether using animals is indeed a sound and ethical idea is questioned by the author.

In the final selection, John Kihlstrom, a renowned psychologist, discusses the validity of psychological experiments. Kihlstrom admonishes his readers to remember that the artificiality of psychological research often undercuts and limits the validity of the results. He reminds us that what we find in the laboratory might not hold in the real world.

The Science of Psychology

Article 1

Why Freud Isn't Dead

by John Horgan, *senior writer*

The anxiety is palapable. Fifty or so psychoanalysts have gathered in a ballroom at New York City's Waldorf-Astoria Hotel to discuss what one of them calls "the survival issue," meaning their rapidly declining status in the mental-health field and in the culture at large. One analyst complains that his daughter's college catalogue does not list a single course on Sigmund Freud, who founded psychoanalysis a century ago. Another expresses amazement that psychoanalysis "has managed to get itself so marginalized in such a short period of time." "Maybe it's time for me to retire," sighs a therapist from southern California having trouble enlisting new patients.

Some paranoiacs, the old joke goes, really do have enemies. Freud's ideas have been challenged since their inception, but in the 1990s the criticism has reached a crescendo. Every year yields more books, such as *Why Freud Was Wrong* and *Freudian Fraud*. Last year the Library of Congress postponed an exhibit on Freud until at least 1998 after protesters—including Freud's own granddaughter—complained that it was too hagiographic.

Market forces are also threatening psychoanalysis. Of the roughly 15 million people in therapy in the U.S., few have the time or money for a treatment that typically lasts years and calls for as many as five one-hour, $100 sessions a week. Many patients—and all health insurers—favor short-term psychotherapies that target specific problems rather than delving deeply into a patient's

past. Two popular approaches are cognitive-behavioral therapy, which seeks to alter unwanted habits of thought and behavior, and interpersonal therapy, which focuses on patients' current relationships with others.

Meanwhile psychiatrists and other M.D.'s are increasingly prescribing medication rather than "talk therapy"—a term that embraces both analysis and all other psychotherapies—for such common ailments as depression and anxiety. Sales of the antidepressant fluoxetine hydrochloride, whose brand name is Prozac, have more than doubled in the past two years, and more than 20 million people worldwide are now taking the drug, according to its manufacturer, Eli Lilly.

Given all these trends, it seems fair to ask, as *Time* magazine did on its cover three years ago, "Is Freud Dead?" Not quite. The meeting at the Waldorf-Astoria provided evidence of that. Some 400 members of the American Psychological Association's psychoanalysis division assembled this past April to trade insights about incest, alcoholism, obesity, obsessive-compulsive disorder and other afflictions. Relatively few of the 75,000 social workers, 60,000 psychologists and 40,000 psychiatrists in the U.S. call themselves psychoanalysts. Still, membership of the American Psychoanalytic Association, which is based in New york City and is the largest society for analysts, has remained surprisingly steady over the past decade at about 3,000. Moreover, the vehement attacks on Freud—which are met with

equally vigorous defenses—demonstrate the astonishing vitality of the Viennese neurologist's ideas.

The Phlogiston Era

So the real question is this: Why is Freudian theory still alive? One explanation may be that his oeuvre, in spite of its flaws, still represents a compelling framework within with to ponder our mysterious selves. Freud's view of human nature "hasn't been matched by any other theory," asserts Peter Gay of Yale University, author of the admiring biography *Freud: A Life for Our Time* (W. W. Norton, 1988). Even such prominent critics as Adolf Grünbaum, a philosopher at the University of Pittsburgh, acknowledge the continuing allure of Freud's ideas. "I wouldn't work hard on a critique of psychoanalysis if I didn't think there was anything in it," he says.

To be sure, specific Freudian hypotheses, such as the Oedipal complex and female penis envy, have fallen out of favor even among psychoanalysts. "There are very few analysts who follow all of Freud's formulations," notes Morris Eagle, president of the psychoanalysis division of the American Psychological Association and a professor at Adelphi University in Garden City, N.Y. Nevertheless, psychotherapists of all stripes still tend to share two of Freud's core beliefs: One is that our behavior, thoughts and emotions stem from unconscious fears and desires, often rooted in childhood experiences. The other is that with the help of a trained therapist, we can

Skeptics continue to challenge Sigmund Freud's ideas about the mind. Yet no unquestionably superior theory or therapy has rendered psychoanalysis completely obsolete

understand the source of our troubles and thereby obtain some relief.

But there is an even more important reason for the persistence of Freud's legacy, and psychoanalysis in particular. Freudians cannot point to unambiguous evidence that psychoanalysis works, but neither can proponents of more modern treatments, whether Jungian analysis, cognitive-behavioral therapy or even medications. Indeed, claims about the "wonder drug" Prozac notwithstanding, numerous independent studies have found that drugs are not significantly more effective than "talking cures" at treating the most common ailments for which people seek treatment, including depression, obsessive-compulsive disorder and panic attacks.

The anti-Freudians argue, in effect, that psychoanalysis has no more scientific standing than phlogiston, the ethereal substance that 18th-century scientist thought gave rise to heat and fire. But the reason scientists do not still debate the phlogiston hypothesis is that advances in chemistry and thermodynamics have rendered it utterly obsolete. A century's worth of research in psychology, neuroscience, pharmacology and other mind-related fields has not yielded a medical paradigm powerful enough to obviate Freud once and for all.

Will scientists ever get past the phlogiston era and create a truly effective treatment for the mind? Jerome D. Frank has his doubts. In his seminal 1961 book *Persuasion and Healing,* the psychiatrist contended that the theoretical framework within which therapists work has little or nothing to do with their ability to "heal" patients. That power stems, rather from the therapist's ability to make patients believe they will improve. In other words, Frank

explains, the placebo effect is the primary active ingredient underlying all psychotherapies and even most drug treatments.

"I do think my views have been borne out," says Frank, now a professor emeritus at the Johns Hopkins University School of Medicine. Frank questions whether science can demonstrate the efficacy—or lack thereof—of psychotherapy, because science cannot pinpoint or measure the qualities that enable a particular therapist to induce the placebo effect in a particular patient. He is therefore bemused by the persistence of the attacks on Freud. "People have been attacking Freud because he wasn't a scientist, but that misses the point. He was a great mythmaker."

Freud-bashing is hardly a novel pastime. The eminent philosopher Karl Popper carped more than 60 years ago that psychoanalysis—derided by one wag as "the treatment of the id by the odd"—was unfalsifiable and therefore unscientific. But Freud was such a dominant figure during the first half of this century, not only within the mental-health community but throughout Western culture, that he and his followers could shrug off such complaints. "Freud turned his back on the whole problem" of empirical testing, says Frederick Crews, a professor emeritus of English at the University of California at Berkeley who has excoriated Freud and his modern descendants in a series of articles in the *New York Review of Books.*

All Must Have Prizes

Only in the 1950s did half a dozen prominent psychoanalytic institutes in New York, Chicago, Boston and elsewhere begin gathering data on patient outcomes. The results, which involved more than 600 patients,

were reviewed in an article in the 1991 *Journal of the American Psychoanalytic Association* (Vol. 39, No. 4) by a group led by Henry Bachrach, a clinical professor of psychiatry at the New York Medical College at Saint Vincents Hospital.

The authors concluded that from 60 to 90 percent of the patients studied had showed "significant" improvement as a result of psychoanalysis. Bachrach and his colleagues acknowledged that the studies were not ideal: investigators admitted only those patients thought likely to benefit from psychoanalysis, a common practice; the assessments of patients' responses were made by their therapists, who might be inclined toward reporting positive outcomes; and there was no control group. But these weaknesses "were no greater than in comparable research about other forms of psychotherapy," Bachrach's team asserted at the 1992 meeting of the American Association for the Advancement of Science.

Indeed, most "outcome" studies supporting alternative talk therapies have also been flawed, according to Robyn M. Dawes, a psychologist at Carnegie Mellon University. In his 1994 book *House of Cards: Psychology and Psychotherapy Built on Myth* (Free Press), Dawes presents a scathing critique not just of psychoanalysis but of all talk therapies. The methods that therapists employ for diagnosing patients and assessing their progress are highly subjective and variable, Dawes charges. He also maintains that therapists' training and mode of therapy have no correlation with patients' outcomes.

Dawes still thinks psychotherapy can work, especially when directed toward specific problems. For example, some reports have indicated that cognitive-behavioral therapy is the best available treatment for panic disorder, a condition marked by extreme, unwarranted fear. But this claim is not corroborated by a rigorous, controlled study carried out recently by M. Katherine Shear, a psychiatrist at the University of Pittsburgh, and three colleagues.

For one group of patients, Shear's team provided 12 sessions of standard cognitive-behavioral therapy, which called for physical and mental exercises designed to help patients control their panic. In the sessions of the control patients, therapists provided only "reflective listening." Both sets of patients responded equally well. These data, Shear and her colleagues concluded in the May 1994 *Archives of General Psychiatry,* "raise questions about the specificity of cognitive-behavioral treatment."

The investigations of Shear, Dawes and others corroborate the so-called

review of more recent efficacy studies, and he is more convinced than ever that the Dodo hypothesis is correct. "There is a huge amount of evidence that psychotherapy works," he emphasizes, but no evidence "across a broad range of samples" that any one mode is superior. Luborsky has also found evidence for what he calls the "allegiance effect," the tendency of researchers to find evidence favoring the therapy that they practice.

Of course, another interpretation of the Dodo hypothesis is that everyone has *lost,* and *none* must have prizes. That is the conclusion of E. Fuller Torrey, a psychiatrist associated with the National Institute of Mental Health in Washington, D.C. In *Freudian Fraud* (HarperCollins, 1992), Torrey blasted psychoanalysis and all other talk therapies as pseudoscience. Freud's ideas took

and other physiological factors. Torrey is confident that sooner or later, drugs, gene therapy and other biological remedies will render talking cures obsolete. In the meantime, he argues, psychotherapy should be excluded from health care coverage.

Torrey's outlook is merely an extreme version of what has become the dominant paradigm within the mental-health community. That was apparent at the annual conference of the American Psychiatric Association held this past May. The contrast between this gathering and the relatively tiny psychoanalysis meeting held at the Waldorf-Astoria Hotel was dramatic: more than 15,000 psychiatrists and other mental-health workers assembled in New York City's gigantic Jacob K. Javits Convention Center.

By far the best-attended sessions were breakfasts and dinners sponsored by the drug companies, during which hundreds of psychiatrists heard talks about the benefits of Prozac for obsessive-compulsive disorder and of Zoloft, another so-called selective serotonin reuptake inhibitor, for depression. Sessions on talk therapy were, in comparison, sparsely attended. One entitled "The Future of Psychotherapy" drew only about 20 people. "At this point, I don't think the future of psychotherapy is very good," lamented Gene L. Usdin, a psychiatrist from the Ochsner Clinic in New Orleans.

Treatments for the Mind: A Lack-of-Progress Report

PSYCHOANALYSIS, which delves into childhood experiences, generally requires three or more sessions a week. No controlled studies of its effectiveness have been conducted.

COGNITIVE-BEHAVIORAL therapy seeks to alleviate specific disorders, such as phobias, through modification of thought and behavior. Although it is increasingly popular, controlled studies have not conclusively demonstrated its superiority to other treatments.

MEDICATIONS such as Prozac have become the most common treatment for depression and other emotional disorders, but they have not been shown to be more effective than talk therapies.

ELECTROCONVULSIVE therapy is increasingly prescribed for intractable depression, although it can cause memory loss. Moreover, relapse rates reportedly run as high as 85 percent.

Dodo hypothesis, first set forth in a classic 1975 paper by the psychologist Lester B. Luborsky and two colleagues. The status of all psychotherapies, Luborsky and his coauthors proposed in the *Archives of General Psychiatry,* could be summed up by the proclamation of the Dodo overseeing a footrace in *Alice's Adventures in Wonderland:* "*Everyone* has won, and *all* must have prizes!"

Luborsky, a professor of psychiatry at the University of Pennsylvania, says he has just completed a

hold not because of their scientific merits, he contends, but because they meshed with the notion— popular among many left-leaning intellectuals—that human nature is highly malleable.

Torrey disputes the underlying assumption of all talk therapies— that the human psyche is shaped by childhood experiences and can be reshaped through psychotherapy. The evidence is overwhelming, he says, that an individual's personality is determined primarily by genes

Drug Trials on Trial

But in an indication that drugs are not the panacea they are sometimes perceived to be, several sessions of the psychiatry meeting were also dedicated to electroconvulsive "shock" therapy. The practice declined in popularity over the past few decades, especially after being depicted as a form of torture in the 1975 movie *One Flew over the Cuckoo's Nest.* But technical improvements have reportedly reduced its major side effect—severe memory loss—and it is now quietly making a comeback as a treatment for patients who suffer from severe depression, schizophrenia and other disorders and who do not respond to drugs.

Indeed, some researchers have challenged the notion that medications represent a great step forward in the treatment of mental illness. The only drug treatments "unambiguously" proved to be superior to talk therapy, contends Martin E. P. Seligman of the University of Pennsylvania, president-elect of the American Psychological Association and an authority on efficacy research, are lithium for manic-depression and tranquilizers such as clozapine for schizophrenia. There is "simply no evidence," he remarks, that Prozac and other drugs are superior to talk therapies for more common disorders, such as depression and obsessive-compulsive disorder.

Seligman's view has been corroborated by three other psychologists, David O. Antonuccio and William G. Danton of the University of Nevada School of Medicine and Garland Y. DeNelsky of the Cleveland Clinic Foundation. In the December 1995 issue of *Professional Psychology*, they presented the results of a meta-analysis of dozens of studies of drugs and psychotherapy. The group concluded that psychological interventions, particularly cognitive-behavioral therapy, are at least as effective as medication in the treatment of depression, even if severe.

Two vociferous critics of the growing use of antidepressants are Seymour Fisher and Roger P. Greenberg, both psychologists at the State University of New York Health Science Center at Syracuse. Fisher and Greenberg have written extensively on Freud's theories, most recently in *Freud Scientifically Reappraised*, published this year by John Wiley & Sons. But they are best known for contending in their 1989 book *The Limits of Biological Treatments for Psychological Distress* (Lawrence Erlbaum) and in numerous articles that anti-

depressants are not nearly as effective as advertised.

After analyzing studies of antidepressants conducted over the past 30 years, they concluded that two thirds of the patients placed on medication either showed no improvement or responded equally well to a placebo as to the antidepressant; drugs produced significantly superior outcomes in only one third of patients. The studies also showed that the effects of medication wane for many patients after the first several months, and those who discontinue treatment have high relapse rates.

Depressing Results

The most serious claim Fisher and Greenberg make is that many ostensibly controlled, double-blind studies of antidepressants are actually biased in favor of showing positive effects. Such studies usually provide the control group with an inert placebo. But because all antidepressants usually cause side effects—such as dry mouth, sweating, constipation and sexual dysfunction—both patients and physicians can often determine who has received the drug, thus triggering an expectation of improvement that becomes self-fulfilling.

To avoid this problem, some drug trials have employed placebos that produce side effects resembling those of the antidepressant, such as dry mouth or sweating. (Atropine, which is often prescribed for motion sickness, is a common substitute.) These studies generally find much less difference between the antidepressant and the placebo than do studies in which the placebo is inert, Fisher and Greenberg note.

Other effects may also skew results, the authors argue. For example, during the course of a study many patients drop out because of unpleasant side effects, an unwillingness to conform to the protocol of the study or other problems. Moreover investigators seeking subjects for a study often exclude those who seem too inarticulate or disor-

ganized or whose depression is accompanied by other physical or mental ailments. In an overview of their findings in the September/October 1995 issue of *Psychology Today*, Fisher and Greenberg concluded that "most past studies of the efficacy of psychotropic drugs are, to unknown degrees, scientifically untrustworthy."

The findings of Fisher and Greenberg have been roundly faulted by psychiatrists, who contend that as psychologists—who cannot prescribe drugs—they are biased in favor of psychotherapy and against medication. But the assertion that the placebo effect might explain much of the effectiveness of medications for emotional disorders has been supported by Walter A. Brown, a psychiatrist at Brown University and an authority on the placebo effect.

It is a tenet of medical lore, Brown elaborates, that patients respond better to new drugs than to older, more established ones. The phenomenon is summed up in a doctor's dictum that dates back to the last century: "Use new drugs quickly, while they still work." The introduction of a novel drug, Brown explains, often generates high hopes among both patients and physicians and thus induces a strong placebo effect: over time, as the drug's novelty fades and its side effects and limitations become more apparent, it becomes less effective.

Unfortunately, neither psychotherapy nor antidepressants are terribly effective at treating depression, according to an ambitious study initiated by the National Institute of Mental Health almost 20 years ago. Called the Treatment of Depression Collaborative Research Program, it involved 239 depressed patients treated at three different hospitals with one of four different methods: cognitive-behavioral therapy; interpersonal therapy; the antidepressant imipramine plus "clinical management," a brief weekly consultation with the drug-dispensing physician; and clinical management with a placebo pill.

The study, the results of which were released in 1989, has been subjected to second-guessing almost since its inception. Earlier this year, in the *Journal of Consulting and Clinical Psychology* (Vol. 64, No. 1), the psychologist Irene Elkin of the University of Chicago and three colleagues reviewed the data in "Science Is Not a Trial (But It Can Sometimes Be a Tribulation)." The findings were not encouraging, the researchers admitted.

Some severely depressed patients, especially those who were functionally impaired, responded better to imipramine than to the psychotherapies. But for the majority of patients, there was little or no significant difference between any of the treatments, including the placebo-plus-clinical-management approach. Only 24 percent of the patients were judged to have recovered and not relapsed for a sustained period. "Although many people improved," Elkin says, "if you look at the total picture, at the number of people who got significantly better and stayed well, that number is low."

One increasingly popular view in mental-health circles is that psychotherapy and drugs can work best in tandem. A notable advocate of this idea is Peter D. Kramer, a psychiatrist at Brown and author of the 1993 best-seller *Listening to Prozac* (Penguin). Although the book is often described as a prodrug, antipsychotherapy tract, Kramer calls himself "a psychotherapist at heart" who thinks drugs can enhance the effects of talk therapy, and vice versa. In the future, he says, "there will be something called psychotherapy that will subsume psychotherapy as it is currently practiced and psychopharmacology."

But the view that psychotherapy-plus-drugs can be more effective than psychotherapy alone was undermined by a survey carried out recently by *Consumer Reports*. The magazine—published by the Consumers Union, a nonprofit group based in Yonkers, N.Y.—asked readers about their experiences seeking help for emotional difficulties. The magazine released the results of its survey, to which 4,000 readers responded, in the November 1995 issue.

The survey had much to comfort talk therapists. Most readers said they had been helped by psychotherapy; in addition, the longer they remained in therapy, the more they felt they had improved. Some observers worried that this finding might reflect the tendency of certain patients to become "therapy addicts." Nevertheless, the American Psychological Association immediately began using the finding to criticize the practice of health insurers to place strict limits on the duration of talk therapy.

A Unified Science of Mind

Psychologists were also delighted that readers who received psychotherapy alone seemed to fare as well as those getting talk therapy in conjunction with drugs such as Prozac. The *Consumer Reports* survey "has provided empirical validation of the effectiveness of psychotherapy," declared Seligman, president-elect of the psychology association, in the December 1995 issue of *American Psychologist*. He acknowledged that the survey had some methodological weaknesses. But these flaws were no more severe than those of more formal comparison studies, he asserted.

On the other hand, the survey also lent support to the Dodo hypothesis. All the therapies seemed to be equally effective—or ineffective. Respondents reported the same degree of satisfaction whether they were treated by social workers, who require only a master's degree; psychologists, who need a doctorate; or psychiatrists, who must complete medical school. Only marriage counselors scored lower than the norm. But readers reported more satisfaction with Alcoholics Anonymous than with any of the mental-health professionals or medications.

Optimists hope that in years to come, the sciences of the mind will coalesce around a new, more powerful paradigm, one that will transcend the schisms—nature versus nurture, drugs versus talk therapy—now rending the mental-health community. One proponent of such a shift is Steven Hyman, a psychiatrist and neuroscientist at Harvard University who was appointed director of the National Institute of Mental Health this past spring. "From the point of view of people who think about the brain and mental health, the traditional dichotomies are simply false," he declares.

Research has shown that traumatic experiences can change the way the brain works, as can talk therapy, Hyman notes. As evidence, he cites an article in the February 1996 *Archives of General Psychiatry* about patients who received cognitive-behavioral therapy for obsessive-compulsive disorder; positron-emission tomography showed that their brains had undergone changes similar to those induced by medication in other obsessive-compulsive patients.

Hyman is confident that genetics, brain imaging and other fields will generate new insights into and treatments for mental illness. Yet he describes himself as an "equal opportunity skeptic," who views not only Freudian theory but also some of the new biological explanations of mental illness as merely "good stories" still lacking empirical substantiation. "We are not going to clone the next serotonin receptor and say we understand the brain," he remarks.

That scholars still debate Freud's ideas, Hyman adds, suggests that science's grasp of the mind is still rather tenuous; after all, experts on infectious diseases do not debate the validity of Louis Pasteur's ideas. "In mature scientific fields," he notes, "one usually doesn't look at writings more than three or four years old." Freud, it seems, may be with us for some time to come.

The Benefits and Ethics of Animal Research

*Experiments on animals are a mainstay
of modern medical and scientific research.
But what are the costs and what are the returns?*

by Andrew N. Rowan

For the past 20 years, we have witnessed an intense but largely unproductive debate over the propriety and value of using animals in medical and scientific research, testing and education. Emotionally evocative images and simple assertions of opinion and fact are the usual fare. But we do not have to accept such low standards of exchange. Sound bites and pithy rhetoric may have their place in the fight for the public's ear, but there is always room for dispassionate analysis and solid scholarship.

When it comes to animal research, there is plenty of reason for legitimate dispute. First, one has to determine what values are being brought to the table. If one believes animals should not be used simply as means to ends, that assumption greatly restricts what animal research one is

willing to accept. Most people, though, believe some form of cost-benefit analysis should be performed to determine whether the use of animals is acceptable. The costs consist mainly of animal pain, distress and death, whereas the benefits include the acquisition of new knowledge and the development of new medical therapies for humans.

There is considerable disagreement among scientists in judging how much pain and suffering occur in the housing and use of research animals. More attention is at last being given to assessing these questions and to finding ways of minimizing such discomfort. Developing techniques that explicitly address and eliminate animal suffering in laboratories will reduce both public and scientific uneasiness about the

ways animals are used in science. At present, indications are that public attention to the animal research issue has declined somewhat; however, the level of concern among scientists, research institutions, animal-rights groups and those who regulate animal use remains high.

There is also much room to challenge the benefits of animal research and much room to defend such research. In the next few pages, you will find a debate between opponents and supporters of animal research.... We leave it to you to judge the case.

ANDREW N. ROWAN is director of the Tufts University Center for Animals and Public Policy.

Animal Research Is Wasteful and Misleading

by Neal D. Barnard and Stephen R. Kaufman

The use of animals for research and testing is only one of many investigative techniques available. We believe that although animal experiments are sometimes intellectually seductive, they are poorly suited to addressing the urgent health problems of our era, such as heart disease, cancer, stroke, AIDS and birth defects. Even worse, animal experiments can mislead researchers or even contribute to illnesses or deaths by failing to predict the toxic effects of drugs. Fortunately, other, more reliable methods that represent a far better investment of research funds can be employed.

The process of scientific discovery often begins with unexpected observations that force researchers to reconsider existing theories and to conceive hypotheses that better explain their findings. Many of the apparent anomalies seen in animal experiments, however, merely reflect the unique biology of the species being studied, the unnatural means by which the disease was induced or the stressful environment of the laboratory. Such irregularities are irrelevant to human pathology, and testing hypotheses derived from these observations wastes considerable time and money.

The majority of animals in laboratories are used as so-called animal models: through genetic manipulation, surgical intervention or injection of foreign substances, researchers produce ailments in these animals that "model" human conditions. This research paradigm is fraught with difficulties, however. Evolutionary pressures have resulted in innumerable subtle, but significant, differences between species. Each species has multiple systems of organs—the cardiovascular and nervous systems, for example—that have complex interactions with one another. A stimulus applied to one particular organ system perturbs the animal's overall physiological functioning in myriad ways that often cannot be predicted or fully understood. Such uncertainty severely undermines the extrapolation of animal data to other species, including humans.

Animal Tests Are Inapplicable

Important medical advances have been delayed because of misleading results derived from animal experiments. David Wiebers and his colleagues at the Mayo Clinic, writing in the journal *Stroke* in 1990, described a study showing that of the 25 compounds that reduced damage from ischemic stroke (caused by lack of blood flow to the brain) in rodents, cats and other animals, none proved efficacious in human trials. The researchers attributed the disappointing results to disparities between how strokes naturally occur in humans and how they were experimentally triggered in the animals. For instance, a healthy animal that experiences a sudden stroke does not undergo the slowly progressive arterial damage that usually plays a crucial role in human strokes.

During the 1920s and 1930s, studies on monkeys led to gross misconceptions that delayed the fight against poliomyelitis. These experiments indicated that the poliovirus infects mainly the nervous system; scientists later learned this was because the viral strains they had administered through the nose had artificially developed an affinity for brain tissue. The erroneous conclusion, which contradicted previous human studies demonstrating that the gastrointestinal system was the primary route of infection, resulted in misdirected preventive measures and delayed the development of a vaccine. Research with human cell cultures in 1949 first showed that the virus could be cultivated on nonneural tissues taken from the intestine and limbs. Yet in the early 1950s, cell cultures from monkeys rather than humans were used for vaccine production; as a result, millions of people were exposed to potentially harmful monkey viruses.

In a striking illustration of the inadequacy of animal research, scientists in the 1960s deduced from numerous animal experiments that inhaled tobacco smoke did not cause lung cancer (tar from the smoke painted on the skin of rodents did cause tumors to develop, but these results were deemed less relevant than the inhalation studies). For many years afterward, the tobacco lobby was able to use these studies to delay government warnings and to discourage physicians from intervening in their patients' smoking habits.

Of course, human population studies provided inescapable evidence of the tobacco-cancer connection, and recent human DNA studies have identified tobacco's "smoking gun," showing how a derivative of the carcinogen benzo(a)-pyrene targets human genes, causing cancer. (It turns out that cancer research is especially sensitive to differences in physiology between humans and other animals. Many animals, particularly rats and mice, synthesize within their bodies approximately 100 times the recommended daily allowance for humans of vitamin C, which is believed to help the body ward off cancer.)

The stress of handling, confinement and isolation alters an animal's physiology and introduces yet another experimental variable that makes extrapolating results to humans even more difficult. Stress on animals in laboratories can increase susceptibility to infectious disease and certain tumors as well as influence levels of hormones and antibodies, which in turn can alter the functioning of various organs.

In addition to medical research, animals are also used in the laboratory to test the safety of drugs and other chemicals; again, these studies are confounded by the fact that tests on different species often provide conflicting results. For instance, in 1988 Lester Lave of Carnegie Mellon University reported in the journal *Nature* that dual experiments to test the carcinogenicity of 214 compounds on both rats and mice agreed with each other only 70 percent of the time. The correlation between rodents and humans could only be lower. David Salsburg of Pfizer Central Research has noted that of 19 chemicals known to cause cancer in humans when ingested, only seven caused cancer in mice and rats using the standards set by the National Cancer Institute.

Indeed, many substances that appeared safe in animal studies and received approval from the U.S. Food and Drug Administration for use in humans later proved dangerous to people. The drug milrinone, which raises cardiac output, increased survival of rats with artificially induced heart failure; humans with severe chronic heart failure taking this drug had a 30 percent increase in mortality. The antiviral drug fialuridine seemed safe in animal trials yet caused liver failure in seven of 15 humans taking the drug (five of these patients died as a result of the medication, and the other two received liver transplants). The commonly used painkiller zomepirac sodium was popular in the early 1980s, but after it was implicated in 14 deaths and hundreds of life-threatening allergic reactions, it was withdrawn from the market. The antidepressant nomifensine, which had minimal toxicity in rats, rabbits, dogs and monkeys, caused liver toxicity and anemia in humans—rare yet severe, and sometimes fatal, effects that forced the manufacturer to withdraw the product a few months after its introduction in 1985.

These frightening mistakes are not mere anecdotes. The U.S. General Accounting Office reviewed 198 of the 209 new drugs marketed between 1976 and 1985 and found that 52 percent had "serious postapproval risks" not predicted by animal tests or limited human trials. These risks were defined as adverse reactions that could lead to hospitalization, disability or death. As a result, these drugs had to be relabeled with new warnings or withdrawn from the market. And of course, it is impossible to estimate how many potentially useful drugs may have been needlessly abandoned because animal tests falsely suggested inefficacy or toxicity.

Better Methods

Researchers have better methods at their disposal. These techniques include epidemiological studies, clinical intervention trials, astute clinical observation aided by laboratory testing, human tissue and cell cultures, autopsy studies, endoscopic examination and biopsy, as well as new imaging methods. And the emerging science of molecular epidemiology, which relates genetic, metabolic and biochemical factors with epidemiological data on disease incidence, offers significant promise for identifying the causes of human disease. Consider the success of research on atherosclerotic heart disease. Initial epidemiological investigations in humans—notably the Framingham Heart Study, started in 1948—revealed the risk factors for heart disease, including high cholesterol levels, smoking and high blood pressure. Researchers then altered these factors in controlled human trials, such as the multicenter Lipid Research Clinics Trial, carried out in the 1970s and 1980s. These studies illustrated, among many other things, that every 1 percent drop in serum cholesterol levels led to at least a 2 percent drop in risk for heart disease. Autopsy results and chemical studies added further links between risk factors and disease, indicating that people consuming high-fat diets acquire arterial changes early in life. And studies of heart disease patients indicated that eating a low-fat vegetarian diet, getting regular mild exercise, quitting smoking and managing stress can reverse atherosclerotic blockages.

Similarly, human population studies of HIV infection elucidated how the virus was transmitted and guided intervention programs. In vitro studies using human cells and serum allowed researchers to identify the AIDS virus and determine how it causes disease. Investigators also used in vitro studies to assess the efficacy and safety of important new AIDS drugs such as AZT, 3TC and protease inhibitors. New leads, such as possible genetic and environmental factors that contribute to the disease or provide resistance to it, are also emerging from human studies.

Many animals have certainly been used in AIDS research, but without much in the way of tangible results. For instance, the widely reported monkey studies using the simian immunodeficiency virus (SIV) under unnatural conditions suggested that oral sex presented a transmission risk. Yet this study did not help elucidate whether oral sex transmitted HIV in humans or not. In other cases, data from animal studies have merely repeated information already established by other experiments. In 1993 and 1994 Gerard J. Nuovo and his colleagues at the State University of New York at Stony Brook determined the route of HIV into the female body (the virus passes through cells in the cervix and then to nearby lymph nodes) using studies of human cervical and lymph node samples. Later, experimenters at New York University placed SIV into the vaginas of rhesus monkeys, then killed the animals and dissected the organs; their paper, published in 1996, arrived at essentially the same conclusion about the virus's path as did the previous human studies.

Research into the causes of birth defects has relied heavily on animal experiments, but these have typically proved to be embarrassingly poor predictors of what can happen in humans. The rates for most birth defects are rising steadily. Epidemiological studies are needed to trace possible genetic and environmental factors associated with birth defects, just as population studies linked lung cancer to smoking and heart disease to cholesterol. Such surveys have already provided some vital information—the connection between neural tube defects and folate deficiency and the identification of fetal alcohol syndrome are notable findings—but much more human population research is needed.

Observations of humans have proved to be invaluable in cancer research as well. Several studies have shown that cancer patients who follow diets low in fat and rich in vegetables and fruit live longer and have a lower risk of recurrence. We now need intervention trials to test which specific diets help with various types of cancers.

The issue of what role, if any, animal experimentation played in past discoveries is not relevant to what is necessary now for research and safety testing. Before scientists developed the cell and tissue cultures common today, animals were routinely used to harbor infectious organisms. But there are few diseases for which this is still the case—modern methods for vaccine production are safer and more efficient. Animal toxicity tests to determine the potency of drugs such as digitalis and insulin have largely been replaced with sophisticated laboratory tests that do not involve animals.

A Rhetorical Device

Animal "models" are, at best, analogous to human conditions, but no theory can be proved or refuted by analogy. Thus, it makes no logical sense to test a theory about humans using animals. Nevertheless, when scientists debate the validity of competing theories in medicine and biology, they often cite animal studies as evidence. In this context, animal experiments serve primarily as rhetorical devices. And by using different kinds of animals in different protocols, experimenters can find evidence in support of virtually any theory. For instance, researchers have used animal experiments to show that cigarettes both do and do not cause cancer.

Harry Harlow's famous monkey experiments, conducted in the 1960s at the University of Wisconsin, involved separating infant monkeys from their mothers and keeping some of them in total isolation for a year. The experiments, which left the animals severely damaged emotionally, served primarily as graphic illustrations of the need for maternal contact—a fact already well established from observations of human infants.

Animal experimenters often defend their work with brief historical accounts of the supposedly pivotal role of animal data in past advances. Such interpretations are easily skewed. For example, proponents of animal use often point to the significance of animals to diabetes research. But human studies by Thomas Cawley, Richard Bright and Appollinaire Bouchardat in the 18th and 19th centuries first revealed the importance of pancreatic damage in diabetes. In addition, human studies by Paul Langerhans in 1869 led to the discovery of insulin-producing islet cells. And although cows and pigs were once the primary sources for insulin to treat diabetes, human insulin is now the standard therapy, revolutionizing how patients manage the disease.

Animal experimenters have also asserted that animal tests could have predicted the birth defects caused by the drug thalidomide. Yet most animal species used in laboratories do not develop the kind of limb defects seen in humans after thalidomide exposure; only rabbits and some primates do. In nearly all animal birth-defect tests, scientists are left scratching their heads as to whether humans are more like the animals who develop birth defects or like those who do not.

In this discussion, we have not broached the ethical objections to animal experimentation. These are critically important issues. In the past few decades, scientists have come to a new appreciation of the tremendous complexity of animals' lives, including their ability to communicate, their social structures and emotional repertoires. But pragmatic issues alone should encourage scientists and governments to put research money elsewhere.

NEAL D. BARNARD and STEPHEN R. KAUFMAN are both practicing physicians. Barnard conducts nutrition research and is president of the Physicians Committee for Responsible Medicine. Kaufman is co-chair of the Medical Research Modernization Committee.

Animal Research Is Vital to Medicine

by Jack H. Botting and Adrian R. Morrison

Experiments using animals have played a crucial role in the development of modern medical treatments, and they will continue to be necessary as researchers seek to alleviate existing ailments and respond to the emergence of new disease. As any medical scientist will readily state, research with animals is but one of several complementary approaches. Some questions, however, can be answered only by animal research. We intend to show exactly where we regard animal research to have been essential in the past and to point to where we think it will be vital in the future. To detail all the progress that relied on animal experimentation would require many times the amount of space allotted to us. Indeed, we cannot think of an area of medical research that does not owe many of its most important advances to animal experiments.

In the mid-19th century, most debilitating diseases resulted from bacterial or viral infections, but at the time, most physicians considered these ailments to be caused by internal derangements of the body. The proof that such diseases did in fact derive from external microorganisms originated with work done by the French chemist Louis Pasteur and his contemporaries, who studied infectious diseases in domestic animals. Because of his knowledge of how contaminants caused wine and beer to spoil, Pasteur became convinced that microorganisms were also responsible for diseases such as chicken cholera and anthrax.

To test his hypothesis, Pasteur examined the contents of the guts of chickens suffering from cholera; he isolated a possible causative microbe and then grew the organism in culture. Samples of the culture given to healthy chickens and rabbits produced cholera, thus proving that Pasteur had correctly identified the offending organism. By chance, he noticed that after a time, cultures of the microorganisms lost their ability to infect. But birds given the ineffective cultures became resistant to fresh batches that were otherwise lethal to untreated birds. Physicians had previously observed that among people who survived a severe attack of certain diseases, recurrence of the disease was rare; Pasteur had found a means of producing this resistance without risk of disease. This experience suggested to him that with the administration of a weakened culture of the disease-causing bacteria, doctors might be able to induce in their patients immunity to infectious diseases.

In similar studies on rabbits and guinea pigs, Pasteur isolated the microbe that causes anthrax and then developed a vaccine against the deadly disease. With the information from animal experiments—obviously of an extent that could never have been carried out on humans—he proved not only that infectious diseases could be produced by microorganisms but also that immunization could protect against these diseases.

Pasteur's findings had a widespread effect. For example, they influenced the views of the prominent British surgeon Joseph Lister, who pioneered the use of carbolic acid to sterilize surgical instruments, sutures and wound dressings, thereby preventing infection of wounds. In 1875 Queen Victoria asked Lister to address the Royal Commission inquiry into vivisection—as the queen put it, "to make some statement in condemnation of these horrible practices." As a Quaker, Lister had spoken publicly against many cruelties of Victorian society, but despite the request of his sovereign, he was unable to condemn vivisection. His testimony to the Royal Commission stated that animal experiments had been essential to his own work on asepsis and that to restrict research with animals would prevent discoveries that would benefit humankind.

Dozens of Vaccines and Antibiotics

Following the work of Pasteur and others, scientists have established causes of and vaccines for dozens of infectious diseases, including diphtheria, tetanus, rabies, whooping cough, tuberculosis, poliomyelitis, measles, mumps and rubella. The investigation of these ailments indisputably relied heavily on animal experimentation: in most cases, researchers identified candidate microorganisms and then administered the microbes to animals to see if they contracted the illness in question.

Similar work continues to this day. Just recently, scientists developed a vaccine against *Hemophilus influenzae* type B (Hib), a major cause of meningitis, which before 1993 resulted in death or severe brain damage in more than 800 children each year in the U.S. Early versions of a vaccine produced only poor, short-lived immunity. But a new vaccine, prepared and tested in rabbits and mice, proved to be powerfully immunogenic and is now in routine use. Within two months of the vaccine's introduction in the U.S. and the U.K., Hib infections fell by 70 percent.

Animal research not only produced new vaccines for the treatment of infectious disease, it also led to the development of antibacterial and antibiotic drugs. In 1935, despite aseptic precautions, trivial wounds could lead to serious infections that resulted in amputation or death. At the same time, in both Europe and the U.S., death from puerperal sepsis (a disease that mothers can contract after childbirth, usually as a result of infection by hemolytic streptococci) occurred in 200 of every 100,000 births. In addition, 60 of every 100,000 men aged 45 to 64 died from lobar pneumonia. When sulfonamide drugs became available, these figures fell dramatically: by 1960 only five out of every 100,000 mothers contracted puerperal sepsis, and only six of every 100,000 middle-aged men succumbed to lobar pneumonia. A range of other infections could also be treated with these drugs.

The story behind the introduction of sulfonamide drugs is instructive. The team investigating these compounds—Gerhard Domagk's group at Bayer Laboratories in Wuppertal-Elberfeld, Germany—insisted that all candidate compounds be screened in infected mice (using the so-called mouse protection test) rather than against bacteria grown on agar plates. Domagk's perspicacity was fortunate: the compound prontosil, for instance, proved to be extremely potent in mice, but it had no effect on bacteria in vitro—the active antibacterial substance, sulfanilamide, was formed from prontosil within the body. Scientists synthesized other, even more powerful sulfonamide drugs and used them successfully against many infections. For his work on antibacterial drugs, Domagk won the Nobel Prize in 1939.

A lack of proper animal experimentation unfortunately delayed for a decade the use of the remarkable antibiotic penicillin: Alexander Fleming, working in 1929, did not use mice to examine the efficacy of his cultures containing crude penicillin (although he did show the cultures had no toxic effects on mice and rabbits). In 1940, however, Howard W. Florey, Ernst B. Chain and others at the University of Oxford finally showed penicillin to be dramatically effective as an antibiotic via the mouse protection test.

Despite the success of vaccines and antibacterial therapy, infectious disease remains the greatest threat to human life worldwide. There is no effective vaccine against malaria or AIDS; physicians increasingly face strains of bacteria resistant to current antibacterial drugs; new infectious diseases continue to emerge. It is hard to envisage how new and better vaccines and medicines against infectious disease can be developed without experiments involving animals.

Research on animals has been vital to numerous other areas in medicine. Open-heart surgery—which saves the lives of an estimated 440,000 people every year in the U.S. alone—is now routine, thanks to 20 years of animal research by scientists such as John Gibbon of Jefferson Medical College in Philadelphia. Replacement heart valves also emerged from years of animal experimentation.

The development of treatments for kidney failure has relied on step-by-step improvement of techniques through animal experiments. Today kidney dialysis and even kidney transplants can save the lives of patients suffering from renal failure as a result of a variety of ailments, including poisoning, severe hemorrhage, hypertension or diabetes. Roughly 200,000 people require dialysis every year in the U.S.; some 11,000 receive a new kidney. Notably, a drug essential for dialysis—heparin—must be extracted from animal tissues and tested for safety on anesthetized animals.

Transplantation of a kidney or any major organ presents a host of complications; animal research has been instrumental in generating solutions to these problems. Experiments on cats helped develop techniques for suturing blood vessels from the host to the donor organ so that the vessels would be strong enough to withstand arterial pressure. Investigators working with rabbits, rodents, dogs and monkeys have also determined ways to suppress the immune system to avoid rejection of the donor organ.

The list continues. Before the introduction of insulin, patients with diabetes typically died from the disease. For more than 50 years, the lifesaving hormone had to be extracted from the pancreas of cattle or pigs; these batches of insulin also had to be tested for safety and efficacy on rabbits or mice.

When we started our scientific careers, the diagnosis of malignant hypertension carried with it a prognosis of death within a year, often preceded by devastating headaches and blindness. Research on anesthetized cats in the 1950s heralded an array of progressively improved antihypertensive medicines, so that today treatment of hypertension is effective and relatively benign. Similarly, gastric ulcers often necessitated surgery with a marked risk of morbidity afterward. Now antiulcer drugs, developed from tests in rats and dogs, can control the condition and may effect a cure if administered with antibiotics to eliminate *Helicobacter pylori* infection.

Common Misconceptions

Much is made in animal-rights propaganda of alleged differences between species in their physiology or responses to drugs that supposedly render animal experiments redundant or misleading. These claims can usually be refuted by proper examination of the literature. For instance, opponents of animal research frequently cite the drug thalidomide as an example of a medicine that was thoroughly tested on animals and showed its teratogenic effect only in humans. But this is not so. Scientists never tested thalidomide in pregnant animals until after fetal deformities were observed in humans. Once they ran these tests, researchers recognized that the drug did in fact cause fetal abnormalities in rabbits, mice, rats, hamsters and several species of monkey. Similarly, some people have claimed that penicillin would not have been used in patients had it first been administered to guinea pigs, because it is inordinately toxic to this species. Guinea pigs, however, respond to penicillin in exactly the same way as do the many patients who contract antibiotic-induced colitis when placed on long-term penicillin therapy. In both guinea pigs and humans, the cause of the colitis is infection with the bacterium *Clostridium difficile.*

In truth, there are no basic differences between the physiology of laboratory animals and humans. Both control their internal biochemistry by releasing endocrine hormones that are all essentially the same; both humans and laboratory animals send out similar chemical transmitters from nerve cells in the central and peripheral nervous systems, and both react in the same way to infection or tissue injury.

Animal models of disease are unjustly criticized by assertions that they are not identical to the conditions studied in humans. But they are not designed to be so; instead such models provide a means to study a particular procedure. Thus, cystic fibrosis in mice may not exactly mimic the human condition (which varies considerably among patients anyway), but it does provide a way to establish the optimal method of administering gene therapy to cure the disease. Opponents of animal experiments also allege that most illness can be avoided by a change of lifestyle; for example, adoption of a vegan diet that avoids all animal products. Whereas we support the promulgation of healthy practices, we do not consider that our examples could be prevented by such measures.

A Black Hole

Our opponents in this debate claim that even if animal experiments have played a part in the development of medical advances, this does not mean that they were essential. Had such techniques been outlawed, the argument goes, researchers would have been forced to be more creative and thus would have invented superior technologies. Others have suggested that there would not be a gaping black hole in place of animal research but instead more careful and respected clinical and cellular research.

In fact, there was a gaping black hole. No outstanding progress in the treatment of disease occurred until biomedical science was placed on a sound, empirical basis through experiments on animals. Early researchers, such as Pasteur and the 17th-century scientist William Harvey, who studied blood circulation in animals, were not drawn to animal experiments as an easy option. Indeed, they drew on all the techniques available at the time to answer their questions: sometimes dissection of a cadaver, sometimes observations of a patient, sometimes examination of bacteria in culture. At other times, though, they considered experimentation on animals to be necessary.

We would like to suggest an interesting exercise for those who hold the view that animal experiments, because of their irrelevance, have retarded progress: take an example of an advance dependent on animal experiments and detail how an alternative procedure could have provided the same material benefit. A suitable example would be treatment of the cardiac condition known as mitral valve insufficiency, caused by a defect in the heart's mitral valve. The production of prosthetic heart valves stemmed from years of development and testing for efficacy in dogs and calves. The artificial valve can be inserted only into a quiescent heart that has been bypassed by a heart-lung machine—an instrument that itself has been perfected after 20 years' experimentation in dogs. If, despite the benefit of 35 years of hindsight, critics of animal research cannot present a convincing scenario to show how effective treatment of mitral valve insufficiency could have developed any other way, their credibility is suspect.

Will animal experiments continue to be necessary to resolve extant medical problems? Transgenic animals with a single mutant gene have already provided a wealth of new information on the functions of proteins and their roles in disease; no doubt they will continue to do so. We also anticipate major progress in the treatment of traumatic injury to the central nervous system. The dogma that it is impossible to restore function to damaged nerve cells in the mammalian spinal cord has to be reassessed in the light of recent animal research indicating that nerve regeneration is indeed possible. It is only a matter of time before treatments begin to work. We find it difficult to envision how progress in this field—and so many others in biological and medical science—can be achieved in the future without animal experiments.

JACK H. BOTTING and ADRIAN R. MORRISON have been active in the defense of animal research since the 1980s. Botting, a retired university lecturer, is the former scientific adviser to the Research Defense Society in London. Morrison is director of the Laboratory for Study of the Brain in Sleep at the University of Pennsylvania School of Veterinary Medicine.

On the Validity of Psychology Experiments

Keynote speaker Kihlstrom discusses the investigator-subject relationship and implications for improving experiment validity

When she introduced John F. Kihlstrom of Yale University as keynote speaker at the opening session of the seventh annual APS convention in New York, Marilynn Brewer admitted a problem:

"Trying to find some thumbnail way to characterize or capture the kind of expertise that John Kihlstrom represents," Brewer said, "I found myself working on one of those tremendously hyphenated things—'John represents neuro-cognitive-social-clinical-personality'—and it was getting longer and longer, when suddenly I stopped myself and said: There is one word that captures the specialization and area of expertise that John represents and that is 'psychology.' He is truly a psychological scientist in the full sense of the broad range to which that applies."

Following are excerpts from Kihlstrom's address, "From a Subject's Point of View: The Experiment as Conversation and Collaboration between Investigator and Subject."

For a speaker and listener to communicate, they have to establish common ground. Each must have some sense of what the other person knows, believes, and supposes to be true, and each must use this knowledge in structuring his or her communication, [as] we know from the work of Stanford University psychologist Herbert Clark. If speaker and listener are not on common ground, they will not understand each other and their interactions cannot go very far.

In order to achieve this mutual understanding, people have to manage their conversations according to what Paul Grice, a linguist at the University of California–Berkeley, has called the cooperative principle: Make your conversational contribution such as is required, at the stage at which it occurs, by the accepted purpose or direction of the talk exchange in which you are engaged.

Of course, you don't need to be a Gricean sociolinguist to think about experiments that way. Harvard University psychologist Martin Orne had the same kind of idea about demand characteristics and the ecological validity of psychological experiments.

Over the years, both notions have been somewhat controversial. The demand characteristics argument got a reputation as a spoiler of experiments. But that's because most people who made the argument failed to appreciate what it was all about. You don't use demand characteristics to discount experiment outcomes—you evaluate them to make your experiments better, more ecologically valid, and more convincing. So I thought I would remind people what the argument was all about, and reflect on its connection to Gricean sociolinguistics, and on the meaning of both for what we do as psychological scientists.

From Orne's point of view, the purpose of laboratory research is to understand the real world, to make the problem simple so that it can be studied effectively, and to control relevant variables so that important relations, especially causal relations, can be revealed. Unfortunately, generalization from the lab to the real world requires an inferential leap: its legitimacy depends on the degree of similarity between the conditions which are obtained in the laboratory and those found in the real world.

The situation is bad enough in animal research, but it is even worse in human research, for the simple reason that human subjects are not reagents in test tubes—passive responders to the experimenter's manipulations. They are sentient, curious creatures, constantly thinking about what is happening to them, evaluating the proceedings, figuring out what they are supposed to do, and planning their responses. These normal human cognitive activities may interact with experimental procedures in unknown ways. At best, they can obscure the effects of a manipulation by adding noise to the system. At worst, they can render an entire experiment invalid.

For Orne, the experiment is a unique form of social encounter, with. roles and rules that are not found anywhere else (except perhaps in doctors' offices). This uniqueness may preclude generalizations from lab to life, which is what Orne means by threats to ecological validity.

In the first place, human subjects are volunteers who, in addition to their desire for remuneration (whether in cash or research participation points) have an emotional investment in research which stems from three goals: to further scientific knowledge, to find out something about themselves, and to present themselves in a positive light.

Second, the experimenter and the subject enter into an implicit contractual arrangement with specifically defined roles. The subject agrees to tolerate deception, discomfort and boredom for the good of science, and the experimenter guarantees the safety and well-being of the subject.

Third, the experiment is by its very nature episodic. In important respects it is divorced from the rest of the subject's life experiences and, in any event, it is time-limited and should have no permanent consequences for the subject.

Fourth, the subjects perceive the experiment in the context of their entire experience. In trying to discern what the experiment is all about and deciding what to do, they pick up on what Orne called the "demand characteristics" of the experiment. By this he meant the totality of cues available in the experimental situation which communicate the experimenter's design, hypotheses, and predictions. Some of these cues are explicitly present in the experimenter's instructions to the subject, but many of them are implicit in the solicitation materials, campus scuttlebutt, incidental remarks made by the research assistants, and hints communicated by the procedures. The important thing to understand is that demand characteristics aren't just communicated by the experimenter. Some demand characteristics are brought into the experiment by the subject, while others arise as the experiment proceeds. In either case, they're everywhere. In the final analysis, they are internal to the subject, they can't be predicted in advance by someone external to the experiments, and, in principle, they cannot be controlled. They can only be evaluated.

The subject's behavior is determined by his or her perceptions of the experimental situation, and those perceptions may be at variance with the experimenter's intentions. If this occurs, the experimenter and the subject are literally participating in two different experiments, and ecological validity is lost.

So in order to make sense of experimental outcomes, the experimenter must attempt to understand the subject's behavior from the subject's point of view. Unfortunately, this understanding is impeded by what Orne called the pact of ignorance implied by the experimental contract. Both parties want the experiment to work. Therefore, the subject agrees not to tell the experimenter that he or she has figured out the experiment, while the experimenter agrees not to force the subject to admit that he or she possesses this forbidden information.

In order to break the pact of ignorance, Orne argued, the experimenter and subject must alter their usual roles, concluding the experimental episode and transforming what once was a subject into a genuine co-investigator, who feels it is legitimate to reflect truthfully and dispassionately on what has gone on before. That's what Orne's real-simulator design was all about. Simulators aren't subjects in the usual sense, because they are only pretending to be in an experiment. They're not controlling for demand characteristics, or indeed for any other experimental variable. They are collaborators of the experimenter, helping to evaluate the experimental design.

All experiments have demand characteristics, and subjects can be guaranteed to pick up on them—threatening the ecological validity of our experiments—and we ignore this possibility, at our peril, as scientists.

Orne was concerned with ecological validity, and with the peculiar character of the experimental situation. To a great extent, he thought that demand characteristics were a problem because of motives that were peculiar to research participants—to help the experimenter, to learn about themselves, and to look good.

Grice reminds us, though, there is another motive which subjects display both in the lab and elsewhere in life. Subjects aren't just motivated to guess and confirm the experimenter's hypothesis. As listeners, that is, as people, they are primarily motivated to make sense of any communicative situation in which they find themselves. In that respect, at least, Orne needn't have worried. For what happens in the laboratory is entirely representative of what goes on in the real world. Because the laboratory is just like the real world after all, it follows that as we establish common ground and collaborate with our subjects we must be careful to follow Grice's maxims: Be cooperative. Be informative. Be true. Be relevant. And be clear.
—John F. Kihlstrom

Unit 2

Key Points to Consider

❖ What do you think contributes most to our psychological makeup and behaviors: the influence of the environment, the expression of genes, or the functioning of the nervous system? How do you think these factors account for psychological characteristics and behaviors? Do you think the importance of the environment changes as we mature? Explain.

❖ What is genetic research? How and why is it done? How much of human behavior are genes responsible for? Give some examples of the influence of genes on human behavior. How does such research help experts in psychology and medicine predict and treat various disorders? How do twins contribute to this type of research? What types of twins are there; how does each type help us understand the development of human behavior?

❖ How does the brain relate to human behavior and psychological characteristics? What functions does the brain control? Do specific parts of the brain control specific behaviors? How do we study the brain? What are some of the types of brain disorders and their symptoms? How do these disorders develop? Are any disorders reversible? How are brain disorders treated?

 **Links** | **www.dushkin.com/online/**

These sites are annotated on pages 4 and 5.

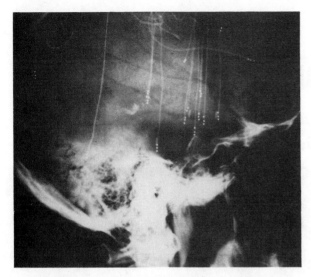

As a child, Nancy vowed she did not want to turn out like either of her parents. Nancy's mother was very passive and acquiescent about her father's drinking. When Dad was drunk, Mom always called his boss to report that Dad was "sick" and then acted as if there was nothing wrong at home. Nancy's childhood was a nightmare. Her father's behavior was erratic and unpredictable. If he drank just a little bit, he was happy. If he drank a lot, which was usually the case, he often became belligerent.

Despite vowing not to become like her father, as an adult Nancy found herself in the alcohol rehabilitation unit of a large hospital. Her employer could no longer tolerate her on-the-job mistakes or her unexplained absences from work, and he referred her to the clinic for help. As Nancy pondered her fate, she wondered whether her genes preordained her to follow in her father's inebriated footsteps or whether the stress of her childhood had brought her to this point in her life. After all, being the child of an alcoholic is not easy.

Just like Nancy, psychologists are concerned with discovering the causes of human behavior. Once the cause is known, treatments for problematic behaviors can be developed. In fact, certain behaviors might even be prevented when the cause is known. But for Nancy, prevention was too late.

One of the paths to understanding humans is to understand the biological underpinnings of their behavior. Genes and chromosomes, the body's chemistry (as found in hormones, neurotransmitters, and enzymes), and the central nervous system comprised of the brain, spinal cord, and nerve cells are all implicated in human behavior. All represent the biological aspects of behavior and ought, therefore, to be worthy of study by psychologists.

Physiological psychologists and psychobiologists examine the role of biology in behavior. The neuroscientist is especially interested in brain functioning; the psychopharmacologist is interested in the effects of various psychopharmacological agents or psychoactive drugs on behavior.

These psychologists often utilize one of three techniques to understand the biology-behavior connection. One technique is animal studies, as reviewed in the first unit, involving manipulation, stimulation, or destruction of certain parts of the brain. A second technique includes the examination of unfortunate individuals whose brains are defective at birth or damaged later by accidents or disease.

We can also use animal models to understand genetics; with animal models we can control reproduction and develop various strains of animals if necessary. Such tactics with humans would be considered extremely unethical. However, the third technique, studying an individual's behavior in comparison to both natural and adoptive parents or studying identical twins reared together or apart, allows psychologists to begin to understand the role of genetics versus that of the environment in human behavior.

This unit is designed to familiarize you with the knowledge that psychologists have gleaned by using these techniques as well as others to study physiological processes and mechanisms in human behavior. I believe each article will interest you and make you more curious about the role of biology in human endeavors.

The first selection in this unit provides a general overview of psychobiological behavior versus environmental issues. In "Nature, Nurture: Not Mutually Exclusive," Beth Azar reviews how genes and the environment interact to affect us and comes to the conclusion that human behavior is probably the complex interplay of many factors related to both nature and nurture.

The next selection examines the role of genes in human behavior. The article, "What We Learn from Twins: The Mirror of Your Soul," reviews why psychologists study twins—to examine the effects of genetics and compare them to environmental effects. The selection does a good job of differentiating between identical and fraternal twins, explaining how each type of twin allows us to understand aspects of the nature-nurture debate. Such twin research is not without controversy.

The next two selections pertain to the brain and the nervous system, the other biological underpinnings of our psychological being. In "Secrets of the Brain," Mark Nichols describes the advances in understanding of the brain and nervous system afforded researchers by new brain-imaging technology. With such technology we are better able to understand brain functions and what parts of the brain control which activities. With this technology, researchers are beginning to understand whether, and under what circumstances, the brain can regenerate itself. In "Revealing the Brain's Secrets" Kathleen Allison explores the role of molecular biology in understanding Alzheimer's disease and other brain disorders. Genetics as well as the environment seem to play a role in these disorders, which means that the job of treating them is made harder.

Biological Bases of Behavior

Nature, nurture: not mutually exclusive

Studies on twins have established that most traits and behaviors are partially influenced by genes.

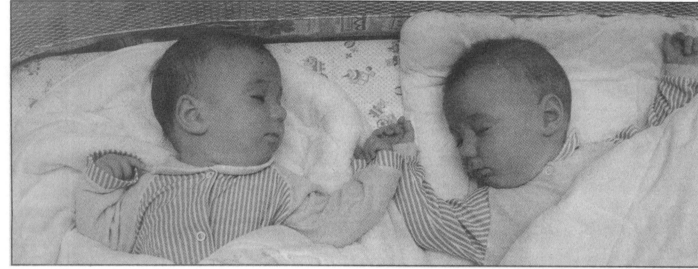

Elizabeth Crews/The Image Works

Beth Azar
Monitor staff

Psychologist Robert Plomin, PhD, would like to see the nature versus nurture debate end. Most human behaviors are not influenced by nature *or* nurture but by nature *and* nurture, he says.

Studies over the past 20 years on twins and adopted children have firmly established that there is a genetic component to just about every human trait and behavior, including personality, general intelligence and behavioral disorders such as schizophrenia and autism.

But the genetic influence on these traits and behaviors is only partial: Genetics account, on average, for half of the variance of most traits. That means the environment accounts for the rest, said Plomin.

"Twin and adoption studies have established that most traits and behaviors are partially influenced by genes," said Thomas Bouchard, PhD, of the University of Minnesota. "Now, using the same techniques, we can ask a lot more detailed and searching questions about the interaction between genes and the environment, between nature and nurture."

Such studies are painting a much more complex picture of development than psychologists had previously conceived. Researchers are finding that the balance between genetic and environmental influences on certain traits change as people age. They also find that genes not only influence behavior directly but may also influence the environment. In other words, our experiences may be influenced in part by our genetic propensities—people may react to us in certain ways because of a genetically influenced personality and we may choose certain experi-

ences because they fit best with out innate preferences.

Such findings imply that the only valid way to study environmental influences on human development is to use genetically sensitive designs, say many researchers.

"If we want to understand things like how the relationships between parents and children affect development, we must conduct genetically informed studies," said psychologist Nathan Brody, PhD, of Wesleyan University. "I'm a generalist, not a behavioral geneticist, but I find that knowing some behavioral genetics is essential as a way of addressing the field."

Increasing inheritance

One way researchers can study the development of traits and behaviors is to measure the influence of genetics

Dolly helps researchers underscore importance of environment

The announcement last winter that researchers successfully cloned a sheep and two monkeys brings up countless ethical conundrums regarding the potential to clone humans.

But it also gives behavioral geneticists an ideal opportunity to emphasize the ultimate importance of the environment to human development.

"As the public is exposed to all this information about cloning and molecular genetics, they may realize, as we have, that while genetics is important, the environment really plays a big role," said Christopher Cunningham, PhD, of the Oregon Health Sciences University. "As soon as the cells of an embryo are implanted [into a surrogate mother], it's unique because its experiences are different."

"The data are in and the environment is important to how people develop," adds psychologist Thomas Bouchard, PhD, of the University of Minnesota. As head of the Minnesota Study of Twins Reared Apart, he's spent most of his career studying twins—a natural study of cloning.

While research has established beyond a doubt that many aspects of human behavior are partly inherited (see article), the same work also affirms the critical importance of environment in shaping who we are, said Bouchard. By environment, researchers are referring to everything from the prenatal environment to the home environment. A person's clone would be more different from him or her than two identical twins are from one another because they would not share such environments, said Robert Plomin, PhD, of the Institute of Psychiatry in London. "Although identical twins are in effect clones,

AP Photo/Paul Clements

Dolly, the cloned sheep, is fueling the nature v. nurture debate.

they're only about 50 percent concordant on most traits" indicating that the environment accounts for the other 50 percent, he said. "That means that real clones will also not be identical—they grow up in a different time with different parents and should be even less similar than identical twins."

Even though genes may influence people's personality and social preferences, in the end, individual experiences will affect which niches they drop into and, in effect, who they become, said Bouchard.

—Beth Azar

throughout the life span. When they do, they find that the genetic influence on several traits increases as people age, said Plomin.

This phenomenon is most apparent in studies of general cognitive ability. The Colorado Adoption Project, for example, found that the resemblance on general cognitive ability between adopted children and their birth parents increased dramatically from ages 3 to 16. In contrast, there was no relationship between the IQ of adopted children at age 16 and their adoptive parents, indicating that the general rearing environment has little impact on IQ, said John DeFries, PhD, a principal investigator on the project.

"This is a striking result," said DeFries, director of the University of Colorado at Boulder's Institute for Be-

havioral Genetics. "Although early on there is a small correlation between adoptive parents and their adopted children, this resemblance fades. I'm convinced that parents do have an impact on their children beyond their genes but such environmental influences do not seem to be correlated with cognitive ability."

Defining the Environment

The results also highlight a distinction behavioral geneticists make between two major sources of environmental influence:

- Shared environmental factors, which are common to children reared together and cause similarities in their behavior; and

- Nonshared environmental factors, which are unique to children reared together and cause differences in their behavior.

For example, parents with two unrelated adopted children provide a common rearing environment—a shared environment that should make the unrelated siblings similar in some respects. But the children also have unique interactions with their parents and distinct perceptions of family encounters that may influence each sibling in different ways.

Behavioral genetics research shows that nonshared environment accounts for most of the environmental influence on children's personalities and moods. The most psychologically relevant environmental influences are those that make children in a family different from, not similar to, one another, said Plomin.

To evaluate which aspects of non-shared environment contribute to child adjustment, several years ago David Reiss, MD, of George Washington University, and several colleagues including Plomin and E. Mavis Heatherington, PhD, of the University of Virginia, began the Nonshared Environment and Adolescent Development (NEAD) project, which included twins as well as full siblings, half-siblings and step-siblings. They expected to pin down some general principles of nonshared environment that affect all people in a similar way. For example, children whose fathers treated them roughly but treated their siblings nicely might all suffer similar developmental problems.

Indeed, the research team found that if parents direct more negative attention toward one child than another, that child is more likely to experience adjustment difficulties, measured as depressive symptoms and antisocial behavior.

However, the correlation between parental treatment and child adjustment virtually disappeared when the researchers accounted for genetic influences on how parents treat their children. Parents' behavior seemed to be highly influenced by each child's genetic propensities, said Reiss, who,

along with his co-investigators, just completed a draft of a book detailing their conclusions about the role of nonshared environment in child development.

This finding—that a seemingly environmental measure such as parental behavior is influenced by genetics—is called "the nature of nurture" and is supported by other recent studies.

For example, the Colorado Adoption Project has found that genetics partially mediate relationships between children's home environment and their psychological development, language development and general cognitive ability.

Several researchers have described three types of gene-environment correlations:

- A passive correlation may occur because parents transmit genes that promote a certain trait and also construct the rearing environment, which will likely support a child's genetic propensities. For example, if we assume musical ability is genetic, musically gifted children will likely have musicly inclined parents who provide them with genes and an environment that promotes the development of musical ability.
- An evocative correlation may occur because genetically distinct people evoke different reactions

from parents, peers and others. For example, teachers may select musically talented children for special opportunities.
- And an active correlation may occur because people may actively select experiences that fit with their genetically influenced preferences. For example, musically gifted children may seek out musical friends and opportunities.

This does not mean that there are no purely environmental effects on behavior. Ken Kendler, MD, of the Medical College of Virginia/Virginia Commonwealth University, and his colleagues found that loss of a parent during childhood is directly correlated with alcoholism in women.

However, if researchers are ever going to unravel the effect of the environment, shared and nonshared, on human traits and behaviors, they must account for the large influence of genes on both behaviors and the environment, said Plomin.

"Research must address the notion that environment is important but, in large measure, may not be independent of genetics," said Reiss. "Developmental researchers must link their work with genetics—it should be a central part of the developmental psychology curriculum, to be used as a fundamental tool."

WHAT WE LEARN FROM TWINS

The mirror of your soul

Familiar question: Are we shaped by our genes, or by what life does to us?
Possible new answer: It isn't as simple as that makes it sound

BARBARA HERBERT, a former council worker living in southern England, discovered after the death of the woman she had thought was her mother that in fact she had been adopted. Among her assumed mother's papers, she found a name and address in Finland. When that produced no answer, she contacted the local newspaper in Finland. A reporter dug up the story. Her real mother had been sent to England, two months pregnant, in 1939. She had given birth, been sent back to Finland, and committed suicide at the age of 24.

Mrs Herbert had a feeling the story was not over. She seemed to recall somebody saying, "There was another one." So she contacted Hammersmith Hospital, where she was born; and, sure enough, there had been twins. The Registrar-General refused to help her contact her twin. She took the Registrar-General to court, and won. That is how she found her sister.

They met at King's Cross station in London. "We just said 'Hi' and walked off together, leaving our husbands standing there," says Mrs Herbert. "It seemed so natural." Mrs Herbert is a bit fatter than her sister, but she can think of no other important difference between them. Their intelligence quotients (IQs) were one point apart. They were tested again a year later; they scored ten points higher, but still only one point apart.

Mrs Herbert and her sister Daphne are gold dust to geneticists. Unlike fraternal twins, who are the product of separate eggs fertilized by different sperm, identical twins are natural clones, produced when a fertilized egg splits in two shortly after conception. Such twins, when separated after birth, are thus a scientific experiment designed jointly by nature and by society. They have the same genes but have been brought up in different environments.

These curiosities are getting rarer. Until the 1960s, twins offered for adoption in the West were often separated at birth, on the argument that two babies would be too much for one mother. That no longer happens. Since only one birth in 300 produces identical twins, and separated pairs are increasingly hard to find, people like Barbara Herbert and her sister are much sought after by scientists eager to study the relative importance of nature and nurture.

These studies provide some of the best clues to the question of how we become who we are—a question which fascinates people in different ways. Ordinary people wonder about the source of their failings and virtues, and would like to know whether they can make their children better, cleverer and happier than they themselves have been. Scientists are gripped, and still largely baffled, by how the human brain and personality are formed. And, in politics, the nature-nurture question lies at the centre of the argument about "social intervention". If our intelligence and our personalities are written into our genes, there is not much that governments can do to improve us.

Since the study of twins generally seems to support the nature side of the argument, it is triumphantly saluted by hereditarians as evidence for their case. "Twins have been used to prove a point, and the point is that we don't become. We are." So writes Lawrence Wright in his new book, "Twins: Genes, Environment and the Mystery of Human Identity". The environmentalists, on the other hand, condemn most studies of twins as methodologically flawed and even dishonest. Actually, what such studies show may be more interesting and mysterious than either side yet realises.

It was Francis Galton, Charles Darwin's cousin, who in the late 19th century first thought of using twins to investigate the differences between people. Galton, who coined the term "eugenics", correctly suggested that twins who looked alike came from one egg, and that those who did not came from different eggs. From that, he worked out a way of using twins to estimate the impact of genes. Look, he suggested, at the similarities between identical twins and those between ordinary ones (who genetically are no more similar than any children of the same parents). Those characteristics which identical twins share more than other twins will, he reasoned, be more caused by the genes the pair brought into the world.

This process, and the study of separated identical twins, are the two main ways of using twins to study the effects of nature and nurture. Galton carried out the first systematic study of twins. The results convinced him of the pre-eminence of genes in human make-up.

Eugenics in disgrace

The idea of eugenics captivated people on both the left and the right of politics in the first half of the 20th century. Fabian social reformers such as Sidney and Beatrice Webb were delighted to think that they would be able to breed a better working class. Josef Mengele, on the other hand, wanted to breed a better race for Hitler.

As Robert Jay Lifton recounts in "The Nazi Doctors", Mengele was obsessed with twins. When a new group of prisoners arrived in the concentration camp at Auschwitz, Mengele would run out to meet them shouting, "Twins out!" Twins lived in a separate block, and were allowed to keep their clothes and their hair. Mengele gave them sweets, and called them his little friends. He weighed them, measured them and logged the colour of their hair and their eyes. And he gave them diseases, to see how long they took to die.

The Nazis' enthusiasm for genetics did the subject no good at all. The left forgot it had ever had any interest in the matter. So did most academics. For a time it became fashionable, instead, to assume that people are chiefly the result of their environment, what they experience after they have been born. This rival view fitted neatly into the social-engineering optimism of most of the world's post-1945 governments.

The posthumous scandal over the work of Cyril Burt seemed to confirm this change of mind. Burt was the main proponent of hereditarian ideas in Britain. His evidence came from studies of separated identical twins. After his death in 1971, it was claimed that much of this evidence had been fabricated. His defenders' attempts to rescue his reputation have been less than conclusive. At best, he was a sloppy scientist; at worst, a fraud.

Still, despite its embarrassments, the hereditarian school began to reassert it-self. In 1969 the Harvard Educational Review published an article by Arthur Jensen called "How much can we boost IQ and scholastic achievement?". Mr Jensen's answer: Not much, because IQ is highly hereditary; so money spent on preschool programmes for poor children is wasted. As Adrian Wooldridge, of *The Economist*, puts it in his book "Measuring the Mind": "The hereditarians felt that the environmentalists had turned into a decadent establishment, smugly self-satisfied but intellectually sloppy."

Hereditarians ascendant

The new hereditarians were assailed, in print and in person; but they were not squashed. Their research won support from, and gave support to, conservative politicians keen to roll back the costly welfare policies of the post-1945 years. "The Bell Curve", by Charles Murray and Richard Herrnstein, published in 1994, is a powerful expression of this alliance. It argues that, since IQ is largely inherited, and people marry people like themselves, the difference between the intelligence of races and classes is liable to grow steadily wider.

The study of twins provided much of the ammunition for the hereditarian counter-attack. Some of it emerged from the first large scale post-Burt study of separated identical twins, run by Thomas Bouchard, a professor at the University of Minnesota. Mr Bouchard saw an article on a pair of reunited identical twins, and decided to make a study of them. It was fun, says Mr Bouchard. Much research work by psychologists involves grumpy students, doing it for the money. The twins, delighted to be reunited, were a pleasure to work with. Mr Bouchard now has a register of 8,000 pairs of twins, some identical, some not, some separated, most reared together.

Another American scientist, Robert Plomin, has been working with 25,000 pairs of identical and non-identical twins in Sweden. Mr Plomin has also set up a study working with 10,000 pairs of identical and non-identical twins in Britain. He now works at the Social, Genetic and Developmental Psychiatry Research Centre at Britain's Institute of Psychiatry.

Over the past couple of decades there has been a clear shift in science's view of the hereditarian argument. These days, no respectable scientist denies the role of genes in forming our brains and characters. The question over which argument continues to rage is just how big that role is.

Studies of twins have examined a range of physical and psychological traits to try to estimate how large a contribution genes make. Some of the work looks at illnesses such as cancer, schizophrenia and alcoholism. Finding the cause of these could help in learning how to cure or contain them. If, for instance, schizophrenia is something you can inherit, then it may be susceptible to gene therapy.

Some of the studies are curiosities. David Lykken, a colleague of Mr Bouchard's, has inquired into the origins of happiness. He concludes that happiness bears almost no relation to wealth, professional standing or marital status, and is 80% inherited. Some other studies have made sceptics' eye brows rise because they appear to show that political conservatism and religious fundamentalism have a genetic basis.

But the most contentious work of all is on IQ. Mr Bouchard's studies suggest that the level of one's intelligence is, in the jargon, "69–78% heritable"—heritability being the proportion of the difference between people that is acquired through the genes, not life itself. Burt's disputed figure is within that range.

Some critics, such as Marcus Feldman, a professor of population genetics at Stanford University, says the work on twins is tainted by politics. The Minnesota research is financed by the Pioneer Fund, a foundation set up in 1937 to help research into heredity and eugenics, including racial differences. The fund has financed work by such controversial figures as Philippe Rushton on the relative size of the genitals and brains of different races. It is accused of but strongly denies, racist motives.

Mr Lykken has played into the critics' hands by arguing that women should be licensed to have children and that children produced by unlicensed breeders should be compulsorily adopted. Mr Bouchard defends Mr Lykken's intellectual freedom. He says he is uneasy about the source of his cash, but insists that the Pioneer Fund has never tried to influence what he does.

What matters in the end, assuming that most of the people involved in this work do it in a properly detached way, is what they find out. It is striking that studies of twins regularly come up with higher levels of heritability than do other sorts of studies. Mr Bouchard's estimate runs up to 78%. That compares with studies of adopted children, and of first- and second-degree relations, which produce figures as low as 30%, and at the highest 50%. A task force of the American Psychological Association, trawling through all the available studies, including those on non-twins, has come up with an average of 50%.

This disparity has led to questions about the reliability of twins studies. One problem is that separated identical twins do not actually provide a perfect nature versus-nurture template. For a start, they do at one time share the same environment—in the womb. If, as some scientists now believe, those nine months are important in deciding how the brain is wired, this would help to explain why non-identical twins, who are no more genetically alike than any brother and sister, have IQS more like each other's than ordinary siblings do. It would also undermine the claims of the separated-twins studies to offer conclusive proof of what genes do.

Moreover, separated identical twins are rarely separated at the moment of birth, and some of them are then reunited before they come under the scientists' eye. If the first six months of a child's life matter as much as most people think they do, then spending even that short time together could influence the result of a twins study. And, when grown-up twins are reunited, they will naturally pay special attention to what they have in common; they may, the professors explain, "mythologise" their relationship. The twins in the Minnesota study had an average of five months together before they were separated, and nearly two years together after their reunion before Mr Bouchard got hold of them.

A subtler concern—voiced by Mr Feldman, himself a father of identical twins—is that the dichotomy between genes and environment is a false one. His own twins, he says, share professions, ideas and friends; their environments, in other words, are much closer than those of most non-identical twins. Maybe Galton's classic twins study was invalid: perhaps you cannot look at the similarities between identical twins, and those between non-identical ones, and conclude that the difference must necessarily be due to genes.

Chickens, eggs and babies

Mr Plomin, the student of those 35,000 pairs of twins, does not deny this. One of the ways in which genes work, he says, is through our tendency to select and design a particular environment. A baby, for instance, may be born happy;

its happiness may make its mother show it more affection; that may reinforce its cheerfulness. Even though that virtuous circle may have originated with the child's genetic tendency, it can be strengthened by what happens after the baby is born. If the child is taken away from its mother and dumped in a children's home, it may not stay happy. Or, if a child with a tendency to be miserable gets an unswervingly affectionate mother, it may cheer up.

And, just as our genes can affect our environment, so our environment may shape the expression of our genes. Height, for instance, is now around 90% heritable in rich countries. In the past the figure was lower because not everybody was well-nourished enough for their genes to express themselves properly. Heritability, in other words, is not a constant; it is affected by whether life is giving people's natural tendencies a chance to flower properly.

Turn the results of the heritability studies on their heads, and there is further cause for reflection. If IQ is 50% or so heritable, then up to another 50% is determined by something other than genes. The same applies to many other parts of our makeup, the figures for which are roughly of the same order of magnitude. But some things seem to be markedly less genetic. Despite the talk of a "breast cancer gene", for instance, this disease seems rarely to be the result of genetic programming. When one identical twin gets breast cancer, the other gets it in only 12% of cases.

Look, too, at sexual orientation. Some studies have suggested that homosexuality is around 50% heritable. Yet a recent study of Australian identical twins who had grown up apart from each other appeared to show that homosexuality was only 20% heritable in men and 24% in women.

So where, if these figures are right, does homosexuality mainly come from? Not, apparently, from growing up in the same family. Across a whole range of measures, including the tendency to homosexuality, if you look at separated identical twins and identical twins who have been brought up together you will find that they are pretty much alike. Belonging to the same family does not, on this evidence, have much effect. This seems to be confirmed by an examination of adopted children, born of different parents, who have been brought up in the same family.

Do they have much more in common with each other than they do with the kids next door? They do not.

There's something else

But that is daft, most people will instinctively say. The experiences we had in our parents' house were surely of vital importance in shaping our lives. The families we grew up in—and the families we ourselves are now creating—cannot be irrelevant to the character of the children they produce. Yet, if this scientific work is to be believed, belonging to the same family apparently has little effect on the way people turn out.

To some extent, of course, the explanation is that parents do not treat their various offspring in the same way. Mr Plomin cites a study which compares parents' and children's accounts of whether one child got the same treatment as his brother or sister. Not surprisingly, the children reported a greater level of difference than did the parents. Yet it is hard to believe that parents commonly treat identical twins so differently that one becomes a homosexual and one a heterosexual.

The bigger part of the explanation may be that except in special cases—the loving mother who manages to warm her genetically miserable child into real-life happiness—what our parents do is not decisively important to the way we grow up. That is the view of Sandra Scarr, a controversial professor of psychology at the University of Virginia. She offers the idea of "good enough" parenting. So long as a child has parents, and so long as they are not seriously brutal, she reckons, one set of parents is just as good as another.

If that is so, the really important variable may be chance. Perhaps it is the small, random event—the instant romance by the swings, the bullying in the corner of the playground—that shifts us imperceptibly towards widely different ends. Or maybe, for those who look at the universe in a different light, it is some higher power. Anyway, those who had feared that the scientists would soon have us neatly dissected on their laboratory tables can take new heart. How we become who we are seems as mysterious as ever. Thank God.

Secrets of the BRAIN

How do people think and learn? Why, faced with danger, do some choose to fight, others to flee?

Mark Nichols

Smith knows he is in trouble. He has problems at home, his job performance has been slipping and his confidence is shot. Now, he has been summoned to the office of that steely-eyed new boss, the one who has left a string of middle-management corpses in his wake since he launched a downsizing shakeup of the firm. At the appointed hour Smith threads his way nervously through a labyrinth of corridors, then climbs a flight of stairs to the more gracious hallway that leads to the boss's office. Suddenly, he is gripped by a fear so total that it nearly freezes his limbs. A voice inside his head screams: "Don't go in there—if you don't go in, he can't fire you." But another part of his brain is telling him that the consequences of running away might be even worse. By now, he is at the boss's door. Fingers trembling, he reaches for the knob and . . .

And what? Does Smith open the door, step inside and face the consequences? Or, consumed by fear, does he draw back and beat an ignominious retreat? What is more—and this is what fascinates scientists—how does the human brain weigh the conflicting claims of intellect and raw animal fear to arrive at a decision? Tony Phillips, who heads the psychology department at the University of British Columbia (UBC) in Vancouver, is trying to solve that riddle. The answer, he says, may lie in an intricate interplay of feedback loops within the brain. And the organ that in the end directs poor Smith to face the boss or flee could be a tiny teardrop-shaped collection of brain cells located behind the frontal lobes called the nucleus accumbens. "Our ability to imagine different courses of action and their consequences is quintessentially human," says Phillips. "Now, we may be close to figuring out the answer to a fundamental puzzle—the nature of the interface between human thought and action."

Scientists around the world are tackling age-old mysteries of the brain and beginning to solve such puzzles as how memory works and why some people's psyches can withstand the kind of horrific experiences that traumatize others. "We are trembling on the edge of an enormous explosion of understanding," says Robert Adamec, a research professor in the psychology department at Memorial University in St. John's, Nfld. "Things are moving so fast right now that in 10 years I may look back on some of the ideas I have now as somewhat foolish."

As researchers venture across one of science's last frontiers, they are boosted by brain-scanning technology that allows them, for the first time, to watch events unfold inside the brain. Alan Evans, who heads the Montreal Neurological Institute's brain-imaging centre, is part of the U.S. Government-sponsored Human Brain Project, dedicated to assembling a comprehensive structural and functional map of the human brain. In Evans's study, technicians are using magnetic resonance imaging (MRI) equipment to peer inside the skulls of 450 people, compare the differences in shapes and sizes of individual anatomies and come up with a diagram of the typical human brain.

Ever since the Montreal brain surgeon Wilder Penfield carried out pioneering experimental work during the 1940s and 1950s, Canadian researchers have been strong contributors to the neurosciences—and today they are playing prominent roles in brain research. One current realm of Canadian specialization is a drive to find out why most brain cells, unlike those in other parts of the human body, do not regenerate after injury. Discovering ways to make neurons grow again in stroke- or disease-damaged brains could pave the way for improved treatments or even cures for such dreaded neurodegenerative conditions as Parkinson's, Huntington's and Lou Gehrig's diseases, which begin in the brain and cripple and kill over time. "We're on the threshold of an era," says William Tatton, director of Dalhousie University's Neuroscience Institute in Halifax, "where for the first time we may be able to intervene effectively in neurological diseases."

Despite cutbacks in government funding, Canadian laboratories are also engaged in studies aimed at understanding the brain's cognitive abilities—the functions that enable humans to think, learn and remember. In a series of dramatic findings during the past decade, Sandra Witelson, a Hamilton-based researcher, has pinpointed structural differences between the brains of men and women, and between heterosexuals and homosexuals (see box "Boys, girls and brainpower"). In Vancouver, psychologist Robert Hare is using MRI to examine the brains of psychopaths, in an effort to find out why they display a stunning absence of conscience.

Exploring the human brain, and comprehending what is going on inside it, is a formidable task. And no wonder, considering the bewildering complexity of the brain, a 3.3–lb. lump of tissue contalning between 50 billion and 100 billion brain cells. In a living brain, individual cells—also known as neurons—routinely make contact with as many as 10,000 other cells in an incredibly complicated electrochemical interplay that scientists are just beginning to grasp.

What is clear is that out of that welter of neuronal activity human consciousness and thought somehow emerge. Much basic brain research is devoted to trying to find out exactly what is happening when electrical impulses flow through a neuron and trigger a discharge of chemicals across the gap—or synapse, between brain cells. It is that synaptic contact that· gives rise to mental activity—by mobilizing millions of brain cells in specific regions that scientists are increasingly linking to specialized roles. The frontal lobes, for example, are the part of the brain that anticipates events and weighs the consequences of behavior, while deeper brain regions, including the seahorse-shaped hippocampus and the nearby amygdala, are associated

THE GOD MACHINE

During the past decade, psychologist Michael Persinger and his assistants have ushered more than 500 volunteers into a soundproof chamber, placed a strange-looking helmet on their heads and then, from a console outside the chamber, exposed their brains to a rhythmic bombardment by low-intensity electromagnetic waves. Persinger, a psychology professor at Laurentian University in Sudbury, Ont., hopes that this unorthodox treatment can be used eventually to help people suffering from such problems as depression, chronic pain and epilepsy by correcting electrical irregularities in the brain. But he is equally interested in the fact that many of his subjects react to the electromagnetic exposure by experiencing unusual auditory and visual sensations. Some people even sense that there is someone or something with them in the chamber, a "presence" they describe as God—or the devil. "Ultimately," says Persinger, "human experience is determined by what is happening in the brain. And the experience of God can be generated by a process that has nothing to do with whether God exists or not."

According to Persinger, electromagnetic brain events of the kind his helmet reproduces may account for many spiritual and paranormal experiences, including visitations by angels, demons or aliens. How can this happen? Persinger says that a person's sense of self arises from language functions, which are usually centered in the left hemisphere. But a variety of factors, including stress, fatigue and depression—and artificial stimulation by Persinger—can alter the brain's normal electrical functioning and produce a sense of "otherness." When this occurs mainly in the left hemisphere, he says, the subject is likely to feel that the presence is benign or god-like. But when the same event is mainly in the right hemisphere, which is concerned with vigilance, the brain is more likely to interpret the presence there as being alien or demonic.

In his experiments, Persinger uses a specially wired motorcycle helmet, which British journalist Ian Cotton donned in 1993 while researching a book on evangelical Christianity entitled *The Hallelujah Revolution*. After Persinger's team provided temple-bell sound effects, reported Cotton, "I was actually in a line of solemn Tibetan monks, grave-eyed, brown cowls around their heads. I too was a Tibetan monk, and what I realized was that I always had been."

Born in Jacksonville, Fla., Persinger—now a Canadian citizen—left the United States in 1969 to avoid being drafted for service in Vietnam. He does not have a high opinion of organized religion. "If you look at the history of human behavior," he says, "it is evident that many wars were caused by rival concepts of God." Reacting to his work, fundamentalist Christians have mounted small protests at Laurentian. Persinger talks at times as though God might be no more than a neurological accident. But he is careful to hedge his bets. "I am interested in the part of the brain that *mediates* the God experience," he says. Does that mean the God experience could be caused by the *presence* of God? Replies Persinger: "It's a possibility."

M.N.

with such things as memory, mood and motivation.

In the case of Smith—the anxiety-ridden employee on his way to see his boss—UBC's Phillips thinks that some brain circuits may be locked in a kind of neural competition in which some can override others. While the hippocampus helps Smith to chart a course through physical space, the amygdala is urgently warning him of possible peril. But that can change if the fear generated

by the amygdala becomes strong enough to somehow override the messages coming from other brain regions.

Outside the boss's office, that very thing threatens to happen. As the amygdala becomes more insistent, the frontal lobes—which perform executive planning functions in the brain—warn that to turn and flee could be even more career-threatening than to face the boss. Phillips thinks that the final decision is made by the nucleus accumbens, perhaps with the help of the frontal lobes. Now, Phillips' research team is trying to find out exactly how that happens by studying rats, whose brains are in many ways scaled-down versions of human ones. "The nucleus accumbens is a very sophisticated switching system," says Phillips. "And somehow, the strongest signal reaching it can determine what orders go out to initiate action."

At Memorial, Adamec is trying to understand why horrific events affect the brains of some people so severely that they develop the condition known as post-traumatic stress disorder—typified by the depression, anxiety and anger that afflicts some war veterans. From human and animal studies, Adamec has concluded that people who have anxious personalities to begin with are probably more likely to suffer lasting damage from involvement in shocking or violent events. "There is something about the way a person's brain is wired that is relevant," says Adamec. "And if an event leads to a lasting increase in anxiousness,

there must be a lasting alteration in some brain circuits."

Using rats, Adamec is now trying to discover which brain circuits are affected—and how. The problem probably involves changes in the flow of several of the 100 or so chemical neurotransmitters that carry messages between brain cells. One of the culprits, says Adamec, may be a neurotransmitter known as CCK, which is associated with panic attacks. The zone in which traumatic events leave their indelible mark may be a circuit involving a number of brain regions, including the amygdala, which is involved in memories of emotion-laden experiences, and the hypothalamus, which regulates bodily functions, including responses to stress. Adamec's ultimate hope: that by understanding how post-traumatic stress disorder arises, scientists may be able to find a way to intervene—after a potentially traumatic shock—with drugs that can prevent permanent changes from occurring in the brain.

Federal cutbacks are putting a strain on brain funding. Ottawa has

announced plans to slice $4.4 million over the next three years from the current $33 million it devotes to brain-related research. At the sam time, federal agencies increasingly are favoring medically oriented discoveries that could help to reduce health-care costs while producing jobs and profits. "I think there is a deliberate attempt by government," says Warren Bull, executive director of the federally backed Canadian NeuroScience Network, "to insist that there be a practical payback."

A discovery by Toronto brain researchers could provide that kind of payback by trimming the estimated $2.3 billion spent treating schizophrenia. The problem with some of the most effective anti-psychotic drugs used to treat the disease, says Shitij Kapur, a research scientist at the Clarke Institute of Psychiatry, "is that the side-effects are so horrible that patients become convinced that the drug is an enemy, and stop taking it." When that happens, patients often lapse into psychosis and have to be hospitalized.

Using PET (for positron emission tomography) brain-scanning technology, Kapur and other scientists at the Institute tracked two widely used anti-psychotic drugs—haloperidol and risperidone—in the brains of schizophrenics. The researchers found that in most cases the drugs worked—and with fewer of the side-effects that can include extreme restlessness and muscular stiffness—when taken at doses well below those often prescribed.

Most scientists believe that schizophrenia is caused by excessive activity of a chemical called dopamine, which helps transmit messages between brain cells—and that anti-psychotic drugs work by blocking receptors that are activated by dopamine. Watching drugs flow through patients' brains, the researchers could see that a drug dose of between two milligrams and six milligrams blocked about 70 per cent of the dopamine receptors, while doses as high as 50 mg only marginally increased the blockage. If Kapur and his colleagues

MAPPING THE MIND

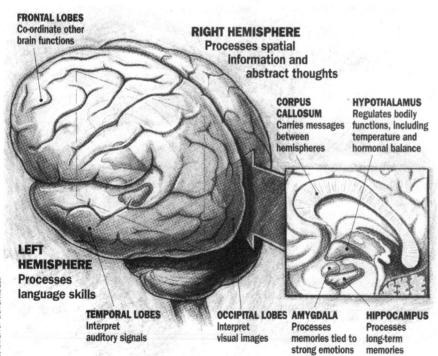

ILLUSTRATION BY STEPHEN MADER

FRONTAL LOBES
Co-ordinate other brain functions

RIGHT HEMISPHERE
Processes spatial information and abstract thoughts

CORPUS CALLOSUM
Carries messages between hemispheres

HYPOTHALAMUS
Regulates bodily functions, including temperature and hormonal balance

LEFT HEMISPHERE
Processes language skills

TEMPORAL LOBES
Interpret auditory signals

OCCIPITAL LOBES
Interpret visual images

AMYGDALA
Processes memories tied to strong emotions

HIPPOCAMPUS
Processes long-term memories

can persuade other scientists that they are right, their finding could improve the lives of schizophrenics while saving millions of dollars by reducing drug and hospital costs.

In another project, Canadian scientists are looking for answers to one of the brain's most painful mysteries—the inability of a damaged brain or spinal cord to heal like a cut finger or a broken bone. There is a period in human development when this is not true: brain cells in unborn babies and infants up to the age of about 2 can regenerate themselves. That is why doctors try to reverse the effects of cell death in Parkinson's disease by transplanting fetal tissue into victims' brains (see box, "The Debate over Fetal Tissue"). But for most people with brain or spinal cord injuries, or other neurodegenerative diseases like Huntington's and Alzheimer's, little can be done to bring dead cells back to life.

About four years ago, Sam Weiss, an associate professor of anatomy and pharmacology at the University of Calgary, and graduate student Brent Reynolds made a discovery that may point to a way of growing new cells in the human brain. They found an inactive cell in the brains of mice that, when prodded into action, behaves like the rapidly reproducing stem cells found in human and animal bone marrow. The burning question now is whether similar cells exist in the human brain.

If they do—and Weiss says there is "some evidence" to support that conclusion—scientists may be able to grow them in a culture to generate millions of new cells, which could be transplanted into the brains of people suffering from neurodegenerative diseases. Even better, adds Weiss, it may be possible "to turn on the stem cells, and persuade them to begin reproducing themselves right inside the brain." To exploit the commercial possibilities of the discovery, the University of Calgary, with the backing of American and Swiss pharmaceutical companies, in 1992 set up a Calgary-based company called NeuroSpheres Ltd., which now employs about 20 people.

John Steeves, a professor of neurobiology at UBC, thinks that a substance called myelin, which forms a coating around neurons that helps speed up communications among cells, may play a role in preventing cell regeneration in damaged brain and spinal cords. Studying the neural circuitry of chickens, Steeves noticed that myelin begins to form about a week before the baby birds are born, just as the spinal cord nerve cells lose their ability to regenerate. Does that mean, Steeves wondered, that one of the roles of myelin is to stabilize neural circuits in a young organism by halting cell replication? If so, he reasoned, then preventing myelin production might encourage cell regeneration.

In an experiment, Steeves and members of his research team injected proteins that suppressed myelin formation into adult chickens whose spinal cords had been severed. "To my amazement," says Steeves, "we got regeneration in about 20 per cent of the damaged cells." It is too early, says Steeves, to try to apply

THE DEBATE OVER FETAL TISSUE

Sometime within the next six weeks, Dr. Ivan Méndez and his surgical team at the Victoria General Hospital in Halifax will pool nerve cells from two, three or perhaps four aborted fetuses and implant them in the brain of a patient with Parkinson's disease. The controversial operation will mark phase two of the team's study of the incurable neurodegenerative disorder. At least nine more patients will follow, with a report expected in late 1997. The theory behind the implants—first tried in Sweden in 1988—is to substitute fetal nerve cells that are capable of growing for damaged adult cells that cannot regenerate. It is, says Méndez, "like replacing a faulty chip in your computer."

Perhaps, but brain surgery has proved nowhere near as simple. Gone is the optimism that greeted fetal-tissue implants in the late 1980s. Inconsistent results have led doctors to believe the implanted neurons—which secrete dopamine, a chemical messenger lacking in Parkinson's patients—will have to be supplemented with other treatments. And no one knows whether the grafts can survive the undiscovered brain-cell killer behind the illness. On top of that, abortion opponents continue to denounce the operations as yet another indignity against the unborn.

Halifax surgeons performed the first fetal-tissue implant in Canada in 1991, followed by four more to complete phase one of their study. In December, 1994, Méndez and company—still the sole Canadian team in the field—announced they would expand their research after all patients showed a lessening in the severity of their symptoms and their deterioration slowed. They all still require medication, however. Unlike phase one, phase two involves implanting cells in two locations of the brain instead of one.

A major stumbling block continues to be cell survivability. "If you don't know how many cells survive, you don't know how much you have to put in." Méndez says. To date, doctors have relied on indirect evidence from brain scans. But last April, *The New England Journal of Medicine* reported on an autopsy that showed implanted fetal cells had survived and grown in the brain of a 59-year-old male Parkinson's patient.

If such surgery proves beneficial to Parkinson's patients, it could eventually be used to treat epilepsy, Huntington's disease or brain and spinal cord injuries. Meanwhile, studies are under way in the United States, Sweden and France that may defuse the controversy over using fetal cells. Scientists are now growing genetically engineered cells in culture, hoping they can provide a limitless supply—and new hope—for victims of brain disease.

DAN HAWALESHKA

Boys, girls and brainpower

The sexes differ in more than appearance

It began almost by accident. In an effort to uncover the causes of dyslexia, psychologist Sandra Witelson decided in 1970 to conduct an experiment involving dyslexic and other children at a Hamilton grade school. Because dyslexia affects mostly males, Witelson planned to use boys only. "But the girls wanted to join in, so they could get to miss some of their regular classes too," says Witelson. "So we included girls." The purpose of the experiment was to see whether some mental functions in dyslexic children—such as language skills or spatial perception—favor one or the other of the two brain hemispheres, as they do in most people. What Witelson found was that dyslexic children have fewer right-left brain differences than other kids—and that, where they exist, the differences were far more pronounced in boys than in girls. That discovery, published in 1976, sent a tremor through the world of brain research. The reason: Witelson's finding suggested that differences between male and female behavior might not be due simply to social conditioning, but rather to biological differences in the brains of men and women.

Certainly there is ample anecdotal evidence to suggest that conclusion. And studies have shown that women often *do* possess superior verbal skills, while men are frequently better at things like mathematics and map reading. But now, the 55-year-old Witelson and a handful of other researchers have begun to produce concrete and mounting evidence of physical differences in the brains of men and women, as well as in the brains of heterosexuals and homosexuals. Typically, in a study published last May, Witelson, a professor in the psychiatry department at Hamilton's McMaster University, reported that in a part of the temporal lobe associated with language skills, women's brains contained up to 11-percent more brain cells than men's brains.

That does not necessarily mean that women are smarter than men—but it does show that they are different. As Witelson notes,—her findings challenge the politically correct dogma that "except for anatomical differences in men's and women's bodies, everything else is supposed to be the same, except where things have been distorted by social forces." If there are physical brain differences between the sexes, adds Witelson, "it may be better to recognize this and deal with it, rather than pretending that we are all the same."

A native of Montreal, Witelson studied psychology at McGill University, where she became interested in childhood learning disabilities. When American researchers in the late 1960s reported that brain regions in the left and right hemispheres often varied in size, Witelson wondered whether the disparities were related to the distribution of brain functions in the two hemispheres. Officials at the U.S. National Institutes of Health in Bethesda, Md., were interested in the same question and, in 1976, they offered to fund scientists to investigate it. Witelson and a McMaster colleague bid on the multimillion-dollar NIH contract—and won.

The three-year grant set the stage for a series of studies by Witelson and her scientific partners that have shed light on the differences between brain hemispheres—and between male and female brains. From the male point of view, one of Witelson's most disturbing discoveries was reported in 1991. She found that as men grow older, the corpus callosum—a brain region that provides communications between the hemispheres—begins shrinking. The biggest surprise was that the study, based on post-mortem examinations of 23 male and 39 female brains, showed virtually no shrinkage of the female corpus callosum. In a current study, Witelson is trying to determine what effect the shrinkage has. "Clearly, whatever is happening in the corpus callosum is not of great consequence for most men," she says. "Lots of men do very well in their later decades."

Witelson and her research partners illustrated another dimension of brain differences in November, 1994. In a study involving 21 people, they showed that part of the corpus callosum in the brains of some homosexual men was 13-percent larger than in the heterosexual men. That might explain why earlier studies, including some by Witelson, have found differences in the cognitive abilities of gay and straight men, including lower scores by gay men on tests of spatial perception. Witelson's findings involving the corpus callosum followed a 1991 U.S. study that reported physical differences between gay and straight men in the hypothalamus, a brain region associated with sexual behavior. Other American researchers have suggested that genetic factors may play a role in homosexuality.

Working in an area of science that is fraught with political implications, Witelson insists that she is interested only in the truth. "I think of myself as a scientist," she says, "not as a male or female scientist." Witelson, who has been married for 35 years to Hamilton eye doctor Henry Witelson, thinks there now is persuasive evidence that men's and women's brains "are actually different in some of the ways they are put together, anatomically and chemically." That will upset some people, she says, "because they assume that biology means things are immutable." But, she adds, "the fact is that upbringing and other environmental factors play a tremendously important role" in shaping the mind—a reminder that biology alone is not destiny.

MARK NICHOLS

---

the finding to humans. But it could point the way to a form of treatment that could help regenerate human neurons at some point in the future.

Over the past seven years, UBC neurobiologist Terry Snutch has made a series of discoveries that could pave the way for better drugs to treat conditions ranging from migraine headaches to manic-depressive illness and schizophrenia. Snutch's specialty is a family of proteins found on the surface of brain cells. The proteins act as channels for calcium, a mineral that plays a vital role inside neurons to trigger the flow of neurotransmitters used in the brain's messaging system. Snutch discovered that calcium channels are located on different parts of neurons—and each channel has a slightly different function.

What that means, says Snutch, is that the amount of calcium, and the flow of neurotransmitters it sets off, "can be controlled to a very fine degree." Some widely prescribed drugs used to treat a variety of illnesses act on calcium channels. Now, by designing drugs to target specific calcium channels, scientists may be able to eliminate some of the unpleasant side-effects—including the nightmares and fatigue caused by some migraine remedies.

Meanwhile, Canadian researchers are trying to solve the mystery of memory—a brain function that Endel Tulving, a Toronto brain researcher, considers to be "the thing that makes us human." Over the years, says Tulving, a senior neuroscientist at Toronto's Rotman Research Institute, investigators have tended to regard memory as a brain function that is simply involved in information storage. Tulving's model is more complicated. First of all, he says, there are two basic memory functions—encoding (taking the information in) and retrieval (getting it back out). In a theory developed over two decades, Tulving has also proposed that there are two different types of memory—semantic, which deals with such factual material as names, dates and the appearance of ordinary physical objects, and episodic memory, which enables people to re-experience the past.

Until recently, there was no way to test many of his ideas. But now Tulving and scientists at Toronto's Clarke Institute are using PET scans to see which parts of the brain handle different memory functions. They have already made an unexpected discovery: although memory is widely distributed throughout the brain, some functions are concentrated in one of the two brain hemispheres. The retrieval of semantic memory, for example, occurs mostly in the left frontal lobe, which makes sense because that side of the brain is strongly associated with language functions.

Tulving's theories may help explain why memories of past events are not always accurate or complete. For example, a bus driver's clever wisecrack might be recorded in an individual's episodic memory, perhaps with details of how the driver looked and the way he talked. At the time of the event, the bus's other passengers did little to engrave themselves in the subject's memory. So when the scene is recalled, the person's brain may sketch in generic passengers based on a general idea of what transit straphangers look like that is drawn from semantic memory.

Tulving admits that many of his ideas about how memory works are just that—ideas that have yet to be proved. "Memory is extraordinarily complicated," he says, "much more so than many people are willing to believe." He thinks that may be true of the brain itself—and that "some day we may discover that the brain works quite differently from what we imagine now." Luckily, one of the glorious paradoxes is that, for all its complexities, it is the human brain itself that may ultimately unlock the mysteries of the mind.

Revealing the Brain's Secrets

Is space truly the final frontier? Not according to scientists who are probing what they call the most complex and challenging structure ever studied: the human brain. "It is the great unexplored frontier of the medical sciences," said neurobiologist John E. Dowling, professor of natural science at Harvard University. Just as space exploration dominated science in the 1960s and 1970s, the human brain is taking center stage in the 1990s.

It may seem odd to compare an organ that weighs only about three pounds to the immensity of the universe. Yet the human brain is as awe-inspiring as the night sky. Its complex array of interconnecting nerve cells chatter incessantly among themselves in languages both chemical and electrical. None of the organ's magical mysteries has been easy to unravel. Until recently, the brain was regarded as a black box whose secrets were frustratingly secure from reach.

Now, an explosion of discoveries in genetics and molecular biology, combined with dramatic new imaging technologies, have pried open the lid and allowed scientists to peek inside. The result is a growing understanding of what can go wrong in the brain, which raises new possibilities for identifying, treating, and perhaps ultimately preventing devastating conditions such as Alzheimer's disease or stroke.

"The laboratory bench is closer to the hospital bed than it has ever been," said neurobiologist Gerald Fischbach, chairman of neurobiology at Harvard Medical School, where the brain and its molecular makeup are a primary focus of research.

One important challenge is to understand the healthy brain. By studying brain cells and the genetic material inside them, scientists are discovering how groups of specialized cells interact to produce memory, language, sensory perception, emotion, and other complex phenomena. Figuring out how the healthy brain goes about its business is an essential platform that researchers need in order to comprehend what goes wrong when a neurological disease strikes.

There have also been great strides toward elucidating some of the common brain disorders that rob people of memory, mobility, and the ability to enjoy life. The most promising of these fall into several broad categories.

- The discovery of disease-producing genetic mutations has made it possible not only to diagnose inherited disorders, but in cases such as Huntington's disease, to predict who will develop them. These findings have also pointed the way toward new therapies.
- Insights into the programmed death of nerve cells may lead to drugs that can halt the progression of degenerative diseases or contain stroke damage.
- Naturally occurring chemicals that protect nerve cells from environmental assaults may hold clues about preventing disease or reversing neurologic injury.
- Information about brain chemistry's role in mood and mental health has already helped people burdened by depression, for example, and is expected to benefit others as well.

Genetics opens a new door

Discovering a gene associated with a disease is like unlocking a storehouse of knowledge. Once researchers have such a gene, they may be able to insert it into experimental systems such as cell cultures or laboratory animals. This makes it easier to discern the basic mechanisms of the disorder, which in turn helps scientists figure out what diagnostic tests or therapies might be best. When a new treatment is proposed, genetically engineered models of human diseases make testing quicker and more efficient.

In recent years, scientists have found abnormal genes associated with Huntington's disease (HD), Alzheimer's disease (AD), amyotrophic lateral sclerosis (ALS or Lou Gehrig's disease), one form of epilepsy, Tay-Sachs disease, two types of muscular dystrophy, and several lesser-known neurological conditions.

A decade-long search for the HD gene ended in 1993, when Harvard researchers Marcy MacDonald and James Gusella, working with scientists at other institutions, identified a sequence of DNA that produces symptoms

Reprinted with permission from the *Harvard Health Letter,* January 1996. pp. 9–12. © 1996 by the President and Fellows of Harvard College.

of the disease if it is repeated enough times. Huntington's is a progressive and ultimately fatal hereditary disorder that affects about 25,000 people in the United States. It typically strikes at midlife, and the researchers discovered that the more copies of the sequence a person inherited, the earlier symptoms show up.

Scientists quickly developed a highly reliable assay that enables people with a family history of HD to find out if they or their unborn fetus harbors the dangerous mutation. But because no cure for the disease exists, few people have rushed to have themselves tested.

Demand might increase, however, if scientists can use the HD gene to design effective treatments. Genes contain the assembly instructions for proteins, the molecules that carry out the day-to-day operations of the body. Scientists strive to identify the protein made by a disease-producing gene and to figure out what it does, which in turn helps them understand the event that initiates the disease process.

The HD gene codes for a protein that appears to contribute to the premature death of certain neurons. It is the loss of these cells that results in the involuntary movements and mental deterioration typical of Huntington's. When researchers know more about this protein, they may be able to develop drugs or other therapies that could slow the onset of symptoms or even block them entirely.

A downward spiral

The gradual extinction of certain brain cells is also the underlying cause of Alzheimer's disease. In this case, the impact is progressive loss of memory, changes in personality, loss of impulse control, and deterioration in reasoning power. Under the microscope, the brains of people who died with AD are studded with abnormalities called amyloid plaques and neurofibrillary tangles. About 20% of all AD cases are inherited, and these people develop symptoms earlier in life than those with the more common form, which typically appears well after age 65.

In recent years, scientists have discovered several different genetic mutations that can cause the unusual, inherited form of AD. One of these abnormal genes has successfully been introduced into mice by researchers at several pharmaceutical companies, and experts believe that this animal model will help them understand how all forms of the disease progress at the cellular and molecular level.

So far, it looks as though some of the animals' brains develop amyloid plaques like the ones that build up in humans. Long-standing doubt about whether plaques cause symptoms may be resolved by future observations of whether these genetically engineered mice show signs of memory loss. If there is a strong correlation between amyloid accumulation and symptom severity, these mice will be used to test drugs that might keep plaques from forming.

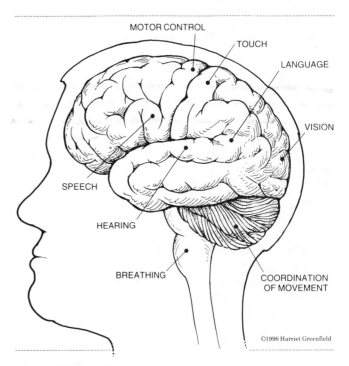

MOTOR CONTROL
TOUCH
LANGUAGE
VISION
SPEECH
HEARING
BREATHING
COORDINATION OF MOVEMENT

©1996 Harriet Greenfield

The cell death story

Unlike other types of cells, nerve cells (neurons) are meant to last a lifetime because they can't reproduce themselves. Struck by the realization that abnormal cell death is the key factor in neurologic problems ranging from Alzheimer's to stroke, scientists have embarked on a crusade aimed at understanding why nerve cells die and how this might be prevented.

It's normal to lose some brain cells gradually. Trouble arises when a large population of cells dies all of a sudden, as in a stroke, or when too many of a certain type die over time, such as in Alzheimer's or Parkinson's (PD) disease. While some scientists remain skeptical that inquiries into cell death will ever lead to effective means for preventing or treating neurodegenerative diseases, many others are enthusiastically pursuing this line of research.

Some scientists are racing to develop *neuroprotective* drugs that could guard brain cells against damage and death or even help them regenerate. There are many different ideas about how to do this.

For example, although Harvard scientists have identified the gene for HD and the protein it makes, they don't understand the mechanisms that lead to symptoms. One theory is that a phenomenon called *excitotoxicity* is responsible, and that Huntington's is only one of many diseases in which this process plays a role.

The idea behind excitotoxicity is that too much of a good thing is bad for cells. Glutamate, for example, is an ordinarily benign chemical messenger that stimulates certain routine cellular activities. Under extraordinary circumstances, however, "cells can be so excited by glutamate that they wear themselves out and die," said John

Penney Jr., a neurologist at Massachusetts General Hospital and a Harvard professor of neurology.

Sending a signal

One of the many types of doorways built into the walls of nerve cells is a structure called an NMDA receptor. One of its functions is to allow small amounts of calcium (a substance usually shut out of the cell) to enter it. This happens when the NMDA receptor is stimulated by glutamate. If excess glutamate is present, too much calcium rushes in—an influx that is lethal to the cell.

Someday it may be possible to halt the advance of Huntington's by injecting drugs which block the NMDA receptor so that calcium can't get in. In animal experiments, scientists have demonstrated that such receptor-blocking agents can keep brain cells from dying. Harvard researchers are seeking approval for a clinical trial that will test such neuroprotective drugs in patients with symptomatic disease. If participants obtain any relief from this treatment, the next step will be to determine whether this approach can prevent symptoms in patients who have the gene but do not have symptoms.

Scientists also hope that neuroprotection can be used to limit brain damage due to stroke. When a stroke shuts down the supply of blood to part of the brain, neurons in the immediate area die within minutes. Over the next several hours, more distant cells in the region are killed as excitotoxic signals spread. In an effort to limit the extent of brain damage, researchers are currently treating small numbers of patients with intravenous doses of experimental agents such as NMDA receptor blockers and free radical scavengers. Other neuroprotective agents under development, include protease inhibitors, nitric oxide inhibitors, and nerve growth factors.

"Our dream is a safe and effective neuroprotectant that can be given to the stroke patient in the ambulance or shortly after arrival in the emergency room," said neurologist Seth Finklestein, an associate professor at Harvard Medical School who conducts basic research at Massachusetts General Hospital. "That's the holy grail of neuroprotective treatment."

Applications for Alzheimer's

Neuroprotection is also making waves in Alzheimer's research, as scientists strive to inhibit the type of cell death that typifies this disease. One group of investigators has identified several *peptides* (small protein molecules) that block the formation of amyloid plaque in the test tube, said neurobiologist Huntington Potter, an associate professor at Harvard Medical School. The researchers hope to test these peptides in humans.

Brain cells manufacture several neuroprotective chemicals on their own, which scientists call *neurotrophic* or nerve growth factors. These small proteins may hold the key to keeping cells alive even in the face of stroke, degenerative diseases, or even spinal cord injury.

For example, several different neurotrophic factors are being tested in the laboratory to determine if they could protect the dopamine-producing cells that die prematurely in people with Parkinson's disease. Other uses are being studied as well, and some researchers anticipate that these chemicals will be tested in humans before the decade draws to a close.

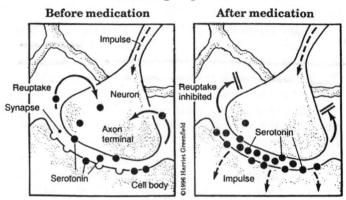

Relieving Depression

People who are depressed have less of the neurotransmitter serotonin than those who aren't. In the picture on the left, the axon terminal of one nerve cell releases serotonin, which travels across the synapse and activates the cell body (receiving cell). Serotonin is then reabsorbed by the sending cell. On the right, a selective serotonin reuptake inhibitor (SSRI), such as the antidepressant Prozac, slows the reabsorption of serotonin, keeping it in the synapse longer and boosting its effect on the receiving cell.

Mood, mind, and brain chemistry

Scientists have discovered that a surprising number of mental disorders, from depression to schizophrenia, are the result of brain chemistry gone awry. And this understanding has led them to design new medications for treating specific mental disorders and behavior problems.

The best known of this new breed of drugs is fluoxetine (Prozac), one of several selective serotonin reuptake inhibitors (SSRIs). It was possible to design these agents, which are widely prescribed to alleviate depression and related disorders, only after scientists came to understand how nerve cells communicate at the molecular level.

Each nerve cell has an *axon,* a long branch that reaches out and touches other nerve cells. A tiny space called a *synapse* separates the axon terminal (which sends a message) and the cell body (that receives it), and this is where the action is. The sending cell releases *neurotransmitters* (chemical messengers) into the synapse which either excite or inhibit a receiving cell that is equipped with the proper receptors. Messages pass from cell to cell in this manner, eventually leading to a physiologic action. In each synapse, the cell that sent the message sops up leftover neurotransmitters and stores them for future use. People who are depressed have less serotonin than those who aren't, and the SSRIs block the reuptake of this chemical, thereby boosting the effect of a small amount on the receiving cell. (*See illustration* "Relieving Depression.")

But Prozac and its relatives are only the tip of the iceberg. As researchers work to understand the roles of different chemical messengers and the highly specific receptors that bind them, a whole new approach to the treatment of mental disorders is evolving. The identification of highly specialized receptors is already paving the way for ever more specific drugs to treat these conditions.

Schizophrenia therapy is a case in point. As devastating as this form of mental illness is, treatments have sometimes appeared worse than the disease. Until very recently, the only drugs that relieved symptoms could also lead to spasmodic, uncontrollable movements known as *tardive dyskinesia*. This is because these agents block all types of receptors for dopamine, a neurotransmitter that is a key player in normal movement as well as in this mental disorder. Now there is a new drug for schizophrenia, clozapine, that blocks only a small subclass of dopamine receptors. It relieves symptoms of the illness in some people without leading to abnormal movements. Still, it can have other serious side effects.

Tailored to fit

The bottom line for the treatment of behavior and emotional disorders may be that drugs will become ever more specialized. Just as computers now help salespeople fit blue jeans to the individual purchasers, it is not inconceivable that psychopharmacologists may someday tailor drugs to the needs of each patient.

What does the future of brain research hold? Dr. Dowling anticipates that medications that can slow the process of degenerative disease, correct the chemical imbalances that cause mental disorders, prevent stroke damage, and repair spinal cord injuries may all be on the horizon. "We have learned so much about the cellular and molecular aspects of the brain," Dr. Dowling said. "We stand at a time of great opportunity, when we can take tremendous advantage of these things and turn them into practical clinical therapies."

—*KATHLEEN CAHILL ALLISON*

Unit 3

Key Points to Consider

❖ Why do psychologists want to study sensation and perception, which are ordinarily the domain of biologists and physicians? Try to rank the senses, that is, place them in a hierarchy of importance. Justify your rankings.

❖ What role does the brain play in sensation and perception? More specifically, what role does the brain play in audition? In touch? In pain? How are touch, audition, and pain related to consciousness? How do touch and hearing relate to our ability to communicate with each other? Can we communicate well if we are blind? If we are deaf? Do the senses interact with each other? Explain your answer.

❖ Do you think the remaining senses, such as smell and balance, are important? Can you give some examples of the ways these senses affect us and why psychologists study them?

❖ What are the problems of dream research? What do dreams mean? Was Freud right, that dreams are repressed wishes? How is the brain involved in dreaming? Do you know of any other parapsychological phenomena or altered states? How could you test for them? If they exist, what does it mean for the individual who is able to participate in them?

 **Links**   **www.dushkin.com/online/**

These sites are annotated on pages 4 and 5.

Susan and her roommate have been friends since freshman year. Because they share so much in common, they decided to become roommates in their sophomore year. They both want to travel abroad one day. Both date men from the same fraternity, major in education, and want to work with young children after graduation. Today they are at the local art museum. As they walk around the galleries, Susan is astonished at her roommate's taste in art. Whatever her roommate likes, Susan hates. The paintings and sculptures that Susan admires are the very ones at which her roommate turns up her nose. "How can our tastes in art be so different?" Susan wonders.

What Susan and her roommate are experiencing is a difference in perception, or the interpretation of the sensory stimulation provided by the artwork. Perception and its sister area of psychology, sensation, are the focus of this unit.

For many years in psychology, it was popular to consider sensation and perception as two distinct processes. Sensation was defined in passive terms as the simple event of some stimulus energy (i.e., a sound wave) impinging on the body or on a specific sense organ, which then reflexively transmits appropriate information to the central nervous system. Both passivity and simple reflexes were stressed in this concept of sensation. Perception, on the other hand, was defined as an integrative and interpretive process that the higher centers of the brain accomplish based on sensory information and available memories for similar events.

The Gestalt psychologists, early German researchers, were convinced that perception was a function of a higher order sensation. They believed that the whole stimulus was more than the sum of its individual sensory parts and that this statement was made true by the process of perception.

For example, when you listen to a song, you hear the words, the loudness, and the harmony as well as the main melody. However, you do not really hear each of these separately; what you hear is a whole song. If the song is pleasant to you, you may say that you like it. If the song is raucous to you, you may perceive that you do not like it. However, even the songs that you do not like on first hearing may become likeable after repeated exposure. Hence perception, according to these early Gestalt psychologists, is a more advanced and complicated process than sensation.

This dichotomy of sensation and perception is no longer widely accepted. The revolution came in the mid-1960s, when a psychologist published a then-radical treatise in which he reasoned that perceptual processes included all sensory events, which he saw as directed by a searching central nervous system. Also, this view provided that certain perceptual patterns, such as recognition of a piece of artwork, may be species-specific. That is, all humans, independent of learning history, should share some of the same perceptual repertoires. This unit on perceptual processes is designed to further your understanding of these complex and interesting processes.

In the first article, "The Senses," Chip Simons introduces one of the main topics of this unit and reviews many of the dominant senses in the human being. He concludes that when we understand the senses, we also understand the brain.

One of the dominant senses in humans is audition or hearing. In the next article, Anita Manning reviews how important hearing is and what contributes to hearing loss as we age. Natural loss contributes to decline, but environmental causes such as noisy workplaces are contributing more and more to deafness in the American population.

The third article in this unit examines another important but often overlooked sense—touch. In an interview with Susan Lederman, a leading psychologist, the importance of skin sensations is outlined. New research on this sense is also revealed.

The final selection in this unit relates to an altered state of consciousness, something outside of normal sensation and perception. Such altered states include extrasensory perception and dreaming. This article is about dreaming, something we all do and something that fascinates most individuals. Jonathan Leonard investigates what dreams mean according to research and how the brain is involved in dreaming.

THE SENSES

They delight, heal, define the boundaries of our world. And they are helping unlock the brain's secrets

To the 19th-century French poet Charles Baudelaire, there was no such thing as a bad smell. What a squeamish, oversensitive bunch he would have deemed the denizens of 20th-century America, where body odors are taboo, strong aromas are immediately suppressed with air freshener, and perfume—long celebrated for its seductive and healing powers—is banned in some places to protect those with multiple chemical sensitivities.

Indeed, in the years since Baudelaire set pen to paper, civilization has played havoc with the natural state of all the human senses, technology providing the ability not only to tame and to mute but also to tease and overstimulate. Artificial fragrances and flavors trick the nose and tongue. Advertisers dazzle the eyes with rapid-fire images. Wailing sirens vie with the beeping of pagers to challenge the ears' ability to cope.

Yet even as we fiddle with the texture and scope of our sensibilities, science is indicating it might behoove us to show them a bit more respect. Growing evidence documents the surprising consequences of depriving or overwhelming the senses. And failing to nurture our natural capabilities, researchers are discovering, can affect health, emotions, even intelligence. Hearing, for example, is intimately connected to emotional circuits: When a nursing infant looks up from the breast, muscles in the middle ear reflexively tighten, readying the child for the pitch of a human voice. The touch of massage can relieve pain and improve concentration. And no matter how we spritz or scrub, every human body produces a natural odor as distinctive as the whorls on the fingertips—an aroma that research is showing to be a critical factor in choosing a sexual partner.

Beyond their capacity to heal and delight, the senses have also opened a window on the workings of the human brain. A flood of studies on smell, sight, hearing, touch and taste in the last two decades have upended most of the theories about how the brain functions. Scientists once believed, for example, that the brain was hard-wired at birth, the trillions of connections that made up its neural circuits genetically predetermined. But a huge proportion of neurons in a newborn infant's brain, it turns out, require input from the senses in order to hook up to one another properly.

Similarly, scientific theory until recently held that the sense organs did the lion's share of processing information about the world: The eye detected movement; the nose recognized smells. But researchers now know that ears, eyes and fingers are only way stations, transmitting signals that are then processed centrally. "The nose doesn't smell—the brain does," says Richard Axel, a molecular biologist at Columbia University. Each of our senses shatters experience into fragments, parsing the world like so many nouns and verbs, then leaving the brain to put the pieces back together and make sense of it all.

In labs across the country, researchers are drafting a picture of the senses that promises not only to unravel the mysterious tangle of nerves in the brain but also to offer reasons to revel in sensuous experience. Cradling a baby not only feels marvelous, scientists are finding, but is absolutely vital to a newborn's emotional and cognitive development. And the results of this research are beginning to translate into practical help for people whose senses are impaired: Researchers in Boston last year unveiled a tiny electronic device called a retinal chip that one day may restore sight to people blinded after childhood. Gradually, this new science of the senses is redefining what it means to be a feeling and thinking human being. One day it may lead to an understanding of consciousness itself.

SIGHT

Seeing is believing, because vision is the body's top intelligence gatherer, at least by the brain's reckoning. A full quarter of

SIGHT

Cells in the retina of the eye are so sensitive they can respond to a single photon, or particle of light.

the cerebral cortex, the brain's crinkled top layer, is devoted to sight, according to a new estimate by neuroscientist David Van Essen of Washington University in St. Louis—almost certainly more than is devoted to any other sense.

It seems fitting, then, that vision has offered scientists their most powerful insights on the brain's structure and operations. Research on sight "has been absolutely fundamental" for understanding the brain, says neurobiologist Semir Zeki of University College in London, in part because the visual system is easier to study than the other senses. The first clues to the workings of the visual system emerged in the 1950s, when Johns Hopkins neurobiologists David Hubel and Torsten Wiesel conducted a series of Nobel Prize–winning experiments. Using hair-thin electrodes implanted in a cat's brain, they recorded the firing of single neurons in the area where vision is processed. When the animal was looking at a diagonal bar of light, one neuron fired. When the bar was at a slightly different angle, a different nerve cell responded.

Hubel and Wiesel's discovery led to a revolutionary idea: While we are perceiving a unified scene, the brain is dissecting the view into many parts, each of which triggers a different set of neurons, called a visual map. One map responds to color and form, another only to motion. There are at least five such maps in the visual system alone, and recent work is showing that other senses are similarly encoded in the brain. In an auditory map, for example, the two sets of neurons that respond to two similar sounds, such as "go" and "ko," are located near each other, while those resonating with the sound "mo" lie at a distance.

Though we think of sensory abilities as independent, researchers are finding that each sense receives help from the others in apprehending the world. In 1995, psycholinguist Michael Tanenhaus of the University of Rochester videotaped people as they listened to sentences about nearby objects. As they listened, the subjects' eyes flicked to the objects. Those movements—so fast the subjects did not realize they'd shifted their gaze—helped them under-

stand the grammar of the sentences, Tanenhaus found. Obviously, vision isn't required to comprehend grammar. But given the chance, the brain integrates visual cues while processing language.

The brain also does much of the heavy lifting for color vision, so much so that some people with brain damage see the world in shades of gray. But the ability to see colors begins with cells in the back of the eyeball called cones. For decades, scientists thought everyone with normal color vision had the same three types of cone cell—for red, green and blue light—and saw the same hues. New research shows, however, that everybody sees a different palette. Last year, Medical College of Wisconsin researchers Maureen Neitz and her husband, Jay, discovered that people have up to nine genes for cones, indicating there may be many kinds of cones. Already, two red cone subtypes have been found. People with one type see red differently from those with the second. Says Maureen Neitz: "That's why people argue about adjusting the color on the TV set."

HEARING

Hearing is the gateway to language, a uniquely human skill. In a normal child, the ears tune themselves to human sounds soon after birth, cementing the neural connections between language, emotions and intelligence. Even a tiny glitch in the way a child processes sound can unhinge development.

About 7 million American children who have normal hearing and intelligence develop intractable problems with language, reading and writing because they cannot decipher certain parcels of language. Research by Paula Tallal, a Rutgers University neurobiologist, has shown that children with language learning disabilities (LLD) fail to distinguish between the "plosive" consonants, such as b, t and p. To them, "bug" sounds like "tug" sounds like "pug." The problem, Tallal has long argued, is that for such kids the sounds come too fast. Vowels resonate for 100 milliseconds or more, but

HEARING

At six months, a baby's brain tunes in to the sounds of its native tongue and tunes out other languages.

plosive consonants last for a mere 40 milli-seconds—not long enough for some children to process them. "These children hear the sound. It just isn't transmitted to the brain normally," she says.

Two years ago, Tallal teamed up with Michael Merzenich, a neurobiologist at the University of California–San Francisco, to create a set of computer games that have produced stunning gains in 29 children with LLD. With William Jenkins and Steve Miller, the neurobiologists wrote computer programs that elongated the plosive consonants, making them louder—"like making a yellow highlighter for the brain," says Tallal. After a month of daily three-hour sessions, children who were one to three years behind their peers in language and reading had leaped forward a full two years. The researchers have formed a company, Scientific Learning Corp., that could make their system available to teachers and professionals within a few years. (See their Web site: *http://www.scilearn.com* or call 415-296-1470.)

An inability to hear the sounds of human speech properly also may contribute to autism, a disorder that leaves children unable to relate emotionally to other people. According to University of Maryland psycho-physiologist Stephen Porges, many autistic children are listening not to the sounds of human speech but instead to frightening noises. He blames the children's fear on a section of the nervous system that controls facial expressions, speech, visceral feelings and the muscles in the middle ear.

These muscles, the tiniest in the body, allow the ear to filter sounds, much the way muscles in the eye focus the eyeball on near or distant objects. In autistic children, the neural system that includes the middle ear is lazy. As a result, these children attend not to the pitch of the human voice but instead to sounds that are much lower: the rumble of traffic, the growl of a vacuum cleaner. In the deep evolutionary past, such noises signaled danger. Porges contends that autistic children feel too anxious to interact emotionally, and the neural system controlling many emotional responses fails to develop.

Porges says that exercising the neural system may help autistic kids gain language and emotional skills. He and his colleagues have begun an experimental treatment consisting of tones and songs altered by computer to filter out low sounds, forcing the middle ear to focus on the pitches of human speech. After five 90-minute sessions, most of the 16 children have made strides that surprised even Porges. Third grader Tomlin Clark, for example, who once spoke only rarely, recently delighted his parents by getting in trouble for talking out of turn in school. And for the first time, he shows a sense of humor. "Listening to sounds seems so simple, doesn't it?" says Porges. "But so does jogging."

TOUCH

The skin, writes pathologist Marc Lappé, "is both literally and metaphorically 'the body's edge' . . . a boundary against an inimical world." Yet the skin also is the organ that speaks the language of love most clearly—and not just in the erogenous zones. The caress of another person releases hormones that can ease pain and clear the mind. Deprive a child of touch, and his brain and body will stop growing.

This new view of the most intimate sense was sparked a decade ago, when child psychologist Tiffany Field showed that premature infants who were massaged for 15 minutes three times a day gained weight 47 percent faster than preemies given standard intensive care nursery treatment: as little touching as possible. The preemies who were massaged weren't eating more; they just processed food more efficiently, says

TOUCH

People with "synesthesia" feel colors, see sounds and taste shapes.

Field, now director of the University of Miami's Touch Research Institute. Field found that massaged preemies were more alert and aware of their surroundings when awake, while their sleep was deeper and more restorative. Eight months later, the massaged infants scored better on mental and motor tests.

SIXTH SENSES

Wish you had that nose?

Folklore abounds with tales of animals possessing exceptional sensory powers, from pigs predicting earthquakes to pets telepathically anticipating their owners' arrival home. In some cases, myth and reality are not so far apart. Nature is full of creatures with superhuman senses: built-in compasses, highly accurate sonar, infrared vision. "Our world-view is limited by our senses," says Dartmouth College psychologist Howard Hughes, "so we are both reluctant to believe that animals can have capabilities beyond ours, and we attribute to them supernatural powers. The truth is somewhere between the two."

In the case of Watson, a Labrador retriever, reality is more impressive than any fiction. For over a year, Watson has reliably pawed his owner, Emily Ramsey, 45 minutes before her epileptic seizures begin, giving her time to move to a safe place. Placed by Canine Partners for Life, Watson has a 97 percent success rate, according to the Ramsey family. No one has formally studied how such dogs can predict seizure onset consistently. But they may smell the chemical changes known to precede epileptic attacks. "Whatever it is," says Harvard University neurologist Steven Schachter, "I think there's something to it."

Scientists have scrutinized other animals for decades, trying to decipher their sensory secrets. Birds, bees, moles and some 80 other creatures are known to sense magnetic fields. But new studies indicate birds have two magnetic detection systems: One seems to translate polarized light into visual patterns that act as a compass; the other is an internal magnet birds use to further orient themselves.

Dolphin sonar so intrigued government researchers that they launched the U.S. Navy marine Mammal Program in 1960, hoping it would lead to more-sophisticated tracking equipment. But the animals still beat the machines, says spokesman Tom LaPuzza. In a murky sea, dolphins can pinpoint a softball two football fields away. A lobe in their forehead focuses their biosonar as a flashlight channels light, beaming 200-decibel clicks.

It took night-vision goggles for humans to replicate the infrared vision snakes come by naturally: A camera-alike device in organs lining their lips lets them see heat patterns made by mammals. And humans can only envy the ability of sharks, skates and rays to feel electric fields through pores in their snouts—perhaps a primordial skill used by Earth's earliest creatures to scout out the new world.

BY ANNA MULRINE

SMELL

A woman's sense of smell is keener than a man's. And smell plays a larger role in sexual attraction for women.

Being touched has healing powers throughout life. Massage, researchers have found, can ease the pain of severely burned children and boost the immune systems of AIDS patients. Field recently showed that office workers who received a 15-minute massage began emitting higher levels of brain waves associated with alertness. After their massage, the workers executed a math test in half their previous time with half the errors.

While such findings may sound touchy-feely, an increasing volume of physiological evidence backs them up. In a recent series of experiments, Swedish physiologist Kerstin Uvnas-Moberg found that gentle stroking can stimulate the body to release oxytocin, sometimes called the love hormone because it helps cement the bond between mothers and their young in many species. "There are deep, deep, physiological connections between touching and love," Uvnas-Moberg says. Oxytocin also blunts pain and dampens the hormones release when a person feels anxious or stressed.

For the babies of any species, touch signals that mother—the source of food, warmth and safety—is near. When she is gone, many young animals show physiological signs of stress and shut down their metabolism—an innate response designed to conserve energy until she returns. Without mother, rat pups do not grow, says Saul Schanberg, a Duke University pharmacologist, even when they are fed and kept warm. Stroking them with a brush in a manner that mimics their mother licking them restores the pups to robust health. "You need the right kind of touch in order to grow," says Schanberg, "even more than vitamins."

SMELL

Long ago in human evolution, smell played a prominent role, signaling who was ready to mate and who ready to fight. But after a while, smell fell into disrepute. Aristotle disparaged it as the most animalistic of the senses, and Immanuel Kant dreamed of losing it. Recent research has restored the nose to some of its former glory. "Odor plays a far more important role in human behavior and physiology than we realize," says Gary Beauchamp, director of Philadelphia's Monell Chemical Senses Center.

A baby recognizes its mother by her odor soon after birth, and studies show that adults can identify clothing worn by their children or spouses by smell alone. In 1995, Beauchamp and colleagues at Monell reported that a woman's scent—genetically determined—changes in pregnancy to reflect a combination of her odor and that of her fetus.

The sense of smell's most celebrated capacity is its power to stir memory. "Hit a tripwire of smell, and memories explode all at once," writes poet Diane Ackerman. The reason, says Monell psychologist Rachel Herz, is that "smells carry an emotional quality." In her latest experiment, Herz showed people a series of evocative paintings. At the same time, the subjects were exposed to another sensory cue—an orange, for example—in different ways. Some saw an orange. Others were given an orange to touch, heard the word "orange" or smelled the fruit. Two days later, when subjects were given the same cue and were asked to recall the painting that matched it, those exposed to the smell of the orange recalled the painting and produced a flood of emotional responses to it.

Herz and others suspect that an aroma's capacity to spark such vivid remembrances arises out of anatomy. An odor's first way station in the brain is the olfactory bulb, two blueberry-sized lumps of cortex from which neurons extend through the skull into the nose. Smell molecules, those wafting off a cinnamon bun, for example, bind to these olfactory neurons, which fire off their signals first to the olfactory bulb and then to the limbic system—the seat of sexual drive, emotions and memory. Connections between the olfactory bulb and the neocortex, or thinking part of the brain, are secondary roads compared to the highways leading to emotional centers.

Scientists once thought all smells were made up of combinations of seven basic odors. But in an elegant series of experiments, research teams led by Columbia's Axel and Linda Buck of Harvard have shown the mechanics of smell to be much more complicated. In 1991, the scientists discovered a family of at least 1,000 genes corresponding to about 1,000 types of olfactory neurons in the nose. Each of these neuronal types responds to one—and only one—type of odor molecule.

The average person, of course, can detect far more than 1,000 odors. That's because a single scent is made up of more than one type of molecule, perhaps even dozens. A rose might stimulate neurons A, B and C, while jasmine sets off neurons B, C and F. "Theoretically, we can detect an astronomical number of smells." says Axel—the

ARE YOU A SUPERTASTER?

All tongues are not created equal. How intense flavors seem is determined by heredity. In this test, devised by Yale University taste experts Linda Bartoshuk and Laurie Lucchina, find out if you are a **nontaster**, an **average taster** or a **supertaster**. Answers on next page.

TASTE BUDS. Punch a hole with a standard hole punch in a square of wax paper. Paint the front of your tongue with a cotton swab dipped in blue food coloring. Put wax paper on the tip of your tongue, just to the right of center. With a flashlight and magnifying glass, count the number of pink, unstained circles. They contain taste buds.

SWEET. Rinse your mouth with water before tasting each sample. Put $\frac{1}{2}$ cup of sugar in a measuring cup, and then add enough water to make 1 cup. Mix. Coat front half of your tongue, including the tip, with a cotton swab dipped in the solution. Wait a few moments. Rate the sweetness according to the scale shown below.

SALT. Put 2 teaspoons of salt in a measuring cup and add enough water to make 1 cup. Repeat the steps listed above, rating how salty the solution is.

SPICY. Add 1 teaspoon of Tabasco sauce to 1 cup of water. Apply with a cotton swab to first half inch of the tongue, including the tip. Keep your tongue out of your mouth until the burn reaches a peak, then rate the pain according to the scale.

equivalent of 10 to the 23rd power. The brain, however, doesn't have the space to keep track of all those possible combinations of molecules, and so it focuses on smells that were relevant in evolution, like the scent of ripe fruit or a sexually receptive mate—about 10,000 odors in all.

Axel and Buck have now discovered that the olfactory bulb contains a "map," similar to those the brain employs for vision and hearing. By implanting a gene into mice, the researchers dyed blue the nerves leading

TASTE

Human beings are genetically hard-wired to crave sweetness; sugar on the lips of a newborn baby will bring a smile.

from the animals' olfactory bulbs to their noses. Tracing the path of these neurons, the researchers discovered that those responsible for detecting a single type of odor molecule all led back to a single point in the olfactory bulb. In other words, the jumble of neurons that exists in the nose is reduced to regimental order in the brain.

Smell maps may one day help anosmics, people who cannot smell. Susan Killorn of Richmond, Va., lost her sense of smell three years ago when she landed on her head while in-line skating and damaged the nerves leading from her nose to her brain. A gourmet cook, Killorn was devastated. "I can remember sitting at the dinner table and begging my husband to describe the meal I'd just cooked," she says. Killorn's ability to detect odors has gradually returned, but nothing smells quite right. One possibility, says Richard Costanzo, a neurophysiologist at Virginia Commonwealth University, is that some of the nerves from her nose have recovered or regenerated but now are hooked up to the wrong spot in her smell map.

Though imperfect, recoveries like Killorn's give researchers hope they may one day be able to stimulate other neurons to regenerate—after a spinal cord injury, for example. Costanzo and others are searching for chemicals made by the body that can act as traffic cops, telling neurons exactly where to grow. In the meantime, Killorn is grateful for every morsel of odor. "I dream at night about onions and garlic," she says, "and they smell like they are supposed to."

TASTE

Human beings will put almost anything into their mouths and consider it food, from stinging nettles to grubs. Fortunately, evolution armed the human tongue with a

set of sensors to keep venturesome members of the species from dying of malnutrition or poison. The four simple flavors—sweet, salty, bitter and sour—tell human beings what's healthy and what's harmful. But as researchers are finding, the sense of taste does far more than keep us from killing ourselves. Each person tastes food differently, a genetically determined sensitivity that can affect diet, weight and health.

In a quest for novelty, people around the world have developed an affinity for foods that cause a modicum of pain. "Humans have the ability to say, 'Oh, that didn't really hurt me—let me try it again,' " says Barry Green, a psychologist at the John B. Pierce Laboratory in New Haven, Conn. Spicy food, Green has found, gives the impression of being painfully hot by stimulating the nerves in the mouth that sense temperature extremes. The bubbles in soda and champagne feel as if they are popping inside the mouth; in reality, carbon dioxide inside the bubbles irritates nerves that sense pain.

One person's spicy meatball, however, is another's bland and tasteless meal. Researchers have long known that certain people have an inherited inability to taste a mildly bitter substance with a tongue-twisting name: propylthiouracil, or PROP, for short. About a quarter of Caucasians are "nontasters," utterly insensitive to PROP, while the vast majority of Asians and Africans can taste it. Now, researchers at Yale University led by psychologist Linda Bartoshuk have discovered a third group of people called "supertasters." So sensitive are supertasters' tongues that they gag on PROP and can detect the merest hint of other bitter compounds in a host of foods, from chocolate and saccharin to vegetables such as broccoli, "which could explain why George Bush hates it," Bartoshuk says. She has recently discovered that supertasters have twice as many taste buds as nontasters and more of the nerve endings that detect the feel of foods. As a consequence, sweets taste sweeter to supertasters, and cream feels creamier. A spicy dish can send a supertaster through the roof.

In an ongoing study, Bartoshuk's group has found that older women who are nontasters tend to prefer sweets and fatty foods—dishes that some of the supertasters find cloying. Not surprisingly, supertasters also tend to be thinner and have lower cholesterol. In their study, the researchers ask subjects to taste cream mixed with oil, a combination Bartoshuk confesses she finds delicious. "I'm a nontaster, and I'm heavy," she says. "I gobble up the test." But tasting ability is not only a matter of cuisine preference and body weight. Monell's Marcia

RESULTS OF TASTE TEST ON PREVIOUS PAGE		
	SUPER-TASTERS	NON-TASTERS
No. of taste buds	25 on average	10
Sweet rating	56 on average	32
Tabasco rating	64 on average	31

Average tasters lie in between. Bartoshuk and Lucchina lack the data to rate salt.

Pelchat and a graduate student recently completed a study indicating that nontasters also may be predisposed to alcoholism.

The human senses detect only a fraction of reality: We can't see the ultraviolet markers that guide a honeybee to nectar; we can't hear most of the noises emitted by a dolphin. In this way, the senses define the boundaries of mental awareness. But the brain also defines the limits of what we perceive. Human beings see, feel, taste, touch and smell not the world around them but a version of the world, one their brains have concocted. "People imagine that they're seeing what's really there, but they're not," says neuroscientist John Maunsell of Baylor College of Medicine in Houston. The eyes take in the light reflecting off objects around us, but the brain only pays attention to part of the scene. Looking for a pen on a messy desk, for example, you can scan the surface without noticing the papers scattered across it.

The word "sentience" derives from the Latin verb *sentire,* meaning "to feel." And research on the senses, especially the discovery of sensory mapping, has taken scientists one step further in understanding the state we call consciousness. Yet even this dramatic advance is only a beginning. "In a way, these sexy maps have seduced us," says Michael Shipley, director of neurosciences at the University of Maryland–Baltimore. "We still haven't answered the question of how do you go from visual maps to recognizing faces, or from an auditory map to recognizing a Mozart sonata played by two different pianists." The challenge for the 21st century will be figuring out how the brain, once it has broken the sensory landscape into pieces, puts them together again.

BY SHANNON BROWNLEE
WITH TRACI WATSON

Gain in years can mean loss in hearing

As the baby boom generation ages, the number of people losing their hearing is rising. And as more women join men in noisy jobs, they will be losing their audio acuity in greater numbers as well.

By Anita Manning
USA TODAY

For Dennis McComb, 54, a Phoenix real estate agent, it started subtly when he was around 38 years old.

"I had joined a company in Phoenix and had to go to a lot of meetings," he says. "There were several people who were mumblers, as I called them. I had to go stand next to them."

He began to suspect it wasn't other people's enunciation that was the problem. He made an appointment with an audiologist, who diagnosed a hearing loss in the middle-range of sound frequency, the range of most human speech.

The audiologist said it's a hereditary condition, but McComb thinks it's the result of months spent in the pressurized cabin of a Navy sub in the late 1960s.

Whatever the cause, the fact of his hearing loss was disturbing. "I thought I was invincible, perfect," he says. "All of a sudden I had a flaw."

But his practical nature took over, and he got fitted for hearing aids. "People wear glasses and nobody says anything," he says. "I don't know why people should be embarrassed to wear a hearing aid."

More than an earful of noise

Any noise at 70 decibels and louder can contribute to hearing impairment.

Aircraft carrier deck: 140 decibels
Jet operation: 140
Jet takeoff (200 ft.): 130
Discotheque: 120
Auto horn (3 ft.): 120
Riveting machine: 110
Garbage truck: 100
N.Y. subway station: 100
Heavy truck (30 ft.): 90
Alarm clock: 80
Freight train (50 ft.): 80
Freeway traffic (50 ft.): 70
Light traffic (100 ft.): 50
Living room, library: 40
Soft whisper (15 ft.): 30

Source: 'Hearing Aids: A User's Guide' by Wayne J. Staab

McComb is one of more than 20 million Americans with hearing loss, a number expected to swell as the population ages. Stephen Lotterman, director of graduate studies in audiology at Gallaudet University, Washington, D.C., says 30% of people over age 65 have hearing loss.

"Part of the aging process includes deterioration in the auditory system, particularly the central nervous system, which carries sound to the brain," Lotterman says. "As changes to the structure of the brain occur, the ability to distinguish sounds changes."

Deterioration in the inner ear reduces the number of receptor cells that carry sound impulses, he says. "It's as if the number of telephone lines available to get information to the brain is reduced.

"Once you reach 30, unknown to you, your hearing is gradually changing," Lotterman says. Historically, more men than women have lost their hearing acuity, because men were in jobs where they were exposed to constant loud noise. That may be changing, he says, as women increasingly work alongside men in noisy jobs.

But at present, more men are hard of hearing than women, and a man at age 65 hears about as well as a women of 75. Men tend to lose high frequency sounds first, while women lose hearing overall, says Manassas, Va., audiologist

Mary Jo Grote. High frequency sounds, she says, include the consonant sounds d, t, sh, s, f and th. People with high-frequency hearing loss would have trouble distinguishing among the words "thin" and "fin."

Phoenix audiologist Wayne J. Staab, author of *Hearing Aids: A User's Guide* (Wayne J. Staab Publisher, $15), writes

that while aging is the most common cause of hearing loss, there are plenty of other causes, including birth trauma, illness—maternal rubella, meningitis or ear infections, for example—and certain drugs.

He categorizes them:

➤**Outer ear causes.** These include infections of the auditory canal lining,

such as "swimmer's ear," which can lead to more serious infections if they're left untreated; malformation of the ear canal or insertion of objects into the ear canal.

➤**Middle ear causes.** Examples are a ruptured eardrum, which can be caused by extreme air pressure changes, a blow to the ear or buildup of fluid due

Several listening devices available

Dramatic improvements in hearing aid technology and in ear surgery are giving hope to people with hearing loss.

Cochlear implantation, the surgical replacement of the inner ear, is a controversial procedure used when the inner ear is not functioning at all. It replaces the damaged cochlea with a device that sends sound signals to the brain.

"It is not as effective as the inner ear," says Stephen Lotterman of Gallaudet University, "but restoration of any sound can be a blessing. Adults and children can often learn to understand speech reasonably well, even though it can be difficult to get used to the difference between what you hear now vs. what you heard before."

For children born deaf, he says, "the earlier they're implanted, the sooner they will acquire speech. The evidence seems strong that young deaf children implanted early do very well in school, can be mainstreamed in regular schools and learn English."

For about 30% of people who are deaf or hard of hearing, hearing aids are of little assistance, Lotterman says, either because the loss is due to central nervous system damage or the nature of destruction within the ear is such that all sounds are distorted. But for most people, hearing aids may be helpful.

Once, hearing aids were fairly clunky gadgets, but new devices have been streamlined, microprocessed and miniaturized to the point where some models fit inside the ear canal.

The job of a hearing aid is to amplify sound in a way that makes it audible to the user. Standard analog hearing aids convert sound signals into an electric current, which is modified in a miniature amplifier and converted back into sound by a receiver.

These devices amplify all sound at the same level, like turning up the volume on a television set. That's a problem for people in busy cafeterias or in crowds because all noise is amplified, including the clatter of dishes and other background din, making the speech of a companion hard to distinguish.

Programmable analog hearing aids have two bands, for high and low frequencies, which allow the audiologist to better tailor the incoming sound to accommodate the individual hearing loss. But they may still have the problem of overall amplification of background noise.

Finding help and information

Audiologist Suzanne Scott recommends these organizations for more information:
➤ The National Information Center on Deafness, phone 202–651–5051 or on the Internet at http://www.gallaudet.edu/ñicd/
➤ American Speech-Language-Hearing Association, 800–638–8255 or on the Internet at http://www.asha.org
➤ Self Help for Hard of Hearing People, 301–657–2248, voice; 301–657–2249, TTY, or on the Internet at http://www.shhh.org

The newest and most high-tech hearing aids are digital. These devices contain tiny computer chips that convert the analog sound impulse into a binary signal through an audio processor.

The digitized sound can be separated into bands, and each band can be adjusted by an audiologist to suit the need of the user.

Among the advantages of digitized sound, manufacturers say, is that the devices can automatically sample the incoming noise and adjust to tone down background noise while boosting the spoken voice of a nearby companion.

Two companies make digital hearing aids: Widex, manufacturer of Senso hearing aids; and Oticon, which makes Digi-Focus. The differences between the two are significant:

➤ Senso separates sound into three programmable bands and makes models small enough to fit inside the ear canal. But they cost $2,900 to $3,700 apiece.

➤ The DigiFocus models, which are larger, split the sound into seven bands, like a graphic equalizer on a stereo system, and are available in behind-the-ear and in-the-ear models. Devices cost about $2,000 to $2,500 each.

Good analog hearing aids cost between $700–$1,500 each, audiologists say. Most advise getting two, since hearing loss is usually equal in both ears.

Dennis McComb of Phoenix has worn Senso digital hearing aids for about six months. He says they're "a quantum leap" ahead of analog hearing aids in terms of sound quality and clarity. Because his hearing loss is only in the middle range, "just about where my wife's voice is," he says, "we engineered (the hearing aids) to leave the low and high bands alone and just amplify the middle band."

That works just fine for him, but, says Gallaudet University audiologist Suzanne Scott, "digital hearing aids are extremely expensive, and I'm not convinced that for the general public they're worth it."

Digital hearing aids may be perfect for one patient, but may not offer much advantage over analog aids for another, she says.

Because the devices are expensive and need to be carefully adjusted to each individual's needs, she says, it's important to find a certified audiologist familiar with a range of listening devices.

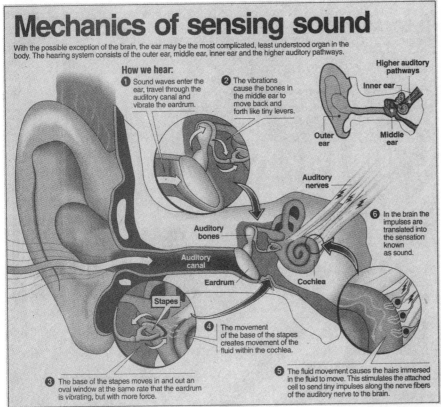

Mechanics of sensing sound

With the possible exception of the brain, the ear may be the most complicated, least understood organ in the body. The hearing system consists of the outer ear, middle ear, inner ear and the higher auditory pathways.

How we hear:

1 Sound waves enter the ear, travel through the auditory canal and vibrate the eardrum.

2 The vibrations cause the bones in the middle ear to move back and forth like tiny levers.

Higher auditory pathways

Inner ear

Outer ear

Middle ear

Auditory nerves

6 In the brain the impulses are translated into the sensation known as sound.

Auditory bones

Auditory canal

Eardrum

Cochlea

Stapes

4 The movement of the base of the stapes creates movement of the fluid within the cochlea.

3 The base of the stapes moves in and out an oval window at the same rate that the eardrum is vibrating, but with more force.

5 The fluid movement causes the hairs immersed in the fluid to move. This stimulates the attached cell to send tiny impulses along the nerve fibers of the auditory nerve to the brain.

Source: *Hearing Aids: A User's Guide* by Wayne J. Staab

By Grant Jerding, USA TODAY

to middle-ear infections; damage to the tiny middle ear bones; tumors and congenital abnormalities.

▶**Inner ear causes.** Damage to the cochlea and the connecting nerves usually causes a greater loss of hearing abil- ity, and that loss is more difficult to correct.

Noise, either loud and prolonged or a single very loud noise like an explosion, is one of the most common causes of hearing loss because of the damage it does to the inner ear.

Intense noise can literally blast away the tiny hairs of the inner ear, which help send sound impulses to the brain. It can also cause a stress reaction that reduces blood circulation to the ears. The resulting oxygen deprivation can make the inner ear hair cells more vulnerable to damage.

At risk for hearing loss are people who work in construction, boilermakers and others who work with heavy, loud machinery. Federal safety regulations require ear protection for workers whose jobs put their hearing in danger, but, Lotterman says, "If you can't hear your boss when he's trying to tell you something, many people would just as soon not wear ear protection."

Most people can recover from occasional evenings next to the speaker at a rock concert, Lotterman says, but repeated assaults on the auditory system will erode hearing, which is why rock musicians often have hearing problems later in life.

"Hearing loss from rock concerts and from turning up music under headphones is going to pay off in future with hearing loss," Lotterman says.

"If I see someone using a jackhammer and not using ear protection, I may as well hand him a business card and say, 'When your hearing loss gets bad enough, give me a call.'"

Don't Take Touch for Granted: An Interview With Susan Lederman

René Verry
Millikin University

Susan Lederman (SL) is an invited member of the International Council of Research Fellows for the Braille Research Center and a Fellow of the Canadian Psychology Association. She was also an Associate of the Canadian Institute for Advanced Research in the Robotics and Artificial Intelligence Programme for 8 years. A Professor in the Departments of Psychology and Computing & Information Science at Queen's University at Kingston (Ontario, Canada), she has written and coauthored numerous articles on tactile, psychophysics, haptic perception and cognition, motor control, and haptic applications in robotics, teleoperation, and virtual environments. She is currently the co-organizer of the Annual Symposium on Haptic Interfaces for Teleoperation and Virtual Environment Systems. René Verry (RV) is a psychology professor at Millikin University (Decatur, IL), where she teaches a variety of courses in the experimental core, including Sensation and Perception. She chose the often-subordinated somatic senses as the focus of her interview, and recruited Susan Lederman as our research specialist.

RV: Many undergraduate texts on sensation and perception note the importance, versatility, and complexity of touch relative to vision and hearing, and yet they typically devote only one chapter to the somatic senses. This seems paradoxical. How would you account for the lack of parallel coverage of the somatic senses relative to the visual and auditory senses even in introductory textbooks?

SL: Quite simply, much less is known about the sense of touch than about either vision or hearing. I can think of a number of reasons why this may be so. When monastic scribes recorded what was then known scientifically about the human body, they were prohibited from writing anything about the skin. Second, North American society has further downplayed the importance of touch by being fairly prudish about using it as a form of nonverbal communication. Touch is often viewed as too erotic or intimate, whether it is to avoid breaking or dirtying an object, or inappropriate public touching. Beginning in early childhood we are given the strong message to deemphasize the very powerful sense of touch. Third, as Frank Geldard so eloquently noted in *The Human Senses* (1972), "Despite the fact that the skin is, from the evolutionary standpoint, the oldest of the sensitive tissues of the body, it has yielded up its secrets reluctantly" (p. 259).

RV: What do you think he meant?

SL: I suspect that Geldard was referring to the lack of commercially available technologies that would have enabled the haptic research community to easily produce, control, and present multidimensional stimuli (e.g., objects or surfaces that vary systematically in texture, compliance, weight, shape, size) to research participants. Unlike vision or auditory researchers, haptic researchers have only recently had access to automated equipment that would allow them to prepare and present complex tactile stimuli to the hand. Finally, it's probably easier to imagine what the loss of vision or hearing would be like, for exam-

From *Teaching of Psychology*, Vol. 25, No. 1, 1998, pp. 64-67. © 1998 by the American Psychological Association. Reprinted by permission of Lawrence Erlbaum Associates, Inc.

ple, by wearing a blindfold or blocking our ears, respectively. Simulating the loss of touch is less straightforward, as for example, when we experience facial or limb numbness from Novocain or excessive nerve pressure. Hence, we tend to take touch for granted.

RV: What are some of the current trends shaping haptic research that those who teach principles of sensation and perception should know and convey to their students?

SL: Like many other fields, somatic research has become highly interdisciplinary due to the increased integration among the neurosciences as well as to greater interactions between basic and applied researchers. As touch scientists attempt to uncover the neural mechanisms and codes underlying complex tactile and haptic experiences, behavioral research on touch has become intimately linked to the neurosciences (e.g., neurophysiology, neuropsychology, medical imaging). Consequently, we know a good deal more now about the skin receptors and their various sensory and, most recently, motor functions than we did even 20 years ago.

RV: How were tactile sensations explained prior to this interdisciplinary neuroscience approach?

SL: We used to explain the function of various encapsulated nerve endings present in the peripheral nervous system in terms of von Frey's proposal formulated around the beginning of the 20th century. Combining logic and empirical testing, von Frey's Specificity Theory suggested that encapsulated and unencapsulated nerve endings (i.e., types of somatic receptors) served different sensory functions. Subsequent anatomical staining and single-cell recording research provided more detailed information showing that von Frey's ideas were largely incorrect. Combining the previously separate fields of psychophysics and neurophysiology is enabling us now to document how the cutaneous and haptic perceptions of various properties of surfaces and objects (e.g., roughness–smoothness, softness–hardness, warmth–cool, small–large, shape) are coded by particular neural mechanisms within the peripheral and central nervous systems.

RV: What is the present state of knowledge about the neurophysiology of the cutaneous and haptic senses?

SL: Currently, researchers have identified four separate neural channels for touch. In the glabrous (hairless) skin of the human hand, the first stage of processing within each channel is performed by a distinct type of mechanoreceptor population whose axons enter and continue up the spinal cord before making their first synapses. In contrast to von Frey's specificity assumptions, all of the different peripheral receptors with encapsulated endings are mechanoreceptors; however, they differ in terms of the distinct features of mechanical stimulation to which they selectively respond.

RV: Can you give an example of how mechanoreceptors differ and the kinds of sensation they produce?

SL: One mechanoreceptor population, the Meissner corpuscles, responds best to low-frequency vibrations, with a peak sensitivity around 40 Hz, and yields a sensation of flutter. Another mechanoreceptor population, the Pacinian corpuscles, responds best to high-frequency vibrations, with a peak sensitivity between 200–300 Hz, and yields a vibratory, buzzing sensation. In addition, both of these mechanoreceptor populations respond most strongly to transient events and are thus characterized as "fast-adapting" tactile units. In contrast, two other mechanoreceptor populations, the Merkel receptors and Ruffini cylinders, respond best to "steady-state" stimulation (static skin deformation) and are characterized as "slowly adapting" units. Further, within each of these two classes of fibers, the relative size of the mechanoreceptors' receptive fields (that area on the skin that produces a change in the neuron's response) differ. The processing distinctions among the different channels are important as they partially determine the cutaneous system's ability to sense and resolve the spatial and temporal details of objects.

RV: You've described the coding of haptic information. How are temperature and pain input coded?

SL: Two other types of receptors with expanded endings, thermoreceptors, appear to be selectively sensitive to changes in temperature. The "cold" receptors are selectively sensitive to decreases in temperature, whereas the "warm" receptors are most sensitive to increases in skin temperature. We think very narrow-diameter unencapsulated fibers (nociceptors) that respond to high-intensity stimulation of any kind are involved in pain perception; however, pain is a very complicated sensory experience that involves more than just the amount of neural response.

RV: How has our present knowledge of somatic neurophysiology changed touch research?

SL: As the story of touch unfolds, we have expanded our study beyond the cutaneous sensitivity and discriminative capacity of the skin to understand how we make judgments about the characteristics of the felt environment. Historically, we investigated these properties by passively stimulating the skin of an observer with a variety of pins and probes. But contrast this with how you normally learn about the world of objects through your hands. As James Gibson noted, we usually employ active manual exploration for purposes of perception. Active exploration involves the haptic system—a neural synthesis of position and movement inputs from the kinesthetic receptors embedded in muscles, tendons, and joints with the mechanical inputs from the skin receptors.

RV: How would this shift be reflected in research strategy?

SL: Roberta Klatzky and I (Lederman & Klatzky, 1987) studied voluntary, manual exploration—what people normally do with their hands—to learn how the haptic system processes information about the properties of surfaces and objects. We believe that haptic versus visual performance differences are partially determined by the choice of haptic "exploratory procedures" (distinct, stereotypical hand-movement patterns such as lateral motion, pressure, contour following), which people use to extract information about the specific properties of objects and surfaces. Our research suggests that these exploratory procedures play a crucial role in explaining why people are so adept at recognizing common objects by touch alone.

RV: How do the senses of touch and vision compare, with respect to how they process object properties?

SL: The haptic system is generally much better (faster and more accurate) than vision at discriminating fine differences in the material properties of objects (e.g., roughness, hardness), whereas vision is far better at differentiating precise details in spatial geometry. In more common perceptual situations where touch and vision often receive and use redundant information, we typically find that touch and vision work in an effective complementary fashion—touch extracts information about material attributes, whereas vision extracts geometric properties.

RV: In addition to new information on somatic receptors, what insights does current research on the cortical organization of the somatosensory system provide?

SL: We are learning that the somatosensory system is surprisingly plastic even in adult animals and humans. For example, research on human phantom limb amputees (Ramachandran, Rogers-Ramachandran, & Stewart, 1992, 1993) and neural stimulation in monkeys (Kaas, Merzenich, & Killacky, 1983) has shown that the somatosensory cortex will reorganize in response to changing (reduced or increased) stimulation. The reorganization consists of a relatively rapid alteration of the cortical map that represents the sensitivity of different parts of the body. These data have caused us to rework our sensory homunculus metaphor, the ubiquitous "little man" of text and lecture that represents the differential sensitivity of specific areas of the body. We must discard the old homunculus, a single unchanging somatosensory map located in the primary sensory area of the parietal lobe, and replace it with multiple flexible sensory homunculi located several times within and again outside the primary sensory area of the parietal lobe.

RV: You also mentioned another trend shaping haptic research today. Would you comment on the developing symbiosis between basic and applied research?

SL: Basic tactile research is now being used to address a variety of real-world problems. Examples include new sensorimotor tests for assessing the extent and recovery of hand function following injury, surgical repair, and rehabilitation; the design of effective raised-graphics displays (e.g., maps, pictures, graphs) for the blind; the further development of breast self-examination strategies for detecting cancerous tissue; and haptic interfaces allowing human operators to control real (teleoperation system) or simulated (virtual-environment system) remote environments using control devices such as a joystick or glove that relay haptic feedback from remote sensors. Whereas the study of haptic perception was historically overlooked, we are now seeing a virtual explosion of interest in processing and representation that expands on the earlier psychophysical work on human cutaneous sensation, while at the same time delves into whole new areas rarely, if ever, considered before. This last area involves psychologists working with people in the fields of computing science, artificial intelligence, mechanical engineering, and medicine (e.g., telemedicine, minimally invasive endoscopic surgery).

RV: When teaching about the senses, there are a variety of compelling demonstrations and labs that can be used to illustrate the fascinating features of vision, audition, olfaction, and gustation. However, it is particularly frustrating that similarly compelling demonstrations and labs are lacking in units on the somatic senses. What kinds of pedagogic tips would you give instructors who want to excite students about the equally interesting research problems in somatic research?

SL: It is a challenge to demonstrate tactile-haptic perceptual phenomena to a large class since touch is not normally a distance sense that can be experienced from afar. With some experimentation, I have developed a strategy that seems to work quite well. I often introduce the topic by contrasting the capabilities and limitations of the haptic system. First, I show how students can identify common objects by touch alone, both quickly and accurately. Then I have some of them try to identify raised two-dimensional outline drawings of those same common objects, a task that they always perform very badly (Klatzky, Lederman, & Metzger, 1985; Lederman, Klatzky, Chataway, & Summers, 1990). This discrepancy in performance enables students to understand and experience the different demands on haptic processing that produce such discrepant results.

RV: Illusions are a powerful way to demonstrate perceptual phenomena. Are there similarly compelling haptic illusions that teachers could demonstrate or use in perception labs?

SL: The size–weight illusion (a small object appears to weigh more than a large object of the same mass; Ellis & Lederman, 1993) is a very robust illusion, whether or not vision is used. It is quite easy to modify different-sized objects so that they weigh the same amount. For example, we have found that you can stuff identical symmetrical containers (film containers or prescription bottles) with appropriate weights, wrapped in cotton batting to prevent movement and to ensure the mass is centered within the container. The raised-line haptic version of the well-known visual horizontal–vertical illusion (the vertical line visually or haptically is perceived as longer than when it is horizontally aligned) is also very powerful. Moreover, because the explanations for the two modalities are quite different, it provides an opportunity for comparing and contrasting perceptual processes across sensory systems (Marchetti & Lederman, 1983).

RV: Many faculty teach large classes, and this is especially true of introductory psychology sections. How do you modify demonstrations for large classes?

SL: If the class is large (e.g., 100 or more), student volunteers can perform the previously mentioned tasks in front of the class. This demonstration can then be followed by individual access to the same materials distributed during class or available at the end of class. Whenever possible, it is preferable to form small groups to allow peer learning. I have also written formal labs on aftereffects (e.g., contingent aftereffects—the orientation-contingent size aftereffect; simple roughness, size, slant aftereffects) and on heightening the perceived roughness of a surface by examining it through an intermediate paper used as a glove. Both of these effects are very robust and therefore work well in class as demonstrations or as formal labs.

RV: You've studied a variety of facets of the somatic senses, including more recent research on robotics, teleoperation, and virtual environments. How did you become interested in this topic?

SL: As an undergraduate, I was particularly attracted by my courses on sensation and perception. But I noticed that there was almost nothing written about the sense of touch. This struck me as odd because touch is our reality sense and is such an important way to communicate. As I read the research that existed at the time, I was struck by how confining the research methods and questions were. As I explained earlier, the observers were always passive, and the experiments focused only on internal, subjective sensations, rather than on the perceptions of the external world around us. This provided the impetus for my doctoral research on how people tactually perceive texture, and subsequently led to my fascination with the nature of haptic perception and manual exploration. I have always been interested in applying the fruits of basic research to real-world problems, and this led to my interest in blindness and in applications of my work to the development of tactile aids for use in education and mobility. Then serendipity struck; a friend provided me with a newspaper article describing how engineers were currently building a new generation of flexible robots that could feel! I immediately wrote the engineer developing these robots and suggested that knowledge of how living systems haptically engage the world might prove useful in his design of tactile systems for robots. He invited me to visit his lab, and we had a wonderful discussion about artificial and living systems and how research in these areas might be integrated to design flexible, sensate robots. From that time on, I deliberately cultivated connections with people in robotics, engineering, and computing science, as it was apparent to me that experimental psychologists could make a unique contribution by blending their knowledge of biological sensorimotor systems with a sophisticated understanding of experimental design, scientific method, and statistical analysis.

RV: What kinds of career opportunities exist for undergraduates who wish to pursue a career in haptic research?

SL: The fact that, as yet, we know so little about the sense of touch offers young researchers the chance to do pioneering work on fascinating and important phenomena. Moreover, applied research opportunities are expanding with the advent of exciting new technological developments in the fields of robotics, teleoperation, and virtual environments. Consequently, there is a variety of different career opportunities for the prepared undergraduate interested in pursuing graduate research on touch. For example, students might work in organizations for the sensory handicapped or with industries that develop tactile aids and prostheses for the blind and deaf. Researchers are also needed for product evaluation of cosmetics, clothing, food, and personal-hygiene products. As I mentioned earlier, there's been a big new push within universities and industries to develop haptic systems for autonomous robotics, as well as haptic interfaces for teleoperation and virtual environment systems that retain the human in the control loop. Experimental psychologists can make a unique and fundamental contribution to these high technology areas. Clearly, a strong science background will help psychology majors successfully compete and communicate with their computing scientist and engineering colleagues on an equal footing.

Resources

Ellis, R. R. & Lederman, S. J. (1993). The role of haptic vs. visual volume cues in the size–weight illusion. *Perception & Psychophysics, 53,* 315–324.

Geldard, F. A. (1972). *The human senses* (2nd ed.). New York: Wiley.

Kaas, J. H., Merzenich, M. M., & Killackey, H. P. (1983). The reorganization of somatosensory cortex following peripheral nerve damage in adult and developing mammals. *Annual Review of Neuroscience, 6,* 325–356.

Klatzky, R. L., Lederman, S. J., & Metzger, V. (1985). Identifying objects by touch: An "expert system." *Perception & Psychophysics, 37,* 299–302.

Lederman, S. J., & Klatzky, R. L. (1987). Hand movements: A window into haptic object recognition. *Cognitive Psychology, 19,* 342–368.

Lederman, S. J., Klatzky, R. L., Chataway, C., & Summers, C. (1990). Visual mediation and the haptic recognition of two-dimensional pictures of common objects. *Perception & Psychophysics, 47,* 54–64.

Marchetti, F. M., & Lederman, S. J. (1983). The haptic radial–tangential effect: Two tests of Wong's (1977) "moments-of-inertia" hypothesis. *Bulletin of the Psychonomic Society, 21,* 43–46.

Ramachandran, V. S., Rogers-Ramachandran, D. C., & Stewart, M. (1992). Perceptual correlates of massive cortical reorganization. *Science, 258,* 1159–1160.

Ramachandran, V. S., Rogers-Ramachandran, D. C., & Stewart, M. (1993). Behavioral and MEG correlates of neural plasticity in the adult human brain. *Proceedings of the National Academy of Sciences, 90,* 10413–10420.

DREAM CATCHERS

Unleashing the genies in the sleeping mind

by Jonathan Leonard

THE DREAMS MOST OF US REMEMBER TEND TO BE ACtion-packed, emotional, and strange. The dreamer is often falling, escaping, or insecure. I recall a dream where I was in a wide sunken walkway or trench with many other people. A lot of pink globes were in the sky, and the mood was festive. All at once I heard an odd sound, looked up, and saw all the pink globes racing toward a distant Cinderella-style castle to my right. I was no longer in the trench but on a green field where the ground sloped upward toward the castle. Many people, perhaps those from the trench, were in the field, and we were all moving toward the castle. I feared what might happen next. I never found out, because just then I awoke. But like innumerable other dreamers, I was impressed by my dream's zany orientation and perplexed as to its cause.

Awhile ago I learned a bit about dreaming from a readable little book called *The Chemistry of Conscious States* that was written by a man named Hobson. Until then I had considered dreams enigmas. Indeed, the cause of dreams seemed fully as mysterious to me as the movement of certain stars must have seemed to medieval astrologers before Copernicus discovered that the earth and planets revolve about the sun. But of course we all love mysteries, a fact that goes a long way toward explaining why, throughout history, we have embraced the mystery of dreams, hiring untold generations of prophets and soothsayers, and more recent generations of psychoanalysts and dream interpreters, to probe the shadows and explain what our dreams really mean.

True knowledge of what causes our nocturnal imaginings has been a long time coming. For most of the twentieth century, the best we could do was agree or disagree with the 1900 dream theory of Sigmund Freud. Freud said, in essence, that dreams arise from a troubled subconscious, contain forbidden wishes we can't bear to acknowledge, and seem bizarre or choppy because a mental censor disguises or removes the forbidden thoughts.

Just where Freud's influential theory came from is unclear. It could have come from the flawed, rudimentary neuroscience of the 1890s, because Freud had studied that; or else, as Freud claimed, he may have developed it by ruthlessly probing his own emotions and earliest memories. Whatever the case, Freud was driven to develop his hypothesis by an awareness of strong similarities between dreams and certain kinds of madness, and by the realization that one might help a lot of people if one could penetrate to the heart of the mystery. Unfortunately, Freud's theory may have been precipitous: although it provided a rich base for development of psychoanalysis, its lack of clear scientific roots presented a slippery slope for those wishing to probe its scientific merit or devise alternative dream theories of their own.

In Freud's day, of course, scientific study of the mind was limited. Natural science was simply not up to revealing the mind's secrets, even though groundwork for later progress was being laid; and resignation on this score finally froze into the pessimistic doctrine of behaviorism—which said science had no business studying mental events and should limit itself to how humans and animals behave.

Even today, remnants of this old pessimism linger, which makes the actual progress to date all the more startling. In fact, especially since the 1950s, we have learned volumes about the human brain—how its roughly 100 billion neurons (nerve cells) receive, process, and transmit messages; how groups of neurons interact; how structures within the brain work with one another; and how the brain's chemistry influences its mental state. Indeed, aided by powerful imaging tools that allow us to penetrate the skull's bony x-ray barrier and watch the mind at work, we now confront a fast-moving river of knowledge that shows promise of unraveling much of the mystery of dreams, learning, memory, thought, and even human consciousness itself.

ONE POWERFUL TRIBUTARY FEEDING THIS GREAT torrent has been biological research on sleep and dreams. Harvard first fostered such research in the 1960s, when it let an unorthodox psychiatry resident named J. Allan Hobson, M.D. '59, split his time between doing animal research at the medical school's physiology department and performing his normal residency duties at the nearby Harvard-affiliated

We all love mysteries, a fact that goes a long way toward explaining why, throughout history, we have embraced the mystery of dreams.

Massachusetts Mental Health Center. In 1968, after completing his residency and getting extensive training in neurobiology, Hobson got a grant from the National Institutes of Health for animal studies, and the head of Harvard's psychiatry department, Bullard professor Jack Ewalt, allocated some of his own discretionary research funds to buy his young colleague equipment. Hobson thereupon created Harvard's Laboratory of Neurophysiology, which he still directs.

Although Hobson's real goal was to learn about the mind, his first research target was REM sleep, the special sleep phase in humans and mammals characterized by "rapid eye movement." Discovered in the 1950s, REM sleep had been associated with rapid heartbeat, fast breathing, special brain-wave patterns, high levels of brain activity, and vivid dreaming. Typically, a sleeping person's brain passes through various nonREM sleep stages, during which its general level of activity decreases, before entering the very active REM stage-a cycle that repeats itself about every 90 minutes. In humans, dream reports indicate that REM sleep dreams are much more likely to be colorful and imaginative, while those occurring at other times tend to be highly repetitive and dull.

Hobson knew from experience that cats were useful subjects for REM sleep research. As he explained later, in *The Chemistry of Conscious States*, "The cat's sleep pattern is strikingly similar to our own. Cats' brain waves, eye movements, and muscle twitches clearly differentiate waking, nonREM, and REM sleep in a manner that is parallel to what people experience." Also, REM sleep seemed to be controlled from the brainstem, an ancient part of the brain, just above the spinal cord, that humans share with all vertebrates. So Hobson decided to probe cat brainstems with microelectrodes in order to detect the firing of individual brainstem neurons and get a better idea of what was happening.

Around this time he was joined by Robert McCarley '59, M.D. '64, a medical resident with a love of neurobiology and a bent for computer programming who met Hobson through one of the latter's seminars, helped him set up the Neurophysiology Laboratory, and thereafter worked closely with him for 16 years. Together they figured out how to immobilize the brain and how to use a grid system to determine where the probe was at any time. They confirmed that their tiny probes could indeed record single nerve cells firing, while the observed cat slept naturally; and by sending the electrical signals to both an audio system and a visual recorder, they could hear these discharges as well as see them. They also confirmed that different nerve cell groups within the brainstem, and elsewhere in the brain, sounded different; and so, by moving from a known group of neurons to some other group, they could proceed to map the brain.

But mapping was not their goal. They wanted to know how the brainstem controlled REM sleep, for which purpose they could draw on a growing body of information. Among other things, they knew the brainstem was a major source of two brain chemicals, norepinephrine and serotonin. They knew these chemicals regulated or slowed the firing rates of certain neurons, played crucial roles in a number of basic brain functions like judgment and learning, and helped govern the entire brain's mental state. They also knew REM sleep was related to bursts of nerve impulses coming up from the brainstem that seemed to excite large parts of the brain. However, the only brain chemical known to cause REM sleep was neither norepinephrine nor serotonin, but rather acetylcholine, which encouraged many of the brain's nerve cells to fire faster. Thus, the exact role of these various brainstem chemicals in generating REM sleep was unclear.

One day in 1973, while exploring a brainstem in Hobson's lab, a researcher named Peter Wyzinski found something interesting. As Hobson relates in another of his books, *The Dreaming Brain*, "Peter Wyzinski called me into the recording room to observe a faintly visible, slowly discharging cell on the oscilloscope screen. . . . The cell . . . was . . . unique in our experience because it stopped firing during REM sleep: it was the first such cell we had ever seen. . . . I instructed Wyzinski not to move the electrode but rather to record this anomalous cell as long as possible. In repeated REM sleep episodes, we found that the cell invariably showed progressive rate decreases during nonREM sleep to a nadir of activity early in the REM period."

In other words, here was a brainstem neuron that did not burst into frenzied activity like many of its companions when REM sleep started. Rather, it slowed its firing rate in REM sleep to almost nothing. This suggested that there were two distinct groups of neurons in the brainstem relating differently to REM sleep—one that turned on around the start of REM sleep and another that turned off.

Later examination showed that Wyzinski's microelectrode had been a hair off the mark. Instead of being at its intended place in the brainstem, where neurons typically turn on in REM sleep, it was in what scientists call the "locus ceruleus," the main area where brainstem neurons take norepinephrine and send it through their long axons to other parts of the brain. More research showed that most neurons in this area turned off as REM sleep started, and so did brainstem neurons elsewhere that distributed either norepinephrine or serotonin.

Working with the information this discovery provided, Hobson and McCarley became convinced that a simple brainstem mechanism caused REM sleep. Accord-

We now confront a fast-moving river of knowledge that shows promise of unraveling much of the mystery of dreams, learning, memory, thought, and even human consciousness itself.

ing to their theory, when a person is awake, brainstem neurons releasing norepinephrine and serotonin suppress those brainstem neurons that distribute acetylcholine, thus dampening down the brainstem's acetylcholine system. But in sleep the brain's general level of activity falls; and after passing through various sleep phases the norepinephrine-serotonin neurons get so inactive that they no longer suppress the acetylcholine generators, unleashing the brainstem's acetylcholine system like a genie released from its lamp. Of course, this genie does not grant wishes. Instead, it sends bursts of acetylcholine through the brain, evoking REM sleep by exciting visual, motor, emotional, and other centers; raising the sleeping brain's general level of arousal; and incidentally sending motor signals to the small muscles of the eyes.

The sleeper doesn't waken because the acetylcholine-driven brain is operating quite differently from when the sleeper is awake: norepinephrine and serotonin are at a low ebb; and the circuits that carry most incoming (sensory) and outgoing (motor) impulses have been blocked by the brainstem, temporarily anesthetizing and paralyzing the sleeper. However, the process is self-limiting. By releasing acetylcholine, the genie excites much of the brain—including the temporarily inactive brainstem cells that had kept it suppressed; and these cells, upon reactivation, release enough norepinephrine and serotonin to suppress it once again. With the genie thus confined, the stimulating rush of acetylcholine eases, the brain's level of activity falls, external circuits unblock, and REM sleep gives way to less exotic rest. In this way the sleeper proceeds, in roughly 90-minute cycles through the night, until waking is induced by a familiar panoply of people, alarm clocks, dawn, the internal prompting of daily (circadian) rhythms, and the complex restorative effects of sleep.

This idea, which Hobson and McCarley called the "reciprocal interaction hypothesis," showed how the brainstem could turn REM sleep on and off, and how REM and other sleep stages could result from a rhythmic chemical dance within the brain. It accounted for why the brain is so active in the REM period without waking, because the chemistry of REM sleep and the waking state are so different. And it explained why judgment and memory seem to work poorly in REM sleep, because the serotonin and norepinephrine shown by other researchers to be necessary for good judgment and memory are lacking.

Beyond that, this concept shed a powerful light on what caused REM dreams—the vivid, bizarre, and colorful dreams that provide much of the fuel for psychoanalysis. Among other things, it indicated that dreams, like much of the brain, are activated in REM sleep by

floods of nerve impulses coming up from the brainstem that release the stimulant acetylcholine. The typical REM-sleep dream is strange because this process calls forth choppy, chaotic bits of internal information that are poorly "synthesized" or stitched together. The dream registers in the dreamer's awareness because the brain is highly active at the time. The dream gets accepted uncritically as reflecting reality because the dreamer's critical faculties lack the serotonin and norepinephrine they need for proper judgment. And the dream is mostly or entirely forgotten because this same chemical shortfall disables memory. The new theory implied that in contrast to what Freud had suggested, dreaming is more akin to a regular, internally generated delirium than it is to neurosis.

HOBSON MADE THIS CONNECTION BETWEEN HIS neurobiology work and dreaming in 1973, just as he was about to address a scientific conference in Scotland. "So," he recalls, "I decided to present the concept to the conference in a lecture entitled 'The Brain as a Dream Machine,' which attracted attention and provoked intense debate."

Part of the debate centered on the source of Hobson's data. He and his colleagues had done virtually all of their experimental work on cats. As noted, while the REM sleep of cats seems quite similar to that of humans, there was no obvious way for Hobson to support his theoretical arguments by eliciting dream reports from cats or assessing the nature of cat dreams.

But the literature of human psychology is full of dream reports. So Hobson and McCarley decided to take collections of human dream reports, give them an old mental-health test known as the "mental status examination," and see if the results fit their theory of brainstem regulation.

Hobson and McCarley realized something else as they entered the world of dream psychology. They knew their dream theory clashed with Freud's old belief that dreams seem strange only because they are "cut" by a hidden censor. As Hobson wrote later, "I differ from Freud in that I think that most dreams are neither obscure nor bowdlerized, but rather transparent and unedited. They contain clearly meaningful, undisguised, highly conflictual impulses worthy of note by the dreamer (and any interpretive assistant). My position echoes Jung's notion of dreams as transparently meaningful. . . ."

As this indicates, the new dream concept, which Hobson and McCarley called the "activation-synthesis hypothesis," was not the first to oppose Freud's. But it was the first one firmly grounded in neurobiology. On the

"I would admit to having created some heat where light might have been more useful," said Hobson later, "but . . . they weren't paying any attention until I turned the heat up a bit."

down side, the theory seemed unlikely to prove either popular or saleable, because it rejected all symbolic dream interpretation schemes out of hand. Furthermore, it seemed likely to suffer benign neglect from psychologists because it was not yet firmly grounded in psychology, was unfamiliar to the psychoanalytic community, and directly contradicted Freud. So the real danger, as Hobson and McCarley saw it, was not that their theory would be rejected, but that it would be ignored.

To keep this from happening, Hobson and McCarley wrote two rigorous articles for the *American Journal of Psychiatry* in 1977 dismissing Freud's old dream theory and offering activation-synthesis as a replacement. For flavoring, Hobson shaped the articles into an overt assault on the foundations of psychoanalysis. The result was encouraging. The pieces generated more letters to the editor, mostly from outraged psychoanalysts, than any articles previously published in the *Journal*. "I would admit to having created some heat where light might have been more useful," said Hobson later, "but I can tell you, they weren't paying any attention until I turned the heat up a bit."

Hobson kept the juices flowing that year by masterminding an art/science exhibit called *Dreamstage: A Multimedia Portrait of the Sleeping Brain*. The main feature of this exhibit, which ran six weeks at Harvard's Carpenter Center, was a person sleeping in a closed room behind a one-way mirror, in plain view of an audience sitting in a darkened room on the other side of the mirror. As in a scientific sleep lab, the sleeper was hooked up to instruments that monitored brain waves, eye movements, and body movements. But instead of applying their data to paper charts, the instruments used it to paint colored waves of laser light on the walls and to run a synthesizer that converted the sleep data into music. When the sleeper shifted or started dreaming, the patterns of light and sound would change, and people would rush in to find out what was happening. The event drew more than 10,000 viewers, received nationwide media coverage, spawned a six-city road show, and served its purpose of announcing to the world that science was starting to learn the truth about sleep and dreams.

Of course, the two Hobson-McCarley theories and *Dreamstage* had their share of critics. Not just psychoanalysts, but a wide range of natural scientists and psychiatrists had reservations. This was only natural, because science demands that new theories be critiqued and tested; sharp disagreement typifies the cognitive sciences; and certain details of the two theories required adjustment. Beyond that, some scientists tended to focus

on details to a point where they rejected these broad theories out of hand and responded to Hobson's open advocacy with name-calling. As one Hobson defender put it, "Allan's an unusual scientist, in that he does propose fairly general theories. I think people who say he's a flimflam artist are the ones who aren't smart enough to do that kind of thing themselves."

But what really exposed Hobson to professional criticism was *Dreamstage*. Like medieval monks, all scientists take an unspoken vow not to pander their wares to laymen. If they break that vow, like former Harvard and Cornell astronomer Carl Sagan, they risk paying for public acclaim with professional discredit. Perhaps because *Dreamstage* was really just one singular happening, Hobson escaped this fate. Nevertheless, when he was granted tenure around this time, one member of the committee making the decision told him, "We decided to grant you tenure despite *Dreamstage*."

Hindsight shows this to have been a good move for Harvard, because the Hobson-McCarley theories proved robust. Not only did the underlying research survive critical review, but no other broad theories based on neurobiology arose to take their place. As Richard Davidson, a leading experimental psychologist at the University of Wisconsin, explains, "By and large, these theories have held up well. Some of the specific details have been revised in the light of modern data. But particularly the activation-synthesis theory of dreaming has provided a framework for relating neurobiologic and mental activity, one that is still a guiding model in all the modern efforts to understand the underlying functional significance of REM sleep and dreaming."

HAVING THUS BUILT A BRIDGE BETWEEN NEUROSCIence and the mind, Hobson set out to reinforce it. He began writing *The Dreaming Brain*, finished and published in 1988, which remains among the best of the scientific books on dreams. While continuing his animal work, he pursued research on human sleep and dreams with whatever tools he had available—including the *Dreamstage* sleep lab when *Dreamstage* was in progress. He used the old *Dreamstage* equipment, once *Dreamstage* was done, to set up a sleep lab at the Massachusetts Mental Health Center. And he invented a simple sleep-charting device, picturesquely dubbed the "Nightcap," to monitor REM sleep and substitute for the relatively costly and cumbersome sleep lab.

This "Nightcap" idea grew out of time-lapse photos that Theodore Spagna, a principal *Dreamstage* collaborator, took of the exhibit's sleepers. These pictures suggested to Hobson, as other evidence confirmed, that

"One day," says Hobson, "he told me if I really wanted to study the mind, then I would have to go to medical school and study the brain."

normal sleepers are likely to change position only when entering or leaving REM sleep. We now know that's because in nonREM sleep the brain is not usually excited enough to cause such movement, while in REM sleep the motor commands that stream toward the spinal cord are blocked, paralyzing the sleeper. It is therefore just at the beginning of REM (before the block is in place), and just at the end (as the block is deactivated), that motor commands from the newly excited or still excited brain are likely to cause a sleeper to shift about.

The Nightcap, which took advantage of this discovery, consisted of a simple piece of headgear wired to a smart pocket-sized recorder. The device reliably detected REM sleep by recording eye movements (indicating REM sleep) plus head movements (indicating the beginning or end of REM sleep and so providing a check on the eye data). At some point the Nightcap's wearer, awakened by an alarm or naturally, would report any dream recalled. In this way, like the sleep lab, the Nightcap was able to track a volunteer's sleep patterns, provide a dream report, and indicate whether the last sleep stage (in which the dream occurred) was REM or nonREM sleep.

This inexpensive and versatile device soon proved its worth. Hobson used it at volunteers' homes to collect masses of dream reports far exceeding any previous collections, with the sleep stage of each report indicated; and other investigators wishing to track sleep patterns found it useful in a wide array of diverse settings where sleep labs couldn't go.

Around the time the Nightcap was emerging, McCarley left Hobson's lab to head up a research facility at the Harvard-affiliated Brockton Veterans' Administration Hospital. (Now professor of psychiatry and head of the hospital's psychiatry department, he is still actively pursuing sleep research, focusing especially on the causes and chemistry of sleep.) Soon there were other changes. Hobson began offering a course at the Extension School (Psychology E1450, "The Biopsychology of Waking, Sleeping, and Dreaming") that he still teaches. He got a MacArthur Foundation Mind-Body Network grant for studying human sleep and dreaming that permitted him to expand the human-research side of his lab's work. And he used his own infectious enthusiasm to recruit volunteers from the extension course and elsewhere. "We've always been very open door," Hobson says. "People hear about us, they like the ideas in the first place, and we're very friendly. So we have extension school students coming, we have Harvard College students coming...."

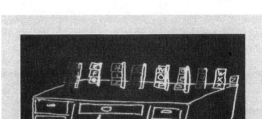

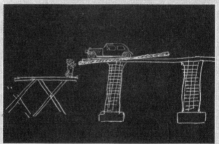

The "Engine Man's" Dream Journal

DREAMS CAN BE CREATIVE. THE DRAWINGS ABOVE COME from the 1930s dream journal of a careful reporter whom Hobson calls the "Engine Man." Top: A desk belonging to a fat man dressed only in a shirt resembling a hospital gown. "Along the back of the desk is fastened an index system of his own invention enabling him to find current quotations almost instantly," apparently a precursor of today's desk-top computer. Middle: A bicycle built for two, with the bachelor dreamer driving and a space available for a companion. Bottom: A car stopped on an unfinished bridge, where the temporary bridge constructed as a stop-gap is lower and must be reached by means of a large plank.

AFTER 1977, MUCH OF THE HOBSON LABORATORY'S dream work focused on strangeness—the odd discontinuities, mismatching elements, or uncertainties that nearly all REM dreams contain. Clearly, these bizarre features accounted for much of the chaotic and choppy nature of REM dreams. Equally clearly, the strangeness in certain cases seemed related to basic sensory or motor problems. For instance, when you dream you are running but getting nowhere, it seems likely that your brain's motor centers (active in REM sleep) are issuing commands to run; but since these commands are blocked by the brainstem and you don't move, your brain perceives running without motion. Likewise, when you dream you are falling endlessly it probably means your brain is receiving no sensory clues to indicate your position. Since your brain always receives such clues except when you are in REM sleep or falling freely with your eyes closed, your brain concludes that you are falling.

In seeking to explain such dream features, Hobson had tended to emphasize the intimate connection between brainstem REM neurons and sensory neurons transmitting information about the body's position. He and his people went to work on such ideas by examining masses of dream reports, classifying their bizarre features, and asking whether these features appeared due to sensorimotor inputs, brain censorship, or something else. They found, as Hobson recounts in *The Dreaming Brain,* that "the trouble arises at or near the sensorimotor level," with most of the strangeness deriving either from bizarre sensorimotor signals or from the brain's efforts to make sense of them. By and large, the findings support the activation-synthesis idea.

Similarly, Hobson's group sought to track REM dream emotions to their neurobiologic roots. Among other things, thoroughgoing examination of dream reports showed that even though emotions were not referred to in all cases, those mentioned were frequently strong and unpleasant. Says Hobson: "Anxiety (most common), elation (next), and anger (next) accounted for about 70 percent of the emotions cited. After that the numbers drop way down, with the rates for shame, guilt, affection, and erotic feelings being very low, all under 5 percent." These results are consistent with activation-synthesis and also with excitement of the brain's prime emotion center, an almond-shaped body called the amygdala, that is known to receive strong stimulation from the brainstem in REM sleep.

While this work was advancing, Hobson had not forgotten that his laboratory's greatest strength was its ability to track mental events all the way from the actions of individual neurons to the broadest reaches of theoretical psychology. Therefore, he continued to direct animal research—work now spearheaded by two assistant professors at the medical school, James Quattrochi and Bernat Kocsis, who are, respectively, studying brain anatomy and key electrophysiologic interactions of certain brain substructures. At the same time, he came to work closely with a number of psychology researchers—among them Edward Pace-Schott and Robert Stickgold '66, both recruited through the extension course. Pace-Schott, an instructor in psychiatry, now oversees Nightcap work. Stickgold, an as-

sistant professor of psychiatry at the medical school, is co-teaching the extension course with Hobson and pursuing research on how sleep affects the mind.

Recently, some of the Hobson-Stickgold work has shown real promise. In one experiment, dream reports containing discontinuities were selected. Half the reports were left intact, while the other half were cut apart and recombined. Judges were then asked to single out the spliced reports.

As Hobson relates with pleasure, "They couldn't do it. I was sure, by the way, that I would be able to do this when it was suggested by Bob Stickgold in a seminar. It turns out you can do it if and only if the splices occur in the midst of continuous action. Otherwise it's hopeless. If you take it scene by scene, there is no objective continuity, even though all who read such reports are convinced it must be there.

"Everyone, including the content-analysis people, have always assumed that dreams are stories, or at least books, or chapters, or something. This work shows they aren't. Indeed, we concluded that most of the integrity that is seen in these reports is projected onto them by the viewer. It's as if what's going on is so difficult to integrate that it just can't be done, and so you get one little story, and then another and another.

"This has profound importance, not just for dream theory but for how people perceive things (how they read, for instance) and how they understand the world. The brain is always trying to make a whole story out of whatever facts are presented. That's the brain's job. You know you couldn't function in the world unless you did that. But with dreams it's a fool's errand. In other words, there is probably a lot more discontinuity and incongruity than we allow ourselves to admit, not just in dreams but in the world in general, because we just can't stand it, we have to be holistic."

IF THE PURPOSE OF DREAMS IS NOT TO RELEASE LIBIDINAL id, as Freud maintained, then what is it? Hobson and many others think it could relate to reorganizing the mind's content and reordering memories. "This is an important shift in emphasis," he says, "one that allows dreams to be nonsensical while the task being done is crucial. The scrambling isn't being done to hide forbidden thoughts, it's being done for some other purpose, and that purpose could be the reordering of memory and the reinforcing of links between memory and emotion.

"What you probably can't have is a 'penny scale' of dream interpretation, a code which says 'This means that.' But you can have so much more. Your brain is doing all this homework for you, getting your mind in order. In this light, dreams may be nonsensical for the same reason that housecleaning tends to make a mess. My housekeeper makes a mess every time she visits, but it's much cleaner when she's done."

Pursuing this line of reasoning, Hobson's team has been investigating how sleep relates to memory and learning. Researchers elsewhere had found that volunteers could "learn" subliminally. They did so by showing their volunteers screens on which a pattern of short lines was flashed briefly. Most of the lines were horizontal, but three were diagonal lines arranged either side by side or one above another. As the patterns were displayed for shorter and shorter times, the volunteers found it progressively harder to tell whether the diagonal lines were arranged vertically or horizontally, and eventually they couldn't tell at all. However, if asked to repeat the tests later, they would typically do better on the second trial—but only if several hours had passed since they first took the test. The conclusion: learning was taking place and being consolidated very slowly, outside of conscious awareness.

Hobson team members, including Stickgold and Vitul Patel '98, decided to test sleep-lab volunteers to see how such learning relates to sleep patterns. So far their work suggests that long, deep sleep ending with a lot of REM sleep helps consolidate such learning, while failure to get proper sleep can wipe it out. This tends to reinforce the long-held suspicions of innumerable undergraduates—that going short on sleep to cram for tests may help pass the tests, but the information "learned" is soon gone. Of course, late-night cramming may provide good general training for the brain, and to date the Hobson team's research appears to be dealing with only one specialized kind of learning. Even so, this work could wind up giving new meaning to the old dictum that education is what's left after you've forgotten everything you learned in school.

Meanwhile, Edward Pace-Schott is coordinating an array of Nightcap projects with other institutions, using the device to monitor the sleep patterns of many groups—including volunteers taking antidepressant drugs, chronic insomniacs receiving anti-insomnia behavior therapy, truck drivers slumbering in their cabs, and astronauts and cosmonauts sleeping on the Mir space station. Surprisingly, as Stickgold recently pointed out, "The Nightcaps on the Mir were some of the only scientific research gear to survive the collision between a supply capsule and the main Mir module housing most of the Mir's scientific experiments. The Nightcaps were not in this module at the time, and so were saved. They are currently still working."

Hobson's sleep lab, containing much of the technical gear inherited from *Dreamstage*, is also still working, because it is needed for tasks like testing volunteers immediately after waking. For most purposes, however, the Nightcap has tended to supplant it. In a like manner, while animal work is still needed for certain kinds of brain research, neurobiology's horizons are being broadened by new scanning techniques, notably PET (positron emission tomography) and MRI (magnetic resonance imaging), that permit researchers to observe the internal workings of a volunteer's brain under controlled conditions. Although Hobson is not directly involved in much of this scanning activity, he is elated because "the work is starting to confirm—with pictures of the human brain—what could previously be surmised only from animal research."

DESPITE ITS ASTONISHING PROGRESS, THE SLEEP and dream revolution is far from over. Many researchers now believe sleep's main functions are to rejuvenate the brain and consolidate memory in various ways, but no one has proven that. Likewise, many think dreams are incidental side-effects of this process that evolution causes us to forget because the forgetting does no harm, while remembering might confuse dreams with reality, threaten our mental balance, and adversely affect survival. But again, nobody knows for sure.

Paradoxically, none of the spectacular advances made to date have much daunted Freudian psychoanalysts or other dream interpreters. What has dethroned psychoanalysis in recent years is an array of powerful psychoactive drugs effective in treating mental illness, most of which mimic or influence the same brainstem chemicals that control REM sleep and dreaming. Meanwhile, humanists' regard for Freud and his dream theory has been only slightly dampened, while public enthusiasm for a wide range of ad hoc dream interpreters is on the rise.

In hindsight, the reason seems clear. People love both mystery and knowledge. Astrology did not vanish when Copernicus and others started learning the truth about the planets; instead, that was merely the place in the road where astronomy and astrology diverged. Similarly, the great strength of Freud's dream theory arose from its appeal to both mystery and reason. That appeal was needed in Freud's day, because the facts could not be known, just as such an appeal is impossible today because we know too much.

Thus, like modern Copernicans, Hobson and other scientific dream-catchers of recent times have passed the place where the road divides, and they cannot go back. They will never rekindle the enthusiasm lit by Freud's dream theory, because they cannot legitimately make his dual appeal. Instead, like Adam after he first bit the Apple of Knowledge, they must settle for the lesser role and lesser fame of those who merely succeed in dispelling ignorance by discovering the truth.

Jonathan Leonard '63, the former editor of an international public-health journal, is a professional writer specializing in medicine and science.

Unit 4

Key Points to Consider

❖ Describe how researchers have proven that fetuses can learn. By what mechanisms do unborn children learn? Is this type of learning important? Do you think the learning they do is different from that of older children?

❖ What is operant conditioning? What principles of learning have we gleaned from the study of operant conditioning and other forms of simple learning? Define reinforcement and punishment and state which approach to behavior is preferable. Why? How can operant principles be practiced or put into effect in everyday life?

❖ Why is memory important? What is forgetting? Why do psychologists want to know about the neuronal mechanisms that underlie learning and memory? To what use can we put this information? Do we learn and remember like a computer does?

❖ Do people remember things that did not happen? Why is this problematic? Can it ever be useful? How can memories be shaped or induced for events that did not happen to us? Why the furor between psychology and law about remembered abuse and eyewitness accuracy?

 **Links** **www.dushkin.com/online/**

These sites are annotated on pages 4 and 5.

Do you remember your first week of classes at college? There were so many new buildings to recognize and people's names to remember. And you had to recall accurately where all your classes were as well as your professors' names. Just remembering your class schedule was problematic enough. For those of you who lived in residence halls, the difficulties multiplied. You had to remember where your residence was, recall the names of individuals living on your floor, and learn how to navigate from your room to other places on campus, such as the dining halls and library. Then came examination time. Did you ever think you would survive college exams? The material in terms of difficulty level and amount was perhaps more than you thought you could manage.

What a stressful time you experienced when you first came to campus! Much of what created the stress was the strain on your learning and memory systems, two complicated processes. Still, most of you survived just fine and with your memories, learning strategies, and mental health intact.

The processes you depended on when beginning college were learning and memory, two of the processes studied the longest by psychologists. Today, with their sophisticated experimental techniques, psychologists have detected several types of memory processes and have discovered what makes learning more complete so that subsequent memory is more accurate. We also have discovered that humans are not the only organisms capable of these processes. All types of animals can learn, even an organism as simple as an earthworm or an amoeba.

Psychologists know, too, that rote learning and practice are not the only forms of learning. For instance, at this point in time in your introductory psychology class, you may be studying operant and classical conditioning, two simple but nonetheless important forms of learning of which both humans and simple organisms are capable. Both types of conditioning can occur without our awareness or active participation. The processes of learning and remembering (or its reciprocal, forgetting) are examined here in some detail.

This unit begins with a look at learning even before life begins. In "Learning Begins Even before Babies Are Born, Scientists Show," Beth Azar discovers that the fetus can indeed learn about sounds and flavors. Such learning comes from the experiences of the mother. Researchers have, with difficulty, discovered clever methods for studying fetal learning in utero.

The second article looks at simple learning—operant conditioning. In "What Constitutes 'Appropriate' Punishment?" Paul DeVito and Ralph Hyatt examine reinforcement and punishment, whose principles come from the study of operant

conditioning. The authors conclude that because punishment is often used, it needs to be applied appropriately. They detail the conditions under which punishment is best used. They conclude that it is better for parents and teachers to reinforce prosocial behaviors than to continually punish negative behaviors.

While the first few articles pertain to learning in its various forms, the remaining articles relate to memory, the process triggered as an adjunct to learning. In the next article, "It's Magical, It's Malleable, It's . . . Memory," Jill Neimark insists that because memory is so important, it behooves us to develop strategies to boost our memory processes. Psychologists have researched a myriad of mnemonic techniques, all designed to improve memory, which are detailed in this article.

There are perhaps times when we would rather not remember something or simply cannot learn or remember despite great effort. On the other hand, psychologists are now discovering that some individuals may remember events that never really happened. One such occasion might occur when an adult individual is motivated to remember child abuse from early life. Whether this actually happened or whether adult memories of abuse are fictional is one of the points of "Memory for a Past That Never Was" by Elizabeth Loftus. Loftus discloses how even the way a lawyer asks a witness a question can distort the content of the witness's memory.

Learning and Remembering

Learning begins even before babies are born, scientists show

The prenatal environment

The fetus learns to interpret sounds, flavors and vibrations, studies have found.

By Beth Azar
Monitor staff

The old metaphor of children as blocks of unmolded clay has lost its relevance over the decades. Research reveals not only that newborns have many genetically based preferences, but some of those preferences may also be the result of fetal learning.

Newborns remember certain aspects of their fetal environment, researchers argue. And research in animals and humans finds that the fetus is capable of rudimentary forms of learning.

This is not to say that parents should start trying to teach their children prenatally, say researchers. Rather, it confirms the importance of prenatal care during a time when the human fetus is developing not only physically but also cognitively. The research may also provide clinicians with a measure they can use to evaluate infant health prenatally.

A memory for sounds

There's no evidence that playing Mozart to an unborn child will encourage musical aptitude, but research does confirm that newborns enter the world with a preference for certain sounds from the fetal world. That world is dominated by two sounds: the mother's heartbeat and her voice. According to research by Columbia University psychologist William Fifer, PhD, and his colleagues, newborns prefer their mother's voice to the voice of other women. They also prefer her voice when it's electronically altered to sound as it did in the uterus, compared with her voice outside the uterus.

In contrast, infants don't prefer their father's voice over the voices of other men, indicating that they have a particular preference for prenatal sounds, not just familiar sounds, says Fifer.

It's likely that it is the cadences, and not the specific words, that the newborns recognize, he adds. One study found that newborns recognize the cadences of rhymes that they heard their mother say repeatedly during the last few weeks of pregnancy, but not the specific words themselves.

"These studies show that there is a mechanism for longterm memory available to the fetus," says Fifer.

The fetus may also have the capacity to remember food flavors available in utero, says Julie Mennella, PhD, of the Monell Chemical Senses Center in Philadelphia. She's found that the fetus has access to flavors, such as garlic, that become present in the amniotic fluid. This flavor transfer from mother to infant can continue after birth as many flavors from the mother's diet are integrated into her breast milk. These early experiences with flavors may form the basis of some food preferences as the child ages, says Mennella, who is beginning experiments to test that theory.

Habituation

Further evidence of fetal learning comes from studies of habituation—the process through which an animal learns, over repeated episodes of stimulation, to give less attention to an increasingly familiar stimulus. To test habituation in the human fetus, researchers apply a stimulus—often a vibrating device—to a pregnant woman's abdomen. By 26 weeks of gestation, a human fetus will reliably move in response to such a stimulus, researchers find. And, after repeated stimulation, a fetus will stop responding, having habituated to the stimulus. However, if a new stimulus is used, the fetus will once again respond.

There's no evidence that playing Mozart to an unborn child will encourage musical aptitude, but research does confirm that newborns enter the world with a preference for certain sounds from the fetal world.

Some researchers argue that habituation is a measure of learning that can predict later cognitive abilities, says psychologist Eugene K. Emory of Emory University.

In particular, Leo Leader, PhD, believes that clinicians can use fetal habituation to evaluate the health and development of the fetus. He's conducted several studies that correlate habituation with later development. Other researchers aren't convinced it's time to start making predictions, but they don't rule out the possibility in the near future.

The National Institute on Child Health and Human Development, which funds much of the fetal research, has hosted two meetings of fetal researchers to discuss the possibility of using data from basic research to begin to inform clinicians.

Fetal learning

Animal researchers can study more specific forms of learning because they can manipulate the fetus in ways impossible to attempt in humans. In rats, researchers can remove an individual pup from its mother's uterus and, keeping it attached to the umbilical cord, keep it alive in small dishes filled with a temperature-regulated water bath that mimics amniotic fluid. The pups can be kept inside the amniotic sac or removed.

Binghamton University psychologist William T. Smotherman, PhD, has taken the lead in fetal learning studies. He's designed a standard conditioned-learning paradigm that he can manipulate to examine specific

questions about fetal learning, including the molecular mechanisms that control it. The paradigm involves one aspect of feeding behavior—learning to respond to a nipple in a way to promote feeding, a behavior we assume is instinctive but that may partly involve learning. Smotherman places an artificial nipple close to the fetus' mouth, and if the fetus grasps the nipple, it receives a squirt of mother's milk into its mouth.

He finds that by around 21 days gestation—equivalent to early in the ninth month of a human pregnancy—the fetuses easily and quickly learn to respond to the nipple as if they were going to receive milk from it.

When researchers examine this response at the molecular level, they find that the milk triggers the release of certain neuropeptides in the brain of the rat fetus, which work to reinforce early feeding behaviors such as suckling. For example, the milk triggers a release of opiates into the fetuses' brains, which reinforces the pups' behavior. When Smotherman and his colleagues block this opiate release, the fetuses no longer become conditioned to the artificial nipple, indicating that the chemicals are necessary for learning.

He's also found that if he exposes fetuses to the nipple and the milk, but not paired in time, they don't become conditioned to respond to the nipple. They have the equivalent amount of experience with the crucial stimuli—the milk and the nipple—but because the two stimuli aren't coupled in time, learning doesn't occur.

This may have implications for premature infants who are fed either intravenously or through a feeding tube. Like the rat fetuses that receive the milk without access to the nipple, these infants may not learn to associate eating with suckling. It may be helpful to pair feeding with some type of non-nutritive suckling, says Smotherman.

Working for warmth

Indiana University psychologist Jeffery Alberts, PhD, agrees that fetal experiences and early newborn experiences help shape early development. Research by him and research scientist April Ronca, PhD, finds that the physical pressures put on the fetus just before and during labor are critical for developmental success and that, after birth, environment can shape early learning.

In one study, the Indiana researchers found that day-old rat pups will work to gain access to heat. Postdoctoral fellow Cynthia Hoffman, PhD, designed an operant conditioning paradigm, taking advantage of the fact that young, immobile pups periodically move their heads from side to side. When the pups in the experiment randomly turned their heads to the left, Hoffman rewarded them with 20 seconds of belly warming—she ran warm water under the plates the pups were lying on. They quickly learned to turn their heads to the left to elicit the belly warming, says Alberts.

"This research shows us how environmental factors, like warmth, can quickly shape behavior very early in life," he says.

Further reading

"Fetal Development: A Psychobiological Perspective," by J. P. Lecanuet, W. Fifer, N. A. Krasnegor, W. Smotherman (Lawrence Erlbaum Associates, Inc., 1995).

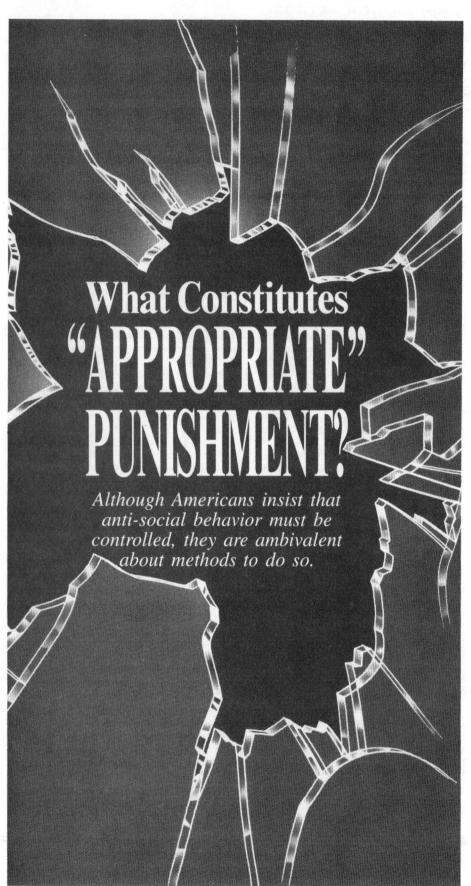

What Constitutes "APPROPRIATE" PUNISHMENT?

Although Americans insist that anti-social behavior must be controlled, they are ambivalent about methods to do so.

Paul L. DeVito and Ralph Hyatt

TAKE A FEW moments to test your philosophy of punishment. Read each of the following situations and write out your responses to the questions that follow them.

• Poverty-stricken teenagers Joey and Art had been dreaming about the rock concert for months, and now that it was in town they only could continue to dream, for they did not have the entrance fee. In desperation, Art sneaked into the kitchen and snatched several dollars from his mother's hiding place in the cupboard. That evening, Joey's father cracked him across the face and accused him of stealing the money. Art, his supposed friend, had lied to his parents and implicated Joey. Art's father complained to Joey's father about the felony. After Joey screamed out the truth, Joey's father angrily approached Art, grasped him around the throat, and quickly got a confession. Art was confined to his room for a week by his parents.

a) Did Joey deserve his whacking?

b) Should Art have been choked?

c) Were Art's parents too lenient?

• Pennsylvania has a unit called "super-max" in its maximum security prisons. This unit houses chronic troublemakers, who totally are segregated from the other inmates. They are given one hour daily of isolated exercise out of their small cells. Many have spent years in super-max.

a) Is it humane to isolate troublesome maximum security prisoners? For such long periods of time?

b) Is this program consistent with rehabilitation?

c) Does the death penalty make more sense?

• Autistic children, although often quite intelligent, do not develop in expected ways. They may be overly active, speech can be delayed, and they do not establish normal human attachments. Many gesture in strange ways and do not make good eye contact. At times, they can be destructive to themselves and others. Some professionals believe that physical restraint is necessary to get their attention as well as a means of helping them to release their pent-up anger. Aversion therapy, a group of methods for treating such individuals, includes paddling and mild electric shock. This mode of treatment also has been used with some success with drug addicts, sexual deviants, and people demonstrating extremely violent behavior.

Dr. DeVito is chairman, Department of Psychology, Saint Joseph's University, Philadelphia, Pa. Dr. Hyatt, Psychology Editor of USA Today, is professor emeritus of psychology, Saint Joseph's University.

a) Should aversion therapy be used as a form of treatment or banned by law?

b) How about physical restraint?

These situations and questions were given to a variety of people on an informal, non-scientific basis. It is safe to say that your particular response—or any of them—is included among those of the group. Respondents replied with a yes, no, and everything in-between to each question. Those at the extremes invariably qualified their answers if additional conditions were to exist. This should come as no surprise since those interviewees who were psychologists, attorneys, correctional employees, and school counselors also had no pat answers.

Recent events bear out the uncertainties people have about meting out punishment, some praying for mercy and forgiveness, others demanding justice—and often blood. Take the caning of Michael Fay, the 18-year-old American visiting Singapore, who was accused of spray-painting and tossing eggs at automobiles, among other acts of vandalism. Prior to his punishment of four cane strokes, which was "mercifully" reduced from six, American sentiment, as revealed by a series of polls, was procaning by a large majority. Even Fay's emotional denials of any wrongdoings other than removing some street signs did not soften their hearts.

Americans, it was hypothesized, had had it up to their eyeballs with teenage social irresponsibility, lack of respect, and gun toting crime. "He deserves it" and "He should have known better" generally expressed their exasperation. Yet, in his hometown in Ohio, 90 days of incarceration and a $750 fine would have taken care of the matter.

It is worth recalling that, in the 1960s, flogging was a form of legal punishment in Delaware. The whipping post still was being used there in 1952. American colonists brought with them and promulgated their array of European penalties—imprisonment, banishment, mutilation, branding, flogging, and execution—despite the forbiddance of "cruel and unusual punishment" in the Constitution!

Many who advocate the death penalty maintain that it could terminate concerns about too few prisons, the cost of incarceration, and the entire mess of rehabilitation and what that means. Yet, the fact is that the death penalty never has succeeded as a deterrent to heinous acts, nor have stiffer sentences.

"The increased severity of the penalties has not reduced crime, it has only increased the prison population," writes former Common Pleas Court judge Lois G. Forer in her book, *A Rage to Punish*. Her non-mandatory sentencing approach runs head-on into Pres. Clinton's "Three strikes and you're out" solution, which throws away the key after a felon's third violent crime. She argues that the crime rate "has not risen materially since 1980 while the prison population and numbers of inmates on death row have soared." She believes in the full use of restitution, fines, education, and counseling. Prior to O.J. Simpson's trial, Americans were in disagreement regarding the appropriateness of the death penalty for him. This occurs in a society that presumes innocence unless proven guilty beyond reasonable doubt.

Defining wrongdoing and setting penalties

There is little wonder that everyone has opinions about punishment. People are subjected to it from the moment they slide out of the womb into a new environment full of strange sounds, temperatures, and pressures. Painful feelings continue from that experience onward: delay in feeding when hungry, soaked diapers, restraint when dressed, scraped knees, sibling rivalry, etc. We are not sure an infant perceives these events as punishment (although "Why is all this happening to me?" may be going through his or her mind), but the concept develops quickly when something like a hot stove is touched: Do the wrong thing and a penalty (pain) follows. Confusion occurs, research has shown, when a penalty does not directly follow wrongdoing or follows it erratically.

The conceptual riddle begins when we try to define "wrong" and "penalty." Wrongdoing, in the first place, may be real or perceived. Someone may believe you did something wrong when, actually, you didn't. Or he or she may accuse you of wrongdoing just to do you in. Also, one can wrong people, property, and God.

Penalties are no less universally agreed upon. There are tongue-lashing, restriction of freedoms, and corporal and capital punishment, not to omit condemnation to hell of sinners. Depending on the occasion, and given a choice, the offender may rather have one form than the other. For example, a kid may prefer to have his rear end smacked in public than hear his mother scream, "Do it again and I'll tell everyone you're a bed-wetter!" Then there is the judgment of how little is little and how big is big. One person's "little" smack is another's "big" one. Is a judge's verdict of one to three years incarceration short or long? What quantity of penalty does a child's "big mouth" deserve? What type of penalty, if any, is suitable for an infant? For doing how much of what?

Insights do not become any less confusing by remembering Proverbs: 13-2: "He that spareth the rod hateth his own son." If one can assume that autistic behaviors such as inattention, aggression, and destructiveness can be improved or eradicated by the use of corporal punishment, should it be permissible? Suppose parents strongly request such "teaching" or "therapeutic" procedures for their autistic child?

Psychologist B.F. Skinner, who condemned the overutilization of punishment, wrote about this issue: "If brief and harmless aversive stimuli, made precisely contingent over self-destructive behavior, suppress the behavior and leave the children free to develop in other ways, I believe it can be justified. When taken out of context, such stimuli may seem less than humane, but they are not to be distinguished from the much more painful stimuli sometimes needed in dentistry and various medical practices. To remain satisfied with punishment without exploring non-punitive alternations is the real mistake."

There is something about punishment that relates it to evil. Do wrong and you get punished; do right and you don't. Does that principle apply to God? Rabbi Harold Kushner's best-seller, *Why Bad Things Happen to Good People*, grapples with that question from a theological perspective. He argues that much of what happens to us—the good and the bad—occurs purely by chance. God does not manage our each and every action, punishing some and rewarding others.

Thomas Hobbes, the 17th-century philosopher, believed that humans are basically solitary, selfish, and practical. They accept socialization primarily to satisfy their needs for safety and protection; otherwise, they wantonly would murder, rape, and pillage. Given the condition of today's world—most prominently in Rwanda, Serbia, and Chechnya, to name a few trouble spots—one is hard put to wave away this negative view, which squarely places Homo sapiens among all other creatures in the universe. Naturalist Charles Darwin, in *Origin of the Species*, espoused the evolutionary theory that solidly links human emotions to lowly organisms.

Sigmund Freud's id theory postulates a self-seeking pleasure instinct in everyone. The superego, an internalized conscience which evolves from early parental scolding and spanking, continually battles the id in order to keep people socialized. Thus, evils lurk inside and outside of individuals, and must be tamed by punishment of some sort.

There are, of course, philosophies and research which deem that humans are basically good. Psychologists have found, for instance, that effective nurturing and love are products of healthy, well-adjusted individuals, not those who are bestial. Kind and helpful children are popular with their peers and self-confident, not isolated and fearful. However, few philosophers, if any, deny the potential malevolence in all people. The enduring question is: What are the most effective methods for socializing humans?

Skinner noted, "We have not yet discovered adequate non-punitive practices to replace the aversive part of our genetic endowment. For example, we are far from abandoning the use of force in international relations or in maintaining domestic order. People living closely together, and that includes teachers and students, therapists and clients, can seldom avoid all forms of punishment."

According to contemporary psychological theory, punishment is included under the domain of behavior modification. Psychologists define it as any procedure that reduces or suppresses an undesirable behavior. The behavior is *not* eradicated or forgotten—just not expressed as it was before. There are both positive and negative forms. "Positive punishment," popularly known as corporal punishment, is exemplified by a child receiving a hand slap after biting his mother's leg. "Negative punishment" is applied, for instance, when a teenager who receives a poor report card is grounded for three weeks. The U.S. criminal justice system largely is based on this form—that is, when one is guilty of some crime, punishment usually is a monetary fine or incarceration. Something painful is applied in positive punishment, whereas something attractive is taken away in negative punishment. Both can have the effect of suppressing an unwanted response.

The alternative is known as reinforcement, where the objective is to increase the likelihood of some desired behavior. As with punishment, there are positive and negative approaches. When Johnny mows the lawn and is told "What a great job!" that is positive reinforcement. He probably will be less resistant to mowing the lawn again. A classic example of negative reinforcement is nagging. When you nag so much that your spouse yields in order to shut you up, that is negative reinforcement. Skinner was a champion of positive reinforcement, and his students coined the phrase "Spare the rod, use behavior mod!"

Experimental studies of positive and negative punishment, with both human and animal subjects, unequivocally demonstrate the effectiveness of these procedures in eliminating unacceptable behaviors. A serious problem, though, is that, in addition to suppressing the behavior, negative punishment often produces undesirable side effects. In a 1953 study, hungry spider monkeys were trained to press a switch for food. Once this response was learned, the experimenters placed a snake in the monkeys' cage whenever they reached for food. This was certain punishment since monkeys are terrified of snakes. After a few such experiences, the monkeys completely stopped pressing the switch for food. However, numerous side effects soon became apparent, including disturbances in eating behavior (loss of 15–25% of body weight), sexual disorders, and a breakdown in social relationships. Most of the monkeys began to develop classic human neurotic and psy-

chotic symptoms, including asthma, facial and muscular tics, and hallucinations.

Do you know a parent who has not experienced a temper tantrum from his or her child? To stop such shenanigans, children have been restricted to their rooms, had cold water thrown in their faces, been yelled at, slapped, ignored, and exposed to countless other "creative" remedies. In a newspaper column, pediatrician T. Berry Brazelton counseled: "Parents are likely to feel manipulated by this kind of behavior, but they miss the purpose of these episodes if they feel they must either eliminate them or punish the child for them. Tantrums are expressions of the child's inner struggle for self-control. It is up to the child to work it out—not the parent." What if the child is throwing hard metal toys against the dining room furniture, though? Or hitting the parents with a stick? Or kicking out the window in the kitchen door? Should he or she be allowed to "work it out"?

The last few decades have shown a rise of disobedience along with violence among children and adolescents. In their vernacular, they seem to be "losing it." Psychologists have become more sensitive to this acting out, and label it "loss of impulse control" when it becomes extreme. One way or another, anti-social behavior must be curbed.

Confusion about punishment reigns in part because of semantics. "Abuse" means unwarranted, inhuman punishment. Child sexual abuse probably has few dissenters in terms of definition, but that is not to say that differences of opinion do not exist. Unless there is a sadomasochistic relationship, spouse abuse also presents relatively few problems in definition. Prisoner abuse, no matter how severe, probably would elicit the fewest disagreements. Discipline, on the other hand, typically evokes multiple meanings and the greatest debates—even between parents.

Are physical restriction, isolation to a room, and being screamed at forms of punishment? Is the current popular technique of "time out," when a child must sit quietly in some corner of the room for an unspecified time, not to be considered punishment? Does anything change when the procedure is described as a lesson in listening? Suppose the child refuses to go into time out, what then? Is the prisoner in super-max being punished or disciplined?

A recent op-ed column in a large city newspaper espoused corporal punishment in the classroom because "using the rod early can help keep some youths from more serious trouble later." The writer continued: "Of course, people warped by the Benjamin Spock school hyperventilate at the slightest mention of paddling. They still believe the Socratic method can be applied to youthful Al Capones. The object lesson for kids is that as they approach adulthood, violation of others' property or property

rights results in punishments much worse than minor taps on the tush."

Children should not grow up with a set of models—parents, teachers, etc.—who are abusive. There is absolutely no argument with that. It is known that the abused tend to become abusers, in turn. The major objective is never to hurt or uncontrollably release anger, but, rather, to curb unacceptable behavior and teach methods of altering it. Infants must *never* be given corporal punishment. Toddlers should be distracted by showing them attractive toys and objects or playing simple games, not slapped.

No matter what it is called—discipline or punishment—good judgment is required. By definition, however, judgment is an opinion, an estimate. It can not be measured or weighed with any scientific accuracy. The hope is that judges, teachers, parents, and others in authority will have sufficient information and self-control to make judgments that are fair, proper, and good. Ordinarily, assessment of their judgments is made after the fact, often when it is too late to alter. Society's task is to make adequate provisions for the training and education of those who are given the responsibility to judge.

Dispensing discipline effectively

Although the following guidelines denote parent-child relationships, the principles apply to all situations: employer-employee, correctional officer-inmate, teacher-student, etc.

• Accentuate the positives. Youngsters should learn behaviors that are acceptable, rather than constantly being told what to avoid. Example: Rather than "Stop yelling," say "Please use a quiet voice."

• Do not label your child. Eliminate name-calling and generalizations. Be specific. Behavior is undesirable, not people. Example: Rather than "You're a liar," say "If you do not tell the truth about going to the movies, your brother no longer will trust you."

• Discipline should follow the unacceptable behavior as closely as possible. *Each* spouse has equal responsibility for disciplining his or her child.

• Setting reasonable limits reflects your values and love. Limits provide the basis of your offspring's self-confidence throughout his or her lifetime.

• When setting limits, ask yourself the following questions:

a) Are they understood? Ask the youngster to state the limit and why it was set.

b) Are they appropriate in this situation?

c) Have too many been set lately?

d) Is the child confused by mixed messages, sometimes having a limit set for a particular misbehavior; at other times, not?

e) Are you ready to enforce a violation of the limit reasonably?

• Discipline is a learning process, never purely a coercive experience to prove your mastery and control.

It's Magical! It's Malleable! It's . . . Memory

So complex and evanescent is memory, our best metaphors fall short, bogged down in materialism.
Yet through the creative blending and reblending of experience and emotion, memory builds that
about us which often seems most solid—our sense of self. We remember, therefore we are.

Jill Neimark

We never know exactly why certain subjects—like certain people—claim us, and do not let us go. Elizabeth Loftus is a research psychologist who has devoted her life to the study of memory, its mystery and malleability. Of late, she has gained ingenious experiments, which have shown repeatedly that about 25 percent of individuals can be easily induced to remember events that never happened to them—false memories that feel absolutely real.

So it was something of a shock when, at a family gathering, an uncle informed the then 44-year-old Loftus that 30 years earlier, when her mother had drowned, she had been the one to discover the body in the pool. Loftus believed she had never seen her mother's dead body; in fact, she remembered little about the death itself.

Almost immediately after her uncle's revelation, "the memories began to drift back," she recalls in her recent book, *The Myth of Repressed Memory* (St. Martin), "like the crisp, piney smoke from evening camp fires. My mother, dressed in her nightgown, was floating face down. . . . I started screaming. I remembered the police cars, their lights flashing. For three days my memory expanded and swelled.

"Then, early one morning, my brother called to tell me that my uncle had made a mistake. Now he remembered (and other relatives confirmed) that Aunt Pearl found my mother's body." Suddenly Loftus understood firsthand what she had been studying for decades. "My own experiment had inadvertently been performed on me! I was left with a sense of wonder at the inherent credulity of even my skeptical mind."

Memory has become a lightning rod of late. This has been a time of fascinating, grisly stories—of recovered memories of satanic cults, butchered babies, and incest that have spawned church scandals, lawsuits, suicides, splintered families, murders, and endless fodder for talk shows. Three major books on the fallibility of memory were reviewed on the front page of the *New York Times Book Review* last spring, and three more were published this fall. The essential nature of memory, which ought by rights to be a scientific debate, has so galvanized the culture that laws have actually been revoked and repealed over it; in Illinois, for example, a law that bars people over 30 from filing lawsuits based on remembered abuse was repealed in 1992, and is now being reinstated.

Memory's ambiguities and paradoxes seem to have suddenly claimed us as they have claimed researchers for decades. This fascination cannot be explained away by the human need to memorialize the past—a need that expresses itself beautifully and indelibly in monuments like the Vietnam memorial or the AIDS quilt, and in projects like Steven Spielberg's ongoing documentary of holocaust survivors.

It's as if we've awakened, at the turn of the millennium, and realized that memory is the bedrock of the self—and that it may be perpetually shifting and terrifically malleable. That image of memory, whose river runs into tabloids and traumas, seems both terrifying and baptismal. If we can repress life-shaping events (such as sexual or physical abuse), or actually invent memories of events that never happened (from UFO abductions to rapes and murders), memory carries a power that promises to utterly reshape the self.

And so it's exciting news that in the past few years, scientists have begun to piece together a picture of memory that is stunning in its specifics:

• Sophisticated PET (positron emission tomography) scans can record the actual firing of the neurons that hold the pictures of our lives, and observe memory move like a current across the brain while it sleeps or wakes.

• How and where the brain lays down and consolidates memory—that is, makes it permanent—is yielding to understanding. As one researcher states, we are seeing "an explosion of knowledge about what parts of the brain are doing what."

• Hormones that help engrave the narrative of our lives into our cells have now been identified.

• Certain drugs block or enhance memory, and they may hold the key to preventing disorders as wide-ranging as Alzheimer's disease and posttraumatic stress disorder (PTSD).

• The well-known "fight-or-flight" response to stress can sear "indelible" memories into the brain.

• Memory is not a single entity residing in a single place. It is the likelihood that the pathway of neurons and connections an experience forges in the brain can be reactivated again. It involves multiple systems in the brain. The emotion associated with a memory, for example, is stored in a different place than the content of the memory itself.

• Some memories occur in a primitive part of the brain, unknown to conscious perception. That part functions "below" the senses, as it were. That is why individuals with brain damage can sometimes learn and remember—without knowing they do so.

• There is a growing understanding that an infant's early experience of emotional attachment can direct the nature and durability of childhood memories and the way they are stored in the brain.

Memory, it turns out, is both far more complex and more primitive than we knew. Ancient parts of the brain can record memory before it even reaches our senses—our sight and hearing, for instance. At the same time, "there are between 200 and 400 billion neurons in the brain and each neuron has about 10,000 connections," notes psychiatrist Daniel Siegel, M.D. "The parallel processing involved in memory is so complex we can't even begin to think how it works."

The one thing that we can say for certain is this: If memory is the bedrock of the self, then even though that self may seem coherent and unchanging, it is built on shifting sands.

13 WAYS OF LOOKING AT THE BRAIN

Moments after being removed from the skull, the brain begins to collapse into a jellylike mass. And yet this wet aspic of tissue contains a fantastic archeology of glands, organs, and lobes, all of which have their own specialized jobs. . . . Much of this archeology is devoted to the complex tasks of memory.

But just what is memory? According to Nobel Prize-winning neuroscientist Gerald Edelman, Ph.D., author of *Bright Air, Brilliant Fire* (Basic Books), memory is the ability to repeat a performance—with mistakes. Without memory, life itself would never have evolved. The genetic code must be able to repeat itself in DNA and RNA; an immune cell must be able to remember an antigen and repeat a highly specific defense next time they meet; a neuron in the brain must be able to send the same signal each time you encounter (for example) a lion escaped from the local zoo. Every living system must be able to remember; but what is most dangerous and wonderful about memory is that it must occasionally make errors. It must be wrong. Mere repetition might explain the way a crystal grows but not the way a brain works. Memory classifies and adapts to our environment. That adaptation requires flexibility. The very ability to make mistakes is precious.

Now you can bravely step into the hall of mirrors that is memory. And though our words to describe this evanescent process are still crude and oversimplistic, here are a few tools to travel with:

Memory can be implicit or explicit. Implicit memory is involved in learning habits—such as riding a bicycle or driving a car. It does not require "conscious" awareness, which is why you can sometimes be lost in thought as you drive and find you've driven home without realizing it. Explicit memory is conscious, and is sometimes called declarative. One form of

declarative memory is autobiographical memory—our ability to tell the story of our life in the context of time.

We often talk of memory storage and retrieval, as if memory were filed in a honeycomb of compartments, but these words are really only metaphors. If memory is the reactivation of a weblike network of neurons that were first activated when an event occurred, each time that network is stimulated the memory is strengthened, or consolidated. Storage, retrieval, consolidation—how comforting and solid they sound; but in fact they consist of electrical charges leaping among a vast tangle of neurons.

In truth, even the simplest memory stimulates complex neural networks at several different sites in the brain. The content (what happened) and meaning (how it felt) of an event are laid down in separate parts of the brain. In fact, research at Yale University by Patricia Goldman-Rakic, Ph.D., has shown that neurons themselves are specialized for different types of memories—features, patterns, location, direction. "The coding is so specific that it can be mapped to different areas . . . in the prefrontal region."

What is activating these myriad connections? We still don't know. Gerald Edelman calls this mystery "the homunculus crisis." Who is thinking? Is memory remembering us? "The intricacy and numerosity of brain connections are extraordinary," writes Edelman. "The layers and loops between them are dynamic, they continually change."

Yet the center holds. The master regulator of memory, the hub at the center of the wheel, is a little seahorse-shaped organ called the hippocampus. Like the rest of the brain, it is lateralized; it exists in both the right and left hemispheres. Without it, we learn and remember nothing—in fact, we are lost to ourselves.

THE SEAHORSE AND THE SELF

"He's 33 years old, and he never remembers that his father is dead. Every time he rediscovers this fact he goes through the whole grieving process again," Mark Gluck, Ph.D., a professor at the Center for Molecular and Behavioral Neuroscience at Rutgers University, says of M.P., a young man who lost his memory after a stroke six years ago. Gluck has been studying M.P. for several years. After his stroke, M.P. forgot that on that very morning he had proposed marriage to his girlfriend. "He can store no new information in his long-term memory. If you tell him a phone number and ask him to repeat it, he will; but if you change the subject and then ask him the number, he can't remember. M.P. is going to be living in the present for the rest of his life. He has lost the essential ability of the self to evolve."

M.P. is uncannily similar to one of the most remarkable and intensively studied patients of all time, a man called H.M., who lost his memory after undergoing brain surgery to treat epilepsy. This type of memory loss, called anterograde amnesia, stops time. It usually results from damage to the hippocampus, which normally processes, discards, or dispatches information by sending signals to other parts of the brain.

"The hippocampus is critical for learning," says Gluck, "and it's also one of the most volatile, unstable parts of the brain—one of the first parts damaged if oxygen is cut off.

Think of it as a highly maneuverable kayak; it has to immediately capture a whole range of information about an event and needs the ability to go rapidly through many changes. We think the hippocampus serves as a filter, learning new associations and deciding what is important and what to ignore or compress. That's why it's critical for learning." The hippocampus is, in a sense, a collating machine, sorting and then sending various packets of information to other parts of the brain.

One of the most exciting advances in neuroscience may lie ahead as researchers begin to actually model the living brain on the computer—creating a new era of artificial intelligence called neural networks. Gluck and researchers at New York University have begun to model the hippocampus, creating "lesions" and watching what happens—in the hope that they can develop specialized tests that will identify Alzheimer's in its early stages, as well as develop machinery that can learn the way a brain does. Thus far their predictions about its role have been borne out—in fact, Gluck is developing applications for the military so that hippocampal-like computers can learn the early signals of engine malfunctions and sound the alarm long before a breakdown.

The hippocampus does not store memories permanently. It is a way station, though a supremely important one. Like a football player in the heat of the game, it passes the ball to other parts of the brain. This takes minutes, or maybe even hours, according to James McGaugh, Ph.D., of the University of California at Irvine. At that point, memories can still be lost. They need to be consolidated; the network of neurons responsible for a memory needs to be strengthened through repeated stimuli, until the memory exists independent of the hippocampus, a process known as long-term potentiation (LTP).

Once again, a word picture of this process is extremely crude. In actuality, Edelman points out, "the circuits of the brain look like no others we have seen before. The neurons have treelike arbors that overlap in myriad ways. Their signaling is like the vast aggregate of interactive events in a jungle."

No one is certain how long it takes to fully consolidate a memory. Days? Weeks? Perhaps it takes even years until the linkages of networks are so deeply engraved that the memory becomes almost crystallized—easy to recall, detailed and clear. Individuals like M.P. seem to lose several years of memory just prior to hippocampal damage; so do Alzheimer's patients, who usually suffer hippocampal damage as their brains begin to malfunction, and who recall their childhood days with fine-etched clarity but find the present blurred.

A MAGIC RHYTHM OF MEMORY?

Just how and when do memories become permanent? Scientists now have direct evidence of what they have long suspected—that consolidation of memories, or LTP, takes place during sleep or during deeply relaxed states. It is then that brain waves slow to a rhythm known as "theta," and perhaps, according to McGaugh, the brain releases chemicals that enhance storage.

In an ingenious experiment reported in the journal *Science* last July, researchers planted electrodes in different cells in rats' hippocampi, and watched each cell fire as the animals explored different parts of a box. After returning to their cages, the rats slept. And during sleep the very same cells fired.

There seems to be a specific brain rhythm dedicated to LTP. "It's the magic rhythm of theta! The theta rhythm is the natural, indigenous rhythm of the hippocampus," exclaims neuroscientist Gary Lynch, Ph.D., of the University of California at Irvine. Lynch is known for his inspiring, if slightly mad, brilliance. His laboratory found that LTP is strongest when stimulation is delivered to the hippocampus in a frequency that corresponds to the slow rhythms of theta, of deep relaxation. Research by James McGaugh seems to confirm this: the more theta waves that appear in an animal's EEG (electroencephalogram), the more it remembers.

No wonder, then, that recent experiments show sleep improves memory in humans—and specifically, the sleep associated with dreaming, REM (rapid eye movement) sleep. In Canada, students who slept after cramming for an exam retained more information than those who pulled an all-nighter. In Israel, researchers Avi Karni and Dov Sagi at the Weizmann Institute found that interrupting REM sleep 60 times in a night completely blocked learning; interrupting non-REM sleep just as often did not. These findings give scientific punch to "superlearning" methods like that of Bulgarian psychiatrist Georgi Lozanov, which utilizes deep relaxation through diaphragmatic breathing and music, combined with rhythmic bursts of information.

THE HAUNTED BRAIN

What happens when memory goes awry? It seems that some memories are so deeply engraved in the brain that they haunt an individual as if he were a character in an Edgar Allen Poe story. How, asks Roger Pittman, M.D., coordinator of research and development at the Manchester (New Hampshire) Veterans Administration Medical Center and associate professor at Harvard Medical School, does the traumatic event "carve its canyons and basins of memory into the living brain?"

In any kind of emotionally arousing experience, the brain takes advantage of the fight-or-flight reaction, which floods cells with two powerful stress hormones, adrenaline and noradrenaline. "We believe that the brain takes advantage of the chemicals released during stress and powerful emotions," says James McGaugh, "to regulate the strength of storage of the memory." These stress hormones stimulate the heart to pump faster and the muscles to tense; they also act on neurons in the brain. A memory associated with emotionally charged information gets seared into the brain. We owe our very lives to this: a dangerous, threatening, or exciting event needs to be recalled well so that we may take precautions when meeting similar danger again.

Scientists are now beginning to understand just how emotional memory works and why it is so powerful. According to Joseph Ledoux, Ph.D., of the Center for Neural Science at New York University, the hormones associated with strong emotion stimulate the amygdala, an almond-shaped organ in the brain's cortex.

It's long been known that when rats are subjected to the sound of a tone and a shock, they soon learn to respond fearfully to the tone alone. The shocker is that when the auditory cortex—the part of the brain that receives sound—is completely destroyed, the rats are still able to learn the exact same fear response. How can a rat learn to be afraid of a sound it cannot hear?

The tone, it appears, is carried directly back to the amygdala, as well as to the auditory cortex. Destroy the amygdala, and even a rat with perfect hearing will never learn to be afraid of the sound. As neurologist Richard Restak, M.D., notes, this "implies that much of our brain's emotional processing occurs unconsciously. The amygdala may process many of our unconscious fear responses." This explains in part why phobias are so difficult to treat by psychotherapy. The brain's memory for emotional experiences is an enduring one.

But the ability of the brain to utilize stress hormones can go badly awry—and a memory can become not simply permanent but intrusive and relentless. "Suppose somebody shoots you and years later you're still waking up in a cold sweat with nightmares," says McGaugh. "The hormonal regulation of memory, when pushed to an extreme in a traumatic situation, may make memories virtually indelible."

Such memories seem so powerful that even an innocuous stimulus can arouse them. Roger Pittman compares the inescapable memories of PTSD, where flashbacks to a nightmarish trauma intrude relentlessly on daily life, to a black hole, "a place in space-time that has such high gravity that even light cannot pass by without being drawn into it."

So with ordinary associations and memories in PTSD: "As all roads lead to Rome, all the patient's thoughts lead to the trauma. A war veteran can't look at his wife's nude body without recalling with revulsion the naked bodies he saw in a burial pit in Vietnam, can't stand the sight of children's dolls because their eyes remind him of the staring eyes of the war dead."

The tragic twist is that, Pittman believes, each time a memory floods in again, the same stress hormones are released, running the same neural paths of that particular memory and binding the victim ever tighter in the noose of the past. Yet in response to the stress of recalling trauma, the body releases a flood of calming opiates. These neurochemicals, which help us meet the immediate demands of stress and trauma, might create a kind of unfortunate biochemical reward for the traumatic memory. "This whole question of an appetitive component to trauma is really fascinating and as yet unexplored," notes Pittman. "It may explain the intrusive, repeating nature of these memories. Maybe, however horrible the trauma, there's something rewarding in the brain chemicals released."

A solution, then, to treating the kind of PTSD we see in war veterans and victims of rape and child abuse, might lie in blocking the action of some of these stress hormones. And perhaps a key to enhancing ordinary learning is to create a judicious amount of stress—excitement, surprise, even a healthy dose of fear (like the kind one may feel before cramming for a demanding final exam).

A landmark study recently reported by James McGaugh and Larry Cahill, in *Nature*, indicates that any emotion, even ordinary emotion, is linked to learning. They gave two groups of college students a drug that blocks the effects of adrenaline and noradrenaline, then showed the students a series of 12 slides that depicted scenes such as a boy crossing the street with his mother or visiting a man at a hospital. A control group was told an ordinary story (son and mother visit the boy's surgeon father) that corresponded to some of the slides. The experimental group heard a story of disaster (boy is hit by car; a surgeon attempts to reattach his severed feet).

Two weeks later, the volunteers were given a surprise memory test. Students who heard the ordinary story recalled all 12 slides poorly. The second group, however, recalled significantly better the slides associated with the story of disaster.

Then, in an ingenious twist, McGaugh and Cahill repeated the experiment with new volunteers. Just before the slide show, the experimental group was given a beta blocker—a drug that acts on nerve cells to block the effect of stress hormones. Two weeks later they could not be distinguished from the control group. They similarly remembered all 12 slides poorly.

The implications of this elegant experiment are far reaching. "Let's suppose," postulates McGaugh, "that a plane crashes near Pittsburgh and you're hired to pick out the body parts. If we give you a beta blocker, we impair your 'emotional' memory, the memory for the trauma, without impairing your normal memory."

Pittman looks forward in the next decade to drugs that not only block PTSD but help ameliorate it. "There seems to be a window of opportunity, up to six hours or so in rats in any case, before memories are consolidated." During that time effective drugs, such as beta blockers, might be administered.

MEMORY LOST AND REGAINED

The stories are legendary. Elizabeth Loftus has found ordinary memory to be so malleable that she can prompt volunteers to "remember nonexistent broken glass and tape recorders; to think of a clean-shaven man as having a mustache, of straight hair as curly, of hammers as screwdrivers, to place a barn in a bucolic scene that contained no buildings at all, to believe in characters who never existed and events that never happened."

Sometimes the memories become so seemingly fantastical that they lead to court cases and ruined lives. "I testified in a case recently in a small town in the state of Washington," Loftus recalls, "where the memories went from, 'Daddy made me play with his penis in the shower' to 'Daddy made me stick my fist up the anus of a horse,' and they were bringing in a veterinarian to talk about just what a horse would do in that circumstance. The father is ill and will be spending close to $100,000 to defend himself."

Nobody is quite sure how memories might be lost to us and then later retrieved—so-called repression. Whatever it is, it is a different process than traumatic amnesia, a well-known phenomenon where a particular horrendous event is forgotten because it was never consolidated in long-term memory in the first place. Such is the amnesia of an accident victim who loses consciousness after injury. Repressed memory, on the other hand, is alleged to involve repeated traumas.

According to UCLA's Daniel Siegel, both amnesia and repression may be due to a malfunction of the hippocampus. In order to recall an explicit memory, and to be able to depict it in words and pictures, the hippocampus must process it first. Perhaps, postulates Siegel, the work of the hippocampus is disrupted during trauma—while other components of memory carry on. We know, for example, that primitive responses like fear or excitement stimulate the amygdala directly; learning can occur without our "knowing" it.

If explicit memory is impaired—you forget what happened to you—but implicit memory is intact, you may still be profoundly influenced by an experience. Siegel thinks that some individuals remove conscious attention during repeated trauma, say from an unbearable event like repeated rapes. In the parlance of the mind trade, they "dissociate."

While his theory may explain repressed memory plausibly, it doesn't suggest how the memory emerges decades later, explicit and intrusive. And it doesn't answer the contention of many researchers that such repression is probably rare, and that the wave of repressed memories we are hearing about today may be due to invention.

It turns out that it's relatively easy to confuse imagery with perception. The work of Stephen Kossyln, Ph.D., a psychologist at Harvard University and author of *Image and Brain* (MIT press), has shown that the exact same centers in the brain are activated by both imagination and perception. "PET studies have shown that, when subjects close their eyes and form visual images, the same areas are activated as if they were actually seeing." The strength of the imagined "signal" (or image) is about half that of a real one. Other research shows that the source of a memory—the time, place, or way the memory began—is the first part to fade. After all, the source of a memory is fragile.

If we concentrate on generating images that then get recorded in the web of neurons as if they were real, we might actually convince ourselves that confabulations are true. (This might also explain how some individuals who lie about an event eventually convince themselves, through repeated lying, that the lie is true.)

The fragility of source memory explains why, in a famous experiment by psychologist John Neisser, John Dean's testimony about Richard Nixon was shown to be both incredibly accurate and hugely inaccurate. "His initial testimony was so impressive that people called him a human tape recorder," recalls psychologist Charles Thompson, Ph.D. "Neisser then compared the actual tapes to his testimony, and found that if you really looked at the specifics, who said what and when, Dean was wrong all over the place. But if you just looked at his general sense of what was going on in the meetings he was right on target. His confusion was about the source." In general, supposes Thompson, this is how memory works. We have an accurate sense of the core truth of an event, but we can easily get the details wrong.

"Memory is more reconstructive than reproductive. As time passes, details are lost. We did a study where we asked people to keep a daily diary for up to a year and a half, and later asked them questions about recorded events. The memory of the core event and its content stayed at a high level of about 70 percent, while the peripheral details dropped quickly."

CAN MEMORY CREATE THE SELF?

From Freud on down, it was believed that memories from infancy or early childhood were repressed and somehow inaccessible—but that their clues, like the bits of bread dropped by Hansel and Gretel in the forest, could be found in dreams or in the pathology of waking life. Now we know better. It's that the brain systems that support declarative memory develop late—two or three years into life.

If we don't actually lay down any memories of our first few years, how can they shape our later life? An intriguing answer can be pieced together from findings by far-flung researchers.

Daniel Siegel plows the field of childhood memory and attachment theory. He finds that memory is profoundly affected in children whose mothers had rejected or avoided them. "We don't know why this happens, but at 10 years old, these children have a unique paucity in the content of their spontaneous autobiographical narratives." As adults, they do not recall childhood family experiences.

It may be that memory storage is impaired in the case of childhood trauma. Or it may be, Siegel suggests, that avoidant parents don't "talk to children about their experiences and memories. Those children don't have much practice in autobiographical narrative. Not only are their memories weak or nonexistent, the sense of self is not as rich. As a psychotherapist, I try to teach people to tell stories about their lives. It helps them develop a richer sense of self."

As far as the biology of the brain goes, this may be no different than training an 18-year-old boy to distinguish between whales and submarines; if the hippocampus is continually fed a stimulus, it will allocate more of the brain's capacities to recording and recognizing that stimulus. In the case of autobiographical narrative, however, what emerges is magical and necessary: the self.

That is almost like saying memory creates the self, and in a sense it does. But memory is also created and recreated by the self. The synergy between the two is like two sticks rubbed together in a forest, creating fire. "We now have a new paradigm of memory," notes Loftus, "where memories are understood as creative blendings of fact and fiction, where images are alchemized by experience and emotion into memories."

"I think it's safe to say we make meaning out of life, and the meaning-making process is shaped by who we are as self," says Siegel. Yet that self is shaped by the nature of memory. "It's this endless feedback loop which maintains itself and allows us to come alive."

When we think of our lives, we become storytellers—heroes of our own narrative, a tale that illumines that precious and mysterious "self" at the center. That "I am" cannot be quantified or conveyed precisely and yet it feels absolute. As Christopher Isherwood wrote long ago in *The Berlin Stories*, "I am a camera." Yet, as the science is showing us, there is no single camera—or if there is, it is more like the impressionist, constantly shifting camera of *Last Year at Marienbad*. Memory is malleable—and so are we.

Memory for a Past That Never Was

Elizabeth F. Loftus[1]

Department of Psychology, University of Washington, Seattle, Washington

For most of this century psychologists have been examining the imperfections of memory. The science of memory has educated us about the kinds of human experiences that Akira Kurosawa expressed in his film *Rashomon,* in which four individuals tried to recall a violent episode that they had previously experienced. Although the recollections differed greatly, each of the various rememberers maintained a strong conviction in his or her own particular version of the past. The history of psychologists' study of memory was well reviewed by Daniel Schacter in the opening chapter of his edited volume on memory distortion, and he used *Rashomon* nicely to ponder the extent to which memory can ever really tell us the truth about what has happened in the past (Schacter, 1995).

The early demonstrations of distorted memory often involved the observation that a true event was remembered, but in a somewhat mistaken way. Visual forms were remembered as being more regular and symmetrical than they really were. Memory of a story was distorted after multiple retellings. Remembered word lists sometimes included words that had not been studied but were strongly associated with words that had been studied (Deese, 1959; see Roediger & McDermott, 1995, for recent demonstrations of this phenomenon).

Later empirical demonstrations showed that people sometimes had an accurate memory but were wrong about the source of that memory. Other work with more complex events showed that people remembered an event itself, but were wrong about some of the details—even details that might be considered critical (see Loftus & Ketcham, 1994).

It is only in the last decade of the 20th century that researchers have seriously turned their attention to the question of how far they can go. Rather than tinkering with a detail here and there, can they actually create entirely false memories for the past? Could they make people believe and remember that they were hospitalized when they were not, or that they were lost and frightened when they had not been? This line of research into false memory shows that it is indeed possible to create complex and elaborate false memories in the minds of research subjects, and that subjects are confident that these false memories are real. Here is how it has been done.

PLANTING CHILDHOOD MEMORIES

Once upon a time, there was a case history involving a 14-year-old boy named Chris. He had been misled to believe and remember that he had been lost in a shopping mall at about the age of 5, that he had been frightened and was crying, and that he had ultimately been rescued by an elderly person and reunited with his family (Loftus, 1993). Chris was partly responsible for inspiring a variety of empirical efforts to create entirely false memories of childhood.

At the University of Washington, my collaborators and I conducted a study using a simple method that was similar to the one Chris had experienced (Loftus, Coan, & Pickrell, 1996; Loftus & Pickrell, 1995). The subjects were 24 individuals who were asked to recall events that were supposedly supplied by a close relative. Three of the events were true, and one was a false event about getting lost in a shopping mall, department store, or other public place. The subjects, who ranged in age from 18 to 53, thought they were taking part in a study of childhood memories. At the outset, each subject completed a booklet said to contain four short stories about events from his or her childhood provided by a parent, sibling, or other older relative. Three events had actually happened, and the fourth, always in the third position, was false. Each event was described in a single paragraph.

The false event was constructed from information provided by the relative, who was asked where the family would have shopped when the subject was about 5 years old, which members of the family usually went along on shopping trips, and what kinds of stores might have attracted the subject's interest. The relative was also asked to verify that the subject had not been lost in a mall around the age of 5. The false events always included the following elements: that the subject (a) was lost in a mall, large department store, or other public place for an extended period of time at about the age of 5, (b) cried, (c) was found and aided by an elderly woman, and (d) was reunited with the family.

Subjects completed the booklets by reading about each event and then writing what they remembered about each event. If they did not remember an event, they were told to write, "I do not remember this."

When the booklets were returned, subjects were called and scheduled for two interviews that occurred approximately 1 to 2 weeks apart. Subjects thought the study was about how their memories compared with those of their relative. Across the interviews, subjects remembered something about 68% of the true events about which they were questioned. The rate of "remembering" the false event was lower: 25% remembered the event, fully or partially.

Could researchers create false memories about events that were more unusual than getting lost? Using a similar procedure, Ira Hyman and his colleagues at Western Washington University successfully implanted in the minds of adult subjects some rather unusual childhood memories (Hyman, Husband, & Billings, 1995). In one study, college

From *Current Directions in Psychological Science,* June 1997, pp. 60-65. © 1997 by the American Psychological Society. Reprinted by permission of Cambridge University Press.

students were asked to recall actual events that had been reported by their parents and one experimenter-crafted false event. The false event was an overnight hospitalization for a high fever and a possible ear infection or else a birthday party with pizza and a clown. Parents confirmed that neither of these events had happened, yet subjects were told that they had experienced one of the false events at about the age of 5.

Subjects tried to recall childhood experiences that they thought had been supplied by their parents, under the belief that the experimenters were interested in how people remember shared experiences differently. All events, both the true ones and the false one, were first cued with an event title (e.g., "family vacation," "overnight hospitalization") and an age. In all, subjects remembered something about over 80% of the true events. As for the creation of false memories, 20% of the subjects adopted the false memory by the time of the second interview. One subject "remembered" that the doctor was a male, but the nurse was female—and also a friend from church.

In a second study, Hyman's group tried to implant memories for three new false events that were unusual, such as attending a wedding reception and accidentally spilling a punch bowl on the parents of the bride. In this study, more intense pressure was exerted on subjects to provide more complete recall. Overall, subjects remembered something about approximately 90% of the true events. Subjects did not remember the false events during the first interview, but approximately 25% did so by the time the third interview was completed. For example, one subject initially had no recall of the wedding accident, stating, "I have no clue. I have never heard that one before." By the second interview, the subject said: "It was an outdoor wedding, and I think we were running around and knocked something over like the punch bowl or something and, um, made a big mess and of course got yelled at for it."

Who is especially susceptible to these sorts of suggestions? One answer came in a study that used the false event involving the punch bowl. False memories—either full or partial—were expressed by 27% of the subjects during the second interview. One subject, for example, remembered extensive detail about the unfortunate man who got punch spilled on him:

> . . . a heavyset man, not like fat but like tall and . . . big beer belly, and I picture him having a dark suit on, like grayish dark, and like having grayish dark hair and balding on top, and, uh, I picture him with a wide square face, and I just

picture him getting up and being kind of irritated or mad. . . .

Two variables related to personal characteristics correlated strongly with the creation of false memories. The first was score on the Dissociative Experiences Scale, which taps into the extent to which a person has lapses in memory and attention or fails to integrate awareness, thought, and memory (Bernstein & Putnam, 1986). Also correlated was score on the Creative Imagination Scale, which is a measure of hypnotizability, and also can be construed as a self-report measure of the vividness of mental imagery (Wilson & Barber, 1978).

Although it happened in the particular studies just cited that 25% of adult subjects accepted the false memory of being lost, 20% accepted the false memory of being hospitalized, and approximately 25% accepted the false memory of knocking over a punch bowl, these studies cannot support any firm claims about the percentage of people in the population who might be able to be misled in this way. It might be higher or lower depending on the particular method used and the characteristics of the sample. For example, Mary Devitt (1995), from the University of North Dakota, found lower percentages of 14- to 24-year-old subjects creating false memories of being lost at age 6 or hospitalized at age 5, with more subjects accepting the hospitalization suggestion than the getting-lost suggestion. Kathy Pezdek (1995), from Claremont University, tried to instill a false memory about getting lost and also a false memory about receiving a rectal enema. She succeeded in the former case (with 15% of subjects accepting the false suggestion about getting lost) but not in the latter (with no subject accepting the false suggestion). What is clear in each of these studies, however, is that false memories took root after strong suggestions, at least in a minority of subjects, showing that researchers are capable of creating quite complex childhood memories in research subjects.

IMPOSSIBLE MEMORIES

One could argue that the suggestions used to plant memories of being lost or hospitalized cause subjects to take some genuine experiences and combine them with other factual details to create distorted memories of true experiences. Perhaps this is so in some instances. A stronger case for implantation of false memories could be made if subjects were induced to remember the impossible. Although there are numerous cases

of people remembering false experiences in the real world, such as being abducted by aliens and transported away on spaceships, memories that many people consider impossible, it would be desirable to demonstrate that impossible memories could be planted experimentally. Recently, researchers have devised some clever ways of getting people to remember experiences that are highly unlikely to be genuine. These studies use various methods to get people to believe that they are remembering episodes from the 1st year of life. Given that adults are exceedingly unlikely to have genuine episodic memories from this period, researchers have confidence that such methods have produced truly false memories.

Remembering Mobiles

A clever procedure for planting false memories was developed by Nick Spanos and his collaborators at Carleton University (Spanos, 1996; Spanos, Burgess, Burgess, Samuels, & Blois, 1997). Subjects were first administered several questionnaires, which were then apparently analyzed by a computer that gave all subjects the same false feedback that they had been classified as "High Positive Cognitive Monitors." This profile suggested that they had specially coordinated eye movements and visual exploration skills that probably were established in the first few days after birth. They were further falsely informed that they had probably been born in hospitals that had special programs in place to hang swinging colored mobiles over the heads of infants to facilitate this eye coordination.

Experimental techniques were then used to "confirm" whether the subjects had been born into such programs. Half were hypnotized and mentally guided back to the day after birth (i.e., age regressed), and asked to describe their experiences. After they were probed for memories of their birth experiences, they were "returned" to their adult age and asked more questions, including questions designed to determine whether they thought the memories they had produced were real or were fantasy. One week later, they came back to the lab for further questioning, having been warned that during the interim they might find that they had been primed by the regression experience to feel itching near the umbilicus or have thoughts and dreams about infancy. During the second lab session, they again discussed and rated the reality of their "memories" and also reported on any interim experiences.

Half the subjects were not hypnotized at all, but engaged in a "guided mnemonic restructuring" procedure, which they were assured would aid them in recalling their infant memories. They were mentally guided back to shortly after birth, and were also actively encouraged to use imagery to recreate experiences from infancy. Otherwise these subjects were treated the same as the hypnotized group, and both were compared with control subjects who did not undergo any memory procedures but simply completed the various other questionnaires.

Spanos and his collaborators found that the vast majority of their subjects were susceptible to these memory-planting procedures. Both the hypnotized subjects and the subjects who engaged in guided mnemonic restructuring reported infant memories, with the latter group doing so somewhat more often than the former (70% vs. 95%). The researchers attempted to hypnotize all the subjects in the group selected for this treatment, regardless of their previously measured levels of hypnotizability.

Both groups remembered the suggested mobile at a relatively high rate (46% of the hypnotized subjects, 56% of the nonhypnotized group). People who had received low scores on the measure of hypnotizability were less likely to include the mobile (31%) in their memory reports than were people with medium and high scores on the measure of hypnotizability (62%).

Did subjects believe they were having real memories, or were they aware that their experiences were fantasies? First, it is worth noting that all control subjects indicated that the experiences were fantasy or else said they were unsure. Second, the hypnotized and guided subjects were far more likely to say that the experiences were truly memories rather than fantasies. Of those who reported memories from infancy, nearly half (49%) classified them as real memories, as opposed to 16% who claimed that they were merely fantasies.

Susan DuBreuil, Maryanne Garry, and I adapted and extended the false-feedback paradigm developed by Spanos (DuBreuil, Garry, & Loftus, in press). Approximately half of our subjects were induced to develop memories of the 1st day of life, as Spanos's group had done, but the rest were induced in a similar fashion to remember specific experiences from the 1st day of kindergarten. We accomplished these inductions with false feedback suggesting that the subjects fit a particular profile; those in the kindergarten group were told that this was probably due to being exposed, on the 1st day of kindergarten, to spiral disks that were hung in the classroom to stimulate coordinated eye movements and visual exploration, and subjects in the infancy group were told what Spanos's group had told their subjects. The infancy subjects were age regressed to ascertain whether they experienced the day after birth and the dangling mobile, and the kindergarten subjects were age regressed to ascertain whether they experienced the spiral disks. The hypothesis was that subjects might be even more readily induced to falsely remember spiral disks from kindergarten than mobiles from infancy because people believe they can remember their early childhood but not their infancy.

The hypothesis was not supported: The results did show that more than 80% of subjects reported remembering some experience at the target age. Approximately 60% of the infancy group claimed some memory of the mobile, and only 25% of the kindergarten group claimed some memory of the spiral disk. Thus, the latter subjects were less likely to create a false memory for the suggested stimulus. One possible reason is that they had some actual memories from the target period that they could describe, so they had something to say, and thus felt less compelled to produce a report about the suggested stimulus.

Many of the false memory reports were quite detailed. An example from a subject in the infancy group gives the flavor of these responses:

> There are little paper baby bottles hanging from the ceiling, and there's a yellow bow tied to somebody's, um, crib, but I don't know why, and the crib I'm in is like, um, a clear plastic thing and there's like, uh, red . . . along the side. And actually I remember there's a mobile. If I'm laying on my back, it's hanging from the left corner. But it seems to be pastel colors. It's nothing bright.

These findings are consistent with the idea that people can be led to experience complex, vivid, detailed false memories via a simple procedure that leads them to expect that they harbor unconscious hidden memories and that special procedures will help unlock these memories. Hypnosis clearly is not a requirement. Even when subjects did not recall the specific mobile that was suggested, many recalled other items—doctors, nurses, bright lights, cribs, bars, masks—just the kinds of things you would expect to encounter in a hospital setting of this kind.

Remembering Early Infancy

Using a very different method, a research group at Ohio University also succeeded in getting reports of "impossible" memories, ones that supposedly occurred in the 1st year of life (Malinoski & Lynn, 1996). In this research, subjects were asked to report their earliest memory, and the instructions emphasized the importance of reported memories being real memories, not memories based on family stories, photos, or other people's accounts. An interviewer allowed each subject 1 min to recall his or her earliest memory; subsequently, the subject reported the memory and rated its clarity and his or her confidence in its accuracy. Next, the experimenter probed for even earlier memories and again obtained subjective ratings of clarity and confidence. The process continued until the subject twice denied having any earlier memories. Next, the subject received misinformation: that most young adults can remember very early events, including their second birthday, if they close their eyes and try hard to visualize, focus, concentrate, and "let themselves go." After a 1-min pause for the subject to visualize, focus, and concentrate, the interviewer asked for the subject's memories of his or her second birthday, with clarity and confidence ratings. If the subject reported having no such memories, the interviewer encouraged him or her to try again.

At the outset, the mean age of earliest memory report was 3.7 years. When instructed to visualize and concentrate, close to 60% of subjects reported a memory of the second birthday. After repeated probes and verbal reinforcement, more than three quarters of the subjects reported memories at or prior to age 24 months, a third reported memories within their first 12 months, and the mean age of earliest memory report was 1.6 years. Early memory reports correlated with hypnotizability; the more hypnotizable a person was, the earlier the memory he or she reported.

Although the researchers could not prove that the memory reports were false, the age of many of the reports makes it doubtful that they were actual memories of events at the claimed age of occurrence. Were subjects simply making things up to please the experimenter? Most subjects explicitly denied doing so. Moreover, confidence ratings indicated that many subjects truly believed in the memories that they reported.

MEMORIES OR MEMORY REPORTS?

The four individuals who tried to recall the violent episode in *Rashomon* gave four different versions. Were these different memories of the same event or simply different reports? Was each narrative consciously constructed to describe an event in a particular way, even if the truth of the event was crystal clear to the teller? Or had each of the four narrators developed a genuine belief in the story he or she was telling?

These questions can be asked not only of *Rashomon,* but also of the subjects who partake in the studies of "false memories." When 25% of subjects say they remember events either fully or partially, how does one know they actually remember the events? Perhaps they learned about the events from family members and later came to remember not the events themselves but the fact that the events happened. Perhaps subjects only claim to remember because they want to be helpful. These are thorny questions for which there are no fully satisfying answers. But researchers in this area have taken steps to determine whether the subjects who say they remember actually do. Are they confident about the memories? In many cases, yes. Do they elaborate upon the memories, providing details that go far beyond what was suggested to them? In many cases, yes. Are they willing to talk about the memories with other individuals they believe are unconnected to the experiment? In certain cases, yes. These are some of the reasons why researchers believe that subjects in the studies of false memories have subjective experiences that feel just like real memories.

FINAL REMARKS

Planting memories is not a particularly difficult thing to do. It can be done not only with strong external suggestion, as in the cases in which relatives helped to convince subjects that they were lost or hospitalized. It can be done with pressure to remember more and more, as in the case in which subjects were convinced they had memories from the 1st year of life. It can also be done in more subtle ways, as when people are induced to simply imagine that they had experiences in the past that they never actually had (Garry, Manning, Loftus, & Sherman, 1996; Goff, 1996; Goff & Roediger, 1996). Researchers still have much to learn about the generalizability of the false memory findings obtained thus far, as well as about the degree of confidence subjects have in these memo-

ries and the characteristics of false memories created in these ways. As research continues, it is probably important to heed the cautionary tale in the data already obtained: Mental health professionals, interviewers, and other investigators need to know how much they can potentially influence participants in research, clinical, and forensic contexts, and take care to avoid that influence when it might be harmful.

Note

1. Address correspondence to Elizabeth Loftus, Department of Psychology, Box 351525, Seattle, WA 98195-1525; e-mail: eloftus@u.washington.edu.

References

Bernstein, E.M., & Putnam, F.W. (1986). Development, reliability, and validity of a dissociation scale. *The Journal of Nervous and Mental Disease, 174,* 727–735.

Deese, J. (1959). On the prediction of occurrence of particular verbal intrusions in immediate recall. *Journal of Experimental Psychology, 58,* 17–22.

Devitt, M.K. (1995). *The effects of time and misinformation on memory for complete events.* Unpublished doctoral dissertation, University of North Dakota, Grand Forks.

DuBreuil, S.C., Garry, M., & Loftus, E.F. (in press). Tales from the crib. In S.J. Lynn & K.M. McConkey (Eds.). *Truth in memory.* New York: Guilford Press.

Garry, M., Manning, C., Loftus, E.F., & Sherman, S.J. (1996). Imagination inflation. *Psychonomic Bulletin & Review, 3,* 208–214.

Goff, L.M. (1996). *Imagination inflation: The effects of number of imaginings on recognition and source monitoring.* Unpublished master's thesis, Rice University, Houston, TX.

Goff, L.M., & Roediger, H.L., III. (1996, November). *Imagination inflation: Multiple imaginings can lead to false recollection of one's actions.* Paper presented at the annual meeting of the Psychonomic Society, Chicago.

Hyman, I.E., Husband, T.H., & Billings, F.J. (1995). False memories of childhood experiences. *Applied Cognitive Psychology, 9,* 181–197.

Loftus, E.F. (1993). The reality of repressed memories. *American Psychologist, 48,* 518–537.

Loftus, E.F., Coan, J.A., & Pickrell, J.E. (1996). Manufacturing false memories using bits of reality. In L. Reder (Ed.), *Implicit memory and metacognition* (pp. 195–220). Mahwah, NJ: Erlbaum.

Loftus, E.F., & Ketcham, K. (1994). *The myth of repressed memory.* New York: St. Martin's Press.

Loftus, E.F., & Pickrell, J.E. (1995). The formation of false memories. *Psychiatric Annals. 25,* 720–725.

Malinoski, P.T., & Lynn, S.J. (1996). *The plasticity of very early memory reports.* Unpublished manuscript. Binghamton University, Binghamton, NY.

Pezdek, K. (1995, July). *Childhood memories: What types of false memories can be suggestively planted?* Paper presented at the biennial meeting of the Society for Applied Research in Memory and Cognition, Vancouver, Canada.

Roediger. H.L., III, & McDermott, K.B. (1995). Creating false memories: Remembering words not presented in lists. *Journal of Experimental Psychology: Learning, Memory, and Cognition, 21,* 803–814.

Schacter, D.L. (1995). Memory distortion: History and current status. In D.L. Schacter (Ed.), *Memory distortion: How minds, brains, and societies reconstruct the past* (pp. 1–43). Cambridge, MA: Harvard University Press.

Spanos, N.P. (1996). *Multiple identities and false memories.* Washington, DC: American Psychological Association.

Spanos, N.P., Burgess, C.A., Burgess, M.F., Samuels, C., & Blois, W.O. (1997). *Creating false memories of infancy with hypnotic and nonhypnotic procedures.* Unpublished manuscript, Carleton University, Ottawa, Canada.

Wilson, S.C., & Barber, T.X. (1978). The Creative Imagination Scale as a measure of hypnotic responsiveness: Applications to experimental and clinical hypnosis. *American Journal of Clinical Hypnosis. 20,* 235–249.

Recommended Reading

Applebaum, P., Elin, M., & Uyehara, L. (Eds). (1996). *Trauma and memory: Clinical and legal controversies.* New York: Oxford University Press.

Hyman, I.E., & Pentland, J. (1996). The role of mental imagery in the creation of false childhood memories. *Journal of Memory and Language, 35,* 101–117.

Loftus, E.F., (1997, September). Creating false memories. *Scientific American, 277,* 70–75.

Loftus, E.F., & Ketcham, K. (1994). (See References)

Schacter, D.L. (Ed.). (1995). *Memory distortion: How minds, brains, and societies reconstruct the past.* Cambridge, MA: Harvard University Press.

Key Points to Consider

❖ What techniques are available for studying the brain in adults and young children? Why is the study of the development of cognitive abilities of interest to psychologists? What exact role does the brain play in cognitive abilities, for example, in language processing?

❖ What is intelligence? How are learning and thinking central to our concepts of intelligence? What are the various types of intelligence described by Howard Gardner? Why is IQ testing controversial? Can you think of people whom you would call "bright" by standards other than the traditional definitions of intelligence? What can we do to teach intelligent individuals to use their brilliance in thoughtful and humanistic ways?

❖ How does the traditional view of intelligence contrast with Gardner's view? What are some of the multiple intelligences? What are some of the myths (and are they true) surrounding the theory of multiple intelligences? How can intelligence be enhanced by education?

❖ Why do psychologists study language and linguistic ability? How is language related to other cognitive abilities? How does the brain process linguistic information? Is language exclusively human? Explain your answer. How are language and communication similar? How are they different?

 **Links** 　　　 **www.dushkin.com/online/**

16. **Chess: Kasparov v. Deep Blue: The Rematch**
    http://www.chess.ibm.com/home/html/b.html

17. **Cognitive Science Article Archive**
    http://www.helsinki.fi/hum/kognitiotiede/archive.html

18. **Introduction to Artificial Intelligence (AI)**
    http://www-formal.stanford.edu/jmc/aiintro/aiintro.html

These sites are annotated on pages 4 and 5.

As Howard watches his 4-month-old baby, he is convinced that the infant possesses a degree of understanding of the world around her. In fact, Howard is sure he has one of the smartest babies in the neighborhood. Although he is indeed a proud father, he keeps these thoughts to himself rather than alienate his neighbors whom he perceives as having less-intelligent babies.

Jack lives in the same neighborhood as Howard. Jack doesn't have any children, but he does own two fox terriers. Despite Jack's most concerted efforts, the dogs never come to him when he calls them. In fact, the dogs have been known to run the opposite way on occasion. Instead of being furious, Jack accepts his dogs' disobedience because he is sure the dogs are just dumb beasts and do not know any better.

These vignettes illustrate important ideas about cognition or thought processes. In the first, Howard ascribes cognitive abilities and high intelligence to his child; in fact, he probably ascribes too much cognitive ability to his 4-month-old. In the other case, Jack assumes that his dogs are incapable of thought, more specifically, incapable of premeditated disobedience, and therefore he forgives them.

Few adults would deny the existence of their cognitive abilities. Some adults, in fact, think about thinking, something which psychologists call metacognition. Cognition is critical to our survival as adults. But are there differences in mentation in adults? And what about other organisms? Can children think? If they can, do they think like adults?

And what about animals: Can they think and solve problems? These and similar questions are related to cognitive psychology and cognitive science, which is showcased in this unit.

Cognitive psychology has grown faster than most other specialties in psychology in the past 20 years in response to new computer technology as well as to the growth of psycholinguistics. Computer technology has prompted an interest in artificial intelligence, the mimicking of human intelligence by machines. Similarly the study of psycholinguistics has prompted the examination of the influence of language on thought and vice versa.

Although interest in these two developments has eclipsed interest in more traditional areas of cognition, such as intelligence, we cannot ignore these traditional areas in this anthology. With regard to intelligence, one persistent problem has been the difficulty of defining just what intelligence is. David Wechsler, author of several of the most popular intelligence tests in current clinical use, defines intelligence as the global capacity of the individual to act purposefully, to think rationally, and to deal effectively with the environment. Other psychologists have proposed more complex definitions. The definitional problem arises when we try to develop tests that validly and reliably measure such concepts. Edward Boring once suggested that we define intelligence as whatever it is that an intelligence test measures.

The first article in this unit offers the reader an introduction to the complex relationship between cognition and the brain. Specifically, this article describes the child's brain and its development and how this development relates to cognitive ability. The child develops language, logic, mathematical ability, and other cognitive skills in systematic ways due to the hard-wiring and maturation of the nervous system.

The next two selections pertain to intelligence. In "To Be Intelligent," John Abbott discusses how learning and thinking are central to our existence. He also describes how we must move beyond formal schooling and other learning environments to teach people how to use these abilities thoughtfully and considerately.

A companion piece, "Reflections on Multiple Intelligence," by Howard Gardner, challenges the above notion of intelligence. Gardner claims that there are many forms of intelligence, not just cognitive intelligence as measured, for example, by vocabulary. In particular, Gardner explores some of the myths about his theory of multiple intelligences. He also discusses how multiple intelligences can be enhanced by various educational strategies.

The final article in this unit is about language, a cognitive ability that may be exclusively possessed by humans. The work of one neuropsychologist who examines brain structures and their relationship to language and cognition is described. In particular, Angela Freiderici's work on vocabulary development and the processing of linguistic information is shared with the reader.

Cognitive Processes

A baby's brain is a work in progress, trillions of neurons waiting to be wired into a mind. The experiences of childhood, pioneering research shows, help form the brain's circuits—for music and math, language and emotion.

Your Child's Brain

Sharon Begley

YOU HOLD YOUR NEWBORN SO his sky-blue eyes are just inches from the brightly patterned wallpaper. *ZZZt:* a neuron from his retina makes an electrical connection with one in his brain's visual cortex. You gently touch his palm with a clothespin; he grasps it, drops it, and you return it to him with soft words and a smile. *Crackle:* neurons from his hand strengthen their connection to those in his sensory-motor cortex. He cries in the night; you feed him, holding his gaze because nature has seen to it that the distance from a parent's crooked elbow to his eyes exactly matches the distance at which a baby focuses. *Zap:* neurons in the brain's amygdala send pulses of electricity through the circuits that control emotion. You hold him on your lap and talk . . . and neurons from his ears start hard-wiring connections to the auditory cortex.

And you thought you were just playing with your kid.

When a baby comes into the world her brain is a jumble of neurons, all waiting to be woven into the intricate tapestry of the mind. Some of the neurons have already been hard-wired, by the genes in the fertilized egg, into circuits that command breathing or control heartbeat, regulate body temperature or produce reflexes. But trillions upon trillions more are like the Pentium chips in a computer before the factory preloads the software. They are pure and of almost infinite potential, unprogrammed circuits that might one day compose rap songs and do calculus, erupt in fury and melt in ecstasy. If the neurons are used they become integrated into the circuitry of the brain by connecting to other neurons; if they are not used, they may die. It is the experiences of childhood, determining which neurons are used, that wire the circuits of the brain as surely as a programmer at a key-board reconfigures the circuits in a computer. Which keys are typed—which experiences a child has—determines whether the child grows up to be intelligent or dull, fearful or self-assured, articulate or tongue-tied. Early experiences are so powerful, says pediatric neurobiologist Harry Chungani of Wayne State University, that "they can completely change the way a person turns out."

By adulthood the brain is crisscrossed with more than 100 billion neurons, each reaching out to thousands of others so that, all told, the brain has more than 100 trillion connections. It is those connections—more than the number of galaxies in the known universe—that give the brain its unrivaled powers. The traditional view was that the wiring diagram is predetermined, like one for a new house, by the genes in the fertilized egg. Unfortunately, even though half the genes—50,000—are involved in the central nervous system in some way, there are not enough of them to specify the brain's incomparably complex wiring. That leaves another possibility: genes might determine only the brain's main circuits, with something else shaping the trillions of finer connections. That something else is the environment, the myriad messages that the brain receives from the outside world. According to the emerging paradigm, "there are two broad stages of brain wiring," says developmental neurobiologist Carla Shatz of the University of California, Berkeley: "an early period, when experience is not required, and a later one, when it is."

Yet, once wired, there are limits to the brain's ability to create itself. Time limits. Called "critical periods," they are windows of opportunity that nature flings open, starting before birth, and then slams shut, one by one, with every additional candle on the child's birthday cake. In the experiments that gave birth to this paradigm in the 1970s, Torsten Wiesel and David Hubel found that sewing shut one eye of a newborn kitten rewired its brain: so few neurons connected from the shut eye to the visual cortex that the animal was blind even after its eye was reopened. Such rewiring did not occur in adult cats

The Logical Brain

SKILL: Math and logic
LEARNING WINDOW: Birth to 4 years
WHAT WE KNOW: Circuits for math reside in the brain's cortex, near those for music. Toddlers taught simple concepts, like one and many, do better in math. Music lessons may help develop spatial skills.
WHAT WE CAN DO ABOUT IT: Play counting games with a toddler. Have him set the table to learn one-to-one relationships—one plate, one fork per person. And, to hedge your bets, turn on a Mozart CD.

The Language Brain

SKILL: Language

LEARNING WINDOW: Birth to 10 years

WHAT WE KNOW: Circuits in the auditory cortex, representing the sounds that form words, are wired by the age of 1. The more words a child hears by 2, the larger her vocabulary will grow. Hearing problems can impair the ability to match sounds to letters.

WHAT WE CAN DO ABOUT IT: Talk to your child—a lot. If you want her to master a second language, introduce it by the age of 10. Protect hearing by treating ear infections promptly.

whose eyes were shut. Conclusion: there is a short, early period when circuits connect the retina to the visual cortex. When brain regions mature dictates how long they stay malleable. Sensory areas mature in early childhood; the emotional limbic system is wired by puberty; the frontal lobes—seat of understanding—develop at least through the age of 16.

The implications of this new understanding are at once promising and disturbing. They suggest that, with the right input at the right time, almost anything is possible. But they imply, too, that if you miss the window you're playing with a handicap. They offer an explanation of why the gains a toddler makes in Head Start are so often evanescent: this intensive instruction begins too late to fundamentally rewire the brain. And they make clear the mistake of postponing instruction in a second language (see box, "Why Do Schools Flunk Biology?"). As Chugani asks, "What idiot decreed that foreign-language instruction not begin until high school?"

Neurobiologists are still at the dawn of understanding exactly which kinds of experiences, or sensory input, wire the brain in which ways. They know a great deal about the circuit for vision. It has a neuron-growth spurt at the age of 2 to 4 months, which corresponds to when babies start to really notice the world, and peaks at 8 months, when each neuron is connected to an astonishing 15,000 other neurons. A baby whose eyes are clouded by cataracts from birth will, despite cataract-removal surgery at the age of 2, be forever blind. For other systems, researchers know what happens, but not—at the level of neurons and molecules—how. They nevertheless remain confident that cognitive abilities work much like sensory ones, for the brain is parsimonious in how it conducts its affairs: a mechanism that works fine for wiring vision is not likely to be abandoned when it comes to circuits for music. "Connections are not forming willy-nilly," says Dale Purves of Duke University, "but are promoted by activity."

Language: Before there are words, in the world of a newborn, there are sounds. In English they are phonemes such as sharp ba's and da's, drawn-out ee's and ll's and sibilant sss's. In Japanese they are different—barked *hi's*, merged rr/ll's. When a child hears a phoneme over and over, neurons from his ear stimulate the formation of dedicated connections in his brain's auditory cortex. This "perceptual map," explains Patricia Kuhl of the University of Washington, reflects the apparent distance—and thus the similarity—between sounds. So in English-speakers, neurons in the auditory cortex that respond to "ra" lie far from those that respond to "la." But for Japanese, where the sounds are nearly identical, neurons that respond to "ra" are practically intertwined, like L.A. freeway spaghetti, with those for "la." As a result, a Japanese-speaker will have trouble distinguishing the two sounds.

Researchers find evidence of these tendencies across many languages. By 6 months of age, Kuhl reports, infants in English-speaking homes already have different auditory maps (as shown by electrical measurements that identify which neurons respond to different sounds) from those in Swedish-speaking homes. Children are functionally deaf to sounds absent from their native tongue. The map is completed by the first birthday. By 12 months," says Kuhl, "infants have lost the ability to discriminate sounds that are not significant in their language. And their babbling has acquired the sound of their language."

Kuhl's findings help explain why learning a second language after, rather than with, the first is so difficult. "The perceptual map of the first language constrains the learning of a second," she says. In other words, the circuits are already wired for Spanish, and the remaining undedicated neurons have lost their ability to form basic new connections for, say, Greek. A child taught a second language after the age of 10 or so is unlikely ever to speak it like a native. Kuhl's work also suggests why related languages such as Spanish and French are easier to learn than unrelated ones: more of the existing circuits can do double duty.

With this basic circuitry established, a baby is primed to turn sounds into words. The more words a child hears, the faster she learns language, according to psychiatrist Janellen Huttenlocher of the University of Chicago. Infants whose mothers spoke to them a lot knew 131 more words at 20 months than did babies of more taciturn, or less involved, mothers; at 24 months, the gap had widened to 295 words. (Presumably the findings would also apply to a father if he were the primary caregiver.) It didn't matter which words the mother used—monosyllables seemed to work. The sound of words, it seems, builds up neural circuitry that can then absorb more words, much as creating a computer file allows the user to fill it with prose. "There is a huge vocabulary to be acquired," says Huttenlocher, "and it can only be acquired through repeated exposure to words."

Music: Last October researchers at the University of Konstanz in Germany reported that exposure to music rewires neural circuits. In the brains of nine string players examined with magnetic resonance imaging, the amount of somatosensory cortex dedicated to the thumb and fifth finger of the left hand—the fingering digits—was significantly larger than in nonplayers. How long the players practiced each day did not affect the cortical map. But the age at which they had been introduced to their muse did: the younger the child when she took up an instrument, the more cortex she devoted to playing it.

Like other circuits formed early in life, the ones for music endure. Wayne State's Chugani played the guitar as a child, then

The Musical Brain

SKILL: Music

LEARNING WINDOW: 3 to 10 years

WHAT WE KNOW: String players have a larger area of their sensory cortex dedicated to the fingering digits on their left hand. Few concert-level performers begin playing later than the age of 10. It is much harder to learn an instrument as an adult.

WHAT WE CAN DO ABOUT IT: Sing songs with children. Play structured, melodic music. If a child shows any musical aptitude or interest, get an instrument into her hand early.

gave it up. A few years ago he started taking piano lessons with his young daughter. She learned easily, but he couldn't get his fingers to follow his wishes. Yet when Chugani recently picked up a guitar, he found to his delight that "the songs are still there," much like the muscle memory for riding a bicycle.

Math and logic: At UC Irvine, Gordon Shaw suspected that all higher-order thinking is characterized by similar patterns of neuron firing. "If you're working with little kids," says Shaw, "you're not going to teach them higher mathematics or chess. But they are interested in and can process music." So Shaw and Frances Rauscher gave 19 preschoolers piano or singing lessons. After eight months, the researchers found, the children "dramatically improved in spatial reasoning," compared with children given no music lessons, as shown in their ability to work mazes, draw geometric figures and copy patterns of two-color blocks. The mechanism behind the "Mozart effect" remains murky, but Shaw suspects that when children exercise cortical neurons by listening to classical music, they are also strengthening circuits used for mathematics. Music, says the UC team, "excites the inherent brain patterns and enhances their use in complex reasoning tasks."

Emotions: The trunk lines for the circuits controlling emotion are laid down before birth. Then parents take over. Perhaps the strongest influence is what psychiatrist Daniel Stern calls attunement—whether caregivers "play back a child's inner feelings." If a baby's squeal of delight at a puppy is met with a smile and hug, if her excitement at seeing a plane overhead is mirrored, circuits for these emotions are reinforced. Apparently, the brain uses the same pathways to generate an emotion as to respond to one. So if an emotion is reciprocated, the electrical and chemical signals that produced it are reinforced. But if emotions are repeatedly met with indifference or a clashing response—Baby is proud of building a skyscraper out of Mom's best pots, and Mom is terminally annoyed—those circuits become confused and fail to strengthen. The key here is "repeatedly": one dismissive harrumph will not scar a child for life. It's the pattern that counts, and it can be very powerful: in one of Stern's studies, a baby whose mother never matched her level of excitement became extremely passive, unable to feel excitement or joy.

Experience can also wire the brain's "calm down" circuit, as Daniel Goleman describes in his best-selling "Emotional Intelligence." One father gently soothes his crying infant, another drops him into his crib; one mother hugs the toddler who just skinned her knee, another screams "It's your own stupid fault!" The first responses are attuned to the child's distress; the others are wildly out of emotional sync. Between 10 and 18 months, a cluster of cells in the ra-

SCHOOLS

Why Do Schools Flunk Biology?

By LynNell Hancock

BIOLOGY IS A STAPLE AT MOST American high schools. Yet when it comes to the biology of the students themselves—how their brains develop and retain knowledge—school officials would rather not pay attention to the lessons. Can first graders handle French? What time should school start? Should music be cut? Biologists have some important evidence to offer. But not only are they ignored, their findings are often turned upside down.

Force of habit rules the hallways and classrooms. Neither brain science nor education research has been able to free the majority of America's schools from their 19th-century roots. If more administrators were tuned into brain research, scientists argue, not only would schedules change, but subjects such as foreign language and geometry would be offered to much younger children. Music and gym would be daily requirements. Lectures, work sheets and rote memorization would be replaced by hands-on materials, drama and project work. And teachers would pay greater attention to children's emotional connections to sub-

jects. "We do more education research than anyone else in the world," says Frank Vellutino, a professor of educational psychology at State University of New York at Albany, "and we ignore more as well."

Plato once said that music "is a more potent instrument than any other for education." Now scientists know why. Music, they believe, trains the brain for higher forms of thinking. Researchers at the University of California, Irvine, studied the power of music by observing two groups of preschoolers. One group took piano lessons and sang daily in chorus. The other did not. After eight months the musical 3-year-olds were expert puzzlemasters, scoring 80 percent higher than their playmates did in spatial intelligence—the ability to visualize the world accurately.

This skill later translates into complex math and engineering skills. "Early music training can enhance a child's ability to reason," says Irvine physicist Gordon Shaw. Yet music education is often the first "frill" to be cut when school budgets shrink. Schools on average have only one music teacher for every 500

The Windows of Opportunity

PRENATAL	BIRTH	1 YEAR OLD	2 YEARS	3 YEAR
	Motor development			
	Emotional control			
	Vision			
	Social attachment			
	Vocabulary			
	Second language			
		Math/logic		
				Musi

tional prefrontal cortex is busy hooking up to the emotion regions. The circuit seems to grow into a control switch, able to calm agitation by infusing reason into emotion. Perhaps parental soothing trains this circuit, strengthening the neural connections that form it, so that the child learns how to calm herself down. This all happens so early that the effects of nurture can be misperceived as innate nature.

children, according to the National Commission on Music Education.

Then there's gym—another expendable hour by most school standards. Only 36 percent of schoolchildren today are required to participate in daily physical education. Yet researchers now know that exercise is good not only for the heart. It also juices up the brain, feeding it nutrients in the form of glucose and increasing nerve connections—all of which make it easier for kids of all ages to learn. Neuroscientist William Greenough confirmed this by watching rats at his University of Illinois at Urbana-Champaign lab. One group did nothing. A second exercised on an automatic treadmill. A third was set loose in a Barnum & Bailey obstacle course requiring the rats to perform acrobatic feats. These "super-smart" rats grew "an enormous amount of gray matter" compared with their sedentary partners, says Greenough.

Of course, children don't ordinarily run such gauntlets; still, Greenough believes, the results are significant. Numerous studies, he says, show that children who exercise regularly do better in school.

The implication for schools goes beyond simple exercise. Children also need to be more physically active in the classroom, not sitting quietly in their seats memorizing subtraction tables. Knowledge is retained longer if children connect not only aurally but emotionally and physically to the material, says University of Oregon education professor Robert Sylwester in "A Celebration of Neurons."

Good teachers know that lecturing on the American Revolution is far less effective than acting out a battle. Angles and dimensions are better understood if children chuck their work sheets and build a complex model to scale. The smell of the glue enters memory through one sensory system, the touch of the wood blocks another, the sight of the finished model still another. The brain then creates a multidimensional mental model of the experience—one easier to retrieve. "Explaining a smell," says Sylwester, "is not as good as actually smelling it."

Scientists argue that children are capable of far more at younger ages than schools generally realize. People obviously continue learning their whole lives, but the optimum "windows of opportunity for learning" last until about the age of 10 or 12, says Harry Chugani of Wayne State University's Children's Hospital of Michigan. Chugani determined this by measuring the brain's consumption of its chief energy source, glucose. (The more glucose it uses, the more active the brain.) Children's brains, he observes, gobble up glucose at twice the adult rate from the age of 4 to puberty. So young brains are as primed as they'll ever be to process new information. Complex subjects such as trigonometry or foreign language shouldn't wait for puberty to be introduced. In fact, Chugani says, it's far easier for an elementary-school child to hear and process a second language—and even speak it without an accent. Yet most U.S. districts wait until junior high to introduce Spanish or French—after the "windows" are closed.

Reform could begin at the beginning. Many sleep researchers now believe that most teens' biological clocks are set later than those of their fellow humans. But high school starts at 7:30 a.m., usually to accommodate bus schedules. The result can be wasted class time for whole groups of kids. Making matters worse, many kids have trouble readjusting their natural sleep rhythm. Dr. Richard Allen of Johns Hopkins University found that teens went to sleep at the same time whether they had to be at school by 7:30 a.m. or 9:30 a.m. The later-to-rise teens not only get more sleep, he says; they also get better grades. The obvious solution would be to start school later when kids hit puberty. But at school, there's what's obvious, and then there's tradition.

Why is this body of research rarely used in most American classrooms? Not many administrators or school-board members know it exists, says Linda Darling-Hammond, professor of education at Columbia University's Teachers College. In most states, neither teachers nor administrators are required to know much about how children learn in order to be certified. What's worse, she says, decisions to cut music or gym are often made by noneducators, whose concerns are more often monetary than educational. "Our school system was invented in the late 1800s, and little has changed," she says. "Can you imagine if the medical profession ran this way?"

With Pat Wingert *and* Mary Hager *in Washington*

Circuits in different regions of the brain mature at different times. As a result, different circuits are most sensitive to life's experiences at different ages. Give your children the stimulation they need when they need it, and anything's possible. Stumble, and all bets are off.

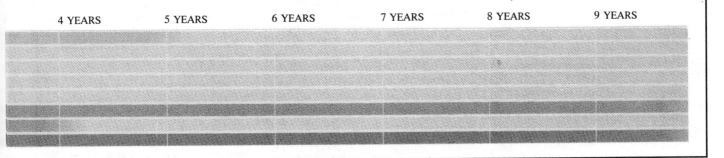

| 4 YEARS | 5 YEARS | 6 YEARS | 7 YEARS | 8 YEARS | 9 YEARS |

Stress and constant threats also rewire emotion circuits. These circuits are centered on the amygdala, a little almond-shaped structure deep in the brain whose job is to scan incoming sights and sounds for emotional content. According to a wiring diagram worked out by Joseph LeDoux of New York University, impulses from eye and ear reach the amygdala before they get to the rational, thoughtful neocortex. If a sight, sound or experience has proved painful before—Dad's drunken arrival home was followed by a beating—then the amygdala floods the circuits with neurochemicals before the higher brain knows what's happening. The more often this pathway is used, the easier it is to trigger: the mere memory of Dad may induce fear. Since the circuits can stay excited for days, the brain remains on high alert. In this state, says neuroscientist Bruce Perry of Baylor College of Medicine, more circuits attend to nonverbal cues—facial expressions, angry noises—that warn of impending danger. As a result, the cortex falls behind in development and has trouble assimilating complex information such as language.

Movement: Fetal movements begin at 7 weeks and peak between the 15th and 17th weeks. That is when regions of the brain controlling movement start to wire up. The critical period lasts a while: it takes up to two years for cells in the cerebellum, which controls posture and movement, to form functional circuits. "A lot of organization takes place using information gleaned from when the child moves about in the world," says William Greenough of the University of Illinois. "If you restrict activity you inhibit the formation of synaptic connections in the cerebellum." The child's initially spastic movements send a signal to the brain's motor cortex; the more the arm, for instance, moves, the stronger the circuit, and the better the brain will become at moving the arm intentionally and fluidly. The window lasts only a few years: a child immobilized in a body cast until the age of 4 will learn to walk eventually, but never smoothly.

THERE ARE MANY MORE CIRcuits to discover, and many more environmental influences to pin down. Still, neuro labs are filled with an unmistakable air of optimism these days. It stems from a growing understanding of how, at the level of nerve cells and molecules, the brain's circuits form. In the beginning, the brain-to-be consists of only a few advance scouts breaking trail: within a week of conception they march out of the embryo's "neural tube," a cylinder of cells extending from head to tail. Multiplying as they go (the brain adds an astonishing 250,000 neurons per minute during gestation), the neurons clump into the brain stem which commands heartbeat and breathing, build the little cerebellum at the back of the head which controls posture and movement, and form the grooved and rumpled cortex wherein thought and perception originate. The neural cells are so small, and the distance so great, that a neuron striking out for what will be the prefrontal cortex migrates a distance equivalent to a human's walking from New York to California, says developmental neurobiologist Mary Beth Hatten of Rockefeller University.

Only when they reach their destinations do these cells become true neurons. They grow a fiber called an axon that carries electrical signals. The axon might reach only to a neuron next door, or it might wend its way clear across to the other side of the brain. It is the axonal connections that form the brain's circuits. Genes determine the main highways along which axons travel to make their connection. But to reach particular target cells, axons follow chemical cues strewn along their path. Some of these chemicals attract: this way to the motor cortex! Some repel: no, *that* way to the olfactory cortex. By the fifth month of gestation most axons have reached their general destination. But like the prettiest girl in the bar, target cells attract way more suitors—axons—than they can accommodate.

How does the wiring get sorted out? The baby neurons fire electrical pulses once a minute, in a fit of what Berkeley's Shatz calls auto-dialing. If cells fire together, the target cells "ring" together. The target cells then release a flood of chemicals, called trophic factors, that strengthen the incipient connections. Active neurons respond better to trophic factors than inactive ones, Barbara Barres of Stanford University reported in October. So neurons that are quiet when others throb lose their grip on the target cell. "Cells that fire together wire together," says Shatz.

The same basic process continues after birth. Now, it is not an auto-dialer that sends signals, but stimuli from the senses. In experiments with rats, Illinois's Greenough found that animals raised with playmates and toys and other stimuli grow 25 percent more synapses than rats deprived of such stimuli.

Rats are not children, but all evidence suggests that the same rules of brain development hold. For decades Head Start has fallen short of the high hopes invested in it: the children's IQ gains fade after about three years. Craig Ramey of the University of Alabama suspected the culprit was timing: Head Start enrolls 2-, 3-, and 4-year-olds. So in 1972 he launched the Abecedarian Project. Children from 20 poor families were assigned to one of four groups: intensive early education in a day-care center from about 4 months to age 8, from 4 months to 5 years, from 5 to 8 years, or none at all. What does it mean to "educate" a 4-month-old? Nothing fancy: blocks, beads, talking to him, playing games such as peek-a-boo. As outlined in the book "Learningames,"* each of the 200-odd activities was designed to enhance cognitive, language, social or motor development. In a recent paper, Ramey and Frances Campbell of the University of North Carolina report that children enrolled in Abecedarian as preschoolers still scored higher in math and reading at the age of 15 than untreated children. The children still retained an average IQ edge of 4.6 points. The earlier the children were enrolled, the more enduring the gain. And intervention after age 5 conferred no IQ or academic benefit.

All of which raises a troubling question. If the windows of the mind close, for the most part, before we're out of elementary school, is all hope lost for children whose parents did not have them count beads to stimulate their math circuits, or babble to them to build their language loops? At one level, no: the brain retains the ability to learn throughout life, as witness anyone who was befuddled by Greek in college only to master it during retirement. But on a deeper level the news is sobering. Children whose neural circuits are not stimulated before kindergarten are never going to be what they could have been. "You want to say that it is never too late," says Joseph Sparling, who designed the Abecedarian curriculum. "But there seems to be something very special about the early years."

And yet . . . there is new evidence that certain kinds of intervention can reach even the older brain and, like a microscopic screwdriver, rewire broken circuits. In January, scientists led by Paula Tallal of Rutgers University and Michael Merzenich of UC San Francisco described a study of children who have "language-based learning disabilities"—reading problems. LLD affects 7 million children in the United States. Tallal has long argued that LLD arises from a child's inability to distinguish short, staccato sounds—such as "d" and "b." Normally, it takes neurons in the auditory cortex something like .015 second to respond to a signal from the ear, calm down and get ready to respond to the next sound; in LLD children, it takes five to 10 times as long. (Merzenich speculates that the defect might be the result of chronic middle-ear infections in infancy: the brain never "hears" sounds clearly and so fails to draw a sharp auditory map.) Short sounds such as "b" and "d" go by too fast—.04 second—to process. Unable to associate sounds with letters, the children develop reading problems.

The scientists drilled the 5- to 10-year-olds three hours a day with computer-produced sound that draws out short consonants, like an LP played too slow. The result: LLD children who were one to three years behind in language ability improved by a full two years after only four weeks. The improvement has lasted. The training, Merzenich suspect, redrew the wiring diagram in the children's auditory cortex to process first sounds. Their reading problems vanished like the sounds of the letters that, before, they never heard.

Such neural rehab may be the ultimate payoff of the discovery that the experiences of life are etched in the bumps and squiggles of the brain. For now, it is enough to know that we are born with a world of potential—potential that will be realized only if it is tapped. And that is challenge enough.

With MARY HAGER

*Joseph Sparling and Isabelle Lewis
(226 pages. Walker. $8.95).

To Be Intelligent

What does it mean to be broadly intelligent?
Our schools and communities need to develop this capacity in our young
people as they face the complex challenges of life today. Research on the
brain and its infinite complexity can help.

John Abbott

John Abbott is President of the 21st Century Learning Initiative, c/o Rothschild Natural Resources, 1101 Connecticut Ave., N.W., Suite 700, Washington, DC 20036 (e-mail: polska@erols.com).

For several summer holidays, when my three sons were young, we had swapped our home just outside Cambridge, England, with friends in Virginia. To our children, America was a land of long summer days, plenty of ice cream, and visits to national parks and historical sites.

Late one evening back in England, we were driving home from a day in the country with the children. My wife played a Garrison Keillor tape—the one describing his fictitious one-room schoolhouse in Minnesota. "At one end of the room there was a portrait of George Washington and at the other end one of Abraham Lincoln, beaming down at us like two long-lost friends," Keillor drawled in his best Lake Wobegon style.

"That's silly," piped up 7-year-old Tom. "They weren't alive at the same time, so how could they have been friends?"

I asked Tom how he knew that. "Well." he said, "when we went to Mount Vernon they said how sad it was that Washington didn't live into the 19th century—and you once told me Lincoln was born after Admiral

Nelson was killed at the Battle of Trafalgar." His logic, and the connections he had built, fascinated me.

Several years later, at a dinner party in Seattle, I recounted that story. "How I wish American elementary schools taught history as well as that!" mused our host, a professor of education.

"That's silly," said our adolescent Tom. "History lessons in school are boring. I just love everything to do with America!"

My wife interjected, "What's your favorite subject?"

"It's math, because my teacher always gets us to think about connections and patterns. That's really interesting; I can see how things come together."

Patterns and relationships, emotions, the need to make sense, intrinsic interest, formal and informal learning, history dates, and mathematical formulas—these elements in Tom's learning defy any logical structure. The process of learning is wondrously spectacular and messy, and it does not easily fit within a closely defined, classroom-based curriculum—particularly for adolescents.

Try as we might to accommodate children's spontaneous questions, too often their natural enthusiasm is dulled by the needs of the system for order. Nevertheless, the capacity for self-organization ("I want to think this out for myself") is valued more and more highly in our society, which

is changing so rapidly that today's questions are answered almost overnight. Some people call such an ability wits. In the north of England, people use an old expression—*nous,* a level of common sense that goes beyond book learning. It's what the brain is all about.

The Complex Workings of the Human Brain

Medical and cognitive sciences, new technologies and pedagogic research are helping us appreciate how the brain works. The human brain is the most complex living organism on Earth. Coveney and Highfield (1995) call it the "Cathedral of Complexity." Although it weighs only about three pounds. it contains billions of cells (neurons). The total length of the "wiring" between the neurons is about 100,000 kilometers (62,150 miles). To illustrate: The total number of neurons is estimated to be greater than all the trees, in all the forests, on the entire Earth's surface. The number of synaptic connections between neurons may be more than all the leaves on those trees. Susan Greenfield, when lecturing a group of 14-year-olds at the Royal Institution in London, compared the memory capability of all those neurons with that of 1,000 CD-ROMs, each one containing an entire *Encarta Encyclopedia.* The brain is, literally, a mind-boggling thought. Every human—including the

From *Educational Leadership,* March 1997, pp. 6-10. © 1997 by the Association for Supervision and Curriculum Development (ASCD). All rights reserved. Reprinted by permission.

most difficult adolescent—has just such a brain.

Biologists can tell us much about brain chemistry; but for educational practice, the concept of complexity helps us understand the layers of organization within the brain that act together, apparently miraculously, to handle not only memory, but also vision, learning, emotion, and consciousness.

The structures and processes of the brain are a direct response to the complexity of environmental factors faced by humans since our species appeared. Until about half a million years ago, the brain changed slowly through evolution. But our brains started to grow more rapidly as we learned to use language. Only within the last 30,000–60,000 years have we developed the capacity to be broadly intelligent.

What does broad intelligence mean? Archaeology and cultural anthropology show that humans developed many discrete skills over about a million years (social intelligence, technological intelligence, natural history intelligence, language intelligence); but only recently—say, in the past 30,000 years—have we been able to combine these skills to create the broad intelligence that now gives us our amazing versatility. The cave paintings discovered by M. Jean-Marie Chauvet in southern France in 1994 date from this period.[1] Highly sophisticated, they bring social, technological, and natural history intelligences together. They seem to have leapt out of nothing—we know of no earlier primitive art. With the emergence of broad intelligence, modern man was created (Mithen 1996). Archaeology is starting to endorse Howard Gardner's call to educators to work with all of children's many forms of intelligence. That is what gives us our creativity.

How the Brain Flows

The brain can handle many situations simultaneously; historical facts are fitted into mathematical patterning when the brain is comfortably challenged in a nonthreatening situation. Psychologists and cognitive scientists call this a state of *flow*—a state you reach when you become so engaged in what you are doing that all tasks seem within your capability (Csikszentmihalyi 1990). This state enables us to react to our environment while also thinking about many abstract matters. The brain handles this complexity through several layers of self-organization and vast interconnecting networks. Once established, traces of these networks appear to survive almost indefinitely and are frequently used as solutions to new problems and as the basis for new ideas. That is how, unconsciously, 7-year-old Tom built up his understanding of historical chronology.

Neurologists can now see some forms of memory in operation. Through magnetic resonance imaging (MRI), they watch specific patterns of activity within the brain light up on a computer screen. To the researchers' surprise, memory exists in many locations in the brain, not just one place. Some people liken memory to a hologram where the whole exists in all the parts. Memory traces seem to follow neural networks that the individuals—at the time of original thought—found most to their advantage, even if only for a short time. Nothing is ever irretrievably lost, though we still do not know how we can access memory more effectively at some life stages than at others. If part of the network is later activated, the brain may well question why it is not being asked to complete the original set of connections.

Going with the Grain of the Brain

All brain activity occurs spontaneously, automatically, in response to challenge. The brain does not have to be taught to learn. To thrive, the brain needs plenty of stimulation, and it needs suitable feedback systems. Effective learning depends on emotional energy. We are driven (the ancestral urges of long ago) as much by emotion as by logic. Children—and adults—who learn about things that matter to them are far more resilient and determined when they face problems than are people who seek external rewards. When in trouble, people with intrinsic motivation search for novel solutions, whereas extrinsically motivated people look for external causes to blame for their failure. The brain is essentially a survival system, and emotional well-being may be more essential for survival than intellectual well-being.

Too much stimulation, however, at any stage in life, turns a challenge into a threat. The brain deals with threat easily. It just turns off—as MRI dramatically shows. Give a person an interesting mental task, and many parts of the brain are seen to light up. Persistently insult that person, and the brain goes into a form of mental defense. The lights literally go out. Downshifting—a phenomenon long recognized by psychologists—is a strictly physiological defense mechanism. Research suggests that working effectively at a challenging task requires significant amounts of reflection—a critical part of brain functioning (Diamond 1995).

No two brains are exactly alike; thus, no enriched environment will completely satisfy any two people for an extended period. Challenge and interactivity are essential. Passive observation is not enough. "Tell me and I forget. Show me and I remember. Let me do it and I understand," says the ancient Chinese proverb.

Learning What Matters

With our new understanding of the brain, we are in an excellent position to make it possible for people to become better learners. The implications of this new knowledge for society and for the economy are massive.

Ernest Hall, a successful English entrepreneur understands the transforming power of learning. He was born in a northern industrial town near Manchester. His parents knew long periods of unemployment in the textile trade. One afternoon, when he was 8 years old, his teacher played a recording of "Apollo's Lyre." Ernest was spellbound; here was a form of beauty that was to transform his life. His family managed to obtain an old piano. By age 12, Ernest played so well that his parents urged him to leave school and earn his living by playing the piano in pubs. "No," said Ernest, "I love music too much to trivialize it. I will make enough money to play the piano properly."

That is exactly what he did. For years he worked in the textile industry, with great success—and continued practicing the piano. By his early 50s, he had bought the closed-down Dean Clough Mills and created an amazing complex that today provides employment for more than 3,000 people in an array of high-tech and other businesses, including a mill—and that reserves a quarter of its space for art galleries, working studios, concert halls, and exhibition spaces. This complex vividly demonstrates that living, learning, and working—beauty and economic productivity—are all deeply interconnected.

To celebrate his 65th birthday, Ernest fulfilled a dream: He performed Bartok's First, Second, and Third Piano Concertos, accompanied by the Leeds Sinfonia Orchestra. His CDs sell alongside those of the greatest pianists of our day.

Ernest believes in the potential of all young people to develop their particular abilities. "I discovered my interest," he says, "before the crushing routines of my little school would have reduced me to a mere cog in a machine. Ability is not innate. It exists like a shadow of ourselves when we are willing to stand in front of a bright light. . . . We must say to every child, 'You are special. You are unique; but to develop your genius you have to work at it, and stick with it year after year.' "

My son Tom comes from a privileged background. Young Ernest certainly did not. But creativity does not depend on privilege, nor does learning necessarily follow from teaching. Thus the old plaint of the teacher: "I taught them everything I ever knew, but they were so uninterested that they learned nothing!" Contrast that with David Perkins (1992), writing in *Smart Schools:* "Learning is a consequence of thinking" (p. 78). We should remind every child of this statement each day.

How Do We Create Intelligence?

The understanding of learning will become the key issue of our time. The creation of intellectual capital has been going on with every generation for millions of years, with perhaps one exception—and that is what has happened over the past five or six generations.

Until the early 1800s, people learned in real-life, on-the-job situations. Then our industrial society required people to develop no more than a range of functional skills (such as reading, writing, and calculation) that allowed them to fit into the dull routines of manufacturing. Schools ignored the more inclusive skills that enabled people to make sense of things for themselves in earlier ages. For much of the past century or more, the spontaneous, deep learning of the Toms and Ernests of this world has existed largely outside the formal education system of Western industrial nations.

The ability to think about your own thinking (metacognition) is essential in a world of continuous change. Through metacognition, we can develop skills that are genuinely transferable. These skills are linked to reflective intelligence, or wits. As never before, the human race needs all the wits it can muster.

Being able to step back as a specialist and reflect—to honestly reevaluate what you are doing from a general perspective—is naturally developed in the rich, collaborative, problem-solving, and uncertain world of the apprentice, as opposed to the tasks, schedules, and measurable activities of the formal classroom. Expertise requires much content

knowledge—and metacognition. This deep reflective capability is what helps us develop new possibilities.

A New Model of Learning

A model of learning that could deliver expertise is ours for the asking. It would work on the basis of the biological concept of weaning—giving very young children plentiful help and direction, and then reducing this direction progressively as children master more and more skills. In this model, as adolescence ends, young people will already have taken full responsibility for directing their own learning. The age of 18 should mark not the beginning of independent learning but the age at which young people perfect that art and know how to exercise it responsibly.

Formal schooling, therefore, must start a dynamic process through which pupils are progressively weaned from their dependence on teachers and institutions and given the confidence to manage their own learning. Surely it should be the child who is tired at the end of the term, and not the teacher.

To achieve this model of learning, we must reappraise the school system and its current use of resources and turn it upside down and inside out. Early childhood learning matters enormously. We must progressively show the youngest children that a lesson about American history, for example, can also be a lesson about how to learn how to learn and remember. As children grow older, they start to become their own teachers. The older the child becomes, the more he or she becomes a productive resource of value to the community (Abbott 1994).

In such a model, we should create smaller classes in the early years of elementary education (using developmentally appropriate styles of teaching) and progressively provide children with an ever richer array of learning resources and situations. Learning need not be confined to an institution—it must become a total community responsibility. It is not merely teachers who can teach, not just pupils who need to learn, and certainly not just the classroom that can be the major access point to knowledge, information, and skills.

Our new understanding about learning is paralleled by radical developments in technology. The technological revolution holds the power to alter our education system, our work, and our culture. Indeed, this revolution puts learning and our traditional, conventional education systems on a collision course. The essence of the coming integrated, universal, multimedia digital network is discovery—the empowerment of the human mind to learn spontaneously, independently, and collaboratively, without coercion.

Such a new learning environment would be highly compatible with the natural functioning of the brain; with what we know about human aspirations; and, in particular, with the adolescent's need to feel involved and of value. It offers the greatest hope for an improvement in people's intelligence and the development of thoughtfulness.

The current crisis in learning has originated not so much in the failure of our classrooms as in the failure of our communities to capture the imagination, involvement, and active participation of young people. A society motivated by a vision of thoughtfulness will quickly recognize that broadly intelligent young people will

revitalize the whole community. We must escape from the 19th-century assumption that learning and schooling are synonymous. Good schools alone will never be good enough—we need communities that think differently, work differently, and are even designed and built differently.[2]

Such communities would make for a better, more exciting world in which living, working, and learning

come together again and recreate vibrant, self-sustaining communities. I would love to live in such a world.

1. The French Ministry of Culture Web site includes photos of the Chauvet cave drawings at http://www.culture.fr/culture/gvpda-en.htm.
2. This article is based on the work of The 21st Century Learning Initiative (draft synthesis, December 1996).

Resources

Abbott, J. (1994). *Learning Makes Sense: Recreating Education for a Changing Future.* London: Education 2000.

Bereiter, C., and M. Scardamalia. (1993). *Surpassing Ourselves: An Inquiry into the Nature and Implications of Expertise.* Chicago: Open Court.

Bruer, J. (1993). *Schools for Thought: A Science of Learning in the Classroom.* Cambridge: Massachusetts Institute of Technology Press.

Caine, R. N., and G. Caine. (1991). *Making Connections: Teaching and the Human Brain.* Alexandria, Va.: ASCD.

Calvin, W. H. (1996). *How Brains Think: Evolving Intelligence, Then and Now.* New York: Basic Books.

Coveney, P., and R. Highfield. (1995). *Frontiers of Complexity: The Search for Order in a Chaotic World.* New York: Fawcett Columbine.

Csikszentmihalyi, M. (1990). *Flow: The Psychology of Optimal Experience.* New York: Harper Perennial.

Diamond, M. (July/September 1995). "The Significance of Enrichment." *The In Report.*

Goleman, D. (1995). *Emotional Intelligence: Why It Can Matter More Than IQ.* London: Bloomsbury.

Greenspan, S. (1996). *The Growth of the Mind, and the Endangered Origins of Intelligence.* New York: Addison Wesley.

Kohn, A. (1993). *Punished by Rewards.* Boston: Houghton Mifflin.

Kotulak. R. (1996). *Inside the Brain.* Chicago: Andrews and McMeel.

Le Doux, J. (1996). *The Emotional Brain: The Mysterious Underpinnings of Emotional Life.* New York: Simon and Schuster.

Mithen, S. (1996). *The Prehistory of the Mind.* London: Thomas and Hudson.

Perkins, D. (1992). *Smart Schools: From Training Memories to Educating Minds.* New York: Free Press.

Perkins, D. (1995). *Outsmarting IQ: The Emerging Science of Learnable Intelligence.* New York: Free Press.

Sylwester, R. (1995). *A Celebration of Neurons: An Educator's Guide to the Human Brain.* Alexandria, Va.: ASCD.

Wills, C. (1993). *The Runaway Brain: The Evolution of Human Uniqueness.* London: Basic Books.

Reflections on Multiple Intelligences

Myths and Messages

Mr. Gardner discusses seven myths that have grown up about multiple intelligences and attempts to set the record straight by presenting seven complementary "realities."

HOWARD GARDNER

HOWARD GARDNER is a professor of education and co-director of Project Zero at the Harvard Graduate School of Education and an adjunct professor of neurology at the Boston University School of Medicine. For their comments on an earlier draft of this article, he wishes to thank Melissa Brand, Patricia Bolanos, Thomas Hatch, Thomas Hoerr, Mara Krechevsky, Mindy Kornhaber, Jerome Murphy, Bruce Torff, Julie Viens, and Ellen Winner. Preparation of this article was supported by the MacArthur Foundation and the Spencer Foundation.

A SILENCE OF A DECADE'S LENGTH is sometimes a good idea. I published *Frames of Mind,* an introduction to the theory of multiple intelligences (MI theory) in 1983.[1] Because I was critical of current views of intelligences within the discipline of psychology, I expected to stir controversy among my fellow psychologists. This expectation was not disappointed.

I was unprepared for the large and mostly positive reaction to the theory among educators. Naturally I was gratified by this response and was stimulated to undertake some projects exploring the implications of MI theory. I also took pleasure from—and was occasionally moved by—the many attempts to institute an MI approach to education in schools and classrooms. By and large, however, except for a few direct responses to criticisms,[2] I did not speak up about new thoughts concerning the theory itself.

In 1993 my self-imposed silence was broken in two ways. My publisher issued a 10th-anniversary edition of *Frames of Mind,* to which I contributed a short, reflective introductory essay. In tandem with that release, the publisher issued *Multiple Intelligences: The Theory in Practice,* a set of articles chronicling some of the experiments undertaken in the wake of MI theory—mostly projects pursued by colleagues at Harvard Project Zero, but also other MI initiatives.[3] This collection gave me the opportunity to answer some other criticisms leveled against MI theory and to respond publicly to some of the most frequently asked questions.

In the 12 years since *Frames of Mind* was published, I have heard, read, and seen several hundred different interpretations of what MI theory is and how it can be applied in the schools.[4] Until now, I have been content to let MI theory take on a life of its own. As I saw it, I had issued an "ensemble of ideas" (or "memes") to the outer world, and I was inclined to let those "memes" fend for themselves.[5] Yet, in light of my own reading and observations I believe that the time has come for me to issue a set of new "memes" of my own.

In the next part of this article, I will discuss seven myths that have grown up about multiple intelligences and, by putting forth seven complementary "realities," I will attempt to set the record straight. Then, in the third part of the article, reflecting on my observations of MI experiments in the schools, I will describe three primary ways in which education can be enhanced by a multiple intelligences perspective.

In what follows, I make no attempt to isolate MI theory from MI practice. "Multiple intelligences" began as a theory but was almost immediately put to practical use. The commerce between theory and practice has been ready, continuous, and, for the most part, productive.

Myths of Multiple Intelligences

Myth 1. Now that seven intelligences have been identified, one can—and perhaps should—create seven tests and secure seven scores.

Reality 1. MI theory represents a critique of "psychometrics-as-usual." A battery of MI tests is inconsistent with the major tenets of the theory.

Comment. My concept of intelligences is an outgrowth of accumulating knowledge about the human brain and about human cultures, not the result of a priori definitions or of factor analyses of test scores. As such, it becomes crucial that intelligences be assessed in ways that are "intelligent-fair," that is, in ways that examine the intelligence directly rather than through the lens of linguistic or logical intelligence (as ordinary paper-and-pencil tests do).

Thus, if one wants to look at spatial intelligence, one should allow an individual to explore a terrain for a while and see whether she can find her way around it reliably. Or if one wants to examine musical intelligence, one should expose an individual to a new melody in a reasonably familiar idiom and see how readily the person can learn to sing it, recognize it, transform it, and the like.

Assessing multiple intelligences is not a high priority in every setting. But when it is necessary or advisable to assess an individual's intelligences, it is best to do so in a comfortable setting with materials (and cultural roles) that are familiar to that individual. These conditions are at variance with our general conception of testing as a decontextualized exercise using materials that are unfamiliar by design, but there is no reason in principle why an "intelligence-fair" set of measures cannot be devised. The production of such useful tools has been our goal in such projects as Spectrum, Arts PROPEL, and Practical Intelligence for School.[6]

Myth 2. An intelligence is the same as a domain or a discipline.

Reality 2. An intelligence is a new kind of construct, and it should not be confused with a domain or a discipline.

Comment. I must shoulder a fair part of the blame for the propagation of the second myth. In writing *Frames of Mind,* I was not as careful as I should have been in distinguishing intelligences from other related concepts. As I have now come to understand, largely through my interactions with Mihaly Csikszentmihalyi and David Feldman,[7] an *intelligence* is a biological and psychological potential; that potential is capable of being realized to a greater or lesser extent as a consequence of the experiential, cultural, and motivational factors that affect a person.

In contrast, a *domain* is an organized set of activities within a culture, one typically characterized by a specific symbol system and its attendant operations. Any cultural activity in which individuals participate on more than a casual basis, and in which degrees of expertise can be identified and nurtured, should be considered a domain. Thus, physics, chess, gardening, and rap music are all domains in Western culture. Any domain can be realized through the use of several intelligences; thus the domain of musical performance involves bodily-kinesthetic and personal as well as musical intelligences. By the same token, a particular intelligence, like spatial intelligence, can be put to work in a myriad of domains, ranging from

sculpture to sailing to neuroanatomical investigations.

Finally, a *field* is the set of individuals and institutions that judge the acceptability and creativity of products fashioned by individuals (with their characteristic intelligences) within established or new domains. Judgments of quality cannot be made apart from the operation of members of a field, though it is worth noting that both the members of a field and the criteria that they employ can and do change over time.

Myth 3. An intelligence is the same as a "learning style," a "cognitive style," or a "working style."

> *The commerce between theory and practice has been continuous and mostly productive.*

Reality 3. The concept of *style* designates a general approach that an individual can apply equally to every conceivable content. In contrast, an *intelligence* is a capacity, with its component processes, that is geared to a specific content in the world (such as musical sounds or spatial patterns).

Comment. To see the difference between an intelligence and a style, consider this contrast. If a person is said to have a "reflective" or an "intuitive" style, this designation assumes that the individual will be reflective or intuitive with all manner of content, ranging from language to music to social analysis. However, such an assertion reflects an empirical assumption that actually needs to be investigated. It might well be the case that an individual is reflective with music but fails to be reflective in a domain that requires mathematical thinking or that a person is highly intuitive in the social domain but not in the least intuitive when it comes to mathematics or mechanics.

In my view, the relation between my concept of intelligence and the various conceptions of style needs to be worked

out empirically, on a style-by-style basis. We cannot assume that "style" means the same thing to Carl Jung, Jerome Kagan, Tony Gregoric, Bernice McCarthy, and other inventors of stylistic terminology.[8] There is little authority for assuming that an individual who evinces a style in one milieu or with one content will necessarily do so with other diverse contents—and even less authority for equating styles with intelligences.

Myth 4. MI Theory is not empirical. (A variant of Myth 4 alleges that MI theory is empirical but has been disproved.)

Reality 4. MI theory is based wholly on empirical evidence and can be revised on the basis of new empirical findings.

Comment. Anyone who puts forth Myth 4 cannot have read *Frames of Mind.* Literally hundreds of empirical studies were reviewed in that book, and the actual intelligences were identified and delineated on the basis of empirical findings. The seven intelligences described in *Frames of Mind* represented my best-faith effort to identify mental abilities of a scale that could be readily discussed and critiqued.

No empirically based theory is ever established permanently. All claims are at risk in the light of new findings. In the last decade, I have collected and reflected on empirical evidence that is relevant to the claims of MI theory, 1983 version. Thus work on the development in children of a "theory of mind," as well as the study of pathologies in which an individual loses a sense of social judgment, has provided fresh evidence for the importance and independence of interpersonal intelligence.[9] In contrast, the finding of a possible link between musical and spatial thinking has caused me to reflect on the possible relations between faculties that had previously been thought to be independent.[10]

Many other lines of evidence could be mentioned here. The important point is that MI theory is constantly being reconceptualized in terms of new findings from the laboratory and from the field (see also Myth 7).

Myth 5. MI theory is incompatible with *g* (general intelligence),[11] with hereditarian accounts, or with environmental accounts of the nature and causes of intelligence.

Reality 5. MI theory questions not the existence but the province and explanatory power of *g*. By the same token, MI theory is neutral on the question of heritability of specific intelligences, instead underscoring the centrality of genetic/environmental interactions.

Comment. Interest in *g* comes chiefly from those who are probing scholastic intelligence and those who traffic in the correlations between test scores. (Recently people have become interested in the possible neurophysiological underpinnings of g^{12} and, sparked by the publication of *The Bell Curve*,[13] in the possible social consequences of "low *g*.") While I have been critical of much of the research in the *g* tradition, I do not consider the study of *g* to be scientifically improper, and I am willing to accept the utility of *g* for certain theoretical purposes. My interest, obviously, centers on those intelligences and intellectual processes that are not covered by $g.^{14}$

While a major animating force in psychology has been the study of the heritability of intelligence(s), my inquiries have not been oriented in this direction. I do not doubt that human abilities—and human differences—have a genetic base. Can any serious scientist question this at the end of the 20th century? And I believe that behavioral genetic studies, particularly of twins reared apart, can illuminate certain issues. However, along with most biologically informed scientists, I reject the "inherited versus learned" dichotomy and instead stress the interaction, from the moment of conception, between genetic and environmental factors.

Myth 6. MI theory so broadens the notion of intelligence that it includes all psychological constructs and thus vitiates the usefulness, as well as the usual connotation, of the term.

Reality 6. This statement is simply wrong. I believe that it is the standard definition of intelligence that narrowly constricts our view, treating a certain form of scholastic performance as if it encompassed the range of human capacities and leading to disdain for those who happen not to be psychometrically bright. Moreover, I reject the distinction between talent and intelligence; in my view, what we call "intelligence" in the vernacular is simply a certain set of "talents" in the linguistic and/or logical-mathematical spheres.

Comment. MI theory is about the intellect, the human mind in its cognitive aspects. I believe that a treatment in terms of a number of semi-independent intelligences presents a more sustainable conception of human thought than one that posits a single "bell curve" of intellect.

Note, however, that MI theory makes no claims whatsoever to deal with issues beyond the intellect. MI

theory is not, and does not pretend to be, about personality, will, morality, attention, motivation, and other psychological constructs. Note as well that MI theory is not connected to any set of morals or values. An intelligence can be put to an ethical or an antisocial use. Poet and playwright Johann Wolfgang von Goethe and Nazi propagandist Joseph Goebbels were both masters of the German language, but how different were the uses to which they put their talents!

> *There is no point in assuming that every topic can be effectively approached in at least seven ways.*

Myth 7. There is an eighth (or ninth or 10th) intelligence.

Reality 7. Not in my writings so far. But I am working on it.

Comment. For the reasons suggested above, I thought it wise not to attempt to revise the principal claims of MI theory before the 1983 version of the theory had been debated. But recently, I have turned my attention to possible additions to the list. If I were to rewrite *Frames of Mind* today, I would probably add an eighth intelligence—the intelligence of the naturalist. It seems to me that the individual who is able readily to recognize flora and fauna, to make other consequential distinctions in the natural world, and to use this ability productively (in hunting, in farming, in biological science) is exercising an important intelligence and one that is not adequately encompassed in the current list. Individuals like Charles Darwin or E. O. Wilson embody the naturalist's intelligence, and, in our consuming culture, youngsters exploit their naturalist's intelligence as they make acute discriminations among cars, sneakers, or hairstyles.

I have read in several secondary sources that there is a spiritual intelligence and, indeed, that I have endorsed a spiritual intelligence. That statement is not true. It is true that I have become interested in understanding better what is meant by "spirituality" and by "spiritual individuals"; as my understanding improves, I expect to write about this topic. Whether or not it proves appropriate to add "spirituality" to the list of intelligences, this human capacity certainly deserves discussion and study in nonfringe psychological circles.

Messages About MI in the Classroom

If one were to continue adding myths to the list, a promising candidate would read: There is a single educational approach based on MI theory.

I trust that I have made it clear over the years that I do not subscribe to this myth.[16] On the contrary, MI theory is in no way an educational prescription. There is always a gulf between psychological claims about how the mind works and educational practices, and such a gulf is especially apparent in a theory that was developed without specific educational goals in mind. Thus, in educational discussions, I have always taken the position that educators are in the best position to determine the uses to which MI theory can and should be put.

Indeed, contrary to much that has been written, MI theory does not incorporate a position on tracking, gifted education, interdisciplinary curricula, the layout of the school day, the length of the school year, or many other "hot button" educational issues. I have tried to encourage certain "applied MI efforts," but in general my advice has echoed the traditional Chinese adage "Let a hundred flowers bloom." And I have often been surprised and delighted by the fragrance of some of these fledgling plants—for example, the use of a "multiple intelligences curriculum" in order to facilitate communication between youngsters drawn from different cultures or the conveying of pivotal principles in biology or social studies through a dramatic performance designed and staged by students.

I have become convinced, however, that while there is no "right way" to conduct a multiple intelligences education, some current efforts go against the spirit of my formulation and embody one or more of the myths sketched above. Let me mention a few applications that have jarred me.

• *The attempt to teach all concepts or subjects using all the intelligences.* As I indicate below, most topics can be powerfully approached in a number of ways. But there is no point in assuming that every topic can be effectively approached in at least seven ways, and it is a waste of effort and time to attempt to do this.

• *The belief that it suffices, in and of itself, just to go through the motions of exercising a certain intelligence.* I have seen classes in which children are encouraged simply to move their arms or to run around, on the assumption that exercising one's body represents in itself some kind of MI statement. Don't read me as saying that exercise is a bad thing; it is not. But random muscular movements have nothing to do with the cultivation of the mind . . . or even of the body!

• *The use of materials associated with an intelligence as background.* In some classes, children are encouraged to read or to carry out math exercises while music is playing in the background. Now I myself like to work with music in the background. But unless I focus on the performance (in which case the composition is no longer serving as background), the music's function is unlikely to be different from that of a dripping faucet or a humming fan.

• *The use of intelligences primarily as mnemonic devices.* It may well be the case that it is easier to remember a list if one sings it or even if one dances while reciting it. I have nothing against such aids to memory. However, these uses of the materials of an intelligence are essentially trivial. What is not trivial—as I argue below—is to think musically or to draw on some of the structural aspects of music in order to illuminate concepts like biological evolution or historical cycles.

• *The conflating of intelligences with other desiderata.* This practice is particularly notorious when it comes to the personal intelligences. Interpersonal intelligence has to do with understanding other people, but it is often distorted as a license for cooperative learning or applied to individuals who are extroverted. Intrapersonal intelligence has to do with understanding oneself, but it is often distorted as a rationale for self-esteem programs or applied to individuals who are loners or introverted. One receives the strong impression that individuals who use the terms in this promiscuous way have never read my writings on intelligence.

When I visit an "MI school," I look for signs of personalization.

• *The direct evaluation (or even grading) of intelligences, without regard to context or content.* Intelligences ought to be seen at work when individuals are carrying out productive activities that are valued in a culture. And that is how reporting of learning and mastery in general should take place. I see little point in grading individuals in terms of how "linguistic" or how "bodily-kinesthetic" they are; such a practice is likely to introduce a new and unnecessary form of tracking and labeling. As a parent (or as a supporter of education living in the community), I am interested in the *uses* to which children's intelligences are put; reporting should have this focus.

Note that it is reasonable, for certain purposes, to indicate that a child seems to have a relative strength in one intelligence and a relative weakness in another. However, these descriptions should be mobilized in order to help students perform better in meaningful activities and perhaps even to show that a label was premature or erroneous.

Having illustrated some problematic applications of MI theory, let me now indicate three more positive ways in which MI can be—and has been—used in the schools.

1. *The cultivation of desired capabilities.* Schools should cultivate those skills and capacities that are valued in the community and in the broader society. Some of these desired roles are likely to highlight specific intelligences, including ones that have usually been given short shrift in the schools. If, say, the community believes

that children should be able to perform on a musical instrument, then the cultivation of musical intelligence toward that end becomes a value of the school. Similarly, emphasis on such capacities as taking into account the feelings of others, being able to plan one's own life in a reflective manner, or being able to find one's way around an unfamiliar terrain are likely to result in an emphasis on the cultivation of interpersonal, intrapersonal, and spatial intelligences respectively.

2. *Approaching a concept, subject matter, or discipline in a variety of ways.* Along with many other school reformers, I am convinced that schools attempt to cover far too much material and that superficial understandings (or nonunderstandings) are the inevitable result. It makes far more sense to spend a significant amount of time on key concepts, generative ideas, and essential questions and to allow students to become thoroughly familiar with these notions and their implications.

Once the decision has been made to dedicate time to particular items, it then becomes possible to approach those topics or notions in a variety of ways. Not necessarily seven ways, but in a number of ways that prove pedagogically appropriate for the topic at hand. Here is where MI theory comes in. As I argue in *The Unschooled Mind*, nearly every topic can be approached in a variety of ways, ranging from the telling of a story, to a formal argument, to an artistic exploration, to some kind of "hands-on" experiment or simulation. Such pluralistic approaches should be encouraged.[17]

When a topic has been approached from a number of perspectives, three desirable outcomes ensue. First, because children do not all learn in the same way, more children will be reached. I term this desirable state of affairs "multiple windows leading into the same room." Second, students secure a sense of what it is like to be an expert when they behold that a teacher can represent knowledge in a number of different ways and discover that they themselves are also capable of more than a single representation of a specified content. Finally, since understanding can also be demonstrated in more than one way, a pluralistic approach opens up the possibility that students can display their new understandings—as well as their continuing difficulties—in ways that are comfortable for them and accessible to others. Performance-based examinations and exhibitions are tailor-made for the foregrounding of a student's multiple intelligences.

3. *The personalization of education.* Without a doubt, one of the reasons that MI theory has attracted attention in the educational community is because of its ringing endorsement of an ensemble of propositions: we are not all the same; we do not all have the same kinds of minds; education works most effectively for most individuals if these differences in mentation and strengths are taken into account rather than denied or ignored. I have always believed that the heart of the MI perspective—in theory and in practice—inheres in taking human differences seriously. At the theoretical level, one acknowledges that all individuals cannot be profitably arrayed on a single intellectual dimension. At the practical level, one acknowledges that any uniform educational approach is likely to serve only a minority of children.

When I visit an "MI school," I look for signs of personalization: evidence that all involved in the educational encounter take such differences among human beings seriously; evidence that they construct curricula, pedagogy, and assessment insofar as possible in the light of these differences. All the MI posters, indeed all the references to me personally, prove to be of little avail if the youngsters continue to be treated in homogenized fashion. By the same token, whether or not members of the staff have even heard of MI theory, I would be happy to send my children to a school with the following characteristics: differences among youngsters are taken seriously, knowledge about differences is shared with children and parents, children gradually assume responsibility for their own learning, and materials that are worth knowing are presented in ways that afford each child the maximum opportunity to master those materials and to show others (and themselves) what they have learned and understood.

Closing Comments

I am often asked for my views about schools that are engaged in MI efforts. The implicit question may well be: "Aren't you upset by some of the applications that are carried out in your name?"

In truth, I do not expect that initial efforts to apply any new ideas are going to be stunning. Human experimentation is slow, difficult, and filled with zigs and zags. Attempts to apply any set of innovative ideas will sometimes be half-hearted, superficial, even wrongheaded.

For me the crucial question concerns what has happened in a school (or class) two, three, or four years after it has made a commitment to an MI approach. Often, the initiative will be long since forgotten—the fate, for better or worse, of most educational experiments. Sometimes, the school has gotten stuck in a rut, repeating the same procedures of the first days without having drawn any positive or negative lessons from this exercise. Needless to say, I am not happy with either of these outcomes.

I cherish an educational setting in which discussions and applications of MI have catalyzed a more fundamental consideration of schooling—its overarching purposes, its conceptions of what a productive life will be like in the future, its pedagogical methods, and its educational outcomes, particularly in the context of the values of that specific community. Such examination generally leads to more thoughtful schooling. Visits with other schools and more extended forms of networking among MI enthusiasts (and critics) constitute important parts of this building process. If as a result of these discussions and experiments, a more personalized education is the outcome, I feel that the heart of MI theory has been embodied. And if this personalization is fused with a commitment to the achievement of worthwhile (and attainable) educational understandings for all children, then the basis for a powerful education has indeed been laid.

The MI endeavor is a continuing and changing one. There have emerged over the years new thoughts about the theory, new understandings and misunderstandings, and new applications, some very inspired, some less so. Especially gratifying to me has been the demonstration that this process is dynamic and interactive: no one, not even its creator, has a monopoly on MI wisdom or foolishness. Practice is enriched by theory, even as theory is transformed in the light of the fruits and frustrations of practice. The burgeoning of a community that takes MI issues seriously is not only a source of pride to me but also the best guarantor that the theory will continue to live in the years ahead.

1. Howard Gardner, *Frames of Mind: The Theory of Multiple Intelligences* (New York: Basic Books, 1983). A 10th-anniversary edition, with a new introduction, was published in 1993.

2. Howard Gardner, "On Discerning New Ideas in Psychology," *New Ideas in Psychology,* vol. 3, 1985, pp. 101–4; and idem, "Symposium on the Theory of Multiple Intelligences," in David N. Perkins, Jack Lochhead, and John C. Bishop, eds., *Thinking: The Second International Conference* (Hillsdale, N.J.: Erlbaum, 1983), pp. 77–101.

3. Howard Gardner, *Multiple Intelligences: The Theory in Practice* (New York: Basic Books, 1993).

4. For a bibliography through 1992, see the appendices to Gardner, *Multiple Intelligences.*

5. The term "memes" is taken from Richard Dawkins, *The Selfish Gene* (Oxford: Oxford University Press, 1976).

6. See Gardner, *Multiple Intelligences.*

7. Mihaly Csikszentmihalyi, "Society, Culture, and Person: A Systems View of Creativity." in Robert J. Sternberg, ed., *The Nature of Creativity* (New York: Cambridge University Press, 1988), pp. 325–39; idem, *Creativity* (New York: HarperCollins, forthcoming); David H. Feldman, "Creativity: Dreams, Insights, and Transformations," in Sternberg, op. cit., pp. 271–97; and David H. Feldman, Mihaly Csikszentmihalyi, and Howard Gardner, *Changing the World: A Framework for the Study of Creativity* (Westport, Conn.: Greenwood, 1994).

8. For a comprehensive discussion of the notion of cognitive style, see Nathan Kogan, "Stylistic Variation in Childhood and Adolescence," in Paul Mussen, ed., *Handbook of Child Psychology,* vol. 3 (New York: Wiley, 1983). pp. 630–706.

9. For writings pertinent to the personal intelligences, see Janet Astington, *The Child's Discovery of the Mind* (Cambridge, Mass.: Harvard University Press, 1993); and Antonio Damasio, *Descartes' Error* (New York: Grosset/Putnam, 1994).

10. On the possible relation between musical and spatial intelligence, see Frances Rauscher, G. L. Shaw, and X. N. Ky, "Music and Spatial Task Performance," *Nature,* 14 October 1993, p. 611.

11. The most thorough exposition of g can be found in the writings of Arthur Jensen. See, for example, *Bias in Mental Testing* (New York: Free Press, 1980). For a critique, see Stephen J. Gould, *The Mismeasure of Man* (New York: Norton, 1981).

12. Interest in the neurophysiological bases of g is found in Arthur Jensen, "Why Is Reaction Time Correlated with Psychometric 'G'?," *Current Directions of Psychological Science,* vol. 2, 1993, pp. 53–56.

13. Richard Herrnstein and Charles Murray. *The Bell Curve* (New York: Free Press, 1994).

14. For my view on intelligences not covered by $g,$ see Howard Gardner, "Review of Richard Herrnstein and Charles Murray, *The Bell Curve,*" *The American Prospect,* Winter 1995, pp. 71–80.

15. On behavioral genetics and psychological research, see Thomas Bouchard and P. Propping, eds., *Twins as a Tool of Behavioral Genetics* (Chichester, England: Wiley, 1993).

16. On the many approaches that can be taken in implementing MI theory, see Mara Krechevsky, Thomas Hoerr, and Howard Gardner, "Complementary Energies: Implementing MI Theory from the Lab and from the Field," in Jeannie Oakes and Karen H. Quartz, eds., *Creating New Educational Communities: Schools and Classrooms Where All Children Can Be Smart: 94th NSSE Yearbook* (Chicago: National Society for the Study of Education, University of Chicago Press, 1995), pp. 166–86.

17. Howard Gardner, *The Unschooled Mind: How Children Learn and How Schools Should Teach* (New York: Basic Books, 1991).

ON THE TRAIL OF LANGUAGE: NEURO-PSYCHOLOGIST ANGELA FRIEDERICI

ANGELA FRIEDERICI, DIRECTOR OF THE LEIPZIG MAX PLANCK INSTITUTE OF COGNITIVE NEUROSCIENCE, IS INVESTIGATING HOW OUR BRAIN UNDERSTANDS LANGUAGE. TOGETHER WITH HER COLLEAGUES, SHE HOPES TO DISCOVER HOW MAN DEVELOPED LANGUAGE: WHAT CHARACTERIZES GRAMMAR? HOW SIGNIFICANT IS VOCABULARY? HOW DOES THE BRAIN PROCESS INFORMATION?

By Andreas Sentker

With building site next to building site and its historical station concealed behind high scaffolding, the city of Leipzig is a vibrating din. At the heart of this construction bedlam lies the Max Planck Institute of Cognitive Neuroscience, founded in 1994. On entering the institute, located on the second floor of a fine old building, one is pleasantly surprised by the generously proportioned rooms and the bright woodwork. Everything has been thoroughly refurbished—perhaps a bit too thoroughly. At first glance, the atmosphere seems as cool and sterile as in an over-sized dentist's practice. Angela Friederici's office is also orderly, almost impersonal. Not a hint of the cosy study. No precarious piles of books, no mountains of manuscripts. Her desk is practically empty. What is more, the language researcher herself contradicts the usual cliché image of the scientist. When the 44-year-old leans back in her chair and scrutinizes her interlocutor, what initially comes to mind is a top level manager. Her elegant suit fits like a glove, the unpretentious jewelry merely intensifying the overall impression of refinement. But once Angela Friederici starts to speak, that impression too has to be corrected. This is not someone who administers research projects, but someone who is fascinated by science and approaches it with a good deal of temperament.

The story of Angela Friederici's career reads like a fairy tale. She received her doctorate at 24 years of age, and qualified to lecture at university ten years later. Since 1944, she has held one of two directoral posts at the Max Planck Institute in Leipzig. She studied German and French, linguistics, psychology and neurobiology at the universities of Bonn, Lausanne, Boston, Geissen

A female scientist who contradicts cliché images

and Berlin. She has carried out research work in Cambridge, San Diego, and Nijmegen in the Netherlands. How does a person cope with all that?

"That's easy," says Friederici. "All my professional life I have been examining one single question: What is language and how is it represented in the brain? The many and varied aspects and activities this involved are just small windows, each presenting one view on the topic. When I examine patients, carry out language experiments with children, test adults, observe behaviors, these are all pieces in a jigsaw puzzle that merge to form an overall image of how language is processed." Her particular field of research is relatively narrow, claims Friederici. She is concerned exclusively with language comprehension.

One thing that soon emerges when speaking with this eloquent neurophychologist is that if you want to understand how language is understood you have to take the broadest possible approach to the topic. What constitutes grammar? How important is vocabulary? What parts of the brain are involved? How do they interact? These questions can only be answered by interdisciplinary teamwork. Tracking down language in the brain required a lot of patience in dealing with test persons, technical knowledge, and above all, lots of imagination for the ingenious experiments this demands. "We have our test persons listen to sentences and measure their brain waves," says Friederici. "Let us take a typical beginning of a sentence. For example, 'The man was sitting in his . . .' Everyone expects a noun like 'armchair' to follow. We simply leave out the noun and introduce the verb right away: 'The man was sitting in his reading the newspaper.' The idea is that the brain should cry out, so to speak." The experiment has been successful. After 160 milliseconds, but be-

Reprinted from *Deutschland*, October 1997, pp. 47-49.

fore the brain recognizes the meaning of the words, it reacts to the mistake in the form of increased cerebral activity.

Angela Friederici distinguishes between three decisive phases in language comprehension. In the first phase, after those 160 milliseconds, the brain analyzes the grammatical structure of the sentence. "The grammatical information constitutes an integral self-repetitive system. The brain is wise to write this knowledge into its hardware, as it were, and not have to think about it again," explains Friederici with reference to the astonishingly high speed of its reaction. The brain's internal lexicon, on the other hand, is not at the ready as quickly. Only in the second phase, after another 200 to 600 milliseconds, are the meanings of the words analyzed. In phase three, after about 700 milliseconds, sentence structure and word meanings are correlated. If the system signals an error, a renewed analysis is initiated.

Piecing together an interdisciplinary jigsaw puzzle to make up a single image

Is this highly developed system an exclusive feature of the human brain? "Syntax and grammar are what characterize human language," believes Angela Friederici. "If any part of language processing is ingrained in the neurones, so to speak, then probably this part. After, all even monkeys and parrots can learn vocabulary."

Is human grammar innate, as some scientists claim? "Grammar itself probably not, but certainly the capacity to learn such a set of rules," replies Angela Friederici. And it is this learning process that is of particular interest to her. She has not been able to detect the swift brain reaction after 160 milliseconds in small children, for example. The signal only arrives after 260 milliseconds, which would seem to suggest that we learn grammar in much the same way as we learn to ride a bike: At some

stage, we stop thinking about the structure of language and simply use it. Working with children demands particular patience and imagination—and can sometimes be full of surprises. "Mom baked a cake," is one of the test sen-

Tracking how vocabulary and grammar are learned

tences. "Wrong," claims one of the young test persons, to the astonishment of the researchers. But what is wrong with the sentence? "That's obvious," explains the little fellow, "you don't bake a cake, you buy it at the supermarket."

The fact that linguistic images mirror our images of the world is something that the researchers in Leipzig are confronted with again and again. It comes as no great surprise that many regard language as the decisive feature that distinguishes man from the animals—allowing him to attain a higher level of consciousness. For many scientists, language and consciousness are inseparably linked. "Should something like consciousness exist, and if we really want to examine it," explains Friederici, "then consciousness would have more to do with self-reflection. And this raises the question as to whether you can think without language? I believe that this is possible. There are certain things in my head that I can conceive of without naming them directly, without having a label for them."

The argument is only partially valid. The American language researcher Hilde Schlesinger has examined the development of deaf children. In their case, certain concepts would seem to be comprehended at a later stage. For example, the principle behind an interrogative sentence remains a puzzle for them for a longer time.

Are abstract language—in whatever form—and the associated concepts of past, present and future, necessary requirements as a basis of consciousness? Is language the precondition for distinguishing between what is real and what is probable? Is it language that renders the nontangible communicable and thus

capable of being experienced? Friederici outlines the dilemma in which we become embroiled by making a seemingly obvious link between language and consciousness: "In my view, it is syntax that distinguishes human language from other systems of communication. Yet this is totally unconscious. So if we claim that man has a particular kind of consciousness because he uses language, and that the decisive feature of human language is unconscious, then something is wrong somehow."

Angela Friederici prefers to focus on examining how the brain processes information. In her view, research on this topic began much too late in Germany. "When I returned to Germany from America with my husband I wondered, what am I going to do here? It's not possible to pursue the kind of research I did in America. That was in 1979/80, the year cognitive science was introduced at the Massachusetts Institute of Technology—a really exciting time."

"So I simply waited patiently and worked, for ten long years." And that patience and diligence paid off. In 1989 Friederici received her first permanent professorial post in Berlin: "Cognitive science was not on the syllabus there so I set up a Cognitive Science Laboratory. When I left, however, that laboratory just disappeared into thin air. Needless to say, that is very frustrating." Despite all the initial promise, is there no future for cognitive science in Germany? "This kind of research is very dependent on the people who carry it out—even in the United States. Things really got going in Germany five years ago, involving a lot of

What distinguishes language from other forms of communication?

young researchers with great ideas."

But there are fewer and fewer work opportunities, and today basic research can no longer offer scientists job security. Is the situation hopeless? "You just have to go on doing what you enjoy doing," says Angela Friederici resolutely, "and develop significant powers of perseverance."

Unit Selections

Key Points to Consider

❖ From where do emotions originate, nature or nurture? Defend your answer. Do you think a person's level of emotionality or overall personality can change with time, or is it somehow fixed early in life? Give examples.

❖ What is emotional intelligence? How does it differ from intelligence as psychologists ordinarily use the term? Which do you think is more important, cognitive or emotional intelligence? How are people with emotional intelligence different from individuals without it?

❖ What is a polygraph? Why is this apparatus of interest to psychologists? Can the polygraph measure lying? If not, what does it measure, if anything? When might a polygraph be useful? Can you think of other ways we can measure a person's emotions?

❖ Does the brain play a role in motivation? Can you give an example? What are endorphins? What is the biology of joy? If you could be in a joyous state forever, would you want to be? How are emotions related to motivation?

❖ How are emotions tied to weight loss or gain? How large a role do you think emotions play in our motivation to eat? To overeat? Why don't some diets work? If you were designing a weight-loss program, what components would you include?

❖ Are people born to be good? What is morality? What elements control whether we are moral or not? Why is it important to include women and minorities in theories of moral behavior?

 **Links** **www.dushkin.com/online/**

These sites are annotated on pages 4 and 5.

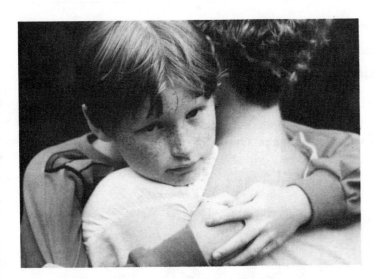

Janet's sister was a working mother and always reminded Janet about how exciting her life was. Janet stayed home because she loved her children, 2-year-old Jennifer, 4-year-old Tommy, and newborn Sara. One day, Janet was having a difficult time with the children. The baby, Sara, had been crying all day. Jennifer and Tommy had been bickering. Janet, realizing that it was already 5:15 and her husband would be home any minute, frantically started preparing dinner. She wanted to fix a nice dinner so that she and her husband could eat after the children went to bed, then relax together.

This was not to be. Janet sat waiting for her no-show husband. When he finally walked in the door at 10:15, she was furious. His excuse, that his boss had invited the whole office for cocktails and dinner, did not reduce Janet's ire. She reasoned that her husband could have called, could have taken 5 minutes to do that. Janet yelled and ranted at him for almost an hour. Her face was taut and red with rage and her voice wavered. Suddenly, bursting into tears, she ran into the living room. Her husband retreated to the safety of their bedroom.

Exhausted and disappointed, Janet sat alone and pondered why she was so angry with her husband. Was she just tired? Was she frustrated by negotiating with young children all day, and did she simply want another adult around once in a while? Was she secretly worried and jealous that her husband was seeing another woman and lied about his whereabouts? Was she combative because her husband's and her sister's lives seemed so much more exciting than her own? Janet was unsure just how she felt and why she had exploded in such rage at her husband, someone she loved dearly.

This sad story, although gender-stereotyped, is not unrealistic when it comes to emotions. There are times when we are moved to deep emotion. At other times, we expect waterfalls of tears but find that our eyes are dry or simply a little misty. What are these strange things we call emotions? What motivates us to rage at someone we love?

These questions and others have inspired psychologists to study emotions and motivation. The episode about Janet and her husband, besides introducing these topics to you, also illustrates why these two topics are usually interrelated in psychology. Some emotions, such as love, pride, and joy, are pleasant, so pleasant that we are motivated to keep them going. Other emotions, such as anger, grief, and jealousy, are terribly draining and oppressive, so negative that we hope they will be over as soon as possible. The relationship of emotions and motivation is the focus of this unit.

The first four articles introduce information about emotions. In the first article, the authors ask whether there are genetic underpinnings to our emotional reactions or, rather, environmental stimuli that trigger emotions. This is an important and difficult question.

The second article discusses a relatively new concept—emotional intelligence. Have you ever noticed how some individuals are expert at detecting and interpreting others' emotions? This is what psychologists have come to label "emotional intelligence" or EQ. Daniel Goleman, the psychologist who developed the concept of emotional intelligence, explains that emotional intelligence is very important; he suggests that it is EQ and not IQ that determines our success in life.

The polygraph or lie detector is one way to measure emotions. The courts and prospective employers embraced this apparatus as a scientific way to detect emotionality, particularly emotions related to lying. Research, however, has demonstrated that the polygraph is very questionable, in fact, so questionable that it is no longer admissible evidence in law courts. A critique of the polygraph is the topic of "A Doubtful Device."

The final article in the series about emotions concerns the emotion joy. Jeremiah Creedon discusses joy and pleasure. He delineates the role that endorphins, types of neurotransmitters, play in our pleasant experiences and emotions.

The remaining two articles pertain to motivation. The first article should be of interest to many American adults. We are the heaviest nation in the world. In "Weight Loss for Grown-Ups," Ann Japenga discusses why Americans are so heavy. In large part she blames our sizeable girths on our inability to manage our emotions. She suggests that any weight-loss program should include ways to teach individuals about emotionality. Thus, this article clearly ties together emotions and motivation.

The final selection describes social scientists' efforts at studying the motive to be moral. Psychologists have recently suggested that, in the end, morality is based on self-interest. However, author Celia Kitzinger suggests that this concep- tualization is rather male-centric. Newer ideas that include women and minorities suggest other reasons for helpfulness and moral behavior.

The wizards of genetics keep closing in on the biological roots of personality. It's not your imagination that one baby seems born cheerful and another morose. But that's not the complete picture. DNA is not destiny; experience plays a powerful role, too.

Shyness, Sadness, Curiosity, Joy.

Is It Nature or Nurture?

By Marc Peyser and Anne Underwood

IF ANY CHILD SEEMED DESTINED TO GROW UP AFRAID OF her shadow and just about anything else that moved, it was 2-year-old Marjorie. She was so painfully shy that she wouldn't talk to or look at a stranger. She was even afraid of friendly cats and dogs. When Jerome Kagan, a Harvard professor who discovered that shyness has a strong genetic component, sent a clown to play with Marjorie, she ran to her mother. "It was as if a cobra entered that room," Kagan says. His diagnosis: Marjorie showed every sign of inherited shyness, a condition in which the brain somehow sends out messages to avoid new experiences. But as Kagan continued to examine her over the years, Marjorie's temperament changed. When she started school, she gained confidence from ballet classes and her good grades, and she began to make friends. Her parents even coaxed her into taking horseback-riding lessons. Marjorie may have been born shy, but she has grown into a bubbly second grader.

For Marjorie, then, biology—more specifically, her genetic inheritance—was not her destiny. And therein lies our tale. In the last few years scientists have identified genes that appear to predict all sorts of emotional behavior, from happiness to aggressiveness to risk-taking. The age-old question of whether nature or nurture determines temperament seems finally to have been decided in favor of Mother Nature and her ever-deepening gene pool. But the answer may not be so simple after all. Scientists are beginning to discover that genetics and environment work together to determine personality as intricately as Astaire and Rogers danced. "If either Fred or Ginger moves too fast, they both stumble," says Stanley Greenspan, a pediatric psychiatrist at George Washington University and the author of "The Growth of the Mind." "Nature affects nurture affects nature and back and forth. Each step influences the next." Many scientists now believe that some experiences can actually alter

61% of all parents believe that differences in behavior between girls and boys are not inborn but a result of the way they're raised

the structure of the brain. An aggressive toddler, under the right circumstances, can essentially be rewired to channel his energy more constructively. Marjorie can overcome her shyness—forever. No child need be held captive to her genetic blueprint. The implications for child rearing—and social policy—are profound.

While Gregor Mendel's pea plants did wonders to explain how humans inherit blue eyes or a bald spot, they turn out to be an inferior model for analyzing something as complex as the brain. The human body contains about 100,000 genes, of which 50,000 to 70,000 are involved in brain function. Genes control the brain's neurotransmitters and receptors, which deliver and accept mental messages like so many cars headed for their assigned parking spaces. But there are billions of roads to each parking lot, and those paths are highly susceptible to environmental factors. In his book "The New View of Self," Dr. Larry Siever, a psychiatry professor at Mount Sinai Medical Center, writes about how the trauma of the Holocaust caused such intense genetic scrambling in some survivors that their children inherited the same stress-related abnormalities. "Perhaps the sense of danger and uncertainty associated with living through such a time is passed on in the family milieu and primes the biological systems of the children as well," says Siever. He added that that might explain why pianist David Helfgott, the subject of the movie "Shine," had his mental breakdown.

A gene is only a probability for a given trait, not a guarantee. For that trait to be expressed, a gene often must be "turned on" by an outside force before it does its job. High levels of stress apparently activate a variety of genes, including those suspected of being involved in fear, shyness and some mental illnesses. Children conceived during a three-month famine in the Netherlands during a Nazi block-

Scientists estimate that genes determine only about 50 percent of a child's personality

ade in 1945 were later found to have twice the rate of schizophrenia as did Dutch children born to parents who were spared the trauma of famine. "Twenty years ago, you couldn't get your research funded if you were looking for a genetic basis for schizophrenia, because everyone knew it was what your mother did to you in the first few years of life, as Freud said," says Robert Plomin, a geneticist at London's Institute of Psychiatry. "Now you can't get funded *unless* you're looking for a genetic basis. Neither extreme is right, and the data show why. There's only a 50 percent concordance between genetics and the development of schizophrenia."

SCIENTISTS HAVE BEEN DEvoting enormous energy to determining what part of a given character trait is "heritable" and what part is the result of socialization. Frank Sulloway's book "Born to Rebel," which analyzes the influence of birth order on personality, opened a huge window on a universal—and largely overlooked—environmental factor. But that's a broad brushstroke. Most studies focus on remarkably precise slivers of human emotions. One study at Allegheny University in Pennsylvania found that the tendency for a person to throw dishes or slam doors when he's angry is 40 percent heritable, while the likelihood a person will yell in anger is only 28 percent heritable. The most common method for determining these statistics is studying twins. If identical twins are more alike in some way than are fraternal twins, that trait is believed to have a higher likelihood of being inherited. But the nature-nurture knot is far from being untied.

The trick, then, is to isolate a given gene and study the different ways environment interacts with it. For instance, scientists believe that people with the longer variety of a dopamine-4 receptor gene are biologically predisposed to be thrill seekers. Because the gene appears to make them less sensitive to pain and physical sensation, the children are more likely to, say, crash their tricycles into a wall, just to see what it feels like. "These are the daredevils," says Greenspan. But

78% of those polled who are in two-parent families say that they share equality when it comes to setting rules for their young child

they need not be. Given strict boundaries, Greenspan says, thrill-seeking kids can be taught to modulate and channel their overactive curiosity. A risk-taking child who likes to pound his fist into hard objects can be taught games that involve hitting softly as well. "If you give them constructive ways to meet their needs," says Greenspan, "they can become charismatic, action-oriented leaders."

Shyness has been studied perhaps more than any other personality trait. Kagan, who has monitored 500 children for more than 17 years at Harvard, can detect telltale signs of shyness in babies even before they're born. He's found that the hearts of shy children in the womb consistently beat faster than 140 times a minute, which is much faster than the heartbeats of other babies. The shy fetus is already highly reactive, wired to overmonitor his environment. But he can also outgrow this predisposition if his parents gently but firmly desensitize him to the situations that cause anxiety, such as encouraging him to play with other children or, as in Marjorie's fear of animals, taking her to the stables and teaching her to ride a horse. Kagan has found that by the age of 4, no more than 20 percent of the previously shy children remain that way.

Will the reprogramming last into adulthood? Because evidence of the role of genes has been discovered only recently, it's still too early to tell. But studies of animals give some indication. Stephen Suomi at the National Institute of Child Health and Human Development works with rhesus monkeys that possess the same genetic predisposition to shyness that affects humans. He's shown that by giving a shy monkey to a foster mother who is an expert caregiver, the baby will outgrow the shyness. Even more surprising, the once shy monkey will become a leader among her peers and an unusually competent parent, just like the foster mom. Though she will likely pass along her shyness genes to her own child, she will teach it how to overcome her predisposition, just as she was taught. And the cycle continues—generations of genetically shy monkeys become not just normal, but superior, adults

and parents. The lesson, says Suomi: "You can't prejudge anyone at birth. No matter what your genetic background, a negative characteristic you're born with may even turn out to be an advantage."

But parents aren't scientists, and it's not always easy to see how experience can influence a child's character. A baby who smiles a lot and makes eye contact is, in part, determining her own environment, which in turn affects her temperament. As her parents coo and smile and wrinkle their noses in delighted response, they are reinforcing their baby's sunny disposition. But what about children who are born with low muscle tone, who at 4 months can barely hold up their own heads, let alone smile? Greenspan has discovered that mothers of these kids smile at the baby for a while, but when the affection isn't returned, they give up. And so does the baby, who over time fails to develop the ability to socialize normally. "If you move in the wrong patterns, the problem is exacerbated," Greenspan says. He has found that if parents respond to nonsmiling babies by being superanimated—like Bob Barker hosting a game show—they can engage their child's interest in the world.

The ramifications of these findings clearly have the potential to revolutionize child-rearing theory and practice. But to an uncertain end. "Our society has a strong belief that what happens in childhood determines your fate. If you have a happy childhood, everything will be all right. That's silly," says Michael Lewis, director of the Institute for the Study of Child Development in New Jersey and the author of "Altering Fate." Lewis estimates that experience ultimately rewrites 90 percent of a child's personality traits, leaving an adult with only one tenth of his inborn temperament. "The idea that early childhood is such a powerful moment to see individual differences in biology or environment is not valid," he says. "We are too open to and modifiable by experience." Some scientists warn that attempting to reprogram even a narrow sliver of childhood emotions can prove to be a daunting task, despite research's fascinating new insights. "Children are not a 24-hour controlled experiment," says C. Robert Cloninger, a professor of psychiatry and genetics at the Washington University School of Medicine in St. Louis. "If you put a child in a Skinner box, *then* maybe you could have substantial influence." So, mindful of the blinding insights of geneticists and grateful for the lingering influences of environment, parents must get on with the business of raising their child, an inexact science if ever there was one.

The EQ Factor

New brain research suggests that emotions, not IQ, may be the true measure of human intelligence

NANCY GIBBS

IT TURNS OUT THAT A SCIENTIST CAN SEE THE future by watching four-year-olds interact with a marshmallow. The researcher invites the children, one by one, into a plain room and begins the gentle torment. You can have this marshmallow right now, he says. But if you wait while I run an errand, you can have two marshmallows when I get back. And then he leaves.

Some children grab for the treat the minute he's out the door. Some last a few minutes before they give in. But others are determined to wait. They cover their eyes; they put their heads down; they sing to themselves; they try to play games or even fall asleep. When the researcher returns he gives the children their hard-earned marshmallows. And then, science waits for them to grow up.

By the time the children reach high school, something remarkable has happened. A survey of the children's parents and teachers found that those who as four-year-olds had the fortitude to hold out for the second marshmallow generally grew up to be better adjusted, more popular, adventurous, confident and dependable teenagers. The children who gave in to temptation early on were more likely to be lonely, easily frustrated and stubborn. They buckled under stress and shied away from challenges. And when some of the students in the two groups took the Scholastic Aptitude Test, the kids who held out longer scored an average of 210 points higher.

When we think of brilliance we see Einstein, deep-eyed, woolly haired, a thinking machine with skin and mismatched socks. High achievers, we imagine, were wired for greatness from birth. But then you have to wonder why, over time, natural talent seems to ignite in some people and dim in others. This is where the marshmallows come in. It seems that the ability to delay gratification is a master skill, a triumph of the reasoning brain over the impulsive one. It is a sign, in short, of emotional intelligence. And it doesn't show up on an IQ test.

For most of this century, scientists have worshiped the hardware of the brain and the software of the mind; the messy powers of the heart were left to the poets. But cognitive theory could simply not explain the questions we wonder about most: why some people just seem to have a gift for living well; why the smartest kid in the class will probably not end up the richest; why we like some people virtually on sight and distrust others; why some people remain buoyant in the face of troubles that would sink a less resilient soul. What qualities of the mind or spirit, in short, determine who succeeds?

The phrase "emotional intelligence" was coined by Yale psychologist Peter Salovey and the University of New Hampshire's John Mayer five years ago to describe qualities like understanding one's own feelings, empathy for the feelings of others and "the regulation of emotion in a way that enhances living." Their notion is about to bound into the national conversation, handily shortened to EQ, thanks to a new book, *Emotional Intelligence* (Bantam; $23.95) by Daniel Goleman. Goleman, a Harvard psychology Ph.D. and a *New York Times* science writer with a gift for making even the chewiest scientific theories digestible to lay readers, has brought together a decade's worth of behavioral research into how the mind processes feelings. His goal, he announces on the cover, is to redefine what it means to be smart. His thesis: when it comes to predict-

ing people's success, brainpower as measured by IQ and standardized achievement tests may actually matter less than the qualities of mind once thought of as "character" before the word began to sound quaint.

At first glance, there would seem to be little that's new here to any close reader of fortune cookies. There may be no less original idea than the notion that our hearts hold dominion over our heads. "I was so angry," we say, "I couldn't think straight." Neither is it surprising that "people skills" are useful, which amounts to saying, it's good to be nice. "It's so true it's trivial," says Dr. Paul McHugh, director of psychiatry at Johns Hopkins University School of Medicine. But if it were that simple, the book would not be quite so interesting or its implications so controversial.

This is no abstract investigation. Goleman is looking for antidotes to restore "civility to our streets and caring to our communal life." He sees practical applications everywhere for how companies should decide whom to hire, how couples can increase the odds that their marriages will last, how parents should raise their children and how schools should teach them. When street gangs substitute for families and schoolyard insults end in stabbings, when more than half of marriages end in divorce, when the majority of the children murdered in this country are killed by parents and stepparents, many of whom say they were trying to discipline the child for behavior like blocking the TV or crying too much, it suggests a demand for remedial emotional education. While children are still young, Goleman argues, there is a "neurological window of opportunity" since the brain's prefrontal circuitry, which regulates how we act on what we feel, probably does not mature until mid-adolescence.

And it is here the arguments will break out. Goleman's highly popularized conclusions, says McHugh, "will chill any veteran scholar of psychotherapy and any neuroscientist who worries about how his research may come to be applied." While many researchers in this relatively new field are glad to see emotional issues finally taken seriously, they fear that a notion as handy as EQ invites misuse. Goleman admits the danger of suggesting that you can assign a numerical yardstick to a person's character as well as his intellect; Goleman never even uses the phrase EQ in his book. But he (begrudgingly) approved an "unscientific" EQ test in *USA Today* with choices like "I am aware of even subtle feelings as I have them," and "I can sense the pulse of a group or relationship and state unspoken feelings."

"You don't want to take an average of your emotional skill," argues Harvard psychology professor Jerome Kagan, a pioneer in child-development research. "That's what's wrong with the concept of intelligence for mental skills too. Some people handle anger well but can't handle fear. Some people can't take joy. So each emotion has to be viewed differently."

EQ is not the opposite of IQ. Some people are blessed with a lot of both, some with little of either. What researchers have been trying to understand is how they complement each other; how one's ability to handle stress, for instance, affects the ability to concentrate and put intelligence to use. Among the ingredients for success, researchers now generally agree that IQ counts for about 20%; the rest depends on everything from class to luck to the neural pathways that have developed in the brain over millions of years of human evolution.

It is actually the neuroscientists and evolutionists who do the best job of explaining the reasons behind the most unreasonable behavior. In the past decade or so, scientists have learned enough about the brain to make judgments about where emotion comes from and why we need it. Primitive emotional responses held the keys to survival: fear drives the blood into the large muscles, making it easier to run; surprise triggers the eyebrows to rise, allowing the eyes to widen their view and gather more information about an unexpected event. Disgust wrinkles up the face and closes the nostrils to keep out foul smells.

Emotional life grows out of an area of the brain called the limbic system, specifically the amygdala, whence come delight and disgust and fear and anger. Millions of years ago, the neocortex was added on, enabling humans to plan, learn and remember. Lust grows from the limbic system; love, from the neocortex. Animals like reptiles that have no neocortex cannot experience anything like maternal love; this is why baby snakes have to hide to avoid being eaten by their parents. Humans, with their capacity for love, will protect their offspring, allowing the brains of the young time to develop. The more connections between limbic system and the neocortex, the more emotional responses are possible.

It was scientists like Joseph LeDoux of New York University who uncovered these cerebral pathways. LeDoux's parents owned a meat market. As a boy in Louisiana, he first learned about his future specialty by cutting up cows' brains for sweetbreads. "I found them the most interesting part of the cow's anatomy," he recalls. "They were visually pleasing—lots of folds, convolutions and patterns. The cerebellum was more interesting to look at than steak." The butchers' son became a neuroscientist, and it was he who discovered the short circuit in the brain that lets emotions drive action before the intellect gets a chance to intervene.

A hiker on a mountain path, for example, sees a long, curved shape in the grass out of the corner of his eye. He leaps out of the way before he realizes it is only a stick that looks like a snake. Then he calms down; his cortex gets the message a few milliseconds after his amygdala and "regulates" its primitive response.

Without these emotional reflexes, rarely conscious but often terribly powerful, we would scarcely be able to function. "Most decisions we make have a vast number of possible outcomes, and any attempt to analyze all of them would never end," says University of Iowa neurologist Antonio Damasio, author of *Descartes' Error: Emotion, Reason and the Human Brain.* "I'd ask you to lunch tomorrow, and when the appointed time arrived, you'd still be thinking about whether you should come." What tips the balance, Damasio contends, is our unconscious assigning of emotional values to some of those choices. Whether we experience a somatic response—a gut feeling of dread or a giddy sense of elation—emotions are helping to limit the field in any choice we have to make. If the prospect of lunch with a neurologist is unnerving or distasteful, Damasio suggests, the invitee will conveniently remember a previous engagement.

When Damasio worked with patients in whom the connection between emotional brain and neocortex had been severed because of damage to the brain, he discovered how central that hidden pathway is to how we live our lives. People who had lost that linkage were just as smart and quick to reason, but their lives often fell apart nonetheless. They could not make decisions because they didn't know how they felt about their choices. They couldn't react to warnings or anger in other people. If they made a mistake, like a bad investment, they felt no regret or shame and so were bound to repeat it.

If there is a cornerstone to emotional intelligence on which most other emotional skills depend, it is a sense of self-awareness, of being smart about what we feel. A person whose day starts badly at home may be grouchy all day at work without quite knowing why. Once an emotional response comes into awareness—or, physiologically, is processed through the neocortex—the chances of handling it appropriately improve. Scientists refer to "metamood," the ability to pull back and recognize that "what I'm feeling is anger," or sorrow, or shame.

Metamood is a difficult skill because emotions so often appear in disguise. A person in mourning may know he is sad, but he may not recognize that he is also angry at the person for dying—because this seems somehow inappropriate. A parent who yells at the child who ran into the street is expressing anger at disobedience, but the degree of anger may owe more to the fear the parent feels at what could have happened.

In Goleman's analysis, self-awareness is perhaps the most crucial ability because it allows us to exercise some self-control. The idea is not to repress feeling (the reaction that has made psychoanalysts rich) but rather to do what Aristotle considered the hard work of the will. "Anyone can become angry—that is easy," he wrote in the *Nicomachean Ethics.* "But to be angry with the right person, to the right degree, at the right time, for the right purpose, and in the right way—that is not easy."

Some impulses seem to be easier to control than others. Anger, not surprisingly, is one of the hardest, perhaps because of its evolutionary value in priming people to action. Researchers believe anger usually arises out of a sense of being trespassed against—the belief that one is being robbed of what is rightfully his. The body's first response is a surge of energy, the release of a cascade of neurotransmitters called catecholamines. If a person is already aroused or under stress, the threshold for release is lower, which helps explain why people's tempers shorten during a hard day.

Scientists are not only discovering where anger comes from; they are also exposing myths about how best to handle it. Popular wisdom argues for "letting it all hang out" and having a good cathartic rant. But Goleman cites studies showing that dwelling on anger actually increases its power; the body needs a chance to process the adrenaline through exercise, relaxation techniques, a well-timed intervention or even the old admonition to count to 10.

Anxiety serves a similar useful purpose, so long as it doesn't spin out of control. Worrying is a rehearsal for danger; the act of fretting focuses the mind on a problem so it can search efficiently for solutions. The danger comes when worrying blocks thinking, becoming an end in itself or a path to resignation instead of perseverance. Over-worrying about failing increases the likelihood of failure; a salesman so concerned about his falling sales that he can't bring himself to pick up the phone guarantees that his sales will fall even further.

But why are some people better able to "snap out of it" and get on with the task at hand? Again, given sufficient self-awareness, people develop coping mechanisms. Sadness and discouragement, for instance, are "low arousal" states, and the dispirited salesman who goes out for a run is triggering a high arousal state that is incompatible with staying blue. Relaxation works better for high energy moods like anger or anxiety. Either way, the idea is to shift to a state of arousal that breaks the destructive cycle of the dominant mood.

The idea of being able to predict which salesmen are most likely to prosper was not an abstraction for Metropolitan Life, which in the mid-'80s was hiring 5,000 salespeople a year and training them at a cost of more than $30,000 each. Half quit the first year, and four out of five within four years. The reason: selling life insurance involves having the door slammed in your face over and over again. Was it possible to identify which people would be better at handling frustration and take each refusal as a challenge rather than a setback?

The head of the company approached psychologist Martin Seligman at the University of Pennsylvania and invited him to test some of his theories about the importance of optimism in people's success. When optimists fail, he has found, they attribute the failure to something they can change, not some innate weakness that they are helpless to overcome. And that confidence in their power to effect change is self-reinforcing. Seligman tracked 15,000 new workers who had taken two tests. One was the company's regular screening exam, the other Seligman's test measuring their levels of optimism. Among the new hires was a group who flunked the screening test but scored as "superoptimists" on Seligman's exam. And sure enough, they did the best of all; they outsold the pessimists in the regular group by 21% in the first year and 57% in the second. For years after that, passing Seligman's test was one way to get hired as a MetLife salesperson.

Perhaps the most visible emotional skills, the ones we recognize most readily, are the "people skills" like empathy, graciousness, the ability to read a social situation. Researchers believe that about 90% of emotional communication is nonverbal. Harvard psychologist Robert Rosenthal developed the PONS test (Profile of Nonverbal Sensitivity) to measure people's ability to read emotional

One Way to Test Your EQ

UNLIKE IQ, WHICH IS GAUGED BY THE FAMOUS STANFORD-Binet tests, EQ does not lend itself to any single numerical measure. Nor should it, say experts. Emotional intelligence is by definition a complex, multifaceted quality representing such intangibles as self-awareness, empathy, persistence and social deftness.

Some aspects of emotional intelligence, however, can be quantified. Optimism, for example, is a handy measure of a person's self-worth. According to Martin Seligman, a University of Pennsylvania psychologist, how people respond to setbacks—optimistically or pessimistically—is a fairly accurate indicator of how well they will succeed in school, in sports and in certain kinds of work. To test his theory, Seligman devised a questionnaire to screen insurance salesmen at MetLife.

In Seligman's test, job applicants were asked to imagine a hypothetical event and then choose the response (A or B) that most closely resembled their own. Some samples from his questionnaire:

You forget your spouse's (boyfriend's/girlfriend's) birthday.
A. I'm not good at remembering birthdays.
B. I was preoccupied with other things.

You owe the library $10 for an overdue book.
A. When I am really involved in what I am reading, I often forget when its due.
B. I was so involved in writing the report, I forgot to return the book.

You lose your temper with a friend.
A. He or she is always nagging me.
B. He or she was in a hostile mood.

You are penalized for returning your income-tax forms late.
A. I always put off doing my taxes.
B. I was lazy about getting my taxes done this year.

You've been feeling run-down.
A. I never get a chance to relax.
B. I was exceptionally busy this week.

A friend says something that hurts your feelings.
A. She always blurts things out without thinking of others.
B. My friend was in a bad mood and took it out on me.

You fall down a great deal while skiing.
A. Skiing is difficult.
B. The trails were icy.

You gain weight over the holidays, and you can't lose it.
A. Diets don't work in the long run.
B. The diet I tried didn't work.

Seligman found that those insurance salesman who answered with more B's than A's were better able to overcome bad sales days, recovered more easily from rejection and were less likely to quit. People with an optimistic view of life tend to treat obstacles and setbacks as temporary (and therefore surmountable). Pessimists take them personally; what others see as fleeting, localized impediments, they view as pervasive and permanent.

The most dramatic proof of his theory, says Seligman, came at the 1988 Olympic Games in Seoul, South Korea, after U.S. swimmer Matt Biondi turned in two disappointing performances in this first two races. Before the Games, Biondi had been favored to win seven golds—as Mark Spitz had done 16 years earlier. After those first two races, most commentators thought Biondi would be unable to recover from his setback. Not Seligman. He had given some members of the U.S. swim team a version of his optimism test before the races; it showed that Biondi possessed an extraordinarily upbeat attitude. Rather than losing heart after turning in a bad time, as others might, Biondi tended to respond by swimming even faster. Sure enough, Biondi bounced right back, winning five gold medals in the next five races.

—By Alice Park

cues. He shows subjects a film of a young woman expressing feelings—anger, love, jealousy, gratitude, seduction—edited so that one or another nonverbal cue is blanked out. In some instances the face is visible but not the body, or the woman's eyes are hidden, so that viewers have to judge the feeling by subtle cues. Once again, people with higher PONS scores tend to be more successful in their work and relationships; children who score well are more popular and successful in school, even [though] their IQs are quite average.

Like other emotional skills, empathy is an innate quality that can be shaped by experience. Infants as young as three months old exhibit empathy when they get upset at the sound of another baby crying. Even very young children learn by imitation; by watching how others act when they see someone in distress, these children acquire a repertoire of sensitive responses. If, on the other hand, the feelings they begin to express are not recognized and reinforced by the adults around them, they not only cease to express those feelings but they also become less able to recognize them in themselves or others.

Empathy too can be seen as a survival skill. Bert Cohler, a University of Chicago psychologist, and Fran Stott, dean of the Erikson Institute for Advanced Study in Child Development in Chicago, have found that children from psychically damaged families frequently become hypervigilant, developing an intense attunement to their parents' moods. One child they studied, Nicholas, had a horrible habit of approaching other kids in his nursery-school class as if he were going to kiss them, then would bite them instead. The scientists went back to study videos of Nicholas at 20 months interacting with his psychotic mother and found that she had responded to his every expression of anger or independence with compulsive kisses. The researchers dubbed them "kisses of death," and their true significance was obvious to Nicholas, who arched his back in horror at her approaching lips—and passed his own rage on to his classmates years later.

Empathy also acts as a buffer to cruelty, and it is a quality conspicuously lacking in child molesters and psychopaths. Goleman cites some chilling research into brutality by Robert Hare, a psychologist at the University of British Columbia. Hare found that psychopaths, when hooked up to electrodes and told they are going to receive a shock, show none of the visceral responses that fear of pain typically triggers: rapid heartbeat, sweating and so on. How could the threat of punishment deter such people from committing crimes?

It is easy to draw the obvious lesson from these test results. How much happier would we be, how much more successful as individuals and civil as a society, if we were more alert to the importance of emotional

Square Pegs in the Oval Office?

IF A HIGH DEGREE OF EMOTIONAL INTELLIGENCE IS A PREREQUISITE FOR OUTSTANDing achievement, there ought to be no better place to find it than in the White House. It turns out, however, that not every man who reached the pinnacle of American leadership was a gleaming example of self-awareness, empathy, impulse control and all the other qualities that mark an elevated EQ.

Oliver Wendell Holmes, who knew intelligence when he saw it, judged Franklin Roosevelt "a second-class intellect, but a first-class temperament." Born and educated as an aristocrat, F.D.R. had polio and needed a wheelchair for most of his adult life. Yet, far from becoming a self-pitying wretch, he developed an unbridled optimism that served him and the country well during the Depression and World War II—this despite, or because of, what Princeton professor Fred Greenstein calls Roosevelt's "tendency toward deviousness and duplicity."

Even a first-class temperament, however, is not a sure predictor of a successful presidency. According to Duke University political scientist James David Barber, the most perfect blend of intellect and warmth of personality in a Chief Executive was the brilliant Thomas Jefferson, who "knew the importance of communication and empathy. He never lost the common touch." Richard Ellis, a professor of politics at Oregon's Willamette University who is skeptical of the whole EQ theory, cites two 19th century Presidents who did not fit the mold. "Martin Van Buren was well adjusted, balanced, empathetic and persuasive, but he was not very successful," says Ellis. "Andrew Jackson was less well adjusted, less balanced, less empathetic and was terrible at controlling his own impulses, but he transformed the presidency."

Lyndon Johnson as Senate majority leader was a brilliant practitioner of the art of political persuasion, yet failed utterly to transfer that gift to the White House. In fact, says Princeton's Greenstein, L.B.J. and Richard Nixon would be labeled "worst cases" on any EQ scale of Presidents. Each was touched with political genius, yet each met with disaster. "To some extent," says Greenstein, "this is a function of the extreme aspects of their psyches; they are the political versions of Van Gogh, who does unbelievable paintings and then cuts off his ear."

History professor William Leuchtenburg of the University of North Carolina at Chapel Hill suggests that the 20th century Presidents with perhaps the highest IQs—Wilson, Hoover and Carter—also had the most trouble connecting with their constituents. Woodrow Wilson, he says, "was very high strung [and] arrogant; he was not willing to strike any middle ground. Herbert Hoover was so locked into certain ideas that you could never convince him otherwise. Jimmy Carter is probably the most puzzling of the three. He didn't have a deficiency of temperament; in fact, he was too temperate. There was an excessive rationalization about Carter's approach."

That was never a problem for John Kennedy and Ronald Reagan. Nobody ever accused them of intellectual genius, yet both radiated qualities of leadership with an infectious confidence and openheartedness that endeared them to the nation. Whether President Clinton will be so endeared remains a puzzle. That he is a Rhodes scholar makes him certifiably brainy, but his emotional intelligence is shaky. He obviously has the knack for establishing rapport with people, but he often appears so eager to please that he looks weak. "As for controlling his impulses," says Willamette's Ellis, "Clinton is terrible." **—By Jesse Birnbaum. Reported by James Carney/Washington and Lisa H. Towle/Raleigh**

intelligence and more adept at teaching it? From kindergartens to business schools to corporations across the country, people are taking seriously the idea that a little more time spent on the "touchy-feely" skills so often derided may in fact pay rich dividends.

In the corporate world, according to personnel executives, IQ gets you hired, but EQ gets you promoted. Goleman likes

to tell of a manager at AT&T's Bell Labs, a think tank for brilliant engineers in New Jersey, who was asked to rank his top performers. They weren't the ones with the highest IQs; they were the ones whose E-mail got answered. Those workers who were good collaborators and networkers and popular with colleagues were more likely to get the cooperation they needed to reach their goals than the socially awkward, lone-wolf geniuses.

When David Campbell and others at the Center for Creative Leadership studied "derailed executives," the rising stars who flamed out, the researchers found that these executives failed most often because of "an interpersonal flaw" rather than a technical inability. Interviews with top executives in the U.S. and Europe turned up nine so-called fatal flaws, many of them classic emotional failings, such as "poor working relations," being "authoritarian" or "too ambitious" and having "conflict with upper management."

At the center's executive-leadership seminars across the country, managers come to get emotionally retooled. "This isn't sensitivity training or Sunday-supplement stuff," says Campbell. "One thing they know when they get through is what other people think of them." And the executives have an incentive to listen. Says Karen Boylston, director of the center's team-leadership group: "Customers are telling businesses, 'I don't care if every member of your staff graduated with honors from Harvard, Stanford and Wharton. I will take my business and go where I am understood and treated with respect.' "

Nowhere is the discussion of emotional intelligence more pressing than in schools, where both the stakes and the opportunities seem greatest. Instead of constant crisis intervention, or declarations of war on drug abuse or teen pregnancy or violence, it is time, Goleman argues, for preventive medicine. "Five years ago, teachers didn't want to think about this," says principal Roberta Kirshbaum of P.S. 75 in New York City. "But when kids are getting killed in high school, we have to deal with it." Five years ago, Kirshbaum's school adopted an emotional literacy program, designed to help children learn to manage anger, frustration, loneliness. Since then, fights at lunchtime have decreased from two or three a day to almost none.

Educators can point to all sorts of data to support this new direction. Students who are depressed or angry literally cannot learn. Children who have trouble being accepted by their classmates are 2 to 8 times as likely to drop out. An inability to distinguish distressing feelings or handle frustration has been linked to eating disorders in girls.

Many school administrators are completely rethinking the weight they have been giving to traditional lessons and standardized tests. Peter Relic, president of the National Association of Independent Schools, would like to junk the SAT completely. "Yes, it may cost a heck of a lot more money to assess someone's EQ rather than using a machine-scored test to measure IQ," he says. "But if we don't, then we're saying that a test score is more important to us than who a child is as a human being. That means an immense loss in terms of human potential because we've defined success too narrowly."

This warm embrace by educators has left some scientists in a bind. On one hand, says Yale psychologist Salovey, "I love the idea that we want to teach people a richer understanding of their emotional life, to help them achieve their goals." But, he adds, "what I would oppose is training conformity to social expectations." The danger is that any campaign to hone emotional skills in children will end up teaching that there is a "right" emotional response for any given situation—laugh at parades, cry at funerals, sit still at church. "You can teach self-control," says Dr. Alvin Poussaint, professor of psychiatry at Harvard Medical School. "You can teach that it's better to talk out your anger and not use violence. But is it good emotional intelligence not to challenge authority?"

SOME PSYCHOLOGISTS GO further and challenge the very idea that emotional skills can or should be taught in any kind of formal, classroom way. Goleman's premise that children can be trained to analyze their feelings strikes Johns Hopkins' McHugh as an effort to reinvent the encounter group: "I consider that an abominable idea, an idea we have seen with adults. That failed, and now he wants to try it with children? Good grief!" He cites the description in Goleman's book of an experimental program at the Nueva Learning Center in San Francisco. In one scene, two fifth-grade boys start to argue over the rules of an exercise, and the teacher breaks in to ask them to talk about what they're feeling. "I appreciate the way you're being assertive in talking with Tucker," she says to one student. "You're not attacking." This strikes McHugh as pure folly. "The author is presuming that someone has the key to the right emotions to be taught to children. We don't even know the right emotions to be taught to adults. Do you really think a child of eight or nine really understands the difference between aggressiveness and assertiveness?"

The problem may be that there is an ingredient missing. Emotional skills, like intellectual ones, are morally neutral. Just as a genius could use his intellect either to cure cancer or engineer a deadly virus, someone with great empathic insight could use it to inspire colleagues or exploit them. Without a moral compass to guide people in how to employ their gifts, emotional intelligence can be used for good or evil. Columbia University psychologist Walter Mischel, who invented the marshmallow test and others like it, observes that the knack for delaying gratification that makes a child one marshmallow richer can help him become a better citizen or—just as easily—an even more brilliant criminal.

Given the passionate arguments that are raging over the state of moral instruction in this country, it is no wonder Goleman chose to focus more on neutral emotional skills than on the values that should govern their use. That's another book—and another debate. **—Reported by Sharon E. Epperson and Lawrence Mondi/New York, James L. Graff/Chicago and Lisa H. Towle/Raleigh**

A Doubtful Device

Lisa Davis

When Anita Hill took a polygraph test [in 1992] in the midst of the Clarence Thomas Pro-Am National Consciousness-Raising Debacle, it would have been hard to find a newspaper that didn't report the fact that she passed. A few months earlier Patricia Bowman, accuser of William Kennedy Smith, passed a lie detector test regarding her allegations—which helped the district attorney decide to file charges of rape. And last May Virginia Governor Douglas Wilder pointed to a failed polygraph test in defending his decision to allow the execution of Roger Coleman, a convicted murderer who protested his innocence until being put to death just 12 hours after the test indicated he lied.

All of this goes on—all the tests, and all their life-changing consequences—despite the fact that for practical purposes the lie detector proves . . .

Nothing.

"An innocent person has about a fifty-fifty chance of failing a polygraph test," says David Lykken, psychologist at the University of Minnesota. "Society would be much better off if the polygraph were retired to a shelf in the Smithsonian."

To be fair, that assessment is offered by the polygraph's most vocal critic in an extremely acrimonious debate. Proponents of the lie-detector hotly dispute Lykken's claims and his statistics. But listen to one of the technique's best-known *supporters,* a researcher who says that under the proper conditions, the polygraph test has an accuracy rate of at least 90 percent.

"There's a great disparity between the potential of the polygraph and the way it's actually used," says University of Utah psychologist David C. Raskin. "As far as I'm concerned, the whole Department of Defense polygraphy department is atrocious—and almost all the federal examiners are trained at the DOD institution. Polygraphers in law enforcement train at private schools, and most of those are terrible," says Raskin. "We're talking about a mess."

In other words, Raskin has complaints about the way the principles of the polygraph are put into practice; Lykken and other critics take on the principles themselves. So first things first. The idea behind the polygraph is a simple one, and compelling: We can lie, we can even do it convincingly—but we can't do it calmly. The awareness of deceit and the fear of detection inevitably produce physiologi-

---

If the lie detector can't tell an honest person from a practiced liar, when what good is it?

---

cal changes such as shallow breathing, surging blood pressure, and the sweaty palms familiar to every schoolchild.

Scientists began trying to assess credibility by measuring such changes as long ago as the late 1800s. The modern polygraph still retains the clumsy look of a proto-technological era: rows of knobs, scrolling paper charts, and trailing wires. The wires are connected to equipment worn by the test subject: a blood-pressure cuff, electrical sensors fitted onto two fin-

gers to measure subtle changes in perspiration, and bands around the chest and abdomen that are sensitive to changes in breathing. As an examiner asks questions—Is your name Joe? Is today Friday? Did you take the diamond ring from the desk?—scribbling pens record the physiological responses.

There's no doubt that the polygraph measures physiological arousal. The question is what that arousal means. According to Leonard Saxe, a City University of New York psychologist who in 1983 led an analysis of the device for Congress, the polygraph simply shows whether a question makes someone anxious, and there are a thousand and one reasons that explain why a person hooked up to a polygraph might become anxious. For instance, you're worried because you're lying about a crime you committed. Or, you're afraid you're going to be convicted for a crime you didn't commit.

There are measures meant to prevent such an unhappy outcome, of course. A pre-test session is designed to reassure suspects about the test's accuracy. The examiner even goes over the questions ahead of time. In a perfect world, all this would leave only the guilty feeling nervous during the test.

As a backup measure in a manifestly imperfect world, polygraphers use what they call control questions. Interspersed with questions about the misbehavior at issue, control questions are intended to make even the innocent test-taker feel like a liar at key moments. Say Joe has been accused of theft. "I need to know whether you're the sort of person who could do this kind of thing," the examiner might say, though he or she is concerned about no such thing. "So I'm going to ask you whether before the age of 21 you ever stole something." If Joe mentions taking nickels from his mother at the age of six, the examiner prods—says, yes, but surely there was nothing *else,* was there?

The purpose of the put-on disapproval is to push Joe into lying, or at least into making a denial he's unsure of, while the polygraph measures the physiological responses during his deceit. It gives the examiner something to use for comparison as Joe answers the central questions of the polygraph test.

But what happens, asks Lykken, when an *innocent* person is more disturbed by a serious accusation than by the control questions? Lykken testified in one such case, in which a woman was eventually cleared of charges of molesting her son. "She failed the polygraph because when she was asked, 'Did you take Tommy's penis in your mouth?' it upset her more than the control question, 'Did you ever lie to stay out of trouble?' " Lykken says. "The jury, fortunately, believed her."

Unfortunately, the jury didn't believe Floyd "Buzz" Fay. Fay was arrested in 1978 for the shooting of a convenience-store clerk in Ohio. Three months later, he was in jail awaiting trial for murder when he was offered the chance to take a lie detector test, and was told that charges would be dropped if he passed. "I thought, hey, great—I can go home tomorrow," says Fay.

But the railroad worker failed the test, and failed a second one as well—results that were entered as evidence during his trial. Fay served nearly three years of a life sentence before an informant revealed the names of the real killers.

Polygraph proponent Raskin examined the test results when Fay, from his jail cell, sent them to polygraph experts. According to Raskin, while one of Fay's tests was unreadable, the other had been improperly scored.

That's not a rare occurrence. Three of the four commonly used scoring systems are subjective, a matter of a polygrapher's deciding whether one response is "dramatically stronger" or merely "significantly stronger" than another.

Such judgments are prey to error, and the mistakes are more likely to be against the innocent than in favor of the guilty, according to Saxe. In Fay's case, says Raskin, the chart was full of difficult calls; and the examiner ruled every questionable response deceitful. "He probably looked at the case facts and said, 'This guy's clearly guilty,' and gave him the minimum guilty score," speculates Raskin.

Polygraph tests are subject to another practical problem. They can be beaten, although it takes some training to do it well. A guilty person can boost his or her physiological response during non-threatening questions by biting the tongue, for instance, or clenching the toes. Done

---

Anita Hill passed the polygraph test, which means she was either telling the truth or a practiced lie.

---

at the right moment, each faked response can make the reaction to crucial questions look mild by comparison. "If I set out to lead a life of crime, I could beat the test time and time again," says Fay, who has campaigned against the use of the polygraph since his release.

In 1989, Congress attempted to limit the opportunities for use or abuse of the polygraph, partly because the study led by psychologist Saxe found neither statistics nor other evidence to support the test's reliability. The Polygraph Protection Act made it illegal for most private businesses to use the device to try to

weed out dishonest job applicants (or, as sometimes happens, applicants of unwanted sexual or political orientation).

But polygraphs are still used, and used frequently. Under certain circumstances, private employers are allowed to use the test during investigations of workplace theft. And according to psychologist Honts, the federal government administers at least 100,000 polygraph tests each year to screen potential employees, or during investigations of transgressions like leaks to the press or espionage.

Moreover, some courts still allow polygraph test results as evidence, under some circumstances. Researchers—both critics of the device and some supporters as well—are particularly worried by a related use. Women who allege that they've been raped have been pressured or even required to prove their truthfulness by passing a polygraph test. "The cards are really stacked against the victim coming across as truthful," Saxe says. "Her anxiety about anything relating to the attack may be so great that she may very easily appear deceptive."

So what does it mean if that woman passes, or if she fails? Or, to return to the well-known cases, what does it mean that Roger Coleman failed his polygraph test? According to Saxe, Raskin, and other experts, it could mean that he was lying about his innocence, or it could mean that *no one* could calmly answer a question carrying the penalty of death.

And what does it mean that Anita Hill passed a polygraph test? It could mean that she was telling the truth. Or, as Saxe points out (for the sake of argument only, since he was convinced by Hill's account), it could mean that Hill's physiological responses had been dampened by the hours of grueling cross-examination she'd already endured.

In other words, the polygraph results mean that Hill was telling either the truth or a practiced lie. Put it another way: The results prove . . . nothing.

THE BIOLOGY OF *Joy*

By Jeremiah Creedon

Scientists are unlocking the secrets of pleasure— and discovering what poets already knew

Pleasure, like fire, is a natural force that from the beginning humans have sought to harness and subdue. We've always sensed that pleasure is somehow crucial to life, perhaps the only tangible payoff for its hardships. And yet many have discovered that unbridled pleasure can also be dangerous, even fatal. Since ancient times, philosophers and spiritual leaders have debated its worth and character, often comparing it unfavorably to its more stable sibling, happiness. No one, however, saint or libertine, has ever doubted which of the pair would be the better first date.

Happiness is a gift for making the most of life. Pleasure is born of the reckless impulse to forget life and give yourself to the moment. Happiness is partly an abstract thing, a moral condition, a social construct: The event most often associated with happiness, some researchers say, is seeing one's children grow up to be happy themselves. How nice. Pleasure, pure pleasure, is a biological reflex, a fleeting "reward" so hot and lovely you might sell your children to get it. Witness the lab rat pressing the pleasure bar until it collapses. Or the sad grin of the crack addict as the molecules of mountain shrub trip a burst of primal gratitude deep in a part of the human brain much like a rat's. Both know all too well that pleasure, uncaged, can eat you alive.

Some scientists claim they're close to knowing what pleasure is, biologically speaking. Their intent is to solve the riddle of pleasure much as an earlier generation unleashed the power of the atom. Splitting pleasure down to its very molecules will have many benefits, they say, including new therapies for treating drug abuse and mental illness. Others note that research on the biology of pleasure is part of a wider trend that's exploding old ideas about the human brain, if not the so-called "Western biomedical paradigm" in general, with its outmoded cleaving of body from mind.

The assumption is that somehow our lives will be better once this mystery has been unraveled. Beneath that is the enduring belief that we can conquer pleasure as we've conquered most everything else, that we can turn it into a docile beast and put it to work. That we've never been able to do so before, and yet keep trying, reveals a lot about who we are, as creatures of a particular age—and species.

Of all the animals that humans have sought to tame, pleasure most resembles the falcon in its tendency to revert to the wild. That's why we're often advised to keep it hooded. The Buddha warned that to seek pleasure is to chase a shadow; it only heightens the unavoidable pain of life, which has to be accepted. Nevertheless, most have chosen to discover that for

From *Utne Reader*, November/December 1997, pp. 66-71, 106. © 1997 by Jeremiah Creedon. Reprinted by permission.

Sensuous
LIKE ME

How I got back in my body through my nose

Some mornings my head is like a little dog panting, whimpering, and straining at his leash. *Let's go, let's go, let's go!* My head gets me up and leads me around all day. Sometimes it's dinnertime before I remember that I have a body.

And the idea that this body can give me pleasure—well, that's a really hard one. I used to think that because I read hip French books about sexual ecstasy I had somehow escaped my Calvinist heritage—the idea that the body is shameful and only a narcissistic lazybones would pay any attention to it. No such luck. My version of Calvinist body-denial was compulsive reading, and the more I read about French people's ecstasies, which are usually pretty cerebral anyway—the more I hid out from my own body. A body that, let's face it, is plumper, paler, and more easily winded than I would prefer.

Falling in love changed things. Intimacy with a woman who was learning to accept and even love her body gave me new eyes to see (and new nerve endings to feel) my own. I started—just started—to think of my body as a means of communication with the world, not a sausage case for Great Thoughts. I wanted to go further.

It was my wife who found Nancy Conger, professor of the five senses. A slender young woman with apparently bottomless reserves of energy and optimism, she lives in an old farmhouse in western Wisconsin, plays the violin, and teaches people how to get out of debt, simplify their lives, and use their senses for entertainment and joy. She even teaches a one-night class called "Sensuous Living." Laurie and I enrolled.

A class in sensuousness. An idea not without irony, amazing that we actually have to study this stuff. Five perfectly sensible-looking adults perched on plastic chairs in a drab little classroom in Minneapolis, with Nancy presiding in a sleeveless black jumpsuit. On two tables toward the front: nasturtiums in a vase, a strip of fur, a piece of sandpaper, a twig, a violin, a seashell.

"Lick your forearm," said Nancy, "and smell yourself."

Lick my forearm and smell myself?

I looked around me. The matronly woman in the purple blouse and matching shoes was licking her forearm. So was the shy, 40ish guy with the salt-and-pepper beard, and the thin, Italian-looking young woman with the big braid. Finally, feeling uncomfortably canine, I licked myself. I sniffed ("Little, short sniffs, like perfumers use," said Nancy). Hmm. A faintly metallic aroma. Sniff, sniff. Beneath it, something breadlike.

Like a wine, I had a bouquet.

themselves. The early Greek hedonists declared pleasure the ultimate good, then immediately began to hedge. Falling in love, for instance, wasn't really a pleasure, given the inevitable pain of falling out of it. The hedonists thought they could be masters of pleasure, not its slaves; yet their culture's literature is a chronicle of impetuous, often unspeakable pleasures to be indulged at any cost.

When the Christians crawled out of the catacombs to make Rome holy, they took revenge on pagan pleasure by sealing it in—then pretended for centuries not to hear its muffled protests. Eclipsed was the Rose Bowl brilliance of the Roman circus, where civic pleasure reached a level of brutal spectacle unmatched until the advent of *Monday Night Football*. Pleasure as a public function seemed to vanish.

The end of the Dark Ages began with the Italian poet Dante, who, for all his obsession with the pains of hell, endures as one of the great, if ambivalent, students of pleasure. His *Inferno* is but a portrait of the enjoyments of his day turned inside out, like a dirty sock. For every kind of illicit bliss possible in the light of the world above, Dante created a diabolically fitting punishment in his theme-park hell below. We can only guess what terrible eternity he has since devised for his countryman, the pleasure-loving Versace, felled in what Dante would have considered the worst of ways—abruptly, without a chance to confess his sins. At the very least he's doomed to wear Armani.

Dante's ability to find a certain glee in the suffering of others—not to mention in the act of writing—goes to the heart of the problem of pleasure. Let's face it: Pleasure has a way of getting twisted. Most people, most of the time, are content with simple pleasures: a walk on the beach, fine wine, roses, cuddling, that sort of thing. But pleasure can also be complicated, jaded, and sick. The darker aspects of pleasure surely lie dormant in many of us, like the Minotaur in the heart of the labyrinth waiting for its yearly meal of pretty flesh. In the words of the Mongol ruler Genghis Khan, "Happiness lies in conquering one's enemies, in driving them in front of oneself, in taking their property, in savoring their despair, in outraging their wives and daughters." He meant pleasure, of course, not happiness—but *you* tell him.

In the Age of Reason, the vain hope that humans could reason with pleasure returned. Thinkers like Jeremy Bentham took up the old Greek idea of devising a "calculus" of pleasure—complex equations for estimating what pleasure really is, in light of the pain often caused by the quest for it. But the would-be moral engineers, rational to a fault, found the masses oddly attached to the older idea of pleasure being a simple sum of parts, usually private parts. As for the foundlings thus multiplied, along with certain wretched venereal ills, well, who would have figured?

The first "scientists of mind" were pretty sure that the secrets of pleasure, and the emotions in general, lay locked beyond their reach, inside our heads. Throughout the 19th century, scientists could only speculate about the human brain and its role as "the organ of consciousness." Even more gall-

Then Nancy got us out of our chairs to wander around and "smell what doesn't seem to have a smell." I put my nose right up next to a big pad of paper on an easel. Faint wheaty aroma like my school tablets in fifth grade. All the sunshiny, chalk-dusty, gentle boredom of elementary school came back, like a tune.

A brick gave off a mysterious musty tang, charged with the past. A quarter smelled sour, a metal door bitter and somehow sad.

"Smell detours right around your thinking brain, back to the limbic system at the bottom of the brain, where memory is," Nancy told us. She also explained that smell can be hugely improved, made more subtle and precise, if you keep sniffing. "Smell dishes. Smell clothes. Smell everything," she exhorted.

I did want to keep on smelling, but we were on to a trust-and-touch experiment. We paired off (I went with the big-braid woman) and took turns blindfolding and leading each other. I put my partner's hand on a brick, a door, a seashell, a twig.

Then I put on the blindfold (it smelled powdery and lusciously feminine), and she led me. Without any visual clues to tell me what things were supposed to feel like, I met each surface with a small thrill of tactile freshness. A metal door, I discovered, was studded with sharp little grains. A twig was as rough as sandpaper, and the sandpaper itself practically made me jump out of my skin. With most of the objects, I enjoyed a few wonderful seconds of pure sensation before the thinking brain clicked in and gave the thing a name. But click in it did; and that's when the magic ended.

The evening concluded with experiments in sound (Nancy played her violin very near each of us so we could feel the vibration in our bodies) and taste (we passed around a loaf of focaccia), but as we drove home I was still hung up on the smell and touch thing.

My nose, which I had mostly used as a passive receiver of pretty large and often alarming signals (skunk crushed on an Iowa road, underarms needing immediate attention, and so on) felt amazingly discriminating, having actually sniffed the difference between a door and a quarter. My fingers still tingled with the thrill of sandpaper and brick and (blessed relief!) fur.

The part of my head that names, makes distinctions, and is vigilant against stupidities pointed out that five middle-class white folks in a certain demographic had just spent three hours rubbing, if not exactly gazing at, their navels.

The honorable side of my Calvinism (as a kid I lived on Calvin Avenue in Grand Rapids, Michigan, just down the street from Calvin College) bridled at the idea of stroking my nerve endings like some French decadent poet, while an entire society—an entire world—splits along economic fault lines.

A third part of me rejoiced: I had discovered the cleverest answer yet to television. It was the exquisite entertainment technology of a body—my body. Anyone's body. It is—or could be—an immediate rebuke and alternative to the technologies of consumerism, which coarsen, obscure, jack up, deny, extend beyond reason, and in general do numbing violence to the subtle, noble equipment for receiving the joys of life that we were all issued at birth.

Anyone can sniff a leaf or reach out to the rough bark of a tree. Anyone can listen for a little while to the world. And anyone can do it now, at the kitchen table, in the schoolroom, at the racetrack, in the hospital bed. And we can keep doing it until we believe again in the wondrous beauty of our own equipment (absolutely no amplification from Sony required).

—Jon Spayde

ing, the era's writers and poets clearly speculated so much better—especially those on drugs.

Two of them, Samuel Taylor Coleridge and Thomas De Quincey, both opium addicts, also may have been early explorers of the brain's inner geography. Images of a giant fountain gushing from a subterranean river in Coleridge's most famous poem—"Kubla Khan; or, A Vision in a Dream" bear an odd resemblance to modern models of brain function, especially brains steeped in mind-altering chemicals. Writing in *The Human Brain* (BasicBooks, 1997), Susan A. Greenfield, professor of pharmacology at Oxford University, describes the "fountainlike" nerve-cell structures that arise in the brain stem and release various chemical messengers into the higher brain areas. As Greenfield notes, and Coleridge perhaps intuited, these geysers of emotion are "often the target of mood-modifying drugs."

De Quincey describes a similar terrain in *Confessions of an English Opium Eater (1821)*. He even suggests that the weird world he envisioned while he was on the drug might have been his own fevered brain projected, a notion he fears will seem "ludicrous to a medical man." Not so. Sherwin B. Nuland, National Book Award winner and clinical professor of surgery at Yale, expresses an updated version of that concept in *The Wisdom of the Body* (Knopf, 1997). In Nuland's view, we may possess an "awareness" distinct from rational thought, a kind of knowledge that rises up from our cells to "imprint itself" on how we interpret the world. "It is by this means that our lives . . . and even our culture come to be influenced by,

and are the reflection of, the conflict that exists within cells," he writes.

Maybe De Quincey really could see his own brain. Maybe that's what many artists see. Think of Dante's downward-spiraling hell, or the Minotaur in the labyrinth, even the cave paintings at Altamira and Lascaux. The first known labyrinth was built in Egypt nearly 4,000 years ago, a convoluted tomb for both a pharaoh's remains and those of the sacred crocodiles teeming in a nearby lake. It's an odd image to find rising up over and over from the mind's sunless sea, of subterranean passages leading ever deeper to an encounter with . . . the Beast. In an age when high-tech imaging devices can generate actual images of the brain at work, it's intriguing to think that artists ventured to the primordial core of that process long ago. And left us maps.

Today, Paul D. MacLean, National Institute of Mental Health scientist and author of *The Triune Brain in Evolution* (Plenum, 1990), describes a similar geography. He theorizes that the human brain is "three-brains-in-one," reflecting its "ancestral relationship to reptiles, early mammals, and recent mammals." Peter C. Whybrow, director of the Neuropsychiatric Institute at UCLA, uses this model to explain what he calls "the anatomical roots of emotion." Writing in *A Mood Apart* (BasicBooks, 1997), his study of depression and other "afflictions of the self," Whybrow notes: "The behavior of human beings is more complicated than that of other animals . . . but nonetheless we share in common with many creatures such behaviors as sexual courtship, pleasure-seeking, aggres-

THE NEW
Pleasure PRINCIPLE

This just in: Pain is not the route to happiness

Don't worry. Be happy.

The philosophy is simple, but living it is not, especially in our achievement-oriented society. According to Los Angeles-based therapist Stella Resnick, that's because we focus on the pain in our lives—getting through it, around it, or over it. Pleasure, the "visceral, body-felt experience of well-being," is a better path to growth and happiness, she contends in her book *The Pleasure Zone* (Conari Press, 1997). If only we knew how to feel it.

Resnick had to learn, too. Her childhood was unpleasant; her father left when she was 5; and, for 10 years, she endured beatings from her stepfather. She hung out on street corners and dated a gang leader. By age 32, she'd had two brief marriages and was involved in another stormy relationship. Although she'd built a successful San Francisco therapy practice, she was lonely and miserable. Nothing helped: not yoga, nor meditation, nor exercise, nor a vegetarian diet. "I was a very unhappy young woman," she recalls. "I'd had the best therapy from the best therapists, but even with all the work I had done on myself, something was missing."

What was missing, she discovered, was the ability to enjoy herself. At 35, after she lost her mother to cancer, she moved to a small house in the Catskill Mountains, where she lived alone for a year and, for the first time, paid attention to what felt good. At first she cried and felt sorry for herself. But by year's end, she was dancing to Vivaldi and the Temptations, and finding creativity in cooking and chopping wood.

She soon realized that most of her patients shared the same pleasure deprivation. "Our whole society diminishes the value of pleasure," she writes. "We think of it as fun and games, an escape from reality—rarely a worthwhile end in itself. Amazingly, we don't make the connection between vitality—the energy that comes from feeling good—and the willingness to take pleasure in moment-by-moment experience."

Therapy too often concentrates on pain and what the mind thinks; Resnick focused on pleasure and what the body feels. But when she first published her ideas in 1978, epithets were hurled: "narcissist," "hedonist," "icon for the Me Decade." It wasn't until research on the positive effects of pleasure and the negative effects of stress began to accumulate in the '80s that people became more receptive. "This is not about creating a society of me-first people," she says of her work. "There's no joy in hoarding all the goodies for our lonesome."

To help people understand pleasure, Resnick divides it into eight "core" categories: primal (the feeling of floating); pain relief (being touched and soothed); elemental (childlike laughter, play, movement, and voice); mental (the fun of learning); emotional (the feeling of love); sensual (the five senses, plus imagination); sexual (arousal, eroticism, orgasm); and spiritual (empathy, morality, and altruism).

Her prescription is body-based and simple. Listen to a fly buzz. Float on your back. Tell a dream. Her number-one tip for falling and staying in love is . . . breathe. Conscious breathing enhances relationships, she claims, because it allows us to let go in

sweet surrender, rather than fighting or resisting ourselves or each other.

Experiencing pleasure opens the body, releasing enormous energy, says Resnick. Ironically, this flow is what scares us, causing us to tense up and shut down, because we don't know what to do with it. We can miss the healing power of great sex, for example, by wanting to release the energy as soon as we get turned on. She advises allowing the excitement to build and circulate so that "it's something you feel in your heart. And in your big toes."

Repressing one's desire for pleasure was once considered virtuous, a sign of moral superiority. But Resnick questions whether it's good to continue in that vein. "We have poor race relations, poor man-woman relations, whole segments of society that have problems with parents and institutions," she says. "Could we do better if we enjoyed our relationships more, if people knew how to encourage and inspire themselves instead of being motivated by shame, guilt, and other negative emotions?"

Resnick doesn't advocate always succumbing to immediate gratification—there's pleasure in yearning—or fear and anger, which can inform and protect us. But using negative means to pursue positive ends simply doesn't work. "The secret to success in all things—business, creativity, art, relationships, family, spirituality—is to be relaxed during challenging times," she says. "Don't hold yourself in, or brace yourself for what might go wrong." And if you don't get it at first, don't worry. Even Resnick has to remind herself to breathe.

—Cathy Madison

---

sion, and the defense of territory. Hence it is safe to conclude that the evolution of human behavior is, in part, reflected in the evolution and hierarchical development of other species."

Deciphering the code of art into the language of modern science took most of two centuries. One discipline after another tried to define what feelings like pleasure were, and from where they arose, only to fall short. Darwin could sense that emotions were important in his evolutionary scheme of things, but he was limited to describing how animals and humans expressed them on the outside, using their bodies, especially faces. William James, in a famous theory published in 1884,

speculated that the brain only translates various sensations originating below the neck into what we think of as, say, joy and fear. Others saw it the other way around—emotions begin in the brain and the bodily reactions follow. Without knowing what pleasure actually is, Freud could see that the inability to feel it is a kind of disease, or at least a symptom, that he traced to (you guessed it) neurotic conflict.

By then, though, many people were fed up with all the talking. The study of mind had reached that point in the movie where the gung-ho types shove aside the hostage negotiator and shout, *We're going in."* And with scalpels drawn, they did. In 1872, Camillo Golgi, a young doctor working at a "home for incurables" in an Italian village, discovered the basic component of brain tissue, the neuron. During the 1920s, German scientist Otto Loewi, working with frog hearts, first identified neurotransmitters: chemical messengers that carry information across the gap between the neurons—the synapse—to receptors on the other side. Meanwhile, the Canadian neurosurgeon Wilder Penfield, operating on conscious patients with severe epilepsy, managed to trigger various emotions and dreamlike memories by electrically stimulating their brains. Such work gave rise to the idea that various mental functions might be "localized" in particular brain areas.

In 1954, psychologists James Olds and Peter Milner made a remarkable breakthrough—by accident. While researching the alerting mechanism in rat brains, they inadvertently placed an electrode in what they soon identified as a rat's pleasure-and-reward center: the so-called limbic system deep inside the brain. When the rats were later wired in a way that let them press a lever and jolt themselves, they did so as many as 5,000 times an hour.

This became the basis for current research on the "biology of reward." Scientists like Kenneth Blum have linked what they call reward deficiency syndrome to various human behavioral disorders: alcoholism, drug abuse, smoking, compulsive eating and gambling. Blum traces these disorders to genetically derived flaws in the neurotransmitters and receptors now associated with pleasure, including the pathways tied to the brain chemicals serotonin and dopamine, and the endorphins. Other researchers aren't so sure.

We all know by now that endorphins are the "body's own natural morphine." The discovery of endorphins in the early '70s marked the start of what some have declared the golden age of modern neuroscience. The impact was clear from the beginning to Candace B. Pert, whose work as a young scientist was crucial to the discovery. A few years earlier, she had helped identify the receptors that the endorphins fit into, as a lock fits a key, thus popping the lid of pleasure. According to Pert, "it didn't matter if you were a lab rat, a First Lady, or a dope addict—everyone had the exact same mechanism in the brain for creating bliss and expanded consciousness." As she recounts in *Molecules of Emotion* (Scribner, 1997), her early success led to a career at the National Institute of Mental Health identifying other such messenger molecules, now known as neuropeptides.

Pert's interest in the natural opiates soon took her into uncharted territory—sexual orgasm. Working with Nancy Ostrowski, a scientist "who had left behind her desire to become a nun and gone on instead to become an expert on the brain mechanisms of animal sex," Pert turned her clinical gaze on the sexual cycle of hamsters. "Nancy would inject the animals with a radioactive opiate before copulation, and then, at various points in the cycle, decapitate them and remove the brains," Pert writes. "We found that blood endorphin levels increased by about 200 percent from the beginning to the end of the sex act." She doesn't say what happened to their own endorphin levels while they watched—but Dante has surely kept a log.

Modern students of pleasure and emotion have their differences. Pert, for instance, having worked so much with neuropeptides, doesn't buy the idea that emotions are localized in certain brain areas. "The hypothalamus, the limbic system, and the amygdala have all been proposed as the center of emotional expression," she writes. "Such traditional formulations view only the brain as important in emotional expressivity, and as such are, from the point of view of my own research, too limited. From my perspective, the emotions are what link body and mind into bodymind."

This apparent reunion of body and mind is, in one sense, Pert's most radical conjecture. And yet, oddly, it's the one idea that many modern researchers do seem to share, implicitly or otherwise, to varying degrees. Most would agree that the process of creating human consciousness is vastly complex. It is also a "wet" system informed and modulated by dozens of neurochemical messengers, perhaps many more, all moving at incredible speeds. Dare we call it a calculus? Not on your life. Any analogy of the brain that summons up a computer is definitely uncool. For now.

There also seems to be a shared sense, not always stated, that some sort of grand synthesis may be, oh, 20 minutes away. In other words, it's only a matter of time before the knowledge of East and West is melded back into oneness, a theory that reunifies body and mind—and, as long as we're at it, everything else. That may be. But given that a similar impulse seems so prevalent throughout the culture, could it be that what we're really seeing is not purely science, but a case of primal yearning, even wishful thinking? A generation of brilliant scientists, their sensibilities formed in the psychedelic '60s, could now be looking back to the vision of mystical union they experienced, or at least heard about over and over again, in their youth. Perhaps they long to reach such a place, abstract though it is, for the same reason a salmon swims to the placid pool where its life began. We, like all creatures, are driven by the hope of an ultimate reward, a pleasure that has no name, a pleasure that in fact may not be ours to feel. Thus, we never conquer pleasure; pleasure conquers us. And for its own reasons, both wondrous and brutal.

None of which makes the alleged new paradigm any less real. As the poets of our day, for better or worse, the modern scientists of mind have already shaped our reality with their words and concepts. Who hasn't heard of the endorphin-driven runner's high, or traced a pang of lover's jealousy to their reptilian brain? On *Star Trek Voyager,* a medical man of the future waves his magic wand over a crewmate emerging from a trance and declares, "His neuropeptides have returned to normal!"

You didn't have to be a Darwin to see that the news gave Captain Janeway a certain . . . pleasure.

Jeremiah Creedon is a senior editor of Utne Reader.

Weight Loss
for Grown-Ups

It's learning to handle your emotions

A promising new program insists
the key to shedding pounds isn't
just eating less or exercising more.

By Ann Japenga

In real life, salvation doesn't usually debut as tidily as it does in the movies. You know, when the heroine peeks in the rearview mirror or glances up at a billboard, and there it is in fiery script: the magic combination that will make her life work.

But that's how it seemed when Sally Shreve's phone rang one morning last winter. Shreve's friend Sue Ann DeBower was on the line, exclaiming over a book that promised deliverance from the weight problems that had bedeviled both women for years. "It's us all over these pages," she enthused. "This is the key, finally."

DeBower wasn't talking about a new diet, a pill with scary side effects, or a grinding exercise regimen. No, the Solution, the program described in the book of the same name, claimed that to lose weight a person merely needs to pause five times each day and ask herself two elementary questions: "How am I feeling?" and "What do I need?"

There was a little more to it. After noting the feelings, she'd have to practice ways of coping with them. And she'd have to adopt some basic healthy eating and exercise patterns as well. But the crucial steps were so simple a child could follow them. In fact, the program was originally developed for overweight children.

A 45-year-old sales executive for a high-tech company, Shreve had tried repeatedly to lose and keep off the 40 extra pounds that had dogged her most of her adult life. Despite her best efforts to eat right and exercise, the weight always came back. Part of the reason may have been genetic; other members of her family had also struggled with excess pounds. But she suspected there was more to the problem. She knew she sometimes ate to buffer herself from emotions she'd rather not face. So the Solution made intuitive sense to her.

Still, when the blinding light appears in the rearview mirror, some people turn away. "No way," Shreve told her friend. "I am not going where this book wants me to go. If I do what the book says, I'm going to start crying and never stop."

THE SOLUTION, a 12-week program newly available at more than 100 hospitals nationwide, is based on the idea that to lose weight people need to grow up. Or, to put it more gently, they must brush up on skills they should have learned as children, such as the ability to comfort themselves when they feel sad or afraid and to set limits on their behavior. Solution founder Laurel Mellin believes people who lack these abilities tend to soothe themselves by eating more than they need. When they are able to master other ways of nurturing themselves, the drive to overeat gets turned off, says Mellin, a dietitian who teaches community medicine and pediatrics at the University of California at San Francisco School of Medicine.

Sounds good. But weight-loss claims are as plentiful as "Seinfeld" reruns. What makes Mellin's concept any more promising than all the others? For one thing, Mellin didn't just materialize on the scene. She has 18 years of experience directing a well-regarded child and adolescent program, Shapedown. This plan, which inspired the Solution, is used in some 400 hospitals around the country and has been shown to help heavy kids lose weight and keep it off.

Mellin recently published a pilot study in the *Journal of The American Dietetic Association* suggesting that Shapedown techniques work for adults as well. Twenty-two adults who completed a Solution course had, on average, kept off 17 pounds two years later. What's more, the participants were exercising an average of three hours more per week than before they enrolled, and 69 percent had sustained a substantial decrease in their blood pressure.

What's most important among these findings, Mellin says, is that the weight stays off long after the lessons are done. In fact, she claims, "This is the first time that a weight-loss treatment has shown long-term maintenance well after the treatment ends."

To today's weary dieters, this would appear to be delicious news. In the past twenty years, obesity rates have jumped 65 percent, with a record 33 percent of the population now overweight. And the standard remedies are of little use. A landmark 1992 National Institutes of Health report confirmed what countless women already knew: Diets don't

WHEN PEOPLE ARE ABLE TO MASTER ALTERNATE WAYS OF NURTURING THEMSELVES, MELLIN SAYS, THE DRIVE TO OVEREAT IS TURNED OFF.

work, because people almost always regain the weight they lost.

More recently, the ballooning masses sought redemption in diet drugs like the combination of fenfluramine and phentermine. But those hopes were dashed last fall when reports of heart valve damage prompted the government to pull fenfluramine off the market.

Into this tableau strolls Laurel Mellin, clutching her small study and a fervent belief that when people learn to look within, they can subdue the urge to overeat. Her approach borrows from existing weight-loss programs and makes use of common psychological techniques. The Solution group carries hints of cognitive therapy (which attempts to uncover and change self-defeating ways of thinking) and dollops of behavioral therapy (which reinforces good habits with rewards). It even weaves in the most venerable strategies of all: eating right and exercising.

But Mellin says none of these traditional approaches alone is enough. That's why the bedrock of her plan is teaching students how to identify their feelings and fulfill their needs by means other than eating. If you automatically head for the refrigerator when you're feeling lonely and blue, for instance, you might try visiting a friend or writing a letter instead. If you overeat when work becomes stressful, you could instead schedule a special treat for yourself, like a day at a spa or a long walk in the country.

For people who make such choices naturally, it's unfathomable that fully functioning

adults would have to take a class to discover their feelings and find ways to act on them. But for Mellin's students, mastering these abilities can feel as foreign as learning to drive on the left side of the road.

This emphasis on feelings is what sets the Solution apart from most weight-loss programs today. But it's not brand new. Mellin is actually reviving a concept that was popular several decades ago.

As she studied the topic of childhood obesity, she kept returning to an idea posited by psychiatrist Hilde Bruch and other researchers in the 1940s and 1950s. These theorists believed that some overweight people were unable to accurately read and respond to their own emotions, interpreting all troubling feelings as hunger and trying to assuage them by eating.

The concept lost favor as evidence for a genetic basis to excess weight piled up. And some critics felt that Bruch's approach unfairly stigmatized overweight people by suggesting they were somehow deficient. But when Mellin unearthed the older theories, she knew from her own experience they made sense; as a teenager she'd sought solace in sweets. The stigma argument didn't stop her from pursuing Bruch's hypothesis. Lots of people lacked self-nurturing and limit-setting skills as far as she could see—skinny people as well as fat. It would be a service to educate them.

In 1979 Mellin began teaching these skills to overweight adolescents. As she got to know the parents of kids in her Shapedown classes, she noticed many of them didn't have these skills themselves. No wonder, then, that their children weren't able to distinguish sadness, say, from the desire for a heap of onion rings. To these kids, and often to their parents, every one of life's jabs and stings felt like hunger. It seemed to Mellin that the parents in the group—and other adults as well—could benefit from her approach.

That hunch was borne out once she tried teaching the Solution to adults. Forty-year-old Northern Californian Pat Cherry, who completed the program two years ago, is one of the 22 people who participated in the pilot study. Cherry still stores Hydrox cookies—her old nemesis—in the pantry. But before indulging she stops and asks herself, "What am I feeling?" Even if she still tosses back a Hydrox or two, she can now distinguish between eating to fill her stomach and eating to appease her heart. Learning the difference helped her lose—and keep off—30 pounds she'd dragged around for years. "I live the Solution every day," she says.

SEVERAL MONTHS after Sue Ann DeBower's phone call, Sally Shreve reconsiders saying no to salvation. Her on-again, off-again engagement to her boyfriend, Dan, is off, and she is beginning to give up hope that she will ever have the family she's always wanted.

Buying her dream house on a quiet leafy lane in a suburb of San Francisco does not revive her spirits. "Sally's afraid to be alone," her friend De Bower says. "With this move, she's really feeling kind of desperate."

It may seem odd that with her personal life troubling her, Shreve is thinking about signing up for a weight-loss program. But she has long been aware of a link between her relationship difficulties and her tendency to overeat. When she was married at age 23, she walked down the aisle at a healthy weight for her five-foot-ten frame. As her unhappiness with the union grew, so did her girth. "Instead of dealing with the issues in my marriage, I'd just stuff it and eat," she says.

When her marriage ended, she tried Weight Watchers, then a program called Thin Within, in which participants recite affirmations as a path to change. She tried even more faddish approaches such as subsisting on nothing but grapefruit and eggs.

"It seems like it just got worse every time I dieted," she says. "If I gained 20 pounds after the last diet, then it was 40 pounds the next time."

"It's not like I don't know what takes weight off. You eat a lot of fruits and vegetables, and you exercise. Duh," she says. "But getting myself to do it has been another story."

Finally Shreve decides to bury her reluctance and signs up for a Solution group at the University of California at San Francisco (cost: $350). On Thursdays, when the group meets, Shreve leaves work early so she can be among the first to arrive. Critical of her own looks, she hates appearing anywhere late and having heads turn to watch her enter the room.

What others see, however, is not what Shreve imagines. Tall, blond, and professionally successful, Shreve has a commanding, sporty presence—as if she might race yachts or play polo on the weekends. She's the sort of woman who could easily inspire envy, if it weren't for the fact that she lavishes warm attention on everyone she meets.

By five-thirty, Shreve and a dozen other women are settled around a conference table cluttered with bottles of mineral water and copies of *The Solution,* each book liberally plastered with stick-on notes.

Tonight, four weeks into the program, there will be little talk of the weight-loss staples of diet and exercise. These topics are explored further in the final weeks, but most class time is focused on self-nurturing and setting limits. Each week the class has been assigned homework to reinforce these skills. The tasks include penning journal entries and writing "feelings letters," a method of expressing painful emotions.

Shreve finds herself resisting Mellin's terminology, saying it sounds "psychobab-

bly." Yet she's been faithfully attempting to keep up with the program. Not that it's been easy. Three weeks each month she travels out of state to meet with clients all day and schmooze over business dinners at night. "I'm going a mile a minute most of the

> SHE'S BEEN STEALING MOMENTS TO ASK, "AM I REALLY HUNGRY?" "WHAT DO I WANT?" MORE OFTEN THAN NOT, SHE DISCOVERS SHE DOESN'T NEED TO EAT.

time," she says. "I barely have time to go to the bathroom. 'What am I feeling?' 'What do I need?' How do I know?"

But she's been stealing moments where she can—in a cab, in an airport lounge—to ask herself the key questions. Before calling for room service, for instance, she makes herself stop and think, Am I really hungry? What is it I want? Nine times out of ten she discovers she doesn't really need to eat. If she's reaching for food because she's feeling tired, she might take a nap instead; if she wants to unwind, she calls a friend.

Still, she tells the group, "All this checking in is so much work that sometimes I want to close my eyes and make it go away."

In this week's class, Shreve learns that other women are also having difficulty monitoring their emotions.

"It's hard, hard, hard," complains an outdoorsy-looking woman in a bright red Synchilla jacket. "I don't think of it. Don't want to do it."

One woman announces to the group that this week has been so stressful she intends to keep comforting herself the only way she knows how: by gorging. Shreve, sitting to her left, pats the woman's forearm sympathetically.

Sensing the mood in the room spiraling downward, Mellin jumps to her feet and initiates a lesson in defining boundaries. After you check in on your feelings and ask yourself what you need, you must follow

through. That means setting clear limits—even in situations where the stakes are high.

Shreve's current dilemma involves Dan, her sometime fiancé. "Dan's a total weightist," Shreve tells the group. She knows she needs to ask Dan to stop making critical comments about her weight, but she's hasn't been able to muster the courage to do it.

Mellin suggests a little role-playing. A woman selected to play Dan looks Shreve over, rolls her eyes, and remarks, "Seems like you've put on some weight."

As in real life, Shreve can't tell Dan how much the judgment hurts. As she struggles to do so, she begins to weep.

Mellin, crouching on the floor near them, gently asks, "Why are you crying?" She presses Shreve to keep focusing on her emotions until she faces what Mellin calls the "essential pain" of confronting Dan. Finally Shreve gulps out her fear that if she tells Dan how she feels, he might leave and she would find herself alone—one of those inevitable losses she's kept out of her thoughts by distracting herself with food.

Then Shreve dabs her face with a borrowed tissue, turns to the woman playing Dan, and says: "I just can't live with the way you treat me about my weight."

The mood in the room breaks as the whole group erupts in cheers.

DURING THE first few weeks of the program, Shreve's weight jogs up and down by one or two pounds. Then, in the final weeks, she drops five pounds. Mellin says once students become comfortable with their newfound skills, they tend to lose about a pound a week.

Yet Mellin advises students not to be too concerned with tallies. "The Solution is not about weighing 100 pounds for life," she says. "The idea is to get within your genetic comfort zone and stay there because the drives to overeat have been turned off."

Ten weeks into the program Shreve is exercising more consistently than she did in the past, when she'd make it to the gym once or twice a week. The practice of limit setting has brought discipline to her workouts, and she now spends an hour a day on the stair stepper or running along the San Francisco Bay.

This is progress, and it's heartening. But will the program really provide the salvation that Shreve and others seek? Is it, as Mellin has said, "the universal solution . . . a way to end the agony forever"?

Obesity experts are reserving judgment. For one thing, many are wary of the notion that there could be a single answer to the problem of excess pounds. "Everyone says they have the solution," says Kelly Brownell, a psychologist and obesity researcher at Yale University. "But obesity is much too complicated to have just one solution."

Complicated, indeed. Studies show that overweight people vary in more ways than they are similar, suggesting that people put on pounds for many reasons. Genetics, obviously, is one of them. (Mellin doesn't deny that heredity is a factor, but she downplays its role, saying that most people have some control over their girth.) Other causes can be as simple as a lack of exercise or an unhealthy diet, completely apart from emotional issues.

Researchers also make the point that Mellin's initial study had no control group, a measure essential to airtight research. And they believe her sample of 22 people is too small to suggest meaningful conclusions.

For these reasons, experts tend to discount Mellin's claim that the Solution is the first treatment documented to lead to long-term weight loss. Until more definitive evidence about the Solution is in, it's not valid to compare it with other weight-loss techniques, says Michael Hamilton, an internist who directs the Duke Diet and Fitness Center in Durham, North Carolina.

Overall, then, the program may not be the universal solution Mellin would like to think it is. But it may well be at least a partial solution for the subset of dieters who resemble Sally Shreve in their eating patterns.

Scientific quibbles aside, the experts do agree that in several ways the program is on solid ground. Like Mellin, many who work with overweight people have observed that some eat to satisfy an emotional rather than physical hunger. Teaching such people to interpret and act on their feelings as a way of breaking unhealthy eating habits, they say, simply makes sense. Then, too, the behavioral and cognitive techniques that Mellin uses are well tested, the nutritional advice that clients receive is sound, and expectations about how much weight they can lose are kept within reasonable bounds.

It's also worth noting that the Solution has no damaging side effects. That alone puts it ahead of many weight-loss products and schemes on the market.

Finally, the Solution fosters skills that are clearly helpful in areas that transcend weight. Regardless of whether she ever loses

another pound, Sally Shreve is learning to be more at ease with her own emotions and to handle relationships more deftly—achievements that must rate at least as important as a slimmer profile.

It's just as well Shreve isn't hearing the experts hem and haw. She's so encouraged by her progress that she's begun a second 12-week course and has lost another five

> ## "I'M BEGINNING TO SEE MY WAY NOW," SHREVE SAYS, "EACH LITTLE VICTORY MAKES ME BELIEVE I CAN MAKE THIS A PART OF MY LIFE."

pounds. For her, the vision of salvation is getting sharper.

"I'm beginning to see my way now, she says. "Each little victory makes me believe I can make this a part of my life."

One such victory is scored on the afternoon Shreve manages to confront her fiancé, Dan, just as she'd practiced in class. Instead of abandoning her, as she had feared, he agrees to try harder to understand her weight problem. He'll start by reading *The Solution*.

Invigorated by her success, Shreve welcomes her father for a weekend visit. Although he was recently diagnosed with Alzheimer's disease, he seems his usual self as he putters around her new home assembling furniture. Only once, when he goes off hunting for a screwdriver, does he become disoriented.

After she hugs her father good-bye, Shreve drives straight to the grocery store

and stocks up on candy and chips. A feelings check or limit-setting exercise never enters her mind; in fact, she's not thinking at all.

Shreve gorges for several days. She abandons her homework and neglects the three phone calls she's supposed to make each week to stay in touch with others in the class.

On the fourth day she forces herself to call a classmate. "The drive to eat is just huge," she tells the woman, her normally robust voice reduced to a shaky whisper. "I'm acting kind of kooky here, and I can't figure out why."

Her classmate suggests that worry over her father may be compelling her to binge. But the connection doesn't click into place for Shreve until the Thursday night meeting. During a letter-writing exercise she finally realizes that her father's frailties terrify her—and make her want to eat.

On the following weekend Shreve opens all the windows of her Cape Cod-style home. Surrounded by birdsongs and the smell of new paint, she sits on her couch and spends two hours alternately crying and writing in her Solution journal, pouring out her feelings about seeing her parents age.

Later in the day, she calls her three brothers and asks them to help her compile a book of family stories to give to their father. "Remember the time Dad bought 25 pounds of spaghetti and wrapped it and put it under the Christmas tree to tease us?" she asks one of her brothers, laughing now.

Shreve initially turned away from the Solution out of fear that if she stopped using food to block her feelings, she'd be overwhelmed by life's inevitable disappointments. What this week's episode teaches her is that she can meet misery head-on, and there will eventually be an end to the crying.

"I really followed the Solution process almost to the letter, and it worked," Shreve says, looking back on the week. "It's not like I can make my fears go away, but now I can do something more constructive with them. I don't have to keep swallowing what I feel."

_____

Ann Japenga is a contributing editor.

Born to be good?

What motivates us to be good, bad or indifferent towards others? **Celia Kitzinger** examines the psychology of morality.

Celia Kitzinger teaches psychology at the University of Loughborough, England.

MANY of us, much of the time, act to benefit others. There are small kindnesses of everyday life—like holding open a door, sharing food or expressing compassion for someone in distress. Things so ordinary that we simply take them for granted.

We are pleased, but not particularly surprised that people commonly care for sick relatives, give money to help famine victims, donate blood to hospitals, or volunteer to assist at hospices. At times what people do for others is truly spectacular. In the US, Lenny Skutnik risked his life diving into the icy waters of the Potomac River to save an airline crash victim; in Nazi Europe many people risked their lives in offering protection to Jews. In both mundane and exceptional ways people often act to help others—which is why psychologists describe human beings not just as 'social' but also as 'pro-social' animals.

But why do people spend so much time and money and effort on others, when we could keep it all for ourselves? One argument is that self-interest lies at the root of all superficially 'moral' behaviour. According to sociobiologists, we are biologically driven towards those forms of altruism—caring for our families, for example—which improve the survival of our genes.[1] Moral actions are simply automatic and instinctive, of no greater or lesser significance than the behaviour of a mother bird putting her own life at risk leading a predator away from her chicks. Helping people who are not genetically related to us can also be in the best interest of our genes if it sets up the expectation that we—or those who share our genes—will be helped in turn.

There are many subtle ways in which helping others can offer rewards which serve our self-interest. These include the praise of onlookers; gratitude from the person being helped; the warm glow of knowing we have done a good deed; and the benefit of avoiding guilt, shame or punishment. Most people agree that some good behaviour can be attributed to self-interest. But is that all there is?

In an ingenious set of experiments, a group of psychologists set out to test the idea that empathy—the ability to imagine ourselves in the place of another and to feel their emotions—can result in genuine altruism.[2] Subjects were encouraged to be empathetic while watching a 'worker' who they believed was reacting badly to a series of uncomfortable electric shocks. They were then given a chance to help the worker by receiving the shocks themselves. If helping were only self-serving egoism, then people who felt empathy for the victim would simply want to escape from the upsetting experience. But researchers found that those with strong empathetic feelings volunteered to take the worker's place, even when told they that they could leave immediately if they refused. The researchers also found that high-empathy people, who were deprived of the opportunity to help, felt just as good when someone else helped instead. This suggests that the offer to help reflected a genuine wish to relieve the victim's suffering, rather than a desire for praise from other people. So it looks as if the cynical view that even good actions have selfish motives may well be wrong. Empathy is common in very small children who often respond to another's distress with crying and sadness, and may attempt to comfort them with a hug or a cuddly toy. Some psychologists believe that behaviour like this signals the start of moral development.[3]

Although empathy may be an important component of moral behaviour, morality cannot rely on empathy alone because this emotion is too circumscribed and partial. It can also lead us to make unfair decisions—taking sides in a dispute, for example. Another explanation for why people behave well is that they are motivated not by emo-tions but by reasoned moral principles. This is what Lawrence Kohlberg proposes in his 'cognitive-development model' theory.[4] Children, he says, begin at a 'preconventional' level in which they see morality in relation to obedience and punishments from adults. At the second, 'conventional' level, reached in late childhood or early adolescence, they are oriented first to pleasing and helping others and later to maintaining the existing social order. At the third and highest stage of moral development—reached by only a small proportion of adults—people begin to define moral values and principles such as human dignity, justice, universal human rights. According to this theory, morality is a matter of cognitive (not emotional) development: it matters not one whit whether we care about or empathize with other people so long as we respect their rights as human beings.

Some critics, notably feminist psychologist Carol Gilligan, have challenged the theory as sexist: men may favour abstract theoretical notions of rights and justice, but women, she says, are more likely to construct morality rooted in their sense of connection with other people, a morality of care and empathy.[5] Others criticize the ethnocentrism of the model, pointing out that Kohlberg has elevated to the highest stage of moral development precisely those views most likely to be held by white, middle-class, educated North Americans.[6]

It's more likely that moral behaviour comes about in a variety of ways: sometimes we may act well in the hope of rewards; other times good behaviour may be motivated by empathy; sometimes it is the outcome of reasoned moral arguments. Crucially, though, neither strong feelings of empathy nor high moral principles guarantee that people will behave well. There is often a gap between moral beliefs and moral action—between how people think and hope they would behave in a situation and how they actually do behave. Some of the classic studies of psychology were prompted by

 From *New Internationalist*, April 1997, pp. 15-17. © 1997 by New Internationalist Publications, Ltd. Reprinted by permission.

situations in which people failed to act in accordance with their moral values.

In the 1960s a young woman named Kitty Genovese was murdered by a man who raped and stabbed her repeatedly for half an

These people were not sadists or psy-chopaths. They were ordinary people

hour in front of 38 residents of a respectable New York City neighbourhood. Nobody went to help her. Only one person finally called the police, after she was dead. This incident prompted a flood of research into what became known as the 'bystander effect' which examined why people don't intervene when others are in pain or in danger.[7] Sometimes people fail to intervene out of callousness or indifference. But more often they fail to act in spite of what they feel they should do, and then feel ashamed afterwards. Why is this?

A common finding is that people are uncertain how to behave because, unsure about what they are seeing, they conform with the behaviour of others, who are equally unsure. Emergencies are rare events which happen suddenly and unexpectedly. How can we know that an emergency is real and is not a prank, a game, or a film being produced? The safest thing is to sit tight and wait to see how others react. If nobody else does anything, then people worry about making fools of themselves. A large group can stand by and do nothing, each lulled into thinking that there is no need to act, each waiting for someone else to make the first move. What looks like callous indifference is actually fear of what other people will think if they make an inappropriate response in an ambiguous situation.

Someone in Kitty Genovese's situation is less likely to be helped if many people are watching than if only one person witnesses the attack. For example, subjects asked to wait in a room before being interviewed

heard a woman in the next room apparently fall, hurt herself, and cry out in distress. Of those waiting alone, 70 per cent went to help her, compared with only 7 per cent of those waiting with a stranger who did nothing. Today's altruist may be tomorrow's passive bystander; it all depends on the social situation because people tend to behave in accordance with socially prescribed roles rather than as individuals.

In a well-known study by Stanley Milgram, subjects were recruited through newspaper advertisements for what was described as 'an experiment in learning'. They were seated in front of a shock machine that could administer up 450 volts to the 'learner', a man strapped into a chair.[8] Each time the 'learner' made a mistake the subject had to pull a lever to give him an electric shock, increasing the voltage each time. (In fact, the lever was a dummy, and the 'learner' was acting out his response). At 150 volts the learner started shouting. At 180 volts, he cried out in pain and pleaded to be released. At 300 volts he screamed with pain and yelled about his heart condition. Later still there was only deathly silence. If subjects wanted to stop giving shocks, the experimenter said only 'the experiment requires that you continue'. No threats, no incentives to go on, just the order. Under these conditions—and contrary to the predictions of psychiatrists who had guessed that virtually no-one would obey to the end—nearly two-thirds of subjects delivered the full range of shocks, proceeding beyond the levers marked 'Danger: Severe Shock' to the ones marked 'XXX'.

These people were not sadists or psychopaths. They were ordinary people who believed that you shouldn't hurt others, who often showed empathy for the learner, and who disliked what they were ordered to do. Virtually all of them complained to the experimenter and asked for permission to stop giving shocks. But when ordered to continue the majority did as they were told. As Milgram says: 'With numbing regularity, good people were seen to knuckle under the demands of authority and perform actions that were callous and severe.' Women were as likely as men to deliver shocks to maximum intensity.

What all these studies illustrate is the extent to which moral behaviour is a social, not an individual issue. In thinking about

why people fail to offer help, why they behave punitively, or why they inflict pain on others, we often resort to explanations which depend on individual characteristics—their personal religious beliefs, their capacity for empathy, their understanding of moral principles, or the kind of upbringing they had. But these explanations overlook the key role of social context. The frightening truth uncovered by these classic psychological studies is that it is not too difficult to set up situations in which most of us behave worse than we could have thought possible, out of conformity, fear of what others might think, loss of individual identity or obedience to authority.

The traditional view of moral behaviour is that people are intrinsically selfish beings whose natural anti-social impulses have been curbed by social structures designed to promote obedience to authority, law and order. An alternative possibility is that people are fundamentally pro-social beings, whose ability to act on altruistic impulses and moral principles is sometimes inhibited by precisely these social pressures. At the very least it is obvious that this is sometimes true, and that we need to develop ways of recognizing and challenging those social pressures which result in apathetic or cruel behaviour in our everyday lives.

Notes

1. Richard Dawkins, *The Selfish Gene,* OUP 1976.
2. CD Batson, *The Altruism Question,* Erlbaum Associates 1991.
3. C Zahn-Waxler & M Radke-Yarrow, 'The Development of Altruism' in N Eisenberg-Berg (ed.) *The Development of Prosocial Behaviour,* Academic Press 1986.
4. L Kohlberg, *The Philosophy of Moral Development,* Harper and Row 1981.
5. C Gilligan, *In a Different Voice,* Harvard University Press 1982.
6. EEL Simpson, 'Moral Development Research: A Case Study of Scientific Cultural Bias', *Human Development 17,* 1974.
7. B Latané & JM Draley, *The Unresponsive Bystander. Why doesn't he help?* Appleton-Century-Croft 1970.
8. S Milgram, 'Some Conditions of Obedience and Disobedience to Authority', *Human Relations 18,* 1965.

Unit Selections

Key Points to Consider

❖ What are the various milestones or developmental landmarks that mark human development? What purpose do these developmental events serve? Can you give examples of some of these events? Why is embryonic life so important? How do the experiences of the fetus affect the child after it is born? How does the fetus acquire experience when it is still inside the mother?

❖ Does parenting matter or do you think that children's development is dictated mostly by genes? Do you think that both nature and nurture affect development? Do you think one of these factors is more important than the other? Which one and why? Do you think it is important for both parents to be present during their child's formative years? Do you think fathers and mothers differ in their interactions with their children? How?

❖ What is puberty? How in adolescence does puberty differ from sexual attraction? Do you think that puberty and first sexual attraction are, in fact, two different stages of adolescent development? Is adolescence one stage of development or several stages of development?

❖ What are the causes and symptoms of Alzheimer's disease? Can we predict who is at risk for Alzheimer's? What are some treatments for Alzheimer's? What is a caregiver? Why might caregiving be stressful?

 **Links**

www.dushkin.com/online/

21. **American Association for Child and Adolescent Psychiatry**
    http://www.aacap.org/factsfam/index.htm
22. **Behavioral Genetics**
    http://www.uams.edu/department_of_psychiatry/slides/ html/genetics/index.htm

These sites are annotated on pages 4 and 5.

The Garcias and the Szubas are parents of newborns. Both sets of parents wander down to the hospital's neonatal nursery where both babies, Jose Garcia and Kimberly Szuba, are cared for by pediatric nurses when the babies are not in their mothers' rooms. Kimberly is alert, active, and often crying and squirming when her parents watch her. On the other hand, Jose is quiet, often asleep, and less attentive to external stimuli when his parents watch him.

Why are these babies so different? Are the differences gender-related? Will these differences disappear as the children develop, or will the differences become exaggerated? What does the future hold for each child? Will Kimberly excel at sports and Jose excel at English? Can Kimberly overcome her parents' poverty and succeed in a professional career? Will Jose become a doctor like his mother or a pharmacist like his father? Will both of these children escape childhood disease, abuse, and the other misfortunes sometimes visited upon children?

Developmental psychologists are concerned with all of the Kimberlys and Joses of our world. Developmental psychologists study age-related changes in language, motor and social skills, cognition, and physical health. They are interested in the common skills shared by all children as well as the differences between children and the events that create these differences.

In general, developmental psychologists are concerned with the forces that guide and direct development. Some developmental theorists argue that the forces that shape a child are found in the environment, in such factors as social class, quality of available stimulation, and parenting style. Other theorists insist that genetics and related physiological factors, such as hormones, underlie the development of humans. A third set of psychologists—in fact many—believe that some combination or interaction of both factors, physiology and environment (or nature and nurture), is responsible for development.

This unit will unfold in a developmental or chronological fashion. In the first selection, "Behaviors of a Newborn Can Be Traced to the Fetus," Beth Azar makes clear that fetal development is crucial to the development of the newborn child. Early experience, even fetal experience provided by the mother, is influential in later life; in fact, it may be crucial for survival.

In "Do Parents Really Matter? Kid Stuff," Annie Murphy Paul asks the critical question that, when interpreted, speaks to whether nurture or environment really make a difference. After pondering much evidence about nature and nurture, Paul infers that parental nurture does matter. She concludes that nurture interacts with nature to affect the developing child.

We move next to some information about adolescence. The first article on puberty and sexual attraction explores exactly what puberty is. The author makes the point that puberty is only one stage of adolescent development and that the adolescent, when first attracted sexually to another person, may be entering a discretely different stage. This notion will make psychologists rethink their various stage theories of adolescence.

The final article is about a tragic disorder of aging—Alzheimer's disease—that afflicts many of our elderly. The article investigates what causes Alzheimer's disease as well as drugs that are being tested that offer promise for a cure or at least a curtailment to the ravages of the disease. The article also offers advice for caregivers who are often the frazzled family members of Alzheimer's patients.

Development

Behaviors of a newborn can be traced to the fetus

The prenatal environment

Fetal research gives scientists unique insight into how behaviors and sensory systems develop.

By Beth Azar
Monitor staff

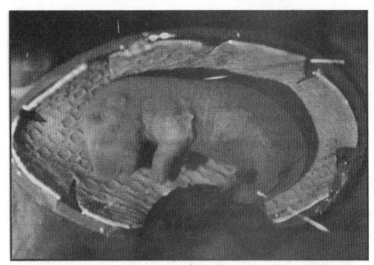

Studies of the rat fetus—kept alive outside its mother—find that touch is imperative to survival.

Some developmental researchers are so curious about how children's brains and behaviors develop that they're pushing the limits of technology to examine development prenatally. And over the past several years their efforts have borne fruit.

Researches are discovering how prenatal experiences affect child development. One of the most remarkable findings, say researchers, is that there isn't a dramatic shift in behavior and abilities from fetus to newborn.

"In some ways the newborn is a 'fetus exutero,'" says Cornell psychologist Steve Robertson, PhD. "Much of the behavior we see in the newborn can be traced directly back to behavior present in the fetus."

For example, Robertson has carefully examined and modeled fetal and then infant movements in humans and animals. He finds that there is a pattern to fetal movement that continues after birth. By age 2 or 3 months, babies' movements begin to appear more intentional. However, the spontaneous fetal movements continue to occur while they sleep.

These movements may play a role in priming animals for coordinated behavior, such as suckling, says Robertson. As part of a continuing collaboration between Robertson and Binghamton University psychologist William Smotherman, PhD, undergraduate students James Reilly and Ben MaClennan found that the waves of spontaneous motor activity seen in the rat fetus predict whether the fetus will respond to an artificial nipple put close to its mouth. "The fluctuations in movement seem to be playing a key role in how the fetus interacts with its environment," says Robertson.

Fetal experiences may also be crucial to survival outside the uterus, according to research by Indiana University psychologists April Ronca, PhD, and Jeffrey Alberts, PhD. In particular, the experience of birth appears to not only jump-start the fetus for the transition to the outside world but also to impart information important to survival, Ronca and Alberts find.

For example, up to 24 hours before a female rat goes into labor, she makes numerous movements, including frequently rearing onto her hind legs, vigorously licking her abdomen and scratching her belly. During this period the fetus is poked, stroked and shaken up, a process that turns out to be critical for development, Ronca and Alberts find.

If the researchers remove a pup from its mother's uterus and "deliver" it very gently, it never starts breathing and dies once the umbilical cord is cut. But when they provide the same tactile stimuli that the pup would receive inside the womb—squeezing it with a simulated uterine contraction, brushing it with an artificial tongue and tilting it to the same degree as when the mother rears—it breathes and develops normally.

Research in humans, including work by University of Miami psychologist Tiffany Field, PhD, finds that premature babies require touch to thrive. Alberts believes that tactile stimulation during and just after birth activates a chemical mechanism that prepares the body for the outside world. And work by researchers such as Saul Schanberg, PhD, MD, are beginning to elucidate those mechanisms.

The birth process may also impart important survival information, says Alberts. Years ago, psychologist Elliot Blass, PhD, now at the University of Massachusetts at Amherst, and his colleagues, found that the smell of the uterine environment is a crucial cue for suckling. When they injected a citrus smell into the amniotic fluid of a pregnant rat beginning 17 days into the pregnancy, her pups would suckle only nipples that were sprayed with citrus.

As an extension of that earlier research, Ronca and graduate student Regina Abel recently found that both smell and tactile stimulation just before birth are critical to suckling. They combined the citrus experiment with the tactile stimulation paradigm—

externalizing fetuses and providing them with tactile stimulation in the presence of citrus or no tactile stimulation in the presence of citrus. They kept the pups that received no tactile stimulation alive by stimulating them postnatally.

The researchers found that around 80 percent of the pups that received both tactile stimulation and citrus successfully attached to their mothers' citrus-scented nipples. But few of the pups in the other group successfully suckled, even though they were exposed to citrus in utero, says Ronca.

"They're unprepared—they don't know what to do to feed themselves," adds Alberts. "This research shows us that experiences intrinsic to the birth process prime us for how we interact with the environment."

Rats in space

The prenatal experience also appears to determine how certain sensory systems develop, Alberts and Ronca find. In particular, they have studied the vestibular system—the sensors in the inner ear that keep track of gravity and body position, providing animals with a sense of balance. They examined how gravity affects the development of balance by studying rats that develop in a weightless environment.

Twice, they joined with a team of researchers funded by the National Institutes of Health and NASA to send a group of pregnant rats up in the space shuttle. The rats lived there in virtual weightlessness for about half of their pregnancy, returning to Earth and gravity soon before delivery. The researchers wanted to test how development might differ if it occurs without the constant gravitational cues experienced by organisms that develop and live on Earth.

The space rats' pups were born on time and were just as healthy as pups born to a group of control rats who stayed on Earth throughout their pregnancies, says Alberts. However, the researchers detected several differences in their sense of balance. For example, if rats are placed on their backs in a tank of warm water, they right themselves as they sink.

But when the researchers dropped the space pups in water, they responded poorly, even landing on their heads when failing to right themselves in time. This problem dissipated quickly, but it indicates that the pups' vestibular system was not initially prepared for the gravity-laden world.

"Examining behavior in the fetus is helping decipher how these sensory and behavioral systems develop and, perhaps, when development might go wrong," says Alberts.

Do Parents Really Matter?

Once, parents were given all the credit—and all the blame—for how their children turned out. Then researchers told us that heredity determines who we are. The latest take: parents can work with their children's innate tendencies to rear happy, healthy kids. It's a message many parents will find reassuring—but it may make others very nervous.

By Annie Murphy Paul

David Reiss, M.D., didn't want to believe it. The George Washington University psychiatrist had worked for more than 12 years on a study of adolescent development—just completed—and its conclusions were a surprise, to say the least. "I'm talking to you seven or eight years after the initial results came out, so I can sound very calm and collected now," says Reiss. "But I was shocked." This, even though other scientists had previously reached similar conclusions in many smaller-scale studies. "We knew about those results, but we didn't believe it," says Reiss, speaking of himself and one of his collaborators, E. Mavis Heatherington, Ph.D. "Now we've done the research ourselves, so . . ." He sighs. "We're not ever going to believe it, but we're going to have to act as if we do."

What Reiss and his colleagues discovered, in one of the longest and most thorough studies of child development ever attempted, was that parents appear to have relatively little effect on how children turn out, once genetic influences are accounted for. "The original objective was to look for environmental differences," says Reiss. "We didn't find many." Instead, it seems that genetic influences are largely responsible for how "adjusted" kids are: how well they do in school, how they get along with their peers, whether they engage in dangerous or delinquent behavior. "If you follow the study's implications through to the end, it's a radical revision of contemporary theories of child development," says Reiss. "I can't even describe what a paradigm shift it is."

The only member of the research team

The way heredity shapes who we are is less like one-way dictation and more like spirited rounds of call and response.

---

who wasn't surprised by the results, Reiss recalls, was Robert Plomin, Ph.D., a researcher at the Institute of Psychiatry in London. Plomin is a behavioral geneticist, and he and others in his field have been saying for years what Reiss has just begun to accept: genes have a much greater influence on our personalities than previously thought, and parenting much less. The work of behavioral geneticists has been the focus of considerable controversy among psychologists, but it has been mostly ignored by parents, despite ample attention from the media. That may be because such coverage has rarely described just how genes are thought to wield their purported influence. Behavioral geneticists don't claim that genes are blueprints that depict every detail of our personality and behavior; rather, they propose that heredity reveals itself through complex interactions with the environment. Their theories are far more subtle, and more persuasive, than the simple idea of heredity as destiny. It is by participating in these very interactions, some scientists now say, that parents exert their own considerable influence—and they can learn to exert even more.

NATURE MEETS NURTURE

As behavioral geneticists understand it, the way heredity shapes who we are is less like one-way dictation and more like spirited rounds of call and response, with each

phrase spoken by heredity summoning an answer from the environment. Scientists' unwieldy name for this exchange is "evocative gene-environment correlations," so called because people's genetic makeup is thought to bring forth particular reactions from others, which in turn influence their personalities. A baby with a sunny disposition will receive more affection than one who is difficult; an attractive child will be smiled at more often than a homely one. And the qualities that prompt such responses from parents are likely to elicit more of the same from others, so that over time a self-image is created and confirmed in others' eyes.

Even as genes are calling forth particular reactions, they're also reaching out for particular kinds of experience. That's because each person's DNA codes for a certain type of nervous system: one that feels alarm at new situations, one that craves strong sensations, or one that is sluggish and slow to react. Given an array of opportunities, some researchers say, children will pick the ones that are most suited to their "genotype," or genetic endowment. As they grow older, they have more chances to choose—friends, interests, jobs, spouses—decisions that both reflect and define personality.

In order for genes and environment to interact in this way, they need to be in constant conversation, back and forth. Since parents usually raise the children to whom they have passed on their genes, that's rarely a problem: they are likely to share and perhaps appreciate the qualities of their offspring. And the environment they provide their children with may further support their natural abilities: highly literate parents might give birth to an equally verbal child, then raise her in a house full of books. Developmental psychologists call this fortunate match "goodness of fit." But problems may arise if nurture and nature aren't on speaking terms—if a child's environment doesn't permit or encourage expression of his natural tendencies. That may happen when children's abilities don't match their parents expectations; when their genetically-influenced temperament clashes with that of their parents; or when their environment offers them few opportunities to express themselves constructively, as is often the case with children who grow up in severe poverty. Research has shown that a poor person-to-environment match can lead to decreased motivation, diminished mental health, and rebellious or antisocial behavior.

The dialogue between genes and environment becomes more complicated when a sibling adds another voice. Although siblings share an average of 50 percent of their genes, the half that is different—and the kaleidoscopic ways that genes can combine—leads their genotypes to ask different

questions and get different answers from what would seem to be the same environment. In fact, siblings create individual environments of their own by seeking out different experiences and by evoking different responses from parents, friends, and others. Like the proverbial blind men touching the leg, the trunk, or the tail of an elephant, they "see" different parts of the same animal. "Our studies show that parents do indeed treat their children differently, but that they are in large measure responding to differences that are already there," says Robert Plomin. "Family environment does have an effect on personality development, but not in the way we've always thought. It's the experiences that siblings *don't* share that matter, not the ones they do."

KIDS IN CHARGE?

One intriguing implication of behavioral genetic research is that children are in many ways driving their own development, through the choices they make, the reactions they elicit, even the friends they pick (see "The Power of Peers"). But parents are crucial collaborators in that process, and that means that their role in shaping their children may actually be larger than it first appears. *How a parent responds to a child's genetically-influenced characteristics may make all the difference in how those traits are expressed,* says David Reiss. In his formulation, the parent-child relationship acts as a sort of translator of genetic influence: the genotype provides the basic plot, but parenting gives it tone and inflection, accent and emphasis. He calls this conception of gene-environment correlation "the relationship code," and says that it returns to parents some of the influence his study would seem to give to genes. "Our data actually give the role of parents a real boost—but it's saying that the story doesn't necessarily start with the parent," says Reiss. "It starts with the kid, and then the parent picks up on it."

To Reiss, parents' role as interpreters of the language of heredity holds out an exciting possibility. "If you could intervene with parents and get them to respond differently to troublesome behavior, you might be able to offset much of the genetic influence" on those traits, he says. In other words, if genes become behavior by way of the environment, then changing the environment might change the expression of the genes. Although such intervention studies are years away from fruition, small-scale research and clinical experience are pointing the way toward working with children's hereditary strengths and weaknesses. Stanley Greenspan, M.D., a pediatric psychiatrist at George Washington Medical School and author of *The Growth*

THE **POWER**
OF peers

IT'S A WORLD OUT OF A FANCIFUL children's book: a place where parents and teachers don't matter, where the company of other kids is most meaningful, where nothing much would change if we left children in their homes and schools "but switched all the parents around." That doesn't describe an imagined never-never land, however, but the environment that every one of us grows up in, contends Judith Rich Harris. The maverick writer and theoretician believes that peers, not parents, determine our personalities, and her unorthodox views have made the very real world of psychology sit up and take notice.

Harris, who is unaffiliated with any university or institution, laid out her radical theory in a 1995 *Psychological Review* paper, which was later cited as one of the year's outstanding articles by the American Psychological Association. Like behavioral geneticists, Harris believes that heredity is a force to be reckoned with. But she sees another powerful force at work: group socialization, or the shaping of one's character by one's peers.

Central to this theory is the idea that behavior is "context-specific": we act in specific ways in specific circumstances. "Children today live in two different worlds: home and the world outside the home," says Harris. "There is little overlap between these two worlds, and the rules for how to behave in them are quite different." Displays of emotion, for example, are often accepted by parents but discouraged by teachers or friends. Rewards and punishments are different too. At home, children may be scolded for their failures and praised for their successes; outside the home, they may be ridiculed when they make a mistake or ignored when they behave appropriately.

As children grow older and peer influence grows stronger, says Harris, they come to prefer the ways of peers over those of their parents. She like to use language as an example: the children of immigrants, she notes, will readily learn to speak the language of the new country without an accent.

They may continue to speak in their parents' tongue when at home, but over time the language of their peers will become their "native" language. Adopting the ways of their contemporaries makes sense, says Harris, because children will live among them, and not among older adults, for the greater part of their lives. "Parents are past, peers are future," she says.

It's evolutionarily adaptive, too. "Humans were designed to live not in nuclear families, but in larger groups," observes Harris. "The individuals who became our ancestors succeeded partly

---

of the Mind, is actively applying the discoveries of genetics to parenting. "Genes do create certain general tendencies, but parents can work with these by tailoring their actions to the nervous system of the child," says Greenspan. He believes that the responses children "naturally" elicit may not

---

**The exact same
temperament that
might predispose a kid
to become a criminal
can also make for
a hot test pilot.**

---

be in their best interests—but that parents can consciously and deliberately give them the ones that are. "You have to pay attention to what you're doing intuitively, and make sure that is what the kids really need," he says.

A baby with a sluggish temperament, for example, won't respond as readily to his parents' advances as a child with a more active nervous system. Disappointed at their offsprings' lack of engagement, parents may respond with dwindling interest and attention. Left to his own devices, the baby may become even more withdrawn, failing to make crucial connections and to master developmental challenges. But if the parents resist their inclinations, and engage the baby with special enthusiasm, Greenspan has found that the child will change his own behavior in response. The same principle of working against the grain of a child's genotype applies to those who are especially active or oversensitive, suggests Greenspan, comparing the process to a right-handed baseball player who practices throwing with his left hand. "It feels funny at first, but gradually you build up strength in an area in which you would naturally be weak," he says.

Of course, honing a right-handed pitch is important, too. Parents can improve on their children's hereditary strengths by encouraging their tendency to seek out experiences in tune with their genes. "Parents should think of themselves as resource providers," says Plomin. "Expose the child to a lot of things, see what they like, what

they're good at, and go with that." By offering opportunities congenial to children's genetic constitutions, parents are in a sense improving their "goodness of fit" with the environment.

WILL YOUR KID GO TO YALE—OR TO JAIL?

For those traits that could easily become either assets or liabilities, parenting may be especially critical to the outcome. "The same temperament that can make for a criminal can also make for a hot test pilot or astronaut," says David Lykken, Ph.D., a behavioral geneticist at the University of Minnesota. "That kind of little boy—aggressive, fearless, impulsive—is hard to handle. It's easy for parents to give up and let him run wild, or turn up the heat and the punishment and thereby alienate him and lose all control. But properly handled, this can be the kid who grows up to break the sound barrier." Lykken believes that especially firm, conscientious, and responsive parents can make the difference—but not all behavioral geneticists agree. David Rowe, Ph.D., a University of Arizona psychologist and author of *The Limits of Family Influence,* claims that "much of the effort of 'superparents' may be wasted, if not because they had the ability to get along with the other members." The group continues to influence us in a number of ways: we identify ourselves with it, and change our behavior to conform to its norms. We define our group by contrasting it with other groups, and seek to distinguish our group by our actions and appearance. Within the group, we compare ourselves to others and jockey for higher status. We may receive labels from our peers, and strive to live up (or down) to them. Finally, we may be most lastingly affected by peers by being rejected by them. People who were rejected as children often report long-term self-esteem problems, poor social skills, and increased rates of psychopathology.

Our personalities become less flexible as we grow older, says Harris, so that "the language and personality acquired in childhood and adolescent peer groups persist, with little modification, for the remainder of the life span." It's a startling conclusion, but Harris claims that her greatest challenge lies not in persuading people that peers matter, but in convincing them that parents don't. She calls the belief in parents' enduring importance "the nurture assumption," and her forthcoming book by that title will argue that it's simply a myth of modern culture. She doesn't deny that children need the care and protection of parents, and acknowledges that mothers and fathers can influence things like religious affiliation and choice of career. But, she maintains, "parental behaviors have no effect on the psychological characteristics their children will have as adults."

In fact, she says, "probably the most important way that parents can influence their children is by determining who their peers are. The immigrants who move their children to another country have provided them with a completely different set of peers. But a less dramatic shift—simply deciding which neighborhood to live in—can also make a difference." From one area to another, she notes, there are substantial variations in the rates of delinquency, truancy, and teen pregnancy—problems parents can try to avoid by surrounding their offspring with suitable friends. Beyond that, however, children will make their own choices. "It's pretty easy to control the social life of a three-year-old," says Harris. "But once the kids are past age 10 or 12, all bets are off."

—A.M.P.

counter-productive." And as for exposing children to a variety of experiences, Rowe thinks that this can give genetically talented children the chance they need, "but not many children have that much potential. This may not be so in Lake Wobegon [where every child is "above average"], but it is true in the rest of the world."

But with an optimism worthy of Garrison Keillor, advocates of parental influence insist that genes aren't the end of the story "The old idea is that you tried to live up to a potential that was set by genes," says Greenspan. "The new idea is that environment helps create potential." His view is supported by recent research that suggests a baby is born with only basic neural "wiring" in place, wiring whose connections are then elaborated by experience. Both sides will have to await the next chapter of genetic research, which may reveal even more complicated interactions between the worlds within and without. In the long-running debate between genes and the environment, neither one has yet had the last word.

Rethinking Puberty: The Development of Sexual Attraction

Martha K. McClintock and Gilbert Herdt[1]

Department of Psychology, The University of Chicago, Chicago, Illinois

A youth remembers a time when he was sitting in the family room with his parents watching the original "Star Trek" television series. He reports that he was 10 years old and had not yet developed any of the obvious signs of puberty. When "Captain Kirk" suddenly peeled off his shirt, the boy was titillated. At 10 years of age, this was his first experience of sexual attraction, and he knew intuitively that, according to the norms of his parents and society, he should not be feeling this same-gender attraction. The youth relating this memory is a self-identified gay 18-year-old in Chicago. He also reports that at age 5 he had an absence of sexual attractions of any kind, and that even by age 8 he had not experienced overt awareness of sexual attraction. By age 10, however, a profound transformation had begun, and it was already completed by the time he entered puberty; sexual attraction to the same gender was so familiar to him (Herdt & Boxer, 1993) that it defined his selfhood.

Recent findings from three distinct and significant studies have pointed to the age of 10 as the mean age of first sexual attraction—well before puberty, which is typically defined as the age when the capacity to procreate is attained (Timiras, 1972). These findings are at odds with previous developmental and social science models of behavioral sexual development in Western countries, which suggested that *gonadarche* (final maturation of the testes or ovaries) is the biological basis for the child's budding interest in sexual matters. Earlier studies postulated that the profound maturational changes during puberty instigate the transition from preadolescent to adult forms of sexuality that involve sexual attraction, fantasy, and behavior (Money & Ehrhardt, 1972). Thus, adult forms of sexuality were thought to develop only after gonadarche, typically around ages 12 for girls and 14 for boys, with early and late bloomers being regarded as "off time" in development (Boxer, Levinson, & Petersen, 1989). But the new findings, which locate the development of sexual attraction before these ages, are forcing researchers to rethink the role of gonadarche in the development of sexual attraction as well as the conceptualization of puberty as simply the product of complete gonadal maturation.

Many researchers have conflated puberty and gonadarche, thinking that the two are synonymous in development. The new research on sexual orientation has provided data that invalidate the old model of gonadarche as the sole biological cause of adult forms of sexuality. To the extent that sexual attraction is affected by hormones, the new data indicate that there should be another significant hormonal event around age 10. Indeed, there is: the maturation of the adrenal glands during middle childhood, termed *adrenarche*. (The adrenal glands[2] are the biggest nongonadal source of sex steroids.) This biological process, distinctively different from gonadarche, may underlie the development not only of sexual attraction, but of cognition, emotions, motivations, and social behavior as well. This observation, in turn, leads to a redefinition of prepubertal and pubertal development.

GONADARCHE IS NOT A SUFFICIENT EXPLANATION

Previous biopsychological models of sexual development have attributed changes in adolescent behavior to changes in hormone levels accompanied by gonadarche (Boxer et al., 1989), presumably because of a focus on the most dramatic features of gonadal development in each gender: menarche in girls and spermarche in boys. If gonadarche were responsible for first sexual attractions, then the mean age of the development of sexual attractions should be around the age of gonadarche. Moreover, one would expect a sex difference in the age of first attraction, corresponding to the sex difference in age of gonadarche: 12 for girls and 14 for boys. Neither of these predictions, however, has been borne out by recent data.

In three studies attempting to illuminate the sources of sexual orientation, adolescents have been asked to recall their earliest sexual thoughts; their answers are surprising. One study (Herdt & Boxer, 1993) investigated the development of sexual identity and social relations in a group of self-identified gay and lesbian teenagers (ages 14–20, with a mean age of 18) from Chicago. The mean age for first same-sex attraction was around age 10 for both males and females. Moreover, sexual attraction marked

From *Current Directions in Psychological Science*, December 1996, pp. 178-183. © 1996 by the American Psychological Society.
Reprinted by permission of Cambridge University Press.

the first event in a developmental sequence: same-sex attraction, same-sex fantasy, and finally same-sex behavior (see Table 1).

This evidence provides a key for understanding sexuality as a process of development, rather than thinking of it as a discrete event, which emerges suddenly at a single moment in time. Virtually all models of adolescent sexual development, from Anna Freud and Erik Erikson up to the present, have been based on the gonadarche model (Boxer et al., 1989). It conceptualizes the development of sexuality as a precipitous, singular, psychological event, fueled by intrinsic changes in hormone levels. Gonadarche is seen as a "switch," turning on desire and attraction, and hence triggering the developmental sequelae of adult sexuality.

Instead, the new data suggest a longer series of intertwined erotic and gender formations that differentiate beginning in middle childhood. Indeed, the psychological sequence of attraction, fantasy, and behavior may parallel the well-known Tanner stages, which are routinely used by clinicians to quantify the process of physical development during puberty (Timiras, 1972). For example, in girls, onset of sexual attraction may co-occur with Tanner Stage II (development of breast buds); sexual fantasy may co-occur with Tanner Stage III (enlargement of mammary glands); and sexual behavior may co-occur with Tanner Stage IV (full breast development), with each psychosexual stage reflecting a different stage of hormonal development. If so, then we may begin to look for a biological mechanism for psychosexual development in the physiological basis for these early Tanner stages that occur prior to the final gonadal maturation that enables procreation.

The generality of these psychological findings is substantiated by two other recent studies that also reported the age of first sexual attraction to be around 10 (see Fig. 1). Pattatucci and Hamer (1995) and Hamer, Hu, Magnuson, Hu, and Pattatucci (1993) asked similar retrospective questions of two distinctive samples

of gay- and lesbian-identified adults in the United States. Unlike the Chicago study (Herdt & Boxer, 1993), these studies gathered information from subjects throughout the United States and interviewed adults who were mostly in their mid-30s (range from 18 to 55). They also used different surveys and interview methodologies. Nevertheless, all three studies pinpointed 10 to 10.5 as the mean age of first sexual attraction. Admittedly, none of the studies was ideal for assessing early development of sexuality; the age of first recalled sexual attraction may not be the actual age. Nonetheless, this work is an essential part of the systematic investigation of same-gender attractions in children.

The question then arises whether there is a similar developmental pattern among heterosexuals. We know of no reason to assume that heterosexuals and homosexuals would have different mechanisms for the activation of sexual attraction and desire. Fortunately, we could test this hypothesis because both Pattatucci's and Hamer's samples had comparison groups of heterosexuals. Indeed, the reported age of first attraction was the same for heterosexually as for homosexually identified adults (only the attraction was toward the opposite sex). Thus, regardless of sexual orientation or gender, the age of initial sexual attraction hovered just over age 10. In sum, the switch mechanism responsible for "turning on" sexual attraction seems to be operating at the same time both for boys and for girls, and regardless of whether their sexual orientation is toward the same or opposite gender.

Thus, we surmise that the maturation of the gonads cannot explain the data found independently by these three studies in different samples and geographic areas. There is no known mechanism that would enable the gonads to supply sufficient levels of hormones at that age to cause sexual attraction, because they are not fully developed. The mean age of sexual attraction is the same in both genders and in both structural forms of sexual orientation; therefore, the biologi-

cal counterpart in both genders and in both structural forms of sexual orientation of sexual attraction is probably the same. These constraints effectively eliminate gonadarche as a candidate to explain the observed findings.

ADRENARCHE IN MIDDLE CHILDHOOD

In the pediatric literature, it is well recognized that children between the ages of 6 and 11 are experiencing a rise in sex steroids. These hormones come from the maturing adrenal glands. Adrenarche is clinically recognized primarily by the onset of pubic hair, but it also includes a growth spurt, increased oil on the skin, changes in the external genitalia, and the development of body odor (New, Levine, & Pang, 1981; Parker, 1991). Nonetheless, both the psychological literature and the institutions of our culture regard this period of middle childhood as hormonally quiescent. Freud's (1905/1965) classic notion of a "latency" period between ages 4 to 6 and puberty perhaps best distills the cultural prejudices. In contrast, we have hypothesized that the rise in adrenal steroid production is critical for understanding interpersonal and intrapsychic development in middle childhood.

Both male and female infants have adult levels of sex steroids during the first days of life, and their adrenal androgens also approach the adult range (see Fig. 2). After a few months, the sex hormone levels begin to fall to a very low level and then remain low until the maturation of the adrenal glands and gonads. When children are between 6 and 8 years of age, their adrenal glands begin to mature. Specifically, the adrenal cortex begins to secrete low levels of androgens, primarily dehydroepiandrosterone (DHEA; see Fig. 2) (Parker, 1991). The metabolism of DHEA leads to both testosterone and estradiol, the primary sex steroids in men and women.

It is noteworthy that both girls and boys experience a rise in androgens, although androgens are typically misidentified as male hormones. Moreover, there is no sex difference in the age at which these androgens begin to rise or the rate at which they do so. After adrenarche, an individual's level of androgens plateaus until around 12 years of age in girls and 14 years of age in boys, whereupon gonadarche triggers a second hormonal rise into the adult range (Parker, 1991).

In adults, the androgens that are produced by the adrenal cortex and their metabolites are known to have psychological effects in a variety of developmental areas relating to aggression,

Table 1. *Ages (years) at which males and females recall having their first same-sex attraction, fantasy, and activity (from Herdt & Boxer, 1993)*

Developmental event	Males			Females		
	M	SD	n	M	SD	n
First same-sex attraction	9.6	3.6	146	10.1	3.7	55
First same-sex fantasy	11.2	3.5	144	11.9	2.9	54
First same-sex activity	13.1	4.3	136	15.2	3.1	49

cognition, perception, attention, emotions, and sexuality. Although adult levels of DHEA are not reached until after gonadarche, levels of this hormone do increase significantly around age 10 (see Fig. 2; De Peretti & Forest, 1976), when they become 10 times the levels experienced by children between 1 and 4 years or age. It is plausible that this marked increase in androgen levels alters the brain, and thus behavior, either by modifying neural function or by permanently altering cellular structure.

WHAT IS SPECIAL ABOUT THE FOURTH GRADE?

We considered the hypothesis that the age of first sexual attraction is similar for boys and girls, both homosexual and heterosexual, because there is some marked change in environmental stimuli, socialization, or cognitive abilities around the age of 10. If so, then the 10-fold rise in DHEA would be only correlated with the emergence of sexuality and should not be considered its direct cause.

A major weakness of the idea that environmental stimuli lead to the emergence of sexual attraction at age 10 is the fact that, in the United States, there is no marked cultural prompt for sexuality in a 10-year-old. Children this age are typically in fourth grade. To our knowledge, there is no overt change in social expectations between Grades 3 and 4, or between Grades 4 and 5, that might account for the developmental emergence of sexual attraction at age 10. In U.S. culture, the typical ages for the so-called rites of passage are 12 to 13, when the adolescent becomes a "teenager," or around 15 to 16, when the driver's license is issued. Perhaps between Grades 5 and 6 (or, depending on the school system, between Grades 6 and 7), we might identify a critical change during the transition from elementary to middle school. Yet all of these culturally more prominent transitions occur later than age 10. Other subtle changes, such as girls wearing ornate earrings or boys forming preteenage groups, may occur around age 10, but these social factors seem too weak to adequately explain the sudden emergence of sexual attraction before anatomical changes are noteworthy in the child.

We also considered the possibility that although the social environment does not change at age 10, sexual attraction arises at this age because of an increase in the child's cognitive capability to perceive and understand the sexual and social environment. When the child becomes cognitively capable of un-

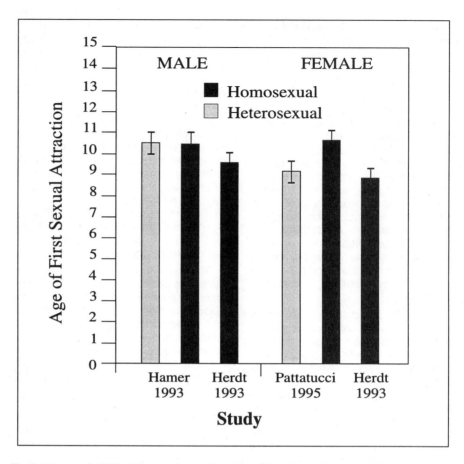

Fig. 1. Mean age (±*SEM*) of first sexual attraction reported by males and females, both homosexual and heterosexual. The data are reported in three studies: Herdt and Boxer (1993), Pattatucci and Hamer (1995), and Hamer, Hu, Magnuson, Hu, and Pattatucci (1993).

derstanding sexual interactions among adults, the child is capable also of imitating and putting into action the behaviors he or she has observed. This may be a plausible explanation for development of an awareness of sexual attraction in heterosexuals, and no doubt plays a role in the development of sexuality (after all, people typically do not develop sexuality in a vacuum). But does the explanation hold for children who are sexually attracted to the same gender?

The simple social-learning hypothesis predicts that as soon as children become aware of a strong cultural taboo on the expression of homosexual feelings, they should inhibit or even extinguish these desires in subsequent sexual development. We would therefore expect to find that homosexuals would reveal same-sex attraction significantly later than the age when heterosexuals reveal opposite-sex attraction. But this is not the case.

If 10-year-old children are simply mimicking the sexual behavior most commonly seen in adults (and the biological ability to actually carry out the behavior will arise only with gonadarche), then, given the predominant culture, all

10-year-old boys should demonstrate sexual attraction toward females, and all 10-year-old girls should show sexual attraction toward males. However, this also is not the case.

Other criticisms of simple learning-theory hypotheses regarding sexual development are well known and need not be repeated here (Abramson & Pinkerton, 1995). However, the Sambia of Papua New Guinea (Herdt, 1981) provide particularly compelling counterevidence to a simple learning theory model. The Sambia provide powerful reinforcement for same-gender relations by institutionalizing the practice of men inseminating boys over a period of many years beginning at age 7 to 10. The goal of the men is to masculinize and "grow" the youths into competent reproductive adult men. This intensive training and reinforcement of sexual relationships between males does not result in exclusive homosexuality in adulthood. Instead, adult Sambia men reveal marked bifurcation of their sexual interest; they generality stop all same-gender relations after marriage and enjoy sexual relations with women.

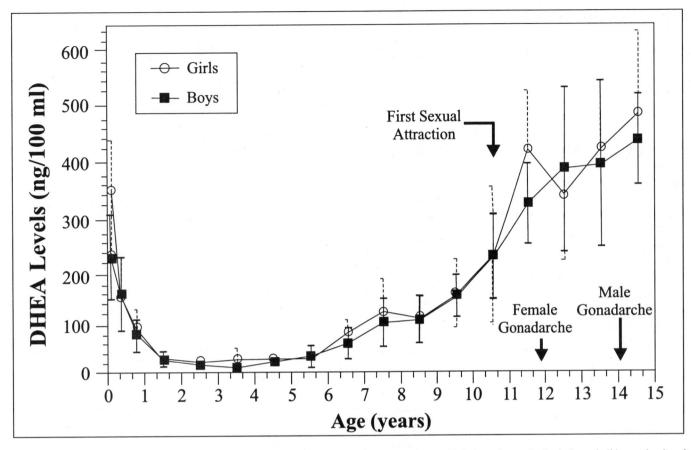

Fig. 2. Mean levels (±*SEM*) of the primary adrenal androgen dehydroepiandrosterone (DHEA) from birth through gonadarche in boys (solid error bars) and girls (dashed error bars). (Data redrawn from De Peretti & Forest, 1976.)

THE RELATIONSHIP BETWEEN ADRENARCHE AND SEXUALITY: CAUSE OR CORRELATION?

Does the inability of the hypotheses of gonadarche and social learning to explain the data imply that adrenarche is the key to the emergence of sexual attraction at age 10? That question cannot yet be answered conclusively. It is entirely possible that the sequential changes in attraction, fantasy, and behavior result from major structural changes in the brain that have their etiology in sources other than sex steroids. However, there has been no documented evidence for such neural structures as of yet. Moreover, if structural changes in the brain do prove to be the cause of the emergence of sexual attraction, modification of all current sexual developmental models and theories will still be needed because they assume that adult desires and behaviors develop from gonadarche.

A change in the nervous system that results from hormones released at adrenarche does took like the most likely developmental mechanism for several reasons. First, girls and boys experience their first sexual attraction, but not gonadarche, at the same age. Second, DHEA, the primary androgen released by the adrenal, is intimately linked with testosterone and estradiol, the major adult sex hormones. Their dynamic relationship is based on the fact that they share many of the fundamental features of steroid function: metabolic pathways that produce the steroids, binding proteins in the blood that carry them to their target tissue, and receptors that enable the cells in the target tissue, including the brain, to change their function in response to the hormonal information. Third, these androgens are known to affect the sexual fantasies and behavior of adolescents and adults, and it is plausible that the same hormones would have similar effects at an earlier age.

RETHINKING PUBERTY: IMPLICATIONS FOR MANY DOMAINS

Given the strong possibility that the currently popular model of puberty is limited, if not incorrect, researchers need to rethink puberty and test the new models in a wide range of psychological disciplines. Adrenarche clearly raises androgens to significant levels, and if these hormones are responsible for the effects seen in sexual attraction, then they are likely to affect a wide range of other behaviors: aggression, cognition, perception, attention, arousal, emotions, and, of course, sexual identity, fantasy, and behavior.

Even if it turns out that hormones released from the adrenal glands are not responsible for the onset of sexual attraction, the behavioral data themselves demonstrate that the concept of puberty must be greatly elaborated and its various stages unpacked. Indeed, Freud's idea of a latency period is seriously flawed. The current behavioral work reinforces the well-established clinical understanding that puberty is composed of at least two separate maturational processes: adrenarche and gonadarche. Any psychosocial research that uses puberty as a stage in development needs to break down the relevant developmental and social behaviors into these two different stages. Researchers need to take into account the hormonal fact that the start of puberty in normal individuals is around ages 6 to 8 and the end of puberty is not until around ages 15 to 17.

The idea of sexuality developing in stages is nothing new to social scientists. But the idea that sexuality is a continuous process that begins from the inside, well before gonadarche, and extends into adulthood is a conceptual advance. These new data from sexual orientation research force a reevaluation of the social and health models of sexual development. No longer can the brain at puberty be treated as a black box, which is suddenly able to process sexual stimuli *de novo* at the time of gonadal change.

Although adrenarche may not be the answer to all the riddles of sexual development, the new data from the developmental and social study of sexual identity have triggered a major conceptual advance in the understanding of both puberty and sexual development as psychobiological phenomena.

Acknowledgements—We extend our profound thanks to Colin Davis, who coordinated the data and helped substantially with manuscript preparation; to Ruvance Pietrz, who edited text and figures; and to Amanda Woodward for her insightful and constructive comments. This work was supported by National Institute of Mental Health MERIT Award R37 MH41788 to Martha K. McClintock.

Notes

1. Address correspondence to Martha K. McClintock, 5730 Woodlawn Ave., Chicago, IL 60637; e-mail: mkml@midway.uchicago.edu.
2. The adrenal glands are small, pyramidal glands located above the kidneys. They produce hormones that affect metabolism, salt regulation, response to stress, and reproductive function, in part by binding in the brain and altering neural function.

References

Abramson, P., & Pinkerton, S. (Eds.). (1995). *Sexual nature, sexual culture.* Chicago: University of Chicago Press.

Boxer, A., Levinson, R. A., & Petersen, A. C. (1989). Adolescent sexuality. In J. Worell & F. Danner (Eds.), *The adolescent as decision-maker* (pp. 209–244). San Diego: Academic Press.

De Peretti, E., & Forest, M. G. (1976). Unconjugated dehydroepiandrosterone plasma levels in normal subjects from birth to adolescence in humans: The use of a sensitive radioimmunoassay. *Journal of Clinical Endocrinology and Metabolism, 43,* 982–991.

Freud, S. (1965). *Three essays on the theory of sexuality.* New York: Basic Books. (Original work published 1905)

Hamer, D. H., Hu, S., Magnuson, V. L., Hu, N., Pattatucci, A. M. L. (1993). A linkage between DNA markers on the X chromosome and male sexual orientation. *Science, 261,* 321–327.

Herdt, G. (1981). *Guardians of the flutes.* New York: McGraw-Hill.

Herdt, G., & Boxer, A. (1993). *Children of horizons.* New York: Beacon Press.

Money, J., & Ehrhardt, A. (1972). *Man, woman, boy, girl.* Baltimore: Johns Hopkins University Press.

New, M. I., Levine, L. S., & Pang, S. (1981). Adrenal androgens and growth. In M. Ritzen (Ed.), *The biology of normal human growth: Transactions of the First Karolinska Institute Nobel Conference* (pp. 285–295). New York: Raven Press.

Parker, L. N. (1991). Adrenarche. *Endocrinology and Metabolism Clinics of North America, 20(1),* 71–83.

Pattatucci, A. M. L., & Hamer, D. H. (1995). Development and familiality of sexual orientation in females. *Behavior Genetics, 25,* 407–420.

Timiras, P. S. (1972). *Developmental physiology and aging.* New York: Macmillan.

Recommended Reading

Becker, J. B., Breedlove, S. M., & Crews, D. (Ed.). (1992). *Behavioral endocrinology.* London: MIT Press.

Boxer, A., & Cohler, B. (1989). The life-course of gay and lesbian youth: An immodest proposal for the study of lives. In G. Herdt (Ed.), *Gay and lesbian youth* (pp. 315–335). New York: Harrington Park Press.

Korth-Schütz, S. S. (1989). Precocious adrenarche. In F. G. Maguelone (Ed.), *Pediatric and adolescent endocrinology* (pp. 226–235). New York: Karger.

Rosenfield, R. L. (1994). Normal and almost normal precocious variations in pubertal development: Premature pubarche and premature thelarche revisited. *Hormone Research, 41,* (Suppl. 2), 7–13.

Slowing down Alzheimer's

New drug treatments offer hope of delaying the disease's progress

BY PEGGY EASTMAN

After years of frustration, medical research is now yielding promising options for ways to treat and even prevent Alzheimer's disease.

Most hopeful is an array of new drug therapies for the brain-wasting disease that affects more than 4 million Americans, most of them over age 65, and costs $100 billion a year.

The accelerated pace of research will fuel "the development of more effective treatments and preventive interventions to reduce the scourge of Alzheimer's disease," Richard J. Hodes, M.D., director of the National Institute on Aging (NIA), told a congressional committee recently.

"In my view we stand at the threshold of a golden age in Alzheimer's disease research," says Edward F. Truschke, president of the Alzheimer's Association, a research and advocacy organization based in Chicago.

But, Truschke adds, a time bomb ticks for potential patients who will need extensive care if the country fails to support basic pharmaceutical research.

Up to 50 percent of people over 85 suffer from dementia—confusion, disorientation and memory loss of recent events. About 60 to 70 percent of these have Alzheimer's disease, an incurable condition in which the ability to learn, reason, remember, control behavior or perform basic tasks of daily life gradually deteriorates.

The disease appears to result from the loss of nerve cells in the brain. While the dead cells cannot be replaced, "medications are being developed that might actually preserve the health of nerve cells—that is, prevent the cells from dying," says Peter J. Whitehouse, M.D., director of the Alzheimer's Center at University Hospitals of Cleveland.

"In the future we hope to be able to identify very early, presymptomatic cases of Alzheimer's disease and treat them to prevent the appearance of symptoms," says Steven T. DeKosky, M.D., director of the Alzheimer's Disease Research Center at the University of Pittsburgh.

New drugs for Alzheimer's are expected to be approved within the next 18 months, while dozens of other drugs are under development in this country and abroad. It takes about 12 years to bring a new drug to market, according to the Pharmaceutical Research and Manufacturers Association (PhRMA).

Scientists are exploring a range of medications. To date, two have been approved to relieve some symptoms of Alzheimer's, but they are only marginally helpful. Tacrine (Cognex) has been in use for several years; donepezil (Aricept) received Food and Drug Administration (FDA) approval in 1996.

"These drugs are not wonder drugs in the sense that they will not reverse or cure the disease, but they represent a vast improvement over drugs we used in the past," says Eric B. Larson, M.D., medical director of the University of Washington Medical Center.

On the horizon—saving nerve cells

Researchers are also seeking compounds that will delay or prevent the death of nerve cells, or neurons, in the brain. And they are discovering that some drugs used for other conditions may be helpful for Alzheimer's.

More than two dozen medications are already being tested, according to PhRMA. About a quarter of these are in Phase III, which means they're being tested for effectiveness and safety in 1,000 to 3,000 human volunteers, the last step before a drug goes to the FDA for approval.

Among the drugs in Phase III testing are several acetylcholine-boosters. (A shortage of acetylcholine, a chemical that helps transmit messages between brain cells, is characteristic of Alzheimer's.)

Promising contender

One promising contender is metrifonate which, like tacrine and donepezil, relieves some symptoms of Alzheimer's. Patients taking low-dose metrifonate in a six-month study scored higher on mental-performance tests than those not taking the drug.

"The results of the study suggest that low doses of metrifonate improved cognitive function," says researcher John C. Morris, M.D., of the Washington University School of Medicine.

Another way to enhance neurotransmission is to stimulate acetylcholine receptors on brain cells with drugs called cholinergic agonists.

Other drug approaches under study:

■ calcium channel blockers, to maintain levels of calcium in cells;

■ ampakines, to boost the response of receptors on neurons;

■ trophic factors, to help brain cells grow and survive;

■ neuropeptides, to enhance memory and communication between neurons; and

■ protease inhibitors, which may stop the production of beta-amyloid, a protein that builds up abnormally and forms plaque in the brains of Alzheimer's patients.

New research on therapies and causes

Even as scientists develop new drugs to combat Alzheimer's disease, they are pursuing clues that may shed light on its causes. Some believe the disease may turn out to have more than one trigger.

Researchers have identified genes on four chromosomes—1, 14, 19 and 21—that appear to increase the risk of Alzheimer's. Genes are thought to play a role in about 5 percent of cases.

The apoE4 gene on chromosome 19 has been linked to late-onset Alzheimer's disease (after age 60), the most common kind; in fact, the gene occurs in about 40 percent of all late-onset cases.

People who inherit two apoE4 genes—one from the mother and one from the father—are at least eight times more likely to develop Alzheimer's than those who inherit two of the more common and less risky apoE3 genes, according to the National Institute on Aging (NIA).

While the technology now exists to test people in families with high rates of Alzheimer's, experts say there's no point in doing it until a preventive treatment is available.

In fact, the test may do more harm than good. People who test positive could encounter discrimination (from insurance companies, for example) or experience unnecessary anxiety (and expense) if they never develop Alzheimer's.

New findings from a small NIA study suggest that brain scans using positron emission tomography (PET) may help predict dementia before symptoms appear.

But large-scale studies are needed, says NIA researcher Pietro Pietrini, M.D., before interventions to slow the disease could be "advised or planned."

Meanwhile, scientists are studying the characteristic plaques and tangles in brains affected by Alzheimer's.

In testing why and how beta-amyloid protein builds up and forms plaques that causes nerve-cell death, one finding indicates the protein forms small channels in cell membranes, letting potentially lethal amounts of calcium into the neurons. Other studies indicate that beta-amyloid may disrupt potassium channels, which could affect calcium levels.

Scientists working at the University of Pennsylvania Medical Center recently discovered plaque-like lesions in brains affected by Alzheimer's that involve a previously unidentified protein and that are rare or absent in other neurodegenerative diseases.

"This is potentially a very significant finding," says Zaven Khachaturian, director of the Alzheimer's Association Ronald and Nancy Reagan Research Institute.

If confirmed, it could offer important clues to the origins and course of the disease and lead to new therapies.

Scientists are also focusing on a protein called *tau,* which usually forms the cross-pieces between microtubules, the long parallel railroad-like tracks in healthy neurons. In Alzheimer's, tangles occur when the neuron structure collapses, and *tau* twists into paired filaments, like two threads wound around one another.

Having identified beta-amyloid in plaques, *tau* in tangles and a new protein lesion, the question now is why proteins turn destructive in Alzheimers disease. The answers could ultimately yield new approaches to combating Alzheimer's disease.

At the Weizmann Institute of Science in Rehovot, Israel, scientists are studying a compound derived from a moss long used in Chinese folk medicine. They found that the substance, called Huperzine A, blocks the enzyme that breaks down acetylcholine.

Double benefits

Some research is focusing on remedies used for other conditions:

■ The NIA-funded Alzheimer's Disease Cooperative Study at 23 U.S. centers showed that vitamin E delayed the effects of Alzheimer's in moderately advanced cases by about seven months and slowed the decline in ordinary functions like handling money, dressing or bathing by about 25 percent.

Vitamin E is an antioxidant that fights free radicals, oxidizing molecules that can damage cells throughout the body. People taking anticoagulants need to consult their doctors before taking vitamin E since it can alter blood-clotting ability. Vitamin E can also have adverse effects on the eye disease retinitis pigmentosa.

■ Selegiline (Eldepryl), normally prescribed for Parkinson's disease, showed similar benefits to vitamin E in the same study. Using the two drugs together is not more effective than using one alone, says researcher Mary Sano, associate professor of clinical neuropsychology at Columbia University College of Physicians and Surgeons.

Selegiline can cause side effects, such as jitteriness, and must be closely monitored, says co-researcher Leon J. Thal, M.D., chairman of the Department of Neurosciences at the University of California in San Diego.

■ Scientists from the NIA and Johns Hopkins University announced that a 15-year study with over 2,300 people indicated that anti-inflammatory drugs such as over-the-counter ibuprofen—taken for as little as two years—seem to lower the risk of Alzheimer's disease.

Some researchers believe the distinctive beta-amyloid plaques of Alzheimer's may be linked to an inflammatory brain response, says Claudia Kawas, M.D., a researcher from the Johns Hopkins School of Medicine.

If that's so, taking ibuprofen may have lowered risk for the disease by reducing brain inflammation.

In this study, aspirin, also a known anti-inflammatory, and acetaminophen, which is not an anti-inflammatory, were not effective against Alzheimer's.

Self-dosing with any of these drugs is not advised, since chronic use can lead to side effects such as impaired kidney function and peptic ulcers.

■ Estrogen replacement therapy—believed to protect women against heart disease and osteoporosis—may also protect them against Alzheimer's.

One study of more than 500 women in the NIA-funded Baltimore Longitudinal Study of Aging showed that the risk for the condition was 54 percent lower among women who had taken estrogen than for women who had not.

It's possible the hormone boosts acetylcholine levels, says Pittsburgh's DeKosky, and enhances antioxidant protection against free radicals in the brain.

One unknown: Did factors other than ERT protect women in studies to date? Estrogen users, for example, were likely to have had more education, a factor that may lower the risk for Alzheimer's.

To answer that question, the Women's Health Initiative (WHI)—a major study funded by the National Institutes of Health—will launch the $16 million WHI Memory Study to determine if ERT can prevent and/or treat Alzheimer's disease.

The memory study will be conducted at 39 U.S. medical centers with 8,000 women age 65 and older and will last for six years. For details, call (800) 549–6636.

■ A key research finding recently revealed a link between the brain damage caused by stroke and Alzheimer's disease.

In a study of 102 elderly Catholic nuns published in the Journal of the American Medical Association (JAMA), researchers from the University of Kentucky's Sanders-Brown Center on Aging found that 61 women showed evidence of Alzheimer's on autopsy.

The prevalence of dementia was 93 percent among those who had had one or more small strokes in certain areas of the brain, compared to 57 percent

among those who had not had such strokes.

Lead researcher David A. Snowdon says that strokes "may play an important role in determining the presence and severity" of Alzheimer's. But, he adds, more study will be needed to determine if preventing strokes can "mute the clinical expression" of the disease.

For the millions of patients and families who live with the disease every day, the scientific sleuthing—on all fronts—can't proceed fast enough.

Advice and support for caregivers

Former first lady Nancy Reagan is one of the thousands of Americans struggling to care for an Alzheimer's patient with love and patience. "Victims and families are suffering with the cruelty of this disease every single hour of every day," she says.

Among the educational and support services for caregivers:

■ Alzheimer's Safe Return, sponsored by the Alzheimer's Association, provides identity bracelets, ID cards and clothing labels for Alzheimer's patients and maintains a national data base connected to U.S. law-enforcement agencies nationwide and a 24-hour toll-free number.

The one-time charge is $25. For a registration form or to learn more about Alzheimer's or the location of the association chapter nearest you, call (800) 272–3900. Visit the group's Web site at **www.alz.org.**

■ Alzheimer's Disease Education and Referral Center (ADEAR) at the National Institute on Aging offers a variety of free information about Alzheimer's studies, drugs, organizations and services. Call (800) 438–4380 and check their Web site at **www.alzheimer's.org/adear.**

■ TriAD (Three for the Management of Alzheimer's Disease), developed by Eisai Inc. and Pfizer Inc.

with the collaboration of the Alzheimer's Association and the National Council on Aging, provides information and support to caregivers and patients. It also offers materials that help caregivers understand Alzheimer's disease and communicate with doctors. Call toll-free (888) 874–2343.

■ The Agency for Health Care Policy and Research Publications Clearinghouse provides free booklets, "Early Alzheimer's Disease" (patient and family guide, 960704) and "Alzheimer's Guideline Overview, 96-R123." Write the clearinghouse at P.O. Box 8547, Silver Spring, Md. 20907.

Unit Selections

30. **The Personality Genes,** J. Madeleine Nash
31. **The Stability of Personality: Observations and Evaluations,**
    Robert R. McCrae and Paul T. Costa Jr.
32. **Are You Shy?** Bernardo J. Carducci with Philip G. Zimbardo
33. **Finding Strength: How to Overcome Anything,** Deborah Blum

Key Points to Consider

❖ What is the study of personality; what is the definition of personality? What are some of the major tenets of most personality theories?

❖ What do you think contributes most to our unique personalities, genes or environment? If you answered genes, what does this imply about the possibility of personality change? If you answered environment, do you think that genes plays any role in personality?

❖ Is personality stable or ever-changing across a lifetime? Explain. What are the advantages of a stable personality? What is the advantage of ever-changing aspects of personality?

❖ From where does the trait of shyness originate? What can shy individuals do to overcome their shyness? What other traits do you think would be important to measure besides shyness? Psychologists have now identified five traits that they think describe all individuals fairly well. Do you think shyness is one of these traits? What are the others?

❖ What is resiliency? Is everyone resilient to some degree or other? Are you resilient? Do you know others who are? What are the types of problems that resilient individuals can easily overcome? What can we do to become resilient if we are not? If an individual is not resilient, how can he or she best cope with daily hassles and with major life traumas?

 **Links**

www.dushkin.com/online/

23. **The Personality Project**
    http://fas.psych.nwu.edu/personality.html

These sites are annotated on pages 4 and 5.

Rashida and Sadie are identical twins. When the girls were young, their parents tried very hard to treat them equally. Whenever Rashida received a present, Sadie received one. Both girls attended dance school and completed early classes in ballet and tap dance. In elementary school, the twins were both placed in the same class. Their teacher also tried to treat them alike.

In junior high school, Sadie became a tomboy. She loved to play rough-and-tumble sports with the neighborhood boys. On the other hand, Rashida remained indoors and practiced on her piano. Rashida was keenly interested in the domestic arts such as sewing and needlepoint. Sadie was more interested in reading science fiction novels and in watching adventure on television.

As the twins matured, they decided it would be best to attend different colleges. Rashida went to a small, quiet college in a rural setting, and Sadie matriculated at a large public university. Rashida majored in English, with a specialty in poetry; Sadie switched majors several times and finally decided on a communications major.

Why, when these twins were exposed to the same childhood environment, did their interests and paths diverge later? What makes even identical twins so unique, so different from one another?

The study of individual differences is the domain of personality. The psychological study of personality has included two major thrusts. The first has focused on the search for the commonalties of human life and development. Its major question would be: How are all humans, especially their personalities, affected by specific events or activities? Personality theories are based on the assumption that a given event, if it is important, will affect almost all people in a similar way, or that the processes by which events affect people are common across events and people. Most psychological research into personality variables has made this assumption. Failures to replicate a research project are often the first clues that differences in individual responses require further investigation.

While some psychologists have focused on personality-related effects that are presumed to be universal among humans, others have devoted their efforts to discovering the bases on which individuals differ in their responses to environmental events. In the beginning, this specialty was called genetic psychology, because most people assumed that individual differences resulted from differences in genetic inheritance. By the 1950s the term genetic psychology had given way to the more current term: the psychology of individual differences.

Does this mean that genetic variables are no longer the key to understanding individual differences? Not at all. For a time, psychologists took up the philosophical debate over whether genetic or environmental factors were more important in determining behaviors. Even today, behavior geneticists compute the heritability coefficients for a number of personality and behavior traits, including intelligence. This is an expression of the degree to which differences in a given trait can be attributed to differences in inherited capacity or ability. Most psychologists, however, accept the principle that both genetic and environmental determinants are important in any area of behavior. These researchers are devoting more of their efforts to discovering how the two sources of influence interact to produce the unique individual. Given the above, the focus of this unit is on personality characteristics and the differences and similarities among individuals.

What is personality? Most researchers in the area define personality as patterns of thoughts, feelings, and behaviors that persist over time and over situations, are characteristic or typical of the individual, and usually distinguish one person from another.

In the first article, "The Personality Genes," the author discovers that DNA might well shape personality and behavior. In other words, we have yet another article investigating the all-important topic of the influence of biology on seemingly psychological processes, in this case, personality.

The second article is also a rather general one about personality. The "Stability of Personality: Observations and Evaluations" features research on individual differences, the crux of personality. This research examines whether people remain the same over a lifetime or change. Robert McCrae and Paul Costa conclude that our personality characteristics remain quite stable across a lifespan.

We next look at several specific aspects of personality, called by some personologists "traits." The first trait is shyness. In their essay on shyness, Bernardo Carducci, with Philip Zimbardo, explains that shy individuals are often misconstrued by others in society; that is, they are often negatively misinterpreted as being snobbish. The authors further elaborate on the causes of and the cures for shyness.

In the final article on personality, one last trait is discussed—resiliency. Psychologists used to almost exclusively study only those individuals with psychological and other types of problems. Now we study individuals who have overcome problems; such individuals are said to have the characteristic of resiliency. This final article explores what resilient individuals are like and how each of us can establish some degree of resiliency in our daily lives.

THE PERSONALITY
GENES

Does DNA shape behavior? A leading researcher's behavior is a case in point

By J. MADELEINE NASH

MOLECULAR BIOLOGIST Dean Hamer has blue eyes, light brown hair and the goofy sense of humor of a stand-up comic. He smokes cigarettes, spends long hours in a cluttered laboratory at the National Institutes of Health, and in his free time clambers up cliffs and points his skis down steep, avalanche-prone slopes. He also happens to be openly, matter-of-factly gay.

What is it that makes Hamer who he is? What, for that matter, accounts for the quirks and foibles, talents and traits that make up anyone's personality? Hamer is not content merely to ask such questions; he is trying to answer them as well. A pioneer in the field of molecular psychology, Hamer is exploring the role genes play in governing the very core of our individuality. To a remarkable extent, his work on what might be called the gay, thrill-seeking and quit-smoking genes reflects his own genetic predispositions.

That work, which has appeared mostly in scientific journals, has been gathered into an accessible and quite readable form in Hamer's provocative new book, *Living with Our Genes* (Doubleday; $24.95). "You have about as much choice in some aspects of your personality," Hamer and coauthor Peter Copeland write in the introductory chapter, "as you do in the shape of your nose or the size of your feet."

Until recently, research into behavioral genetics was dominated by psychiatrists and psychologists, who based their most compelling conclusions about the importance of genes on studies of identical twins. For example, psychologist Michael Bailey of Northwestern University famously demonstrated that if one identical twin is gay, there is about a 50% likelihood that the other will be too. Seven years ago, Hamer picked up where the twin studies left off, homing in on specific strips of DNA that appear to influence everything from mood to sexual orientation.

Hamer switched to behavioral genetics from basic research; after receiving his Ph.D. from Harvard, he spent more then a decade studying the biochemistry of metallothionein, a protein that cells use to metabolize heavy metals like copper and zinc. As he was about to turn 40, however, Hammer suddenly realized he had learned as much about metallothionein as he cared to. "Frankly, I was bored," he remembers, "and ready for something new."

Instrumental in Hamer's decision to switch fields was Charles Darwin's *The Descent of Man, and Selection in Relation to Sex*. "I was fascinated to learn that Darwin seemed so convinced that behavior was partially inherited," he remembers, "even though when he was writing, genes had not been discovered, let alone DNA." Homosexual behavior, in particular, seemed ripe for exploration because few scientists had dared tackle such an emotionally and politically charged subject. "I'm gay," Hamer says with

Nature or Nurture?
Many aspects of personality may have a genetic component—such as sexual orientation, anxiety, a tendency to take chances and ...

IMPULSIVENESS

OPENNESS

a shrug, "but that was not a major motivation. It was more of a question of intellectual curiosity—and the fact that no one else was doing this sort of research."

The results of Hamer's first foray into behavioral genetics, published by the journal *Science* in 1993, ignited a furor that has yet to die down. According to Hamer and his colleagues, male homosexuality appeared to be linked to a stretch of DNA at the very tip of the X chromosome, the chromosome men inherit from their mothers. Three years later, in 1996, Hamer and his collaborators at NIH seconded an Israeli group's finding that linked a gene on chromosome 11 to the personality trait psychologists called novelty seeking. That same year Hamer's lab helped pinpoint another gene, this time on chromosome 17, that appears to play a role in regulating anxiety.

Unlike the genes that are responsible for physical traits, Hamer emphasizes, these genes do not cause people to become homosexuals, thrill-seeking rock climbers or anxiety-ridden worrywarts. The biology of personality is much more complicated than that. Rather, what genes appear to do, says Hamer, is subtly bias the psyche so that different individuals react to similar experiences in surprisingly different ways.

Intriguing as these findings are, other experts caution that none has been unequivocally replicated by other research teams. Why? One possibility is that, despite all of Hamer's work, the links between these genes and these particular personality traits do not, in fact, exist. There is, however, another, more tantalizing possibility. Consider the genes that give tomatoes their flavor, suggests Hamer's colleague Dr. Dennis Murphy of the National Institute of Mental Health. Even a simple trait like acidity is controlled not by a single gene but by as many as 30 that operate in concert. In the same way, he

speculates, many genes are involved in setting up temperamental traits and psychological vulnerabilities; each gene contributes just a little bit to the overall effect.

Hunting down the genes that influence personality remains a dauntingly difficult business. Although DNA is constructed out of a mere four chemicals—adenine, guanine, cytosine, thymine—it can take as many as a million combinations to spell out a single human gene. Most of these genes vary from individual to individual by only one chemical letter in a thousand, and it is precisely these minute differences that Hamer and his colleagues are trying to identify. Of particular interest are variations that may affect the operation of such brain chemicals as dopamine and serotonin, which are well-known modulators of mood. The so-called novelty-seeking gene, for example, is thought to affect how efficiently nerve cells absorb dopamine. The so-called anxiety gene is postulated to affect serotonin's action.

How can this be? After all, as Hamer and Copeland observe in their book, " . . . genes are not switches that say 'shy' or 'outgoing' or 'happy' or 'sad.' Genes are simply chemicals that direct the combination of more chemicals." What genes do is order up the production of proteins in organs like the kidney, the skin and also the brain. Thus, Hamer speculates, one version of the novelty-seeking gene may make a protein that is less efficient at absorbing dopamine. Since dopamine is the chemical that creates sensations of pleasure in response to intense experiences, people who inherit this gene might seek to stimulate its production by seeking out thrills.

Still, as critics emphasize and Hamer himself acknowledges, genes alone do not control the chemistry of the brain. Ultimately, it is the environment that determines how these genes will express themselves. In

another setting, for example, it is easy to imagine that Hamer might have become a high school dropout rather than a scientist. For while he grew up in an affluent household in Montclair, N.J., he was hardly a model child. "Today," he chuckles, "I probably would have been diagnosed with attention-deficit disorder and put on Ritalin." In his senior year in high school, though, Hamer discovered organic chemistry and went from being an unruly adolescent to a first-rate student. What people are born with, Hamer says, are temperamental traits. What they can acquire through experience is the ability to control these traits by exercising that intangible part of personality called character.

Over the coming decade, Hamer predicts, scientists will identify thousands of genes that directly and indirectly influence behavior. A peek inside the locked freezer in the hallway outside his own lab reveals a rapidly expanding stash of plastic tubes that contain DNA samples form more than 1,760 volunteers. Among them: gay men and their heterosexual brothers, a random assortment of novelty seekers and novelty avoiders, shy children and now a growing collection of cigarette smokers.

Indeed, while Hamer has maintained a professional distance from his studies, it is impossible to believe he is not also driven by a desire for self-discovery. Soon, in fact, his lab will publish a paper about a gene that makes it harder or easier for people to stop smoking. Judging by the pack of cigarettes poking out of his shirt pocket, Hamer would seem to have drawn the wrong end of that genetic stick. He has tried to stop smoking and failed, he confesses, dozens of times. "If I quit," he says, "it will be an exercise of character." And not, it goes without saying, of his genes.

ILLUSTRATIONS FOR TIME BY SCOTT MENCHIN

The Stability of Personality: Observations and Evaluations

Robert R. McCrae and
Paul T. Costa, Jr.

Robert R. McCrae is Research Psychologist and **Paul T. Costa, Jr.,** is Chief, Laboratory of Personality and Cognition, both at the Gerontology Research Center, National Institute on Aging, National Institutes of Health. Address correspondence to Robert R. McCrae, Personality, Stress and Coping Section, Gerontology Research Center, 4940 Eastern Ave., Baltimore, MD 21224.

"There is an optical illusion about every person we meet," Ralph Waldo Emerson wrote in his essay on "Experience":

In truth, they are all creatures of given temperament, which will appear in a given character, whose boundaries they will never pass: but we look at them, they seem alive, and we presume there is impulse in them. In the moment it seems impulse; in the year, in the lifetime, it turns out to be a certain uniform tune which the revolving barrel of the music-box must play.[1]

In this brief passage, Emerson anticipated modern findings about the stability of personality and pointed out an illusion to which both laypersons and psychologists are prone. He was also perhaps the first to decry personality stability as the enemy of freedom, creativity, and growth, objecting that "temperament puts all divinity to rout." In this article, we summarize evidence in support of Emerson's observations but offer arguments against his evaluation of them.[2]

EVIDENCE FOR THE STABILITY OF ADULT PERSONALITY

Emerson used the term temperament to refer to the basic tendencies of the individual, dispositions that we call personality traits. It is these traits, measured by such instruments as the Minnesota Multiphasic Personality Inventory and the NEO Personality Inventory, that have been investigated in a score of longitudinal studies over the past 20 years. Despite a wide variety of samples, instruments, and designs, the results of these studies have been remarkably consistent, and they are easily summarized.

1. The mean levels of personality traits change with development, but reach final adult levels at about age 30. Between 20 and 30, both men and women become somewhat less emotional and thrill-seeking and somewhat more cooperative and self-disciplined—changes we might interpret as evidence of increased maturity. After age 30, there are few and subtle changes, of which the most consistent is a small decline in activity level with advancing age. Except among individuals with dementia, stereotypes that depict older people as being withdrawn, depressed, or rigid are unfounded.
2. Individual differences in personality traits, which show at least some continuity from early childhood on, are also essentially fixed by age 30.

Stability coefficients (test-retest correlations over substantial time intervals) are typically in the range of .60 to .80, even over intervals of as long as 30 years, although there is some decline in magnitude with increasing retest interval. Given that most personality scales have short-term retest reliabilities in the range from .70 to .90, it is clear that by far the greatest part of the reliable variance (i.e., variance not due to measurement error) in personality traits is stable.
3. Stability appears to characterize all five of the major domains of personality—neuroticism, extraversion, openness to experience, agreeableness, and conscientiousness. This finding suggests that an adult's personality profile as a whole will change little over time, and studies of the stability of configural measures of personality support that view.
4. Generalizations about stability apply to virtually everyone. Men and women, healthy and sick people, blacks and whites all show the same pattern. When asked, most adults will say that their personality has not changed much in adulthood, but even those who claim to have had major changes show little objective evidence of change on repeated administrations of personality questionnaires. Important exceptions to this generalization include people suffering from dementia and certain

From *Current Directions in Psychological Science*, December 1994, pp. 173–175. Reprinted by permission of Cambridge University Press.

categories of psychiatric patients who respond to therapy, but no moderators of stability among healthy adults have yet been identified.[3]

When researchers first began to publish these conclusions, they were greeted with considerable skepticism—"I distrust the facts and the inferences" Emerson had written—and many studies were designed to test alternative hypotheses. For example, some researchers contended that consistent responses to personality questionnaires were due to memory of past responses, but retrospective studies showed that people could not accurately recall how they had previously responded even when instructed to do so. Other researchers argued that temporal consistency in self-reports merely meant that individuals had a fixed idea of themselves, a crystallized self-concept that failed to keep pace with real changes in personality. But studies using spouse and peer raters showed equally high levels of stability.[4]

The general conclusion that personality traits are stable is now widely accepted. Some researchers continue to look for change in special circumstances and populations; some attempt to account for stability by examining genetic and environmental influences on personality. Finally, others take the view that there is much more to personality than traits, and seek to trace the adult developmental course of personality perceptions or identity formation or life narratives.

These latter studies are worthwhile, because people undoubtedly do change across the life span. Marriages end in divorce, professional careers are started in mid-life, fashions and attitudes change with the times. Yet often the same traits can be seen in new guises: Intellectual curiosity merely shifts from one field to another, avid gardening replaces avid tennis, one abusive relationship is followed by another. Many of these changes are best regarded as variations on the "uniform tune" played by individuals' enduring dispositions.

ILLUSORY ATTRIBUTIONS IN TEMPORAL PERSPECTIVE

Social and personality psychologists have debated for some time the accuracy of attributions of the causes of behavior to persons or situations. The "optical illusion" in person perception that Emerson pointed to was somewhat different. He felt that people attribute behavior to the live and spontaneous person who freely creates responses to the situation, when in fact behavior reveals only the mechanical operation of lifeless and static temperament. We may (and we will!) take exception to this disparaging, if common, view of traits, but we must first concur with the basic observation that personality processes often appear different when viewed in longitudinal perspective: "The years teach much which the days never know."

Consider happiness. If one asks individuals why they are happy or unhappy, they are almost certain to point to environmental circumstances of the moment: a rewarding job, a difficult relationship, a threat to health, a new car. It would seem that levels of happiness ought to mirror quality of life, and that changes in circumstances would result in changes in subjective well-being. It would be easy to demonstrate this pattern in a controlled laboratory experiment: Give subjects $1,000 each and ask how they feel!

But survey researchers who have measured the objective quality of life by such indicators as wealth, education, and health find precious little association with subjective well-being, and longitudinal researchers have found surprising stability in individual differences in happiness, even among people whose life circumstances have changed markedly. The explanation is simple: People adapt to their circumstances rapidly, getting used to the bad and taking for granted the good. In the long run, happiness is largely a matter of enduring personality traits.[5] "Temper prevails over everything of time, place, and condition, and . . . fix[es] the measure of activity and of enjoyment."

A few years ago, William Swann and Craig Hill provided an ingenious demonstration of the errors to which too narrow a temporal perspective can lead. A number of experiments had shown that it was relatively easy to induce changes in the self-concept by providing self-discrepant feedback. Introverts told that they were really extraverts rated themselves higher in extraversion than they had before. Such studies supported the view that the self-concept is highly malleable, a mirror of the evaluation of the immediate environment.

Swann and Hill replicated this finding, but extended it by inviting subjects back a few days later. By that time, the effects of the manipulation had disappeared, and subjects had returned to their initial self-concepts. The implication is that any one-shot experiment may give a seriously misleading view of personality processes.[6]

The relations between coping and adaptation provide a final example. Cross-sectional studies show that individuals who use such coping mechanisms as self-blame, wishful thinking, and hostile reactions toward other people score lower on measures of well-being than people who do not use these mechanisms. It would be easy to infer that these coping mechanisms detract from adaptation, and in fact the very people who use them admit that they are ineffective. But the correlations vanish when the effects of prior neuroticism scores are removed; an alternative interpretation of the data is thus that individuals who score high on this personality factor use poor coping strategies and also have low well-being: The association between coping and well-being may be entirely attributable to this third variable.[7]

Psychologists have long been aware of the problems of inferring causes from correlational data, but they have not recognized the pervasiveness of the bias that Emerson warned about. People tend to understand behavior and experience as the result of the immediate context, whether intrapsychic or environmental. Only by looking over time can one see the persistent effects of personality traits.

THE EVALUATION OF STABILITY

If few findings in psychology are more robust than the stability of personality, even fewer are more unpopular. Gerontologists often see stability as an affront to their commitment to continuing adult development; psychotherapists sometimes view it as an alarming challenge to their ability to help patients;[8] humanistic psychologists and transcendental philosophers think it degrades human nature. A popular account in *The Idaho Statesman* ran under the disheartening headline "Your Personality—You're Stuck With It."

In our view, these evaluations are based on misunderstandings: At worst, stability is a mixed blessing. Those individuals who are anxious, quarrelsome, and lazy might be understandably distressed to think that they are likely to stay that way, but surely those who are imaginative, affectionate, and carefree at age 30 should be glad to hear that they will probably be imaginative, affectionate, and carefree at age 90.

Because personality is stable, life is to some extent predictable. People can make vocational and retirement choices with some confidence that their current interests and enthusiasms will not desert them. They can choose friends and mates with whom they are likely to remain compatible. They can vote on the basis of candidates' records, with some assurance that future policies will resemble past ones. They can learn which co-workers they can depend on, and which they cannot. The personal and social utility of personality stability is enormous.

But it is precisely this predictability that so offends many critics. ("I had fancied that the value of life lay in its inscrutable possibilities," Emerson complained.) These critics view traits as mechanical and static habits and believe that the stability of personality traits dooms human beings to lifeless monotony as puppets controlled by inexorable forces. This is a misunderstanding on several levels.

First, personality traits are not repetitive habits, but inherently dynamic dispositions that interact with the opportunities and challenges of the moment.[9] Antagonistic people do not yell at everyone; some people they flatter, some they scorn, some they threaten. Just as the same intelligence is applied to a lifetime of changing problems, so the same personality traits can be expressed in an infinite variety of ways, each suited to the situation.

Second, there are such things as spontaneity and impulse in human life, but they are stable traits. Individuals who are open to experience actively seek out new places to go, provocative ideas to ponder, and exotic sights, sounds, and tastes to experience. Extraverts show a different kind of spontaneity, making friends, seeking thrills, and jumping at every chance to have a good time. People who are introverted and closed to experience have more measured and monotonous lives, but this is the kind of life they choose.

Finally, personality traits are not inexorable forces that control our fate, nor are they, in psychodynamic language, ego alien. Our traits characterize us; they are our very selves;[10] we act most freely when we express our enduring dispositions. Individuals sometimes fight against their own tendencies, trying perhaps to overcome shyness or curb a bad temper. But most people acknowledge even these failings as their own, and it is well that they do. A person's recognition of the inevitability of his or her one and only personality is a large part of what Erik Erikson called ego integrity, the culminating wisdom of a lifetime.

Notes

1. All quotations are from "Experience," in *Essays: First and Second Series,* R.W. Emerson (Vintage, New York, 1990) (original work published 1844).

2. For recent and sometimes divergent treatments of this topic, see R.R. McCrae and P.T. Costa, Jr., *Personality in Adulthood* (Guilford, New York, 1990); D. C. Funder, R.D. Parke, C. Tomlinson-Keasey and K. Widaman, Eds., *Studying Lives Through Time: Personality and Development* (American Psychological Association, Washington, DC, 1993); T. Heatherton and J. Weinberger, *Can Personality Change?* (American Psychological Association, Washington, DC, 1994).

3. L.C. Siegler, K.A. Welsh, D.V. Dawson, G.G. Fillenbaum, N.L. Earl, E.B. Kaplan, and C.M. Clark, Ratings of personality change in patients being evaluated for memory disorders, *Alzheimer Disease and Associated Disorders, 5,* 240–250 (1991); R.M.A. Hirschfeld, G.L. Klerman, P. Clayton, M.B. Keller, P. McDonald-Scott, and B. Larkin, Assessing personality: Effects of depressive state on trait measurement, *American Journal of Psychiatry, 140,* 695–699 (1983); R.R. McCrae, Mediated analyses of longitudinal personality stability, *Journal of Personality and Social Psychology, 65,* 577–585 (1993).

4. D. Woodruff, The role of memory in personality continuity: A 25 year follow-up, *Experimental Aging Research, 9,* 31–34 (1983); P.T. Costa, Jr., and R.R. McCrae, Trait psychology comes of age, in *Nebraska Symposium on Motivation: Psychology and Aging,* T.B. Sonderegger, Ed. (University of Nebraska Press, Lincoln, 1992).

5. P.T. Costa, Jr., and R.R. McCrae, Influence of extraversion and neuroticism on subjective well-being: Happy and unhappy people, *Journal of Personality and Social Psychology, 38,* 668–678 (1980).

6. The study is summarized in W.B. Swann, Jr., and C.A. Hill, When our identities are mistaken: Reaffirming self-conceptions through social interactions, *Journal of Personality and Social Psychology, 43,* 59–66 (1982). Dangers of single-occasion research are also discussed in J.R. Council, Context effects in personality research, *Current Directions in Psychological Science, 2,* 31–34 (1993).

7. R.R. McCrae and P.T. Costa, Jr., Personality, coping, and coping effectiveness in an adult sample, *Journal of Personality, 54,* 385–405 (1986).

8. Observations in nonpatient samples show what happens over time under typical life circumstances; they do not rule out the possibility that psychotherapeutic interventions can change personality. Whether or not such change is possible, in practice much of psychotherapy consists of helping people learn to live with their limitations, and this may be a more realistic goal than "cure" for many patients. See P.T. Costa, Jr., and R.R. McCrae, Personality stability and its implications for clinical psychology, *Clinical Psychology Review, 6,* 407–423 (1986).

9. A. Tellegen, Personality traits: Issues of definition, evidence and assessment, in *Thinking Clearly About Psychology: Essays in Honor of Paul E. Meehl,* Vol. 2, W. Grove and D. Cicchetti, Eds. (University of Minnesota Press, Minneapolis, 1991).

10. R.R. McCrae and P.T. Costa, Jr., Age, personality, and the spontaneous self-concept, *Journals of Gerontology: Social Sciences, 43,* S177–S185 (1988).

ARE YOU SHY?

*You have lots of company. Nearly one of two Americans claims to be shy.
What's more, the incidence is rising, and technology may be turning ours into
a culture of shyness.*

Bernardo J. Carducci, Ph.D.,
with Philip G. Zimbardo, Ph.D.

In sharp contrast to the flamboyant life-style getting under way at dance clubs across the country, another, quieter, picture of Americans was emerging from psychological research. Its focus: those on the sidelines of the dance floor. In 1975 *Psychology Today* published a ground-breaking article by Stanford University psychologist Philip Zimbardo, Ph.D., entitled "The Social Disease Called Shyness." The article revealed what Zimbardo had found in a survey conducted at several American colleges: An astonishing 40 percent of the 800 questioned currently considered themselves to be shy.

In addition to documenting the pervasiveness of shyness, the article presented a surprising portrait of those with the condition. Their mild-mannered exterior conceals roiling turmoil inside. The shy disclosed that they are excessively self-conscious, constantly sizing themselves up negatively, and overwhelmingly preoccupied with what others think of them. While everyone else is meeting and greeting, they are developing plans to manage their public impression (*If I stand at the far end of the room and pretend to be examining the painting on the wall, I'll look like I'm interested in art but won't have to talk to anybody*). They are consumed by the misery of the social setting (*I'm having a horrible time at this party because I don't know what to say and everyone seems to be staring at me*). All the while their hearts are pounding, their pulses are speeding, and butterflies are swarming in their stomach—physiological symptoms of genuine distress.

The article catalogued the painful consequences of shyness. There are social problems, such as difficulty meeting people and making new friends, which may leave the shy woefully isolated and subject to loneliness and depression. There are cognitive problems; unable to think clearly in the presence of others, the shy tend to freeze up in conversation, confusing others who are trying to respond to them. They can appear snobbish or disinterested in others, when they are in fact just plain nervous. Excessively egocentric, they are relentlessly preoccupied with every aspect of their own appearance and behavior. They live trapped between two fears: being invisible and insignificant to others, and being visible but worthless.

The response to the article was overwhelming. A record number of letters to the editor screamed HELP ME!, surprising considering that then, as now, PT readers were generally well-educated, self-aware, and open-minded—not a recipe for shyness.

The article launched a whole new field of study. In the past 20 years, a variety of researchers and clinicians, including myself, have been scrutinizing shyness. To celebrate the 20th anniversary of PTs epochal report, we decided to spotlight recent advances in understanding this social disease:

• Research in my laboratory and elsewhere suggests that, courtesy of changing cultural conditions, the incidence of shyness in the U.S. may now be as high as 48 per-cent—and rising.

• Most shyness is hidden. Only a small percentage of the shy appear to be obviously ill at ease. But all suffer internally.

• Some people are born with a temperamental tilt to shyness. But even that inheritance doesn't doom one to a life of averting others' eyes. A lot depends on parenting.

• Most shyness is acquired through life experiences.

• There is a neurobiology of shyness. At least three brain centers that mediate fear and anxiety orchestrate the whole-body response we recognize as shyness. Think of it as an over-generalized fear response.

• The incidence of shyness varies among countries. Israelis seem to be the least shy inhabitants of the world. A major contributing factor: cultural styles of assigning praise and blame to kids.

• Shyness has huge costs to individuals at all ages, especially in Western cultures.

• Shyness does have survival value.

• Despite the biological hold of shyness, there are now specific and well-documented ways to overcome its crippling effects.

Shy on the Sly

How is it possible that 40 to 50 percent of Americans—some of your friends, no doubt—are shy? Because while some people are obviously, publicly shy, a much larger percentage are privately shy. Their shyness, and its pain, is invisible to everyone but themselves.

Only 15 to 20 percent of shy people actually fit the stereotype of the ill-at-ease person. They use every excuse in the book to avoid social events. If they are unlucky enough to find themselves in casual conversation, they can't quite manage to make eye contact, to reply to questions without stumbling over their words, or to keep up their end of the conversation; they seldom smile. They are easy to pick

Reprinted with permission from *Psychology Today*, November/December 1995, pp. 34–40, 64, 66, 68, 70, 78, 82. © 1995 by Sussex Publishers, Inc.

out of a crowd because their shyness is expressed behaviorally.

The other 80 to 85 percent are privately shy, according to University of Pittsburgh psychologist Paul Pilkonis, Ph.D. Though their shyness leaves no behavioral traces—it's felt subjectively—it wreaks personal havoc. They feel their shyness in a pounding heart and pouring sweat. While they may seem at ease and confident in conversation, they are actually engaging in a self-deprecating inner dialogue, chiding themselves for being inept and questioning whether the person they are talking to really likes them. "Even though these people do fairly well socially, they have a lot of negative self-thought going on in their heads," explains Pilkonis. Their shyness has emotional components as well. When the conversation is over, they feel upset or defeated.

"There are a lot of people who have private aspects of shyness who are willing to say they are shy but don't quite jibe with the people we can see trembling or blushing," notes Pilkonis.

The Natural History of Shyness

Shyness has not always been a source of pain. Being shy or inhibited serves a very protective function: it breeds caution. No doubt shyness has pulled *H. sapiens* out of some pretty tight spots over the eons.

Originally, shyness served as protective armor around the physical self. After all, only after an animal has fully acquainted itself with a new environment is it safe to behave in a more natural, relaxed manner and explore around. The process of habituation is one of the most fundamental characteristics of all organisms.

As conscious awareness has increased, the primary threat is now to the psychological self—embarrassment. Most people show some degree of social inhibition; they think about what they are going to say or do before hand, as well as the consequences of saying or doing it. It keeps us from making fools of ourselves or hurting the feelings of others.

According to Wellesley psychologist Jonathan Cheek, Ph.D., situational shyness "can help to facilitate cooperative living; it inhibits behaviors that are socially unacceptable." So, a little bit of shyness may be good for you and society. But too much benefits no one.

Shyness can lurk in unlikely hosts—even those of the talk show variety. Take David Letterman, king of late-night TV. Although his performance in front of a live studio audience and countless viewers seems relaxed and spontaneous, Letterman is known to be relentless in the planning and orchestration of each nightly performance down to the last detail. Like Johnny Carson, he spends little time socializing outside a very small circle of friends and rarely attends social functions.

Letterman is the perfect example of what Zimbardo calls the shy extrovert: the cool, calm, and collected type whose insides are in fact churning. A subset of the privately shy, shy extroverts may be politicians, entertainers, and teachers. They have learned to act outgoing—as long as they are in a controlled environment. A politician who can speak from a prepared script at a mass political rally really may get tongue-tied during a question-and-answer period. A professor may be comfortable as long as she is talking about her area of expertise; put in a social gathering where she may have to make small talk, she clams up.

Zimbardo's short list of notable shy extroverts: funny lady Carol Burnett, singer Johnny Mathis, television reporter Barbara Walters, and international opera star Joan Sutherland. These stars are not introverts, a term often confused with shyness. Introverts have the conversational skills and self esteem necessary for interacting successfully with others but prefer to be alone. Shy people want very much to be with others but lack the social skills and self-esteem.

What unites the shy of any type is acute self-consciousness. The shy are even self-conscious about their self-consciousness. Theirs is a twisted egocentricity. They spend so much time focusing on themselves and their weaknesses, they have little time or inclination to look outward.

Wired for Shyness?

According to developmental psychologist Jerome Kagan, Ph.D., and colleagues at Harvard University, up to a third of shy adults were born with a temperament that inclined them to it. The team has been able to identify shyness in young infants before environmental conditions make an impact.

In his longitudinal studies, 400 four-month-old infants were brought into the lab and subjected to such stimuli as moving mobiles, a whiff of a Q-Tip dipped in alcohol, and a tape recording of the human voice. Then they were brought back at a later age for further study. From countless hours of observation, rerun on videotapes, Kagan, along with Harvard psychologists Nancy Snidman, Ph.D, and Doreen Arcus, Ph.D., have nailed down the behavioral manifestations of shyness in infants.

About 20 percent of infants display a pattern of extreme nervous-system reactivity to such common stimuli. These infants grow distressed when faced with unfamiliar people, objects, and events. They momentarily extend their arms and legs spastically, they vigorously wave their arms and kick their legs, and, on occasion, arch their backs. They also show signs of distress in the form of excessive fretting and crying, usually at a high pitch and sustained tension that communicates urgency. Later on, they cling to their parents in a new play situation.

In contrast, 40 percent of all infants exposed to the same stimuli occasionally move an arm or leg but do not show the motor outbursts or fretting and crying typical of their highly reactive brethren. When the low-reactive infants do muster up a crying spell, it is nothing out of the ordinary.

Lab studies indicate that highly reactive infants have an easily excitable sympathetic nervous system. This neural network regulates not only many vital organs, including the heart, but the brain response of fear. With their high-strung, hair-trigger temperament, even the suggestion of danger—a stranger, a new environment—launches the psychological and physiologic arousal of fear and anxiety.

One of the first components of this reaction is an increased heart rate. Remarkably, studies show that high-reactive infants have a higher-than-normal heart rate—and it can he detected even before birth, while the infant is still *in utero*. At 14 months, such infants have over-large heart rate acceleration in response to a neutral stimulus such as a sour taste.

Four years later, the same kids show another sign of sympathetic arousal—a cooler temperature reading in their right ring finger than in their left ring finger while watching emotionally evocative film clips. Too, as children they show more brain wave activity in the right frontal lobe; by contrast, normally reactive children display more brain wave activity in the left frontal area. From other studies it is known that the right side of the brain is more involved in the expression of anxiety and distress.

The infant patterns point to an inborn variation in the response threshold of the amygdala, an almond-shaped brain structure linked to the expression of fear and anxiety (see "The Shy Brain"). This neural hypersensitivity eventually inclines such children to avoid situations that give rise to anxiety and fear—meeting new people or being thrown into new environments. In such circumstances they are behaviorally inhibited.

Though it might sound strange, there may even be a season for shyness—specifically early fall. Kagan and Harvard sociologist Stephen Gortmaker, Ph.D., have found that women who conceive in August or

September are particularly likely to bear shy children. During these months, light is waning and the body is producing increasing amounts of melatonin, a hormone known to be neurally active; for example, it helps set our biological clocks. As it passes through the placenta to the developing fetal brain, Kagan surmises, the melatonin may act on cells to create the hyperaroused, easily agitated temperament of the shy.

Further evidence of a biological contribution to shyness is a pattern of inheritance suggesting direct genetic transmission from one generation to the next. Parents and grandparents of inhibited infants are more likely to report being shy as children than the relatives of uninhibited children, Snidman found in one study. Kagan and company are looking for stronger proof—such as, say, an elevated incidence of panic disorder (acute episodes of severe anxiety) and depression in the parents of inhibited children. So far he has found that among preschool children whose parents were diagnosed with panic attack or depression, one-third showed inhibited behavior. By contrast, among children whose parents experience neither panic disorder nor depression, only about five percent displayed the inhibited reactive profile.

Are inhibited infants preordained to become shy adults? Not necessarily, Doreen Arcus finds. A lot has to do with how such children are handled by their parents. Those who are overprotected, she found from in-home interviews she conducted, never get a chance to find some comfortable level of accommodation to the world; they grow up anxious and shy. Those whose parents do not shield them from stressful situations overcome their inhibition.

Snidman, along with Harvard psychiatrist Carl Schwartz, M.D., examined the staying power of shyness into adolescence. They observed 13- and 14-year-olds who were identified as inhibited at two or three years of age. During the laboratory interview, the adolescents with a history of inhibition tended to smile less, made fewer spontaneous comments, and reported being more shy than those who were identified as uninhibited infants.

Taken over a lifetime, gender doesn't figure much into shyness. Girls are more apt to be shy from infancy through adolescence, perhaps because parents are more protective of them than boys, who are encouraged to be more explorative. Yet in adolescence, boys report that shyness is more painful than do girls. This discomfort is likely related to sex-role expectations that boys must be bold and outgoing, especially with girls, to gear up for their role as head of family and breadwinner. But once into adulthood, gender differences in shyness disappear.

Bringing Biology Home

If only 15 to 20 percent of infants are born shy and nearly 50 percent of us are shy in adulthood, where do all the shy adults come from? The only logical answer is that shyness is acquired along the way.

One powerful source is the nature of the emotional bond parents forge with their children in the earliest years of life. According to Paul Pilkonis, children whose parenting was such that it gave rise to an insecure attachment are more likely to end up shy. Children form attachments to their caregivers from the routine experiences of care, feeding, and caressing. When caretaking is inconsistent and unreliable, parents fail to satisfy the child's need for security, affection, and comfort, resulting in insecure bonds. As the first relationship, attachment becomes the blueprint for all later relationships. Although there are no longitudinal studies spotlighting the development of

Helping Others Beat Shyness

You may not be shy, but one out of two people are. Be sensitive to the fact that others may not be as outgoing and confident. It's your job to make others comfortable around you. Be a host to humanity.

• Make sure no one person at a social gathering—including yourself—is the focus of attention. That makes it possible for everyone to have some of the attention some of the time.

• Like the host of any party, make it your job to bring out the best in others, in any situation. At school, teachers should make it a point to call on kids who are reluctant to speak up. At work, bosses should seek out employees who don't comment in meetings; encouragement to express ideas and creativity will improve any company. At parties, break the ice by approaching someone who is standing alone.

• Help others put their best foot forward. Socially competent people feel comfortable because they tend to steer conversation to their own interests. Find out what the shy person next to you is interested in; introduce the topic.

• Help others keep the conversation going. Shy people often don't speak up in ongoing conversations. Ask a shy person his or her opinion next time you are in a lively discussion.

shyness from toddlerhood to adulthood, there is research showing that insecure early attachment can predict shyness later on.

"The most damnable part of it is that this insecure attachment seems to become self-fulfilling," observes Pilkonis. Because of a difficult relationship to their parents, children internalize a sense of themselves as having problems with all relationships. They generalize the experience—and come to expect that teachers, coaches, and peers won't like them very much.

These are the narcissistically vulnerable—the wound to the self is early and deep, and easily evoked. They are quick to become disappointed in relationships, quick to feel rejection, shame, ridicule. They are relentlessly self-defeating, interpreting even success as failure. "They have negative perceptions of themselves and of themselves in relation to others that they hold onto at all costs," says Pilkonis. The narcissistically vulnerable are among the privately shy—they are seemingly at ease socially but torture themselves beneath the surface. Theirs is a shyness that is difficult to ameliorate, even with psychotherapy.

Shyness can also be acquired later on, instigated at times of developmental transition when children face new challenges in their relationships with their peers. For instance, entering the academic and social whirl of elementary school may leave them feeling awkward or inept with their peers. Teachers label them as shy and it sticks; they begin to see themselves that way—and act it.

Adolescence is another hurdle that can kick off shyness. Not only are adolescents' bodies changing but their social and emotional playing fields are redefining them. Their challenge is to integrate sexuality and intimacy into a world of relationships that used to be defined only by friendship and relatives. A complicated task!

Nor are adults immune. Shyness may result from tail-spinning life upheavals. Divorce at mid-life might be one. "A whole new set of problems kick in with a failure of a relationship, especially if you are interested in establishing new relationships," says Pilkonis. For highly successful, career-defined people, being fired from a long-held job can be similarly debilitating, especially in the interviewing process.

Count in the Culture

Biology and relationship history are not the sole creators of shyness. Culture counts, too. Shyness exists universally, although it is not experienced or defined the same way from culture to culture. Even Zimbardo's earliest surveys hinted at cultural differences in shyness: Japanese and Taiwanese students consistently expressed the highest level of shyness, Jewish stu-

We Shall Overcome

1. Overcoming the Anxiety: To tame your racing heart and churning stomach, learn how to relax. Use simple breathing exercises that involve inhaling and exhaling deeply and slowly.

You can ride out the acute discomfort by staying around for a while. If you give into your distress and flee a party after only five minutes, you guarantee yourself a bad time. Stick around.

2. Getting Your Feet Wet: Nothing breeds success like success. Set up a nonthreatening social interaction that has a high probability of success and build from there. Call a radio show with a prepared comment or question. Call some sort of information line.

3. Face to Face: Then tackle the art of very, very small talk face-to-face. Start a casual, quick exchange with the person next to you, or the cashier, in the supermarket checkout line. Most people in such situations would be very responsive to passing the time in light conversation. Since half the battle is having something to say, prepare. Scan the newspaper for conversation topics, and practice what you are going to say a few times.

5. Smile and Make Eye Contact: When you smile you project a benign social force around you; people will be more likely to notice you and smile back. If you frown or look at your feet, you don't exist for people, or worse, you project a negative presence. Once you have smiled and made eye contact, you have opened up a window for the casual "This elevator is so slow"–type comment. Always maintain eye contact in conversation; it signals that you are listening and interested.

6. Compliment: The shortest route to social success is via a compliment. It's a way to make other people feel good about themselves and about talking to you. Compliment someone every day.

7. Know How to Receive Compliments: Thank the person right away. Then return the compliment: "That's great coming from you, I've always admired the way you dress." Use this as a jumping-off point for a real conversation. Elaborate, ask him where he gets his ties or shops for suits.

8. Stop Assuming the Worst: In expecting the worst of every situation, shy people undermine themselves—they get nervous, start to stutter, and forget what they wanted to say. Chances are that once you actually throw yourself into that dreaded interaction it will be much easier than you thought. Only then will you realize how ridiculous your doomsday predictions are. Ask your workmate if he likes his job. Just do it.

9. Stop Whipping Yourself: Thoughts about how stupid you sound or how nobody really likes you run through your head in every conversation. No one would judge your performance as harshly as you do. Search for evidence to refute your beliefs about yourself. Don't get upset that you didn't ask someone to dance; focus on the fact that you talked to a woman you wanted to meet.

Don't overgeneralize your social mishaps. Say you start to stutter in conversation with someone at a party. Don't punish yourself by assuming that every other interaction that night or in your life will go the same way.

10. Lose the Perfectionism: Your jokes have to be hilarious, your remarks insightful and ironic. Truth is, you set standards so impossible they spawn performance anxiety and doom you to failure. Set more realistic standards.

11. Learn to Take Rejection: Rejection is one of the risks *everyone* takes in social interaction. Try not to take it personally; it may have nothing to do with you.

12. Find Your Comfort Zone: Not all social situations are for everybody. Go where your interests are. You might be happier at an art gallery, book club, or on a volleyball team than at a bar.

13. Comfort Is Not Enough: The goal in overcoming shyness is to break through your self-centeredness. In an interaction, focus on the other person. Make other people's comfort and happiness your main priority. If people think to themselves, "I really enjoyed being with her," when they leave you, then you have transformed your shyness into social competence. Congratulations.

dents the lowest. With these clues, Zimbardo took himself to Japan, Israel, and Taiwan to study college students. The cross-cultural studies turned up even greater cultural differences than the American survey. In Israel, only 30 percent of college-age students report being shy—versus 60 percent in Japan and Taiwan.

From conversations with foreign colleagues and parents, Zimbardo acquired unprecedented insights into how culture shapes behavior in general, and more specifically the cultural roots of shyness. The key is in the way parents attribute blame or praise in the performance of their children. When a child tries and fails at a task, who gets the blame? And when a child tries and succeeds, who gets the credit?

In Japan, if a child tries and succeeds, the parents get the credit. So do the grandparents, teachers, coaches, even Buddha. If there's any left over, only then is it given to the child. But if the child tries and fails, the child is fully culpable and cannot blame anyone else. An "I can't win" belief takes hold, so that children of the culture never take a chance or do anything that will make them stand out. As the Japanese proverb states, "the nail that stands out is pounded down." The upshot is a low-key interpersonal style. Kids are likely to be modest and quiet; they do little to call attention to themselves. In fact, in studies of American college students' individuation tendencies—the endorsement of behaviors that will make a person stand out, unique, or noticed—Asian students tend to score the lowest. They are much less likely to speak or act up in a social gathering for fear of calling attention to themselves.

In Israel, the attributional style is just the opposite. A child who tries gets rewarded, regardless of the outcome. Consider the Yiddish expression *kvell*, which means to engage in an outsize display of pride. If a child tries to make a kite, people *kvell* by pointing out what a great kite it is. And if it doesn't fly, parents blame it on the wind. If a child tries and fails in a competitive setting, parents and others might reproach the coach for not giving the child enough training. In such a supportive environment, a child senses that failure does not have a high price—and so is willing to take a risk. With such a belief system, a person is highly likely to develop *chutzpah*, a type of audacity whereby one always take a chance or risk—with or without the talent. Children of such a value system are more apt to speak up or ask someone to dance at a party without overwhelming self-consciousness.

Shyness, then, is a relative, culture-bound label. It's a safe bet that a shy Israeli would not be considered shy in Japan. Nancy Snidman brings the point home. In studying four-month-olds in Ireland and the U.S., she found no differences in degree of nervous system reactivity. But at age five, the Irish kids did not talk as much nor were they as loud as the American kids. The difference lies in the cultural expectations expressed in child-rearing. Using American norms of social behavior as the standard of comparison, the normal Irish child would be labeled shy. But, in their own culture, with their own norms of behavior, they are not. By the same token, American kids may be perceived as boorish by the Irish.

The Scarlet S

Shyness is un-American. We are, after all, the land of the free and the home of the brave. From the first settlers and explorers who came to the New World 500 years ago to our leadership in space exploration, America has always been associated with courageous and adventurous people ready to boldly go where others fear to tread. Our culture still values rugged individualism and the conquering of new environments, whether in outer space or in overseas markets. Personal attributes held high in our social esteem are leadership, assertiveness, dominance, independence, and risk-taking. Hence a stigma surrounding shyness.

The people given the most attention in our society are expressive, active, and sociable. We single out as heroes actors, athletes, politicians, television personalities, and rock stars—people expert at calling attention to themselves: Madonna, Rosanne, Howard Stern. People who are most likely to be successful are those who are able to obtain attention and feel comfortable with it.

What shy people don't want, above all else, is to be the focus of attention. Thus, in elementary school, the shy child may not even ask the teacher for help. In college, the shy student is reluctant to ask a question in class. In adulthood, the shy employee is too embarrassed to make a formal presentation to those who grant promotions. In every case, shyness undermines the ability to access the attention of others who would increase the likelihood of success. In a culture where everybody loves a winner, shyness is like entering a foot race with lead insoles.

Consider the findings of Stanford Business School professor Thomas Harrell. To figure out the best predictors of success in business, he gathered the records of Stanford B-School graduates, including their transcripts and letters of recommendation. Ten years out of school, the graduates were ranked from most to least successful based on the quality of their jobs. The only consistent and significant variable that could predict success (among students who were admittedly bright to start with) was verbal fluency—exactly what the typically tongue-

The Shy Brain

We all take time to get used to (or habituate to) a new stimulus (a job interview, a party) before we begin to explore the unfamiliar. After all, a novel stimulus may serve as a signal for something dangerous or important. But shy individuals sense danger where it does not exist. Their nervous system does not accommodate easily to the new. Animal studies by Michael Davis, Ph.D., of Yale University, indicate that the nerve pathways of shyness involve parts of the brain involved in the learning and expression of fear and anxiety.

Both fear and anxiety trigger similar physiologic reactions: muscle tension, increased heart rate, and blood pressure, all very handy in the event an animal has to fight or flee sudden danger. But there are important differences. Fear is an emotional reaction to a specific stimulus; it's quick to appear, and just as quick to dissipate when the stimulus passes. Anxiety is a more generalized response that takes much longer to dissipate.

Studies of cue conditioning implicate the **amygdala** as a central switchboard in both the association of a specific stimulus with the emotion of fear and the expression of that fear. Sitting atop the brain stem, the amygdala is crucial for relaying nerve signals related to emotions and stress. When faced with certain stimuli—notably strangers, authority figures, members of the opposite sex—the shy associate them with fearful reactions.

In contrast to such "explicit" conditioning is a process of "contextual" conditioning. It appears more slowly, lasts much longer. It is often set off by the context in which fear takes place. Exposure to that environment then produces anxiety-like feelings of general apprehension. Through contextual conditioning, shy people come to associate general environments—parties, group discussions where they will be expected to interact socially—with unpleasant feelings, even before the spe-

cific feared stimulus is present.

Contextual conditioning is a joint venture between the amygdala and the **hippocampus,** the sea horse–shaped cell cluster near the amygdala, which is essential to memory and spatial learning. Contextual conditioning can be seen as a kind of learning about unpleasant places.

But a crucial third party participates in contextual conditioning. It's the **bed nucleus of the stria terminalis (BNST).** The long arms of its cells reach to many other areas of the brain, notably the **hypothalamus** and the brain stem, both of which spread the word of fear and anxiety to other parts of the body. The BNST is principally involved in the generalized emotional-behavioral arousal characteristic of anxiety. The BNST may be set off by the neurotransmitter corticotropin releasing factor (CRF).

Once alerted, the hypothalamus triggers the sympathetic nervous system, culminating in the symptoms of inner turmoil experienced by the shy—from rapid heartbeat to sweaty paleness. Another pathway of information, from the amygdala to the brain stem, freezes movement of the mouth.

The shy brain is not different in structure from yours and mine; it's just that certain parts are more sensitive. Everyone has a "shyness thermostat," set by genes and other factors. The pinpointing of brain structures and neurochemicals involved in shyness holds out the promise that specific treatment may eventually be developed to curb its most debilitating forms.

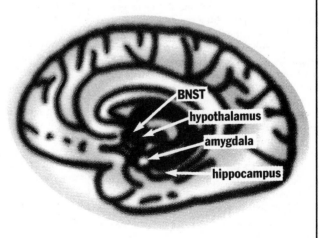

145

tied shy person can't muster. The verbally fluent are able to sell themselves, their services, and their companies—all critical skills for running a corporation; think of Lee Iacocca. Shy people are probably those behind the scenes designing the cars, programs, and computers—impressive feats, but they don't pay as much as CEO.

The costs of shyness cut deeper than material success, and they take on different forms over a lifetime.

• A shy childhood may be a series of lost opportunities. Think of the child who wants so much to wear a soccer uniform and play just like all the other kids but can't muster the wherewithal to become part of a group. And if the parents do not find a way to help a child overcome feelings of nervousness and apprehension around others, the child may slip into more solitary activities, even though he really wants to be social. The self-selection into solitary activities further reduces the likelihood of the child developing social skills and self-confidence.

• Shy kids also have to endure teasing and peer rejection. Because of their general disposition for high reactivity, shy children make prime targets for bullies. Who better to tease and taunt than someone who gets scared easily and cries?

• Whether inherited or acquired, shyness predisposes to loneliness. It is the natural consequence of decades spent shunning others due to the angst of socializing. Reams of research show that loneliness and isolation can lead to mental and physical decline, even a hastened death.

• Without a circle of close friends or relatives, people are more vulnerable to risk. Lacking the opportunity to share feelings and fears with others, isolated people allow them to fester or escalate. What's more, they are prone to paranoia; there's no one around to correct their faulty thinking, no checks and balances on their beliefs. We all need someone to tell us when our thinking is ridiculous, that there is no Mafia in suburban Ohio, that no one is out to get you, that you've just hit a spate of bad luck.

• Shyness brings with it a potential for abusing alcohol and drugs as social lubricants. In Zimbardo's studies, shy adolescents report feeling greater peer pressure to drink or use drugs than do less shy adolescents. They also confide that they use drugs and alcohol to feel less self-conscious and to achieve a greater sense of acceptance.

• Call it the Hugh Grant Effect. Shyness is linked to sexual, uh, difficulties. Shy people have a hard time expressing themselves to begin with; communicating sexual needs and desires is especially difficult. Shy men may turn to prostitutes just to avoid the awkwardness of intimate negotiations. When Zimbardo asked them to describe their typical client, 20 San Francisco prostitutes said that the men who frequented them were shy and couldn't communicate

Helping Shy Kids

Infants with a touchy temperament are not necessarily doomed to become shy adults. Much depends on the parenting they receive.

Do not overprotect or overindulge: Although it may sound counterintuitive, you can help your child cope more effectively with shyness by allowing him or her to experience moderate amounts of anxiety in response to challenges. Rather than rush to your child's aid to soothe away every sign of distress, provide indirect support. Gradually expose your child to new objects, people, and places so that the child will learn to cope with his own unique level of sensitivity to novelty. Nudge, don't push, your child to continue to explore new things.

Show respect and understanding: Your children have private emotional lives separate from yours. It is important to show your shy child that you can understand and sympathize with her shyness, by talking with the child about her feelings of nervousness and being afraid. Then talk with her about what might be gained by trying new experiences *in spite of* being afraid. Revealing related experiences from your own childhood is a natural way to start the ball rolling. Overcoming fears and anxieties is not an easy process; the feelings may remain even after specific shy behaviors have been overcome. Key ingredients are sympathy, patience, and persistence.

Ease the tease: Shy children are especially sensitive to embarrassment. Compared to other children, they need extra attention, comfort, and reassurance after being teased and more encouragement to develop positive self-regard.

Help build friendships: Invite one or two playmates over to let the child gain experience in playing with different kids in the security of familiar surroundings. But allow them as much freedom as possible in structuring play routines. Shy kids sometimes do better when playing with slightly younger children.

Talk to teachers: Teachers often overlook a shy child or mistake quiet-

ness and passivity for disinterest or a lack of intelligence. Discuss what measure[s] might be taken in the classroom or playground.

Prepare the child for new experiences: You can help to reduce fears and anxieties by helping your child get familiar with upcoming novel experiences. Take the child to a new school before classes actually start. Help rehearse activities likely to be performed in new situations, such as practicing for show-and-tell. Also role play with the child any anticipated anxiety-provoking situations, such as how to ask someone to dance at a party (if they'll let you) or speak up in a group at summer camp.

Find appropriate activities: Encourage your child to get involved in after-school activities as a means of developing a network of friends and social skills.

Provide indirect support: Ask the child the degree to which he wants you to be involved in his activities. For some kids, a parent cheering in the bleachers is humiliating. Better is indirect support—discussing the child's interests with him and letting him know of your pleasure and pride in him for participating.

Fit not fight: It's not as important to overcome shyness as to find a comfort zone consistent with your child's shyness. Rather than try to make your daughter outgoing, help her find a level of interaction that is comfortable and consistent with her temperament.

Own your temperament: Think how your own personality or interaction style operates in conjunction with your child's. If you aren't shy, understand that your child may need more time to feel comfortable before entering a novel situation or joining a social group. If you are shy, you may need to address your own shyness as a bridge to helping your child with hers.

Bottom Line: Talk, listen, support, and love shy children for who they are, not how outgoing you would like them to be.

their sexual desires to wives or girlfriends. And the shy guys made distinctive customers. They circled a block over and over again in their car before getting the nerve to stop and talk to the prostitute. To shy

men, the allure of a prostitute is simple—she asks what you want, slaps on a price, and performs. No humiliation, no awkwardness.

Performance anxiety may also make the prospect of sex overwhelming. And because shy people avoid seeking help, any problems created by embarrassment or self-doubt will likely go untreated.

• Another cost—time. Shy people waste time deliberating and hesitating in social situations that others can pull off in an instant. Part of their problem is that they don't live in the present, observes Zimbardo, who is currently focusing on the psychology of time perspective. "Shy people live too much in their heads," obsessed with the past, the future, or both. A shy person in conversation is not apt to think about what is being said at the moment, but about how past conversations have initially gone well and then deteriorated—just as the current one threatens to. Says Zimbardo: "These are people who cannot enjoy that moment because everything is packaged in worries from the past—a Smithsonian archive of all the bad—that restructure the present."

Or shy people may focus all their thoughts and feelings on future consequences: If I say this, will he laugh at me? If I ask him something simple like where he is from, he'll be bored and think I'm a lousy conversationalist, so why bother anyway? The internal decision trees are vast and twisted. "Concern for consequences always makes you feel somewhat anxious. And that anxiety will impair the shy person's performance," says Zimbardo.

Factoring in past and future is wise, but obsession with either is undermining. Shy people need to focus on the now—the person you are talking to or dancing with—to appreciate any experience. "Dancing is a good example of being completely of the moment," comments Zimbardo. "It is not something you plan, or that you remember, you are just doing it." And enjoying it.

If the costs of shyness are paid by shy people, the benefits of shyness are reaped by others—parents, teachers, friends, and society as a whole.

Yet shy people are often gifted listeners. If they can get over their self-induced pressures for witty repartee, shy people can be great at conversation because they may actually be paying attention. (The hard part comes when a response is expected.) According to Harvard's Doreen Arcus, shy kids are apt to be especially empathic. Parents of the children she studies tell her that "even in infancy, the shy child seemed to be sensitive, empathic, and a good listener. They seem to make really good friends and their friends are very loyal to them and value them quite a bit." Even among children, friendships need someone who will talk and someone who will listen.

For any society to function well, a variety of roles need to be played. There is a place for the quiet, more reflective shy individual who does not jump in where angels fear to tread or attempt to steal the limelight from others. Yet as a culture we have devalued these in favor of boldness and expressiveness as a means of measuring worth.

The Future of Shyness

To put it bluntly, the future of shyness is bleak. My studies have documented that since 1975 its prevalence has risen from 40 percent to 48 percent. There are many reasons to expect the numbers to climb in the decades ahead.

Most significantly, technology is continually redefining how we communicate. We are engaging in a diminishing number of face-to-face interactions on a daily basis. When was the last time you talked to a bank teller? Or a gas station attendant? How often do you call friends or colleagues when you know they aren't in just so you can leave a message on their machine? Voice mail, faxes, and E-mail give us the illusion of being "in touch" but what's to touch but the keyboard? This is not a Luddite view of technology but a sane look at its deepest costs.

The electronic age was supposed to give us more time, but ironically it has stolen it from us. Technology has made us time-efficient—and redefined our sense of time and its value. It is not to be wasted, but to be used quickly and with a purpose.

Office encounters have become barren of social interaction. They are information-driven, problem-oriented, solution-based. No pleasantries. No backs slapped. We cut to the chase: I need this from you. Says Zimbardo, "You have to have an agenda."

Some people don't even bother to show at the office at all; they telecommute.

The dwindling opportunities for face-to-face interaction put shy people at an increasing disadvantage. They no longer get to practice social skills within the comfort of daily routine. Dropping by a colleague's office to chat becomes increasingly awkward as you do it less and less. Social life has shrunk so much it can now be entirely encapsulated in a single, near-pejorative phrase: "face time," denoting the time employees may engage in eyeball-to-eyeball conversation. It's commonly relegated to morning meetings and after 4:00 P.M.

Electronic hand-held video games played solo now crowd out the time-honored social games of childhood. Even electronically simulated social interactions can't substitute—they do not permit people to learn the necessary give and take that is at the heart of all interpersonal relationships.

Technology is not the only culprit. The rise of organized sports for kids and the fall of informal sidewalk games robs kids of the chance to learn to work out their own relationship problems. Instead, the coach and the referee do it.

If technology is ushering in a culture of shyness, it is also the perfect medium for the shy. The Internet and World Wide Web are conduits for the shy to interact with others; electronic communication removes many of the barriers that inhibit the shy. You prepare what you want to say. Nobody knows what you look like. The danger, however, is that technology will become a hiding place for those who dread social interaction.

The first generation to go from cradle to grave with in-home computers, faxes, and the Internet is a long way from adulthood. We will have to wait at least another 20 years to accurately assess shyness in the wake of the new electronic age. But to do so, we must find a group of infants—shy and nonshy—and follow them through their life, rather than observe different people, from different generations, in different periods of their lives. Only then will we see the course of shyness over a lifetime. Stay tuned for PT's next shyness article, in 2015.

FINDING STRENGTH

How to Overcome Anything

Are some of us born more resilient than others? Can strength be taught? Here, a breakthrough report detailing what only decades of research can show—how people overcome terrible trauma, and just what it takes to survive and thrive. Start believing in yourself—now!

By Deborah Blum

For most of us, high-voltage transmission lines are blots on the landscape. They slice up the sky and emit a sinister little hum of energy that translates into "Stay back if you want to see tomorrow. So, for David Miller to like power lines so much—to see in them uplift and promise and future—well, you first have to understand the landscape of a child whose mother decided not to keep him.

He was born in 1960, in Reidsville, North Carolina, in a neighborhood of small, neat ranch houses—in the African-American-only part of town. This was, after all, the deep South of almost forty years ago. He lived with his grandparents. His mother left him

there; she couldn't do it, everyone knew that. She was 24, pregnant by mistake. "It's not that I didn't see my mother," Miller says, "but my grandparents raised me." Yet because his grandparents both worked—his grandfather at a dry cleaners, his grandmother as a laundry attendant—"I was a latchkey kid before the coin was termed."

And when they were home, they had little patience for a small boy's antics. "My grandmother would save up my spankings all week," says Miller. "Friday was judgment day." If the offense was grave enough, he ended up with welts across his back.

You might imagine that he was a child standing on a slippery hillside, his birth merely the first skidding step downward. In his spare time, though, he used to walk under the power lines. "It seemed like hours and miles," he recalls, "but I was pretty small." And he'd follow them with his feet and then his eyes until they disappeared into the clouded edges of the sky. And he'd think about where they went and wonder about the world beyond.

Miller is 37 now and an assistant professor of social work at Case Western Reserve University in Cleveland. He's chosen to study resilience—the ability, let's say, to stand steady on such treacherous hillsides, even to climb them—among other at-risk children, young African-Americans from the poor and drug-overrun neighborhoods of the inner city.

"I'm interested in strengths," he says. "What strengths allow you to deal with the violence, and the guns held to your head, and the fear of being molested? What is it that allows children to grow up in that and not be immobilized?" And when he talks to teenagers there, he remembers his own climb. "I do see myself as resilient. I always believed in my own abilities. I wasn't handcuffed by where I grew up. I'm happy with my life."

And when he travels to New York or Miami or into the power-line neighborhoods of Cleveland, where he lives, he still looks up and watches that unexpected flight of utility hardware to the horizon. And he thinks, "Oh, this is where they were taking me."

WHEN THE RED BALL BOUNCES

Could there be a research field more personal than that of resilience? When we all know that life, even for those who have had the best of childhoods, promises challenge after challenge, year after year? Who doesn't want to know where resilience comes from, how to transcend pain and grief, surmount obstacles and frustrations—to dream along the power lines, if you will? I began thinking about it as a parent. There were days I hated: finding my son standing by a wall in the schoolyard, eyes filling with tears, unwanted by his playmates at that moment. I wanted, oh, I

TRIUMPH OVER TORTURE

I HAD NEVER READ A BOOK AS PITI-less, terrifying, and inspiring in my life: a Tibetan woman's account of twenty-seven years of torture in labor camps for resisting China's occupation of her homeland. *Ama Adhe: The Voice That Remembers* (Wisdom Publications) is a memoir that describes—with unutterable calm—acts of unthinkable evil, and the unwavering spirit of the woman who withstood them. But meeting her was the true shock: when I sat with Adhe in my home, she took my hands in hers—strong, vital, calloused, caressing—and it was I, the baby boomer American journalist, who drew strength from her.

She was dressed in typical Tibetan garb—peasant style—and counted her prayer beads from time to time. Now in her sixties, Adhe lives in exile in India under the protection of the Dalai Lama. She has remarried, and speaks reverently of "waking each morning and realizing that I am in freedom, living in the same town that his Holiness the Dalai Lama lives in, and then I am very happy."

The facts: In 1954, when Adhe's son was just a year old, and she was pregnant with her second child, her husband was poisoned and died in front of her. Her husband's mother died soon afterward, of grief. In 1958, nine armed men came to Adhe's home, beat her in front of her children, and arrested her. Several months of physical torture followed, and finally she was brought before a large crowd and forced to watch as her brother-in-law was shot in front of her. "Pieces of his brain and his blood splashed on my dress," Adhe recalls. Her sister, his wife, lost her mind and died soon after.

Adhe, however, was not killed. "They said, 'We want you to suffer for the rest of your life. Now you see who has won.' " Almost three decades of imprisonment, forced labor, near starvation, and beatings followed. Moved from prison to prison, Adhe was not allowed to change or wash her only dress—known in Tibetan as a *chupa*—for years. When she menstruated, she let the blood dry and scraped it off. At one point she fainted while carrying stones; she was believed to be dead and was put in a hut that held the bodies of other dead prisoners. "The bodies looked like skeletons," says Adhe. "The eyes had blackened, the cheekbones were protruding. The sickening smell was overwhelming."

Over time, Adhe became something of a cause célèbre and was finally allowed to visit friends and family in 1979, twenty-one years after she was first imprisoned. She discovered that a friend had raised her daughter, but her son had gone insane after her arrest and one day fell into a river and drowned. "My surviving friends came to see me in the night," she says, "and told me of the fates of most of the women who had worked with me in the resistance. Now they were dead." That may have been Adhe's darkest moment: "There was nothing left. All these years I had been living for nothing, and now I didn't have to try anymore. A terrible restlessness came over me, and I began to wander around muttering to myself, totally unaware of my immediate surroundings."

How does one even use the word "resilience" in this context? It seems too small. There is a quality of indestructible strength and joy in Adhe that seems inborn. However, in her story, one does find the common traits of resilience that researchers have pointed out. For instance, perhaps the cardinal finding about the resilient is that they do not survive alone. Too weak to say her daily prayers (or even to remember them), Adhe sought the advice of an imprisoned monk who crafted her a shortened version of the prayer. Mourning the deaths of fellow women prisoners, Adhe began to make a quilt from their old dresses, and after a few years, it was large enough to sleep on. To this day she keeps the quilt: "My daughter used to beg me to get rid of it, saying, 'I can't stand it. Please throw it in the river.' But somehow I couldn't. It is with me even today."

Later, Adhe was sent food by her brother, and when prison officials wanted to take it away from her, a Chinese doctor at the labor camp who had taken an interest in Adhe's welfare intervened. "He said he would keep the food and give it to me slowly. 'If you overeat at this point, you will die.' " Adhe asked the doctor to use the food to prepare a special soup for all the prisoners. In her memoir, she recalls: "All the prisoners were so happy in getting their share that although it was still very hot, they drank it immediately. You could see their faces glowing red. Some licked the cups, then put in some water, shook the cup, and drank again. Some kissed my hand. They said, 'At least before we die, we are having our native food.' " One Tibetan, a man too weak to walk or stand, gave her his hat, in which a tiny portrait of the Dalai Lama was tied with thread. "After that, I always wore the hat. The most precious gift gave me hope."

When asked how she survived, Adhe says it was through daily prayer. Today, she lives in two rooms with her husband, in Dharmshala, India. She wakes at dawn, makes an offering at her altar, and prays until noon. She then goes to meet and help new Tibetan refugees. She says that though the jailers, labor camps, and suffering of her fellow prisoners comes back to her constantly in dreams, every morning, as soon as she awakens, she is happy again.

The Chinese told her long ago, as they shot her brother-in-law to death in front of her, "Now you see who has won." Yes, now we see who has won.

---

wanted revenge, although that was pure, lunatic fantasy. I wanted to bundle my son away in some cozy little world without hurt. An even greater fantasy.

Most of all, I wanted to know if I could teach him to bounce back. We all tumble. If we pick ourselves up, and learn from it, and go on with only superficial injury, well—I wanted to know if I could give my son that wonderful ability—that bounce.

I had a powerful visual image of the process. Not Miller's power lines, but the neat, clean, and quick bounce of a ball. The slap, the sting of being down, and then the easy rise, arching into a brighter air. It was a lovely image, really. It made me think of Paul Simon's old lyric about coming back from a failed love affair: "The morning sun is shining like a red rubber ball."

It was such a terrific thought. And this is what I wanted science to tell me: can resilience be deliberately acquired, or must we be born a David Miller, with some marvelous inner ability to see beyond where we stand?

It turns out to be a good time to ask those questions, because so many re-searchers are also asking them, in a professional capacity. Scientists now study resilience, it seems, in every possible niche: inner cities, tropical islands, families fleeing war or trying to live with it, children coping with the loss of a parent, entire families struggling with the loss of a home. It's part of what American Psychological Association President Martin Seligman, Ph.D., believes is a sea change in psychology, away from focusing on what damages people toward trying to understand what makes them strong.

The first finding, to my chagrin, is that I'm going to have to tuck my red rubber ball image back into the lore of pop-rock. There's no: "Hey, the kid went down, but look, he bounced, he's fine" ending to this story. The ability to rebound is part of the process, sure, but it's not magically pain-free or instantaneous. Psychologists want that message out there. In fact, a professional alarm sounded last year when a national news magazine (okay, *U.S. News and World Report*) published a cover story about resilience research titled "Invincible Children."

"It is a primary example of what I have been calling the myth of the "superkid," who walks between raindrops, confronts any challenge and emerges unscarred and unscathed, never experiences a moment's pain," says Washington, D.C., psychologist Sybil Wolin, Ph.D., who, with husband and clinical psychiatrist Steve Wolin, M.D., co-authored the popular book, *The Resilient Self.*

> One's upbringing does not build a lifelong prison. "The first, biggest surprise to me," says Emmy Werner, Ph.D., "is that so many people recovered" from traumatic childhoods.

"The notion we try to put forth is that resilience embodies a paradox," she says. "We're talking about the capacity to rebound from experience, mixed with all the damage and problems that adversity can cause. It's not an either/or thing. And this 'media resilience' does kids who are struggling no good, does professionals no good in understanding them, has downright dangerous policy implications, and frankly, gives resilience research a bad name."

THE ROCKY CLIMB

Resilience research is often not bright and shiny at all. If you're going to study people climbing upward, you have to start at the very rocky bottom. "I decided to look at adults who'd had traumatic childhoods because I knew some very neat people who had come from that background," said John DeFrain, Ph.D., a professor of family studies at the University of Nebraska. "I thought it would be all warm and fuzzy-feeling. But these were people who were sometimes just

barely hanging on. They were surviving as children, but just."

He found that it was in adulthood that people really began to transcend the difficulties of childhood and to rebuild. One man, beaten as a child by his father with belts, razor strops, and tree branches, reached a point in his mid-twenties, when he decided to die. He wrote a suicide note, put the gun to his head, and then suddenly thought, "I'm not going to die because of what someone else did to me." That day for the first time, he called a psychologist and went into counseling.

That dramatically emphasizes one of several key aspects of resilience research:

•**There is no timeline, no set period, for finding strength**, resilient behaviors and coping skills. People do best if they develop strong coping skills as children, and some researchers suggest the first ten years are optimum. But the ability to turn around is always there.

•**About one-third of poor neglected, abused children are capably building better lives** by the time they are teenagers, according to all resilience studies. They are doing well in school, working toward careers, often helping to support their siblings.

•**Faith—be it in the future, the world at the end of the power lines, or in a higher power—is an essential ingredient.** Ability to perceive bad times as temporary times gets great emphasis from Seligman as an essential strength.

•**Most resilient people don't do it alone—in fact, they don't even try.** One of the standout findings of resilience research is that people who cope well with adversity, if they don't have a strong family support system, are able to ask for help or recruit others to help them. This is true for children and adults; resilient adults, for instance, are far more likely to talk to friends and even co-workers about events in their lives.

•**Setting goals and planning for the future** is a strong factor in dealing with adversity. In fact, as University of California-Davis psychologist Emmy Werner, Ph.D., points out, it may minimize the adversity itself. For instance, Werner found that when Hurricane Iniki battered Hawaii in 1993, islanders who were previously identified as resilient reported less property damage than others in the study. Why? They'd prepared more, boarded up windows, invested in good insurance.

•**Believing in oneself and recognizing one's strengths is important.** University of Alabama psychologist Ernestine Brown, Ph.D., discovered that when children of depressed, barely functioning mothers took pride in helping take care of the family, they didn't feel as trapped. "You pick yourself up, give yourself value," Brown says. "If you can't change a bad situation, you can at least nurture yourself. Make yourself a place for intelligence and competence, surround yourself with things that help you stabilize, and remember what you're trying to do."

•**And it's equally important to actually recognize one's own strengths.** Many people don't. Teaching them such self-recognition is a major part of the approach that the Wolins try when helping adults build

> An astonishing one-third of children who grow up neglected, poor, or abused, are capable of building better lives by the time they are teenagers.

a newly resilient approach to life. They are among a small group of professionals testing the idea that resilience can be taught, perhaps by training counselors and psychologists to focus on building strengths in their clients.

A WHOLE NEW VIEW OF STRENGTH

Steve Wolin tells a story about one of his clients, a woman whose father—if he felt threatened or challenged in any way—would batter the offender. The woman, who was whipped throughout her childhood, saw herself as helpless. But Wolin encouraged her to see it differently: she was smart; she had learned how to recognize and respond to her father's moods; she was an accomplished strategist. "We encourage people to reframe the way they see themselves," he says. "We call this Survivor's Pride." Insight is only one of the abilities that he tries to persuade his clients to value. Others include humor, independence, initiative, creativity, and morality.

Edith Grotberg, who heads an international resilience project, tries to help people organize their strengths into three simple categories: I have (which includes strong relationships, structure and rules at home, role models); I am (a person who has hope and faith, cares about others, is proud of oneself); and I can (ability to communicate, solve problems, gauge the temperament of others, seek good relationships). She finds, by the way, that men tend to draw most confidence from the "I can" category and women from the "I am."

"But all people have the capacity for resilience," says Grotberg, Ph.D., from the University of Alabama, Birmingham. "We just have to learn to draw it out and to support them."

This is, without hyperbole, a breathtaking change from the approach of psychology just a few decades ago. Seligman describes the old

> # I HAVE—strong relationships and role models; I AM—a person who has hope, faith, pride, and cares about others; I CAN—communicate, solve problems, and seek good relationships.

approach—which he says took over after World War II—as victimology, an emphasis on psychological damage driven by the parallel emphasis of the same period on nurture over nature. Psychologists believed that people were shaped by environment—a harmful environment would inevitably result in a bent or skewed or non-functional person.

So powerful was this notion that when Norman Garmezy, Ph.D., of the University of Minnesota, studied children of severely depressed mothers and found that some of them seemed healthy and capable, his first response was that he had misdiagnosed the mothers. Michael Rutter, Ph.D., of the Institute of Psychiatry in London, tracked children of drug-addicted mothers, and reported the same, I-must-have-screwed-up reaction. But their findings—that at least one-fourth of the children seemed both confident and capable—wouldn't go away. Garmezy and Rutter refocused on the coping skills of people in troubled families. Their work laid the foundation for today's entire generation of resilience researchers. This year's annual American Psychological Association meeting is focused on recognizing human strengths.

Garmezy gives credit to Emmy Werner for nurturing the field. "Mother Resilience" is his favorite nickname for her, and it makes her laugh. "Maybe at the age of 68, it needs to be changed to 'Grandmother Resilience,'" she jokes.

Her primary work for the last thirty years, a longitudinal study of native Hawaiians, does provide a terrific case study of resilience research in motion. Werner has followed the same group of islanders from late adolescence into middle age. She titled her last book about them *Overcoming the Odds.*

There are 505 people in Werner's study, born in 1955 on the small and beautiful island of Kauai. About half were born into poverty, mostly the children of sugar plantation workers. It should be noted, from the beginning, that this is almost a guaran-

tee of poverty; the island sugarcane industry has been falling away almost since these children were born. Not surprisingly, many of them grew up in homes dominated by fears of even greater poverty, where alcoholism and anger and abuse were just the way of life.

As Werner says, victim-theory would have predicted that by the time those children reached their twenties, they would have simply sunk into a swamp of crime and unemployment. And most did. Yet there was still that startling number: one-third never seemed to sink at all; they did well in school, began promising careers and—most important—defined themselves as capable and competent adults.

One woman profiled, Leilani, is a working mother of three sons; she is in her thirties, and put it like this: "I am proud of myself as a person now. I have received so much fulfillment in being a wife, mother, and worker. I feel I've finally grown up."

YOUR PAST IS NOT A PRISON

The ground breaking point in Werner's work—which Garmezy calls "the best single study" on resilience in children—is that one's upbringing does not build a lifelong prison. "The first, biggest surprise to me was that so many recovered," Werner said. And when she went back and looked at the islanders in their thirties and forties, she found that even more had determined not to repeat their parents lives. More than half had fallen, as teenagers, into petty crime. Of that group, only 10 percent of the females and one-fourth of males still had criminal records in their thirties. The majority had struggled, but had moved on.

One of the unexpected spinoffs of resilience research, then, is that it has begun breaking down myths of failure—that having a bad beginning makes one a bad person; that abused children grow up to be abusers. In fact, the statistics are very comparable to Werner's resilience study. New studies show that a clear one-third of abused children grow up determined never to lay a hand on their children, and they don't.

And they can choose that even after childhoods that seem to hang on the dark edge of nightmare. John DeFrain and his colleagues—Nikki DeFrain, Linda Ernst, and Jean Jones—have compiled a horrific

portrait of an abusive childhood, based on interviews with forty adults identified as growing up in traumatic family situations.

Consider a typical description from their study: "One time I remember sitting at the dinner table when I was six or seven. My sister was told to say grace and when she finished, my dad slapped her across the face. He told her she said it wrong and to do it over. She started again and he slapped her again. This went on and on, over and over, faster and faster, for what seemed like half an hour. I remember sitting there across from her, paralyzed. I just kept praying, 'Get it right.' The problem was, she was doing it right, just the way we learned it in Sunday School."

Or this one: "I learned to survive by letting myself go. I taught myself how to go numb, to have no feeling. I can feel myself floating out of my body and look down on a little girl screaming. A little dark-eyed girl sits in a big over-stuffed chair. She does not move or whimper, but prays that her mother will forget she is angry at her. 'I'm sorry, I'm sorry' keeps playing in her ears, but she can't remember what for. 'I did my homework,' she reminds herself. 'I made my bed this morning and didn't forget to clean my room.' And then she loses herself in the cracks in the ceiling with the first blows to her head."

No one just bounces back in that type of situation, and DeFrain emphasizes this with great intensity: "I think if society comes to the conclusion that there are some magical little children out there who are somehow inoculated against savagery and violence, we will look the other way as children continue to be traumatized."

But as his work also emphasizes, if a family situation is insane, most people will build, within it, their own sanctuary and sanity.

They learn the tricks of mental distance, as did the little girl in the big chair. They

> # Eighty-three percent of adults had transcended troubled childhoods and were proud of it.

escape: into music and books. Skills aren't only a way to build a better future, they are a safe house. "I took piano and sang in the church choir as well as the school choir," one woman said. "At home, I was quiet and stayed in my room most of the time. Away from home, I was cheerful and upbeat." Many braced themselves with religious faith; in DeFrain's study, people almost unanimously said that they had received little help from people in the church—56 percent said they had no one to talk to—but that they held to the idea of guardian angels or a God who, as one man puts it, "will always love me and forgive me."

DeFrain and his colleagues asked every person in their study if childhood still hurt. "If you're an eight-year-old girl and you're getting pounded every day and all you have is a belief that there's a God out there who loves you, is that a wonderful story?" he asks. Not one person in his study said that they had left their childhood unscarred. Eleven percent said they considered themselves bare survivors, but an astonishing 83 percent said they had moved past, were transcending their childhood, building an adult life they could be proud of.

Ann S. Masten, Ph.D., a professor of psychology at the University of Minnesota, reports a similar balancing of pain and determination in a study of Khmer-American teenagers in Minnesota, children of families who fled Cambodia.

"During the Pol Pot years, from 1975 to 1979," says Masten, "they were very young children, and most lived for many years afterwards under difficult conditions in Thai refugee camps. These children have lived through the unspeakable horrors of war. And most of them have witnessed torture and the death of family and friends from awful violence and starvation, or forced labor and other terribly traumatic events."

There's no arguing that many still suffer the consequences, Masten concedes. "They still have nightmares, periods when they are jumpy and cannot concentrate, or get depressed and anxious. For instance, when the Persian Gulf War was broadcast live on television, many Cambodians experienced an upsurge of the symptoms of trauma from their own wartime experiences."

"Yet these young people are living in Minnesota, getting on with their lives, worrying about what they are going to wear to the prom, or what college they are going to. They are absolute, living testimony to the human capacity for resilience."

RECRUITING HELP: THE MAGIC AND THE MYSTERY

Can one do that on their own, rise above the terrifying parent, the terrible neighborhood, or the trauma of living in a war zone? Resilience researchers find—anecdotally at least—that there are individuals who possess an extraordinary will to transcend, to make their lives work. David Miller, who is studying African-American teenagers living in the drug-plagued neighborhoods of Cleveland, tells of one boy who made up

More than half of resilient people hold to the idea of guardian angels or a God who will always love them.

his mind that he would not do drugs, not join a gang, not fall like his friends around him.

"They wanted him to, but he refused," says Miller. "He was threatened and he was beaten up and he steadfastly remained outside. He took the beatings, and he fought back. He said, 'I'm not doing this.' Eventually they left him alone. He's now a freshman in college."

Can you teach that kind of inner resolve? "No, I don't think so," Miller says. "You can teach people to understand consequences; you can teach them ways to go at life, so that when trauma strikes, they don't become overwhelmed. You can teach them ways to find strength. After all, it doesn't take strength to go the wrong way. It doesn't require any effort."

Miller—and, really, everyone in the field of resilience—emphasizes the importance of someone else's presence. Parents, first and best of all, who believe in you, and, if that fails, neighbors, friends, teachers. The foremost element in transcending trouble is not having to do it alone. Emmy Werner found that many islanders in her study group pulled their lives together when they married. There's an element of obvious common sense here—we all need love and hope and help. At an informational meeting for members of Congress in March 1996, Masten put it like this: "The most important message I have for you today is that there is no magic here."

But Steve Wolin points out that people who emerge successfully from tough times tend to be very good at recruiting people into a support system. He gives the example of a high school boy living in his girlfriend's basement. The boy's parents were drug addicts; his home life was awful, and the girl's mother, who liked him, had offered him a temporary home. He told Wolin that he courted the mother, studying the foods she liked best, bringing gifts like spaghetti sauce and loaves of French bread.

"I want people to see that this is not being manipulative," Wolin said. "This child was not a user. This is a strength." The boy was working after school to provide food for his younger brothers. He was also considering dropping out and taking a second job, to get them better clothes.

Peg Heinzer, who holds joint nursing appointments at LaSalle University in

Pennsylvania and Albert Einstein School of Medicine in New York, studied the ways in which children cope with the death of a parent. Heinzer began by trying to help her own five children. Her husband, their father, died a decade ago of lymphoma. Her children ranged from eight to 17 at the time. One of her sons wrote a school paper on role models that began: "The person I most admire is no longer alive."

Determined to provide a strong and loving, single-parent home, she set out to explore whether love really made a difference. To her surprise, the child's attachment to the surviving parent did not directly predict a strong recovery. But children who came from supportive homes had a great ability to build extended networks; they were likable and considerate of others. "They were all delightful," she recalls. "I went into 89 homes and, in every case, the teenagers offered me something to drink or eat and made sure I was comfortable."

And that quality, she thinks, made them good at asking for help. "We need to be able to talk about the hard times," she says. "And I think we can teach people that it's okay to ask for help."

The ability to read at grade level by age ten is a startling predictor of resilience in poor and neglected children.

Miller can still remember the names of everyone on his grandparent's street: there was Mr. Sam and Miss Bertha and the Harrisons and the Watts. Those neighbors hired him to do chores, invited him to drop in for snacks, and urged him on to a better life. He recalls people constantly advising him on good manners, good grades. "It's as if you attract it. People see possibility in you. They would say to me, 'David, you be someone.' It's as if you just attract people who believe in you."

And if one is not a born recruiter, it turns out, organized programs can still make a remarkable difference. For example, a 1996 analysis of the Big Brother/Big Sister Program conducted by Public/Private Ventures provided some remarkable statistics of success: The study looked at children from poor, single-parent homes where there was a high incidence of violence. Among children involved in the Big Brother/Big Sister program, first-time drug use was 46 percent lower, school absenteeism was 52 percent lower, and violent behavior was 33 percent lower.

WHY SCHOOL COUNTS

Education remains one of the most important factors in resilience; its greatest side effect is the belief that one is building a roadway out of despair. One girl in Miller's study, the daughter of drug addicts, told him she felt completely isolated, except for school. There she felt competent. She is also now in college, he says. Werner found, in fact, that the ability to read at grade level by age ten was a startling predictor of whether or not poor children would engage in juvenile crime; at least 70 percent of youthful offenders were in need of remedial education by the fourth grade.

This has led some researchers to suggest that intelligence is a key factor in resilient behavior. But Werner argues that we should turn that around: if scholastic competence is important in rising above adversity, then, she says, that suggests we should put more effort into teaching children well in those early years. We don't have to fully understand resilience to concentrate on basics, such as fostering competence in school, learning to find help, learning to plan and set goals.

Peg Heinzer recalls that after her husband died—in a period when she felt that she might simply wash away in grief—she set tiny goals for herself. On her drive to graduate school, there was one particular intersection where she would begin to weep every day. She'd arrive in class with her lap drenched with tears. The first day that she made it through that intersection without weeping, she took as a measure of healing—that she was going to be all right.

"It's more than just surviving," she says now. "I built a new life. I raised five caring and close children. I'm proud of myself. I'm happy."

People who've overcome adversity often try to make the world better. It's a kind of antidote to pain.

JOY: THE SILVER LINING

Actually, here is one place where we could let the red rubber ball back in. There can be a real joyfulness to the rebound. I've seen it in my son when he goes back to school the next day, plays with his friends again, and that day, partly by pure contrast, is just a wonderful day.

There's a triumph to overcoming the odds, one that doesn't come when you begin on high and stable ground. And many people, once they've made it through, have strong faith in themselves and their strengths, more so than those who have not been tried so hard. "The key person is me," one man told DeFrain. "In some ways I was fortunate to learn to rely on myself. I knew I had to make the change. No one else could do it for me."

DeFrain and his colleagues found that more than 80 percent of the people they talked to, while hating their childhoods, believed they'd become better people because of it: stronger, kinder, and quicker to care for and help others. People who've overcome adversity often try to make the world a better place. One of Steve Wolin's clients came breathlessly to a session after unhesitatingly jumping between an elderly woman and a group of muggers.

"We hear it all the time," Wolin says. "I've been tested and I've prevailed and I'm better for it. We think that kind of reaction fits right into Survivor's Pride, and that it's an antidote to the pain. And that's part of it too. These are people who have struggled mightily and who have wounds to show for it. No one's story is a clean one; we are all a checkerboard of strengths and scars."

Certainly, Miller sees himself that way. He recognizes how far determination has brought him: "I'll work and work to achieve something. I said that to a friend once, that there are people out there who are smarter than I am, but no one who will work harder." There are still things that come hard for Miller, though. His marriage failed; his wife and 13-year-old daughter live in another state. "Yes," he says, slowly, "there are things I wish I did better, that I work on still."

And his voice falls away from the pure confidence that it holds when he describes his work.

Resilience, as Werner points out, is many different things. It is multifaceted. We all respond differently to different challenges. And no one yet understands how the facets come together; no one can predict when we will be strong or when our strengths will fail us. On that point, there is rare unanimity among researchers: "We aren't there yet," says Peg Heinzer; "We need to evaluate," explains Emmy Werner; "We need more research," replies Ernestine Brown. "We don't want to think we're studying invincibility."

A child may dream along the power lines, if that's the only avenue. And the fact that the child follows the dreams? Does that come from an inner strength we don't understand or one that we do? Miller himself recognizes that his childhood led him, not simply to the town of Cleveland, but far beyond, to begin to map the power of the human soul.

Deborah Blum is a Pulitzer Prize-winning science writer and a professor in the School of Journalism at the University of Wisconsin.

Unit Selections

Key Points to Consider

❖ What causes criminality? How does family life relate to violence? Discuss whether or not violent crimes can be prevented. What are predictors that place an individual at risk of becoming violent or a criminal?

❖ What is bias? How are bias and prejudice related to cognitive processing? Are most thoughts processed automatically? Are stereotypes processed automatically? Can we overcome our prejudices if they are merely automatic cognitions? How?

❖ Under what circumstances do we laugh? What are the differences between children and adults in what they think is humorous? Between men and women? List some of the differences. What are some of the consequences of these communication differences? What can men and women do in order to communicate better with one another?

 **Links**   **www.dushkin.com/online/**

24. **National Clearinghouse for Alcohol and Drug Information**
   http://www.health.org

These sites are annotated on pages 4 and 5.

Everywhere we look there are groups of people. Your general psychology class is a group. It is what social psychologists would call a secondary group, a group that comes together for a particular, somewhat contractual reason and then disbands after its goals have been met. Other secondary groups include athletic teams, church associations, juries, and committees.

There are other types of groups, too. One other type is a primary group. A primary group has much face-to-face contact, and there is often a sense of "we-ness" (cohesiveness, as social psychologists would call it) in the group. Examples of primary groups include families, suite mates, sororities, and fraternities.

Collectives are loosely knit, large groups of people. A bleacher full of football fans would be a collective. A line of people waiting to get into a rock concert would also be a collective. As you might guess, collectives behave differently from primary and secondary groups.

Mainstream American society and any other large group that shares common rules and norms is also a group, albeit an extremely large group. While we might not always think about our society and how it shapes our behavior and our attitudes, society and culture nonetheless have a measureless influence on us. Psychologists, anthropologists, and sociologists alike are all interested in studying the effects of a culture on its members.

The first two articles are general and concern mainstream American culture and society. Patrick Fagan, in the first article, assesses why violence is occurring more frequently in American society. He blames not race but the disintegration of the American family. Fagan says that both black and white children whose nuclear families have fallen apart are more apt to commit violent crimes than children whose families are intact.

The next article on American society is "Where Bias Begins: The Truth about Stereotypes." The author attributes racial prejudice or racial bias and the stereotypes that accompany prejudice to unconscioius cognitive patterns to which we all fall prey. The article discusses briefly what we can do

to replace automatic thought processing with conscious, unpredjudiced beliefs.

We turn next to some interesting and subtle social differences between men and women. In "Laughter May Be No Laughing Matter," Rebecca Clay describes male and female differences in what each sex finds humorous. She also suggests that men and women use humor differently in their social interactions. For example, women laugh more than men. Interestingly, Clay also asserts that laughter is more mundane than what psychologists thought in the past. That is, the stimuli that trigger laughter are not jokes and pratfalls but rather small, everyday incidents.

In the final article of this unit, "Brain Sex and the Language of Love," by Robert Nadeau, men and women are again the subject. Men and women communicate differently; these differences can lead to miscommunication, which, in turn, can lead to sour relationships. Fortunately, the article also suggests ways that men and women can improve their relationships.

Disintegration of the Family

VIOLENT

" . . . The popular assumption that there is an association between race and crime is false. Illegitimacy, not race, is the key factor. It is the absence of marriage and the failure to maintain intact families that explain the incidence of crime among whites as well as blacks."

Patrick F. Fagan

SOCIAL SCIENTISTS, criminologists, and many other observers at long last are coming to recognize the connection between the breakdown of families and various social problems that have plagued American society. In the debate over welfare reform, for instance, it now is a widely accepted premise that children

Mr. Fagan is William H. G. Fitzgerald Fellow for Family and Cultural Studies, Heritage Foundation, Washington, D.C. This article is based on a Hillsdale (Mich.) College Center for Constructive Alternatives seminar on "Crime in America: Fighting Back with Moral and Market Virtues."

born into single-parent families are much more likely than those in intact families to fall into poverty and welfare dependency.

While the link between the family and chronic welfare dependency is understood much better these days, there is another link—between the family and crime—that deserves more attention. Entire communities, particularly in urban areas, are being torn apart by crime. We desperately need to uncover the real root cause of criminal behavior and learn how criminals are formed in order to be able to fight this situation.

There is a wealth of evidence in the professional literature of criminology and sociology to suggest that the breakdown of family is the real root cause of crime in the U.S. Yet,

the orthodox thinking in official Washington assumes that it is caused by material conditions, such as poor employment opportunities and a shortage of adequately funded state and Federal social programs.

The Violent Crime Control and Law Enforcement Act of 1994, supported by the Clinton Administration, perfectly embodies Washington's view of crime. It provides for billions of dollars in new spending, adding 15 social programs on top of a welfare system that has cost taxpayers five trillion dollars since the War on Poverty was declared in 1965. There is no reason to suppose that increased spending and new programs will have any significant positive impact. Since 1965, welfare spending has grown 800% in real terms, while the number of major felo-

From *USA Today Magazine*, May 1996, pp. 36–38. © 1996 by the Society for the Advancement of Education. Reprinted by permission.

Is the Real Root Cause of

CRIME

nies per capita today is roughly three times the rate prior to 1960. As Sen. Phil Gramm (R.-Tex.) rightly observes, "If social spending stopped crime, America would be the safest country in the world."

Still, Federal bureaucrats and lawmakers persist in arguing that poverty is the primary cause of crime. In its simplest form, this contention is absurd; if it were true, there would have been more crime in the past, when more people were poorer. Moreover, in less-developed nations, the crime rates would be higher than in the U.S. History defies the assumption that deteriorating economic circumstances breed crime and improving conditions reduce it. America's crime rate actually rose during the long period of economic growth in the

early 20th century. As the Great Depression set in and incomes dropped, the crime rate also fell. It went up again between 1965 and 1974, when incomes rose. Most recently, during the recession of 1982, there was a slight dip in crime, not an increase.

Washington also believes that race is the second most important cause of crime. The large disparity in crime rates between whites and blacks often is cited as proof. However, a closer look at the data shows that the real variable is not race, but family structure and all that it implies in terms of commitment and love between adults and children.

A 1988 study of 11,000 individuals found that "the percentage of single-parent households with children between the ages of 12 and 20 is significantly as-

sociated with rates of violent crime and burglary." The same study makes it clear that the popular assumption that there is an association between race and crime is false. Illegitimacy, not race, is the key factor. It is the absence of marriage and the failure to form and maintain intact families that explains the incidence of crime among whites as well as blacks.

There is a strong, well-documented pattern of circumstances and social evolution in the life of a future violent criminal. The pattern may be summarized in five basic stages:

Stage one: Parental neglect and abandonment of the child in early home life. When the future violent criminal is born, his father already has abandoned the mother. If his parents are married, they are likely to divorce by the third year of his life. He is raised in a neighborhood with a high concentration of single-parent families. He does not become securely attached to his mother during the critical early years. His child care frequently changes.

The adults in his life often quarrel and vent their frustrations physically. He, or a member of his family, may suffer one or more forms of abuse, including sexual. There is much harshness in his home, and he is deprived of affection.

He becomes hostile, anxious, and hyperactive. He is difficult to manage at age three and is labeled a "behavior problem." Lacking his father's presence and attention, he becomes increasingly aggressive.

Stage two: The embryonic gang becomes a place for him to belong. His behavior continues to deteriorate at a rapid rate. He satisfies his needs by exploiting others. At age five or six, he hits his mother. In first grade, his aggressive behavior causes problems for other children. He is difficult for school officials to handle.

He is rejected socially at school by "normal" children. He searches for and finds acceptance among similarly aggressive and hostile youngsters. He and his friends are slower at school. They fail at verbal tasks that demand abstract thinking and at learning social and moral concepts. His reading scores trail behind the rest of his class. He has lessening interest in school, teachers, and learning.

By now, he and his friends have low educational and life expectations for themselves. These are reinforced by teachers and family members. Poor supervision at home continues. His father, or father substitute, still is absent. His life primarily is characterized by aggressive behavior by himself and his peers and a hostile home life.

Stage three: He joins a delinquent gang. At age 11, his bad habits and attitudes are well-established. By age 15, he engages in criminal behavior. The earlier he commits his first delinquent act, the longer he will be likely to lead a life of crime.

His companions are the main source of his personal identity and his sense of belonging. Life with his delinquent friends is hidden from adults. The number of delinquent acts increases in the year before he and his friends drop out of school.

His delinquent girlfriends have poor relationships with their mothers, as well as with "normal" girls in school. A number of his peers use drugs. Many, especially the girls, run away from home or just drift away.

Stage four: He commits violent crime and the full-fledged criminal gang emerges. High violence grows in his community with the increase in the number of single-parent families. He purchases a gun, at first mainly for self-defense. He and his peers begin to use violence for exploitation. The violent young men in his delinquent peer group are arrested more than the non-violent criminals, but most of them do not get caught at all.

Gradually, different friends specialize in different types of crime—violence or theft. Some are more versatile than others. The girls are involved in prostitution, while he and the other boys are members of criminal gangs.

Stage five: A new child—and a new generation of criminals—is born. His 16-year-old girlfriend is pregnant. He has no thought of marrying her; among his peers this simply isn't done. They stay together for awhile until the shouting and hitting start. He leaves her and does not see the baby anymore.

One or two of his criminal friends are experts in their field. Only a few members of the group to which he now belongs—career criminals—are caught. They commit hundreds of crimes per year. Most of those he and his friends commit are in their own neighborhood.

For the future violent criminal, each of these five stages is characterized by the absence of the love, affection, and dedication of his parents. The ordinary tasks of growing up are a series of perverse exercises, frustrating his needs, stunting his capacity for empathy as well as his ability to belong, and increasing the risk of his becoming a twisted young adult. This experience is in stark contrast to the investment of love and dedication by two parents normally needed to make compassionate, competent adults out of their offspring.

The impact of violent crime

When one considers some of the alarming statistics that make headlines today, the future of our society appears bleak. In the mid 1980s, the chancellor of the New York City school system warned: "We are in a situation now where 12,000 of our 60,000 kindergartners have mothers who are still in their teenage years and where 40% of our students come from single-parent households."

Today, this crisis is not confined to New York; it afflicts even small, rural communities. Worse yet, the national illegitimacy rate is predicted to reach 50% within the next 12–20 years. As a result, violence in school is becoming worse. The Centers for Disease Control recently reported that more than four percent of high school students surveyed had brought a firearm at least once to school. Many of them, in fact, were regular gun carriers.

The old injunction clearly is true—violence begets violence. Violent families are producing violent youths, and violent youths are producing violent communities. The future violent criminal is likely to have witnessed numerous conflicts between his parents. He may have been physically or sexually abused. His parents, brothers, and sisters also may be criminals, and thus his family may have a disproportionate negative impact on the community. Moreover, British and American studies show that fewer than five percent of all criminals account for 50% of all criminal convictions. Over all, there has been an extraordinary increase in community violence in most major American cities.

Government agencies are powerless to make men and women marry or stay wed. They are powerless to guarantee that parents will love and care for their children. They are powerless to persuade anyone to make and keep promises. In fact, government agencies often do more harm than good by enforcing policies that undermine stable families and by misdiagnosing the real root cause of such social problems as violent crime.

Nevertheless, ordinary American[s] are not powerless. They know full well how to fight crime effectively. They do not need to survey the current social science literature to know that a family life of affection, cohesion, and parental involvement prevents delinquency. They instinctively realize that paternal and maternal affection and the father's presence in the home are among the critical elements in raising well-balanced children. They acknowledge that parents should encourage the moral development of their offspring—an act that best is accomplished within the context of religious belief and practice.

None of this is to say that fighting crime or rebuilding stable families and communities will be easy. What is easy is deciding what we must do at the outset. Begin by affirming four simple principles: First, marriage is vital. Second, parents must love and nurture their children in spiritual as well as physical ways. Third, children must be taught how to relate to and empathize with others. Finally, the backbone of strong neighborhoods and communities is friendship and cooperation among families.

These principles constitute the real root solution to the problem of violent crime. We should do everything in our power to apply them in our own lives and the life of the nation, not just for our sake, but for that of our children.

WHERE BIAS BEGINS:
THE TRUTH ABOUT STEREOTYPES

Psychologists once believed that only bigoted people used stereotypes. Now the study of unconscious bias is revealing the unsettling truth: We all use stereotypes, all the time, without knowing it. We have met the enemy of equality, and the enemy is us.

By Annie Murphy Paul

Mahzarin Banaji doesn't fit anybody's idea of a racist. A psychology professor at Yale University, she studies stereotypes for a living. And as a woman and a member of a minority ethnic group, she has felt firsthand the sting of discrimination. Yet when she took one of her own tests of unconscious bias, "I showed very strong prejudices," she says. "It was truly a disconcerting experience." And an illuminating one. When Banaji was in graduate school in the early 1980s, theories about stereotypes were concerned only with their explicit expression: outright and unabashed racism, sexism, anti-Semitism. But in the years since, a new approach to stereotypes has shattered that simple notion. The bias Banaji and her colleagues are studying is something far more subtle, and more insidious: what's known as automatic or implicit stereotyping, which, they find, we do all the time without knowing it. Though out-and-out bigotry may be on the decline, says Banaji, "if anything, stereotyping is a bigger problem than we ever imagined."

Previously researchers who studied stereotyping had simply asked people to record their feelings about minority groups and had used their answers as an index of their attitudes. Psychologists now understand that these conscious replies are only half the story. How progressive a person seems to be on the surface bears little or no relation to how prejudiced he or she is on an unconscious level—so that a bleeding-heart liberal might harbor just as many biases as a neo-Nazi skinhead.

As surprising as these findings are, they confirmed the hunches of many students of human behavior. "Twenty years ago, we hypothesized that there were people who said they were not prejudiced but who really did have unconscious negative stereotypes and beliefs," says psychologist Jack Dovidio, Ph.D., of Colgate University "It was like theorizing about the existence of a virus, and then one day seeing it under a microscope."

The test that exposed Banaji's hidden biases—and that this writer took as well, with equally dismaying results—is typical of the ones used by automatic stereotype researchers. It presents the subject with a series of positive or negative adjectives, each paired with a characteristically "white" or "black" name. As the name and word appear together on a computer screen, the person taking the test presses a key, indicating whether the word is good or bad. Meanwhile, the computer records the speed of each response.

A glance at subjects' response times reveals a startling phenomenon: Most people who participate in the experiment—even some African-Americans—respond more quickly when a positive word is paired with a white name or a negative word with a black name. Because our minds are more accustomed to making these associations, says Banaji, they process them more rapidly. Though the words and names aren't subliminal, they are presented so quickly that a subject's ability to make deliberate choices is diminished—allowing his or her underlying assumptions to show through. The same technique can be used to measure stereotypes about many different social groups, such as homosexuals, women, and the elderly.

THE UNCONSCIOUS COMES INTO FOCUS

From these tiny differences in reaction speed—a matter of a few hundred milliseconds—the study of automatic stereotyping was born. Its immediate ancestor was the cognitive revolution of the 1970s, an explosion of psychological research into the way people think. After decades dominated by the study of observable behavior, scientists wanted a closer look at the more mysterious operation of the human brain. And the development of computers—which enabled scientists to display information

LIKE THE CULTURE, OUR MINDS ARE SPLIT ON THE SUBJECTS OF RACE, GENDER, SEXUAL ORIENTATION.

very quickly and to measure minute discrepancies in reaction time—permitted a peek into the unconscious.

At the same time, the study of cognition was also illuminating the nature of stereotypes themselves. Research done after World War II—mostly by European émigrés struggling to understand how the Holocaust had happened—concluded that stereotypes were used only by a particular type of person: rigid, repressed, authoritarian. Borrowing from the psychoanalytic perspective then in vogue, these theorists suggested that biased behavior emerged out of internal conflicts caused by inadequate parenting.

The cognitive approach refused to let the rest of us off the hook. It made the simple but profound point that we all use categories—of people, places, things—to make sense of the world around us. "Our ability to categorize and evaluate is an important part of human intelligence," says Banaji. "Without it, we couldn't survive." But stereotypes are too much of a good thing. In the course of stereotyping, a useful category—say women—becomes freighted with additional associations, usually negative. "Stereotypes are categories that have gone too far," says John Bargh, Ph.D., of New York University "When we use stereotypes, we take in the gender, the age, the color of the skin of the person before us, and our minds respond with messages that say hostile, stupid, slow, weak. Those qualities aren't out there in the environment. They don't reflect reality."

Bargh thinks that stereotypes may emerge from what social psychologists call in-group/out-group dynamics. Humans, like other species, need to feel that they are part of a group, and as villages, clans, and other traditional groupings have broken down, our identities have attached themselves to more ambiguous classifications, such as race and class. We want to feel good about the group we belong to—and one way of doing so is to denigrate all those who aren't in it. And while we tend to see members of our own group as individuals, we view those in out-groups as an undifferentiated—stereotyped—mass. The categories we use have changed, but it seems that stereotyping itself is bred in the bone.

Though a small minority of scientists argues that stereotypes are usually accurate and can be relied upon without reservations, most disagree—and vehemently. "Even if there is a kernel of truth in the stereotype, you're still applying a generalization about a group to an individual, which is always incorrect," says Bargh. Accuracy aside, some believe that the use of stereotypes is simply unjust. "In a democratic society people should be judged as individuals and not as members of a group," Banaji argues. "Stereotyping flies in the face of that ideal."

PREDISPOSED TO PREJUDICE

The problem, as Banaji's own research shows, is that people can't seem to help it. A recent experiment provides a good illustration. Banaji and her colleague, Anthony Greenwald, Ph.D., showed people a list of names—some famous, some not. The next day the subjects returned to the lab and were shown a second list, which mixed names from the first list with new ones. Asked to identify which were famous, they picked out the Margaret Meads and the Miles Davises—but they also chose some of the names on the first list, which retained a lingering familiarity that they mistook for fame. (Psychologists call this the "famous overnight-effect.") By a margin of two-to-one, these suddenly "famous" people were male.

Participants weren't aware that they were preferring male names to female names, Banaji stresses. They were simply drawing on an unconscious stereotype of men as more important and influential than women. Something similar happened when she showed subjects a list of people who might be criminals: without knowing they were doing so, participants picked out an overwhelming number of African-American names. Banaji calls this kind of stereotyping *implicit*, because people know they are making a judgment—but just aren't aware of the basis upon which they are making it.

Even further below awareness is something that psychologists call automatic processing, in which stereotypes are trig-gered by the slightest interaction or encounter. An experiment conducted by Bargh required a group of white participants to perform a tedious computer task. While performing the task, some of the participants were subliminally exposed to pictures of African-Americans with neutral expressions. When the subjects were then asked to do the task over again, the ones who had been exposed to the faces reacted with more hostility to the request—because, Bargh believes, they were responding in kind to the hostility which is part of the African-American stereotype. Bargh calls this the "immediate hostile reaction," which he believes can have a real effect on race relations. When African-Americans accurately perceive the hostile expressions that their white counterparts are unaware of, they may respond with hostility of their own—thereby perpetuating the stereotype.

Of course, we aren't completely under the sway of our unconscious. Scientists think that the automatic activation of a stereotype is immediately followed by a conscious check on unacceptable thoughts—at least in people who think that they are not prejudiced. This internal censor successfully restrains overtly biased responses. But there's still the danger of leakage, which often shows up in nonverbal behavior: our expressions, our stance, how far away we stand, how much eye contact we make.

The gap between what we say and what we do can lead African-Americans and whites to come away with very different impressions of the same encounter, says Jack Dovidio. "If I'm a white person talking to an African-American, I'm probably monitoring my conscious beliefs very carefully and making sure everything I say agrees with all the positive things I want to express," he says. "And I usually believe I'm pretty successful because I hear the right words coming out of my mouth." The listener who is paying attention to non-verbal behavior, however, may be getting quite the opposite message. An African-American student of Dovidio's recently told him that when she was growing up, her mother had taught her to observe how white people moved to gauge their true feelings toward blacks. "Her mother was a very astute ama-

THE CATEGORIES WE USE HAVE CHANGED, BUT STEREOTYPING ITSELF SEEMS TO BE BRED IN THE BONE.

WE HAVE TO CHANGE HOW WE THINK WE CAN INFLUENCE PEOPLE'S BEHAVIORS. IT WOULD BE NAIVE TO THINK THAT EXHORTATION IS ENOUGH.

teur psychologist—and about 20 years ahead of me," he remarks.

WHERE DOES BIAS BEGIN?

So where exactly do these stealth stereotypes come from? Though automatic-stereotype researchers often refer to the unconscious, they don't mean the Freudian notion of a seething mass of thoughts and desires, only some of which are deemed presentable enough to be admitted to the conscious mind. In fact, the cognitive model holds that information flows in exactly the opposite direction: connections made often enough in the conscious mind eventually become unconscious. Says Bargh: "If conscious choice and decision making are not needed, they go away. Ideas recede from consciousness into the unconscious over time."

Much of what enters our consciousness, of course, comes from the culture around us. And like the culture, it seems that our minds are split on the subjects of race, gender, class, sexual orientation. "We not only mirror the ambivalence we see in society, but also mirror it in precisely the same way," says Dovidio. Our society talks out loud about justice, equality, and egalitarianism, and most Americans accept these values as their own. At the same time, such equality exists only as an ideal, and that fact is not lost on our unconscious. Images of women as sex objects, footage of African-American criminals on the six o'clock news,—"this is knowledge we cannot escape," explains Banaji. "We didn't choose to know it, but it still affects our behavior."

We learn the subtext of our culture's messages early. By five years of age, says Margo Monteith, Ph.D., many children have definite and entrenched stereotypes about blacks, women, and other social groups. Adds Monteith, professor of psychology at the University of Kentucky: "Children don't have a choice about accepting or rejecting these conceptions, since they're acquired well before they have the cognitive abilities or experiences to form their own beliefs." And no matter how progressive the parents, they must compete with all the forces that would promote and perpetuate these stereotypes: peer pressure, mass media, the actual balance of power in society. In fact, prejudice may be as much a result as a cause of this imbalance. We

create stereotypes—African-Americans are lazy, women are emotional—to explain why things are the way they are. As Dovidio notes, "Stereotypes don't have to be true to serve a purpose."

WHY CAN'T WE ALL GET ALONG?

The idea of unconscious bias does clear up some nettlesome contradictions. "It accounts or a lot of people's ambivalence toward others who are different, a lot of their inconsistencies in behavior," says Dovidio. "It helps explain how good people can do bad things." But it also prompts some uncomfortable realizations. Because our conscious and unconscious beliefs may be very different—and because behavior often follows the lead of the latter—"good intentions aren't enough," as John Bargh puts it. In fact, he believes that they count for very little. "I don't think free will exists," he says, bluntly—because what feels like the exercise of free will may be only the application of unconscious assumptions.

Not only may we be unable to control our biased responses, we may not even be aware that we have them. "We have to rely on our memories and our awareness of what we're doing to have a connection to reality," says Bargh. "But when it comes to automatic processing, those cues can be deceptive." Likewise, we can't always be sure how biased others are. "We all have this belief that the important thing about prejudice is the external expression of it," says Banaji. "That's going to be hard to give up."

One thing is certain: We can't claim that we've eradicated prejudice just because its outright expression has waned. What's more, the strategies that were so effective in reducing that sort of bias won't work on unconscious beliefs. "What this research is saying is that we are going to have to change dramatically the way we think we can influence people's behaviors," says Banaji. "It would be naive to think that exhortation is enough." Exhortation, education, political protest—all of these hammer away at our conscious beliefs while leaving the bedrock below untouched. Banaji notes, however, that one traditional remedy for discrimination—affirmative action—may still be effective since it bypasses our unconsciously compromised judgment.

But some stereotype researchers think that the solution to automatic stereotyping lies in the process itself. Through practice, they say people can weaken the mental links that connect minorities to negative stereotypes and strengthen the ones that connect them to positive conscious beliefs. Margo Monteith explains how it might work. "Suppose you're at a party and someone tells a racist joke—and you laugh," she says. "Then you realize that you shouldn't have laughed at the joke. You feel guilty and become focused on your thought processes. Also, all sorts of cues become associated with laughing at the racist joke: the person who told the joke, the act of telling jokes, being at a party drinking." The next time you encounter these cues, "a warning signal of sorts should go off—'wait, didn't you mess up in this situation before?'—and your responses will be slowed and executed with greater restraint."

That slight pause in the processing of a stereotype gives conscious, unprejudiced beliefs a chance to take over. With time, the tendency to prevent automatic stereotyping may itself become automatic. Monteith's research suggests that, given enough motivation, people may be able to teach themselves to inhibit prejudice so well that even their tests of implicit bias come clean.

The success of this process of "deautomatization" comes with a few caveats, however. First, even its proponents concede that it works only for people disturbed by the discrepancy between their conscious and unconscious beliefs, since unapologetic racists or sexists have no motivation to change. Second, some studies have shown that attempts to suppress stereotypes may actually cause them to return later, stronger than ever. And finally, the results that Monteith and other researchers have achieved in the laboratory may not stick in the real world, where people must struggle to maintain their commitment to equality under less-than-ideal conditions.

Challenging though that task might be, it is not as daunting as the alternative researchers suggest: changing society itself. Bargh, who likens de-automatization to closing the barn door once the horses have escaped, says that "it's clear that the way to get rid of stereotypes is by the roots, by where they come from in the first place." The study of culture may someday tell us where the seeds of prejudice originated; for now the study of the unconscious shows us just how deeply they're planted.

Laughter may be no laughing matter

Laughter signals mirth as well as dominance and submission.

By Rebecca A. Clay

Deep in the mountainous rain forests of Rwanda, Dian Fossey occasionally came across gorillas frolicking, tickling each other and making raspy vocalizations she described as chuckles. Jane Goodall noted similar behavior in the chimpanzees she studied at the Gombe Stream Research Centre in Tanzania.

Psychologist Robert R. Provine, PhD, studies primate laughter much closer to home. Eavesdropping on more than 1,200 conversations at shopping malls, classrooms and other public places, he has made important discoveries about this universal human behavior. Noting that virtually all the literature on laughter focuses on audiences' responses to humor, he has made the subject of everyday laughter his own. He has examined such topics as the rules that govern laughter, gender differences in laughter and even the sonic structure of laughter.

And while Provine describes his work as purely descriptive, he and other researchers offer clues about why such an odd behavior evolved in the first place. Their theories about laughter's role in signaling dominance, submission and other conditions suggest that laughter is nothing to laugh about.

Laughing at nothing

"If you went to the zoo and heard animals performing some of their species-typical calls, you might point and laugh and think how extraordinary they are," says Provine, a psychology professor and director of the neuroscience program at the University of Maryland Baltimore County.

"But those animals are looking out at you and witnessing behavior that's no less strange. We have a tendency of trivializing the commonplace, such as people getting together in groups and going 'Ha-ha-ha' every once in a while. We don't appreciate that, because we see it all around us."

What surprised Provine most when he first started looking at the phenomenon was the fact that most of the things people laugh at simply aren't funny. In fact, jokes, stories and other recognizable attempts at humor generated less than 20 percent of the laughter he observed. Most laughter, he discovered, occurs immediately after such banalities as "Got to go now," "I see your point" and "It was nice meeting you."

Although laughter typically occurs in playful settings, says Provine, most laughter is not a response to comedy but rather an attempt to set a positive emotional tone and enhance feelings of group belonging. Because laughter isn't consciously controlled, he adds, people usually don't even realize that they're laughing at comments that aren't humorous in the least.

Of course, laughter isn't always good-humored. Consider the difference between laughing at someone and laughing with them, says Provine. In some cases, he says, laughter may be a way of signaling dominance or submission, rejection or acceptance. An audience may laugh politely to signal acceptance of a speaker's message or give an indignant "ha!" to signal rejection, for example. Or a speaker may use laughter to buffer the impact of what he or she is saying.

What's surprising, says Provine, is the fact that the average speaker laughs 46 percent more than the people he or she is speaking to. There are important gender differences as well. When a woman addresses a

From *APA Monitor,* September 1997, p. 16. © 1997 by the American Psychological Association. Reprinted by permission.

male audience, for instance, she typically laughs a whopping 127 percent more than her listeners. In contrast, a man addressing a female audience typically laughs 7 percent less than they do. Cross-cultural evidence has confirmed that men are typically humor-producers and women laughers, says Provine.

Vying for status

Moving from the unconscious motor act that is laughter to the cognitive behavior that is humor, other researchers see evolutionary forces at work.

To ethologist Glenn E. Weisfeld, PhD, an associate professor of psychology at Wayne State University in Detroit, laughter is a way of rewarding people who provide valuable information to listeners. Just as tickling teaches children how to protect vulnerable parts of their bodies, he says, humor transmits important information about how to avoid social *faux pas* of various kinds.

Jokes—which often focus on public failure or embarrassment—show us what not to do, says Weisfeld, pointing out that professional comedians are often accompanied by stooges who serve as the butt of their jokes. Puns and other forms of wordplay teach us about words and language in general.

"The subject matter of humor often pertains to ticklish situations," says Weisfeld. "Lots of humor pertains to sexual situations or aggressive, competitive situations in which someone gets hurt. It makes sense that we would be especially interested in learning about these aspects of life."

Weisfeld rejects explanations of humor that focus on the ways in which it helps people get along or enhances group functioning. Evolutionary theory, he says, requires that a particular behavior benefit individuals, not the group. In his view, humor offers advantages to both the humorist and the humor recipient: The recipient learns valuable lessons and rewards the humorist with the nonverbal gesture of appreciation that is laughter—and with invitations to parties that offer food, drink and potential mates.

Richard D. Alexander, PhD, the Hubbell professor of evolutionary biology at the University of Michigan in Ann Arbor, makes a similar point. Describing team sports as practice for warfare, he sees humor as practice for the high-stakes realm of ensuring reproductive success. Humor, he speculates, is simply a way of asserting the humorist's social status and putting others in their place.

Alexander challenges students in his classes to come up with a joke that doesn't put someone down. So far, no one's been able to find one. The skit on David Letterman's show called "Everything is Funnier When Someone Gets Hurt" is only the most obvious example, says Alexander.

Similarly, jokes that put down ethnic or other types of groups attempt to raise the joke-teller's prestige at the expense of others. Puns and intellectual wordplay demonstrate the joke-teller's cleverness while suggesting the listener's inability to get the joke. Even "Why did the chicken cross the road?" is a put-down, says Alexander, because the listener feels foolish for overlooking the obvious answer, "To get to the other side."

The groans that often greet a punch line or a pun signal the listeners' awareness of their lower status, says Alexander, while their laughter confers status to the humorist. The fact that most people laugh at their bosses' jokes only underlines the fact that laughter is often a signal of submission, he says.

"This is a bleak way to look at laughter," he adds. "But it's one I can't escape."

Rebecca A. Clay is a freelance writer in Washington, D.C.

BRAIN SEX AND THE LANGUAGE OF LOVE

Robert L. Nadeau

If we can believe the experts, the standard for healthy intimacy in love relationships between men and women is female, and maleness is a disease in desperate need of a cure. Men, say social scientists, have a "trained incapacity to share" and have learned to overvalue independence and to fear emotional involvement. Female friendships, claim the intimacy experts, are based on emotional bonding and mutual support, and male friendships on competition, emotional inhibition, and aggression.[1] Social scientists have also pathologized maleness because men typically view love as action, or doing things for another, while women view love as talking and acknowledging feelings.

In fairness to the intimacy experts, what they say about differences in the behavior of men and women has been well documented. Numerous studies have shown that men feel close to other men when working or playing side by side, while women feel close to other women when talking face to face.[2] Male group behavior is characterized by an emphasis on space, privacy, and autonomy, and female group behavior by a need to feel included, connected, and attached.[3] Male conversation tends to center around activities (sports, politics, work), and personal matters are discussed in terms of strengths and achievements. Female conversation, in contrast, is more likely to center around feelings and relationships, and there is considerably less reluctance to reveal fears and weaknesses.

Men and women also appear to experience intimacy in disparate ways. In men's relationships with other men, the index of intimacy is the degree of comfort and relaxation felt when engaged in activities, such as helping a friend move furniture or repair cars. Even when men comfort one another in crisis situations, like the loss of a family member or a spouse, it is physical presence, rather than intimate talk, that tends to be most valued.[4]

The index for intimacy among women is the extent to which personal feelings can be shared in a climate of mutual support and trust. What tends to be most valued in these interactions is confirmation of feelings as opposed to constructive criticism and advice. When women are asked to describe the benefits of such conversations with other women, they typically mention relief from

1. Mirra Komarovsky, *Blue-collar Marriage* (New York: Vintage, 1964).

2. D. Goleman, "Two Views of Marriage Explored: His and Hers," *New York Times,* 1 Apr. 1989.

3. C. Gilligan, *In a Different Voice* (Cambridge, Mass.: Harvard University Press, 1982).

4. Scott Swain, "Covert Intimacy: Closeness in Men's Friendship," in B. J. Reisman and P. Schwartz, eds., *Gender in Intimate Relations* (Belmont, Calif.: Wadsworth, 1989).

This article originally appeared in *The World & I,* November 1997, pp. 330-339. Reprinted by permission of *The World & I,* a publication of the Washington Times Corporation. © 1997.

The human brain, like the human body, is sexed, and differences in the sex-specific human brain condition a wide range of behaviors that we typically associate with maleness or femaleness.

anxiety and stress, feeling better, and a more enhanced sense of self-worth. Although women also express intimacy by doing things for other women, the doing is typically viewed as an occasion for verbal intimacy.[5]

The response of males to depression also favors action, or a tendency to "run" when overcome with sadness, anxiety, or dread. And when men talk about their depression in therapy, they typically "rush through" an account of their emotions and describe depression with action metaphors, such as "running in place," "running wide open," and "pushing the edge."[6] When women are clinically depressed, they are more willing to talk about their feelings, to find opportunities to do so with other women, and to seek help in talk therapy. Women also typically disclose the sources of depression in detailed narratives that represent and analyze experience. And while men tend to respond to clinical depression by running or moving, women tend to respond with sedentary activities like uncontrollable crying, staying in bed, and compulsive eating.

The sex-specific patterns that lie beneath the diversity of these behaviors reduce to a male orientation toward action and a female orientation toward talking. Why is this the case? According to the intimacy experts, it is entirely a product of learning and one of the primary sources of male pathology. As psychologist Carol

Tavris puts it, "The doing-versus-talking distinction in the emotional styles of males and females begins in childhood, when boys begin to develop what psychologists call 'side by side' relationships, in which intimacy means sharing the same activity—sports, games, watching a movie or a sports event together." Girls, in contrast, "tend to prefer 'face to face' relationships, in which intimacy means revealing ideas and emotions in a heart-to-heart exchange."[7]

The problem is not, as a best-selling book would have us believe, that women are from Venus and men from Mars. It is that we have only recently come to realize something about the legacy of the evolution of our species on planet Earth. Throughout virtually all of our evolutionary history, men and women lived in small tribes of hunter-gatherers where the terms for survival were not the same. We have long recognized that the different terms for survival, along with mate selection, account for sexual differences in the human body. But only in the last few decades have we discovered that the legacy of our evolutionary past is also apparent in the human brain. The human brain, like the human body, is sexed, and differences in the sex-specific human brain condition a wide range of behaviors that we typically associate with maleness or femaleness.

THE LEGACY OF THE HUNTER-GATHERERS

The family album containing the record of our hunter-gatherer evolutionary past is DNA, and the legacy of that past begins to

unfold following the union of sperm and ovum. Normal females have two long X chromosomes, contributed by each biological parent, that closely resemble one another. Normal males have a long X chromosome, contributed by the mother, and a short Y chromosome, contributed by the father. Although each sperm and ovum contributes half of the full complement of forty-six chromosomes, the ovum provides all of the cytoplasmic DNA.

A fetus will develop with a female brain unless a gene on the Y chromosome, known as SRY, is expressed about the sixth week of pregnancy and triggers the release of testosterone in the gonads. The testosterone transforms the developing fetus into a male by interacting with genes that regulate or are regulated by the expression of SRY. The result is a kind of chain reaction in which genes involved in the determination of maleness are activated in a large number of cells. But since the levels of hormones vary across individual brains, the response of brain regions to the presence of hormones is highly variable.

Many of the sex-specific differences in the human brain are located in more primitive brain regions, and they condition male and female copulatory behavior, sexual orientation, and cyclic biological processes like menstruation. Sex-specific differences also exist, however, in the more recently evolved neocortex or in the higher brain regions. The neocortex looks like a redundantly folded sheet and contains 70 percent of the neurons in the central nervous system. It is divided into two hemispheres that process different kinds of information fairly independently, and each communicates with the

[5] Robin Lakoff, *Talking Power: The Politics of Language* (New York: Basic Books, 1990).

[6] Catherine Riessman, *Divorce Talk: Women and Men Make Sense of Personal Relationships* (New Brunswick, N.J.: Rutgers University Press, 1990).

[7] Carol Tavris, *The Mismeasure of Women* (New York: Simon & Schuster, 1992), 251–52.

While males talk about their status in terms of simple descriptions of individual skills and achievements, Tannen says, females do so with complicated descriptions of overall character.

other via a 200-million-fiber network called the corpus callosum. While the symmetry is not exact, structures in one hemisphere are mirrored in the other. Thus we have two parietal lobes, two occipital lobes, and so on.

In people with normal hemispheric dominance, the left hemisphere has executive control. This hemisphere manages linguistic analysis and expression, as well as sequential motor responses or body movements. The right hemisphere is responsible for perception of spatial relationships, faces, emotional stimuli, and prosody (vocal intonations that modify the literal meaning of a

word).[8] The two frontal lobes of each hemisphere, located behind the forehead, integrate inputs from other brain regions and are closely associated with conscious decision making. This portion of our brain, which occupies 29 percent of the cortex, has undergone the most recent evolutionary expansion.

One piece of evidence that suggests why the brains of women and men tend to process information differently involves the corpus callosum, or the network of fibers connecting the two hemispheres. A subregion of this network, the splenium, is significantly larger in women than in men and more bulbous in shape.[9] More connections between the hemispheres in female brains could be a partial explanation for another significant discovery—both hemispheres are normally more active in the brains of females.

Computer-based imaging systems, such as positron emission tomography (PET) and magnetic resonance imaging (MRI), allow scientists to assess which areas of the brains of conscious subjects are active. All of these systems use advanced computers to construct three-dimensional images of brains as they process various kinds of information. Studies based on advanced imaging systems have revealed that cognitive tasks in the female brain tend to be localized in both hemispheres,[10] and that the same tasks in the male brain tend to be localized in one hemisphere.[11] Other recent studies using this technology have revealed sex-specific differences in the brain regions used to process language and sex-specific differences in feedback from more-primitive brain regions.[12] What this research suggests is that differences in the

communication styles of men and women are not simply the product of learning.[13] They are also conditioned by differences in the sex-specific human brain.[14]

YOU JUST DON'T UNDERSTAND ME

While none of the intimacy experts, to my knowledge, attribute differences in the conversation styles of men and women to the sex-specific human brain, there is a growing consensus that it is extremely difficult to eliminate these differences. In the best-seller *You Just Don't Understand: Women and Men in Conversation*, Deborah Tannen claims that while men use conversation "to preserve their independence and negotiate and maintain status in a hierarchical social order," women use conversation as "a way of establishing connections and negotiating relationships."[15] Based on this assumption, Tannen makes the case that there are some large differences in the languages of men and women.

Men, she says, are more comfortable with public speaking, or "report talk," and women are more comfortable with private or "rapport talk." Men use language that is abstract and categorical, or communicate in "messages," and women use language that conveys subtle nuances and hidden meanings, or communicate in "metamessages." Similarly, men respond to problems with concrete solutions and suggestions, and women respond with empathy and an emphasis on community.

Competitive males, claims Tannen, favor "commands," or statements that indicate what should be done without qualification, while

8. S. F. Wietelson, "Neural Sexual Mosaicism: Sexual Differentiation of the Human Temporo-Parietal Region for Functional Asymmetry," *Psychoneuroendochrinology* 16:1–3 (1991): 131–55.

9. Wietelson, "Neural Sexual Mosaicism," 137–38.

10. I. Jibiki, H. Matsuda, et al., "Quantitative Assessment of Regional Blood Flow with 1231–IMP in Normal Adult Subjects," *Acta-Neurol-Napoli* 15:1 (1993): 7–15, and F. Okada, Y. Tokumitsu, et al., "Gender and Handedness-Related Differences of Forebrain Oxygenation and Hemodynamics," *Brain Research* 601:1–2 (1993): 337–47.

11. S. P. Springer and G. Deutsch, *Left Brain, Right Brain* (San Francisco: W. H. Friedman Co., 1985).

12. Ruben Gur, quoted in Gina Kolata, "Men's World, Women's World? Brain Studies Point to Differences," *New York Times*, 28 Feb. 1995, C1.

13. Melissa Hines, "Gonadal Hormones and Human Cognitive Development," in Jacques Balthazart, ed., *Hormones, Brain and Behavior in Vertebrates* (Basel, Switz.: Karger, 1990), 51–63.

14. Susan Phillips, Susan Steele, and Christine Tanz, eds., *Language, Gender and Sex in Comparative Perspective* (Cambridge, Eng.: Cambridge University Press, 1987); and David Martin and H. D. Hoover, "Sex Differences in Educational Achievement: A Longitudinal Study," *Journal of Early Adolescence* 7 (1987): 65–83.

15. Deborah Tannen, *You Just Don't Understand: Women and Men in Conversation* (New York: Ballantine Books, 1990), 77.

Men may perceive commands, as opposed to requests, as more consistent with their sense of the real and as a more expedient way to solve problems.

consensus-building females favor "conditional propositions," or statements prefaced with words like "let's," "we could," and "maybe." And while males talk about their status in terms of simple descriptions of individual skills and achievements, Tannen says, females do so with complicated descriptions of overall character.

This sparse theoretical framework, however, does not account for the enormous popularity of Tannen's book. What most impresses readers are the conversations that Tannen uses to illustrate the distinctive character of the languages used by men and women. The following exchange occurs when a husband indicates that he did not get enough sleep:

He: I'm really tired. I didn't sleep well last night.
She: I didn't sleep well either. I never do.
He: Why are you trying to belittle me?
She: I'm not! I'm just trying to show you I understand!

"This woman," says Tannen, "was not only hurt by her husband's reaction; she was mystified by it. How could he think she was belittling him? By 'belittle me,' he meant 'belittle my experience.' He was filtering her attempts to establish connection through his concern with preserving independence and avoiding being put down."[16]

In a discussion of the differences between messages and metamessages, Tannen quotes from Anne Tyler's novel *The Accidental Tourist*. At

16. Tannen, *You Just Don't Understand*, 51.
17. Quoted in Tannen, *You Just Don't Understand*, 175.

this point in the narrative the character Macon has left his wife and moved in with a woman named Muriel. The conversation begins when Macon makes an observation about Muriel's son:

"I don't think Alexander's getting a proper education," he said to her one evening.
"Oh, he's okay."
"I asked him to figure what change they'd give back when we bought the milk today, and he didn't have the faintest idea. He didn't even know he'd have to subtract."
"Well, he's only in second grade," Muriel said.
"I think he ought to go to private school."
"Private schools cost money."
"So? I'll pay."
She stopped flipping the bacon and looked over at him. "What are you saying?" she said.
"Pardon?"
"What are you saying, Macon? Are you saying you're committed?"

Muriel then tells Macon that he must decide whether he wants to divorce his wife and marry her, and that she will not put her son in a new school when he could be forced to leave if Macon returns to his wife. Confused and frustrated by Muriel's attack, Macon responds, "But I just want him to learn to subtract." The problem, writes Tannen, is that "Macon is concerned with the message, the simple matter of Alexander's learning math. But Muriel is concerned with the metamessage. What would it say about the relationship if he began paying for her son's education?"[17]

Some reviewers of Tannen's book have rightly complained that these differences are made to appear too

categorical. But they also concede, along with the majority of other reviewers, that Tannen has disclosed some actual disparities in the languages used by men and women. How, then, does Tannen account for these remarkable differences in the manner in which men and women linguistically construct reality? She claims that younger children "learn" these languages from older children in single-sex groups on the playground.

WHY MEN CAN'T ALWAYS TALK LIKE WOMEN

When we examine what Tannen says about differences in the languages used by men and women in the light of what we know about the sex-specific human brain, it seems clear the differences are not simply learned. Report talk and messages may reflect the orientation toward action associated with higher reliance on the primitive region of the limbic system in the male brain and with an orientation toward linear movement in abstract map space in the neocortex.

Although the usual biological explanation for the male tendency to give commands is higher levels of aggression, this linguistic habit also seems consistent with the manner in which reality tends to be constructed in the male brain. Commands may reflect the bias toward action and the organization of particulars in terms of movement between points in map space. All of which suggests that men may perceive commands, as opposed to requests, as more consistent with their sense of the real and as a more expedient way to solve problems.

When divorced women are asked to explain the failure of a marriage, the common refrain is "lack of communication," or the unwillingness of the ex-husband to talk about or share feelings.

The relationship between the two hemispheres in the female brain tends to be more symmetric, and there is a greater degree of interaction between these hemispheres. Since linguistic reality in the brains of women seems to invoke a wider range of right-brain cognitive functions, this may enhance awareness of emotionally relevant details, visual clues, verbal nuances, and hidden meanings. This suggests that the female brain tends to construct linguistic reality in terms of more extensive and interrelated cognitive and emotional contexts. If this is the case, all aspects of experience may appear more interdependent and interconnected, and this could contribute to the tendency to perceive people and events in a complex web of relation. Perhaps this is why the language of women tends to feature a more profound sense of identification with others, or why this language seems more "consensual."

Rapport talk may reflect this sense of identification and satisfy the need to feel interconnected. And metamessages, which allow analysis of single events to be extended through a complex web of relation, also seem consistent with the manner in which the female brain tends to construct reality. Since this reality seems more consensual, women may be more inclined to regard decision making as consensual and to prefer "us" instead of "I." Higher reliance in the female brain on the portion of the limbic system associated with symbolic action could also contribute to these tendencies.

Since the male brain tends to construct reality in terms of abstract solutions and sequential movements in map space, men probably perceive action as more commensurate with their sense of the real. If action in the reality of males seems more

"actual" than talking, this could explain, in part at least, why men are more inclined to associate intimacy with shared activities, to respond to depression with action, and to describe feelings with action metaphors.

Neuroscience also suggests why women seem to believe that emotions are conveyed more through talking than action. If reality as it is constructed in the female brain features a more extended network of perceptions, memories, associations, and feelings, then the real could be more closely associated with language. This could also explain why women favor "rapport talk," or conversations about the personal and the private. If this talk is more commensurate with the actual character of reality in the female brain, women more than men might depend on conversation to reinforce their reality.

More emotional content in female constructions of reality could also explain why women are more inclined to equate talking with feeling, and to view caring actions that are not accompanied by verbal expressions of feeling as less than authentic. And if linguistic constructions of reality in the female brain feature a broader range of emotional experience, women may have less difficulty, on average, disclosing, describing, and contextualizing feelings.

A NEW VIEW OF THE LANGUAGE OF LOVE

The use of qualifiers like "on average," "tends," "may," "probably," and "might" in the description of behavior associated with the sex-specific human brain is not a concession to political correctness. It is the

only way to fairly characterize the differences. There is nothing in this research that argues for a direct causal connection between sex-specific brains and the behavior of men and women. Every human brain is unique and becomes more so as a result of learning, and there is more variation between same-sex brains than opposite-sex brains. What is most striking in virtually all of the research on the sex-specific human brain is not differences between the emotional and cognitive processes of men and women but the amazing degree of overlap, or sameness. And while nature may play a larger role in conditioning same-sex behavior than we previously realized, nurture, or learning, remains the most vital part of the equation.

Although many of the behaviors in the litany of male pathology are obviously learned and subject to change, the tendencies associated with the sex-specific male brain cannot be erased in the learning process. This means that the assumption that love is not love unless men must think, feel, and behave like women in love relationships is not, in the vast majority of instances, realistic. Consider, for example, the primary reason why women seek a divorce. When divorced women are asked to explain the failure of a marriage, the common refrain is "lack of communication," or the unwillingness of the ex-husband to talk about or share feelings.[18] In one recent study, over two-thirds of the women surveyed felt that men would never un-

---

18. Thomas Wills, Robert Weiss, and Gerald Patterson, "A Behavioral Analysis of the Determinants of Marital Separation," *Journal of Consulting and Clinical Psychology* 42 (1974): 802–11.

derstand them, or that the men in their lives would remain forever clueless about the lives of women.[19] And yet numerous studies have also shown that women view men who deviate from the masculine norm by displaying or talking openly about emotions as "too feminine" and "poorly adjusted."[20]

[19.] Survey by Yankelovitch Partners, 1993.

[20.] See, for example, John Robertson and Louise Fitzgerald, "The (Mis)treatment of Men: Effects of Client Gender Role and Lifestyle on Diagnosis and Attribution of Pathology," *Journal of Counseling Psychology* 37 (1990): 3–9.

Recognizing discrepancies in reality as it "tends" to be constructed in the brains of men and women does not frustrate the desire of men and women to communicate better with their partners. In fact, the opposite is true. Awareness of the discrepancies makes it much easier to negotiate differences and to communicate to our partners how they might better satisfy our expectations and desires without recourse to blame and anger. And this could lead to a greater willingness to embrace two additional assumptions about human reality that have been grandly reinforced by brain science—the total reality is that of both men and women, and the overlap or sameness of the realities of men and women is far greater than the differences.

Robert L. Nadeau is a professor at George Mason University. This article is based on his most recent book, S/he Brain: Science, Sexual Politics and the Feminist Movement *(Praeger, 1996).*

Unit Selections

Key Points to Consider

❖ Why do some professionals believe that mental illness is a myth? Do you believe that everyone has the potential for developing a mental disorder? What circumstances lead an individual to mental illness? Do you think that mental disorders are biological or psychological? If we discover that most mental disorders are caused by something physiological, do you think they will remain the purview of psychology? Why or why not?

❖ What is attention deficit disorder? What do you think it would be like to live with a child with this diagnosis? With what other childhood disorders might this be confused? What are the symptoms and causes of attention deficit disorder? Why is this a prevalent diagnosis today?

❖ Do we all suffer from anxiety? How then is an anxiety disorder different from everyday anxiety? What are the causes of anxiety disorder? What are some possible treatments for anxiety disorders? How can we tame normal anxiety?

❖ What is domestic violence? How common is it? What type of women are victimized by domestic violence? How would you profile the abuser? How can we break the cycle of violence? How can we assist the victims? Why do some women choose to stay with the abuser?

❖ What is schizophrenia? What are the symptoms of schizophrenia? What usually happens to the families of the schizophrenics? What are some of the more common treatments for schizophrenia?

 **Links** | **www.dushkin.com/online/**

These sites are annotated on pages 4 and 5.

Jay and Harry were two brothers who owned a service station. They were the middle children of four. The other two children were sisters, the oldest of whom had married and moved out of the family home. The service station that these young men operated was once owned by their father, who had retired and turned the business over to his sons.

Harry and Jay had a good working relationship. Harry was the "up-front" man. Taking customer orders, accepting payments, and working with parts distributors, Harry was the individual who dealt most directly with the customers and others. Jay worked behind the scenes. While Harry made the mechanical diagnoses, Jay was the one who did the corrective work. Some of his friends thought Jay was a mechanical genius.

Preferring to spend time by himself, Jay had always been a little odd and a bit of a loner. His emotions had been more inappropriate and intense than other people's. Harry was the stalwart in the family. He was the acknowledged leader and decision-maker when it came to family finances.

One day Jay did not show up for work on time. When he did, he was dressed in the most garish outfit and was laughing hysterically and talking to himself. Harry at first suspected that his brother had taken some illegal drugs. However, Jay's condition persisted. Out of concern, his family took him to the their physician who immediately sent Jay and his family to a psychiatrist. The diagnosis—schizophrenia. Jay's uncle had also been schizophrenic. The family grimly left the psychiatrist's office. After several other appointments with the psychiatrist, they traveled to the local pharmacy to fill a prescription for antipsychotic medications that Jay would probably have to take for the rest of his life.

What caused Jay's drastic and rather sudden change in mental health? Was Jay destined to be schizophrenic because of his family genes? Did competitiveness with his brother and the feeling that he was a less-revered family member than Harry cause Jay's descent into mental disorder? How can psychiatrists and clinical psychologists make accurate diagnoses? Once a diagnosis of mental disorder is made, can the individual ever completely recover?

These and other questions are the emphasis of this unit. Mental disorder has fascinated and, on the other hand, terrified us for centuries. At various times in our history, those who suffered from these disorders were persecuted as witches, tortured to drive out possessing spirits, punished as sinners, jailed as a danger to society, confined to insane asylums, or, at best, hospitalized for simply being too ill to care for themselves.

Today, psychologists propose that the view of mental disorders as "illnesses" has outlived its usefulness. We should think of mental disorders as either biochemical disturbances or disorders of learning in which the person develops a maladaptive pattern of behavior that is then maintained by an inappropriate environment. At the

same time, we need to recognize that these reactions to stressors in the environment or to inappropriate learning situations may be genetically preordained; some people may more easily develop the disorders than others. Serious disorders are serious problems and not only for the individual who is the patient or client. The impact of mental disorders on the family (just as for Jay's family) and friends deserves our full attention, too. Diagnosis, treatment and the implications of mental disorders are covered in some of the articles in this unit. Unit 11 further explores the treatment of mental disorders.

The first article in this unit offers a general introduction to the concept of mental disorder and its causes. Lisa Cool asks a very cogent question: Is mental illness catching? If the root cause of mental disorder is a virus, then perhaps mental illnesses are contagious. What this would mean for the mentally disordered is also included in this interesting article.

We next look at some specific disorders. The first is attention deficit disorder. Children are frequently diagnosed with this disorder. The disorder can be problematic for the child, the family, and the teacher. "Mother's Little Helper" details symptoms of this disorder and popular treatments for it.

The next article provides information on anxiety disorder. We all suffer from anxiety at one time or another. Some individuals, however, suffer from extreme anxiety that interferes with their daily lives. "Why Worry?" helps the reader understand the differences between day-to-day anxiety and anxiety disorder. Causes and treatments for the disorder are also explained.

Two other problems are reviewed next. One is, unfortunately, a common problem—domestic violence. In domestic violence the woman is often the abused person while the boyfriend or husband is the abuser. We do know, however, that women can also abuse their partners. In "Patterns of Abuse," the authors examine why women stay or leave the abusive relationship and where such women can seek help if the abuse continues. This powerful article also discusses why abusers commit abuse.

The final selection pertains to schizophrenia, one of the most bizarre and mysterious of mental disorders. Schizophrenia is a form of psychosis in which the sufferer often has hallucinations and loses touch with reality in other ways. In this article, the reader is introduced to E. Fuller Torrey who has long studied this baffling disorder. Again the possible causes and treatments for the disorder are highlighted.

Is Mental Illness Catching?

It may sound incredible, but there's evidence that psychological conditions such as depression, obsessive-compulsive disorder and schizophrenia can be caused by strep throat, the flu and other illnesses. Finally, startling proof that mental disorders are not all in the head.

By Lisa Collier Cool

Like many kids, Enid Rose of Tucker, GA, suffered recurrent strep throat infections. But neither her parents nor her doctors saw any reason to link these infections with the far more disabling symptoms that led to her being labeled "the weird kid in school," and that, when she grew up, limited her ability to work. "I've always had obsessive thoughts," says Rose, now age 30. "If I see a knife or anything sharp—even a pencil—I get scared it will somehow poke my eyes out or cut my Achilles tendons." Rose also has such a horror of dirt that she spends hours each day scouring her already immaculate kitchen and bathroom. She even vacuums her bed daily.

It wasn't until 1995 that she was diagnosed with obsessive-compulsive disorder, a condition that affects over 2% of Americans. Marked by the presence of persistent obsessive thoughts and worries, as well as compulsive rituals such as repeated handwashing or constantly checking that the stove is turned off, the illness was once thought to be brought on by destructive parenting practices, such as harsh toilet training. But recent, groundbreaking studies at the National Institute of Mental Health (NIMH) in Bethesda, MD, have revealed a surprising cause for OCD: an abnormal immune response to strep throat or flu-like infections.

The Infection Connection While the idea that you can "catch" a mental illness in the same way that you catch a cold may sound improbable, there's increasing evidence that psychological conditions such as depression, OCD and schizophrenia have biological roots. "What most people don't realize is that psychiatric disorders like OCD and schizophrenia are also true medical illnesses," says Susan Swedo, M.D., scien-

Is It All in Your Head?

Depression, anxiety and other emotional symptoms can, in some cases, be caused by a wide range of physical conditions. Consider your symptoms and the possible psychological and physical causes, then consult your doctor for a diagnosis.

Depression

Symptoms: Persistent sadness, fatigue, change in eating or sleeping patterns, loss of interest or pleasure in daily activities, suicidal thoughts, chronic body aches, memory problems
Other Conditions That Can Produce These Symptoms: Thyroid disease, stroke, chronic fatigue syndrome, lupus, mononucleosis, cancer, heart disease, diabetes

Obsessive-Compulsive Disorder

Symptoms: Repeated intrusive thoughts and worries; involuntary, senseless rituals or checking routines like compulsive cleaning or forever checking that a door is locked
Other Conditions That Can Produce These Symptoms: Irritable bowel disorder, adrenal gland disease, autoimmune disorders, brain injury or infection, neurological diseases

Schizophrenia

Symptoms: Delusional beliefs, lack of appropriate emotional responses or behavior, hallucinations, incoherent speech, paranoia
Other Conditions That Can Produce These Symptoms: Adrenal gland or thyroid disease, brain tumor, substance abuse (especially of LSD, PCP or cocaine), reaction to steroids

tific director of the NIMH and coauthor of *It's Not All in Your Head.* "Not only can a predisposition to mental illness run in a family, just as heart disease or breast cancer can, but it also may be sparked by the very same infections that trigger other diseases."

Dr. Swedo and her colleagues first suspected the connection among strep throat, OCD and Tourette's syndrome (a neurological disorder that causes vocal and physical tics), when earlier studies of patients with rheumatic fever (a strep throat complication that can damage the heart) showed that some also developed OCD-like obsessions and a movement disorder similar to Tourette's known as Sydenham's chorea. "So far," says Dr. Swedo, "we've found 75 children whose parents told us that their perfectly well-adjusted kid woke up one morning after having an inadvertently untreated strep infection locked in obsessive-compulsive rituals, or that their child's mild OCD or Tourette's exploded in intensity after having had strep or a flu-like illness." So far, there's no evidence that strep infection triggers OCD in adults.

Though the NIMH study is small, it *is* revolutionary, and experts believe it could lead to fundamental changes in the treatment of mental disorders. For instance, researchers are now experimenting with giving penicillin on a continuing basis to kids with mild, strep-triggered OCD to prevent a recurrence of strep that could make their symptoms worse. They're also testing drugs that act on the immune system, based on the theory that when the immune system produces antibodies to fight strep, it also attacks a part of the brain that seems related to OCD. All the children in the NIMH study improved dramatically after such treatments, which suggests that their diseases are no more "psychological" than rheumatic fever is.

Of course, the vast majority of kids don't go on to develop OCD after a bout of strep throat, and more research is needed before penicillin and immune-altering therapies are routinely prescribed for OCD and Tourette's. But it's important to take your child to the doctor if you suspect she has strep (symptoms include fever, swollen glands, sore throat and pus on the tonsils).

A Flu in the Mind

Until the late sixties, when the genetic link to schizophrenia was first discovered, parents took the rap for causing the disease, which affects about 1% of Americans and can cause delusions, paranoia and disordered thinking, among other symptoms. Mental health experts typically blamed the disorder on hostile mothers in particular, who supposedly warped their children's minds by constantly putting

---

Old Think/New Think

Here are some of the more pervasive myths about common psychological disorders, along with a good dose of reality.

Obsessive-Compulsive Disorder Old Think: Caused by excessively harsh toilet training. **New Think:** Can result from an abnormal immune response to strep throat or a flu-like infection.

Schizophrenia Old Think: Caused by poor parenting. **New Think:** May result from biological and environmental factors, or when a fetus is exposed to its mother's illness in the womb.

Depression Old Think: People with depression can cheer up if they really want to. **New Think:** Results from chemical imbalances, such as abnormal levels of certain brain chemicals or thyroid dysfunction.

---

them in stressful, no-win situations. Now there's evidence that a virus, *not* bad parenting, may play a role in triggering this devastating disease.

In a study of people born in the nine months after the 1957 Asian flu epidemic in Finland, University of Southern California psychology professor Sarnoff Mednick, Ph.D., found that the children whose mothers had the flu during their second trimester of pregnancy had a far higher than normal rate of schizophrenia later in life. This is the first time that schizophrenia, and perhaps any psychiatric disorder, has been connected to a maternal infection. Since then, studies suggest that prenatal exposure to other disorders, including toxoplasmosis (a parasitic infection), positive-negative blood incompatibility between a mother and her unborn baby, and even cold viruses may also increase a person's chances of developing schizophrenia.

Still, the exact role that viral infections play in causing schizophrenia remains unclear; most people who are exposed to viruses while in the womb don't go on to develop the disease. Like other mental illnesses, schizophrenia is thought to be caused by a variety of biological and environmental triggers. But there's no doubt that the damage to the brain that causes this illness occurs very early on. Babies who eventually develop schizophrenia (which typically occurs during adolescence) tend to sit up later and lag slightly behind other kids in speech and overall motor development, according to Kathryn Kotrla, M.D., assistant professor of psychiatry at Baylor College of Medicine in Houston. "It's clear," she says, "that these children are different from birth."

Depression: A Surprising Link

After Debbie Harris, 42, of Fairborn, OH, was diagnosed with Graves' disease, a disorder of the thyroid gland, she found herself crying at the drop of a hat. She continued to feel extremely depressed after treatment with radioactive iodine and thyroid supplements and repeatedly asked her endocrinologist if her thyroid problems might be the cause. Each time he reassured her that, though her hormone levels were a bit low, they were within the normal range. Harris endured six years of misery before a psychiatrist advised her physician to increase her thyroid dose, which rapidly restored her former disposition.

According to preliminary findings by Robert Stern, Ph.D., associate professor of psychiatry and neurology at Brown University in Providence, RI, women who tested just slightly below normal in thyroid function seemed to be more susceptible to episodes of depression than women whose hormone levels were normal. There are other intriguing links between thyroid function and depression. "Lab tests reveal that 5% to 20% of people with depression have a slightly overactive thyroid, even though they show no thyroid symptoms," notes Dr. Stern. "And though we don't know why, some depressed patients with normal thyroid function don't respond to antidepressants unless they're also given thyroid hormones."

Scientists from the Free University of Berlin have found that the Borna disease virus, which causes horses and cats to act apathetic and listless, is also present in some depression patients. Since evidence of this virus appeared either during or before the time when these patients became depressed, it's possible that it triggers depression in people who are genetically predisposed to the disorder.

Shattering Stigmas As scientists focus on the organic rather than emotional underpinnings of these diseases, the 30 million to 45 million Americans with psychological ailments might finally feel free to step out of the shadows and get help. "One hundred years ago, the most common 'mental illnesses' were tuberculosis, epilepsy and syphilis," says James Hudson, M.D., an associate professor of psychiatry at Harvard Medical School in Boston. People with epilepsy, for instance, were sent to sanatoriums because they were considered to be too emotionally fragile to withstand the stress of industrial society—a theory that didn't die out until doctors discovered the characteristic brain-wave abnormalities for epilepsy in the mid-20th century. "Similarly," says Dr. Hudson, "we might one day find the idea that diseases like schizophrenia, depression, and OCD were ever viewed as 'emotional problems' just as laughable."

That would be a good thing, since 80% of people who currently suffer from psychological illnesses still don't get treatment. "There's so much shame surrounding mental illness that many people wait until they break down completely before they get help," says Victor Reus, M.D., a professor of psychiatry at the University of California at San Francisco School of Medicine. The truth is, mental illnesses are as real as any other disease, as the wealth of new findings makes clear. They're no different—and no more shameful—than having breast cancer or diabetes.

Lisa Collier Cool is a health writer living in Pelham, NY.

Where to Get Help

• **Depression** For information on mood disorders, send an SASE with $1.01 in postage to: National Foundation for Depressive Illness, P.O. Box 2257, New York, NY 10016; call 800-239-1293; or visit the NFDI's Website at http://www.depression.org.

• **OCD** For a list of doctors and support groups in your area and a newsletter, write to the Obsessive-Compulsive Foundation, P.O. Box 70, Milford, CT 06460; call 203-878-5669; or check out the group's Website at http://pages.prodigy.com/alwilen/ocf.html.

• **Schizophrenia** For brochures, treatment information and a newsletter on the latest research developments on the disease, contact: NARSAD Research, 60 Cutter Mill Road, Suite 404, Great Neck, NY 11021; call 800-829-8289; or visit its Website at http://www.mhsource.com.

More than 1 million American children take Ritalin regularly to help them with Attention Deficit Disorder, an increase of two and a half times since 1990. Do we have a miracle cure—or overmedicated kids?

Mother's Little Helper

I T IS ANOTHER MEDICATION MORNING AT Winnebago Elementary School in the middle-class Chicago suburb of Bloomingdale. Three pings sound precisely over the intercom at 11:45 a.m. Principal Mark Wagener opens a locked file cabinet and withdraws a giant Tupperware container filled with plastic prescription vials. Nearly a dozen students scramble to the office for their Ritalin, a drug that calms the agitated by stimulating the brain. These children—all ages, mostly boys—have been diagnosed with Attention-Deficit/Hyperactivity Disorder, a complex neurological impairment that takes the brakes off brains and derails concentration. The school nurse places the pills, one by one, in the children's mouths, a rite

THIS STORY WAS WRITTEN by LynNell Hancock and reported by Pat Wingert and Mary Hager in Washington, Claudia Kalb in Boston, Karen Springen in Chicago and Dante Chinni in New York

of safe passage before lunch. "Let me see . . . ," says nurse Pat Nazos, as she checks under each child's tongue for a stray, unswallowed capsule.

A decade ago, Wagener remembers, only two Winnebago students lined up for Ritalin. He is uncertain how many more "take their meds," as some students say. Some take time-released pills before school. Others take their doses at off-hours. One boy's jogging watch is timed to beep for Ritalin at 10 a.m. and 2 p.m. Like many administrators, Wagener is not sure what to make of it. Are doctors just catching this disabling affliction more often? Or has our culture gone so high-baud haywire that we have lost patience with the demanding quirks of our children? For some students, Wagener observes, Ritalin can make the crucial difference between failing a test or sitting still long enough to pass it. But for others, he laments, "they've just got an excuse to be bad."

The Ritalin riddle, a brain teaser for the '90s, confounds doctors, parents and, sometimes, children. The stimulant can be a god-

send for those who truly need it. Pharmaceutically speaking, "Ritalin is one of the raving successes in psychiatry," says Dr. Laurence Greenhill of Columbia University medical school. Now it's a routinely prescribed drug at distinguished institutions from Johns Hopkins to the Mayo Clinic, a pill that allows children and a growing number of adults to focus their minds and rein in their rampaging attention spans.

But for those who don't need it, Ritalin and its generic twins can be useless, or can even backfire. There is no X-ray, no blood test, no CT scan to determine who needs it; diagnosing attention deficit remains as much art as science. There are no definitive long-term studies to reassure parents that this stimulant isn't causing some hidden havoc to their child. Critics dismiss the drug as just a behavioral "quick fix" for children forced to live in an impatient culture that feeds on deadlines, due dates, sound bites and megabytes. "It takes time for parents and teachers to sit down and talk to kids," says Dr. Sharon Collins, a pediatrician in Cedar Rapids,

Iowa, where reportedly 8 percent of the children are on Ritalin. "It takes less time to get a child a pill."

WHAT'S CLEAR AMID THE DEBATE is that a remarkable revolution has taken place in the care and treatment of America's children. ADHD has become America's No. 1 childhood psychiatric disorder. Experts believe that more than 2 million children (or 3 to 5 percent) have the disorder. According to an estimate by the National Institute of Mental Health, about one student in every classroom is believed to experience it. Since 1990, Dr. Daniel Safer of Johns Hopkins University School of Medicine calculates, the number of kids taking Ritalin has grown 2½ times. Among today's 38 million children at the ages of 5 to 14, he reports, 1.3 million take it regularly. Sales of the drug last year alone topped $350 million.

This is, beyond question, an American phenomenon. The rate of Ritalin use in the United States is at least five times higher than in the rest of the world, according to federal studies. It's so common in some upscale precincts that a mini black market has emerged in a handful of playgrounds and campuses. "Vitamin R"—one of its recreational names—sells for $3 to $15 per pill, to be crushed and snorted for a cheap and relatively modest buzz.

Ritalin is the brand name of the drug known as methylphenidate. Doctors have discovered that this and other stimulants work like an antenna adjuster for children whose brains crackle with static interference, as if a dozen stations are coming in on one channel. Technically, the stimulant appears to increase the level of dopamine in the frontal lobe of the brain, where it regulates attention and impulsivity. It is a powerful drug, and one that the U.S. Drug Enforcement Administration has classified as a Schedule II controlled substance, in the same category as cocaine, methadone and methamphetamine. Parent groups are now lobbying to ease the restrictions on Ritalin to avoid monthly doctor's visits. The DEA is opposing them, going so far last month as to enlist the help of the International Narcotics Control Board.

For all the success they've had in treating ADHD, many doctors are convinced that Ritalin is overprescribed. "I fear that ADHD is suffering from the 'disease of the month' syndrome," says Dr. Peter S. Jensen, chief of the Child and Adolescent Disorders Research Branch of NIMH. Teachers—even in preschool—are known to pull parents of active kids aside and suggest Ritalin. Overwhelmed with referrals, school psychologists (averaging one for every 2,100 students) say they feel pressed to recommend pills first before they have time to begin an evaluation. Psychiatrists nationwide say that about half the children who show up in their offices as ADHD referrals are actually suffering from a variety of other ailments, such as learning disabilities, depression or anxiety—disorders that look like ADHD, but do not need Ritalin. Some seem to be just regular kids. A St. Petersburg, Fla., pediatrician says parents of normal children have actually asked him for Ritalin just to improve their grades. "When I won't give it to them, they switch doctors," says Dr. Bruce Epstein. "They can find someone who will."

Finding someone who will is distressingly easy. Doctors themselves admit their methods are too often hasty. Almost half the pediatricians surveyed for a recent report in the Archives of Pediatric and Adolescent Medicine said they send ADHD children home in an hour. With such a rapid turnaround, many doctors never talk to teachers, review the child's educational levels, nor do any kind of psychological work-up—all essential diagnostic elements (see ADHD Checklist chart). Most children only get a prescription.

Making matters worse is that, ADHD experts now say, most children need behavior-modification therapy and special help in school. But most of the surveyed pediatricians said they rarely recommend anything more than pills. "A lot of doctors," says Dr. F. Xavier Castellanos, an ADHD researcher at NIMH, "are lulled into complacency. They

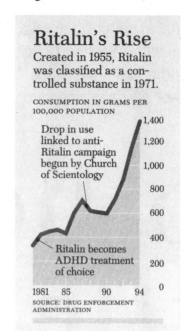

Ritalin's Rise

Created in 1955, Ritalin was classified as a controlled substance in 1971.

CONSUMPTION IN GRAMS PER 100,000 POPULATION

Drop in use linked to anti-Ritalin campaign begun by Church of Scientology

Ritalin becomes ADHD treatment of choice

1,400
1,200
1,000
800
600
400
200
0

1981   85   90   94

SOURCE: DRUG ENFORCEMENT ADMINISTRATION

ADHD Checklist

Professionals will base their diagnosis of ADHD on the following guidelines. From each list, six or more of the following symptoms need to exist in a way that significantly impairs the child:

Inattention

✔ pays little attention to details; makes careless mistakes
✔ has short attention span
✔ does not listen when spoken to directly
✔ does not follow instructions; fails to finish tasks
✔ has difficulty organizing tasks
✔ avoids tasks that require sustained mental effort
✔ loses things
✔ is easily distracted
✔ is forgetful in daily activities

Hyperactivity, impulsivity

HYPERACTIVITY
✔ fidgets; squirms in seat
✔ leaves seat in classroom when remaining seated is expected
✔ runs about or climbs excessively at inappropriate times
✔ has difficulty playing quietly
✔ acts as if "driven by a motor"
✔ talks excessively
IMPULSIVITY
✔ blurts out answers before questions are completed

SOURCE: AMERICAN PSYCHIATRIC ASSOCIATION

The Road to Ritalin

Step 1: Adult observations

PARENTS: Parents are often the first to notice extreme (with an emphasis on extreme) behavior: trouble following simple instructions and controlling temper; hyperactivity. Parents may compare observations with the child's teacher.

TEACHER: If the teacher thinks the student has unusual trouble sitting still or concentrating, a school psychologist may be called in (if one is available) to examine, test the child and gather behavioral history from the parents.

think that by giving a child Ritalin, the likelihood of helping him is high and the downside is low."

What is ADHD? The disorder is almost as elusive as its name. More than a century ago, these children were known as "fidgety Phils." In the '50s, they were "hyperkinetic." The term Attention Deficit Disorder was coined in 1980. "Hyperactivity" was added in 1987 to describe the vast majority. (Roughly 20 percent suffer ADD without the hyperactivity.) But the label still isn't quite right. "It's not that they are not paying attention," says Sally L. Smith, founder of The Lab School of Washington, a private K-12 institution for children with learning disabilities. "They are paying too much attention, to too many things."

CHILDREN WITH ATTENTION PROBLEMS are "lost in space and time," says Smith. Boys are afflicted up to three times as often as girls. They tend to be bright, but are poor students. These are the children who can't wait their turn. They blurt out answers before questions are asked. They can't stop wiggling their legs, tapping their pencils. They lose their bookbags, their homework, their tempers ... not sometimes, but *constantly*. Decades ago "these children were the outcasts, the losers, the zoned-out kids," says Castellanos. Many just left school. "I had an uncle who dropped out in the fourth grade," says Dr. Martha Denckla, director of cognitive neurology at Johns Hopkins. "The explanation was, 'Milton was not a student'." She is convinced he was ADHD. The difference is, today's schools can't afford to give up on them.

It's not that these kids are purposely defiant. They simply can't control themselves.

Debbie Mans realized that her twin boys were more than just rambunctious when they reached preschool. Alex, the wilder of the two, couldn't handle being with 18 children in his nursery-school class. He would hit the kids, the teacher, and then hurl himself around the room. "The teachers told me he was everything from colorblind to dumb to just plain bad," says Mans.

She knew intelligence wasn't the issue: this was a boy who at the age of 3 could put a broken telephone back together. After taking a host of tests, Alex and his twin,

> ## To make an ADHD diagnosis, doctors take family histories, observe behavior, give abstract cognitive tests and ask questions. It would be a lot easier if science could isolate a flaw in the brain.

Sam, were diagnosed with learning disabilities and ADHD. They had trouble following directions because they could neither perceive them properly nor pay attention long enough to try. The twins, now 7, were given Ritalin to help untangle the gibberish. It has, but no single pill will fix everything. Attention deficit is often only a fraction of a child's problems. Like the Mans twins, many have additional learning disabilities.

If doctors believe they have found a treatment, they do not pretend to fully comprehend the disorder. For now, scientists know ADHD is not the result of brain damage, wrong diet or bad parenting, as previously

surmised. Instead, they have a new set of suspects. Dr. James Swanson, a psychologist at the University of California, Irvine, believes it may be the result of something gone awry in pregnancy, anything from fetal distress to alcohol or exposure to lead in utero. Dr. Lawrence Greenberg, a Minnesota ADHD specialist, estimates that as many as a quarter of surviving premature infants may have ADHD. Other researchers blame heredity. ADHD researcher Dr. Russell Barkley, of the University of Massachusetts, reports that nearly half the ADHD children have a

parent, and more than one third have a sibling, with the disorder.

That's no surprise to the Schmidt family of Rochester, Minn. Over the past three years, all five have been diagnosed with attention deficit. The first case was Stephen, 8, who appeared to be hypersensitive and hard of hearing. "You would look straight at him, and say something, and he'd always say 'What?' " says Joan, 40, his mom. The psychiatrist determined that Stephen, Dennis, 37, and Daniel, 10, all had ADHD. Joan and her daughter, Maggie, 5, were found to have ADD, without the hyperactivity. One child takes Ritalin, another the antidepressant

---

There are many different kinds of doctors and types of tests parents may choose if they suspect their child has ADHD.

Parents should explore as many options as possible before medication is tried. One ideal scenario:

   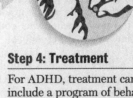

Step 2: Medical exam

PEDIATRICIAN: The doctor looks for physical conditions that can explain the child's problem: vision or hearing difficulties, allergies, etc. Should consult with other specialists, but too often writes a prescription instead.

Step 3: Specialists' observations

PSYCHIATRIST, NEUROLOGIST: This specialist looks for emotional disorders and evaluates the family situation. Takes testimony from other adults: teachers, scout leaders, etc. Does the child have ADHD or severe anxiety or depression?

DEVELOPMENTAL SPECIALIST: A speech pathologist or occupational therapist testS for even more subtle problems. Searches for learning disabilities and perception problems that can be marked by inattention.

Step 4: Treatment

For ADHD, treatment can include a program of behavior modification, imposing more structure and removing distractions; medication, usually Ritalin, to help the child focus. Doctors will monitor the child's progress.

Wellbutrin. The rest take daily combinations of Ritalin for ADHD, plus antidepressants (Prozac, Wellbutrin or Paxil) for accompanying depression.

There are three distinctive signals of ADHD: inattention, impulsivity and hyperactivity. But all can be part of an ordinary child's modus operandi, too. Most kids get distracted during the day, do impulsive things and bounce off walls. So, how can doctors tell when the behavior means "normal kid" and when it means trouble?

Doctors should take family histories, observe behavior, give cognitive tests and a battery of behavioral exams. They rule out other diseases. And they ask questions. Dr. Edward Hallowell, a child psychiatrist and coauthor of "Driven to Distraction," asks: "How does he get dressed in the morning? How does he behave at dinner, in restaurants, with other kids?" Eventually physicians make a judgment. "Parents need to make sure their child has a full evaluation before the first pill is put in their child's mouth," says Dr. Stanley Greenspan, psychiatrist and author of "The Challenging Child."

Noticing ADD is even trickier. These children are the lethargic daydreamers, "little absent-minded professors," says Barkley in his book, "Taking Charge of ADHD." They neither finish their work nor cause a fuss. Many are girls. "People think children with ADD look like baby gorillas, ripping wallpaper off the wall," says Dr. Betsy Busch, a pediatrician in Chestnut Hill, Mass.

This would all be a lot easier if science could isolate a flaw in the brain to aid diagnosis. Several studies indicate that ADHD brains may look and function slightly differently from "normal" brains. PET (positron emission tomograph) scans indicate that ADHD brains use less glucose—meaning less energy—in the prefrontal-lobe control center for attention and impulsivity. Other tests show less electrical activity in the same zone directly behind the forehead. In the most recent study, NIMH researchers measured the brains of ADHD boys using an MRI (magnetic resonance imaging). Preliminary findings show slightly smaller areas in the frontal lobe in boys who have attention deficit than those who don't. These are important pieces to the puzzle, but pieces, nonetheless.

After the tests, the anxiety and the judgment comes the pill. It's ubiquitously called Ritalin, even though the patent expired 23 years ago and generic methylphenidate is widely sold. For Ciba-Geigy, the Swiss pharmaceutical giant which last week announced a proposed merger with Sandoz, another drug goliath, Ritalin remains a glittering profit center. And for patients, a benefit if not a panacea. NIMH experts report that this stimulant is a positive treatment for nine out of 10 ADHD children who require medication. (Two other stimulants, Dexedrine and Cylert, are prescribed less often.) Older children testify to its effects. "Ritalin is like my training wheels," says Dylan MaGowan, a junior at The Lab School of Washington. "It helps keep me on track."

Researchers believe methylphenidate juices up the central nervous system. The drug appears to have its own attention deficit, taking effect in 30 minutes and then petering out after three or four hours. Kids

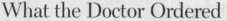

What the Doctor Ordered

In a recent survey, almost half of the pediatricians said they spent less than an hour evaluating children before prescribing Ritalin.

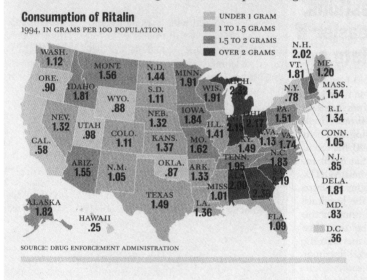

Consumption of Ritalin
1994, IN GRAMS PER 100 POPULATION

UNDER 1 GRAM
1 TO 1.5 GRAMS
1.5 TO 2 GRAMS
OVER 2 GRAMS

WASH. 1.12
ORE. .90
MONT. 1.56
IDAHO 1.81
N.D. 1.44
MINN. 1.91
WIS. 1.91
N.H. 2.02
VT. 1.81
ME. 1.20
S.D. 1.11
WYO. .88
N.Y. .78
MASS. 1.54
NEV. 1.32
UTAH .98
NEB. 1.32
IOWA 1.84
PA. 1.51
R.I. 1.34
COLO. 1.11
ILL. 1.41
KY. 1.13 VA. 1.74
CONN. 1.05
CAL. .58
KANS. 1.37
MO. 1.62
TENN. 1.95
N.C. 1.83
N.J. .85
ARIZ. 1.55
N.M. 1.05
OKLA. .87
ARK. 1.33
MISS. 1.01
2.19
DELA. 1.81
ALASKA 1.82
TEXAS 1.49
LA. 1.36
FLA. 1.09
MD. .83
HAWAII .25
D.C. .36

SOURCE: DRUG ENFORCEMENT ADMINISTRATION

usually take five to 10 mg three times a day for prime-time schoolwork. They often take "drug holidays" on the weekends and every few months.

Most experts believe that Ritalin is risk-free, having witnessed no permanent disabilities. "Stimulants have been used since the late '30s," says the NIMH's Jensen, "with no evidence of long-term damage." But studies are still inconclusive. Adding a flurry of doubts to the debate, the Food and Drug Administration last month released a study of mice that found Ritalin may have the potential to cause a rare form of liver cancer. Since there has been no comparative rise in hepatoblastoma among those on the drug over the decades, the FDA still regards Ritalin as "safe and effective."

Another story emerges, however, when the drug is abused on the playground. High doses, snorted or injected, can become addictive. The DEA warns that the "smart drug" may become a problem "street drug" in the near future. But aside from one death due to Ritalin overdose last April, the numbers of abusers seem to be next to negligible. Scientists believe it will have a tough time making an appearance on the favorite-party-drug list. Ritalin is too complex to manufacture illegally. It doesn't create anything near the euphoria of cocaine. Kids on prescribed doses, more often than not, want to stop when they get older. They get tired of the hassle and are often embarrassed by being different. "It's the opposite reaction to addiction," says Denckla.

Some side effects have been spotted, even when correct doses are followed. Children often complain of loss of sleep, stomach pains and irritability, particularly when the dose is wearing off. The most distressing, though still fairly rare, problem is facial tics.

N INE-YEAR-OLD John White, as he asks to be called, experienced the worst aspects of Ritalin, from conflicting diagnoses to near disaster. At first, nothing but a taste for Jarlsberg and an exceptional intelligence distinguished the child from others. Then he transferred to a more structured school in the middle of first grade. Within weeks the new teacher was complaining that John was talking out of turn; he wouldn't concentrate on his assignments. After a battery of tests, a neurologist declared him to be borderline ADHD. "I knew that if we didn't accept some kind of diagnosis, we wouldn't get help from the school," says his mother, Sarah.

Soon after his first Ritalin dose, John began losing his appetite. He stopped sleeping. He would explode with laughter one minute, shed tears the next. "It was scary," says Sarah. Then, the facial tics developed: eye tics, mouth tics, vocal tics. A hair-pulling habit—one that continued months after she pulled him off Ritalin—left a bald spot on the back of his head. Sarah enrolled him in biofeedback therapy and schooled her son at home for some months. Three years later John is thriving, Ritalin-free. "We choose to look at him as just a very bright child," says Sarah, "with some quirks."

When she talks about Ritalin, Sally Smith likes to hold up a ruler. "This is how much Ritalin does for you," says Smith, pointing to the one-inch mark. "Ritalin makes you available to learn. You and your parents and teachers have to work on all the rest." Smith's Lab School in Washington works with the most severe cases of ADHD and learning disabilities. And her staff has developed all sorts of clever strategies to help children get through their days. Teachers put down masking tape in the hallways so the kids will be reminded of where they should stand. Others will divide desk tops into different colored segments: one side for work, the other for storage. Children earn points for self-control and can cash them in for pizza slices or free time.

But The Lab School, and others like it, are extraordinary—and expensive. Most families can't afford $15,000-a-year tuitions. Experts believe that many kids are languishing in classes that are way too big, on medication that is not quite right. Peter Briger, 7, has spun through several different drugs and as many different classroom settings in the past six months. Ritalin didn't work. Cylert was no better. Now imipramine, an antidepressant, may be causing breathing problems. It does seem to calm him. Without special attention from teachers, he has yet to demonstrate much focus. Peter spends half his day in Manhattan's PS 191 in a class of

The Medicine Cabinet

Doctors have more than one choice when prescribing for patients with ADHD.

Stimulants

These drugs enhance the flow of dopamine in the brain, which can increase impulse control and attention span.

Ritalin *(Methylphenidate)*
Dexedrine *(Dextroamphetamine)*
Cylert *(Pemoline)*

POSSIBLE SIDE EFFECTS: Insomnia, weight loss, irritability, nausea, dizziness, headaches.

Antidepressants

Besides treating depression, they can decrease hyperactivity and aggression in some patients.

Tofranil *(Imipramine)*
Norpramin *(Desipramine)*
Elavil *(Amitriptyline)*

POSSIBLE SIDE EFFECTS: Dizziness, drowsiness, dry mouth, excessive sweating, weight gain, fatigue. May also affect blood pressure and heart rate. Avoid if there is a family history of seizures or heart attack.

SOURCE: "THE HANDBOOK OF PSYCHIATRIC DRUGS," HENRY HOLT AND CO.; "BEYOND RITALIN," VILLARD BOOKS

more than 20 second graders. On a typical day recently, he sat on top of his desk, headed for the drinking fountain and banged his head with a three-ring binder. His notebooks were filled with scribbles, decorated intermittently with half-written assignments. "He's lost so much time," says Millie Morales, the aunt who has cared for Peter since his mom died and his dad went to prison.

To researchers, it's a classic "pay now or pay more later" situation. "Studies indicate that those with untreated ADHD are more likely to become alcoholics, smokers or drug abusers than the general population," says Castellanos of NIMH. More than one third drop out of school, says Barkley of the University of Massachusetts. And, he says, about one tenth of ADHD adults attempt suicide.

In the end, what makes all this debate so urgent is its subject: the nation's children. The fear, simply put, is that too many who need help may be going unnoticed, untreated, while too many who don't are getting pills instead of proper care. But there is glory here, too. Children who otherwise would be cast aside are receiving world-class treatment. Obviously, we need more of the latter, less of the former. And to do that, parents, doctors, therapists and teachers need to exercise care. It may be a truism, but one that can too easily be forgotten in a rush to diagnosis.

WHY
worry?

One in four of us will suffer from an anxiety disorder in our lifetime. And the rest of us will worry, fuss, and fret far more than we need to. Now, in this excerpt from his new book, Worry, the psychiatrist who helped put attention deficit disorder on the map offers his treatment program for brooders.

BY EDWARD M. HALLOWELL, M.D.

Worry gives a small thing a big shadow.
—Swedish Proverb.

WORRY IS LIKE blood pressure: you need a certain level to live, but too much can kill you. At its worst, worry is insidious, invisible, a relentless scavenger roaming the corners of your mind, feeding on anything it finds. It sets upon you unwanted and unbidden, feasting on the infinite array of negative possibilities in life, diminishing your enjoyment of friends, family, achievements, and physical being—all because you live in fear of what might go wrong. People who worry too much suffer. For all their hard work, for all their humor and willingness to laugh at themselves, for all their self-awareness, worriers just cannot achieve peace of mind.

Worry is amazingly common. At least one in four of us—about 65 million Americans—will meet the criteria for an anxiety disorder at some point in our lifetime. Even those individuals whose lives are going well may worry excessively on occasion.

And yet, worry is a very treatable condition. Most people today are not aware of all that we have learned about worry in the last 50 years. Just as rainstorms may strike in different ways—sudden thunderstorms, lingering drizzle, occasional showers—so does worry attack its victims variously. We've come to understand the many distinctly different types of worry and the underlying triggers. Worry may accompany simple shyness, depression, generalized anxiety disorder, or even post-traumatic stress disorder. Each kind of worry responds to specific and powerful techniques, from cognitive therapy to medication to regular exercise.

WHAT IS WORRY?

Worry is a special form of fear. It is what humans do with simple fear once it reaches the part of their brain called the cerebral cortex. We make fear complex, adding anticipation, memory, imagination, and emotion.

Worry takes many forms, but it almost always stems from an overwhelming sense of vulnerability and powerlessness. Many of us locate the source of worry outside ourselves, believing it is triggered purely by life experiences: "What is going on in the world to make me feel this way?" Such thoughts only increase our feeling of vulnerability. And, as anyone who has worried knows all too well, even when the world is right, worry surfaces. Rational reassurances get no farther into the psyche of the worrier than words spoken in Martian. "Honey, everything will be fine. We are not about to go broke." "There really is no reason to obsess about your boss. He just told you that you were doing a great job!" "Truly, that mole on your back is not malignant melanoma!" The worrier may be momentarily calmed, but the fire soon flares again.

Why does the worrier go on worrying? His mind has, in effect, gone into a spasm, a grip that can't relax and accept good news. He is suffering a kind of "brain burn," because his system is continually pumping out a huge bolus of adrenaline under high pressure.

Today, we are finally beginning to understand the biology of worry to pinpoint what is happening in the nerve cells of the worrier, rather than his soul. It turns out that some of us may be born worriers. Our autonomic nervous systems are cranked up higher, and our blood pressure, pulse, and respiratory rate may be higher. And we may be less sensitive than others to the brain's natural stress modulators, which are activated by the neurotransmitter GABA (gamma-amino butyric acid). People who have a good supply of GABA, or brains that are especially responsive to it, may be innately cool and calm. By contrast, a fascinating 1996 study actually linked a gene (called SLC6A4) to individuals who are highly susceptible to anxiety, pessimism, and negative thinking. Other pioneering research, by Jerome Kagan, Ph.D., has revealed that children who are high-strung and highly aroused early on often become tense, shy, worrying adults. And brain scans have shown that people who ruminate have excess activity in a part of their brains called the cingulate cortex.

Our new knowledge has enabled us to stop blaming worriers for their woes, and begin helping them to get better. One of our newest and most powerful findings is that brains are adaptable and flexible. You cannot give yourself a new brain but you can be redirected, retrained, reassured, and reset. You can change.

BROKEN BONDS

Many people who worry too much do so out of broken trust or loss of faith. If these people share what they really feel in their hearts, their story will reveal the deep trauma underlying their worry.

Allison Barnes came to see me at a crisis point in her life. She had a good marriage and wonderful children, and had once loved her work as a physician, "But now I'm terrified," she confessed. "I worry every day about someone trying to sue me for malpractice."

Allison's worry was rooted in the reality of today's world. She *had* been sued five years earlier, by a patient named Jim whom she thought of as a friend. "We exchanged family pictures," she told me. "When his son Simon had leukemia, I gave blood and so did my whole family." Then Simon died, and a year later Jim came in for a headache workup. "I spent an hour with him, then

sent him off for some tests. He said I dismissed him without giving him the time he needed, so he went to another doctor, who diagnosed a benign tumor." Jim filed a lawsuit against her for malpractice. Although Allison won the suit, she lost her peace of mind. "He took out his anger about the death of his son on me," she told me. "Now everyone who walks in the door I see as a potential adversary. I can't stand it."

Allison's faith in the world had been shattered. She admitted she felt ashamed of her worry and afraid to talk to her husband about it. And so the worry had spread like brushfire: "Now I can find worry in a cigarette butt on the sidewalk."

My job with Allison was to apply metaphorical cold towels to her forehead and to strengthen her with hot chicken soup for the soul. I also gave her techniques to retrain her brain, which I explain in detail later.

But the most important part of her treatment did not depend on me at all. Allison was living alone inside her worry. She needed to increase the amount of support in her life, to develop deeper connections to others, from her husband to friends, extended family, colleagues, and other physicians. Life is scary and insecure. But many people suffer excessively because they don't know how or where to get support. The sum of our meaningful connections, our connectedness, is the key to emotional health and the surest protection we have against the psychological ravages of worry (see "Weaving a Web of Life"). By promoting connectedness in your life, you will increase your feeling of power and greatly reduce your sense of vulnerability. There is strength in numbers.

GNAWING OLD BONES

One of the original meanings of worry is "to gnaw." Like a dog with a bone, the worrier chews all day long, and sometimes it is a very old bone the worrier gnaws. The bone gets buried and dug up, buried and dug up, as the same old pain gets reworried ceaselessly. The only way to let go of that bone once and for all is to feel the original pain through and through.

Liz Brightman was preoccupied with a multitude of problems in her life, significant as well as trivial. But the real source of her worry was decades old. As I listened to Liz tell me her father had committed suicide in a mental hospital when she was 10, I thought to myself, "The sadness she has not felt has become the worry she continues to feel." Liz told me that after the funeral, her mother took the family to a carnival "to have some fun and forget." Her mother never talked about her father again. "Then she met my stepfather, and we went on. My father kept receding into the past,

like a rowboat that had fallen off the big ship. I never even cried."

Many people's worries are really masked grief, still buried at home. People may even use worry as a psychological defense against feeling this long-buried pain. Often, the worrier knows what the pain is. Every day a little voice inside says that the answer to your worry lies in traveling north but still you spend your whole life deliberately going in every direction except north.

In Liz's case, going north meant talking about her father. She needed to remember and cry. For many, people this is the act they fear the most. Crying feels humiliating, too out of control, too vulnerable, possibly overpowering. But Liz needed to let it out in front of another person and in front of herself, to discover that her world would not fall apart when she did it and that there was no shame in it.

How Liz and I worked on this together would make another book. It is not a simple matter, like saying, "Okay, Liz, cry." But once she had heaved up the big thing, it amazed her how the little things shrunk back down to size. She had gone north and she came back a whole person.

BUT WHAT IF?

Worry sometimes begins with a negative possibility, a mere "What if?" Then it burgeons up out of information that originally was neutral or innocuous. One of my patients, Becky, calls these endless "What ifs?" SBPOWs, which stands for "spontaneously branching polymers of worry." (She pronounces SBPOWs as "spouse" because she claims her husband is the source of most of them.)

"A little worry can branch spontaneously with a vengeance," she explains. "It's like a pattern of frost that shoots across a cold pane of glass. In seconds I am fighting with an enormous net of dangerous, intricate detail. You can't believe how quickly I go from dealing with one worry to having a jumbled mess of them."

This kind of worrier broods incessantly. When the mind obsesses over negative outcomes at the mere hint of one, the worrier is suffering from a type of obsessive-compulsive disorder (OCD). About 5 million Americans are afflicted with OCD, and though we do not have a cure, we do have excellent treatments which can drastically reduce the severity of the symptoms.

In OCD, worry rules the mind like a sorcerer. The individual even resorts to superstitious rituals in the hope that the rituals will magically rid him of the dangers he senses and fears. I once treated a man who had to hop on one foot whenever he

WEAVING A WEB OF LIFE:
A Talk with Edward Hallowell, M.D.

PSYCHOLOGY TODAY: You're known as the man who helped bring attention deficit disorder to national attention. Why have you turned now to the subject of worry?

EDWARD HALLOWELL: Because I'm such a worrier. I attribute my worrying to my chaotic childhood. I tell people I'm from the WASP triad of alcoholism, mental illness, and politeness. I had an alcoholic mother and a psychotic father, and as much as I love my parents dearly, they provided me with no stability. It seems a minor miracle that I've done as well as I have. And I really attribute it to the power of connectedness. I've seen that, time and again, personal happiness depends on the richness and depth of our connections. The connected person is much stronger and able to deal with adversity than the disconnected person.

PT: There's been a lot of research recently looking at anxiety and social connectedness. But how does one go about getting connected?

EH: Number one is the family you're born into; it's our biological connectedness. Many people these days have very little contact with grandparents, cousins, aunts, uncles. They tend to feel less secure.

PT: How to you stay connected if you've got a chaotic family, as in your case?

EH: You can replace [the family connection] with a strong set of friends, which also can be a security network. People today have a host of acquaintances, but don't have someone they can pour their heart and soul out to. A friend in the old-fashioned sense can be very sustaining. A related kind of connectedness is to institutions and organizations, and this is really threatened these days. The world of Dilbert is the world of the disconnected employee, the employee who feels cynical, exploited, about to be downsized at any moment.

PT: You also talk about connection to information and ideas. But can't the world of ideas isolate you from people?

was waiting in line, because he felt he would be in extreme danger otherwise. The sufferer of OCD is obsessed with a variety of intrusive, unwanted thoughts. He also feels compelled to act out certain rituals in an attempt to stave off (imagined) dire consequences associated with his unwanted thoughts.

Treatment for OCD has been revolutionized by our recent discoveries about the brain. We now know that there is a physical basis to OCD. We have even found differences in brain scans of individuals with OCD. Only two decades ago the standard treatment for OCD was to try to ferret out the psychological conflict that must be causing such bizarre behavior. People would stay in psychotherapy for years, while still suffering from OCD. Today we know that a combination of medication and therapy works best in this kind of obsessive worrying.

PANIC ATTACKS

Sometimes the brain's alarm system misreads danger signals, like a vast sprinkler misreading cigarette smoke as a fire, drenching everyone right in the middle of the grand ball. This alarm system, regulated by a group of nerves deep in your brain called the locus ceruleus, can simply go berserk. The name of this problem is panic disorder. And worry can be one of its cardinal symptoms. In panic disorder, a specific stimulus sets off a flood of terror.

Everyone who has felt panic knows how it hijacks the body: the rapid breathing and racing pulse, the burning waves of fear coursing through the body, the desperate feeling of needing to break free. Panic is the nervous system's turbo-charged means of escape. When panic strikes at the wrong time, however, it's like having an airplane take off in your living room.

Adrienne was standing in line at her bank one day when panic struck. "Suddenly, I became terrified. I felt as if I were being dragged to the edge of a cliff where someone was going to push me off. I broke out into a sweat, started to shake, then my legs gave out and I just collapsed to the floor."

"Do you have any idea what triggered this episode?" I asked her when she came to see me a few weeks later.

"I usually have no idea when an attack will hit," she replied. "It just happens. Sometimes I have three attacks in one week. It's crippling me."

Adrienne had begun to put off doing the most routine errands, saying she felt too nervous to go outside. She was developing agoraphobia, a condition that accompanies panic disorder up to 50 percent of the time. Agoraphobia is characterized by an intense fear of, and avoidance of, places or situations in which escape may be difficult or one imagines a panic attack may occur.

Panic disorder may show itself as social phobia, fear of public speaking, or of being the center of attention. It responds well to medication, as well as to desensitization techniques and cognitive therapy. By a variety of methods, those with the disorder are gradually and safely exposed to the source of their panic and worry. The intensity of the stimulus is slowly increased, and homework is often prescribed. This therapy alone has a success rate of 60 to 80 percent.

There is another kind of worry that is characterized by panic. But it is rarely focused on a single topic. It is called generalized anxiety disorder (GAD), and there is usually no apparent cause for the anxiety. It is free-floating. When GAD underlies worry, the thoughts can seem like mosquitoes. This means that they should be no big deal: just slap them away. But if you are surrounded by them, slapping them away constantly becomes, at best, tiring. Furthermore, they leave bites that itch and must be scratched. Like panic disorder, GAD can be treated successfully.

TAMING YOUR WORRIES

The medications we have developed to treat toxic forms of worry mark a major breakthrough in healing human distress. While we must take care not to overuse medications, I am glad we have the option of using them when necessary. Listen to what my patient Jane wrote me, after she began taking Prozac: "My response to Prozac was dramatic. Within several weeks I stopped feeling depressed. I did not, however, expect that I would also stop worrying, but I did. I began to expect that problems would be resolved, and I resolved them." Psychotherapy, a program of exercise, and Prozac were the solutions to a lifetime problem for Jane.

We now have many safe and effective medications to treat worry:

• **Benzodiazepines**, such as Valium, are the most common group of medications used to treat anxiety and worry. They shut down the alarm system in the brain, but can be habit-forming, even addictive, and some interact dangerously with alcohol. They are used best as part of a short-term intervention.

• **Beta-blockers**, such as Propranolol (Inderal) can be useful for worry associated with specific situations, such as stage fright, or fear of public speaking. Taking a low dose an hour or so before a performance or speech can curtail tremor, palpitations, and sweating. Beta-blockers have some side effects, and cannot be used in people who have asthma.

• **Buspirone** (BuSpar) is a new antianxiety agent that does not seem sedating

EH: It can, but done properly it has just the opposite effect: It throws you into the world of other minds. It's important to develop a comfortable relationship with information and ideas.

Historical connectedness is also important. If you have no awareness of the past, you're cutting yourself off from something significant. I named my daughter after my great-great-great-great-grandmother, who fought to free slaves and supported women's rights. That name will deepen her sense of where she came from—a strong woman from another century.

And finally, there is connectedness to what is beyond knowledge—God, your sense of the transcendent. Those six spheres of connectedness—to family, friends, the past, information, institutions, and the transcendent—give you a psychological armor that can sustain you through life.

PT: Even if you put all the connectedness into place, isn't there a vulnerability you're going to carry with you from a difficult childhood?

EH: Absolutely. I will never be able to have the bedrock security that someone who had a different kind of childhood would have. But I can come very close. Yes, I'll always be a little bit haunted by what was missing in my childhood. But no matter where you're coming from, you can get to a better place with these simple techniques. One of the real bits of good news from the neurosciences is that as much as you can burn the brain, you can heal it, too.

PT: You "come out" as a practicing Christian in your book, which is a risk for someone of such renown in the psychiatric community.

EH: It's a risk that I take knowing that some people will dismiss me, but I think it's worth it. When I wrote *Driven to Distraction,* some people said, "You can't say you have attention deficit disorder. You'll be dismissed as some kind of a nut." I said, "How can I tell people not to be ashamed of it if I can't even say I have it myself?" I feel the same way about writing about God. How can I say to people, "You ought to develop a spiritual life," if I don't dare acknowledge my own? I think doctors, and certainly psychiatrists, have not known what to do with spirituality. As a result they've just ignored it, which to me is a huge mistake. It's a very powerful part of the mind, and at least as powerful a part of one's life as sexuality. In my case, a relationship with God is another source of connection. And ultimately, it makes sense of my life in ways that nothing else can. But that's just me.

or addictive—but is also less potent than benzodiazepenes.

• **Antidepressants** play an important role in the treatment of worry. By far the most famous antidepressants are the selective serotonin reuptake inhibitors (SSRIs), such as Prozac and Zoloft. For people who brood endlessly, an SSRI can break the cycle. This change is not mind-altering so much as it is mind-healing. Ruminations are like severe headaches. If they go away, you feel like a new person, although you are in fact no different at all. You are the healthy version of yourself. The SSRIs have also become the first choice in panic disorder, and can help OCD. An older antidepressant, Chlomipramine (Anafranil) is still the first choice for OCD, but its side effects are worse.

• **Wellbutrin** is an unusual antidepressant that increases two neurotransmitters, dopamine and norepinephrine. It's a good choice for worry that is associated with depression.

• **MAO Inhibitors** such as Nardil require dietary changes (users must avoid wine, cheese, and chocolate) but are very effective for worry tied to a fear of rejection, or to post-traumatic stress.

FACING WORRY HEAD-ON

Medications are only part of a treatment program for worry and often they are not necessary at all. First, you must understand the pattern of your worrying. Is it based in anxiety, depression, unhealed trauma? Whatever your diagnosis, learn as much about it as you can.

Then develop a treatment plan. One of the most powerful methods to decrease worry is through gradual exposure. If heights make you nervous, you might start by imagining you are standing at a certain height, looking down. Then in your imagination, and in the presence of a therapist, start going up, a few floors at a time. After you feel comfortable being exposed to heights in your imagination, try it in reality, using the same graduated process.

Similarly, a therapist may deliberately recreate the physical sensations accompanying worry to help you get more comfortable with them. I helped my patient Adrienne recreate the feelings of panic within herself—breathlessness, dizziness, rapid heartbeat. She'd exercise until her heart raced, then talk herself through the feeling, noting that nothing bad was happening. Then we tackled her dizziness: she sat in a chair and I spun her around a few times. In this way she began to take apart her worried state until she got comfortable with each individual piece. When she experienced them all together, in the stew of worry, she was less afraid of their impact.

RETRAINING YOUR BRAIN

Most of the worriers I treat need to retrain their minds and learn new mental skills. It's like training your muscles to learn the pattern of a golf or tennis swing, so that the correct swing becomes automatic. You can train your brain to learn effective ways of dealing with situations that arise again and again, such as financial worries or fears of failure.

There is a window of opportunity that lasts about a minute, during which you can sever the tentacle of a toxic worry before it grips you totally. Your brain has not yet gone into spasm. That is the time to defuse worry.

Talk to yourself in a useful way. Most worriers talk to themselves in half-phrases of imagined doom, little punches and jabs of negativity. Try to erase those old, automatic patterns by deliberately distracting yourself. Whistle or sing. Snap your fingers. Insert a positive thought. One positive thought at a time can gradually shift the balance of your thinking from negative to positive.

Monitor your automatic thoughts whenever you get bad news or perceive danger of some sort. It's helpful to write them down. Often you can see immediately how wildly exaggerated they actually are. Then examine these thoughts for errors in logic. Create alternative hypotheses that are more logical.

You may find that these automatic thoughts and errors in logic grow out of the fundamental way you look at life and at yourself, your self-schema. Do you fear that the deck of life is irretrievably stacked against you? Are you afraid that nobody will ever find you attractive? Whatever your self-schema might be, you can change consciously. Over time, self-questioning begins to replace reflexive self-flagellation.

Become creative in finding ways of quenching worry. Allison Barnes would blow into the palms of her hands sometimes before going into a meeting and say she had just "blown off" her worries. She bought an ugly-looking toad figurine, which she kept in her purse ready to deposit on a shelf whenever she needed a reminder that her worries could be put aside. You have to be willing to play along and suspend your disbelief for this method to work, but if you are willing it can work very well.

Worry paralyzes the sufferer and prevents him from taking action. My brain-training program teaches you to make concrete plans, eliminating unnecessary worry before it occurs. I call this program EPR: evaluate, plan, remediate. Evaluate a possible problem rationally, set up a plan to take care of it, then act on the plan. Turn worry into action. I recommend that worriers make a list of three—and only three—changes they want to make in their life.

They might be as simple as making a dentist appointment or consolidating their credit cards. Persist until all three tasks are done. Then make a new list of three, and only three, changes you want to make in your life. After six months to a year, you will have dramatically changed your life for the better. And you will worry less, because you will be safer. Structure reduces risk.

WORKING OUT WORRY

As simple as it sounds, exercise is the best natural anti-anxiety agent we have. Exercise reduces tension, drains off excess aggression and frustration, enhances well-being, improves sleep, curbs the tendency to overeat, aids in concentration, and reduces distractability. It is healing to the body, and therefore to the mind. Getting exercise at least every other day should be part of your plan to reduce anxiety and control worry. But you can also exercise on the spot to reduce acute worry. If you are having a bad day at the office, try walking up and down a flight of stairs five times. Your mind will be less troubled when you come back to your desk. The change in physiology induced by exercise calms the mind.

DON'T WRING YOUR HANDS: CLASP THEM

Prayer or meditation can change the state of your brain as well. Talk to God when you feel worried. If you are not religious, learn how to meditate. Brain scans and EEG monitors show beneficial changes in the brain during meditation and prayer. These changes correlate with most of our measures of improved health, including longevity and reduced incidence of illness. And extended worry subsides with regular prayer or meditation.

WORRY WISELY

I was playing squash one Sunday morning with Jeff Sutton, a neuroscientist and good friend, when I told him I was writing about people who worry too much. He instantly responded, "But worry is good! You have to worry to survive!" He then went on to talk about worry in the most animated, unworried tones, as he whipped the ball against the wall with a sharp smack. "Fear is wired in. Deeper than any other feeling." Smack! "Worry is good! If you don't want to worry, be a plant!" Smack! "Worry gives successful people an edge."

Jeff, of course, is right. There is such a thing as wise worry. It is our reaction to worry that counts. For winners, worry is a reason to take positive action. They use fear as a fuel.

Imagine the bow of a violin as life experience and the strings of the violin as our biological makeup. The bow of life's experience draws across the violin strings of biology to produce the music of life. What kind of music we make depends on both the bow and violin. And now with advances in medicine, psychotherapy, and other techniques, the music wafting from that violin is truly in your own hands.

Patterns of Abuse

Two million women are beaten every year, one every 16 seconds. Who's at risk, why does violence escalate—and when should a woman fear for her life?

THE STORIES SPILL OUT FROM behind bedroom walls and onto the front pages. Back in 1983, before talk shows dissolved into daily confessionals, actor David Soul offered up the stunning admission that he'd abused his wife, Patti. Two years later, John Fedders, the chief regulator of the Securities and Exchange Commission, resigned after he acknowledged that he'd broken his wife's eardrum, wrenched her neck and left her with black eyes and bruises. In 1988, the nation sat mesmerized by Hedda Nussbaum and her testimony about being systematically beaten by her companion, a brooding New York lawyer named Joel Steinberg, who also struck the blows that killed their adopted daughter, Lisa. Now America is riveted again, this time by the accumulating evidence of O.J. Simpson's brutality against his wife, Nicole. Yet, for all the horror, there is a measure of futility in these tales: one moment, they ignite mass outrage; then the topic fades from the screen.

Americans often shrug off domestic violence as if it were no more harmful than Ralph Kramden hoisting a fist and threatening: "One of these days, Alice . . . Pow! Right in the kisser!" But there's nothing funny about it—and the phenomenon of abuse is just as complicated as it is common. About 1,400 women are killed by their husbands, ex-husbands and boyfriends each year and about 2 million are beaten—on average, one every 16 seconds. Although some research shows women are just as likely as men to start a fight, Justice Department figures released last February reveal that

women are the victims 11 times more often than men. Battering is also a problem among gay couples: the National Coalition on Domestic Violence estimates that almost one in three same-sex relationships are abusive, seemingly more than among heterosexual couples. But violence against women is so entrenched that in 1992 the U.S. Surgeon General ranked abuse by husbands and partners as the leading cause of injuries to women aged 15 to 44. Despite more hot lines and shelters and heightened awareness, the number of assaults against women has remained about the same over the last decade.

A disturbing double standard also remains. "If O.J. Simpson had assaulted Al Cowlings nine times and if A.C. called the police, O.J. couldn't have told them, 'This is a family matter'," says Mariah Burton Nelson, author of the book "The Stronger Women Get the More Men Love Football." "Hertz and NBC would have dropped him and said, 'This man has a terrible problem.' But family violence is accepted as no big deal." New York University law professor Holly Maguigan says wife-beating was actually once sanctioned by the so-called Rule of Thumb—English common law, first cited in America in an 1824 Mississippi Supreme Court decision, that said a man could physically chastise his wife as long as the stick he used was no wider than his thumb. Even now, Maguigan says, "we're not very far removed from a time when the criminal-justice system saw its task as setting limits on the amount of force a man could use, instead of saying that using force against your wife is a crime."

Changing attitudes is difficult. Although advocacy groups are already claiming that Nicole Simpson's case can do for spousal abuse what Rock Hudson did for AIDS and Anita Hill did for sexual harassment, that may be more rhetoric than reality; there is great ambivalence about family violence. Americans cling to a "zone of privacy"—the

unwritten code that a man's home is his castle and what happens inside should stay there. It helps explain why, in some states, a man who strikes his wife is guilty only of a misdemeanor, but if he attacks a stranger, it's a felony. It helps explain why a woman can walk away from a friend who says she got her black eye walking into a door. And it helps explain why men retreat when a buddy dismisses brutality as the ups and downs that "all" marriages go through.

So many look away because they don't know what constitutes domestic violence. Who's a victim? Who's an abuser? Most people believe that, unless a woman looks as pathetic as Hedda Nussbaum did—her nose flattened, her face swollen—she couldn't possibly be a victim. And despite highly publicized cases of abuse, celebrity still bestows credibility. What's more, it's hard for many to comprehend how anything short of daily brutality can be wife-beating. Even Nicole's sister fell into the trap. "My definition of a battered woman is somebody who gets beat up all the time," Denise Brown told The New York Times last week. "I don't want people to think it was like that. I know Nicole. She was a very strong-willed person. If she was beaten up, she wouldn't have stayed with him. That wasn't her." Or was it? The patterns of abuse—who's likely to be at risk, why women take action and when battering turns deadly—can often be surprising, as paradoxical as the fact that love can coexist with violence.

WHO IS MOST AT RISK

EXPERTS USED TO THINK THAT BATTERED women were "asking for it"—somehow masochistically provoking abuse from their men. Mercifully, that idea has now been discredited. But researchers do say that women who are less educated, un-

MICHELE INGRASSIA AND MELINDA BECK, WITH REPORTING BY GINNY CARROLL, NINA ARCHER BIDDLE, KAREN SPRINGEN, PATRICK ROGERS, JOHN McCORMICK, JEANNE GORDON, ALLISON SAMUELS AND MARY HAGER.

Ten Risk Factors

Previous domestic violence is the highest risk factor for future abuse. Homes with two of these others show twice as much violence as those with none. In those with seven or more factors, the violence rate is 40 times higher.

- **Male unemployed**
- **Male uses illicit drugs at least once each year**
- **Male and female have different religious backgrounds**
- **Male saw father hit mother**
- **Male and female cohabit and are not married**
- **Male has blue-collar occupation, if employed**
- **Male did not graduate from high school**
- **Male is between 18 and 30 years of age**
- **Male or female use severe violence toward children in home**
- **Total family income is below the poverty line**

SOURCE: RISK-MARKERS OF MEN WHO BATTER, A 1994 ANALYSIS BY RICHARD J. GELLES, REGINA LACKNER AND GLENN D. WOLFNER

employed, young and poor may be more likely to have abusive relationships than others. Pregnant women seem to make particular targets: according to one survey, approximately one in six is abused; another survey cites one in three. There are other common characteristics: "Look for low self-esteem, a background in an abusive family, alcohol and drug abuse, passivity in relationships, dependency, isolation and a high need for approval, attention and affection," says psychologist Robert Geffner, president of the Family Violence and Sexual Assault Institute in Tyler, Texas. "The more risk factors a woman has, the more likely she is to become a candidate."

But not all women fit that profile: statistically, one woman in four will be physically assaulted by a partner or ex-partner during her lifetime, so it's not surprising that abuse cuts across racial, ethnic, religious and socioeconomic lines. "I'm treating physicians, attorneys, a judge and professors who are, or were, battered women," says Geffner. "Intelligent people let this happen, too. What goes on inside the home does not relate to what's outside."

And what's outside is often deceiving. Dazzling blond Nicole Simpson didn't look like someone who could have low self-esteem. But she met O.J. when she was just 18, and devoted herself to being his wife. In her 1992 divorce papers, she claimed that O.J. forced her to quit junior college and be with him all the time. She said she'd do anything to keep him from being angry: "I've always told O.J. what he wants to hear. I've always let him . . . it's hard to explain." For all their jet-setting, she was isolated—and reluctant to discuss what was happening at home, even though some friends say they had known. "She would wear unsuitable clothing to cover the bruises, or sunglasses to hide another shiner," says one. "She was trapped. She didn't have any training to do anything, and he knew that and he used it."

But even feisty women with their own careers can get involved with violent men. Earlier this month, Lisa (Left Eye) Lopes, a singer with the hip-hop group TLC, allegedly burned down the $800,000 home of her boyfriend, Atlanta Falcons' wide receiver Andre Rison. Police say the barely 5-foot, 100-pound Lopes appeared bruised and beaten when they arrived on the scene; friends say it was an open secret that she was abused. (Rison denies the allegations.) Curiously, the lyrics of Lopes's debut album are peppered with references about standing up to men: "I have my own control/I can't be bought or sold/And I never have to do what I'm told. . . ." Was that just a tough act to mask insecurity? Jacquelyn Campbell, a researcher in domestic violence at Johns Hopkins University, concludes that a woman's risk of being battered "has little to do with her and everything to do with who she marries or dates."

WHO BECOMES AN ABUSER

WHAT KIND OF MAN HEAPS physical and emotional abuse on his wife? It's only in the last decade that researchers have begun asking. But one thing they agree on is the abuser's need to control. "There is no better way of making people compliant than beating them up on an intermittent basis," says Richard Gelles, director of the Family Violence Research Program at the University of Rhode Island. Although Gelles says men who have less education and are living close to the poverty line are more likely to be abusers, many white-collar men—doctors, lawyers and accountants—also beat their partners.

"Amy," a 50-year-old Colorado woman, spent 23 years married to one of them. Her husband was an attorney, well heeled, well groomed, a pillar of the community. She says he hit her, threw her down the stairs, tried to run her over. "One night in Vail, when he had one of his insane fits, the police came and put him in handcuffs," says Amy, who asked that her real name not be used. "My arms were still red from where he'd

Striking a wife can be a misdeameanor while hitting a stranger is a felony

trapped them in the car window, but somehow, he talked his way out of it." Lenore Walker, director of the Domestic Violence Institute in Denver, sees the pattern all the time. "It's like Jekyll and Hyde—wonderful one minute, dark and terrifying the next."

Indiana University psychologist Amy Holtzworth-Munroe divides abusers into three behavioral types. The majority of men who hit their wives do so infrequently and their violence doesn't escalate. They look ordinary, and they're most likely to feel remorse after an attack. "When they use violence, it reflects some lack of communication skills, combined with a dependence on the wife," she says.

A second group of men are intensely jealous of their wives and fear abandonment. Most likely, they grew up with psychological and sexual abuse. Like those in the first group, these men's dependence on their wives is as important as their need to control them—if she even talks to another man, "he

For women aged 15 to 44, domestic abuse is the leading cause of injury

thinks she's leaving or sleeping around," says Holtzworth-Munroe. The smallest—and most dangerous—group encompasses men with an antisocial personality disorder. Their battering fits into a larger pattern of violence and getting in trouble with the law. Neil S. Jacobson, a marital therapist at the University of Washington, likens such men to serial murderers. Rather than becoming more agitated during an attack, he says, they become calmer, their heart rates drop. "They're like cobras. They're just like criminals who beat up anybody else when they're not getting what they want."

Avoiding Abuse

Battered women use a range of desperate methods to discourage partners from injuring them, from running away to fighting back.

STRATEGIES USED BY WOMEN TO END SEVERE SPOUSAL VIOLENCE

Avoid him or avoid certain topics	69%
Talking him out of it	59
Get him to promise no more violence	57
Threaten to get a divorce	54
Physically fight back	52
Hide or go away	37
Threaten to call the police	36
Leave home for two or more days	32

SOURCE; INTIMATE VIOLENCE, BY RICHARD J. GELLES AND MURRAY A. STRAUS (DATA FROM A 1985 STUDY)

Men who batter share something else: they deny what they've done, minimize their attacks and always blame the victims. Evan Stark, codirector of the Domestic Violence Training Project in New Haven, Conn., was intrigued by Simpson's so-called suicide note. "He never takes responsibility for the abuse. These are just marital squabbles. Then he blames her—'I felt like a battered husband'." Twenty-nine-year-old "Fidel" once felt the same way. When he began getting counseling in Houston's Pivot Project, he blamed everyone else for his violence—especially his new wife, who, he discovered, was pregnant by another man. "When I came here, I couldn't believe I had a problem," he says. "I always thought of myself as a well-mannered person."

WHY WOMEN STAY

I T LOOKS SO SIMPLE FROM THE OUTSIDE. Many women think that if a mate ever hit them, they'd pack up and leave immediately. But women who have been in abusive relationships say it isn't that easy. The violence starts slowly, doesn't happen every day and by the time a pattern has emerged there may be children, and financial and emotional bonds that are difficult to break. "I know when I took my marriage vows, I meant 'for better or for worse'," G. L. Bundow, a South Carolina physician, wrote in The Journal of the American Medical Association, describing her own abusive relationship. "But when 'until death do us part' suddenly became a frightening reality, I was faced with some terrifying decisions."

With more women working and greater availability of shelters, financial dependence is less of a factor than it used to be. The emotional dependence is often stronger. "Women are trained to think that we can save these men, that they can change," says Angela Caputi, a professor of American Studies at the University of New Mexico. That mythology, she notes, is on full display in "Beauty and the Beast": the monster smashing furniture will turn into a prince if only the woman he's trapped will love him.

Many abusers *can* be charming—and abused women often fall for their softer side. Denver's Lenore Walker says there are three parts to the abuse cycle that are repeat[ed] over and over—a phase where tension is building and the woman tries desperately to keep the man calm; an explosion with acute battering, and then a period where the batterer is loving and contrite. "During this last phase, they listen to the woman, pay attention, buy her flowers—they become the ideal guy," Walker says. Geffner adds that in this part of the relationship, "they make love, the sex is good. And that also keeps them going."

Eventually, however, the repeated cycles wear women down until some are so physically and mentally exhausted that leaving is almost impossible. The man gradually takes control of the woman's psyche and destroys her ability to think clearly. Even the memory of past abuse keeps the woman in fear and in check. "You can't underestimate the terror and brainwashing that takes place in battering relationships," says psychiatrist Elaine Carmen of the Solomon Carter Fuller Mental Health Center in Boston. "She really comes to believe that she deserves the abuse and is incompetent."

WHEN WOMEN TAKE ACTION

T HE TURNING POINT MAY COME WHEN a woman can no longer hide the scars and bruises. Or when her own financial resources improve, when the kids grow up—or when she begins to fear for their safety. Sometimes, neighbors hear screaming and call police—or a doctor challenges a woman's made-up story about how she got those broken ribs. "There are different moments of truth," says psychiatrist Carmen. "Acting on them partly depends on how safe it is to get up and leave." Walker says that women decide to get help when the pain of staying in a relationship outweighs the emotional, sexual or financial benefits.

For "Emma," a bank teller, the final straw came the day she returned from work to find that her husband hadn't mowed the lawn as she asked. "You promised me you'd mow the lawn," she said, then dropped the issue. Later they were seated calmly on the couch, when suddenly he was standing on the coffee table, coming down on her with his fists. He beat her into the wall until plaster fell down. "I was dragged through the house by my hair. At some point I began thinking I don't want to live anymore. If it hadn't been for this tiny voice in the background saying, 'Mama, please don't die,' I would have surrendered." Emma finally crawled to the car but couldn't see to drive, so her grandmother took her to the emergency room, where the doctor didn't believe her story about being mugged. "He said, 'You're not fine. You're bleeding internally. You've got a concussion.' He got a mirror and showed me my face. I looked like a monster in a horror movie. It was the first time I recognized how bad things had gotten." For a while, though, life got even harder. "When I arrived in Chicago, I had two children, two suitcases and $1,500 in my pocket to start a new life." She found it running a coalition that provides shelter for more than 700 battered women.

When women do take action, it can run the gamut from calling a hot line, seeking counseling, filing for divorce or seeking a court order of protection. Often those measures soothe the abuser—but only temporarily. "They think he's changed. Then it starts three months later," says Chicago divorce attorney David Mattenson. Some women weaken, too: they may lock the doors, check the shadows—but still let him have the keys to the house. Emma herself briefly returned to her husband when he begged and pleaded. "The same week I went back, he was beating me again."

WHEN COPS AND COURTS STEP IN

B LUNTLY PUT, COPS HATE DOMESTIC calls—in part because they are so unpredictable. A neighbor may simply report a disturbance and cops have no idea what they will find on the scene. The parties may have cooled down and be sitting in stony silence. Or one may be holding the other hostage, or the kids. Sometimes, warring spouses even turn on cops—which is why many police forces send them in pairs and tell them to maintain eye contact with each other at all times. But dangerous as family combat is, many cops still don't see such calls as real police work, says Jerome Storch, a professor of law and

STOPPING ABUSE: WHAT WORKS

Can a man who batters his partner learn to stop? Can psychotherapy turn an abuser into a respectful companion? Specialized treatment programs have proliferated in recent years, most of them aimed at teaching wife-beaters to manage their anger. But abusive men tend to resist treatment, and there are no proven formulas for reforming them. "We don't have any research that tells us any particular intervention is effective in a particular situation," says Eve Lipchik, a private therapist in Milwaukee. "We have nothing to go on."

Some abusers are less treatable than others. Researchers have identified a hard core, perhaps 10 to 20 percent, who seem beyond the reach of therapy. Experts differ on how best to handle the rest, but they agree that abusers shouldn't be coddled, even if they have grown up as victims themselves. "These men need to be confronted," says New York psychologist Matthew Campbell,

who runs a treatment program in Suffolk County. "Giving them TLC just endangers women. The man has to take full responsibility. He has to learn to say, 'I can leave. I can express upset. But I cannot be abusive'."

Some therapists favor counseling abusers and victims as couples, provided the beating has stopped and the relationship has a healthy dimension to build on. But couples therapy is controversial, especially among feminists. In fact, several states have outlawed it. "Couples therapy says to the victim, 'If you change, this won't happen'," says Campbell. "That's dangerous."

To avoid that message, most clinics deal exclusively with abusers, often having them confront each other in groups. During a typical session at Houston's Pivot Project, a private, not-for-profit counseling agency, batterers take turns recounting the past week's conflicts. (As a reminder that women aren't property,

the participants must refer to their partners by name. Anyone using the phrase "my wife" has to hold a stuffed donkey.) As each man testifies, his peers offer criticism. Therapist Toby Myers says one client recently boasted that he had avoided punching his wife by ramming his fist through a wall. Instead of praising him, a counselor asked the other participants what message the gesture had sent to the man's wife. A group member's reply: "It says she better be careful or she's next."

There's no question that such exercises can change men's behavior. At the Domestic Abuse Project in Minneapolis, follow-up studies suggest that two out of three clients haven't battered their partners 18 months after finishing treatment. Unfortunately, few abusers get that far: Only half of the men who register at the Abuse Project show up, even though most are under court orders. And only half of those who start treatment see it through.

Drug treatment may some day provide another tool. Preliminary findings suggest that Prozac-style antidepressants, which enhance a brain chemical called serotonin, help curb some men's aggressiveness. Neither counseling nor drug treatment is a cure-all. "We need psychological services," says Campbell, the New York psychologist. "But services mean nothing without sanctions. Men need to know that if they don't change, they'll go to jail."

Not every abuser is sensitive to that threat. Dr. Roland Maiuro, director of the Harborview Anger Management and Domestic Violence Program in Seattle, notes that some men simply become more bitter—and more dangerous—after they're arrested. But until treatment becomes a surer science, keeping those men behind bars may be the best way to keep their victims alive.

GEOFFREY COWLEY *with* GINNY CARROLL *in Houston and bureau reports*

---

police science at John Jay College of Criminal Justice in New York. "There's this thing in the back of the [cops'] mind that it's a domestic matter, not criminal activity."

Many cities have started training programs to make police take domestic-violence calls more sensitively—and seriously. For several years, the San Diego Police Department has even used details of O.J. Simpson's 1989 arrest for spousal battery as an example to recruits not to be intimidated by a famous name or face. Laws requiring police to make arrests in domestic cases are on the books in 15 states. But compliance is another matter. Since 1979, New York City has had a mandatory-arrest law, which also requires cops to report every domestic call. Yet a 1993 study found that reports were filed in only 30 percent of approximately 200,000 annual domestic-violence calls, and arrests

were made in only 7 percent of the cases. Many cops insist they need to be able to use their own judgment. "If there's a minor assault, are you going to make an arrest just because it's 'a domestic crime'?" asks Storch. "Then if you take it to court and the judge says, 'This is minor,' it's dismissed. If you place mandates on the police, you must place them on the courts."

Prosecutors are just as frustrated. Testimony is often his word against hers; defense attorneys scare off victims with repeated delays and many victims decline to cooperate or press charges. "When women call the police, they don't call because they want to prosecute," says Mimi Rose, chief of the Family Violence and Assault Unit at the Philadelphia District Attorney's Office. "They are scared and want the violence to stop. Ten days later when they get the sub-

poena to appear in court, the situation has changed. The idea of putting someone you live with in jail becomes impossible." Pressing charges is just the first step. The victim is faced with a range of potential legal remedies: orders of protection, criminal prosecution, family-court prosecution, divorce, a child-custody agreement. Each step is complex and time-consuming, requiring frequent court appearances by the victim—and the abuser, if he'll show up.

Courts around the country have made an effort to streamline the procedures; more than 500 bills on domestic violence were introduced in state legislatures last year, and 100 of them became law. In California alone, new bills are pending that would impose mandatory minimum jail sentences and long-term counseling for abusers, set up computer registries for restraining orders, ban abusers from carrying firearms, mandate training for judges—and even raise the "domestic-violence surcharge" on marriage licenses by $4 to be used for shelter services. On the national level, women's groups are pushing for the $1.8 million Violence Against Women act that would set up a national hot line, provide police training, toughen penalties and aid shelters and prevention programs. But those in the field say the question is whether the justice system can solve a highly complex social problem. "We need to rethink what we're doing," says Rose. "Prosecution isn't a panacea. It's like a tourniquet. We put it on when there is an emergency and we keep it on as long as necessary. But the question is, then what?"

WHEN ABUSE TURNS DEADLY

AFTER YEARS OF ABUSE, LEAVING IS often the most dangerous thing a woman can do. Probably the first thing a battered wife learns in counseling is that orders of protection aren't bulletproof. Severing ties signals the abuser that he's no longer in control, and he often responds in the only way be knows how—by escalating the violence. Husbands threaten to

One third of women in prison for homicide have killed an inmate

"hunt them down and kill them," says Margaret Byrne, who directs the Illinois Clemency Project for Battered Women. One man, she recalled, told his wife he would find her shelter and burn it down, with her in it. "It's this male sense of entitlement—'If I can't have her, no one can'," says University of Illinois sociologist Pauline Bart. Friends claim O.J. made similar threats to Nicole.

Although conventional wisdom has it that women are most vulnerable in the first two years after they separate, researcher Campbell is suspicious of limiting danger to a particular time. Typically, she says, women report they're harassed for about a year after a breakup, "but we think the really obsessed guys remain that way much longer." In the last 16 years, the rate of homicides in domestic-abuse cases has actually gone down slightly—particularly for black women—according to an analysis of FBI data by James Fox, dean of the College of Criminal Justice at Northeastern University. Fox is not certain why. "More and more women are apparently getting out of a relationship before it's too late."

Or perhaps women are getting to the family gun first. While studying some 22,000 Chicago murders since 1965, researcher Carolyn Block of the Illinois Criminal Justice Information Authority discovered that among black couples, women were more likely to kill men in domestic-abuse situations than the other way round. In white relationships, by contrast, only about 25 percent of the victims were male. Nationwide, about one third of the women in prison for homicide have killed an intimate, according to the Bureau of Justice Statistics. While judges and juries are increasingly sympathetic to "Burning Bed" tales of longtime abuse, the vast majority don't get off.

Whatever the numbers, men and women kill their partners for very different reasons. For men, it's usually an escalation of violence. For women, killing is often the last resort. "The woman who is feisty and strong would have left," says Geffner. "The one who murders her husband is squashed, terrified by, 'You're never going to get away from me, I'm going to take the kids.' There's nothing left for her. To protect herself or her kids, she ends up killing the batterer."

WHAT HAPPENS TO THE KIDS

THE CHILDREN OF O.J. AND NICOLE Simpson were reportedly with their maternal grandparents in Orange County, Calif., last week, riding their bikes and playing with cousins on the beach. Sydney, 9, and Justin, 5, know their mother is dead, but they reportedly have not been told that their father has been charged in her murder. Even if their family unplugs the TV and hides the newspapers, the scars may already be too deep.

"The worst thing that can happen to kids is to grow up in an abusive family," says Gelles. Research has shown that children reared amid violence risk more problems in school and an increased likelihood of drug and alcohol abuse. And, of course, they risk repeating the pattern when they become parents. Former surgeon general C. Everett Koop says domestic violence is often three-generational: in families in which a grandparent is abused, the most likely assailant is the daughter—who's likely to he married to a man who abuses her. Together, they abuse their children. "If you are going to break the chain," Koop says, "you have to break it at the child level."

The effects of violence can play out in many ways. Some boys get angry when they watch their father beat their mother, as Bill Clinton did as a teenager. Other children rebel and withdraw from attachment. All of them, says Northwestern University child psychiatrist David Zinn, suffer by trying to hide their family's dirty little secret. As a result, they feel isolated and unlike other kids. Sadly, it's a good bet the Simpsons' children will never again feel like everyone else. "The worst of all tragedies is to become social orphans—they lost their mother through a horrific crime and now their father has been turned into Mephistopheles," says Gelles. It's difficult enough for any child to overcome the legacy of domestic violence; having it play out on a national stage may make it all but impossible.

In October 1995 Orenthal James Simpson was acquitted in the June 1994 brutal stabbing of his ex-wife, Nicole Brown Simpson, and her friend, Ronald Goldman.
—**Ed.**

With an afflicted sister,
E. Fuller Torrey has long had reason to find a cure.
Now he may have the means.

Schizophrenia's Most Zealous Foe

By Michael Winerip

"WE WON'T BE GETTING ANY BRAINS IN THE MAIL today," the nation's best-known schizophrenia researcher says as he hurries to a meeting at his Washington laboratory. "They don't mail them over the weekend. We'll probably get some fresh brains Fed Exed tomorrow." Dr. E. Fuller Torrey, a psychiatrist, has had many grand passions during his three-decade crusade to cure schizophrenia, but none greater than his new human brain bank. For years, a major obstacle for scientists researching the neurological roots of serious mental illnesses—schizophrenia, manic depression, depression—has been the lack of first-rate human brains to study. "The only schizophrenic brains available have been very old and not in very good shape," Torrey says. They came from state hospitals and nursing homes, from patients so elderly that by the time they died the brain had atrophied. "We wanted to be in position to get better brains, brains of people younger and not dead long." Brains that would be full of unaltered proteins and neurotransmitters, viruses and cytokines that might hold the answers to schizophrenia's cause.

As has so often happened when Torrey needed something done that no one else would do, he did it himself. "He'll talk about it," says Ted Stanley, the philanthropist who has financed the brain bank, "then suddenly, he's done it." In the 1970's, while others were complaining that the seriously mentally ill had no lobbying group, Tor-

rey helped build the National Alliance for the Mentally Ill into a powerful political force that now has 170,000 members. When a literary agent couldn't find a publisher for Torrey's books, Torrey served as his own agent. (His "Surviving Schizophrenia," published in 1983, has sold 250,000 copies; his biography of Ezra Pound, "The Roots of Treason," was a nominee for the National Book Critics Circle award that same year.)

And when, in the mid-1980's, he was too outspoken for the psychiatry establishment and was demoted from his supervisory post at the National Institute of Mental Health, Torrey quit and became an independent researcher. Today he runs the mental health branch of a private foundation, which gives out so much research money that it rivals the Federal Government. Scientists from all over seek out the onetime renegade, requesting research funds. "It is amazing," Torrey says. For the first time, he has all the money he needs to chase his dream. In recent months, the 60-year-old Torrey has cut back his speaking engagements and his advocacy work to devote himself to searching for a cure for schizophrenia. "I think we can do it in the next 5 to 10 years," he says. "If we do, I'll die happy."

The brain bank is central to his grand plan. In 1994, he began contacting medical examiners' offices and has since built a national network that collects brains of mentally ill people who died in their 20's, 30's and 40's, from suicide and heart failure, in car crashes and fires. Torrey has employed a half-dozen pathologists around the country, paying them as much as $100,000 a year, to work full-time hunting brains. Within 48 hours of death, the brain is frozen at minus-70 degrees and shipped to Torrey. "We're up to 226 brains," Torrey says. "We have 44 freezers here just full of brain." While Torrey uses some tissue samples himself, most are distributed free to researchers worldwide. "Scientists historically have not shared their sources," says Dr. Stanley J. Watson, a University of Michigan professor who leased a truck in December to pick up 20,000 brain sections from Torrey's lab. "His attitude has been, the more horsepower, the faster we can all move ahead."

Once a week, Torrey and his staff sit down to review incoming and outgoing brain shipments. "I have the pre-deed, today the standard treatment is anti-psychotic medications that control excess brain chemicals known as neurotransmitters.

From the beginning, Torrey was at war with much of his profession. Well into the 1970's, many Freudian psychiatrists still believed that a particular type of bad mother—the "schizophrenogenic mother"—caused schizophrenia in their children. Torrey's 1974 book, "The Death of Psychiatry," was a broadside that many colleagues still resent. "A lot of us were very upset by that book," says Dr. Herbert Pardes, dean of the faculty of medicine at Columbia University.

The feelings were mutual: Torrey quit the American Psychiatric Association and never rejoined. As an administrator at the National Institute of Mental Health in the 1970's, he criticized his peers for flocking into lucrative private practices to serve the "worried well," proposing that psychiatrists either spend two years working in underserved

Torrey has cut back his advocacy work, focusing on one last push for a cure. 'I think we can do it in the next 5 to 10 years,' he says. 'If we do, I'll die happy.'

frontal pulled for Lenox," said Dr. Maree Webster at a recent meeting, discussing a load for Dr. Robert H. Lenox at the University of Florida. "I have anterior cingulate for him, too."

"How many samples for Xing and how many for Zhang?" asked Torrey.

"Xing's 20, Zhang's 15."

"That will please them enormously," Torrey said. "Does that take care of all the frontals? O.K., we are on to the hippocampus, then."

HE KNEW FROM CHILDHOOD THAT HE WANTED TO study medicine, but it was 40 years ago, as a Princeton sophomore, that E. Fuller Torrey decided psychiatry would be his specialty. He got a call from his mother in upstate New York, saying that his younger sister, Rhoda, an attractive, smart high-school senior, was acting peculiar. "She was lying out in the front yard," Torrey recalls, "yelling, 'The British are coming.' " Actually, what was coming was schizophrenia. Torrey accompanied his sister and widowed mother to America's best medical centers and what he heard seemed crazy. "At the Mass. General, they said the schizophrenia had been brought on by the shock of my father's death when my sister was young," Torrey says. "It made no more sense to me than the man in the moon. Why didn't *I* have schizophrenia if that's what caused it?" What did make sense to him was that schizophrenia—which affects 1 percent of adults, emerges in the late teens to mid-20's and often causes the afflicted to hear voices and hallucinate—was a brain disease, like multiple sclerosis and Alzheimer's are brain diseases. In-areas or repay the money that the Government had invested in their training.

They came after him. Chairmen of 15 university psychiatry departments descended on Washington demanding that he be fired. Though they were unsuccessful, his policy was never implemented. (Torrey himself has practiced medicine in the South Bronx and on a remote Alaskan island and, for 15 years, has volunteered at Washington homeless clinics.)

In 1983, Torrey reached a low point in his 20 years of Government service. He was overseeing a dozen wards at St. Elizabeths, the Federal mental hospital in Washington, and had become intrigued by the story of Ezra Pound. The poet had spent 1946 to 1958 at the hospital, supposedly insane and unable to stand trial for treason in connection with his pro-Fascist, anti-Semitic wartime radio broadcasts from Italy. Torrey kept hearing that Pound, while eccentric, had been perfectly sane, but that the superintendent of St. Elizabeths had admired the poet and lied about his medical condition to protect him. Torrey got hold of Pound's records and in "The Roots of Treason" laid out the story. Both Pound and the hospital superintendent who had protected him, Dr. Winfred Overholser, were dead by then. But Overholser was a former president of the American Psychiatric Association and still had powerful friends. "There was a story about the book in The Washington Post," Torrey says. "The next Monday I was demoted to ward psychiatrist, overseeing 25 patients."

Two years later, he retired from Government. But Torrey was about to be catapulted to the forefront of psychiatry by a series of enormous changes. Powerful machines capable of taking sophisticated pictures of the brain—

M.R.I.'s and PET scans—opened up a new world for researchers. A fresh generation of scientists saw Freud as a historical figure and the brain as the body's last frontier. To them, Torrey's emphasis on mental illness as brain disease made perfect sense. To them, psychiatry was a neuroscience.

Torrey's theories also made sense to families in the growing advocacy movement. While traditional psychiatry blamed them for their children's disorders, Torrey told them they had no more role in causing a teen-ager's schizophrenia or manic depression than in bringing about a parent's Alzheimer's. "Fuller spoke for us when no one in the medical community world," says Laurie Flynn, executive director of the National Alliance for the Mentally Ill. Year after year, Torrey crisscrossed the country speaking to NAMI groups. "Surviving Schizophrenia" became the primer for families learning about the diseases, and he donated the hardcover royalties to NAMI—$110,000 to date.

Torrey became the social conscience of the movement. In 1986, he created an annual survey ranking each state's programs for the mentally ill and then used it to shame state officials. After he lambasted Nevada for being at the bottom of the list, the Legislature enacted a 38 percent budget increase for mental health care. Nevada's administrator of mental health, Carlos Brandenburg, recently called to thank Torrey. "People know Dr. Torrey says it the way it is," Brandenburg says.

Pity the theorist Torrey doesn't like. Of Dr. Thomas Szasz, the once-influential social thinker who argues that mental illness is an invention of psychiatrists, Torrey wrote, "Szasz has produced more erudite nonsense on the subject of serious mental illness than any man alive." Of Dr. Theodore Lidz, still publishing research into the 1990's on the link between bad parenting and schizophrenia, Torrey wrote, "This book completes 45 years of pumpkin-headed research by Dr. Lidz."

Torrey has always been hard to peg politically. While he says he mostly votes for Democrats because they have a better history of looking out for the disadvantaged, he regularly attacks civil libertarians for being too slow to commit the untreated mentally ill on the streets. "If a person with Alzheimer's wanted to go outside with no shoes in the winter, we wouldn't say, 'That's fine, he should have free choice.' But that is precisely what those wonderful people at the Civil Liberties Union say if the person has schizophrenia. I find it easier to get a conservative at the Heritage Foundation like Stuart Butler to understand what we mean when we say schizophrenia's a brain disease like multiple sclerosis than a well-meaning person like Rosalynn Carter, who would say that a woman having trouble with teen-age children is no different from someone with schizophrenia."

It was Torrey's directness that appealed to Vada and Ted Stanley, a Connecticut couple who made their fortune marketing collectibles like a leather-bound "greatest books" series and Princess Di dolls. The Stanleys, who have had experience with mental illness in their family, were so impressed by "Surviving Schizophrenia" that they called Torrey in 1989, saying they wanted to donate $50,000. He suggested they hire a lobbyist for NAMI. Soon after, they wanted to take him to dinner at a nice Washington restaurant. "I had to research that one," says Torrey, who carries a bag lunch and works out of an office so narrow that two people can't stand shoulder to shoulder in it. At dinner, the Stanleys told him they wanted to donate $1 million. This year, the Stanleys will give out $20 million for mental health research. Torrey estimates that they will spend more on manic depression research than the Federal Government and about a fifth of what the Government spends on schizophrenia research.

Torrey, meanwhile, has been the motor driving the effort, creating projects like the brain bank and an internship program to inspire young scientists to enter the field. He distributes about 100 grants a year, a third of them to researchers outside the United States. Though it is a full-time job, he and his wife of 30 years, Barbara, an administrator at the National Academy of Sciences, decided he would take no salary. "I get $35,000 a year from my retirement and another $15,000 in book royalties," Torrey says. "My wife has a good job. We have what we need. If the Stanleys are generous enough to donate millions for research, I should donate my time to make sure it's spent well."

Friends warn Torrey that he is in danger of becoming respectable. Indeed, he was invited to give a lecture at Columbia last year and was warmly introduced by the medical-school dean, Pardes—one of the men, Torrey says, who once tried to get him fired from his Federal post. (Pardes says he has no recollection of the incident.)

TORREY IS WORKING ON HIS 16TH AND 17th books, one tracking the rise of lunacy in industrialized society, the other a cartoon guide to the brain. House guests say that when they go to bed he heads downstairs to write; when they wake, he is already up writing. A couple of times a week, he rises before dawn to play hockey in a senior league. Like many researchers, he is kept going by an incurable optimism. In 1996, he was invited to debate Szasz, author of "The Myth of Mental Illness." The debate was surreal. There was no common ground; it was as if the two men came from different centuries: *The Man Who Kept Saying Schizophrenia Was Just a Word Made Up by Psychiatrists* vs. *the Man With the M.R.I.'s of Cerebral Ventricles Enlarged by Schizophrenia.* I wondered why Torrey had bothered. "I have this idea," Torrey said recently, "that I can get him to admit there is mental illness—I almost got him at the end of the debate."

Today, medications control schizophrenia's worst symptoms but rarely restore the person to full health. Relapses are common—Torrey's sister, who lives in a group home, has been hospitalized six times in the past two years. Doctors often test one anti-psychotic drug after another on patients. "My sister's medical records are three feet high," Torrey says.

Her condition has helped keep him focused on a cure. Torrey's one splurge with the Stanley money has been to put together a team of seven researchers at John Hopkins University to pursue his own theory on schizophrenia's cause: that a virus, as yet unidentified, invades the hippocampus, a central structure of the brain crucial to processing sensory information, and then lays dormant for years before doing its damage.

Even his theory on schizophrenia is optimistic. "If it is a virus," he says, "a vaccine could be developed. This could be a disease of the past!" Though the evidence is mainly circumstantial, he is taking a long shot and gearing up to test antiviral medications on schizophrenics, starting with drugs that control the H.I.V. virus.

Many scientists view Torrey's viral theory with skepticism. Dr. Daniel Weinberger, a research chief at the National Institute of Mental Health, is an admirer of Torrey; still, he says, "the scientific evidence is lacking" for much of Torrey's virus theory. Weinberger and his colleagues have done some of the most intriguing schizophrenia research. They began by damaging cells in the hippocampus of newborn rats and monkeys. The animals were relatively normal until young adulthood, when late-developing areas of the brain that communicate with the hippocampus mature. At that point, the animals began behaving abnormally—a striking parallel to schizophrenia. This has led researchers to wonder if the cause of schizophrenia might be a trauma inflicted on a human fetus's brain while the hippocampus is forming in the womb. The damage to the hippocampus might result from any injury to the mother, a nutritional problem, an infection, an exposure to a toxin, a virus or a random misalignment of the developing brain cells. If so, the prognosis would be bleak. It would mean that life's infinite perils are at the root of schizophrenia, and there will never be a vaccine for that.

SINCE HIS MOTHER DIED 15 YEARS AGO, TORREY has been his sister Rhoda's only family. He phones her regularly, pays a woman to take her out every Saturday and visits her a few times a year in Rome, N.Y., at her group home. One morning last month, he arrived before 9. There was a foot of snow on the ground and the sky was a brilliant blue. He had the day all planned. They would go to Herb Philipson's to get Rhoda new duck boots, to Friendly's for lunch, then to a meeting with counselors from her day program.

Rhoda was standing on the porch waiting. He could see at a glance she wasn't well. Her hair hadn't been done; she wasn't wearing her glasses or her teeth. "Rhoda, how are you?" he said, hugging her and leading her back inside. Linda Sheppard, the group home's cook, and Torrey stood in the front hallway discussing Rhoda. Rhoda stood beside them, gazing at the floor. "She's not right," Sheppard said. "She's not right."

"Screaming at night?" Torrey asked.

"All day," said the cook. "Hallucinations have been bad. She's been seeing rats on her bed."

"My teeth aren't in," Rhoda said.

"I see," her brother said. "I'm more worried about your glasses." She is practically blind without them.

"I don't like to wear them because I might lose them," Rhoda said.

"She'll sit and talk to herself for hours," the cook said. "That's not Rhoda."

"We're going to see about changing her meds," Torrey said. "O.K., Rhoda, hang on to my arm—it's slippery." They walked onto the porch and down the steps. "Oh, Rhoda, look at the sun," he said. "It's going to be a beautiful day."

Michael Winerip, a staff writer for The New York Times Magazine, is the author of "9 Highland Road: Sane Living for the Mentally Ill."

Unit Selections

Key Points to Consider

❖ What varieties of psychotherapy are available? Discuss whether or not psychotherapy works. Do you think that laypersons can be effective therapists? Is professional assistance for psychological problems always necessary? Can you give some examples of people who successfully changed themselves? When is professional help needed? What can be changed successfully? What problems seem immune to change?

❖ What types of medications are now available for use by people with psychological disorders? Do you think these and other drugs make our society too drug dependent? What would you prefer, psychotherapy or medication? What are the problems inherent in psychopharmalogic research? Can you think of other ways to conduct such research? What role does ethics play in such research; do ethical problems limit the way we can conduct such research?

❖ How does clinical depression differ from the everyday blues we sometimes experience? What are some of the treatments for severe depression? What is Prozac and how does it work? What are some of its side effects and disadvantages? If you were a psychiatrist, would your first line of treatment for depression be Prozac? Why or why not?

❖ What is schizophrenia and why is it so hard to treat? Discuss some of the newer treatments for schizophrenia.

 **Links**

www.dushkin.com/online/

These sites are annotated on pages 4 and 5.

Have you ever had the nightmare that you are trapped in a dark, dismal place? No one will let you out. Your pleas for freedom go unanswered and, in fact, are suppressed or ignored by domineering authority figures around you. You keep begging for mercy but to no avail. What a nightmare! You are fortunate to awake to your normal bedroom and to the realities of your daily life. For the mentally ill, the nightmare of institutionalization, where individuals can be held against their will in what are sometimes terribly dreary, restrictive surroundings, is a reality. Have you ever wondered what would happen if we took perfectly normal individuals and institutionalized them? In one well-known and remarkable study, that is exactly what was done.

In 1973, eight people, including a pediatrician, a psychiatrist, and some psychologists, presented themselves to psychiatric hospitals. Each claimed that he or she was hearing voices. The voices, they reported, seemed unclear but appeared to be saying "empty" or "thud." Each of these individuals was admitted to a mental hospital, and most were diagnosed as being schizophrenic. Upon admission, the fake patients gave truthful information and thereafter acted like their usual, normal selves.

Their hospital stays lasted anywhere from 7 to 52 days. The nurses, doctors, psychologists, and other staff members treated them as if they really were schizophrenic and never saw through their trickery. Some of the real patients in the hospital did recognize, however, that the pseudopatients were

perfectly normal. Upon discharge almost all of the pseudopatients received the diagnosis of "schizophrenic in remission," meaning that they were still clearly construed as schizophrenic; they just weren't exhibiting any of the symptoms at the time.

What does this study demonstrate about mental illness? Is true mental illness readily detectable? If we can't always detect mental disorders, the more professionally accepted term for mental illness, how can we treat them? What treatments are available, and which work better for various diagnoses? The treatment of mental disorders is a challenge. The array of available treatments is ever-increasing and can be downright bewildering—and not just to the patient or client! In order to demystify and simplify your understanding of various treatments, we will look at them in this unit.

We commence with two general articles on treatment. In the first, renowned psychologist Martin Seligman discusses what we can hope to accomplish if we attempt reform. Some individuals have successfully shed weight, overcome anxiety and phobias, or quit smoking, either by themselves or with professional assistance. Seligman takes a realistic look at such efforts in "What You Can Change and What You Cannot Change."

In "Prescriptions for Happiness," authors Seymour Fisher and Roger Greenberg write about the plethora of drugs available to control our psychological states. In particular, they question the validity of research on these drugs because of the problems built into this kind of research.

Depression afflicts many of us. Some individuals suffer from chronic and intense depression, known as clinical depression. The third article, "The Quest for a Cure," not only details the symptoms of depression, but also provides a good discussion of the possible treatments for severe depression. In particular, the revolutionary drug, Prozac, is showcased.

The final article of this unit and of the book looks at treatments for schizophrenia. The problems schizophrenia creates for its victims and their families were described earlier. In this final article, new and old treatments for schizophrenia are outlined. Because we now believe that schizophrenia is the result of a neurochemical problem, many of these new treatments affect brain chemistry.

What You Can Change & What You Cannot Change

There are things we can change about ourselves and things we cannot. Concentrate your energy on what is possible—too much time has been wasted.

Martin E. P. Seligman, Ph.D.

This is the age of psychotherapy and the age of self-improvement. Millions are struggling to change: We diet, we jog, we meditate. We adopt new modes of thought to counteract our depressions. We practice relaxation to curtail stress. We exercise to expand our memory and to quadruple our reading speed. We adopt draconian regimens to give up smoking. We raise our little boys and girls to androgyny. We come out of the closet and we try to become heterosexual. We seek to lose our taste for alcohol. We seek more meaning in life. We try to extend our life span.

Sometimes it works. But distressingly often, self-improvement and psychotherapy fail. The cost is enormous. We think we are worthless. We feel guilty and ashamed. We believe we have no willpower and that we are failures. We give up trying to change.

On the other hand, this is not only the age of self-improvement and therapy, but also the age of biological psychiatry. The human genome will be nearly mapped be-

fore the millennium is over. The brain systems underlying sex, hearing, memory, left-handedness, and sadness are now known. Psychoactive drugs quiet our fears, relieve our blues, bring us bliss, dampen our mania, and dissolve our delusions more effectively than we can on our own.

Our very personality—our intelligence and musical talent, even our religiousness, our conscience (or its absence), our politics, and our exuberance—turns out to be more the product of our genes than almost anyone would have believed a decade ago. The underlying message of the age of biological psychiatry is that our biology frequently makes changing, in spite of all our efforts, impossible.

But the view that all is genetic and biochemical and therefore unchangeable is also very often wrong. Many people surpass their IQs, fail to "respond" to drugs, make sweeping changes in their lives, live on when their cancer is "terminal," or defy the hormones and brain circuitry that "dictate" lust, femininity, or memory loss.

The ideologies of biological psychiatry and self-improvement are obviously colliding. Nevertheless, a resolution is apparent. There are some things about ourselves that can be changed, others that cannot, and some that can be changed only with extreme difficulty.

What can we succeed in changing about ourselves? What can we not? When can we overcome our biology? And when is our biology our destiny?

I want to provide an understanding of what you can and what you can't change about yourself so that you can concentrate your limited time and energy on what is possible. So much time has been wasted. So much needless frustration has been endured. So much of therapy, so much of child rearing, so much of self-improving, and even some of the great social movements in our century have come to nothing because they tried to change the unchangeable. Too often we have wrongly thought we were weak-willed failures, when the changes we wanted to make in ourselves

From *Psychology Today*, May/June 1994, pp. 34–41, 70, 72–74, 84. Excerpted from *What You Can Change and What You Can't* by Martin E. P. Seligman. © 1993 by Martin E. P. Seligman. Reprinted by permission of Alfred A. Knopf, Inc.

So much child rearing, therapy, and self-improvement have come to nothing.

were just not possible. But all this effort was necessary: Because there have been so many failures, we are now able to see the boundaries of the unchangeable; this in turn allows us to see clearly for the first time the boundaries of what *is* changeable.

With this knowledge, we can use our precious time to make the many rewarding changes that are possible. We can live with less self-reproach and less remorse. We can live with greater confidence. This knowledge is a new understanding of who we are and where we are going.

CATASTROPHIC THINKING: PANIC

S. J. Rachman, one of the world's leading clinical researchers and one of the founders of behavior therapy, was on the phone. He was proposing that I be the "discussant" at a conference about panic disorder sponsored by the National Institute of Mental Health (NIMH).

"Why even bother, Jack?" I responded. "Everyone knows that panic is biological and that the only thing that works is drugs."

"Don't refuse so quickly, Marty. There is a breakthrough you haven't yet heard about."

Breakthrough was a word I had never heard Jack use before.

"What's the breakthrough?" I asked.

"If you come, you can find out."

So I went.

I had known about and seen panic patients for many years, and had read the literature with mounting excitement during the 1980s. I knew that panic disorder is a frightening condition that consists of recurrent attacks, each much worse than anything experienced before. Without prior warning, you feel as if you are going to die. Here is a typical case history:

The first time Celia had a panic attack, she was working at McDonald's. It was two days before her 20th birthday. As she was handing a customer a Big Mac, she had the worst experience of her life. The earth seemed to open up beneath her. Her heart began to pound, she felt she was smothering, and she was sure she was going to have a heart attack and die. After about 20 minutes of terror, the panic subsided. Trembling, she got in her car, raced home and barely left the house for the next three months.

Since then, Celia has had about three attacks a month. She does not know when they are coming. She always thinks she is going to die.

Panic attacks are not subtle, and you need no quiz to find out if you or someone you love has them. As many as five percent of American adults probably do. The defining feature of the disorder is simple: recurrent awful attacks of panic that come out of the blue, last for a few minutes, and then subside. The attacks consist of chest pains, sweating, nausea, dizziness, choking, smothering, or trembling. They are accompanied by feelings of overwhelming dread and thoughts that you are having a heart attack, that you are losing control, or that you are going crazy.

THE BIOLOGY OF PANIC

There are four questions that bear on whether a mental problem is primarily "biological" as opposed to "psychological":

- Can it be induced biologically?
- Is it genetically heritable?
- Are specific brain functions involved?
- Does a drug relieve it?

Inducing panic. Panic attacks can be created by a biological agent. For example, patients who have a history of panic attacks are hooked up to an intravenous line. Sodium lactate, a chemical that normally produces rapid, shallow breathing and heart palpitations, is slowly infused into their bloodstream. Within a few minutes, about 60 to 90 percent of these patients have a panic attack. Normal controls—subjects with no history of panic—rarely have attacks when infused with lactate.

Genetics of panic. There may be some heritability of panic. If one of two identical twins has panic attacks, 31 percent of the cotwins also have them. But if one of two fraternal twins has panic attacks, none of the cotwins are so afflicted.

Panic and the brain. The brains of people with panic disorders look somewhat unusual upon close scrutiny. Their neurochemistry shows abnormalities in the system that turns on, then dampens, fear. In addition, the PET scan (positron-emission tomography), a technique that looks at how much blood and oxygen different parts of the brain use, shows that patients who panic from the infusion of lactate have

We are now able to see the boundaries of the unchangeable.

What Can We Change?

When we survey all the problems, personality types, patterns of behavior, and the weak influence of childhood on adult life, we see a puzzling array of how much change occurs. From the things that are easiest to those that are the most difficult, this rough array emerges:

Panic	Curable
Specific Phobias	Almost Curable
Sexual Dysfunctions	Marked Relief
Social Phobia	Moderate Relief
Agoraphobia	Moderate Relief
Depression	Moderate Relief
Sex Role Change	Moderate
Obsessive-Compulsive Disorder	Moderate Mild Relief
Sexual Preferences	Moderate Mild Change
Anger	Mild Moderate Relief
Everyday Anxiety	Mild Moderate Relief
Alcoholism	Mild Relief
Overweight	Temporary Change
Posttraumatic Stress Disorder (PTSD)	Marginal Relief
Sexual Orientation	Probably Unchangeable
Sexual Identity	Unchangeable

higher blood flow and oxygen use in relevant parts of their brain than patients who don't panic.

Drugs. Two kinds of drugs relieve panic: tricyclic antidepressants and the anti-anxiety drug Xanax, and both work better than placebos. Panic attacks are dampened, and sometimes even eliminated. General anxiety and depression also decrease.

Since these four questions had already been answered "yes" when Jack Rachman called, I thought the issue had already been settled. Panic disorder was simply a biological illness, a disease of the body that could be relieved only by drugs.

A few months later I was in Bethesda, Maryland, listening once again to the same four lines of biological evidence. An inconspicuous figure in a brown suit sat hunched over the table. At the first break, Jack introduced me to him—David Clark, a young psychologist from Oxford. Soon after, Clark began his address.

"Consider, if you will, an alternative theory, a cognitive theory." He reminded all of us that almost all panickers believe that they are going to die during an attack. Most commonly, they believe that they are having heart attacks. Perhaps, Clark suggested, this is more than just a mere symptom. Perhaps it is the root cause. Panic may simply be the *catastrophic misinterpretation of bodily sensations.*

For example, when you panic, your heart starts to race. You notice this, and you see it as a possible heart attack. This makes you very anxious, which means that your heart pounds more. You now notice that your heart is *really* pounding. You are now *sure* it's a heart attack. This terrifies you, and you break into a sweat, feel nauseated, short of breath—all symptoms of terror, but for you, they're confirmation of a heart attack. A full-blown panic attack is under way, and at the root of it is your misinterpretation of the symptoms of anxiety as symptoms of impending death.

I was listening closely now as Clark argued that an obvious sign of a disorder, easily dismissed as a symptom, is the disorder itself. If he was right, this was a historic occasion. All Clark had done so far, how-

---

Issues of the soul can barely be changed by psychotherapy or drugs.

---

ever, was to show that the four lines of evidence for a biological view of panic could fit equally well with a misinterpretation view. But Clark soon told us about a series of experiments he and his colleague Paul Salkovskis had done at Oxford.

First, they compared panic patients with patients who had other anxiety disorders and with normals. All the subjects read the following sentences aloud, but the last word was presented blurred. For example:

dying
If I had palpitations, I could be
excited

choking
If I were breathless, I could be
unfit

When the sentences were about bodily sensations, the panic patients, but no one else, saw the catastrophic endings fastest. This showed that panic patients possess the habit of thinking Clark had postulated.

Self-Analysis Questionnaire

Is your life dominated by anxiety? Read each statement and then mark the appropriate number to indicate how you generally feel. There are no right or wrong answers.

1. I am a steady person.

Almost never	Sometimes	Often	Almost always
4	3	2	1

2. I am satisfied with myself.

Almost never	Sometimes	Often	Almost always
4	3	2	1

3. I feel nervous and restless.

Almost never	Sometimes	Often	Almost always
1	2	3	4

4. I wish I could be as happy as others seem to be.

Almost never	Sometimes	Often	Almost always
1	2	3	4

5. I feel like a failure.

Almost never	Sometimes	Often	Almost always
1	2	3	4

6. I get in a state of tension and turmoil as I think over my recent concerns and interests.

Almost never	Sometimes	Often	Almost always
1	2	3	4

7. I feel secure.

Almost never	Sometimes	Often	Almost always
4	3	2	1

8. I have self-confidence.

Almost never	Sometimes	Often	Almost always
4	3	2	1

9. I feel inadequate.

Almost never	Sometimes	Often	Almost always
1	2	3	4

10. I worry too much over something that does not matter.

Almost never	Sometimes	Often	Almost always
1	2	3	4

To score, simply add up the numbers under your answers. Notice that some of the rows of numbers go up and others go down. The higher your total, the more the trait of anxiety dominates your life. If your score was:

10–11, you are in the lowest 10 percent of anxiety.

13–14, you are in the lowest quarter.

16–17, your anxiety level is about average.

19–20, your anxiety level is around the 75th percentile.

22–24 (and you are male) your anxiety level is around the 90th percentile.

24–26 (and you are female) your anxiety level is around the 90th percentile.

25 (and you are male) your anxiety level is at the 95th percentile.

27 (and you are female) your anxiety level is at the 95th percentile.

Should you try to change your anxiety level? Here are my rules of thumb:

- If your score is at the 90th percentile or above, you can probably improve the quality of your life by lowering your general anxiety level—regardless of paralysis and irrationality.

- If your score is at the 75th percentile or above, and you feel that anxiety is either paralyzing you or that it is unfounded, you should probably try to lower your general anxiety level.

- If your score is 18 or above, and you feel that anxiety is unfounded and paralyzing, you should probably try to lower your general anxiety level.

Next, Clark and his colleagues asked if activating this habit with words would induce panic. All the subjects read a series of word pairs aloud. When panic patients got to "breathlessness-suffocation" and "palpitations-dying," 75 percent suffered a full-blown panic attack right there in the laboratory. No normal people had panic attacks, no recovered panic patients (I'll tell you more in a moment about how they got better) had attacks, and only 17 percent of other anxious patients had attacks.

The final thing Clark told us was the "breakthrough" that Rachman had promised.

"We have developed and tested a rather novel therapy for panic," Clark continued in his understated, disarming way. He explained that if catastrophic misinterpretations of bodily sensation are the cause of a panic attack, then changing the tendency to misinterpret should cure the disorder. His new therapy was straightforward and brief:

Patients are told that panic results when they mistake normal symptoms of mounting anxiety for symptoms of heart attack, going crazy, or dying. Anxiety itself, they are informed, produces shortness of breath, chest pain, and sweating. Once they misinterpret these normal bodily sensations as an imminent heart attack, their symptoms become even more pronounced because the misinterpretation changes their anxiety into terror. A vicious circle culminates in a full-blown panic attack.

Patients are taught to reinterpret the symptoms realistically as mere anxiety symptoms. Then they are given practice right in the office, breathing rapidly into a paper bag. This causes a buildup of carbon dioxide and shortness of breath, mimicking the sensations that provoke a panic attack. The therapist points out that the symptoms the patient is experiencing—shortness of breath and heart racing—are harmless, simply the result of overbreathing, not a sign of a heart attack. The patient learns to interpret the symptoms correctly.

"This simple therapy appears to be a cure," Clark told us. "Ninety to 100 percent of the patients are panic free at the end of therapy. One year later, only one person had had another panic attack."

This, indeed, was a breakthrough: a simple, brief psychotherapy with no side effects showing a 90-percent cure rate of a disorder that a decade ago was thought to be incurable. In a controlled study of 64 patients comparing cognitive therapy to drugs to relaxation to no treatment, Clark and his colleagues found that cognitive therapy is markedly better than drugs or relaxation, both of which are better than nothing. Such a high cure rate is unprecedented.

How does cognitive therapy for panic compare with drugs? It is more effective and less dangerous. Both the antidepressants and Xanax produce marked reduction in panic in most patients, but drugs must be taken forever; once the drug is stopped, panic rebounds to where it was before therapy began for perhaps half the patients. The drugs also sometimes have severe side effects, including drowsiness, lethargy, pregnancy complications, and addictions.

After this bombshell, my own "discussion" was an anticlimax. I did make one point that Clark took to heart. "Creating a cognitive therapy that works, even one that works as well as this apparently does, is not enough to show that the *cause* of panic is cognitive." I was niggling. "The biological theory doesn't deny that some other therapy might work well on panic. It merely claims that panic is caused at the bottom by some biochemical problem."

Two years later, Clark carried out a crucial experiment that tested the biological theory against the cognitive theory. He gave

---

Anxiety scans your life for imperfections. When it finds one, it won't let go.

---

the usual lactate infusion to 10 panic patients, and nine of them panicked. He did the same thing with another 10 patients, but added special instructions to allay the misinterpretation of the sensations. He simply told them: "Lactate is a natural bodily substance that produces sensations similar to exercise or alcohol. It is normal to experience intense sensations during infusion, but these do not indicate an adverse reaction." Only three out of the 10 panicked. This confirmed the theory crucially.

The therapy works very well, as it did for Celia, whose story has a happy ending. She first tried Xanax, which reduced the intensity and the frequency of her panic attacks. But she was too drowsy to work and she was still having about one attack every six weeks. She was then referred to Audrey, a cognitive therapist who explained that Celia was misinterpreting her heart racing and shortness of breath as symptoms of a heart attack, that they were actually just symptoms of mounting anxiety, nothing more harmful. Audrey taught Celia progressive relaxation, and then she demonstrated the harmlessness of Celia's symptoms of overbreathing. Celia then relaxed in the presence of the symptoms and found that they gradually subsided. After several more practice sessions, therapy termi-

nated. Celia has gone two years without another panic attack.

EVERYDAY ANXIETY

Attend to your tongue—right now. What is it doing? Mine is swishing around near my lower right molars. It has just found a minute fragment of last night's popcorn (debris from *Terminator 2*). Like a dog at a bone, it is worrying the firmly wedged flake.

Attend to your hand—right now. What's it up to? My left hand is boring in on an itch it discovered under my earlobe.

Your tongue and your hands have, for the most part, a life of their own. You can bring them under voluntary control by consciously calling them out of their "default" mode to carry out your commands: "Pick up the phone" or "Stop picking that pimple." But most of the time they are on their own. They are seeking out small imperfections. They scan your entire mouth and skin surface, probing for anything going wrong. They are marvelous, nonstop grooming devices. They, not the more fashionable immune system, are your first line of defense against invaders.

Anxiety is your mental tongue. Its default mode is to search for what may be about to go wrong. It continually, and without your conscious consent, scans your life—yes, even when you are asleep, in dreams and nightmares. It reviews your work, your love, your play—until it finds an imperfection. When it finds one, it worries it. It tries to pull it out from its hiding place, where it is wedged inconspicuously under some rock. It will not let go. If the imperfection is threatening enough, anxiety calls your attention to it by making you uncomfortable. If you do not act, it yells more insistently—disturbing your sleep and your appetite.

You can reduce daily, mild anxiety. You can numb it with alcohol, Valium, or marijuana. You can take the edge off with meditation or progressive relaxation. You can beat it down by becoming more conscious of the automatic thoughts of danger that trigger anxiety and then disputing them effectively.

But do not overlook what your anxiety is trying to do for you. In return for the pain it brings, it prevents larger ordeals by making you aware of their possibility and goading you into planning for and forestalling them. It may even help you avoid them altogether. Think of your anxiety as the "low oil" light flashing on the dashboard of your car. Disconnect it and you will be less distracted and more comfortable for a while. But this may cost you a burned-up engine. Our *dysphoria*, or bad feeling, should, some of the time, be tolerated, attended to, even cherished.

GUIDELINES FOR WHEN TO TRY TO CHANGE ANXIETY

Some of our everyday anxiety, depression, and anger go beyond their useful function. Most adaptive traits fall along a normal spectrum of distribution, and the capacity for internal bad weather for everyone some of the time means that some of us may have terrible weather all of the time. In general, when the hurt is pointless and recurrent—when, for example, anxiety insists we formulate a plan but no plan will work—it is time to take action to relieve the hurt. There are three hallmarks indicating that anxiety has become a burden that wants relieving:

First, is it *irrational?*

We must calibrate our bad weather inside against the real weather outside. Is what you are anxious about out of proportion to the reality of the danger? Here are some examples that may help you answer this question. All of the following are not irrational:

- A fire fighter trying to smother a raging oil well burning in Kuwait repeatedly wakes up at four in the morning because of flaming terror dreams.
- A mother of three smells perfume on her husband's shirts and, consumed by jealousy, broods about his infidelity, reviewing the list of possible women over and over.
- A student who had failed two of his midterm exams finds, as finals approach, that he can't get to sleep for worrying. He has diarrhea most of the time.

The only good thing that can be said about such fears is that they are well-founded.

In contrast, all of the following are irrational, out of proportion to the danger:

- An elderly man, having been in a fender bender, broods about travel and will no longer take cars, trains, or airplanes.
- An eight-year-old child, his parents having been through an ugly divorce, wets his bed at night. He is haunted with visions of his bedroom ceiling collapsing on him.
- A housewife who has an MBA and who accumulated a decade of experience as a financial vice president before her twins were born is sure her job search will be fruitless. She delays preparing her résumés for a month.

The second hallmark of anxiety out of control is *paralysis*. Anxiety intends action: Plan, rehearse, look into shadows for lurking dangers, change your life. When anxiety becomes strong, it is unproductive; no problem-solving occurs. And when anxiety is extreme, it paralyzes you. Has your anxiety crossed this line? Some examples:

- A woman finds herself housebound because she fears that if she goes out, she will be bitten by a cat.
- A salesman broods about the next customer hanging up on him and makes no more cold calls.
- A writer, afraid of the next rejection slip, stops writing.

'Dieting below your natural weight is a necessary condition for bulimia. Returning to your natural weight will cure it.'

The final hallmark is *intensity*. Is your life dominated by anxiety? Dr. Charles Spielberger, one of the world's foremost testers of emotion, has developed well-validated scales for calibrating how severe anxiety is. To find out how anxious *you* are, use the self-analysis questionnaire.

LOWERING YOUR EVERYDAY ANXIETY

Everyday anxiety level is not a category to which psychologists have devoted a great deal of attention. Enough research has been done, however, for me to recommend two techniques that quite reliably lower everyday anxiety levels. Both techniques are cumulative, rather than one-shot fixes. They require 20 to 40 minutes a day of your valuable time.

The first is *progressive relaxation*, done once or, better, twice a day for at least 10 minutes. In this technique, you tighten and then turn off each of the major muscle groups of your body until you are wholly flaccid. It is not easy to be highly anxious when your body feels like Jell-O. More formally, relaxation engages a response system that competes with anxious arousal.

The second technique is regular *meditation*. Transcendental meditation ™ is one useful, widely available version of this. You can ignore the cosmology in which it is packaged if you wish, and treat it simply as the beneficial technique it is. Twice a day for 20 minutes, in a quiet setting, you close your eyes and repeat a *mantra* (a syllable whose "sonic properties are known")

to yourself. Meditation works by blocking thoughts that produce anxiety. It complements relaxation, which blocks the motor components of anxiety but leaves the anxious thoughts untouched.

Done regularly, meditation usually induces a peaceful state of mind. Anxiety at other times of the day wanes, and hyperarousal from bad events is dampened. Done religiously, TM probably works better than relaxation alone.

There's also a quick fix. The minor tranquilizers—Valium, Dalmane, Librium, and their cousins—relieve everyday anxiety. So does alcohol. The advantage of all these is that they work within minutes and require no discipline to use. Their disadvantages outweigh their advantages, however. The minor tranquilizers make you fuzzy and somewhat uncoordinated as they work (a not uncommon side effect is an automobile accident). Tranquilizers soon lose their effect when taken regularly, and they are habit-forming—probably addictive. Alcohol, in addition, produces gross cognitive and motor disability in lockstep with its anxiety relief. Taken regularly over long periods, deadly damage to liver and brain ensue.

If you crave quick and temporary relief from acute anxiety, either alcohol or minor tranquilizers, taken in small amounts and only occasionally, will do the job. They are, however, a distant second-best to progressive relaxation and meditation, which are each worth trying before you seek out psychotherapy or in conjunction with therapy. Unlike tranquilizers and alcohol, neither of these techniques is likely to do you any harm.

Weigh your everyday anxiety. If it is not intense, or if it is moderate and not irrational or paralyzing, act now to reduce it. In spite of its deep evolutionary roots, intense everyday anxiety is often changeable. Meditation and progressive relaxation practiced regularly can change it forever.

DIETING: A WAIST IS A TERRIBLE THING TO MIND

I have been watching my weight and restricting my intake—except for an occasional binge like this—since I was 20. I weighed about 175 pounds then, maybe 15 pounds over my official "ideal" weight. I weigh 199 pounds now, 30 years later, about 25 pounds over the ideal. I have tried about a dozen regimes—fasting, the Beverly Hills Diet, no carbohydrates, Metrecal for lunch, 1,200 calories a day, low fat, no lunch, no starches, skipping every other dinner. I lost 10 or 15 pounds on each in about a month. The pounds always came back, though, and I have gained a net of about a pound a year—inexorably.

This is the most consistent failure in my life. It's also a failure I can't just put out of mind. I have spent the last few years reading the scientific literature, not the parade of best-selling diet books or the flood of women's magazine articles on the latest way to slim down. The scientific findings look clear to me, but there is not yet a consensus. I am going to go out on a limb, because I see so many signs all pointing in one direction. What I have concluded will, I believe, soon be the consensus of the scientists. The conclusions surprise me. They will probably surprise you, too, and they may change your life.

Here is what the picture looks like to me:

- Dieting doesn't work.
- Dieting may make overweight worse, not better.
- Dieting may be bad for health.
- Dieting may cause eating disorders—including bulimia and anorexia.

ARE YOU OVERWEIGHT?

Are you above the ideal weight for your sex, height, and age? If so, you are "overweight." What does this really mean? Ideal weight is arrived at simply. Four million people, now dead, who were insured by the major American life-insurance companies, were once weighed and had their height measured. At what weight on average do people of a given height turn out to live longest? That weight is called ideal. Anything wrong with that?

You bet. The real use of a weight table, and the reason your doctor takes it seriously, is that an ideal weight implies that, on average, if you slim down to yours, you will live longer. This is the crucial claim. Lighter people indeed live longer, on average, than heavier people, but how much longer is hotly debated.

But the crucial claim is unsound because weight (at any given height) has a normal distribution, *normal* both in a statistical sense and in the biological sense. In the biological sense, couch potatoes who overeat and never exercise can legitimately be called overweight, but the buxom, "heavy-boned" slow people deemed overweight by the ideal table are at their natural and healthiest weight. If you are a 155-pound woman and 64 inches in height, for example, you are "overweight" by around 15 pounds. This means nothing more than that the average 140-pound, 64-inch-tall woman lives somewhat longer than the average 155-pound woman of your height. It does not follow that if you slim down to 125 pounds, *you* will stand any better chance of living longer.

In spite of the insouciance with which dieting advice is dispensed, no one has properly investigated the question of whether slimming down to "ideal" weight produces longer life. The proper study would compare the longevity of people who are at their ideal weight without dieting to people who achieve their ideal weight by dieting. Without this study the common medical advice to diet down to your ideal weight is simply unfounded.

This is not a quibble; there is evidence that dieting damages your health and that this damage may shorten your life.

MYTHS OF OVERWEIGHT

The advice to diet down to your ideal weight to live longer is one myth of overweight. Here are some others:

- *Overweight people overeat.* Wrong. Nineteen out of 20 studies show that obese people consume no more calories each day than nonobese people. Telling a fat person that if she would change her eating habits and eat "normally" she would lose weight is a lie. To lose weight and stay there, she will need to eat excruciatingly less than a normal person, probably for the rest of her life.
- *Overweight people have an overweight personality.* Wrong. Extensive research on personality and fatness has proved little. Obese people do not differ in any major personality style from nonobese people.
- *Physical inactivity is a major cause of obesity.* Probably not. Fat people are indeed less active than thin people, but the inactivity is probably caused more by the fatness than the other way around.
- *Overweight shows a lack of willpower.* This is the granddaddy of all the myths. Fatness is seen as shameful because we hold people responsible for their weight. Being overweight equates with being a weak-willed slob. We believe this primarily because we have seen people decide to lose weight and do so in a matter of weeks.

But almost everyone returns to the old weight after shedding pounds. Your body has a natural weight that it defends vigorously against dieting. The more diets tried, the harder the body works to defeat the next diet. Weight is in large part genetic. All this gives the lie to the "weak-willed" interpretations of overweight. More accurately, dieting is the conscious will of the individual against a more vigilant opponent: the species' biological defense against starvation. The body can't tell the difference between self-imposed starvation and actual famine, so it defends its weight by refusing to release fat, by lowering its me-

tabolism, and by demanding food. The harder the creature tries not to eat, the more vigorous the defenses become.

BULIMIA AND NATURAL WEIGHT

A concept that makes sense of your body's vigorous defense against weight loss is *natural weight*. When your body screams "I'm hungry," makes you lethargic, stores fat, craves sweets and renders them more delicious than ever, and makes you obsessed with food, what it is defending is your natural weight. It is signaling that you have dropped into a range it will not accept. Natural weight prevents you from gaining too much weight or losing too much. When you eat too much for too long, the opposite defenses are activated and make long-term weight gain difficult.

There is also a strong genetic contribution to your natural weight. Identical twins reared apart weigh almost the same throughout their lives. When identical twins are overfed, they gain weight and add fat in lockstep and in the same places. The fatness or thinness of adopted children resembles their biological parents—particularly their mother—very closely but does not at all resemble their adoptive parents. This suggests that you have a genetically given natural weight that your body wants to maintain.

The idea of natural weight may help cure the new disorder that is sweeping young America. Hundreds of thousands of young women have contracted it. It consists of bouts of binge eating and purging alternating with days of undereating. These young women are usually normal in weight or a bit on the thin side, but they are terrified of becoming fat. So they diet. They exercise. They take laxatives by the cup. They gorge. Then they vomit and take more laxatives. This malady is called *bulimia nervosa* (bulimia, for short).

Therapists are puzzled by bulimia, its causes, and treatment. Debate rages about whether it is an equivalent of depression, or an expression of a thwarted desire for control, or a symbolic rejection of the feminine role. Almost every psychotherapy has been tried. Antidepressants and other drugs have been administered with some effect but little success has been reported.

I don't think that bulimia is mysterious, and I think that it will be curable. I believe that bulimia is caused by dieting. The bulimic goes on a diet, and her body attempts to defend its natural weight. With repeated dieting, this defense becomes more vigorous. Her body is in massive revolt—insistently demanding food, storing fat, craving sweets, and lowering metabolism. Periodically, these biological defenses will overcome her extraordinary willpower (and extraordinary it must be to even approach an ideal weight, say, 20 pounds lighter than her natural weight). She will then binge. Horrified by what this will do to her figure, she vomits and takes laxatives to purge calories. Thus, bulimia is a natural consequence of self-starvation to lose weight in the midst of abundant food.

The therapist's task is to get the patient to stop dieting and become comfortable with her natural weight. He should first convince the patient that her binge eating is caused by her body's reaction to her diet. Then he must confront her with a question: Which is more important, staying thin or getting rid of bulimia? By stopping the diet, he will tell her, she can get rid of the uncontrollable binge-purge cycle. Her body will now settle at her natural weight, and she need not worry that she will balloon beyond that point. For some patients, therapy will end there because they would rather be bulimic than "loathsomely fat." For these patients, the central issue—ideal weight versus natural weight—can now at least become the focus of therapy. For others, defying the social and sexual pressure to be thin will be possible, dieting will be abandoned, weight will be gained, and bulimia should end quickly.

These are the central moves of the cognitive-behavioral treatment of bulimia. There are more than a dozen outcome studies of this approach, and the results are good. There is about 60 percent reduction in binging and purging (about the same as with antidepressant drugs). But unlike drugs, there is little relapse after treatment. Attitudes toward weight and shape relax, and dieting withers.

Of course, the dieting theory cannot fully explain bulimia. Many people who diet don't become bulimic; some can avoid it because their natural weight is close to their ideal weight, and therefore the diet they adopt does not starve them. In addition, bulimics are often depressed, since binging-purging leads to self-loathing. Depression may worsen bulimia by making it easier to give in to temptation. Further, dieting may just be another symptom of bulimia, not a cause. Other factors aside, I can speculate that dieting below your natural weight is a necessary condition for bulimia, and that returning to your natural weight and accepting that weight will cure bulimia.

OVERWEIGHT VS. DIETING: THE HEALTH DAMAGE

Being heavy carries some health risk. There is no definite answer to how much, because there is a swamp of inconsistent findings. But even if you could just wish pounds away, never to return, it is not certain you should. Being somewhat above your "ideal" weight may actually be your healthiest natural condition, best for your particular constitution and your particular metabolism. Of course you can diet, but the odds are overwhelming that most of the weight will return, and that you will have to diet again and again. From a health and mortality perspective, should you? *There is, probably, a serious health risk from losing weight and regaining it.*

In one study, more than five thousand men and women from Framingham, Massachusetts, were observed for 32 years. People whose weight fluctuated over the years had 30 to 100 percent greater risk of death from heart disease than people whose weight was stable. When corrected for smoking, exercise, cholesterol level, and blood pressure, the findings became more convincing, suggesting that weight fluctuation (the primary cause of which is presumably dieting) may itself increase the risk of heart disease.

If this result is replicated, and if dieting is shown to be the primary cause of weight cycling, it will convince me that you should not diet to reduce your risk of heart disease.

DEPRESSION AND DIETING

Depression is yet another cost of dieting, because two root causes of depression are failure and helplessness. Dieting sets you up for failure. Because the goal of slimming down to your ideal weight pits your fallible willpower against untiring biological defenses, you will often fail. At first you will lose weight and feel pretty good about it. Any depression you had about your figure will disappear. Ultimately, however, you will probably not reach your goal; and then you will be dismayed as the pounds return. Every time you look in the mirror or vacillate over a white chocolate mousse, you will be reminded of your failure, which in turn brings depression.

On the other hand, if you are one of the fortunate few who can keep the weight from coming back, you will probably have to stay on an unsatisfying low-calorie diet for the rest of your life. A side effect of prolonged malnutrition is depression. Either way you are more vulnerable to it.

If you scan the list of cultures that have a thin ideal for women, you will be struck by something fascinating. All thin-ideal cultures also have eating disorders. They also have roughly twice as much depression in women as in men. (Women diet twice as much as men. The best estimate is that 13 percent of adult men and 25 percent of adult women are now on a diet.) The cultures without the thin ideal have no eating disorders, and the amount of depression in women and men in these cultures is the same. This suggests that around the world, the thin ideal and dieting not only cause eating disorders, but they may also cause women to be more depressed than men.

THE BOTTOM LINE

I have been dieting off and on for 30 years because I want to be more attractive, healthier, and more in control. How do these goals stack up against the facts?

Attractiveness. If your attractiveness is a high-enough priority to convince you to diet, keep three drawbacks in mind. First, the attractiveness you gain will be temporary. All the weight you lose and maybe more will likely come back in a few years. This will depress you. Then you will have to lose it again and it will be harder the second time. Or you will have to resign yourself to being less attractive. Second, when women choose the silhouette figure they want to achieve, it turns out to be thinner than the silhouette that men label most attractive. Third, you may well become bulimic particularly if your natural weight is substantially more than your ideal weight. On balance, if short-term attractiveness is your overriding goal, diet. But be prepared for the costs.

Health. No one has ever shown that losing weight will increase my longevity. On balance, the health goal does not warrant dieting.

Control. For many people, getting to an ideal weight and staying there is just as biologically impossible as going with much less sleep. This fact tells me not to diet, and defuses my feeling of shame. My bottom line is clear: I am not going to diet anymore.

DEPTH AND CHANGE: THE THEORY

Clearly, we have not yet developed drugs or psychotherapies that can change all the problems, personality types, and patterns of behavior in adult life. But I believe that success and failure stems from something other than inadequate treatment. Rather, it stems from the depth of the problem.

We all have experience of psychological states of different depths. For example, if you ask someone, out of the blue, to answer quickly, "Who are you?" they will usually tell you—roughly in this order—their name, their sex, their profession, whether they have children, and their religion or race. Underlying this is a continuum of depth from surface to soul—with all manner of psychic material in between.

I believe that issues of the soul can barely be changed by psychotherapy or by drugs. Problems and behavior patterns somewhere between soul and surface can be changed somewhat. Surface problems can be changed easily, even cured. What is changeable, by therapy or drugs, I speculate, varies with the depth of the problem.

My theory says that it does not matter *when* problems, habits, and personality are acquired; their depth derives only from their biology, their evidence, and their power. Some childhood traits, for example, are deep and unchangeable but not because they were learned early and therefore have a privileged place.

Rather, those traits that resist change do so either because they are evolutionarily prepared or because they acquire great power by virtue of becoming the framework around which later learning crystallizes. In this way, the theory of depth carries the optimistic message that we are not prisoners of our past.

When you have understood this message, you will never look at your life in the same way again. Right now there are a number of things that you do not like about yourself and that you want to change: your short fuse, your waistline, your shyness, your drinking, your glumness. You have decided to change, but you do not know what you should work on first. Formerly you would have probably selected the one that hurts the most. Now you will also ask yourself which attempt is most likely to repay your efforts and which is most likely to lead to further frustration. Now you know your shyness and your anger are much more likely to change than your drinking, which you now know is more likely to change than your waistline.

Some of what does change is under your control, and some is not. You can best prepare yourself to change by learning as much as you can about what you can change and how to make those changes. Like all true education, learning about change is not easy; harder yet is surrendering some of our hopes. It is certainly not my purpose to destroy your optimism about change. But it is also not my purpose to assure everybody they can change in every way. My purpose is to instill a new, warranted optimism about the parts of your life you can change and so help you focus your limited time, money, and effort on making actual what is truly within your reach.

Life is a long period of change. What you have been able to change and what has resisted your highest resolve might seem chaotic to you: for some of what you are never changes no matter how hard you try, and other aspects change readily. My hope is that this essay has been the beginning of wisdom about the difference.

PROZAC. ZOLOFT. PAXIL. WELLBUTRIN.

Prescriptions for Happiness?

The biological approach to treating unhappiness is booming. But is it all it's cracked up to be? Two noted researchers demonstrate that the "scientific" studies that underpin claims of drug effectiveness are seriously flawed—undone by signals from our bodies. Perhaps the studies really prove the power of placebo—and the absurdity of drawing any line between what is biological and what is psychological.

Seymour Fisher, Ph.D., and Roger P. Greenberg, Ph.D.

The air is filled with declarations and advertisements of the power of biological psychiatry to relieve people of their psychological distress. Some biological psychiatrists are so convinced of the superiority of their position that they are recommending young psychiatrists no longer be taught the essentials of doing psychotherapy. Feature stories in such magazines as Newsweek and Time have portrayed drugs like Prozac as possessing almost a mystical potency. The best-selling book Listening to Prozac by psychiatrist Peter Kramer, M.D., projects the idyllic possibility that psychotropic drugs may eventually be capable of correcting a spectrum of personality quirks and lacks.

As longtime faculty members of a number of psychiatry departments, we have personally witnessed the gradual but steadily accelerated dedication to the idea that "mental illness" can be mastered with biologically based substances. Yet a careful sifting of the pertinent literature indicates that modesty and skepticism would be more appropriate responses to the research accumulated thus far.

In 1989, we first raised radical questions about such biological claims in a book, The Limits of Biological Treatments for Psychological Distress: Comparisons with Psychotherapy and Placebo (Lawrence Erlbaum). Our approach has been to filter the studies that presumably anchor them through a series of logical and quantitative (meta-analytic) appraisals.

How Effective Are Antidepressant Drugs?

Antidepressants, one of the major weapons in the biological therapeutic arsenal, illustrate well the largely unacknowledged uncertainty that exists in the biological approach to psychopathology. We suggest that, at present, no one actually knows how effective antidepressants are. Confident declarations about their potency go well beyond the existing evidence.

To get an understanding of the scientific status of antidepressants, we analyzed how much more effective the antidepressants are than inert pills called "placebos." That is, if antidepressants are given to one depressed group and a placebo to another group, how much greater is the recovery of those taking the active drug as compared to those taking the inactive placebo? Generous claims that antidepressants usually produce improvement in about 60 to 70 percent of patients are not infrequent, whereas placebos are said to benefit 25 to 30 percent. If antidepressants were, indeed, so superior to placebos, this would be a persuasive advertisement for the biological approach.

We found 15 major reviews of the antidepressant literature. Surprisingly, even the most positive reviews indicate that 30 to 40 percent of studies show no significant difference in response to drug versus placebo! The reviews indicate overall that one-third of patients do not improve with antidepressant treatment, one-third improve with placebos, and an additional third show a response to medication they would not have attained with placebos. In the most optimistic view of such findings, two-thirds of the cases (placebo responders and those who do not respond to anything) do as well with placebo as with active medication.

We also found two large-scale quantitative evaluations (meta-analyses) integrating the outcomes of multiple studies of antidepressants. They clearly indicated, on the average, quite modest therapeutic power.

We were particularly impressed by the large variation in outcomes of studies conducted at multiple clinical sites or centers. Consider a study that compared the effectiveness of an antidepressant among patients at five different research centers. Although the pooled results demonstrate that the drug was generally more effective than placebo, the results from individual centers reveal much variation. After six weeks of treatment, every one of the six measures of effectiveness showed the antidepressant (imipramine) to be merely equivalent to placebo in two or more of the centers. In two of the settings, a difference favoring the medication was detected on only one of 12 outcome comparisons.

In other words, the pooled, apparently favorable, outcome data conceal that dramatically different results could be obtained as a function of who conducted the study and the specific conditions at each locale. We can only conclude that a good deal of fragility characterized the apparent superiority of drug over placebo. The scientific literature is replete with analogous examples.

Incidentally, we also looked at whether modern studies, which are presumably better protected against bias, use higher doses, and often involve longer treatment periods, show a greater superiority of the antidepressant than did earlier studies. The literature frequently asserts that failures to demonstrate antidepressant superiority are due to such methodological failures as not using high enough doses, and so forth.

We examined this issue in a pool of 16 studies assembled by psychiatrists John Kane and Jeffrey Lieberman in 1984. These studies all compare a standard drug, such as imipramine or amitriptyline, to a newer drug and a placebo. They use clearer diagnostic definitions of depression than did the older studies and also adopt currently accepted standards for dosage levels and treatment duration. When we examined the data, we discovered that the advantage of drug over placebo was modest. Twenty-one percent more of the patients receiving

a drug improved as compared to those on placebo. Actually, most of the studies showed no difference in the percentage of patients significantly improved by drugs. There was no indication that these studies, using more careful methodology, achieved better outcomes than older studies.

Finally, it is crucial to recognize that several studies have established that there is a high rate of relapse among those who have responded positively to an antidepressant but then are taken off treatment. The relapse rate may be 60 percent or more during the first year after treatment cessation. Many studies also show that any benefits of antidepressants wane in a few months, even while the drugs are still being taken. This highlights the complexity of evaluating antidepressants. They may be effective initially, but lose all value over a longer period.

Are Drug Trials Biased?

As we burrowed deeper into the antidepressant literature, we learned that there are also crucial problems in the methodology used to evaluate psychotropic drugs. Most central is the question of whether this methodology properly shields drug trials from bias. Studies have shown that the more open to bias a drug trial is, the greater the apparent superiority of the drug over placebo. So questions about the trustworthiness of a given drug-testing procedure invite skepticism about the results.

The question of potential bias first came to our attention in studies comparing inactive placebos to active drugs. In the classic double-blind design, neither patient nor researcher knows who is receiving drug or placebo. We were struck by the fact that the presumed protection provided by the double-blind design was undermined by the use of placebos that simply do not arouse as many body sensations as do active drugs. Research shows that patients learn to discriminate between drug and placebo largely from body sensations and symptoms.

A substance like imipramine, one of the most frequently studied antidepressants, usually causes clearly defined sensations, such as dry mouth, tremor, sweating, constipation. Inactive placebos used in studies of antidepressants also apparently initiate some body sensations, but they are fewer,

more inconsistent, and less intense as indicated by the fact that they are less often cited by patients as a source of discomfort causing them to drop out of treatment.

Vivid differences between the body sensations of drug and placebo groups could signal to patients as to whether they are receiving an active or inactive agent. Further, they could supply discriminating cues to those responsible for the patients' day-to-day treatment. Nurses, for example, might adopt different attitudes toward patients they identify as being "on" versus "off" active treatment and consequently communicate contrasting expectations.

The Body Of Evidence

This is more than theoretical. Researchers have reported that in a double-blind study of imipramine, it was possible by means of side effects to identify a significant number of the patients taking the active drug. Those patients receiving a placebo have fewer signals (from self and others) indicating they are being actively treated and should be improving. By the same token, patients taking an active drug receive multiple signals that may well amplify potential placebo effects linked to the therapeutic context. Indeed, a doctor's strong belief in the power of the active drug enhances the apparent therapeutic power of the drug or placebo.

Is it possible that a large proportion of the difference in effectiveness often reported between antidepressants and placebos can be explained as a function of body sensation discrepancies? It is conceivable, and fortunately there are research findings that shed light on the matter.

Consider an analysis by New Zealand psychologist Richard Thomson. He reviewed double-blind, placebo-controlled studies of antidepressants completed between 1958 and 1972. Sixty-eight had employed an inert placebo and seven an active one (atropine) that produced a variety of body sensations. The antidepressant had a superior therapeutic effect in 59 percent of the studies using inert placebo—but in only one study (14 percent) using the active placebo. The active placebo eliminated any therapeutic advantage for the antidepressants, apparently because it convinced patients they were getting real medication.

Vivid differences between the body sensations of drug and placebo could signal to patients whether they are receiving an active or inactive agent.

A patient's attitude toward the therapist is just as biological in nature as a patient's response to an antidepressant drug.

How Blind Is Double-Blind?

Our concerns about the effects of inactive placebos on the double-blind design led us to ask just how blind the double-blind really is. By the 1950s reports were already surfacing that for psychoactive drugs, the double-blind design is not as scientifically objective as originally assumed. In 1993 we searched the world literature and found 31 reports in which patients and researchers involved in studies were asked to guess who was receiving the active psychotropic drug and who the placebo. In 28 instances the guesses were significantly better than chance—and at times they were surprisingly accurate. In one double-blind study that called for administering either imipramine, phenelzine, or placebo to depressed patients, 78 percent of patients and 87 percent of psychiatrists correctly distinguished drug from placebo.

One particularly systematic report in the literature involved the administration of alprazolam, imipramine, and placebo over an eight-week period to groups of patients who experienced panic attacks. Halfway through the treatment and also at the end, the physicians and the patients were asked to judge independently whether each patient was receiving an active drug or a placebo. If they thought an active drug was being administered, they had to decide whether it was alprazolam or imipramine. Both physicians (with an 88 percent success rate) and patients (83 percent) substantially exceeded chance in the correctness of their judgments. Furthermore, the physicians could distinguish alprazolam from imipramine significantly better than chance. The researchers concluded that "double-blind studies of these pharmacological treatments for panic disorder are not really 'blind.' "

Yet the vast majority of psychiatric drug efficacy studies have simply *assumed* that the double-blind design is effective; they did not test the blindness by determining whether patients and researchers were able to differentiate drug from placebo.

We take the somewhat radical view that this means most past studies of the efficacy of psychotropic drugs are, to unknown degrees, scientifically untrustworthy. At the least, we can no longer speak with confidence about the true differences in therapeutic power between active psychotropic drugs and placebos. We must suspend judgment until future studies are completed with more adequate controls for the defects of the double-blind paradigm.

Other bothersome questions arose as we scanned the cascade of studies focused on antidepressants. Of particular concern is how unrepresentative the patients are who end up in the clinical trials. There are the usual sampling problems having to do with which persons seek treatment for their discomfort, and, in addition, volunteer as subjects for a study. But there are others. Most prominent is the relatively high proportion of patients who "drop out" before the completion of their treatment programs.

Numerous dropouts occur in response to unpleasant side effects. In many published studies, 35 percent or more of patients fail to complete the research protocol. Various procedures have been developed to deal fairly with the question of how to classify the therapeutic outcomes of dropouts, but none can vitiate the simple fact that the final sample of fully treated patients has often been drastically reduced.

There are still other filters that increase sample selectivity. For example, studies often lose sizable segments of their samples by not including patients who are too depressed to speak, much less participate in a research protocol, or who are too disorganized to participate in formal psychological testing. We also found decisions not to permit particular racial or age groups to be represented in samples or to avoid using persons below a certain educational level. Additionally, researchers typically recruit patients whose depression is not accompanied by any other type of physical or mental disorder, a situation that does not hold for the depressed in the general population.

So we end up wondering about the final survivors in the average drug trial. To what degree do they typify the average individual in real life who seeks treatment? How much can be generalized from a sample made up of the "leftovers" from multiple depleting processes? Are we left with a relatively narrow band of those most willing to conform to the rather rigid demands of the research establishment? Are the survivors those most accepting of a dependent role?

The truth is that there are probably multiple kinds of survivors, depending upon the specific local conditions prevailing where the study was carried out. We would guess that some of the striking differences in results that appear in multicenter drug studies could be traced to specific forms of sampling bias. We do not know how psychologically unique the persons are who get recruited into, and stick with, drug research enterprises. We are not the first to raise this question, but we are relatively more alarmed about the potential implications.

Researcher Motivation And Outcome

We recently conducted an analysis that further demonstrates how drug effectiveness diminishes as the opportunity for bias in research design wanes. This analysis in which a newer antidepressant is compared (under double-blind conditions) with an older, standard antidepressant and a placebo. In such a context the efficacy of the newer drug (which the drug company hopes to introduce) is of central interest to the researcher, and the effectiveness of the older drug of peripheral import. Therefore, if the double-blind is breached (as is likely), there would presumably be less bias to enhance the efficacy of the older drug than occurred in the original trials of that drug.

We predicted that the old drug would appear significantly less powerful in the newer studies than it had in earlier designs, where it was of central interest of the researcher. To test this hypothesis, we located 22 double-blind studies in which newer antidepressants were compared with an older antidepressant drug (usually imipramine) and a placebo. Our meta-analysis revealed, as predicted, that the efficacy rates, based on clinicians' judgments of outcome, were quite modest for the older antidepressants. In fact, they were approximately one-half to one-quarter the average size of the effects reported in earlier studies when the older drug was the only agent appraised.

Let us be very clear as to what this signifies: When researchers were evaluating the antidepressant in a context where they were no longer interested in proving its therapeutic power, there was a dramatic decrease in that apparent power, as compared to an earlier context when they were enthusiastically interested in demonstrating the drug's potency. A change in researcher motivation was enough to change outcome. Obviously this means too that the present double-blind design for testing drug efficacy is exquisitely vulnerable to bias.

Another matter of pertinence to the presumed biological rationale for the efficacy of antidepressants is that no consistent links have been demonstrated between the concentration of drug in blood and its efficacy. Studies have found significant correlations for some drugs, but of low magnitude. Efforts to link plasma levels to therapeutic outcome have been disappointing.

Similarly, few data show a relationship between antidepressant dosage levels and their therapeutic efficacy. That is, large doses of the drug do not necessarily have greater effects than low doses. These inconsistencies are a bit jarring against the context of a biological explanatory framework.

We have led you through a detailed critique of the difficulties and problems that prevail in the body of research testing the power of the antidepressants. We conclude that it would be wise to be relatively modest in claims about their efficacy. Uncertainty and doubt are inescapable.

While we have chosen the research on the antidepressants to illustrate the uncertainties attached to biological treatments of psychological distress, reviews of other classes of psychotropic drugs yield similar findings. After a survey of anti-anxiety drugs, psychologist Ronald Lipman concluded there is little consistent evidence that they help patients with anxiety disorders: "Although it seems natural to assume that the anxiolytic medications would be the most effective psychotropic medications for the treatment of anxiety disorders, the evidence does not support this assumption."

BIOLOGICAL VERSUS PSYCHOLOGICAL?

The faith in the biological approach has been fueled by a great burst of research. Thousands of papers have appeared probing the efficacy of psychotropic drugs. A good deal of basic research has attacked fundamental issues related to the nature of brain functioning in those who display psychopathology. Researchers in these areas are dedicated and often do excellent work. However, in their zeal, in their commitment to the so-called biological, they are at times overcome by their expectations. Their hopes become rigidifying boundaries. Their vocabulary too easily becomes a jargon that camouflages over-simplified assumptions.

A good example of such oversimplification is the way in which the term "biological" is conceptualized. It is too often viewed as a realm distinctly different from

the psychological. Those invested in the biological approach all too often practice the ancient Cartesian distinction between somatic-stuff and soul-stuff. In so doing they depreciate the scientific significance of the phenomena they exile to the soul-stuff category.

But paradoxically, they put a lot of interesting phenomena out of bounds to their prime methodology and restrict themselves to a narrowed domain. For example, if talk therapy is labeled as a "psychological" thing—not biological—this implies that biological research can only hover at the periphery of what psychotherapists do. A sizable block of behavior becomes off limits to the biologically dedicated.

In fact, if we adopt the view that the biological and psychological are equivalent (biological monism), there is no convincing real-versus-unreal differentiation between the so-called psychological and biological. It *all* occurs in tissue and one is not more "real" than the other. A patient's attitude toward the therapist is just as biological in nature as a patient's response to an antidepressant. A response to a placebo is just as biological as a response to an anti-psychotic drug. This may be an obvious point, but it has not yet been incorporated into the world views of either the biologically or psychologically oriented.

Take a look at a few examples in the research literature that highlight the overlap or identity of what is so often split apart. In 1992, psychiatrist Lewis Baxter and colleagues showed that successful psychotherapy of obsessive-compulsive patients results in brain imagery changes equivalent to those produced by successful drug treatment. The brain apparently responds in equivalent ways to both the talk and drug approaches. Even more dramatic is a finding that instilling in the elderly the illusion of being in control of one's surroundings (by putting them in charge of some plants) significantly increased their life span compared to a control group. What could be a clearer demonstration of the biological nature of what is labeled as a psychological expectation than the postponement of death?

Why are we focusing on this historic Cartesian confusion? Because so many who pursue the so-called biological approach are by virtue of their tunnel vision motivated to overlook the psychosocial variables that mediate the administration of such agents as psychotropic drugs and electroconvulsive therapy. They do not permit

themselves to seriously grasp that psychosocial variables are just as biological as a capsule containing an antidepressant. It is the failure to understand this that results in treating placebo effects as if they were extraneous or less of a biological reality than a chemical agent.

PLACEBO EFFECTS

Indeed, placebos have been shown to initiate certain effects usually thought to be reserved for active drugs. For example, placebos clearly show dose-level effects. A larger dose of a placebo will have a greater impact than a lower dose. Placebos can also create addictions. Patients will poignantly declare that they cannot stop taking a particular placebo substance (which they assume is an active drug) because to do so causes them too much distress and discomfort.

Placebos can produce toxic effects such as rashes, apparent memory loss, fever, headaches, and more. These "toxic" effects may be painful and even overwhelming in their intensity. The placebo literature is clear: Placebos are powerful body-altering substances, especially considering the wide range of body systems they can influence.

Actually, the power of the placebo complicates all efforts to test the therapeutic efficacy of psychotropic drugs. When placebos alone can produce positive curative effects in the 40 to 50 percent range (occasionally even up to 70–80 percent), the active drug being tested is hard-pressed to demonstrate its superiority. Even if the active drug exceeds the placebo in potency, the question remains whether the advantage is at least partially due to the superior potential of the active drug itself to mobilize placebo effects because it is an active substance that stirs vivid body sensations. Because it is almost always an inactive substance (sugar pill) that arouses fewer genuine body sensations, the placebo is less convincingly perceived as having therapeutic prowess.

Drug researchers have tried, in vain, to rid themselves of placebo effects, but these effects are forever present and frustrate efforts to demonstrate that psychoactive drugs have an independent "pure" biological impact. This state of affairs dramatically testifies that the labels "psychological" and "biological" refer largely to different per-

---

Administering a therapeutic drug is not simply a medical, biological act. It is also a complex social act, its effectiveness mediated by the patient's expectations.

If a stimulant drug is administered with the deceptive instruction that it is a sedative, it can initiate a physiological response characteristice of a sedative, such as decreased heart rate.

spectives on events that all occur in tissue. At present, it is somewhat illusory to separate the so-called biological and psychological effects of drugs used to treat emotional distress.

The literature is surprisingly full of instances of how social and attitudinal factors modify the effects of active drugs. Anti-psychotic medications are more effective if the patient likes rather than dislikes the physician administering them. An antipsychotic drug is less effective if patients are led to believe they are only taking an inactive placebo. Perhaps even more impressive, if a stimulant drug is administered with the deceptive instruction that it is a sedative, it can initiate a pattern of physiological response, such as decreased heart rate, that is sedative rather than arousing in nature. Such findings reaffirm how fine the line is between social and somatic domains.

What are the practical implications for distressed individuals and their physicians? Administering a drug is not simply a medical (biological) act. It is, in addition, a complex social act whose effectiveness will be mediated by such factors as the patient's expectations of the drug and reactions to the body sensations created by that drug, and the physician's friendliness and degree of personal confidence in the drug's power. Practitioners who dispense psychotropic medications should become thoroughly acquainted with the psychological variables modifying the therapeutic impact of such drugs and tailor their own behavior accordingly. By the same token, distressed people seeking drug treatment should keep in mind that their probability of benefiting may depend in part on whether they choose a practitioner they truly like and respect. And remember this: You are the ultimate arbiter of a drug's efficacy.

How to go about mastering unhappiness, which ranges from "feeling blue" to despairing depression, puzzles everyone. Such popular quick fixes as alcohol, conversion to a new faith, and other splendid distractions have proven only partially helpful. When antidepressant drugs hit the shelves with their seeming scientific aura, they were easily seized upon. Apparently serious unhappiness (depression) could now be chemically neutralized in the way one banishes a toothache.

But the more we learn about the various states of unhappiness, the more we recognize that they are not simply "symptoms" awaiting removal. Depressed feelings have complex origins and functions. In numerous contexts—for example, chronic conflict with a spouse—depression may indicate a realistic appraisal of a troubling problem and motivate a serious effort to devise a solution.

While it is true that deep despair may interfere with sensible problem-solving, the fact is that, more and more, individuals are being instructed to take antidepressants at the earliest signs of depressive distress and this could interfere with the potentially constructive signaling value of such distress. Emotions are feelings full of information. Unhappiness is an emotion, and despite its negativity, should not be classified single-mindedly as a thing to tune out. This in no way implies that one should submit passively to the discomfort of feeling unhappy. Actually, we all learn to experiment with a variety of strategies for making ourselves feel better, but the ultimate aim is long-term effective action rather than a depersonalized "I feel fine."

Seymour Fisher, Ph.D., [was] professor of psychology and coordinator of research training in the Department of Psychiatry and Behavioral Sciences at the University of New York Health Science Center, Syracuse.

Roger P. Greenberg, Ph.D., is professor and head of the Division of Clinical Psychology, as well as director of psychology internship training, at the University of New York Health Science Center, Syracuse.

THE QUEST FOR A CURE

BY MARK NICHOLS

Every few weeks, several teenage girls arrive at Halifax's Queen Elizabeth II Health Sciences Centre to take part in a study that may someday ease the crippling misery of depression. For two nights, the girls, a different group each time, bunk down in a sleep laboratory with tiny electrodes attached to their heads. Through the night, electronic equipment monitors their brain activity as they pass through the various stages of sleep, including the periods of rapid eye movement (REM) when dreaming occurs. Half of the roughly 80 girls who will take part in the study have no family history of depression. The others do—their mothers have had major depression and researchers know that these girls have a 30 percent chance of being victims,

introduced a product called Prozac almost 10 years ago. The first of a new class of drugs that can alleviate depression without the same nasty side effects of many older antidepressants, it profoundly improved the quality of life for millions of people. Thanks to Prozac and drugs like it, says Dr. Sid Kennedy, head of the mood disorders program at Toronto's Clarke Institute of Psychiatry, "depressed people are able to live normal, productive lives in a way that wouldn't have been possible 10 years ago."

Now, drugs that are potentially even better are undergoing tests, while researchers study the intricate universe of the brain in search of clues that could someday banish depression entirely. "Things are really moving quickly,"

New drugs and therapies join the battle against depression

too. Dr. Stan Kutcher, a Dalhousie University psychiatrist who is involved in the study, wants to see whether a feature of sleep in depressed adults—they reach the REM stage faster than others—shows up in the kids. If it does, doctors for the first time would have a way of predicting depression and starting treatment early. Kutcher has been working with troubled youngsters most of his life. "It's a tremendous feeling to be able to help kids get better," he says. "It's a privilege to be let into their lives."

A pioneer in studying and treating adolescent depression, Kutcher is part of an army of medical researchers whose efforts are bringing new drugs, new therapies and new ways of thinking to bear in the war on the debilitating disorder. One of the biggest breakthroughs came in capsule form when Indianapolis's Eli Lilly and Co.

says Dr. Trevor Young, a neuroscientist at McMaster University in Hamilton. "They're really getting close to understanding the biochemical changes that occur in depressed brains."

And doctors are coming closer to the time when they may be able to start treatment, in some cases, even before depression takes hold. After the Dalhousie researchers finish their current series of tests early next year, they will keep track of their young subjects for five years to see whether their REM sleep patterns pinpoint which of them will become depressed. If they do, then doctors in the future may be able to test children from families with a history of depression, and identify potential victims. One possibility, says Kutcher, would be to begin treating those children with antidepressants even before the first bout of depression occurred—in the hope that it never will.

Underpinning the new wave of research is a quiet revolution that has transformed thinking about depression over the past two decades. As recently as in the 1960s, when Sigmund Freud's psychoanalytic philosophy was still pervasive, depression and most other forms of mental illness were regarded as the consequences of emotional turmoil in childhood. Now, scientists have clear evidence that inherited flaws in the brain's biochemistry are to blame for many mental problems, including manic-depressive illness—with its violent swings between depressive lows and manic highs—and, according to some experts, recurring severe depression. Beyond that, many experts think that damaging events in childhood-sexual or physical abuse, poisoned parental relationships and other blows to the child's psyche—may cause depression later by disrupting development of crucial chemical pathways in the brain. "Losses early in life," says Dr. Jane Garland, director of the mood and anxiety clinic at the British Columbia Children's Hospital in Vancouver, "can raise the brain's level of stress hormones that are associated with depression."

When the dark curtain of depression descends, today's victims have access to quick and effective treatment. Short-term "talk therapies" now in use can help haul a patient out of depression in as little as four months—as opposed to years on a psychoanalyst's couch. The purpose of such therapy, says Dr. Marie Corral, a psychiatrist at the British Columbia Women's Hospital in Vancouver, is "to deal with the skewed thinking that develops when a person has been depressed for a long time." The most widely used methods: interpersonal therapy, which focuses on specific people-related problems, and cognitive therapy, which tries to counter the feelings of worthlessness and hopelessness that plague depressed people. "We try to show the patient that much of this thinking may be unfounded," says Zindel Segal, a Toronto psychologist.

But along with the new approaches to dealing with depression, a treatment introduced nearly 60 years ago that has earned a grim public image-electroconvulsive therapy (ECT)—is still a mainstay. Popularly known as shock treatment, it remains "one of our most potent forms of therapy" for severely depressed patients who do not respond to other treatment, says Dr. David Goldbloom, chief of staff at Toronto's Clarke Institute. ECT is routinely used every year on thousands of depressed Canadians, including older patients who cannot tolerate some of the side-effects of drug therapies.

ECT's bad reputation owes much to the 1975 movie *One Flew over the Cuckoo's Nest*, in which staff members of a mental institution punish a rebellious patient, played by Jack Nicholson, with repeated ECT sessions. Patients *did* endure painful ordeals in the early days of ECT when larger electrical shocks were used to induce a limb-shaking seizure in unanesthetized patients. Electroconvulsive

treatment is gentler now. Doctors administer a muscle relaxant and a general anesthetic before subjecting the patient's brain to the amount of current needed to light a 60-watt bulb for one second.

ECT's aftereffects can include painful headaches lasting half an hour or so, and some memory loss. ECT does its job, they add, by altering the brain's electrical and chemical activity. The therapy has some bitter opponents, who claim that it can cause lasting memory loss and impair other brain functions, such as concentration. "ECT damages people's brains—that's really the whole point of it," says Wendy Funk, a 41-year-old Cranbrook, B.C., housewife. Funk says that after receiving electroconvulsive therapy for depression in 1989 and 1990, she lost virtually all memory—she could not recall even her own name or that she was married and had two children.

Meanwhile, for the approximately 70 per cent of patients who respond to them, Prozac and the family of drugs it spawned—Paxil, Zoloft, Luvox and Serzone—are making life far more bearable. Collectively, the drugs are known as SSRIs (for selective serotonin reuptake inhibitors) because they increase the brain's supply of the chemical messenger serotonin. The SSRIs have foes: the Internet bristles with accusations that the drugs can cause panic attacks, aggressive behavior and suicidal tendencies. But most doctors have nothing but praise for the drugs. It's not that they are better than their predecessors at relieving depression—most physicians say they are not.

But SSRIs are easier to live with than some older antidepressants, which often caused dry mouth, daytime sleepiness, constipation, vision problems and other unpleasant side effects. "The SSRIs are better tolerated," says Dr. Russell Joffe, dean of health sciences at McMaster University, "and it is much harder to overdose on them than the older drugs"—a vital consideration in treating people who may be at risk from suicide. The SSRIs can have side effects of their own, including insomnia and a diminished interest in sex that sometimes persuade patients to stop taking them. "You just don't get sexually aroused," says Giselle, a 41-year-old Manitoba resident who requested anonymity. "There's just nothing there."

Another problem with the SSRIs is that patients usually have to take them for three weeks or more before they start to work. The reason: when an SSRI increases the flow of serotonin in the brain, the thermostat-like mechanism that normally controls the flow of the chemical shuts down—and then takes three to six weeks to adapt and allow serotonin to flow again. "If you have a severely depressed patient who may be thinking about suicide," says Dr. Pierre Blier, a professor of psychiatry at Montreal's McGill University, "telling him he may have to wait that long for relief isn't good enough."

After studying the problem exhaustively, Blier and another McGill psychiatrist, Dr. Claude deMontigny, proposed in 1993 that the SSRIs would probably take effect more rapidly if used in conjunction with another drug that could block the brain mechanism causing the delay. Such a drug, a hypertension medication called Pindolol, existed. And the following year, a Spanish physician tried the combination—and found that it worked. Since then, studies have shown that the Pindolol-SSRI combination can cut the waiting time for SSRIs to take effect to about 10 days. Working with that knowledge, several major drug companies now are trying to develop a new generation of fast-acting SSRIs.

Meanwhile, efforts to lay bare the roots of depression are being pursued by a number of Canadian research teams:

• While most antidepressants concentrate on two of the brain's chemical messengers—serotonin and noradrenaline—a research team at the University of Alberta in Edmonton headed by neurochemist Glen Baker is studying a substance called GABA. Another of the brain's neurotransmitters, GABA appears to play a role in quelling the panic attacks that often accompany depression. GABA (for gamma-aminobutyric acid) seems to work in the brain by preventing selected nerve cells from sending signals down the line. To find out more, Baker's team is

tify which defective chemical pathways make that happen. "Once we know more about these things," says Young, "we may be able to correct the problems with drugs."

• In Toronto, a Clarke Institute team co-headed by psychiatrists Sid Kennedy and Franco Vaccarino is using high-tech imaging equipment to look at brain functioning before and after treatment with antidepressants. Images produced by a PET scan machine show that, in depressed people, some parts of the brain's pre-frontal region—an area associated with emotion—are less active than normal. Surprisingly, when antidepressant drugs start acting on the brain, those areas be come even *less* active. Kennedy thinks that may be because in depression, the brain deliberately dampens down pre-frontal activity to cope with high levels of stress, and antidepressants may help the process by reducing activity even further. Kennedy hopes next to study brains in people who had remained well on antidepressants for at least a year, and thinks "we may find that by then activity in the pre-frontal areas has returned to something normal"—meaning that the brain's overstressed condition has been corrected.

Most doctors praise the Prozac-like drugs

studying the action of two older antidepressants that are used to treat panic, imipramine and phenelzine. They want to find out whether the drugs work by increasing GABA activity in the brain. A possible payoff: a new class of drugs that could some day stem panic by boosting the flow of GABA in the brain.

• At McMaster, Young's team is focusing on manic-depressive illness in an effort to discover which brain chemicals are involved. One approach to the puzzle involves dosing rats—which have many of the same genes as humans—with antidepressants or mood stabilizers and examining tissue samples to see which genes are activated. Eventually, Young hopes to learn more about the signalling process inside the brain that can go awry and lead to depression or mania. He also wants to iden-

The best antidepressants can banish depression—but they do not necessarily protect patients from relapses. Susan Boning, who organizes volunteer services for the Society for Depression and Manic Depression of Manitoba at its Winnipeg headquarters, had been taking Prozac for two years when she felt her mood "dipping" last March. Her condition worsened to the point where she made what she calls "a suicidal gesture" by drinking half a bottle of rum and passing out on her living-room floor. Boning, 37, has stopped taking Prozac and has turned to three other drugs, including Serzone. Boning's experience, like countless others, shows that while medical science is making rapid progress in treating depression, for many in the remorseless grip of the disease it is still not fast enough.

New Treatments for Schizophrenia—Part I

The first major revolution in the treatment of schizophrenia occurred in the 1950s, when effective antipsychotic drugs were introduced. By relieving hallucinations and delusions and suppressing bizarre behavior, they allowed most schizophrenic patients to leave mental hospitals. But the drugs had many limitations and side effects, and most people with schizophrenia remained severely disabled. Along with the opportunities for psychological and social rehabilitation created by the emptying of mental hospitals came many serious problems, including homelessness, suicide, and substance abuse. In the last ten years, pharmacologists and psychiatrists have introduced new antipsychotic drugs that work in different ways and seem to be more effective than the older medications. At the same time, 40 years of experience are giving people with schizophrenia and the people who care for them a better sense of how to seize the opportunities and solve the problems created by community living.

Older drug treatments

Drugs of the first generation suppressed so-called positive symptoms (hallucinations, delusions, disordered thinking) but had less effect on the more persistent negative symptoms—lack of initiative, limited speech, social withdrawal, and emotional unresponsiveness. Even when they took their drugs faithfully, schizophrenic patients had difficulty caring for themselves, finding and keeping work, and maintaining a social life. The drugs themselves had many side effects, including drowsiness, constipation, dry mouth, blurred vision and dizziness from postural hypotension (a rush of the blood to the feet on standing). By raising levels of the hormone prolactin, the drugs could cause overproduction of breast milk, menstrual irregularities, and possibly infertility in women. They could also interfere with sexual functioning in both sexes.

An even more serious problem was abnormal involuntary body movements. Some of these movements, known as extrapyramidal symptoms (a reference to the brain system involved), occur early in the course of treatment: acute dystonia (muscle spasms or cramps); akathisia ("restless legs," pacing or fidgeting), and parkinsonism (tremors, slow and stiff movements, rigid facial expression, abnormal posture and shuffling gait resembling Parkinson's disease). These symptoms, especially akathisia, make many patients so uncomfortable that they refuse to take the drugs. Relief is provided by lowering the dose or by adding antiparkinsonian medications, but these unfortunately have side effects of their own. Controlling the abnormal body movements can be difficult.

Extrapyramidal symptoms often fade after a few months, but they may be succeeded by tardive ("belated") dyskinesia, a more persistent and disabling condition that includes facial tics, tongue rolling, and spasmodic and writhing motions of the arms, legs, and neck. About a third of patients treated for long periods with conventional drugs develop some signs of tardive dyskinesia. Usually the symptoms are minor, but they can be difficult and sometimes seemingly impossible to treat. In a small proportion of patients, they are disfiguring or socially incapacitating.

New drugs

The new drugs, already in widespread use, are still sometimes called "atypical," a term that may soon become obsolete. In general, they have fewer neurological side effects than the older drugs and are probably more helpful for negative symptoms and negative deficiencies. They may also be more effective in reducing depression and preventing relapse. Their higher present cost, research suggests, is probably made up by savings from lower rates of hospitalization and fewer visits to emergency rooms and doctors' offices. Some of these drugs will be still more valuable when they become available in depot ("deposit") form for slow absorption by intramuscular injection once a month—a technique that can

From *The Harvard Mental Health Letter*, April 1998, pp. 1-3. © 1998 by the President and Fellows of Harvard College. Reprinted by permission.

be helpful when patients will not consistently take a daily dose on their own.

Clozapine (Clozaril) is the first substantial qualitative advance in the drug treatment of schizophrenia since the 1950s. It has proved moderately but distinctly superior to conventional drugs in 14 controlled studies; some patients do so well that they seem almost to have fully recovered. Clozapine may improve some negative symptoms and relieve deficiencies in memory and attention. It is the only drug that has been proved effective for patients who do not respond to the older drugs. It does not raise prolactin levels. It has little effect on body movements and may even improve symptoms of tardive dyskinesia in some patients. Unfortunately, clozapine has many other side effects, including dizziness, drowsiness, drooling, lowered blood pressure, weight gain, and occasionally seizures. The greatest danger is agranulocytosis, a potentially deadly decrease in the capacity to manufacture white blood cells. With careful monitoring, it occurs in less than 1% of patients and can be corrected if it is discovered early. The death rate has been very low—about one in 10,000—but the need for periodic blood testing makes clozapine expensive and cumbersome to use.

Risperidone (Risperdal), already one of the most widely prescribed antipsychotic drugs, has some of the virtues of clozapine without the risk of agranulocytosis. Like clozapine, it may be useful in the treatment of positive and negative symptoms as well as thinking deficiencies. Its most common side effects are dizziness, fatigue, a dry mouth, a rapid heart beat, and lowered blood pressure. Unlike clozapine, risperidone raises prolactin levels and has some modest effect on body movements.

Olanzapine (Zyprexa) has recently outperformed the traditional medication haloperidol (Haldol) in two large controlled experiments. Like risperidone, it appears to be effective for both positive and negative symptoms, and researchers are now studying its effects on thinking. Patients often prefer it because of its unusually low rate of side effects (the most common are drowsiness, constipation, and weight gain). It affects body movements slightly, does not significantly raise prolactin levels, and is unlikely to cause seizures. Little is known about its long-term effectiveness.

Quetiapine (Seroquel) is useful for both positive and negative symptoms and has few significant side effects. It does not raise prolactin levels and has almost no effect on body movements. Some animals given high doses of quetiapine have developed cataracts. Although it is not clear that this can occur in human beings at therapeutic doses, the manufacturer recommends regular eye examinations for patients taking the drug.

Ziprasidone (Zeldox) is expected to be available soon as a prescription drug. It has little effect on sexual functions or body movements and does not cause weight gain. The main side effects are headache, nausea, constipation, and insomnia.

The development of new antipsychotic drugs has been stimulated by advances in our knowledge of the brain's chemical transmitters and the receptor sites on neurons where they lodge to regulate the passage of nerve impulses. All the older drugs relieve positive symptoms by preventing the neurotransmitter dopamine from acting at D2 nerve receptors in the limbic region of the brain, which governs emotional responses. They disturb body movements by affecting the same type of receptor in the extrapyramidal system. The new drugs work differently, each in its own way. Some block D2 receptors chiefly in the limbic region. Others may act at D1, D3, or D4 receptors and influence patterns of interaction among receptors for other transmitters, including norepinephrine, serotonin, and glutamate. Some authorities believe that malfunctioning of neurotransmitter systems in the prefrontal cortex, the seat of planning and social judgment, is the ultimate cause of negative schizophrenic symptoms. Low activity in that region may cause positive symptoms by weakening inhibitions against excessive dopamine activity in the limbic system. New drugs that seem to relieve negative symptoms may be acting indirectly on the prefrontal region by altering the balance of neurotransmitters elsewhere in the brain. Their relative lack of extrapyramidal activity presumably explains why they cause fewer abnormal body movements.

When schizophrenic symptoms first appear, drug treatment is often put off because the nature of the illness is unclear or because the patient cannot be persuaded to seek help. A year's delay between the first psychotic symptoms and the first use of antipsychotic drugs is common. Recent studies suggest that delay makes for slower recovery from the first episode and a poorer long-term prognosis. The alienating and isolating effects of prolonged psychotic episodes make it increasingly difficult to recover a normal personal and social life after each one. And each psychotic episode may heighten the brain's vulnerability to further psychosis, in the same way that an epileptic seizure can further irritate its focus (originating point) in the brain and raise the likelihood of later seizures. For these reasons, many authorities are now putting special emphasis on the need to detect and treat schizophrenia early. Psychiatrists have often been reluctant to prescribe antipsychotic drugs immediately because of their concern about side effects, but the new drugs should change that attitude.

Cognitive and behavioral support

Although most schizophrenic patients need antipsychotic medication to benefit from any other help, the drugs by themselves are far from sufficient; psychiatric care and social rehabilitation are just as important. Depending on the severity of their symptoms, patients may need help in understanding the illness, taking their drugs regularly, responding to signs of relapse, securing housing, jobs, and medical care, even caring for their basic physical needs and coping with everyday social situations and personal relations.

Behavioral techniques, including social skills training, are one widely used form of help. Schizophrenic patients are coached, prompted and corrected as they rehearse behavior and observe others as models. They are shown how to cash checks, prepare for interviews, sustain a conversation, and even clean and dress themselves. Research has shown that social skills training can be effective. In two recent meta-analyses (combined statistical analyses of many studies), this training has been found to reduce relapse rates for up to a year. But the results are difficult to transfer to real life, and they often dissipate over time.

Some mental health professionals are now trying to teach what could be called thinking and emotional skills. Patients are lectured and coached on how to monitor their thoughts, overcome tendencies to withdraw, paranoia, and loss of concentration, and cope with guilt, sadness, feelings of humiliation, and aggressive impulses. They may also work to improve memory, planning, and decision-making. A cognitive-behavioral program for hospitalized patients, integrated psychological therapy, uses word problems and games to practice conversation and the interpretation of social situations. Cognitive training can be time-consuming and expensive, and there is some question whether its effects carry over into daily life. Some believe that thinking exercises have limited potential for the damaged brains of schizophrenic patients. In one recent study, patients given integrated psychological therapy showed improvement on tests of attention after 18 months, but their capacity for complex thinking remained low, and they still lacked the skills needed for independent living.

Another cognitive approach emphasizes the content of thoughts rather than the process of thinking. Patients are taught to evaluate and correct their delusional ideas and hallucinatory perceptions. The therapist finds out when the most disabling psychotic symptoms occur, how seriously they interfere with the patient's life, and how the patient copes with them. The patient practices these methods and is helped to develop new ones. What little evidence there is suggests that this technique may be somewhat effective for delusions but does not affect hallucinations or the more common negative symptoms.

FOR FURTHER READING

Patricia Backlar. The Family Face of Schizophrenia: Practical Counsel from America's Leading Experts. *New York: Jeremy P. Tarcher/Putnam, 1994.*

John Michael Kane. Schizophrenia. *New England Journal of Medicine 334:34–41 (January 4, 1996).*

Kim T. Mueser and Susan Gingerich. Coping With Schizophrenia: A Guide for Families. *Oakland, CA: New Harbinger Publications, 1994.*

David L. Penn and Kim T. Mueser. Research update on the psychosocial treatment of schizophrenia. *American Journal of Psychiatry 153:607–617 (May 1996).*

This glossary of psychology terms is included to provide you with a convenient and ready reference as you encounter general terms in your study of psychology and personal growth and behavior that are unfamiliar or require a review. It is not intended to be comprehensive, but taken together with the many definitions included in the articles themselves, it should prove to be quite useful.

abnormal behavior Behavior that contributes to maladaptiveness; is considered deviant by the culture; or that leads to personal psychological distress.

absolute threshold The minimum amount of physical energy required to produce a sensation.

accommodation Process in cognitive development; involves altering or reorganizing the mental picture to make room for a new experience or idea.

acculturation The process of becoming part of a new cultural environment.

acetylcholine A neurotransmitter involved in memory.

achievement drive The need to attain self-esteem, success, or status. Society's expectations strongly influence the achievement motive.

achievement style The way people behave in achievement situations; achievement styles include the direct, instrumental, and relational styles.

acquired immune deficiency syndrome (AIDS) A fatal disease of the immune system.

acquisition In conditioning, forming associations in first learning a task.

actor-observer bias Tendency to attribute the behavior of other people to internal causes and our own behavior to external causes.

acupuncture Oriental practice involving the insertion of needles into the body to control pain.

adaptation The process of responding to changes in the environment by altering responses to keep a person's behavior appropriate to environmental demands.

adjustment How we react to stress; some change that we make in response to the demands placed upon us.

adrenal glands Endocrine glands involved in stress and energy regulation.

adrenaline A hormone produced by the adrenal glands that is involved in physiological arousal; adrenaline is also called epinephrine.

affective flattening Individuals with schizophrenia who do not exhibit any emotional arousal.

aggression Behavior intended to harm another member of the same species.

agoraphobia Anxiety disorder in which an individual is excessively afraid of places or situations from which it would be difficult or embarrassing to escape.

alarm reaction The first stage of Hans Selye's general adaptation syndrome. The alarm reaction is the immediate response to stress; adrenaline is released and digestion slows. The alarm reaction prepares the body for an emergency.

all-or-none law The principle that states that a neuron only fires when a stimulus is above a certain minimum strength (threshold), and when it fires, it does so at full strength.

alogia Individuals with schizophrenia that show a reduction in speech.

alpha Brain-wave activity that indicates that a person is relaxed and resting quietly; 8–12 Hz.

altered state of consciousness (ASC) A state of consciousness in which there is a redirection of attention, a change in the aspects of the world that occupy a person's thoughts, and a change in the stimuli to which a person responds.

ambivalent attachment Type of infant-parent attachment in which the infant seeks contact but resists once the contact is made.

amphetamine A strong stimulant; increases arousal of the central nervous system.

amygdala A part of the limbic system involved in fear, aggression, and other social behaviors.

anal stage Psychosexual stage during which, according to Sigmund Freud, the child experiences the first restrictions on his or her impulses.

analytical psychology The personality theory of Carl Jung.

anorexia nervosa Eating disorder in which an individual becomes severely underweight because of self-imposed restrictions on eating.

antisocial personality disorder Personality disorder in which individuals who engage in antisocial behavior experience no guilt or anxiety about their actions; sometimes called sociopathy or psychopathy.

anxiety disorder Fairly long-lasting disruption of a person's ability to deal with stress; often accompanied by feelings of fear and apprehension.

applied psychology The area of psychology that is most immediately concerned with helping to solve practical problems; includes clinical and counseling psychology as well as industrial, environmental, and legal psychology.

approach-approach conflict When we are attracted to two equally desirable goals that are incompatible.

approach-avoidance conflict When we are faced with a single goal that has positive and negative aspects.

aptitude test Any test designed to predict what a person with the proper training can accomplish in the future.

archetypes In Carl Jung's personality theory, unconscious universal ideas shared by all humans.

arousal theory Theory that focuses on the energy (arousal) aspect of motivation; it states that we are motivated to initiate behaviors that help to regulate overall arousal level.

asocial phase Phase in attachment development in which the neonate does not distinguish people from objects.

assertiveness training Training that helps individuals stand up for their rights while not denying rights of other people.

assimilation Process in cognitive development; occurs when something new is taken into the child's mental picture.

associationism A theory of learning suggesting that once two stimuli are presented together, one of them will remind a person of the other. Ideas are learned by association with sensory experiences and are not innate.

attachment Process in which the individual shows behaviors that promote proximity with a specific object or person.

attention Process of focusing on particular stimuli in the environment.

attention deficit disorder Hyperactivity; inability to concentrate.

attitude Learned disposition that actively guides us toward specific behaviors; attitudes consist of feelings, beliefs, and behavioral tendencies.

attribution The cognitive process of determining the motives of someone's behavior, and whether they are internal or external.

autism A personality disorder in which a child does not respond socially to people.

autokinetic effect Perception of movement of a stationary spot of light in a darkened room.

autonomic nervous system The part of the peripheral nervous system that carries messages from the central nervous system to the endocrine glands, the smooth muscles controlling the heart, and the primarily involuntary muscles controlling internal processes; includes the sympathetic and parasympathetic nervous systems.

aversion therapy A counterconditioning therapy in which unwanted responses are paired with unpleasant consequences.

avoidance conditioning Learning situation in which a subject avoids a stimulus by learning to respond appropriately before the stimulus begins.

avoidant attachment Type of infant-parent attachment in which the infant avoids the parent.

avolition Individuals with schizophrenia who lack motivation to follow through on an activity.

backward conditioning A procedure in classical conditioning in which the US is presented and terminated before the termination of the CS; very ineffective procedure.

basic research Research conducted to obtain information for its own sake.

behavior Anything you do or think, including various bodily reactions. Behavior includes physical and mental responses.

behavior genetics How genes influence behavior.

behavior modification Another term for behavior therapy; the modification of behavior through psychological techniques; often the application of conditioning principles to alter behavior.

behaviorism The school of thought founded by John Watson; it studied only observable behavior.

belongingness and love needs Third level of motives in Maslow's hierarchy; includes love and affection, friends, and social contact.

biological motives Motives that have a definite physiological basis and are biologically necessary for survival of the individual or species.

biological response system Systems of the body that are important in behavioral responding; includes the senses, muscles, endocrine system, and the nervous system.

biological therapy Treatment of behavior problems through biological techniques; major biological therapies include drug therapy, psychosurgery, and electroconvulsive therapy.

bipolar disorder Mood disorder characterized by extreme mood swings from sad depression to joyful mania; sometimes called manic-depression.

blinding technique In an experiment, a control for bias in which the assignment of a subject to the experimental or control group is unknown to the subject or experimenter or both (a double-blind experiment).

body dysmorphic disorder Somatoform disorder characterized by a preoccupation with an imaginary defect in the physical appearance of a physically healthy person.

body language Communication through position and movement of the body.

bottom-up processing The psychoanalytic process of understanding communication by listening to words, then interpreting phrases, and finally understanding ideas.

brief psychodynamic therapy A therapy developed for individuals with strong egos to resolve a core conflict.

bulimia nervosa Eating disorder in which an individual eats large amounts of calorie-rich food in a short time and then purges the food by vomiting or using laxatives.

bystander effect Phenomenon in an emergency situation in which a person is more likely to help when alone than when in a group of people.

California Psychological Inventory (CPI) An objective personality test used to study normal populations.

Cannon-Bard theory of emotion Theory of emotion that states that the emotional feeling and the physiological arousal occur at the same time.

cardinal traits In Gordon Allport's personality theory, the traits of an individual that are so dominant that they are expressed in everything the person does; few people possess cardinal traits.

catatonic schizophrenia A type of schizophrenia that is characterized by periods of complete immobility and the apparent absence of will to move or speak.

causal attribution Process of determining whether a person's behavior is due to internal or external motives.

central nervous system The part of the human nervous system that interprets and stores messages from the sense organs, decides what behavior to exhibit, and sends appropriate messages to the muscles and glands; includes the brain and spinal cord.

central tendency In statistics, measures of central tendency give a number that represents the entire group or sample.

central traits In Gordon Allport's personality theory, the traits of an individual that form the core of the personality; they are developed through experience.

cerebellum The part of the hindbrain that is involved in balance and muscle coordination.

cerebral cortex The outermost layer of the cerebrum of the brain where higher mental functions occur. The cerebral cortex is divided into sections, or lobes, which control various activities.

cerebrum (cerebral hemisphere) Largest part of the forebrain involved in cognitive functions; the cerebrum consists of two hemispheres connected by the corpus callosum.

chromosome Bodies in the cell nucleus that contain the genes.

chunking Process of combining stimuli in order to increase memory capacity.

classical conditioning The form of learning in which a stimulus is associated with another stimulus that causes a particular response. Sometimes called Pavlovian conditioning or respondent conditioning.

clinical psychology Subfield in which psychologists assess psychological problems and treat people with behavior problems using psychological techniques (called psychotherapy).

cognition Mental processes, such as perception, attention, memory, language, thinking, and problem solving; cognition involves the acquisition, storage, retrieval, and utilization of knowledge.

cognitive behavior therapy A form of behavior therapy that identifies self-defeating attitudes and thoughts in a subject, and then helps the subject to replace these with positive, supportive thoughts.

cognitive development Changes over time in mental processes such as thinking, memory, language, and problem solving.

cognitive dissonance Leon Festinger's theory of attitude change that states that, when people hold two psychologically inconsistent ideas, they experience tension that forces them to reconcile the conflicting ideas.

cognitive expectancy The condition in which an individual learns that certain behaviors lead to particular goals; cognitive expectancy motivates the individual to exhibit goal-directed behaviors.

cognitive learning Type of learning that theorizes that the learner utilizes cognitive structures in memory to make decisions about behaviors.

cognitive psychology The area of psychology that includes the study of mental activities involved in perception, memory, language, thought, and problem solving.

cognitive restructuring The modification of the client's thoughts and perceptions that are contributing to his or her maladjustments.

cognitive therapy Therapy developed by Aaron Beck in which an individual's negative, self-defeating thoughts are restructured in a positive way.

cognitive-motivational-relational theory of emotion A theory of emotion proposed by Richard Lazarus that includes cognitive appraisal, motivational goals, and relationships between an individual and the environment.

collective unconscious Carl Jung's representation of the thoughts shared by all humans.

collectivistic cultures Cultures in which the greatest emphasis is on the loyalty of each individual to the group.

comparative psychology Subfield in which experimental psychologists study and compare the behavior of different species of animals.

compulsions Rituals performed excessively such as checking doors or washing hands to reduce anxiety.

concept formation (concept learning) The development of the ability to respond to common features of categories of objects or events.

concrete operations period Stage in cognitive development; from 7 to 11 years, the time in which the child's ability to solve problems with reasoning greatly increases.

conditioned response (CR) The response or behavior that occurs when the conditioned stimulus is presented (after the CS has been associated with the US).

conditioned stimulus (CS) An originally neutral stimulus that is associated with an unconditioned stimulus and takes on the latter's capability of eliciting a particular reaction.

conditioned taste aversion (CTA) An aversion to particular tastes associated with stomach distress; usually considered a unique form of classical conditioning because of the extremely long interstimulus intervals involved.

conditioning A term applied to two types of learning (classical and operant). Conditioning refers to the scientific aspect of the type of learning.

conflict Situation that occurs when we experience incompatible demands or desires; the outcome when one individual or group perceives that another individual or group has caused or will cause harm.

conformity Type of social influence in which an individual changes his or her behavior to fit social norms or expectations.

connectionism Recent approach to problem solving; the development of neural connections allows us to think and solve problems.

conscientiousness The dimension in the five-factor personality theory that includes traits such as practical, cautious, serious, reliable, careful, and ambitious; also called dependability.

conscious Being aware of experiencing sensations, thoughts, and feelings at any given point in time.

conscious mind In Sigmund Freud's psychoanalytic theory of personality, the part of personality that we are aware of in everyday life.

consciousness The processing of information at various levels of awareness; state in which a person is aware of sensations, thoughts, and feelings.

consensus In causal attribution, the extent to which other people react as the subject does in a particular situation.

conservation The ability to recognize that something stays the same even if it takes on a different form; Piaget tested conservation of mass, number, length, and volume.

consistency In causal attribution, the extent to which the subject always behaves in the same way in a situation.

consolidation The biological neural process of making memories permanent; possibly short-term memory is electrically coded and long-term memory is chemically coded.

contingency model A theory that specific types of situations need particular types of leaders.

continuum of preparedness Martin Seligman's proposal that animals are biologically prepared to learn certain responses more readily than they are prepared to learn others.

control group Subjects in an experiment who do not receive the independent variable; the control group determines the effectiveness of the independent variable.

conventional morality Level II in Lawrence Kohlberg's theory, in which moral reasoning is based on conformity and social standards.

convergence Binocular depth cue in which we detect distance by interpreting the kinesthetic sensations produced by the muscles of the eyeballs.

conversion disorder Somatoform disorder in which a person displays obvious disturbance in the nervous system without a physical basis for the problem.

correlation Statistical technique to determine the degree of relationship that exists between two variables.

counterconditioning A behavior therapy in which an unwanted response is replaced by conditioning a new response that is incompatible with it.

creativity A process of coming up with new or unusual responses to familiar circumstances.

critical period hypothesis Period of time during development in which particular learning or experiences normally occur; if learning does not occur, the individual has a difficult time learning it later.

culture-bound The idea that a test's usefulness is limited to the culture in which it was written and utilized.

cumulative response curve Graphed curve that results when responses for a subject are added to one another over time; if subjects respond once every 5 minutes, they will have a cumulative response curve value of 12 after an hour.

curiosity motive Motive that causes the individual to seek out a certain amount of novelty.

cyclothymia disorder A moderately severe problem with numerous periods of hypomanic episodes and depressive symptoms.

death instinct (also called Thanatos) Freud's term for an instinct that is destructive to the individual or species; aggression is a major expression of death instinct.

decay Theory of forgetting in which sensory impressions leave memory traces that fade away with time.

defense mechanisms Psychological techniques to help protect ourselves from stress and anxiety, to resolve conflicts, and to preserve our self-esteem.

delayed conditioning A procedure in classical conditioning in which the presentation of the CS precedes the onset of the US and the termination of the CS is delayed until the US is presented; most effective procedure.

delusion The holding of obviously false beliefs; for example, imagining someone is trying to kill you.

dependent variable In psychology, the behavior or response that is measured; it is dependent on the independent variable.

depersonalization disorder Dissociative disorder in which the individual escapes from his or her own personality by believing that he or she does not exist or that his or her environment is not real.

depolarization Any change in which the internal electrical charge becomes more positive.

depression A temporary emotional state that normal individuals experience or a persistent state that may be considered a psychological disorder. Characterized by sadness and low self-esteem.

descriptive statistics Techniques that help summarize large amounts of data information.

developmental psychology Study of physical and mental growth and behavioral changes in individuals from conception to death.

Diagnostic and Statistic Manual of Mental Disorders (DSM) Published by the American Psychiatric Association in 1952, and revised in 1968, 1980, 1987, and 1994, this manual was provided to develop a set of diagnoses of abnormal behavior patterns.

diffusion of responsibility Finding that groups tend to inhibit helping behavior; responsibility is shared equally by members of the group so that no one individual feels a strong commitment.

disorganized schizophrenia A type of schizophrenia that is characterized by a severe personality disintegration; the individual often displays bizarre behavior.

displacement Defense mechanism by which the individual directs his or her aggression or hostility toward a person or object other than the one it should be directed toward; in Freud's dream theory, the process of reassigning emotional feelings from one object to another one.

dissociative disorder Psychological disorder that involves a disturbance in the memory, consciousness, or identity of an individual; types include multiple personality disorder, depersonalization disorder, psychogenic amnesia, and psychogenic fugue.

dissociative fugue Individuals who have lost their memory, relocated to a new geographical area, and started a new life as someone else.

dissociative identity disorder (multiple personality disorder) Dissociative disorder in which several personalities are present in the same individual.

distinctiveness In causal attribution, the extent to which the subject reacts the same way in other situations.

Down syndrome Form of mental retardation caused by having three number 21 chromosomes (trisomy 21).

dream analysis Psychoanalytic technique in which a patient's dreams are reviewed and analyzed to discover true feelings.

drive Motivational concept used to describe the internal forces that push an organism toward a goal; sometimes identified as psychological arousal arising from a physiological need.

dyssomnia Sleep disorder in which the chief symptom is a disturbance in the amount and quality of sleep; they include insomnia and hypersomnia.

dysthymic disorder Mood disorder in which the person suffers moderate depression much of the time for at least two years.

ego Sigmund Freud's term for an individual's sense of reality.

egocentric Seeing the world only from your perspective.

eidetic imagery Photographic memory; ability to recall great detail accurately after briefly viewing something.

Electra complex The Freudian idea that the young girl feels inferior to boys because she lacks a penis.

electroconvulsive therapy (ECT) A type of biological therapy in which electricity is applied to the brain in order to relieve severe depression.

emotion A response to a stimulus that involves physiological arousal, subjective feeling, cognitive interpretation, and overt behavior.

empiricism The view that behavior is learned through experience.

encoding The process of putting information into the memory system.

encounter group As in a sensitivity training group, a therapy where people become aware of themselves in meeting others.

endorphins Several neuropeptides that function as neurotransmitters. The opiate-like endorphins are involved in pain, reinforcement, and memory.

engineering psychology Area of psychology that is concerned with how work is performed, design of equipment, and work environment; also called human factors psychology.

engram The physical memory trace or neural circuit that holds memory; also called memory trace.

episodic memory Highest memory system; includes information about personal experiences.

Eros Sigmund Freud's term for an instinct that helps the individual or species survive; also called life instinct.

esteem needs Fourth level of motives in Abraham Maslow's hierarchy; includes high evaluation of oneself, self-respect, self-esteem, and respect of others.

eustress Stress that results from pleasant and satisfying experiences; earning a high grade or achieving success produces eustress.

excitement phase First phase in the human sexual response cycle; the beginning of sexual arousal.

experimental group Subjects in an experiment who receive the independent variable.

experimental psychology Subfield in which psychologists research the fundamental causes of behavior. Many experimental psychologists conduct experiments in basic research.

experimenter bias Source of potential error in an experiment from the action or expectancy of the experimenter; might influence the experimental results in ways that mask the true outcome.

external locus of control In Julian Rotter's personality theory, the perception that reinforcement is independent of a person's behavior.

extraversion The dimension in the five-factor personality theory that includes traits such as sociability, talkativeness, boldness, fun-lovingness, adventurousness, and assertiveness; also called surgency. The personality concept of Carl Jung in which the personal energy of the individual is directed externally.

factor analysis A statistical procedure used to determine the relationship among variables.

false memories Memories believed to be real, but the events never occurred.

fast mapping A process by which children can utilize a word after a single exposure.

fetal alcohol syndrome (FAS) Condition in which defects in the newborn child are caused by the mother's excessive alcohol intake.

five-factor model of personality tracts A trait theory of personality that includes the factors of extraversion, agreeableness, conscientiousness, emotional stability, and openness.

fixed action pattern (FAP) Unlearned, inherited, stereotyped behaviors that are shown by all members of a species; term used in ethology.

fixed interval (FI) schedule Schedule of reinforcement where the subject receives reinforcement for a correct response given after a specified time interval.

fixed ratio (FR) schedule Schedule of reinforcement in which the subject is reinforced after a certain number of responses.

flashbulb memory Memory of an event that is so important that significant details are vividly remembered for life.

forgetting In memory, not being able to retrieve the original learning. The part of the original learning that cannot be retrieved is said to be forgotten.

formal operations period Period in cognitive development; at 11 years, the adolescent begins abstract thinking and reasoning. This period continues throughout the rest of life.

free association Psychoanalytic technique in which the patient says everything that comes to mind.

free recall A verbal learning procedure in which the order of presentation of the stimuli is varied and the subject can learn the items in any order.

frequency theory of hearing Theory of hearing that states that the frequency of vibrations at the basilar membrane determines the frequency of firing of neurons carrying impulses to the brain.

frustration A cause of stress that results from the blocking of a person's goal-oriented behavior.

frustration-drive theory of aggression Theory of aggression that states that it is caused by frustration.

functionalism School of thought that studied the functional value of consciousness and behavior.

fundamental attribution error Attribution bias in which people overestimate the role of internal disposition and underestimate the role of external situation.

gate-control theory of pain Theory of pain that proposes that there is a gate that allows pain impulses to travel from the spinal cord to the brain.

gender-identity disorder (GID) Incongruence between assigned sex and gender identity.

gender-identity/role Term that incorporates gender identity (the private perception of one's sex) and gender role (the public expression of one's gender identity).

gene The basic unit of heredity; the gene is composed of deoxyribonucleic acid (DNA).

general adaptation syndrome (GAS) Hans Selye's theory of how the body responds to stress over time. GAS includes alarm reaction, resistance, and exhaustion.

generalized anxiety disorder Anxiety disorder in which the individual lives in a state of constant severe tension, continuous fear, and apprehension.

genetics The study of heredity; genetics is the science of discovering how traits are passed along generations.

genotype The complete set of genes inherited by an individual from his or her parents.

Gestalt psychology A school of thought that studied whole or complete perceptions.

Gestalt therapy Insight therapy designed to help people become more aware of themselves in the here and now and to take responsibility for their own actions.

grandiose delusion Distortion of reality; one's belief that he or she is extremely important or powerful.

group therapy Treatment of several patients at the same time.

groupthink When group members are so committed to, and optimistic about, the group that they feel it is invulnerable; they become so concerned with maintaining consensus that criticism is muted.

growth The normal quantitative changes that occur in the physical and psychological aspects of a healthy child with the passage of time.

GSR (galvanic skin response) A measure of autonomic nervous system activity; a slight electric current is passed over the skin, and the more nervous a subject is, the easier the current will flow.

hallucinations A sensory impression reported when no external stimulus exists to justify the report; often hallucinations are a symptom of mental illness.

hallucinogens Psychedelic drugs that result in hallucinations at high doses, and other effects on behavior and perception in mild doses.

halo effect The finding that once we form a general impression of someone, we tend to interpret additional information about the person in a consistent manner.

haptic Relating to or based on the sense of touch. Also, a predilection for the sense of touch.

Hawthorne effect The finding that behavior can be influenced just by participation in a research study.

health psychology Field of psychology that studies psychological influences on people's health, including how they stay healthy, why they become ill, and how their behavior relates to their state of health.

heuristic Problem-solving strategy; a person tests solutions most likely to be correct.

hierarchy of needs Abraham Maslow's list of motives in humans, arranged from the biological to the uniquely human.

higher order conditioning Learning to make associations with stimuli that have been learned previously.

hippocampus Brain structure in the limbic system that is important in learning and memory.

homeostasis The state of equilibrium that maintains a balance in the internal body environment.

hormones Chemicals produced by the endocrine glands that regulate activity of certain bodily processes.

humanistic psychology Psychological school of thought that believes that people are unique beings who cannot be broken down into parts.

hyperphagia Disorder in which the individual continues to eat until he or she is obese; can be caused by damage to ventromedial hypothalamus.

hypersomnia Sleep disorder in which an individual falls asleep at inappropriate times; narcolepsy is a form of hypersomnia.

hypnosis Altered state of consciousness characterized by heightened suggestibility.

hypochondriasis Somatoform disorder in which the individual is obsessed with fears of having a serious medical disease.

hypothalamus Part of the brain's limbic system; involved in motivational behaviors, including eating, drinking, and sex.

hypothesis In the scientific method, an educated guess or prediction about future observable events.

iconic memory Visual information that is encoded into the sensory memory store.

id Sigmund Freud's representation of the basic instinctual drives; the id always seeks pleasure.

identification The process in which children adopt the attitudes, values, and behaviors of their parents.

identity diffusion In Marcia's adolescent identity theory, the status of individuals who have failed to make a commitment to values and roles.

illusion An incorrect perception that occurs when sensation is distorted.

imitation The copying of another's behavior; learned through the process of observation.

impression formation Developing an evaluation of another person from your perceptions; first, or initial, impressions are often very important.

imprinting A form of early learning in which birds follow a moving stimulus (often the mother); may be similar to attachment in mammals.

independent variable The condition in an experiment that is controlled and manipulated by the experimenter; it is a stimulus that will cause a response.

indiscriminate attachment phase Stage of attachment in which babies prefer humans to nonhumans, but do not discriminate among individual people.

individuation Carl Jung's concept of the process leading to the unification of all parts of the personality.

inferential statistics Techniques that help researchers make generalizations about a finding based on a limited number of subjects.

inferiority complex Adler's personality concept that states that because children are dependent on adults and cannot meet the standards set for themselves they feel inferior.

inhibition Restraint of an impulse, desire, activity, or drive.

insight A sudden grasping of the means necessary to achieve a goal; important in the Gestalt approach to problem solving.

insight therapy Therapy based on the assumption that behavior is abnormal because people do not adequately understand the motivation causing their behavior.

instinct Highly stereotyped behavior common to all members of a species that often appears in virtually complete form in the absence of any obvious opportunities to learn it.

instrumental conditioning Operant conditioning.

intelligence Capacity to learn and behave adaptively.

intelligence quotient (IQ) An index of a person's performance on an intelligence test relative to others in the culture; ratio of a person's mental age to chronological age.

interference Theory of forgetting in which information that was learned before (proactive interference) or after (retroactive interference) causes the learner to be unable to remember the material of interest.

internal locus of control In Rotter's personality theory, the perception that reinforcement is contingent upon behavior.

interstimulus interval Time interval between two stimuli; in classical conditioning, it is the elapsed time between the CS and the US.

intrinsic motivation Motivation inside the individual; we do something because we receive satisfaction from it.

introspection Method in which a subject gives a self-report of his or her immediate experience.

introversion The personality concept of Carl Jung in which the personal energy of the individual is directed inward; characterized by introspection, seriousness, inhibition, and restraint.

James-Lange theory of emotion Theory of emotion that states that the physiological arousal and behavior come before the subjective experience of an emotion.

just noticeable difference (JND) Difference threshold: minimum amount of energy required to produce a difference in sensation.

kinesthesis The sense of bodily movement.

labeling of arousal Experiments suggest that an individual experiencing physical arousal that cannot be explained will interpret those feelings in terms of the situation she or he is in and will use environmental and contextual cues.

language acquisition device (LAD) Hypothesized biological structure that accounts for the relative ease of acquiring language, according to Noam Chomsky.

latent dream content In Sigmund Freud's dream theory, the true thoughts in the unconsciousness; the true meaning of the dream.

latent learning Learning that occurs when an individual acquires knowledge of something but does not show it until motivated to do so.

law of effect Edward Thorndike's law that if a response produces satisfaction it will be repeated; reinforcement.

learned helplessness Condition in which a person learns that his or her behavior has no effect on his or her environment; when an individual gives up and stops trying.

learned social motives Social motives that are learned; include achievement and affiliation.

learning The relatively permanent change in behavior or behavioral ability of an individual that occurs as a result of experience.

learning styles The preferences students have for learning; theories of learning styles include personality differences, styles of information processing, and instructional preferences.

life instinct (also called Eros) Sigmund Freud's term for an instinct that helps the individual or species survive; sex is the major expression of life instinct.

life structure In Daniel Levinson's theory of adult personality development, the underlying pattern of an individual's life at any particular time; seasonal cycles include preadulthood, early adulthood, middle adulthood, and late adulthood.

linguistic relativity hypothesis Proposal that the perception of reality differs according to the language of the observer.

locus of control Julian Rotter's theory in which a person's beliefs about reinforcement are classified as internal or external.

long-term memory The permanent memory where rehearsed information is stored.

love An emotion characterized by knowing, liking, and becoming intimate with someone.

low-ball procedure The compliance technique of presenting an attractive proposal to someone and then switching it to a more unattractive proposal.

magic number 7 The finding that most people can remember about seven items of information for a short time (in short-term memory).

magnetic resonance imaging (MRI) A method of studying brain activity using magnetic field imaging.

major depressive disorder Severe mood disorder in which a person experiences one or more major depressive episodes; sometimes referred to simply as depression.

maladjustment Condition that occurs when a person utilizes inappropriate abilities to respond to demands placed upon him or her.

manic depressive reaction A form of mental illness marked by alternations of extreme phases of elation (manic phase) and depression.

manifest dream content In Sigmund Freud's dream theory, what is remembered about a dream upon waking; a disguised representation of the unconscious wishes.

massed practice Learning as much material as possible in long continuous stretches.

maturation The genetically controlled process of growth that results in orderly changes in behavior.

mean The arithmetic average, in which the sum of scores is divided by the number of scores.

median The middle score in a group of scores that are arranged from lowest to highest.

meditation The practice of some form of relaxed concentration while ignoring other sensory stimuli.

memory The process of storing information so that it can be retrieved and used later.

memory attributes The critical features of an event that are used when the experience is encoded or retrieved.

mental age The age level on which a person is capable of performing; used in determining intelligence.

mental set Condition in which a person's thinking becomes so standardized that he or she approaches new problems in fixed ways.

Minnesota Multiphasic Personality Inventory (MMPI-2) An objective personality test that was originally devised to identify personality disorders.

mnemonic technique Method of improving memory by combining and relating chunks of information.

modeling A process of learning by imitation in a therapeutic situation.

mood disorder Psychological disorder in which a person experiences a severe disruption in mood or emotional balance.

moral development Development of individuals as they adopt their society's standards of right and wrong; development of awareness of ethical behavior.

motivated forgetting (repression) Theory that suggests that people want to forget unpleasant events.

motivation The forces that initiate and direct behavior, and the variables that determine the intensity and persistence of the behavior.

motivator needs In Frederick Herzberg's theory, the factors that lead to job satisfaction; they include responsibility, the nature of the work, advancement, and recognition.

motive Anything that arouses the individual and directs his or her behavior toward some goal. Three categories of motives include biological, stimulus, and learned social.

Müller-Lyer illusion A well-known illusion, in which two horizontal lines have end lines either going in or out; the line with the end lines going in appears longer.

multiple approach-avoidance conflict Conflict that occurs when an individual has two or more goals, both of which have positive and negative aspects.

multiple attachment phase Later attachment stage in which the baby begins to form attachments to people other than the primary caretaker.

multiple intelligences Howard Gardner's theory that there exists several different kinds of intelligence.

Myers-Briggs Type Indicator (MBTI) Objective personality test based on Carl Jung's type theory.

narcotic analgesics Drugs that have an effect on the body similar to morphine; these relieve pain and suppress coughing.

naturalistic observation Research method in which behavior of people or animals in their normal environment is accurately recorded.

Necker cube A visual illusion. The Necker cube is a drawing of a cube designed so that it is difficult to determine which side is toward you.

negative reinforcement Removing something unpleasant to increase the probability that the preceding behavior will be repeated.

NEO Personality Inventory (NEO-PI) An objective personality test developed by Paul Costa Jr. and Robert McCrae to measure the five major factors in personality; consists of 181 questions.

neodissociation theory Idea that consciousness can be split into several streams of thought that are partially independent of each other.

neuron A specialized cell that functions to conduct messages throughout the body.

neurosis A Freudian term that was used to describe abnormal behavior caused by anxiety; it has been eliminated from *DSM-IV*.

neutral stimulus A stimulus that does not cause the response of interest; the individual may show some response to the stimulus but not the associated behavior.

norm A sample of scores representative of a population.

normal curve When scores of a large number of random cases are plotted on a graph, they often fall into a bell-shaped curve; as many cases on the curve are above the mean as below it.

observational learning In social learning theory, learning by observing someone else behave; people observe and imitate in learning socialization.

obsessions Fears that involve the inability to control impulses.

obsessive compulsive disorder Anxiety disorder in which the individual has repetitive thoughts (obsessions) that lead to constant urges (compulsions) to engage in meaningless rituals.

object permanence The ability to realize that objects continue to exist even if we can no longer see them.

Oedipus complex The Freudian idea that the young boy has sexual feelings for his mother and is jealous of his father and must identify with his father to resolve the conflict.

olfaction The smell sense.

openness The dimension in the five-factor personality theory that includes traits such as imagination, creativity, perception, knowledge, artistic ability, curiosity, and analytical ability; also called culture or intellect.

operant conditioning Form of learning in which behavior followed by reinforcement (satisfaction) increases in frequency.

opponent-process theory Theory that when one emotion is experienced, the other is suppressed.

optimum level of arousal Motivation theory that states that the individual will seek a level of arousal that is comfortable.

organic mental disorders Psychological disorders that involve physical damage to the nervous system; can be caused by disease or by an accident.

organizational psychology Area of industrial psychology that focuses on worker attitudes and motivation; derived primarily from personality and social psychology.

orgasm The climax of intense sexual excitement; release from building sexual tension, usually accompanied by ejaculation in men.

paired-associate learning A verbal learning procedure in which the subject is presented with a series of pairs of items to be remembered.

panic disorder Anxiety disorder characterized by the occurrence of specific periods of intense fear.

paranoid schizophrenia A type of schizophrenia in which the individual often has delusions of grandeur and persecution, thinking that someone is out to get him or her.

partial reinforcement Any schedule of reinforcement in which reinforcement follows only some of the correct responses.

partial reinforcement effect The finding that partial reinforcement produces a response that takes longer to extinguish than continuous reinforcement.

pattern recognition Memory process in which information attended to is compared with information already permanently stored in memory.

Pavlovian conditioning A bond or association between a neutral stimulus and a response; this type of learning is called classical conditioning.

perception The active process in which the sensory information that is carried through the nervous system to the brain is organized and interpreted; the interpretation of sensation.

persecutory delusion A delusion in which the individual has a distortion of reality; the belief that other people are out to get one.

person perception The process of using the information we gather in forming impressions of people to make evaluations of others.

personal unconscious Carl Jung's representation of the individual's repressed thoughts and memories.

personality disorder Psychological disorder in which there are problems in the basic personality structure of the individual.

phantom-limb pain Phenomenon in which people who have lost an arm or leg feel pain in the missing limb.

phobias Acute excessive fears of specific situations or objects that have no convincing basis in reality.

physiological needs First level of motives in Abraham Maslow's hierarchy; includes the biological needs of hunger, thirst, sex, exercise, and rest.

placebo An inert or inactive substance given to control subjects to test for bias effects.

plateau phase Second phase in the human sexual response cycle, during which the physiological arousal becomes more intense.

pleasure principle In Freudian theory, the idea that the instinctual drives of the id unconsciously and impulsively seek immediate pleasure.

positive reinforcement Presenting a subject something pleasant to increase the probability that the preceding behavior will be repeated.

postconventional morality Level III in Lawrence Kohlberg's theory, in which moral reasoning is based on personal standards and beliefs; highest level of moral thinking.

posttraumatic stress disorder (PTSD) Condition that can occur when a person experiences a severely distressing event; characterized by constant memories of the event, avoidance of anything associated with it, and general arousal.

Prägnanz (law of) Gestalt psychology law that states that people have a tendency to group stimuli according to rules, and that people do this whenever possible.

preconscious mind In Sigmund Freud's psychoanalytic theory of personality, the part of personality that contains information that we have learned but that we are not thinking about at the present time.

preconventional morality Level I of Lawrence Kohlberg's theory, in which moral reasoning is largely due to the expectation of rewards and punishments.

prejudice An unjustified fixed, usually negative, way of thinking about a person or object.

Premack principle Principle that states that, of any two responses, the one that is more likely to occur can be used to reinforce the response that is less likely to occur.

preoperational thought period Period in cognitive development; from two to seven years, the period during which the child learns to represent the environment with objects and symbols.

primacy effect Phenomenon where items are remembered because they come at the beginning of a list.

primary appraisal Activity of determining whether a new stimulus event is positive, neutral, or negative; first step in appraisal of stress.

primary narcissism A Freudian term that refers to the oral phase before the ego has developed; the individual constantly seeks pleasure.

primary reinforcement Reinforcement that is effective without having been associated with other reinforcers; sometimes called unconditioned reinforcement.

probability (p) In inferential statistics, the likelihood that the difference between the experimental and control groups is due to the independent variable.

procedural memory The most basic type of long-term memory; involves the formation of associations between stimuli and responses.

projection Defense mechanism in which a person attributes his or her unacceptable characteristics or motives to others rather than himself or herself.

projective personality test A personality test that presents ambiguous stimuli to which subjects are expected to respond with projections of their own personality.

proximity Closeness in time and space. In perception, it is the Gestalt perceptual principle in which stimuli next to one another are included together.

psyche According to Carl Jung, the thoughts and feelings (conscious and unconscious) of an individual.

psychoactive drug A drug that produces changes in behavior and cognition through modification of conscious awareness.

psychoanalysis The school of thought founded by Sigmund Freud that stressed unconscious motivation. In therapy, a patient's unconscious motivation is intensively explored in order to bring repressed conflicts up to consciousness; psychoanalysis usually takes a long time to accomplish.

psychobiology (also called biological psychology or physiological psychology) The subfield of experimental psychology concerned with the influence of heredity and the biological response systems on behavior.

psychogenic amnesia A dissociative disorder in which an individual loses his or her sense of identity.

psychogenic fugue A dissociative disorder in which an individual loses his or her sense of identity and goes to a new geographic location, forgetting all of the unpleasant emotions connected with the old life.

psychographics A technique used in consumer psychology to identify the attitudes of buyers and their preferences for particular products.

psycholinguistics The psychological study of how people convert the sounds of a language into meaningful symbols that can be used to communicate with others.

psychological dependence Situation in which a person craves a drug even though it is not biologically needed by the body.

psychological disorder A diagnosis of abnormal behavior; syndrome of abnormal adjustment, classified in *DSM*.

psychological types Carl Jung's term for different personality profiles; Jung combined two attitudes and four functions to produce eight psychological types.

psychopharmacology Study of effects of psychoactive drugs on behavior.

psychophysics An area of psychology in which researchers compare the physical energy of a stimulus with the sensation reported.

psychosexual stages Sigmund Freud's theoretical stages in personality development.

psychosomatic disorders A variety of body reactions that are closely related to psychological events.

psychotherapy Treatment of behavioral disorders through psychological techniques; major psychotherapies include insight therapy, behavior therapy, and group therapy.

psychotic disorders The more severe categories of abnormal behavior.

puberty Sexual maturation; the time at which the individual is able to perform sexually and to reproduce.

punishment Any event that decreases the likelihood that the behavior preceding it will be repeated.

quantitative trait loci (QTLs) Genes that collectively contribute to a trait for high intelligence.

rational-emotive therapy A cognitive behavior modification technique in which a person is taught to identify irrational, self-defeating beliefs and then to overcome them.

reaction formation Defense mechanism in which a person masks an unconsciously distressing or unacceptable trait by assuming an opposite attitude or behavior pattern.

reality principle In Freudian theory, the idea that the drives of the ego try to find socially acceptable ways to gratify the id.

reciprocal determinism The concept proposed by Albert Bandura that the behavior, the individual, and the situation interact and influence each other.

reciprocal inhibition Concept of Joseph Wolpe that states that it is possible to break the bond between anxiety-provoking stimuli and responses manifesting anxiety by facing those stimuli in a state antagonistic to anxiety.

reflex An automatic movement that occurs in direct response to a stimulus.

regression Defense mechanism in which a person retreats to an earlier, more immature form of behavior.

reinforcement Any event that increases the probability that the behavior that precedes it will be repeated; also called a reinforcer; similar to a reward.

reinforcement therapy A behavior therapy in which reinforcement is used to modify behavior. Techniques in reinforcement therapy include shaping, extinction, and token economy.

releaser (sign stimulus) Specific environmental cues that stimulate a stereotyped behavior to occur; releasers cause fixed action patterns.

repression Defense mechanism in which painful memories and unacceptable thoughts and motives are conveniently forgotten so that they will not have to be dealt with.

residual schizophrenia Type of schizophrenia in which the individual currently does not have symptoms but has had a schizophrenic episode in the past.

resistance Psychoanalytic term used when a patient avoids a painful area of conflict.

resolution phase The last phase in the human sexual response cycle; the time after orgasm that the body gradually returns to the unaroused state.

Restricted Environmental Stimulation Technique (REST) Research technique in which environmental stimuli available to an individual are reduced drastically; formerly called sensory deprivation.

retroactive interference Interference caused by information learned after the material of interest.

retrograde amnesia Forgetting information recently learned because of a disruptive stimulus such as an electric shock.

reversible figure In perception, a situation in which the figure and ground seem to reverse themselves; an illusion in which objects alternate as the main figure.

risky-shift The tendency for groups to make riskier decisions than individuals.

Rorschach Inkblot Test A projective personality test in which subjects are asked to discuss what they see in cards containing blots of ink.

safety needs Second level of motives in Abraham Maslow's hierarchy; includes security, stability, dependency, protection, freedom from fear and anxiety, and the need for structure and order.

Schachter-Singer theory of emotion Theory of emotion that states that we interpret our arousal according to our environment and label our emotions accordingly.

scheme A unit of knowledge that the person possesses; used in Jean Piaget's cognitive development theory.

schizophrenia Severe psychotic disorder that is characterized by disruptions in thinking, perception, and emotion.

scientific method An attitude and procedure that scientists use to conduct research. The steps include stating the problem, forming the hypothesis, collecting the information, evaluating the information, and drawing conclusions.

secondary appraisal In appraisal of stress, this is the evaluation that an individual's abilities and resources are sufficient to meet the demands of a stressful event.

secondary reinforcement Reinforcement that is effective only after it has been associated with a primary reinforcer; also called conditioned reinforcement.

secondary traits In Gordon Allport's personality theory, the less important situation-specific traits that help round out personality; they include attitudes, skills, and behavior patterns.

secure attachment Type of infant-parent attachment in which the infant actively seeks contact with the parent.

self-actualization A humanistic term describing the state in which all of an individual's capacities are developed fully. Fifth and highest level of motives in Abraham Maslow's hierarchy; this level, the realization of one's potential, is rarely reached.

self-efficacy An individual's sense of self-worth and success in adjusting to the world.

self-evaluation maintenance model (SEM) Tesser's theory of how we maintain a positive self-image despite the success of others close to us.

self-handicapping strategy A strategy that people use to prepare for failure; people behave in ways that produce obstacles to success so that when they do fail they can place the blame on the obstacle.

self-serving bias An attribution bias in which an individual attributes success to his or her own behavior but failure to external environmental causes.

semantic memory Type of long-term memory that can use cognitive activities, such as everyday knowledge.

sensation The passive process in which stimuli are received by sense receptors and transformed into neural impulses that can be carried through the nervous system; first stage in becoming aware of environment.

sensitivity training group (T-group) Therapy group that has the goal of making participants more aware of themselves and their ideas.

sensorimotor period Period in cognitive development; first two years, during which the infant learns to coordinate sensory experiences with motor activities.

sensory adaptation Tendency of the sense organs to adjust to continuous stimulation by reducing their functioning; a stimulus that once caused sensation and no longer does.

sensory deprivation Situation in which normal environmental sensory stimuli available to an individual are reduced drastically; also called REST (Restricted Environmental Stimulation Technique).

serial learning A verbal learning procedure in which the stimuli are always presented in the same order, and the subject has to learn them in the order in which they are presented.

sex roles The set of behaviors and attitudes that are determined to be appropriate for one sex or the other in a society.

shaping In operant conditioning, the gradual process of reinforcing behaviors that get closer to some final desired behavior. Shaping is also called successive approximation.

signal detection theory Research approach in which the subject's behavior in detecting a threshold is treated as a form of decision making.

similarity Gestalt principle in which similar stimuli are perceived as a unit.

simple phobia Excessive irrational fear that does not fall into other specific categories, such as fear of dogs, insects, snakes, or closed-in places.

simultaneous conditioning A procedure in classical conditioning in which the CS and US are presented at exactly the same time.

Sixteen Personality Factor Questionnaire (16PF) Raymond Cattell's personality test to measure source traits.

Skinner box B. F. Skinner's animal cage with a lever that triggers reinforcement for a subject.

sleep terror disorder (pavor nocturnus) Nonrapid-eye-movement (NREM) sleep disorder in which the person (usually a child) wakes up screaming and terrified, but cannot recall why.

sleepwalking (somnambulism) NREM sleep disorder in which the person walks in his or her sleep.

social cognition The process of understanding other people and ourselves by forming and utilizing information about the social world.

social cognitive theory Albert Bandura's approach to personality that proposes that individuals use observation, imitation, and cognition to develop personality.

social comparison Theory proposed by Leon Festinger that we tend to compare our behavior to others to ensure that we are conforming.

social exchange theory Theory of interpersonal relationships that states that people evaluate the costs and rewards of their relationships and act accordingly.

social facilitation Phenomenon in which the presence of others increases dominant behavior patterns in an individual; Richard Zajonc's theory states that the presence of others enhances the emission of the dominant response of the individual.

social influence Influence designed to change the attitudes or behavior of other people; includes conformity, compliance, and obedience.

social learning theory An approach to social psychology that emphasizes observation and modeling; states that reinforcement is involved in motivation rather than in learning, and proposes that aggression is a form of learned behavior.

social phobia Excessive irrational fear and embarrassment when interacting with other people. Social phobias may include fear of assertive behavior, fear of making mistakes, or fear of public speaking.

social psychology The study of how an individual's behavior, thoughts, and feelings are influenced by other people.

sociobiology Study of the genetic basis of social behavior.

sociocultural Emphasizes the importance of culture, gender, and ethnicity in how we think, feel, and act.

somatic nervous system The part of the peripheral nervous system that carries messages from the sense organs and relays information that directs the voluntary movements of the skeletal muscles.

somatization disorder Somatoform disorder in which a person has medical complaints without physical cause.

somatoform disorders Psychological disorders characterized by physical symptoms for which there are no obvious physical causes.

specific attachment phase Stage at about six months of age, in which the baby becomes attached to a specific person.

split-brain research Popular name for Roger Sperry's research on the syndrome of hemisphere deconnection; research on individuals with the corpus callosum severed. Normal functioning breaks down in split-brain subjects when different information is presented to each hemisphere.

SQ5R A technique to improve learning and memory. Components include survey, question, read, record, recite, review, and reflect.

stage of exhaustion Third stage in Hans Selye's general adaptation syndrome. As the body continues to resist stress, it depletes its energy resources and the person becomes exhausted.

stage of resistance Second stage in Hans Selye's general adaptation syndrome. When stress is prolonged, the body builds some resistance to the effects of stress.

standardization The process of obtaining a representative sample of scores in the population so that a particular score can be interpreted correctly.

Stanford-Binet Intelligence Scale An intelligence test first revised by Lewis Terman at Stanford University in 1916; still a popular test used today.

state-dependent learning Situation in which what is learned in one state can only be remembered when the person is in that state of mind.

statistically significant In inferential statistics, a finding that the independent variable did influence greatly the outcome of the experimental and control group.

stereotype An exaggerated and rigid mental image of a particular class of persons or objects.

stimulus A unit of the environment that causes a response in an individual; a physical or chemical agent acting on an appropriate sense receptor.

stimulus discrimination Responding to relevant stimuli.

stimulus generalization Responding to stimuli similar to the stimulus that had caused the response.

stimulus motives Motivating factors that are internal and unlearned, but do not appear to have a physiological basis; stimulus motives cause an individual to seek out sensory stimulation through interaction with the environment.

stimulus trace The perceptual persistence of a stimulus after it is no longer present.

strange situation procedure A measure of attachment developed by Mary Ainsworth that consists of eight phases during which the infant is increasingly stressed.

stress Anything that produces demands on us to adjust and threatens our well-being.

Strong Interest Inventory An objective personality test that compares people's personalities to groups that achieve success in certain occupations.

structuralism First school of thought in psychology; studied conscious experience to discover the structure of the mind.

subject bias Source of potential error in an experiment from the action or expectancy of a subject; a subject might influence the experimental results in ways that mask the true outcome.

subjective organization Long-term memory procedures in which the individual provides a personal method of organizing information to be memorized.

sublimation Defense mechanism; a person redirects his or her socially undesirable urges into socially acceptable behavior.

successive approximation Shaping; in operant conditioning, the gradual process of reinforcing behaviors that get closer to some final desired behavior.

sudden infant death syndrome (SIDS) Situation in which a seemingly healthy infant dies suddenly in its sleep; also called crib death.

superego Sigmund Freud's representation of conscience.

surface traits In Raymond Cattell's personality theory, the observable characteristics of a person's behavior and personality.

symbolization In Sigmund Freud's dream theory, the process of converting the latent content of a dream into manifest symbols.

systematic desensitization Application of counterconditioning, in which the individual overcomes anxiety by learning to relax in the presence of stimuli that had once made him or her unbearably nervous.

task-oriented coping Adjustment responses in which the person evaluates a stressful situation objectively and then formulates a plan with which to solve the problem.

test of significance An inferential statistical technique used to determine whether the difference in scores between the experimental and control groups is really due to the effects of the independent variable or to random chance. If the probability of an outcome is extremely low, we say that outcome is significant.

Thanatos Sigmund Freud's term for a destructive instinct such as aggression; also called death instinct.

Thematic Apperception Test (TAT) Projective personality test in which subjects are shown pictures of people in everyday settings; subjects must make up a story about the people portrayed.

theory of social impact Latané's theory of social behavior; it states that each member of a group shares the responsibility equally.

Theory X Douglas McGregor's theory that states that the worker dislikes work and must be forced to do it.

Theory Y Douglas McGregor's theory that states that work is natural and can be a source of satisfaction, and, when it is, the worker can be highly committed and motivated.

therapy In psychology, the treatment of behavior problems; two major types of therapy include psychotherapy and biological therapy.

time and motion studies In engineering psychology, studies that analyze the time it takes to perform an action and the movements that go into the action.

tip-of-the-tongue phenomenon A phenomenon in which the closer a person comes to recalling something, the more accurately he or she can remember details, such as the number of syllables or letters.

token economy A behavior therapy in which desired behaviors are reinforced immediately with tokens that can be exchanged at a later time for desired rewards, such as food or recreational privileges.

trace conditioning A procedure in classical conditioning in which the CS is a discrete event that is presented and terminated before the US is presented.

trait A distinctive and stable attribute in people.

trait anxiety Anxiety that is long-lasting; a relatively stable personality characteristic.

transference Psychoanalytic term used when a patient projects his feelings onto the therapist.

transsexualism A condition in which a person feels trapped in the body of the wrong sex.

trial and error learning Trying various behaviors in a situation until the solution is found.

triangular theory of love Robert Sternberg's theory that states that love consists of intimacy, passion, and decision/commitment.

triarchic theory of intelligence Robert Sternberg's theory of intelligence that states that it consists of three parts: componential, experiential, and contextual subtheories.

Type-A behavior Behavior shown by a particular type of individual; a personality pattern of behavior that can lead to stress and heart disease.

unconditional positive regard Part of Carl Rogers's personality theory; occurs when we accept someone regardless of what he or she does or says.

unconditioned response (UR) An automatic reaction elicited by a stimulus.

unconditioned stimulus (US) Any stimulus that elicits an automatic or reflexive reaction in an individual; it does not have to be learned in the present situation.

unconscious mind In Sigmund Freud's psychoanalytic theory of personality, the part of personality that is unavailable to us; Freud suggests that instincts and unpleasant memories are stored in the unconscious mind.

undifferentiated schizophrenia Type of schizophrenia that does not fit into any particular category, or fits into more than one category.

validity The degree to which you actually measure what you intend to measure.

variability In statistics, variability measures the range of the scores.

variable interval (VI) schedule Schedule of reinforcement in which the subject is reinforced for the first response given after a certain time interval, with the interval being different for each trial.

variable ratio (VR) schedule Schedule of reinforcement in which the subject is given reinforcement after a varying number of responses; the number of responses required for reinforcement is different for every trial.

vestibular sense Sense that helps keep our balance.

visuo-spatial sketch pad Responsible for visual images involved in geographical orientation and spatial task.

vulnerability-stress model Theory of schizophrenia that states that some people have a biological tendency to develop schizophrenia if they are stressed enough by their environment.

Weber's Law Ernst Weber's law that states that the difference threshold depends on the ratio of the intensity of one stimulus to another rather than on an absolute difference.

Wechsler Adult Intelligence Scale (WAIS) An intelligence test for adults, first published by David Wechsler in 1955; it contains verbal and performance subscales.

Wechsler Intelligence Scale for Children (WISC-III) Similar to the Wechsler Adult Intelligence Scale, except that it is designed for children ages 6 through 16, and helps diagnose certain childhood disorders, such as dyslexia and other learning disabilities.

Wechsler Preschool and Primary Scale of Intelligence (WPPSI-R) Designed for children between the ages of 4 and 7; helps diagnose certain childhood disorders, such as dyslexia and other learning disabilities.

withdrawal Unpleasant physical reactions that a drug-dependent user experiences when he or she stops taking the drug.

within-subject experiment An experimental design in which each subject is given all treatments, including the control condition; subjects serve in both experimental and control groups.

working memory The memory store, with a capacity of about 7 items and enduring for up to 30 seconds, that handles current information.

Yerkes-Dodson Law Popular idea that performance is best when arousal is at a medium level.

Sources for the Glossary:

The majority of terms in this glossary are from Psychology: A ConnecText, 4th Edition, Terry F. Pettijohn. ©1999 Dushkin/McGraw-Hill, Guilford, CT 06437. The remaining terms were developed by the Annual Editions staff.

AE Article Review Form

We encourage you to photocopy and use this page as a tool to assess how the articles in **Annual Editions** expand on the information in your textbook. By reflecting on the articles you will gain enhanced text information. You can also access this useful form on a product's book support Web site at ***http://www.dushkin.com/online/***.

NAME: _____ DATE: _____

TITLE AND NUMBER OF ARTICLE:
_____

BRIEFLY STATE THE MAIN IDEA OF THIS ARTICLE:
_____

LIST THREE IMPORTANT FACTS THAT THE AUTHOR USES TO SUPPORT THE MAIN IDEA:

_____

WHAT INFORMATION OR IDEAS DISCUSSED IN THIS ARTICLE ARE ALSO DISCUSSED IN YOUR TEXTBOOK OR OTHER READINGS THAT YOU HAVE DONE? LIST THE TEXTBOOK CHAPTERS AND PAGE NUMBERS:

_____

LIST ANY EXAMPLES OF BIAS OR FAULTY REASONING THAT YOU FOUND IN THE ARTICLE:

_____

LIST ANY NEW TERMS/CONCEPTS THAT WERE DISCUSSED IN THE ARTICLE, AND WRITE A SHORT DEFINITION:

_____

ANNUAL EDITIONS revisions depend on two major opinion sources: one is our Advisory Board, listed in the front of this volume, which works with us in scanning the thousands of articles published in the public press each year; the other is you—the person actually using the book. Please help us and the users of the next edition by completing the prepaid article rating form on this page and returning it to us. Thank you for your help!

ANNUAL EDITIONS: PSYCHOLOGY 99/00

ARTICLE RATING FORM

Here is an opportunity for you to have direct input into the next revision of this volume. We would like you to rate each of the 46 articles listed below, using the following scale:

1. Excellent: should definitely be retained
2. Above average: should probably be retained
3. Below average: should probably be deleted
4. Poor: should definitely be deleted

Your ratings will play a vital part in the next revision. So please mail this prepaid form to us just as soon as you complete it. Thanks for your help!

RATING

ARTICLE

1. Why Freud Isn't Dead
2. The Benefits and Ethics of Animal Research
3. On the Validity of Psychology Experiments
4. Nature, Nurture: Not Mutually Exclusive
5. What We Learn from Twins: The Mirror of Your Soul
6. Secrets of the Brain
7. Revealing the Brain's Secrets
8. The Senses
9. Gain in Years Can Mean Loss in Hearing
10. Don't Take Touch for Granted: An Interview with Susan Lederman
11. Dream Catchers
12. Learning Begins Even before Babies Are Born, Scientists Show
13. What Constitutes "Appropriate" Punishment?
14. It's Magical! It's Malleable! It's . . . Memory
15. Memory for a Past That Never Was
16. Your Child's Brain
17. To Be Intelligent
18. Reflections on Multiple Intelligences: Myths and Messages
19. On the Trail of Language: Neuropsychologist Angela Friederici
20. Is It Nature or Nurture?
21. The EQ Factor
22. A Doubtful Device
23. The Biology of Joy

RATING

ARTICLE

24. Weight Loss for Grown-Ups
25. Born to Be Good?
26. Behaviors of a Newborn Can Be Traced to the Fetus
27. Do Parents Really Matter? Kid Stuff
28. Rethinking Puberty: The Development of Sexual Attraction
29. Slowing Down Alzheimer's
30. The Personality Genes
31. The Stability of Personality: Observations and Evaluations
32. Are You Shy?
33. Finding Strength: How to Overcome Anything
34. Disintegration of the Family Is the Real Root Cause of Violent Crime
35. Where Bias Begins: The Truth about Stereotypes
36. Laughter May Be No Laughing Matter
37. Brain Sex and the Language of Love
38. Is Mental Illness Catching?
39. Mother's Little Helper
40. Why Worry?
41. Patterns of Abuse
42. Schizophrenia's Most Zealous Foe
43. What You Can Change and What You Cannot Change
44. Prescriptions for Happiness?
45. The Quest for a Cure
46. New Treatments for Schizophrenia—Part I

(Continued on next page)

We Want Your Advice

ANNUAL EDITIONS: PSYCHOLOGY 99/00

ABOUT YOU

Name

Date

Are you a teacher? ☐   A student? ☐

Your school's name

Department

Address

City

State

Zip

School telephone #

YOUR COMMENTS ARE IMPORTANT TO US !

Please fill in the following information:

For which course did you use this book?

Did you use a text with this *ANNUAL EDITION*?   ☐ yes   ☐ no

What was the title of the text?

What are your general reactions to the *Annual Editions* concept?

Have you read any particular articles recently that you think should be included in the next edition?

Are there any articles you feel should be replaced in the next edition? Why?

Are there any World Wide Web sites you feel should be included in the next edition? Please annotate.

May we contact you for editorial input?   ☐ yes   ☐ no

May we quote your comments?   ☐ yes   ☐ no